THE TEACHINGS OF
EZRA TAFT BENSON

THE TEACHINGS OF
EZRA TAFT BENSON

Ezra Taft Benson

BOOKCRAFT
Salt Lake City, Utah

Library of Congress Catalog Card Number: 88-72239

ISBN 0-88494-639-8

2ND PRINTING, 1988

Printed in the United States of America

President Ezra Taft Benson is the thirteenth President of The Church of Jesus Christ of Latter-day Saints. As the Prophet, Seer, and Revelator, his inspired words are considered by members of the Church to be the word of God.

President Benson has been uniquely prepared by the Lord to serve as His mouthpiece to the whole world. For forty-two years he was a member of the Quorum of the Twelve Apostles, twelve years of which he served as its president. Twice he served as European Mission president, once immediately following World War II administering to the needs of the Saints in those war-torn countries. Twice he served as stake president—once in Boise, Idaho, and again as the first stake president in the Washington, D.C., area.

By the time he came to the Presidency of the Church, he had personally known many heads of state and had received broad formal education. He served in the Cabinet of the President of the United States for eight years, and is highly respected in the nation and the world. He is the recipient of several honorary doctorate degrees, and has served on the boards of numerous national and international organizations.

Through all of these experiences, President Benson has been in great demand as a speaker. He has delivered thousands of speeches, both formally and informally, around the world. His audiences have ranged from the tens of thousands to a gathering in a neighborhood home.

His subject matter has also had a broad range that includes church and civic affairs, the home, and his profession of agriculture.

Previous selections of some of his talks covering three general areas can be found in his book *God, Family, Country* (1974). Excerpts from his talks spanning a wide range of subjects can be found in his earlier book *So Shall Ye Reap* (1960).

For the purpose of this book, the emphasis will be particularly on the gospel and the Church.

For those who would like more of his agricultural messages, he is the author of the books *Farmers at the Crossroads* (1956) and *Freedom to Farm* (1960). As the United States Secretary of Agriculture, he delivered hundreds of addresses on agricultural subjects. Those talks must await the skills of a future compiler.

For those who would like more of his civic messages, these can be found in his books *The Red Carpet* (1962), *Title of Liberty* (1964), *An Enemy Hath Done This* (1969), and *This Nation Shall Endure* (1977).

He is also the author of the books *Come unto Christ* (1983) and *A Witness and a Warning* (1988).

Some of his teachings may also be found in various biographies of his life. *Ezra Taft Benson* (1987) covers his entire life. *Crossfire: The Eight Years with Eisenhower* (1962) covers his years in the Cabinet. *On Wings of Faith* (1972) covers his presidency of the European Mission following World War II.

The excerpts that make up this teachings volume have come from his speeches or public writings after he was called to the apostleship and sustained as a Prophet, Seer, and Revelator.

President Benson personally reviewed the entire manuscript, as did his counselors in the First Presidency.

It has been the hope and prayer of President Benson over the years to do only those things that are "best for the kingdom of God" and lead men to Christ. May this volume contribute to that end and bless the lives of our Father's children.

Contents

Part 2
The Church

Part 3
The Gospel in Our Lives

Part 4
Family and Home

Part 5
Country

Sources, References, and Abbreviations

Each excerpt shows a source reference.

References for some of the speeches given to small or private groups show simply location and date.

The abbreviation CR in the references stands for Conference Report.

The references show full publication detail for all books except those written by Ezra Taft Benson. For the latter, the references show only the titles.

Excerpts are included from the following books by President Benson:

Farmers at the Crossroads (Devin-Adair, 1956)

Freedom to Farm (Doubleday, 1960)

So Shall Ye Reap (Deseret Book, 1960)

Crossfire: The Eight Years with Eisenhower (Doubleday, 1962)

The Red Carpet (Bookcraft, 1962)

Title of Liberty (Deseret Book, 1964)

An Enemy Hath Done This (Parliament, 1969)

God, Family, Country: Our Three Great Loyalties (Deseret Book, 1974)

This Nation Shall Endure (Deseret Book, 1977)

Come unto Christ (Deseret Book, 1983)

The Constitution: A Heavenly Banner (Deseret Book, 1986)

A Witness and a Warning (Deseret Book, 1988)

Acknowledgments

Several people have been involved in varying degrees in the large task of selecting, editing, and typing the material included in the manuscript for this volume. Appreciation is extended to them for their much-needed help. Particular thanks go to various members of the Benson family and to Frank Alan Bruno, V. Dennis Wardle, and Religious Education at Brigham Young University.

PART 1

GOSPEL PRINCIPLES AND DOCTRINES

GOSPEL PRINCIPLES AND DOCTRINES

The Godhead

A basic and important doctrine of The Church of Jesus Christ of Latter-day Saints is this: "We believe in God, the Eternal Father, and in His Son, Jesus Christ, and in the Holy Ghost" (Article of Faith 1). We accept these three personages without reservation "as the supreme governing council in the heavens. The Father and the Son have tabernacles of flesh and bones, and the Holy Ghost is a personage of Spirit. We worship the Father in the name of the Son, who is the Mediator between God and man, and his is the only name given whereby man can be saved. We accept Jesus as the Only Begotten Son of the Father in the flesh, although we are all his offspring in the spirit, and therefore his children." (Joseph Fielding Smith, *Doctrines of Salvation*, 1:1.)

An understanding of these basic truths is of the utmost importance. Knowledge is power, but all knowledge is not of equal value. That knowledge which deals with the personality and attributes of God the Father and man's relationship to Him is of supreme importance. (Youth Fireside Series for the Church, Washington, D.C., 27 September 1960.)

The Savior declared that life eternal is to know the only true God, and His Son Jesus Christ (John 17:3). If this is true, and I bear you my solemn witness that it is true, then we must ask how we come to know God. The process of adding one godly attribute to another, as described by Peter, becomes the key to gaining this knowledge that leads to eternal life. Note Peter's promise which immediately follows the process described: "For if these things be in you, and abound, they make you that ye shall neither be barren nor unfruitful in the knowledge of our Lord Jesus Christ" (2 Peter 1:8). (CR October 1986, *Ensign* 16 [November 1986]: 48.)

From the days of the ancient Apostles to the restoration of the gospel, there has been doubt, confusion, and conflict regarding the character, nature, and personality of God and the Godhead. Instead of accepting God as He has declared Himself to be, the Christian sects have sought by human reason and wisdom to describe God. Some have gone so far as to declare that man makes his own god and that the God of the ancient patriarchs—of the time of Moses or of the early Christian era—is not the God of today. Surely, there is no place in Christian faith for such heresy. (Youth Fireside Series for the Church, Washington, D.C., 27 September 1960.)

Joseph Smith, a prophet of God, restored the knowledge of God. Joseph's first vision clearly revealed that the Father and Son are separate personages, having bodies as tangible as man's. Later it was also revealed that the Holy Ghost is a personage of Spirit, separate and distinct from the personalities of the Father and the Son. (See D&C 130:22.) This all-important truth shocked the world even though sustained by the Bible. ("Basic Doctrines of Church Explained to Youth Firesides," *Church News* [20 May 1961]: 14.)

God the Father

We believe God to be the personal Heavenly Father to all mankind, that all mortal beings are literally His spirit offspring. We worship God as a personal, all-knowing, all-powerful being, endowed with all the attributes of perfection. As God's literal offspring, we believe man to be His only creation blessed with His image and His likeness (see D&C 20:18). (*This Nation Shall Endure*, pp. 100–101.)

Our doctrine of God is clear. He is our Heavenly and Eternal Father. We are His literal children. Through righteous living according to His plan we can see God and become like Him. ("Basic Doctrines of Church Explained to Youth Firesides," *Church News* [20 May 1961]: 14.)

The first and second commandments stipulate our worship and belief in God: "Thou shalt have no other gods before me," and "Thou shalt not make unto thee any graven image" (Exodus 20:3–4). Worship of and belief in God have been basic to America's collective progress for two hundred years. It is the foundation to its Judaic-Christian culture. Its coins bear the inscription "In God We Trust." Citizens pledge allegiance to the republic that is one nation "under God." Its officials take oaths of office before God. Yet today that worship and belief are waning. Efforts are even being made to remove the references to God from the coins, the Pledge of Allegiance, and other public ceremonies. Today we see man walking in his own way, after the image of his own god (see D&C 1:16), an image that bears the stamp of worldliness, lust, greed, and power. As Abraham Lincoln pronounced during the Civil War, so now may we say, "We have forgotten God!" ("The Ten Commandments," *New Era* 8 [July 1978]: 36.)

Mormon philosophy, based on the revelations of God, assures us that our Heavenly Father is the supreme scientist of the universe. He is the supreme authority of the humanities. God is the supreme authority on politics, on economics, on sociology. He knows what works best in human relations. He is the master teacher, with a glorious plan based on freedom of choice, for the building of godlike men and women. He stands today ready to help us reach out and tap that great unseen power as we heed the counsel of His living mouthpiece, a true prophet of God. (*An Enemy Hath Done This*, pp. 280–81.)

God our Father does live. The evidence of history and tradition declares that He lives. The evidence of human reason declares that He lives. The conclusive evidence of direct revelation from God Himself declares that He lives. Holy writ declares in unmistakable evidence that He lives and that we, His children, are created in His image. Here is one example from the Apostle Paul: "Furthermore we have had fathers of our flesh which corrected us, and we gave them reverence: shall we not much rather be in subjection unto the

Father of spirits, and live?'' (Hebrews 12:9.) Yes, He is our Father —the father of our spirits. We are His spirit offspring. (''Basic Doctrines of Church Explained to Youth Firesides,'' *Church News* [20 May 1961]: 14.)

Jesus Christ

Jesus Christ was and is the Lord God Omnipotent (see Mosiah 3:5). He was chosen before He was born. He was the all-powerful Creator of the heavens and the earth. He is the source of life and light to all things. His word is the law by which all things are governed in the universe. All things created and made by Him are subject to His infinite power. (*Come unto Christ*, p. 128.)

Jesus was a God in the premortal existence. Our Father in Heaven gave Him a name above all others—the Christ. We have a volume of scripture whose major mission is to convince the world that Jesus is the Christ. It is the Book of Mormon. It is another testament of Jesus Christ. In its pages we read ''that there shall be no other name given nor any other way nor means whereby salvation can come unto the children of men, only in and through the name of Christ, the Lord Omnipotent'' (Mosiah 3:17).

As far as man is concerned, we must build ''upon the rock of our Redeemer, who is Christ'' (Helaman 5:12). The first and great commandment is to love Him and His Father. Jesus Christ is ''the Father of heaven and earth, the Creator of all things from the beginning'' (Mosiah 3:8).

''Wherefore,'' declared Jacob in the Book of Mormon, ''if God being able to speak and the world was, and to speak and man was created, O then, why not able to command the earth, or the workmanship of his hands upon the face of it, according to his will and pleasure?'' (Jacob 4:9.) God, the Creator, commands His creations even at this very moment. (''Joy in Christ,'' *Ensign* 16 [March 1986]: 3.)

A fundamental doctrine of true Christianity is the divine birth of the child Jesus. This doctrine is not generally comprehended by the world. The paternity of Jesus Christ is one of the ''mysteries of godliness'' comprehended only by the spiritually minded. (See 1 Timothy 3:16; D&C 19:10.)

The Apostle Matthew recorded: "Now the birth of Jesus Christ was on this wise: When as his mother Mary was espoused to Joseph, before they came together, she was found with child of the Holy Ghost" (Matthew 1:18).

Luke rendered a plainer meaning to the divine conception. He quoted the angel Gabriel's words to Mary: "The Holy Ghost shall come upon thee, and the power of the Highest shall overshadow thee: therefore also that holy [being] which shall be born of thee shall be called the Son of God" (Luke 1:35).

Some six hundred years before Jesus was born, an ancient prophet had a vision. He saw Mary and described her as "a virgin, most beautiful and fair above all other virgins." He then saw her "carried away in the Spirit . . . for the space of a time." When she returned, she was "bearing a child in her arms . . . even the Son of the Eternal Father." (1 Nephi 11:15, 19–21.)

Thus the testimonies of appointed witnesses leave no question as to the paternity of Jesus Christ. God was the Father of Jesus' mortal tabernacle, and Mary, a mortal woman, was His mother. He is therefore the only person born who rightfully deserved the title "the Only Begotten Son of God." (*Come unto Christ*, pp. 2–3.)

The Church of Jesus Christ of Latter-day Saints proclaims that Jesus Christ is the Son of God in the most literal sense. The body in which He performed His mission in the flesh was sired by that same Holy Being we worship as God, our Eternal Father. Jesus was not the son of Joseph, nor was He begotten by the Holy Ghost. He is the Son of the Eternal Father. (*Come unto Christ*, p. 4.)

He was the Only Begotten Son of our Heavenly Father in the flesh—the only child whose mortal body was begotten by our Heavenly Father. His mortal mother, Mary, was called a virgin, both before and after she gave birth. (See 1 Nephi 11:20.) ("Joy in Christ," *Ensign* 16 [March 1986]: 3–4.)

Jesus Christ is the Son of God. He came to this earth at a fore-appointed time through a royal birthright that preserved His godhood. Combined in His nature were the human attributes of His mortal mother and the divine attributes and power of His Eternal Father. As the Son of God, He inherited powers and intelligence that no human has ever had before or since. He was literally Immanuel, which means "God with us." (*Come unto Christ*, p. 128.)

Nearly two thousand years ago a perfect Man walked the earth —Jesus the Christ. He was the Son of a Heavenly Father and an earthly mother. He is the God of this world, under the Father. In His life, all the virtues were lived and kept in perfect balance; He taught men truth—that they might be free; His example and precepts provide the great standard—the only sure way—for all mankind. Among us He became the first and only one who had the power to reunite His body with His spirit after death. By His power all men who have died shall be resurrected. Before Him one day we all must stand to be judged by His laws. He lives today, and in the not too distant future shall return, in triumph, to subdue His enemies, to reward men according to their deeds, and to assume His rightful role to rule and reign in righteousness over the entire earth. (*An Enemy Hath Done This*, pp. 52–53.)

To qualify as the Redeemer of all our Father's children, Jesus had to be perfectly obedient to all the laws of God. Because He subjected Himself to the will of the Father, He grew from "grace to grace, until He received a fulness" of the Father's power. Thus He had "all power, both in heaven and on earth." (D&C 93:13, 17.)
Once this truth about the One we worship as the Son of God is understood, we can more readily comprehend how He had power to heal the sick, cure all manner of diseases, raise the dead, and command the elements. Even devils, whom He cast out, were subject to Him and acknowledged His divinity. (See Matthew 8:28–32.) (*Come unto Christ*, pp. 128–29.)

Even though He was God's Son sent to earth, the divine plan of the Father required that Jesus be subjected to all the difficulties and tribulations of mortality. Thus He became subject to "temptations, . . . hunger, thirst, and fatigue" (Mosiah 3:7). (*Come unto Christ*, p. 128.)

Today some unbelievers among us spread seeds of heresy, claiming that Jesus could not cast out evil spirits and did not walk on water nor heal the sick nor miraculously feed five thousand nor calm storms nor raise the dead. These would have us believe that such claims are fantastic and that there is a natural explanation for each alleged miracle. Some have gone so far as to publish psychological explanations for His reported miracles. But Jesus' entire ministry was a mark of His divinity. He spoke as God, He acted as God, and He performed works that only God Himself can do. His works bear testimony to His divinity. (*Come unto Christ*, p. 6.)

Because His Father was God, Jesus Christ had power that no other human had before or since. He was God in the flesh—even the Son of God. He therefore, as scripture records, had power to do many miracles: raise the dead, cause the lame to walk and the blind to receive their sight, and cast out evil spirits (see Mosiah 3:5-6).

He provided His gospel as a source of constant sustenance and nourishment to keep each individual's spirituality alive forever. His own testimony is: "Whosoever drinketh of the water that I shall give him shall never thirst; but the water that I shall give him shall be in him a well of water springing up into everlasting life" (John 4:14). (*Come unto Christ*, pp. 75-76.)

As the great Lawgiver, He gave laws and commandments for the benefit of all our Heavenly Father's children. Indeed, His law fulfilled all previous covenants with the house of Israel. Said He: "Behold, I am the law, and the light. Look unto me, and endure to the end, and ye shall live; for unto him that endureth to the end will I give eternal life." (3 Nephi 15:9.) (*Come unto Christ*, p. 129.)

Several years ago, a number of prominent theologians were asked the question, What do you think of Jesus? Their replies startled many professed Christians. One asserted that a "true Christian" must reject the Resurrection. Another admitted that New Testament scholars were so divided on the question that one cannot say anything certain about the historical Jesus. Another scholar and teacher of Jesuit priests explained, "It is difficult to say in our age what the divinity of Jesus can mean. We are groping now for a way to express it—we just don't know." ("Easter 1966 —A Quest for the True Jesus," *Newsweek*, April 11, 1966, p. 72.)

In a public opinion poll conducted by George Gallup, Jr., seven in ten adult American respondents said they believed in the divinity of Christ. But 90 percent of these said that Jesus is divine only in the sense that He embodies the best that is in all men (*Church News*, October 23, 1983). The Church of Jesus Christ of Latter-day Saints consents to no such ambiguity in relation to our position regarding the divinity of Jesus Christ. (*Come unto Christ*, p. 2.)

The question is sometimes asked, "Are Mormons Christians?" We declare the divinity of Jesus Christ. We look to Him as the only source of our salvation. We strive to live His teachings, and we look forward to the time that He shall come again on this earth to rule and reign as King of Kings and Lord of Lords. In the words of a Book of Mormon prophet, we say to men today, "There [is] no other name given nor any other way nor means whereby salvation can come unto the children of men, only in and through the name of Christ, the Lord Omnipotent" (Mosiah 3:17). ("A Promised Lord—A Promised Land—A Promised People," Wichita, Kansas, 11 November 1976.)

As witnesses of the Lord Jesus Christ we proclaim that He truly is the Savior of all. He whose birth the Christian world celebrates is indeed the Son of God, the Redeemer, the Promised Messiah. No message is more significant than the one He brought. No event is of greater importance than His atoning sacrifice and subsequent resurrection. And no mortal tongue can express sufficient thanks for all that Jesus has done for us. ("First Presidency—Christmas Message," *Church News* [15 December 1985]: 3.)

We need to know that Christ invites us to come unto Him. "Behold, he sendeth an invitation unto all men, for the arms of mercy are extended towards them, . . . Yea he saith: Come unto me and ye shall partake of the fruit of the tree of life." (Alma 5:33–34.)

Come, for he stands "with open arms to receive you" (Mormon 6:17).

Come, for "he will console you in your afflictions, and he will plead your cause" (Jacob 3:1).

"Come unto him, and offer your whole souls as an offering unto him" (Omni 1:26).

As Moroni closed the record of the Jaredite civilization, he wrote, "I would commend you to seek this Jesus of whom the prophets and apostles have written" (Ether 12:41).

In Moroni's closing words written toward the end of the Nephite civilization, he said, "Yea, come unto Christ, and be perfected in him, . . . and if ye shall deny yourselves of all ungodliness, and love God with all your might, mind and strength, then is his grace sufficient for you" (Moroni 10:32).

Those who are committed to Christ "stand as witnesses of God at all times and in all things, and in all places" that they may be in "even until death" (Mosiah 18:9). They "retain the name" of Christ "written always" in their hearts (Mosiah 5:12). They take upon themselves "the name of Christ, having a determination to serve him to the end" (Moroni 6:3).

When we live a Christ-centered life, "we talk of Christ, we rejoice in Christ, we preach of Christ" (2 Nephi 25:26). We "receive the pleasing word of God, and feast upon his love" (Jacob 3:2). Even when Nephi's soul was grieved because of his iniquities, he said, "I know in whom I have trusted. My God hath been my support." (2 Nephi 4:19–20.)

We remember Alma's counsel: "Let all thy doings be unto the Lord, and whithersoever thou goest let it be in the Lord; yea, let all thy thoughts be directed unto the Lord; yea, let the affections of thy heart be placed upon the Lord forever. Counsel with the Lord in all thy doings." (Alma 37:36–37.)

"Remember, remember," said Helaman, "that it is upon the rock of our Redeemer, who is Christ, . . . that ye must build your foundation; that when the devil shall send forth his mighty winds, . . . they shall have no power over you to drag you down to the gulf of misery" (Helaman 5:12).

Nephi said, the Lord "hath filled me with his love, even unto the consuming of my flesh" (2 Nephi 4:21). Those who are consumed in Christ "are made alive in Christ" (2 Nephi 25:25). They "suffer no manner of affliction, save it were swallowed up in the joy of Christ" (Alma 31:38). They are "clasped in the arms of Jesus" (Mormon 5:11). Nephi said, "I glory in my Jesus, for he hath redeemed my soul" (2 Nephi 33:6). Lehi said, "I am encircled about eternally in the arms of his love" (2 Nephi 1:15).

Now, my beloved brethren and sisters, let us read the Book of Mormon and be convinced that Jesus is the Christ. Let us continually reread the Book of Mormon so that we might more fully come to Christ, be committed to Him, centered in Him, and consumed in Him. (CR October 1987, *Ensign* 17 [November 1987]: 84–85.)

We should like to reaffirm to all the world that The Church of Jesus Christ of Latter-day Saints is led by our Lord and Savior, Jesus Christ. We believe in Christ. We accept and affirm His teachings as revealed truths from God. We know Him to be the literal Son of God. We love Him as our resurrected Lord and Savior. We believe there is "none other name under heaven given among men, whereby we must be saved" (see Acts 4:12).

We invite all men, as the Book of Mormon declares, to "come unto Christ, and be perfected in him, and deny yourselves of all ungodliness; . . . and love God with all your might, mind and strength" (Moroni 10:32). (Statement upon becoming President of the Church, 11 November 1985.)

Without Christ there would be no Christmas, and without Christ there can be no fulness of joy. ("Keeping Christ in Christmas," Christmas Devotional, Salt Lake City, Utah, 1 December 1985.)

The babe of Bethlehem became the Nazarene, the Man of Galilee, the Life and Light of the world, the Savior and Redeemer of mankind, the miracle of all time. More books have been written about Him, more buildings have been erected to His honor, more men have died with His name on their lips than any other person who ever lived. (*God, Family, Country*, p. 12.)

I bear witness to you that Jesus is the Christ, the Savior and Redeemer of the world—the very Son of God. He was born the babe of Bethlehem. He lived and ministered among men. He was crucified on Calvary. His friends deserted Him. His closest associates did not fully understand His mission, and they doubted. One of the most trusted denied knowing Him.

A pagan governor, struggling with his conscience after consenting to Jesus' death, caused a sign to be erected over the cross proclaiming Him "JESUS OF NAZARETH THE KING OF THE JEWS" (John 19:19). He asked forgiveness for His tormentors and then willingly gave up His life. His body was laid in a borrowed tomb. An immense stone was placed over the opening. In the minds of His stunned followers over and over echoed some of His last words, "Be of good cheer; I have overcome the world" (John 16:33).

On the third day there was a great earthquake. The stone was rolled back from the door of the tomb. Some of the women, among the most devoted of His followers, came to the place with spices "and found not the body of the Lord Jesus" (Luke 24:3). Angels appeared and said simply, "Why seek ye the living among the dead? He is not here, but is risen." (Luke 24:5–6.) There is nothing in history to equal that dramatic announcement: "He is not here, but is risen." (CR April 1964, *Improvement Era* 67 [June 1964]: 503–4.)

No other single influence has had so great an impact on this earth as the life of Jesus the Christ. We cannot conceive of our lives without His teachings. Without Him we would be lost in a mirage of beliefs and worships, born in fear and darkness where the sensual and materialistic hold sway. We are far short of the goal He set for us, but we must never lose sight of it; nor must we forget that our great climb toward the light, toward perfection, would not be possible except for His teachings, His life, His death, and His resurrection. (CR April 1971, *Ensign* 1 [June 1971]: 33.)

I testify that Christ is the light to all mankind. He has pointed, marked out, and lighted the way. Sadly, many individuals and nations have extinguished that light and have attempted to supplant His gospel with coercion and the sword. But even to those who reject Him, He is "the light which shineth in the darkness" (John 1:5). ("The Light of Christmas," Temple Square Christmas Lighting Ceremony, Salt Lake City, Utah, 26 November 1982.)

To be like the Savior—what a challenge for any person! He is a member of the Godhead. He is the Savior and Redeemer. He was perfect in every aspect of His life. There was no flaw or failing in Him. Is it possible for us as priesthood holders to be even as He is? The answer is yes. Not only can we, but that is our charge. (3 Nephi 27:27.) He would not give us that commandment if He did not mean for us to do it. (CR October 1986, *Ensign* 16 [4 October 1986]: 45.)

May we be convinced that Jesus is the Christ, choose to follow Him, be changed for Him, captained by Him, consumed in Him, and born again. (CR October 1985, *Ensign* 15 [November 1985]: 7.)

Atonement. The Lord testified, "I came into the world to do the will of my Father, because my Father sent me. And my Father sent me that I might be lifted up upon the cross." (3 Nephi 27:13– 14.) And so He was. In Gethsemane and on Calvary, He worked out the infinite and eternal atonement. It was the greatest single act of love in recorded history. Thus He became our Redeemer— redeeming all of us from physical death, and redeeming those of us from spiritual death who will obey the laws and ordinances of the gospel. ("Keeping Christ in Christmas," Christmas Devotional, Salt Lake City, Utah, 1 December 1985.)

On the night Jesus was betrayed, He took three of the Twelve and went into the place called Gethsemane. There He suffered the pains of all men. He suffered as only God could suffer, bearing our griefs, carrying our sorrows, being wounded for our transgressions, voluntarily submitting Himself to the iniquity of us all, just as Isaiah prophesied (see Isaiah 53:4–6).

It was in Gethsemane that Jesus took on Himself the sins of the world, in Gethsemane that His pain was equivalent to the cumulative burden of all men, in Gethsemane that He descended below all things so that all could repent and come to Him. The mortal mind fails to fathom, the tongue cannot express, the pen of man cannot describe the breadth, the depth, the height of the suffering of our Lord—nor His infinite love for us. (*Come unto Christ*, pp. 6–7.)

Because He was God—even the Son of God—He could carry the weight and burden of other men's sins on Himself. Isaiah prophesied our Savior's willingness to do this in these words: "Surely he has borne our griefs, and carried our sorrows. He was wounded for our transgressions, he was bruised for our iniquities: the chastisement of our peace was upon him; and with his stripes we are healed." (Isaiah 53:4–5.)

That holy, unselfish act of voluntarily taking on Himself the sins of all other men is called the Atonement. How one could bear the sins for all is beyond the comprehension of mortal man. But this I know: He did take on Himself the sins of all and did so out of His infinite love for each of us. He has said: "For behold, I,

God, have suffered these things for all, that they might not suffer if they would repent; . . . Which suffering caused myself, even God, the greatest of all, to tremble because of pain, and to bleed at every pore, and to suffer both body and spirit—and would that I might not drink the bitter cup, and shrink." (D&C 19:16, 18.)

In spite of that excruciating ordeal, He took the cup and drank. He suffered the pains of all men so we would not have to suffer. He endured the humiliation and insults of His persecutors without complaint or retaliation. He bore the flogging and then the ignominy of the brutal execution—the cross. ("Jesus Christ: Our Savior, Our God," San Diego, California, 21 December 1979.)

No mortal being had the power or capability to redeem all other mortals from their lost and fallen condition, nor could any other voluntarily forfeit His life and thereby bring to pass a universal resurrection for all other mortals. Only Jesus Christ was able and willing to accomplish such a redeeming act of love. (*Come unto Christ*, p. 130.)

As was so characteristic of His entire mortal experience, the Savior submitted to our Father's will and took the bitter cup and drank. He suffered the pains of all men in Gethsemane so they would not have to suffer if they would repent. Only then did He voluntarily submit to death. Again, He explained: "No man taketh [my life] from me, but I lay it down of myself. I have power to lay it down, and I have power to take it again. This commandment have I received of my Father." (John 10:18.) (*Come unto Christ*, p. 130.)

We may never understand nor comprehend in mortality how He accomplished what He did, but we must not fail to understand why He did what He did. All that He did was prompted by His unselfish, infinite love for us. (*Come unto Christ*, p. 130.)

Resurrection. The greatest events of history are those which affect the greatest number for the longest periods. By this standard, no event could be more important to individuals or nations than the resurrection of the Master. The eventual resurrection of every soul who has lived and died on earth is a scriptural certainty. And surely there is no event for which one should make more careful preparation.

Nothing is more absolutely universal than the Resurrection. Every living being will be resurrected. "As in Adam all die, even so in Christ shall all be made alive" (1 Corinthians 15:22). Yes, the resurrection of Jesus Christ is a glorious reality. He became the first fruits of them that slept. He truly rose from the tomb the third day, as He and His prophets foretold, and became, in very deed, "the resurrection and the life" (John 11:25). He broke the bonds of death for all of us. We, too, will be resurrected—our spirits will be reunited with our bodies. (*So Shall Ye Reap*, p. 4.)

If we live good lives on earth and keep the commandments of the Lord, life on the other side of the veil will be glorious. The Lord described it as paradise—a place where there is much joy and happiness instead of worries and heartaches. But as beautiful as the spirit world is for those who are righteous, life does not endlessly continue there. In time, our spirits must be joined again to our bodies to obtain complete joy. This is called the resurrection.

Three days after Jesus' body was laid in a tomb, He took His body up again. By doing so He overcame death for every other individual so that we, too, will live after this life. This is what He meant when He said that "because I live, ye shall live also" (John 14:19). ("He Is Risen," *Friend* 11 [April 1981]: 6.)

Christ's resurrection was abundantly verified. The witnesses are many. Throughout the forty days following His resurrection the Lord manifested Himself at intervals and gave instructions in the things pertaining to the kingdom of God. Much that He said and did is not written, but such things as are of record, John assures us, "are written, that ye might believe that Jesus is the Christ, the Son of God; and that believing ye might have life through his name" (John 20:31). (CR April 1964, *Improvement Era* 67 [June 1964]: 504.)

And when Christ and the disciples had gone "as far as to Bethany," where Mary, Martha, and Lazarus lived, the Lord lifted up His hands and blessed them. And while He yet spoke He rose from their midst until a cloud received Him out of their sight.

As the Apostles stood gazing steadfastly upward, two person-ages, clothed in white apparel, appeared by them; these spoke unto the eleven, saying: "Ye men of Galilee, why stand ye gazing up into heaven? This same Jesus, which is taken up from you into heaven, shall so come in like manner as ye have seen him go into heaven." (Acts 1:9–11; also Luke 24:50–51.)

Worshipfully and with great joy the Apostles returned to Jeru-salem. The Lord's ascension was accomplished. It was as truly a literal departure of a material being as His resurrection had been an actual return of His spirit to His own physical body. Now the disciples began to comprehend more fully that He had truly "over-come the world"—not that He had displaced Caesar, or even Pi-late who ruled over Judea (see John 16:33). The great majority of the world's peoples had still not even heard of Him. But there was victory over the grave. (*So Shall Ye Reap*, p. 5.)

The Book of Mormon records the resurrected Lord's appear-ance on the American continent. To those people He said, "Be-hold, I am Jesus Christ, whom the prophets testified shall come into the world. Arise and come forth unto me, that ye may thrust your hands into my side, and also that ye may feel the prints of the nails in my hands and in my feet, that ye may know that I am the God of Israel, and the God of the whole earth, and have been slain for the sins of the world." One by one, about twenty-five hundred people "thrust their hands into his side, and did feel the prints of the nails in his hands and in his feet." And they did "cry out with one accord, saying: Hosanna! Blessed be the name of the Most High God! And they did fall down at the feet of Jesus, and did worship Him." (3 Nephi 11:10–17.) ("Keeping Christ in Christ-mas," Christmas Devotional, Salt Lake City, Utah, 1 December 1985.)

Since the day of resurrection when Jesus became the "first-fruits of them that slept" (1 Corinthians 15:20), there have been those who disbelieve and scoff. They maintain there is no life be-yond mortal existence. Some have even written books that contain their fanciful heresies to suggest how Jesus' disciples perpetrated the hoax of His resurrection. I give you my testimony: The resur-rection of Jesus Christ is the greatest historical event in the world to date. He lives! He lives with a resurrected body. There is no truth or fact of which I am more assured than the truth of the literal resurrection of our Lord. (*Come unto Christ*, pp. 9–10.)

There has been considerable publicity and media coverage recently on the reporting of experiences that seemingly verify that "life after life" is a reality. The ancient prophet's question asked centuries ago has been revived: "If a man die, shall he live again" (Job 14:14)? In other words, what happens to a person once he dies? A definite answer to that question is provided by the Savior's ministry in the spirit world following His crucifixion, death, and burial (see D&C 138). (*Come unto Christ*, p. 117.)

This great thing that we refer to as the Resurrection has partly been accomplished. Part of those who have been in the graves arose at the time the Master broke the bonds of death. There are some who feel that the resurrection is going on continually and has been since that time. That is not scripturally true, but we do know that it is possible for our Father to call from the graves those whom He needs to perform special missions and special service. For example, we know of at least three who have been called up since the resurrection of the Master and since that first mass resurrection when the graves were opened and many of the Saints arose.

Peter and James who came and laid their hands upon the Prophet Joseph and ordained him to the Melchizedek Priesthood were resurrected beings who lived and ministered after the time that the Master was upon the earth. Moroni, who lived and died many years after the time of the resurrection of the Master, was a resurrected being. So we know that there are some that have been resurrected, and we know that certain promises are made that if the Lord needs the help of certain special messengers they may be called up. We are trying to live so that we will be worthy to come forth in the morning of this resurrection that will come preceding the great millennial period. The righteous will be caught up to meet the Savior as He comes in glory and makes His second appearance to rule and reign here in the earth when the millennial period will begin. (Washington D.C. Stake Conference, 8 March 1959.)

This power to revive His own life was possible because Jesus Christ was God—even the Son of God. Because He had the power to overcome death, all mankind will be resurrected. "Because I live, ye shall live also," He testified (John 14:19). (*Come unto Christ*, p. 130.)

Second Coming. This is the last and great dispensation in which the great consummation of God's purposes will be made, the only dispensation in which the Lord has promised that sin will not prevail. The Church will not be taken from the earth again. It is here to stay. The Lord has promised it and you are a part of that Church and kingdom—the nucleus around which will be builded the great kingdom of God on the earth. The kingdom of heaven and the kingdom of God on the earth will be combined together at Christ's coming—and that time is not far distant. How I wish we could get the vision of this work, the genius of it, and realize the nearness of that great event. I am sure it would have a sobering effect upon us if we realized what is before us. ("I'll Go Where You Want Me to Go," *Church News* [23 November 1946]: 8.)

I solemnly declare that the Lord has established His latter-day kingdom upon the earth in fulfillment of prophecies uttered by His ancient prophets and Apostles. Holy angels have again communed with men on the earth. God has again revealed Himself from heaven and restored to the earth His holy priesthood with power to administer in all the sacred ordinances necessary for the exaltation of His children. His Church has been reestablished among men with all the spiritual gifts enjoyed anciently. All this is done in preparation for Christ's second coming. The great and dreadful day of the Lord is near at hand. In preparation for this great event and as a means of escaping the impending judgments, inspired messengers have gone forth to the nations of the earth carrying this testimony and warning. (Stockholm Sweden Area Conference, 18 August 1974.)

This great time is drawing near. There is every evidence that His second coming is near at hand. I do not say that wars are over. I wish I could tell you that permanent peace is with us. I wish you would read that revelation given to Joseph Smith on Christmas day in 1832 regarding wars to come and in which the Civil War of my own country was predicted—in which it is recorded that war will continue to be poured out until nations will be no more (see D&C 87). Then the great theocracy, with Christ at the head, will be established. ("I'll Go Where You Want Me to Go," *Church News* [23 November 1946]: 8.)

Not many years hence Christ will come again. He will come in power and might as King of Kings and Lord of Lords. And ultimately "every knee shall bow and every tongue confess that Jesus is the Christ" (Romans 14:11; D&C 88:104; Mosiah 27:31). ("Joy in Christ," *Ensign* 16 [March 1986]: 5.)

All nations will see Him "in the clouds of heaven, clothed with power and great glory; with all the holy angels. . . . And the Lord shall utter his voice, and all the ends of the earth shall hear it; and the nations of the earth shall mourn, and they that have laughed shall see their folly. And calamity shall cover the mocker, and the scorner shall be consumed; and they that have watched for iniquity shall be hewn down and cast into the fire." (D&C 45:44, 49–50.)

When the Savior spoke of these signs and prophecies to His disciples in Jerusalem, they were apprehensive. He said to them, "Be not troubled, for, when all these things shall come to pass, ye may know that the promises which have been made unto you shall be fulfilled" (D&C 45:35). Do we realize we are living in the days of the fulfillment of these signs and wonders? We are among those who will see many of these prophecies fulfilled. Just as certain as was the destruction of the temple at Jerusalem and the scattering of the Jews, so shall these words of the Savior be certain to our generation. We know not the day nor the hour of His coming, but of this we may feel assured: We stand close to the great day of the Lord! (*Come unto Christ*, pp. 114–15.)

The Plan of Salvation

The scriptures teach that man was created in the image and likeness of his Creator (Genesis 1:26–27). Fundamental to the theology of The Church of Jesus Christ of Latter-day Saints is the belief that the purpose of man's whole existence is to grow into the likeness and image of God. We accept quite literally the Savior's mandate: "Be ye therefore perfect, even as your Father which is in heaven is perfect" (Matthew 5:48; see 3 Nephi 12:48). (*This Nation Shall Endure*, p. 100.)

As eternal beings, we each have in us a spark of divinity. (CR April 1971, *Ensign* 1 [June 1971]: 32.)

As God's offspring, we have His attributes in us. We are gods in embryo, and thus have an unlimited potential for progress and attainment. (Miami, Florida, 19 March 1976.)

This is our first interest as a Church—to save and exalt the souls of the children of men. There is no richer program anywhere in the world than we have in the Church today for the building of men and women and providing the answers to the problems that face parents, families, and individuals. (*God, Family, Country*, p. 43.)

To fulfill the purpose of His omniscient design, our Heavenly Father foreordained certain valiant spirit children and assigned them to come to earth at specific times and places to fulfill their appointments. The greatest of these spirits He reserved to come as prophets and priesthood leaders in His kingdom. "Every man," said the Prophet Joseph Smith, "who has a calling to minister to the inhabitants of the world was ordained to that very purpose in the Grand Council of Heaven before this world was" (*Teachings of the Prophet Joseph Smith*, p. 365).

Other good and valiant spirits were foreappointed to lay the foundation for man's liberty through their service in political matters. The Founding Fathers of this American nation were in this category. President Wilford Woodruff said, "They are the best spirits the God of Heaven could find on the face of the earth. They were choice spirits." They were held in reserve to collectively come in the time and at the place when one of history's greatest crises demanded their talents. ("The Crises of Our Constitution," Salt Lake Valley Utah Central Area Special Interest Lecture Series, 8 September 1977.)

The calling and testing of men for assignment of responsibility in the great work of salvation is, no doubt, going on on both sides of the veil. The calling of men to sacred office is not confined to earth life only. There is organization, direction, and assignment in preearth life and in postearth life also. (*God, Family, Country*, p. 30.)

Truth pertaining to man's relationship to Deity, the purpose of earth life, and our immortal destiny is of paramount importance to you as you face a doubting world. You will find such an anchor invaluable. You will not live to the fullest without its support. These glorious, unchanging, and ultimate truths pertain to our guidance here and eventually to our salvation and exaltation. Be not ashamed to believe and proclaim that God lives, that He is the Father of our spirits; that Jesus is the Christ, the Redeemer of the world; that the Resurrection is a reality; that we lived as spirits before mortal birth and will live again as immortal beings through the eternities to come. ("Concerning Principles and Standards," *Church News* [4 June 1947]: 5.)

I don't know that it is very important to our eternal exaltation as to just how far we are able to reach out into space. I don't know that our salvation is going to be dependent upon whether we can get a missile into orbit around the moon or the sun, but there are certain things that we do know are important to our salvation and exaltation. These things are not mysterious. They are not way out in space. They are close at hand, easy to understand. They are basic fundamental principles which never change. They pertain not only to our spiritual salvation and exaltation, they pertain to our living here. They pertain to government. Some of them are written as moral principles, spiritual principles. (Washington D.C. Stake Conference, 8 March 1959.)

We are in very deed living today a part of eternity. The great plan of salvation is operating, not only here in this world but also throughout the many worlds which our Heavenly Father has created, not only on this side of the veil but on the other side also. The Church is organized over there. The priesthood is functioning over there. The missionary work is going on over there. It makes very little difference whether we serve on one side of the veil or the other, so long as our service is actuated by a spirit of devotion, a spirit of loyalty, a spirit of love, and is in line with these eternal principles which our Heavenly Father has been kind enough to reveal unto us. (Washington D.C. Stake Conference, 8 March 1959.)

The Church of Jesus Christ of Latter-day Saints proclaims that life is eternal, that it has purpose. We believe we lived as intelligent beings in a world of progress before this mortal life. Our life on this earth is a probation, a testing period, an opportunity for growth and experience in a physical world. It is all part of the plan of our Heavenly Father for the benefit and blessing of us, His children. This is to be done through a great and all-wise plan—the gospel of Jesus Christ. This master plan, if lived, will build men of character, men of strength, men of deep spirituality, Godlike men. (CR October 1966, *Improvement Era* 69 [December 1966]: 1144.)

Premortal Life

It is a fundamental of our religion that we had a pre-earthly existence. That we are the literal offspring of God has been a cardinal teaching of the Lord's prophets in all ages. (Miami, Florida, 19 March 1976.)

We have sung the carol "Joy to the world, the Lord is come," as well we should (*Hymns*, 1985, no. 201). In our premortal state we shouted for joy as the plan of salvation was unfolded to our view (see Job 38:7). It was there our elder brother Jesus, the first-born in the spirit of our Father's children, volunteered to redeem us from our sins. He became our foreordained Savior, the Lamb "slain from the foundation of the world" (Moses 7:47). ("Keeping Christ in Christmas," Christmas Devotional, Salt Lake City, Utah, 1 December 1985.)

We understand that the purpose of the Council in Heaven was to announce and present the plan of redemption for the salvation of all of God's children. The council was called so that every man and woman could sustain the provisions of the Father's plan, which required that all people obtain mortal bodies, be tried and proven in all things, and have opportunity to choose of their own free will to obey the laws and ordinances essential to their exaltation.

Because a fallen condition was an essential part of this plan, an infinite, eternal sacrifice was also required to redeem us from this state. We are all familiar with the facts: how Lucifer—a personage of prominence—sought to amend the plan, while Jehovah sustained the plan. The central issue in that council, then, was: Shall the children of God have untrammeled agency to choose the course they should follow, whether good or evil, or shall they be coerced and forced to be obedient? Christ and all who followed Him stood for the former proposition—freedom of choice; Satan stood for the latter—coercion and force. Because Satan and those who stood with him would not accept the vote of the council, but rose up in rebellion, they were cast down to the earth, where they have continued to foster the same plan. The war that began in heaven is not yet over. The conflict continues on the battlefield of mortality. And one of Lucifer's primary strategies has been to restrict our agency through the power of earthly governments. Proof of this is found in the long history of humanity (see *Teachings of the Prophet Joseph Smith*, p. 357). (*The Constitution: A Heavenly Banner*, pp. 2–3.)

We once knew well our Elder Brother and our Father in Heaven. We rejoiced at the prospects of earth life that could make it possible for us to have a fulness of joy. We could hardly wait to demonstrate to our Father and our Brother, the Lord, how much we loved them and how we would be obedient to them in spite of the earthly opposition of the evil one. Now we are here. Our memories are veiled. We are showing God and ourselves what we can do. Nothing is going to startle us more when we pass through the veil to the other side than to realize how well we know our Father and how familiar His face is to us. ("Jesus Christ—Gifts and Expectations," Christmas Devotional, Salt Lake City, Utah, 7 December 1986.)

Mortal Probation

This earth on which we stand was created for man. Not only is it a residence to us while in this "second estate," but it provides us with the schooling, the experience, and the tests by which we may work out our salvation. (See Abraham 3:25–26.) Free agency has been given to all of us to make important decisions that will have bearing on our salvation. Those decisions affect our happiness in eternity. As President Spencer W. Kimball has said, "Man will suffer or enjoy his future according to his life's works in mortality." (Miami, Florida, 19 March 1976.)

Man is the crowning achievement of creation. All wholesome things, both seen and unseen, are provided for his development and blessing. These afford him opportunities for experience and growth. The individual is the key to family, community, and national greatness. (*The Red Carpet*, p. 259.)

Mortality was provided to man as a probationary period to test him. God decreed its purpose in these words: "We will prove them [mankind] herewith, to see if they will do all things whatsoever the Lord their God shall command them" (Abraham 3:25). (Miami, Florida, 19 March 1976.)

When our Heavenly Father placed Adam and Eve on this earth, He did so with the purpose in mind of teaching them how to regain His presence. Our Father promised a Savior to redeem them from their fallen condition. He gave them the plan of salvation and told them to teach their children faith in Jesus Christ and repentance. Further, Adam and his posterity were commanded by God to be baptized, to receive the Holy Ghost, and to enter into the order of the Son of God. (See Moses 6.) To enter into the order of the Son of God is the equivalent today of entering into the fulness of the Melchizedek Priesthood, which is only received in the house of the Lord. ("What I Hope You Will Teach Your Children About the Temple," *Ensign* 15 [August 1985]: 8.)

We are not at home here in mortality. We are spirit children of Heavenly Parentage and the righteous long for that homecoming to their Eternal Parents. This is why the revelations teach that holy men "confessed that they were strangers and pilgrims on the earth" (Hebrews 11:13; see D&C 45:13). (Asenath S. Conklin Funeral Service, Salt Lake City, Utah, 7 August 1982.)

You are now in the midst of your life's mission, earning today the blessings you will hereafter inherit. Now is your day of opportunity. You are striving for the greatest prize ever offered to any person in all the world. You are face to face with the supreme period of your existence. To fail is unthinkable. Then, know who you are. ("The Greatest Leadership," BYU Student Leadership Conference, Sun Valley, Idaho, September 1959.)

Our affections are often too highly placed upon the paltry perishable objects. Material treasures of earth are merely to provide
us, as it were, room and board while we are here at school. It is for
us to place gold, silver, houses, stocks, lands, cattle, and other
earthly possessions in their proper place. Yes, this is but a place of
temporary duration. We are here to learn the first lesson toward
exaltation—obedience to the Lord's gospel plan. (CR April 1971,
Ensign 1 [June 1971]: 33.)

God has had a hand in the history of mankind. His purpose is
to bring to pass the immortality of all of His children, and eternal
life to those of His children who willingly comply with His commandments. You will notice that I have made a distinction between the terms *immortality* and *eternal life*. Immortality is a free
gift to all men because of the resurrection of Jesus Christ. Eternal
life is the quality of life enjoyed by our Heavenly Father. Those
who fully comply with His commandments believe the promise
that they will have this quality of life. ("A Promised Lord—A
Promised Land—A Promised People," Wichita, Kansas, 11
November 1976.)

God bless all of us that we may follow the course laid out for us
by our Heavenly Father and our greatest example—the Lord,
Jesus Christ. May we do so regardless of what the world may say
or do, that we may hold fast to the iron rod, that we may be true to
the faith, that we may maintain the standards set for us and follow
this course to safety and exaltation (see 1 Nephi 8:19). The door is
open. The plan is here on earth. It is the Lord's plan. The authority and power are here. It is now up to you. ("Stand Firm in the
Faith," BYU Graduation Exercises, Provo, Utah, 17 August
1979.)

Our Heavenly Father expects the youth and all members of His
Church to become exalted in the celestial kingdom. We are not
striving for the lower kingdoms; we are not candidates for the telestial or terrestrial kingdoms. The young people of this Church
are candidates for the celestial kingdom and the highest glory in
that kingdom. That requires a great deal, a great deal that has to
do with our day-to-day standards. This means not just going to

Church, not just holding the priesthood, not just being happy, as measured by the world. It means living every standard of the Church fully. (Scandinavia and Finland Area Conference, 16–18 August 1974.)

Gospel Plan

Our Heavenly Father has given us a plan for our happiness. That plan is His gospel, and it is in His Church. God's authority and power are here. When you follow that plan, you will be happy, you will be successful, and you will be exalted in the celestial kingdom with all your worthy loved ones. (London England Area Conference, 19–20 June 1976.)

Life has a fourfold purpose. First of all, we come to this mortal life to receive a physical, mortal body. Without a physical body man is limited in his progression and only with a spirit and a body united together permanently can man receive a fulness of joy; so we are living today part of eternity. We accepted that plan in the spirit world before we came here, and we rejoiced at the opportunity of coming here.

Second, we came here to gain experience—experience with a physical, mortal world.

The third purpose of life is to give us an opportunity to prove ourselves (Abraham 3:25). To prove that even in the presence of evil and sin we can live a good life. To prove that in spite of temptation that we have the strength and the character to adhere to the principles of the gospel.

And fourth, this life is intended to provide an opportunity to help our Father in Heaven with His great plan, and we do that through honorable parenthood. We cooperate with our Heavenly Father in helping to prepare tabernacles to house spirits of His other children. So the matter of marriage, the home, and the family is a vital part of the plan of our Heavenly Father, and by keeping this fourfold purpose of life in mind constantly and carrying out these purposes faithfully we receive a fulness of joy here, insofar as it is possible to have a fulness of joy in mortal life, and we prepare ourselves for exaltation in the celestial kingdom where we will receive a fulness of joy. So the whole purpose of the Church is to help and assist us in carrying out these purposes in life. (Tokyo, Japan, 27 October 1957.)

I am deeply concerned about what we are doing to teach the Saints at all levels the gospel of Jesus Christ as completely and authoritatively as do the Book of Mormon and the Doctrine and Covenants. By this I mean teaching the "great plan of the Eternal God," to use the words of Amulek (Alma 34:9). Are we using the messages and the method of teaching found in the Book of Mormon and other scriptures of the Restoration to teach this great plan of the Eternal God?

There are many examples of teaching this great plan, but I will quote just one. It is Mormon's summary statement of Aaron's work as a missionary:

> And it came to pass that when Aaron saw that the king would believe his words, he began from the creation of Adam, reading the scriptures unto the king—how God created man after his own image, and that God gave him commandments, and that because of transgression, man had fallen.
>
> And Aaron did expound unto him the scriptures from the creation of Adam, laying the fall of man before him, and their carnal state and also the plan of redemption, which was prepared from the foundation of the world, through Christ, for all whosoever would believe on his name.
>
> And since man had fallen he could not merit anything of himself; but the sufferings and death of Christ atone for their sins, through faith and repentance. (Alma 22:12–14.)

The Book of Mormon Saints knew that the plan of redemption must start with the account of the fall of Adam. In the words of Moroni, "By Adam came the fall of man. And because of the fall of man came Jesus Christ . . . and because of Jesus Christ came the redemption of man." (Mormon 9:12.)

Just as a man does not really desire food until he is hungry, so he does not desire the salvation of Christ until he knows why he needs Christ. No one adequately and properly knows why he needs Christ until he understands and accepts the doctrine of the Fall and its effect upon all mankind. And no other book in the world explains this vital doctrine nearly as well as the Book of Mormon.

We all need to take a careful inventory of our performance and also the performance of those over whom we preside to be sure that we are teaching the "great plan of the Eternal God" to the Saints. Are we accepting and teaching what the revelations tell us about the Creation, Adam and the fall of man, and redemption from that fall through the atonement of Christ? Do we frequently review the crucial questions which Alma asks the members of the Church in the fifth chapter of Alma in the Book of Mormon? Do we understand and are we effective in teaching and preaching the Atonement? What personal meaning does the Lord's suffering in Gethsemane and on Calvary have for each of us? What does redemption from the Fall mean to us? In the words of Alma, do we "sing the song of redeeming love" (Alma 5:26)?

What should be the source for teaching the great plan of the Eternal God? The scriptures, of course—particularly the Book of Mormon. This should also include the other modern-day revelations. These should be coupled with the words of the Apostles and prophets and the promptings of the Spirit. Alma "commanded them that they should teach nothing save it were the things which he had taught, and which had been spoken by the mouth of the holy prophets" (Mosiah 18:19). The Doctrine and Covenants states: "Let them journey from thence preaching the word by the way, saying none other things than that which the prophets and apostles have written, and that which is taught them by the Comforter through the prayer of faith" (D&C 52:9).

Now, after we teach the great plan of the Eternal God, we must personally bear our testimonies of its truthfulness. Alma, after giving a great message to the Saints about being born again and the need for them to experience a "mighty change" in their hearts, sealed his teachings with his testimony in these words:

> And this is not all. Do ye not suppose that I know of these things myself? Behold, I testify unto you that I do know that these things whereof I have spoken are true. And how do ye suppose that I know of their surety?
>
> Behold, I say unto you they are made known unto me by the Holy Spirit of God. Behold, I have fasted and prayed many days that I might know these things of myself. And now I do know of myself that they are true; for the Lord God hath made them manifest unto me by his Holy Spirit; and this is the spirit of revelation which is in me. (Alma 5:45–46.)

(CR April 1987, *Ensign* 17 [May 1987]: 84–85.)

The gospel can be viewed from two perspectives. In the broadest sense, the gospel embraces all truth, all light, all revealed knowledge to mankind. In a more restrictive sense, the gospel means the doctrine of the Fall, the consequences of the fall of man that brought into the world physical and spiritual death, the atonement of Jesus Christ which brings to pass immortality and eternal life, and the ordinances of salvation.

When the Savior referred to His gospel, He meant the great plan of redemption by which immortality and eternal life come. He meant the laws, covenants, and ordinances that men must comply with to work out their salvation. He meant faith in the Lord Jesus Christ, repentance from all sin, baptism by immersion by a legal administrator for the remission of our sins, and the receipt of the gift of the Holy Ghost which may entitle one to the constant companionship of the Holy Ghost, and finally He meant that one should be valiant in his testimony of Jesus until the end of his days. This is the gospel Jesus preached, and this is the plan of redemption we are commissioned to preach. (Salt Lake City, Utah, 2 October 1985.)

Death

Another of the purposes of man's mortal probation is to pass through the experience we call death. This experience is necessary "to fulfill the merciful plan of the great Creator" (2 Nephi 9:6). In death, the body returns to the earth or the elements from which it was created, and the spirit goes into the world of spirits—there to wait the day of resurrection. (Miami, Florida, 19 March 1976.)

"Life is real! life is earnest!/And the grave is not its goal;/Dust thou art, to dust returnest,/Was not spoken of the soul." (Henry Longfellow, "A Psalm of Life.") We are eternal beings and I am so grateful for the rich blessings which are mine. God lives and He is not dead, He hears and answers prayers and He can be as close to us with His Spirit as we permit Him to be. (Grantsville Utah Stake Conference, 1 September 1974.)

There is always a great tendency for us to feel when we talk about people who have passed beyond, who have passed through the change called death, that they have gone some great distance away onto another planet or into another world. It is difficult for us to realize that the spirit world is close by, that it is all part of the operation here on this earth. President Brigham Young asked the question: "Where is this spirit world?" He answers his own question in these words: "It is right here. Do spirits go beyond the boundaries of the organized earth? No, they do not. They are brought forth upon this earth for the express purpose of inhabiting it through all eternity. When the spirits leave our bodies they are in the presence of our Father and God. They are prepared then to see, hear, and understand spiritual things. If the Lord would permit it, and it was His will that it should be done, you could see the spirits that have departed from this world as plainly as you now see bodies with your natural eyes." (See *Journal of Discourses*, 3:368–69.)

The Prophet Joseph taught that ofttimes those who go before, our loved ones particularly, are permitted to look down and view the activities of this world, to view the activities of their own loved ones and often are pained because of our misdeeds and our mistakes and our neglect. (Washington D.C. Stake Conference, 8 March 1959.)

Indisputably there is life after death. Mortality is a place of temporary duration—and so is the spirit world. As inevitable as death is to mortals, so also is an eventual resurrection to those in the spirit world. (Clare Middlemiss Funeral Service, Salt Lake City, Utah, 11 March 1983.)

I am sure many of you know that the veil can be very thin— that there are people over there who are pulling for us—people who have faith in us and who have great hopes for us, who are hoping and praying that we will measure up—our loved ones (parents, grandparents, brothers, sisters, and friends) who have passed on. (Salt Lake Utah Emigration Stake Conference, 2 February 1975.)

In recent years, several of our faithful brethren have passed to the other side of the veil. My sentiments were well expressed by

President Wilford Woodruff: "I have felt of late as if our brethren on the other side of the vail had held a council, and that they had said to this one, and that one, 'Cease thy work on earth, come hence, we need help,' and they have called this man and that man. It has appeared so to me in seeing the many men who have been called from our midst lately." (*Journal of Discourses*, 22:334.) Whether we work on this side of the veil or on the other side makes little difference. Before the Lord it is all one great program. ("Spencer W. Kimball: Star of the First Magnitude," *Ensign* 15 [December 1985]: 33.)

Jacob, a Book of Mormon prophet, declared: "Death hath passed upon all men, to fulfil the merciful plan of the great Creator" (2 Nephi 9:6). To the righteous, death is a door through which we must pass in order to obtain greater joy; for, as revealed by another Book of Mormon prophet, "the spirits of those who are righteous are received into a state of happiness, which is called paradise, a state of rest, a state of peace, where they shall rest from all their troubles and from all care, and sorrow" (Alma 40:12). (Ernest L. Wilkinson Funeral Service, Salt Lake City, Utah, 10 April 1978.)

Funerals truly are for the living, not the deceased. On these occasions we have mingled feelings of humility because we never know when death is going to overtake any of us, and sadness because we have been called upon to part with one whom we love deeply. The sadness brings tears to our eyes, but the Lord expected that. He said, "Thou shalt live together in love, insomuch that thou shalt weep for the loss of them that die" (D&C 42:45). And so it is fitting that we should have sadness in our hearts and should weep at the passing of one we love, and one whom the Lord loves and has magnified. (Elder O. Leslie Stone Funeral Service, Salt Lake City, Utah, 30 April 1986.)

Death is fundamental to our eternal progression. We are reminded by the Psalmist that "precious in the sight of the Lord is the death of his saints" (Psalm 116:15). Isaiah has also declared that the Savior will "swallow up death in victory; and the Lord God will wipe away tears from all faces" (Isaiah 25:8). (Asenath S. Conklin Funeral Service, Salt Lake City, 7 August 1982.)

The death of a righteous individual is both an honorable release and a call to new labors. (President Nathan Eldon Tanner Funeral Service, Salt Lake City, Utah, 30 November 1982.)

We should remember that on the other side there is a great family reunion and much rejoicing. This farewell and our separation is their reunion and homecoming. Appropriately we "weep for the loss of them that die," for the Lord has so commanded us (see D&C 42:45). But we also take great consolation through the Comforter that those who die in the Lord "shall not taste of death, for it shall be sweet unto them" (D&C 42:46). (Asenath S. Conklin Funeral Service, Salt Lake City, Utah, 7 August 1982.)

When a man's life is completed, it is not how much money he has made, how many of the honors of men he has attained, or personal attainments acquired that reveal the nobility of the man. It is rather, was he faithful to God, to his priesthood callings, to the Church? Did he love and serve his fellowman? And was he loyal to his family? (Ernest L. Wilkinson Funeral Service, Salt Lake City, Utah, 10 April 1978.)

Did the God of Heaven who created and intended marriage and family to be the source of man's greatest joy, his dearest possession while on this earth, intend that it end at death? Do marriage and families pertain only to this transitory state? Are all our sympathies, affections, and love for each other a thing of naught, to be cast off in death? We testify that Joseph Smith was a prophet raised up by God to restore many great truths which had been lost because of the absence of revelation. Through him God revealed the eternity of the marriage covenant and the timelessness of the family. ("America's Strength—The Family," Seattle, Washington, 23 November 1976.)

Those who die in the Lord do not taste of death. Rest assured that you will be together again. Such is the destiny of the faithful, over whom death has no power or victory. God bless and comfort you in your temporary separation. (Alvin R. Dyer Funeral Service, Salt Lake City, Utah, 9 March 1977.)

There is the ever-expectancy of death, but in reality there is no death—no permanent parting. The Resurrection is a reality. The scriptures are replete with evidence. Almost immediately after the glorious resurrection of the Lord, Matthew records: "And the graves were opened; and many bodies of the saints which slept arose, and came out of the graves after his resurrection, and went into the holy city, and appeared unto many." (Matthew 27:52–53.) The Apostle John on the Isle of Patmos "saw the dead, small and great, stand before God" (Revelation 20:12). (CR April 1971, *Ensign* 1 [June 1971]: 33.)

Life does not end with death. As our mortal life is a place of temporary duration, so is the spirit world. The time is not far distant when the righteous in the world of spirits will come forth in the glorious morning of the first resurrection, clothed with honor, glory, and priesthood power. (Ernest L. Wilkinson Funeral Service, Salt Lake City, Utah, 10 April 1978.)

Yes, life is eternal. We live on and on after earth-life, even though we ofttimes lose sight of that great basic truth. (CR April 1971, *Ensign* 1 [June 1971]: 33.)

The Veil Is Thin

When I was a freshman at Utah State, living in the home of my grandmother, Louise Ballif Benson, who spent most of her time working on genealogical research and temple work, I remember coming home from a party about midnight. As I entered the door, I could hear someone speaking in Grandmother's room and I wondered who could be there at that time of the night. As I got closer and heard her voice, I realized that she was praying, thanking the Lord that He had extended her life for a few years after her husband had gone on so she could complete the family temple work. She also prayed that she might see the last of her thirteen children married in the temple. This had now been accomplished and she would now like to go to her husband if it was pleasing to the Lord.

As I left for a mission a few months later and as I shook her hand, I had the distinct impression I would not see her again in mortal life. A few months later in England, I got an impression that Grandmother had passed away. I mentioned it to my companion. He said, "She has been ill, you are just worried about it." "No, she has not been sick," I replied. Ten days later I received a letter from Father saying that she had passed peacefully away. As near as I could tell, it was the same day on which I received that impression. Yes, the veil is very thin, brothers and sisters. ("Temple Memories," Ogden Utah Temple Dedication, 18 January 1972.)

Later in that same community I formed an acquaintance with another great temple worker, my mother-in-law, Barbara Smith Amussen. She had spent twenty-three years officiating at the Logan Temple. So thin is the veil that this good woman knew the time she was going to leave. She announced on Thursday or Friday that the following Thursday she would be leaving mortal life. She had had a dream or a vision of her husband telling her it was her time to go. It is my feeling that every good and righteous person has a specific time to go. I don't think it applies to everyone. ("Temple Memories," Ogden Utah Temple Dedication, 18 January 1972.)

Visitors, seen and unseen, from the world beyond, are often close to us. This is part of eternity which we are living today—part of God's plan. There is no veil to the Lord. ("Temple Blessings and Covenants," Temple Presidents Seminar, Salt Lake City, Utah, 28 September 1982.)

Sometimes actions here, by the priesthood of God, the First Presidency and the Twelve, as we meet in the temple, have been planned and influenced by leaders of the priesthood on the other side. I am sure of that. We have evidence of it. (Salt Lake Utah Emigration Stake Conference, 2 February 1975.)

On the other side of the veil, the righteous are taught their duties preparatory to the time when they will return with the Son of Man to earth when He comes again, this time to judge every man according to his works. These righteous spirits are close by us. They are organized according to priesthood order in family organizations as we are here; only there they exist in a more perfect order. This was revealed to the Prophet Joseph. (Ernest L. Wilkinson Funeral Service, Salt Lake City, Utah, 10 April 1978.)

One of the great responsibilities that we have is in connection with temple work—work for the living as well as the dead, because to our Father all of His children are living whether they are here in mortality or have passed on to the spirit world. All of them must receive the gospel or have the opportunity to receive it. This means, of course, that missionary work is going on on the other side of the veil. ("The Church," Paris, France, 7 August 1960.)

The work to be done on the other side of the veil is far more extensive than here. There, billions must hear the gospel preached. Joseph F. Smith, sixth President of the Church, received this revelation: "I beheld that the faithful elders of this dispensation, when they depart from mortal life, continue their labors in the preaching of the gospel of repentance and redemption, through the sacrifice of the Only Begotten Son of God, among those who are in darkness and under the bondage of sin in the great world of the spirits of the dead" (D&C 138:57). Bruce R. McConkie will continue his ministry there—only on a much more enlarged and expanded scale.

Amelia and family members, I pray the benediction of our Heavenly Father's Spirit on all of you that you may have the perfect peace and assurance that our Heavenly Father's will was done in the calling of your husband and father to the other side of the veil. His ministry will carry forward as he now joins with other prophets of this dispensation in furthering the work of the Lord which he loves so much. (Bruce R. McConkie Funeral Service, Salt Lake City, Utah, 23 April 1985.)

No men anywhere have a greater love for our Father's children than those who hold and honor the priesthood. We are all in it together—yes, on both sides of the veil, because I feel sure there is organization and wise delegation of authority over there, and most important decisions also. (*God, Family, Country*, p. 130.)

The glorious work of salvation and exaltation goes on over there with the knowledge and, at least to some extent, the direction of the work here on this side of the veil. And in this direction the Prophet Joseph Smith, head of the greatest and last gospel dispensation, occupies a sacred place. (*God, Family, Country*, p. 31.)

Postmortal Life

The great purpose of God throughout the history of mankind has been to bring His children to eternal life. It is a purpose motivated out of His infinite love which He has for all of us, His children. ("A Promised Lord—A Promised Land—A Promised People," Wichita, Kansas, 11 November 1976.)

Even though death may come to our loved ones and friends, we know that in the spirit world they are happy, removed from the sorrows and tears of mortal life. They now understand much more clearly the purpose of our Heavenly Father's plan and that they will live eternally. Someday we will know them again, for we all will come forth as Jesus did with perfected bodies. ("He Is Risen," *Friend* 11 [April 1981]: 7.)

Even before the fall of Adam, which ushered death into this world, our Heavenly Father had prepared a place for the spirits who would eventually depart this mortal life. At the time of Jesus' death, the spirit world was occupied by hosts of our Father's children who had died—from Adam's posterity to the death of Jesus —both the righteous and the wicked.

There were two grand divisions in the world of spirits. Spirits of the righteous (the just) had gone to paradise, a state of happiness, peace, and restful work. The spirits of the wicked (the unjust) had gone to prison, a state of darkness and misery. (See Alma 40:12–15.) Jesus went only to the righteous—to paradise. (*Come unto Christ*, pp. 117–18.)

Through the resurrection of our Lord and by revelations given to the Prophet Joseph Smith and other modern prophets, we know that life does not end at death when our bodies are buried in the earth. But our spirits, which give life to our bodies, continue to live in the spirit world, where we may associate again with family and friends. In the world of spirits the gospel is preached to millions of people who never had an opportunity to hear it while on the earth. The preaching of the gospel there is a more intense activity than it is here, and the ministers of the Lord number in the tens of thousands. ("He Is Risen," *Friend* 11 [April 1981]: 6.)

The Resurrection is a reality. Activity to help promote our Father's work is going forward among the disembodied spirits who have left this life. It will continue to go forward until every one of God's children has had an opportunity to receive the gospel, to hear it and to have it explained to them. And then at the end of that millennial period we will all stand judgment. There is a partial judgment before, but the final judgment will be at the end. Then this earth will undergo a change and receive its paradisiacal glory and will be made a fit abode for the celestial beings. Those who live to inherit the celestial kingdom will live on this earth eternally. This is made very clear in the scriptures. (Washington D.C. Stake Conference, 8 March 1959.)

I share with you a vision of your eternal possibilities. The celestial kingdom, residence of God, our Eternal Father, is comprised of men and women who have complied with divine law and who were not deceived by the craftiness of men or the doctrines of devils. They are just men made perfect through the mediation and atonement of Jesus Christ (see D&C 76:69). They are obedient to celestial law; for, as the Lord has said, he who is not able to abide the law of a celestial kingdom cannot abide a celestial glory (D&C 88:22). ("A Vision and a Hope for the Youth of Zion," in *1977 Devotional Speeches of the Year* [Provo, Utah: BYU, 1978], p. 73.)

Speaking of those who will eventually receive the blessings of the celestial kingdom, the Lord said to Joseph Smith: "They are they who received the testimony of Jesus, and believed on his name and were baptized after the manner of his burial, being buried in the water in his name, and this according to the commandment which he has given" (D&C 76:51).

These are they who are valiant in their testimony of Jesus, who, as the Lord has declared, "overcome by faith, and are sealed by the Holy Spirit of promise, which the Father sheds forth upon all those who are just and true" (D&C 76:53).

"Those who are just and true." What an apt expression for those valiant in the testimony of Jesus! They are courageous in defending truth and righteousness. These are members of the Church who magnify their callings in the Church (see D&C 84:33), pay their tithes and offerings, live morally clean lives, sustain their Church leaders by word and action, keep the Sabbath as a holy day, and obey all the commandments of God.

To these the Lord has promised that "all thrones and dominions, principalities and powers, shall be revealed and set forth upon all who have endured valiantly for the gospel of Jesus Christ" (D&C 121:29). ("Valiant in the Testimony of Jesus," *Ensign* 17 [February 1987]: 2.)

The Scriptures

We live in a world where the philosophies and practices of man surround us. The only way we can keep a spiritual outlook is to invest time to determine the Lord's mind and will for us.

Concerning the scriptures, Jesus Christ has said: "These words are not of men nor of man, but of me; wherefore, you shall testify they are of me and not of man; for it is my voice which speaketh them unto you; for they are given by my Spirit unto you, and by my power you can read them one to another; and save it were by my power you could not have them. Wherefore, you can testify that you have heard my voice and know my words." (D&C 18:34–36.) (*Come unto Christ*, pp. 35–36.)

Studying and searching the scriptures is not a burden laid upon Saints by the Lord, but a marvelous blessing and opportunity. Note what the Lord Himself has said about the benefits of studying His word. To the great prophet-leader Joshua, He said: "This book of the law shall not depart out of thy mouth; but thou shalt meditate therein day and night, that thou mayest observe to do according to all that is written therein; for then thou shalt make thy way prosperous, and then thou shalt have good success" (Joshua 1:8). The Lord was not promising Joshua material wealth and fame, but that his life would prosper in righteousness and that he would have success in that which matters most in life, namely the quest to find true joy (see 2 Nephi 2:25). ("The Power of the Word," CR April 1986, *Ensign* 16 [May 1986]: 81.)

The more we are familiar with the scriptures, the closer we become to the mind and will of the Lord. It will be easier for us to allow the truths of eternity to rest on our minds. (*Come unto Christ*, p. 20.)

Fortunately, today we are not left in darkness. We have a guide —not only the Holy Bible, but added modern scriptures. And of the utmost importance for us today, we have the counsel and direction of living oracles. This counsel, this direction—in fact, the message of the fulness of the restored gospel—is being carried to the world by ambassadors of the Lord Jesus Christ. (*Title of Liberty*, pp. 107–8.)

Many a man in his hour of trial has turned to the Book of Mormon and been enlightened, enlivened, and comforted. The psalms in the Old Testament have a special food for the soul of one in distress. In our day we are blessed with the Doctrine and Covenants, modern revelation. The words of the prophets, particularly the living President of the Church, are crucial reading and can give direction and comfort in an hour when one is down. (CR October 1974, *Ensign* 4 [November 1974]: 66.)

"I would commend you," urged Moroni, "to seek this Jesus of whom the prophets and apostles have written" (Ether 12:41). And God has provided the means—the holy scriptures, particularly the Book of Mormon—that all who seek may know that Jesus is the Christ. ("Joy in Christ," *Ensign* 16 [March 1986]: 4–5.)

The Book of Mormon and the Doctrine and Covenants are bound together as revelations from Israel's God to gather and prepare His people for the second coming of the Lord. The bringing forth of these sacred volumes of scripture "for the salvation of a ruined world" cost "the best blood of the nineteenth century"— that of Joseph Smith and his brother Hyrum (D&C 135:6).

Each divine witness contains a great proclamation to all the world—the title page of the Book of Mormon and section 1, the

Lord's preface to the Doctrine and Covenants. "This generation," said the Lord to Joseph Smith, "shall have my word through you" (D&C 5:10). And so it has through the Book of Mormon, the Doctrine and Covenants, and other modern revelations.

The Book of Mormon and Doctrine and Covenants testify of each other. You cannot believe one and not the other. The Book of Mormon testifies of modern books of scripture. It refers to them as "other books" and "last records" which "establish the truth" of the Bible and make known the "plain and precious things which have been taken away" from the Bible (1 Nephi 13:39–40).

Excluding the witnesses to the Book of Mormon, the Doctrine and Covenants is by far the greatest external witness and evidence which we have from the Lord that the Book of Mormon is true. At least thirteen sections in the Doctrine and Covenants give us confirming knowledge and divine witness that the Book of Mormon is the word of God (see D&C 1; 3; 5; 8; 10; 11; 17; 18; 20; 27; 42; 84; 135).

The Doctrine and Covenants is the binding link between the Book of Mormon and the continuing work of the Restoration through the Prophet Joseph Smith and his successors. In the Doctrine and Covenants we learn of temple work, eternal families, the degrees of glory, Church organization, and many other great truths of the Restoration. "Search these commandments," said the Lord of the Doctrine and Covenants, "for they are true and faithful, and the prophecies and promises which are in them shall all be fulfilled. What I the Lord have spoken, I have spoken, and I excuse not myself; and though the heavens and the earth pass away, my word shall not pass away, but shall all be fulfilled, whether by mine own voice or by the voice of my servants, it is the same." (D&C 1:37–38.) The Book of Mormon brings men to Christ. The Doctrine and Covenants brings men to Christ's kingdom, even The Church of Jesus Christ of Latter-day Saints, "the only true and living church upon the face of the whole earth" (verse 30). I know that.

The Book of Mormon is the "keystone" of our religion, and the Doctrine and Covenants is the capstone, with continuing latter-day revelation. The Lord has placed His stamp of approval on both the keystone and the capstone. (CR April 1987, *Ensign* 17 [May 1987]: 83.)

Virtually every page of both the Doctrine and Covenants and the Book of Mormon teaches about the Master—His great love for His children and His atoning sacrifice—and teaches us how to live so that we can return to Him and our Heavenly Father.

Each of these two great latter-day books of scripture contains the knowledge and the power to help us live better lives in a time of great wickedness and evil. Anyone who carefully and prayerfully searches the pages of these books will find comfort, counsel, guidance, and the quiet power to improve their lives. (CR October 1986, *Ensign* 16 [November 1986]: 79.)

We must diligently study the scriptures. The Book of Mormon, Brigham Young said, was written on the tablets of his heart and no doubt helped save him from being deceived. The Book of Mormon has a lot to say about America, freedom, and secret combinations.

The Doctrine and Covenants is important because it contains the revelations which helped lay the foundation of this great latter-day work. It speaks of many things. Government should hold inviolate the right and control of property (see D&C 134:2). This makes important reading in a day when government controls are increasing and people are losing the right to control their own property. (*God, Family, Country*, pp. 338–39.)

Do we, as Saints of the Most High God, treasure the word He has preserved for us at so great a cost? Are we using these books of latter-day revelation to bless our lives and resist the powers of the evil one? This is the purpose for which they were given. How can we not stand condemned before the Lord if we treat them lightly by letting them do no more than gather dust on our shelves? (See D&C 84:54.) I bear my solemn witness that the Book of Mormon and Doctrine and Covenants contain the mind and the will of the Lord for us in these days of trial and tribulation. They stand with the Bible to give witness of the Lord and His work. These books contain the voice of the Lord to us in these latter days. May we turn to them with full purpose of heart and use them in the way the Lord wishes them to be used. (CR October 1986, *Ensign* 16 [November 1986]: 80.)

God bless us all to use all the scriptures, but in particular the instrument He designed to bring us to Christ—the Book of Mormon, the keystone of our religion—along with its companion volume, the capstone, the Doctrine and Covenants, the instrument to bring us to Christ's kingdom, The Church of Jesus Christ of Latter-day Saints. (CR April 1987, *Ensign* 17 [May 1987]: 85.)

Children, support your parents in their efforts to have daily family scripture study. Pray for them as they pray for you. The adversary does not want scripture study to take place in our homes, and so he will create problems if he can. But we must persist. Perhaps each family member can take a turn reading a verse at a time. Comments could follow. Maybe you can study by subject. Perhaps assignments might be made. (CR April 1986, *Ensign* 16 [May 1986]: 78.)

We should make daily study of the scriptures a lifetime pursuit. (CR October 1986, *Ensign* 16 [November 1986]: 47.)

Elder LeGrand Richards will ever be remembered among his colleagues as one of the purest souls—never any pretense or guile. His only aim was the promotion of truth. How we appreciated his frankness, unpretentiousness, total and energetic dedication, and sparkling humor. He truly loved and understood the scriptures. He had memorized scores of passages. We today can take a lesson from the pages of his life and study the scriptures and commit passages to memory that will uplift, inspire, and give reason for our faith. (Elder LeGrand Richards Funeral Service, Salt Lake City, Utah, 14 January 1983.)

More than at any time in our history we have need for greater spirituality. The way to develop greater spirituality is to feast on the words of Christ as revealed in the scriptures. One of the most significant happenings in recent Church history is the publication of the new editions of the standard works with the new footnotes and other helps. I think we can say without exaggeration that never before in any dispensation have the Saints been so abundantly blessed with the words of the Lord and His prophets. Now our challenge is to do as the Lord commanded: "Study my word which hath gone forth among the children of men" (D&C 11:22). (CR April 1984, *Ensign* 14 [May 1984]: 7.)

Bend your efforts and your activities to stimulating meaningful scripture study among the members of the Church. Often we spend great effort in trying to increase the activity levels in our stakes. We work diligently to raise the percentages of those attending sacrament meetings. We labor to get a higher percentage of our young men on missions. We strive to improve the numbers of those marrying in the temple. All of these are commendable efforts and important to the growth of the kingdom. But when individual members and families immerse themselves in the scriptures regularly and consistently, these other areas of activity will automatically come. Testimonies will increase. Commitment will be strengthened. Families will be fortified. Personal revelation will flow. ("The Power of the Word," CR April 1986, *Ensign* 16 [May 1986]: 81.)

I now add my voice to these wise and inspired brethren and say to you that one of the most important things you can do as priesthood leaders is to immerse yourselves in the scriptures. Search them diligently (see D&C 1:37; 3 Nephi 23:1). Feast upon the words of Christ (see 2 Nephi 31:20; 32:3). Learn the doctrine. Master the principles that are found therein. There are few other efforts that will bring greater dividends to your calling. There are few ways to gain greater inspiration as you serve. ("The Power of the Word," CR April 1986, *Ensign* 16 [May 1986]: 81.)

The word of God, as found in the scriptures, in the words of living prophets, and in personal revelation, has the power to fortify the Saints and arm them with the Spirit so they can resist evil, hold fast to the good and find joy in this life. ("The Power of the Word," CR April 1986, *Ensign* 16 [May 1986]: 80.)

Let us not treat lightly the great things we have received from the hand of the Lord. His word is one of the most valuable gifts He has given us. I urge you to recommit yourselves to a study of the scriptures. Immerse yourselves in them daily so you will have the power of the Spirit to attend you in your calling. Read them in your families and teach your children to love and treasure them. Then prayerfully and in counsel with others, seek every way possible to encourage the members of the Church to follow your example. ("The Power of the Word," CR April 1986, *Ensign* 16 [May 1986]: 82.)

Bible

I love the Bible, both the Old and the New Testaments. It is a source of great truth. It teaches us about the life and ministry of the Master. From its pages we learn of the hand of God in directing the affairs of His people from the very beginning of the earth's history. It would be difficult to overestimate the impact the Bible has had on the history of the world. Its pages have blessed the lives of generations.

But as generation followed generation, no additional scripture came forth to the children of men. Without additional revelation to guide them, men began to interpret the Bible differently. Numerous churches and creeds developed, each using the Bible as their authoritative source.

But this in no way lessens the worth of the Bible. That sacred and holy book has been of inestimable worth to the children of men. In fact, it was a passage from the Bible that inspired the Prophet Joseph Smith to go to a grove of trees near his home and kneel in prayer (see James 1:5). What followed was the glorious vision which commenced the restoration of the fulness of the gospel of Jesus Christ to the earth. That vision also began the process of bringing forth new scripture to stand shoulder to shoulder with the Bible in bearing witness to a wicked world that Jesus is the Christ and that God lives and loves His children and is still intimately involved in their salvation and exaltation. (CR October 1986, *Ensign* 16 [November 1986]: 78.)

The Founding Fathers knew that "where the spirit of the Lord is, there is liberty" (2 Corinthians 3:17). The United States of America began and lives as a result of faith in God. The Bible has been and is the foundation for this faith. "It is impossible to govern the world without the Bible," said George Washington. The fathers of our country had to turn to religion in order that their new experiment make sense. (*Title of Liberty*, p. 105.)

Doctrine and Covenants

The Doctrine and Covenants is a glorious book of scripture given directly to our generation. It contains the will of the Lord for us in these last days that precede the second coming of Christ. It contains many truths and doctrines not fully revealed in other scripture. Like the Book of Mormon, it will strengthen those who carefully and prayerfully study from its pages. (CR October 1986, *Ensign* 16 [November 1986]: 80.)

When the elders of the Church were assembled in conference to determine whether the revelations should be published to the world, the Lord gave a revelation to the Church which He referred to as His "preface" to His book of revelations. This revelation, section 1 of the Doctrine and Covenants, prepares the reader, as a preface to a book should, with an explanation of the purpose of the Author in giving the revelations contained in it. The Author of the Doctrine and Covenants is the Lord Jesus Christ, through the instrumentality of the Prophet Joseph Smith. The Doctrine and Covenants is unique among the standard works of the Church not only in its authorship, but it is a modern book of scripture. ("A Voice of Warning," Hiram Ohio Branch Chapel Groundbreaking Service, 22 March 1986.)

The Doctrine and Covenants is true, for its author is Jesus Christ and His message is for all men. ("A Voice of Warning," Hiram Ohio Branch Chapel Groundbreaking Service, 22 March 1986.)

Book of Mormon

History. On the evening of 21 September 1823, an angel appeared to the Prophet Joseph Smith. The angel's name was Moroni. He was the last of a long line of ancient prophets of two great civilizations who lived here on the American continent centuries ago. The angel told Joseph Smith that a history of these early inhabitants of America was written on metallic plates and lay buried in a hill nearby. (See Joseph Smith—History 1:29–35.)

These records covered a period of American history from the time of the Tower of Babel until about A.D. 421. Part of these cumulative records engraved and handed down from generation to generation were abridged by Moroni's father, Mormon. Moroni added some additional writings and then laid the records in the earth where they remained until he delivered them to Joseph Smith. Under the inspiration of God, Joseph Smith translated part of these records and this is known today as the Book of Mormon. Besides Joseph Smith there were other witnesses who saw the angel and the plates and whose written testimony you will find printed in the front of each copy of the Book of Mormon. As the Bible is a scriptural account of God's dealings with His children in the Old World, so also is the Book of Mormon a scriptural account of God's dealings with His children in the Americas. (*An Enemy Hath Done This*, p. 329.)

I hold in my hand one of the sacred volumes of scripture which we as Latter-day Saints love—the Book of Mormon. It is a companion volume to the Bible. It is the sacred record, an inspired record, of the people who lived on this hemisphere between the period roughly six hundred years before Christ and four hundred years after Christ—a thousand-year history. It substantiates the Bible. It is an added witness to the divine mission of the Christ who appeared on this hemisphere as a resurrected being. It tells of the wars and the contention and the strife, the wickedness and the righteousness of the people who lived here, of which the American Indians are but a remnant. I commend it to you, my brothers and sisters and friends, as a new witness for Christ. I commend it to you as a new volume of scripture, written and translated under the inspiration of heaven by a young prophet of God who knew nothing in the field of languages or history. A farm boy who under the inspiration of heaven translated this sacred record so that we have it today as an added witness to the divine mission of the Master, and an added witness to the divinity of the Holy Bible. (Short Hills, New Jersey, 15 January 1961.)

The ancient preparation of the Book of Mormon, its preservation, and its publication verify Nephi's words that "the Lord knoweth all things from the beginning; wherefore, he prepareth a way to accomplish all his works among the children of men; for behold, he hath all power unto the fulfilling of all his words" (1 Nephi 9:6). We are not required to prove that the Book of Mormon is true or is an authentic record through external evidences—though there are many. It never has been the case, nor is it so now, that the studies of the learned will prove the Book of Mormon true or false. The origin, preparation, translation, and verification of the truth of the Book of Mormon have all been retained in the hands of the Lord, and the Lord makes no mistakes. You can be assured of that.

God has built in His own proof system of the Book of Mormon as found in Moroni, chapter 10, and in the testimonies of the Three and the Eight Witnesses and in various sections of the Doctrine and Covenants. We each need to get our own testimony of the Book of Mormon through the Holy Ghost. Then our testimony, coupled with the Book of Mormon, should be shared with others so that they, too, can know through the Holy Ghost of its truthfulness.

Nephi testifies that the Book of Mormon contains the "words of Christ" and that if people "believe in Christ" they will believe in the Book of Mormon (2 Nephi 33:10). It is important in our teaching we make use of the language of holy writ. Alma said, "I . . . do command you in the language of him who hath commanded me" (Alma 5:61). The words and the way they are used in the Book of Mormon by the Lord should become our source of understanding and should be used by us in teaching gospel principles.

God uses the power of the word of the Book of Mormon as an instrument to change people's lives: "As the preaching of the word had a great tendency to lead the people to do that which was just—yea, it had had more powerful effect upon the minds of the people than the sword, or anything else, which had happened unto them—therefore Alma thought it was expedient that they should try the virtue of the word of God" (Alma 31:5).

Alma reminded his brethren of the Church how God delivered their fathers' souls from hell: "Behold, he changed their hearts; yea, he awakened them out of a deep sleep, and they awoke unto God. Behold, they were in the midst of darkness; nevertheless, their souls were illuminated by the light of the everlasting word."

(Alma 5:7.) We need to use the everlasting word to awaken those in deep sleep so they will awake "unto God." (CR April 1987, *Ensign* 17 [May 1987]: 83–84.)

A powerful testimony to the importance of the Book of Mormon is to note where the Lord placed its coming forth in the timetable of the unfolding Restoration. The only thing that preceded it was the First Vision. In that marvelous manifestation, the Prophet Joseph Smith learned the true nature of God and that God had a work for him to do. The coming forth of the Book of Mormon was the next thing to follow. Think of that in terms of what it implies. The coming forth of the Book of Mormon preceded the restoration of the priesthood. It was published just a few days before the Church was organized. The Saints were given the Book of Mormon to read before they were given the revelations outlining such great doctrines as the three degrees of glory, celestial marriage, or work for the dead. It came before priesthood quorums and Church organization. Doesn't this tell us something about how the Lord views this sacred work? (CR October 1986, *Ensign* 16 [November 1986]: 4.)

The first and most central theme of the Book of Mormon is that Jesus is the promised Messiah, our Lord and Redeemer. He came to redeem mankind from a lost and fallen condition brought about by Adam's transgression. Nearly all Christian churches accepted this truth as a fundamental to their faith when the Book of Mormon was published to the world in 1830. The fact that another book had come forth as a second witness to Christ's divinity was regarded by many churches as being both superfluous and spurious. They said, "We already have a Bible, why do we need another?" (2 Nephi 29:3.)

But the nineteenth century was not the twentieth. Who but God and inspired prophets could have foreseen the need for an additional witness for the divinity of His Son. Who but God and inspired prophets could have foreseen the time when self-evident truths in the Bible were made obscure by virtue of modern translations—translations made by scholars who seriously challenged the divinity of Jesus Christ as the Son of God. Who but God and inspired prophets could have foreseen the day when ministers of prominent denominations would openly challenge the divinity of Jesus Christ. ("A Promised Lord—A Promised Land—A Promised People," Wichita, Kansas, 11 November 1976.)

Upon hearing the story of golden plates delivered by an angel, some people today ask: "Where are the plates now?" They seem to think if they could see the plates, it would make the testimony of the witnesses more credible. But this is not the way the Lord works. He operates through a law called the law of witnesses. This law provides that in the mouth of two or three witnesses shall the truth of His word be established in all ages (see D&C 6:28; 2 Nephi 27:12–14). ("Martin Harris—A Special Witness," Martin Harris Memorial Amphitheater Dedication, Clarkston, Utah, 6 August 1983.)

The Lord says that He gave Joseph Smith "power from on high . . . to translate the Book of Mormon; Which contains . . . the fulness of the gospel of Jesus Christ . . . Which was given by inspiration" (D&C 20:8–10). Nephi, one of the prophet-writers of the Book of Mormon, testifies that the book contains "the words of Christ" (2 Nephi 33:10), and Moroni, the last writer in the book, testifies that "these things are true" (Moroni 7:35). This same Moroni, as an angelic being sent from God, showed these ancient records to three witnesses in our day. Their testimony of the records is contained in the front of the Book of Mormon. They state: "We also know that they have been translated by the gift and power of God for his voice hath declared it unto us; wherefore we know of a surety that the work is true." ("The Book of Mormon Is the Word of God," Regional Representatives Seminar, Salt Lake City, Utah, 4 April 1986.)

Ancient American prophets, six hundred years before Christ, foresaw the coming of Columbus and those who followed. These prophets saw the establishment of the colonies, the War for Independence, and predicted the outcome. These prophecies are contained in a volume of scripture called the Book of Mormon. This sacred record, a companion to the Holy Bible which it confirms, is an added witness to the divine mission of Jesus as the Son of God and Redeemer of the world. How I wish every American and every living soul would read the Book of Mormon. I testify to you that it is true. It tells about the prophetic history and mission of America. (*Title of Liberty*, p. 87.)

As I participated in the Mexico City Temple dedication, I received the distinct impression that God is not pleased with our neglect of the Book of Mormon. The object of studying the Book of Mormon is to learn from the experiences of those who have gone before us that blessings come by keeping the commandments of God and that tragedy is the result of disobedience. By learning from the lessons of the past, mistakes need not be repeated in our own lives. You will gain a firm and unshakable testimony of Jesus Christ and the absolute knowledge that the origin of the Book of Mormon, as described by Joseph Smith, is true. Reading and pondering the Book of Mormon and other scriptures brings spiritual-mindedness. The Lord has instructed: "Let the solemnities of eternity rest upon your mind" (D&C 43:34), and "treasure up in your minds continually the words of life" (D&C 84:85). ("Lord, Increase Our Faith," Provo Utah Tabernacle Rededication, 21 September 1986.)

In our day, the Lord has revealed the need to reemphasize the Book of Mormon to get the Church and all the children of Zion out from under condemnation—the scourge and judgment (see D&C 84:54–58). This message must be carried to the members of the Church throughout the world. (CR April 1986, *Ensign* 16 [May 1986]: 78.)

Keystone and Additional Testament. I would like to speak about one of the most significant gifts given to the world in modern times. The gift I am thinking of is more important than any of the inventions that have come out of the industrial and technological revolutions. This is a gift of greater value to mankind than even the many wonderful advances we have seen in modern medicine. It is of greater worth to mankind than the development of flight or space travel. I speak of the gift of the Book of Mormon.

This gift was prepared by the hand of the Lord over a period of more than a thousand years, then hidden up by Him so that it would be preserved in its purity for our generation. Perhaps there is nothing that testifies more clearly of the importance of this mod-

ern book of scripture than what the Lord Himself has said about
it.

By His own mouth He has borne witness that it is true (D&C
17:6); that it contains the truth and His words (D&C 19:26); that it
was translated by power from on high (D&C 20:8); that it contains
the fulness of the gospel of Jesus Christ (D&C 20:9; 42:12); that it
was given by inspiration and confirmed by the ministering of angels (D&C 20:10); that it gives evidence that the holy scriptures are
true (D&C 20:11); and that those who receive it in faith shall receive eternal life (D&C 20:14). (CR October 1986, *Ensign* 16 [No-
vember 1986]: 4.)

Once we realize how the Lord feels about this book it should
not surprise us that He also gives us solemn warnings about how
we receive it. After indicating that those who receive the Book of
Mormon with faith, working righteousness, will receive a crown of
eternal glory (see D&C 20:14), the Lord follows with this warning:
"But those who harden their hearts in unbelief, and reject it, it
shall turn to their own condemnation" (D&C 20:15).

In 1829, the Lord warned the Saints that they are not to "trifle
with sacred things" (D&C 6:12). Surely the Book of Mormon is a
sacred thing, and yet many trifle with it, or in other words, take it
lightly, treat it as though it is of little importance. In 1832, as some
early missionaries returned from their fields of labor, the Lord re-
proved them for treating the Book of Mormon lightly. As a result
of that attitude, He said their minds had been darkened. Not only
had treating this sacred book lightly brought a loss of light to
themselves, it had also brought the whole Church under condemnation, even all the children of Zion. And then the Lord said,
"And they shall remain under this condemnation until they repent
and remember the new covenant, even the Book of Mormon"
(D&C 84:54–57).

Has the fact that we have had the Book of Mormon with us for
over a century and a half made it seem less significant to us today?
Do we remember the new covenant, even the Book of Mormon? In
the Bible we have the Old Testament and the New Testament. The
word *testament* is the English rendering of a Greek word that can
also be translated as "covenant" (see *Unger's Bible Dictionary*,
s.v. *testament*). Is this what the Lord meant when He called the
Book of Mormon the "new covenant"? It is indeed another testa-

ment or witness of Jesus. This is one of the reasons why we have recently added the words "Another Testament of Jesus Christ" to the title of the Book of Mormon. (CR October 1986, *Ensign* 16 [November 1986]: 4.)

The Book of Mormon is the keystone of our religion. This was the Prophet Joseph Smith's statement. He testified that "the Book of Mormon was the most correct of any book on the earth, and the keystone of our religion" (Book of Mormon Introduction). A keystone is the central stone in an arch. It holds all the other stones in place, and if it is removed the arch crumbles.

There are three ways in which the Book of Mormon is the keystone of our religion. It is the keystone in our witness of Christ. It is the keystone of our doctrine. It is the keystone of testimony.

The Book of Mormon is the keystone in our witness of Jesus Christ, who is Himself the cornerstone of everything we do. It bears witness of His reality with power and clarity. Unlike the Bible, which passed through generations of copyists, translators and corrupt religionists who tampered with the text, the Book of Mormon came from writer to reader in just one inspired step of translation. Therefore its testimony of the Master is clear, undiluted, and full of power.

But it does even more. Much of the Christian world today rejects the divinity of the Savior. They question His miraculous birth, His perfect life, and the reality of His glorious resurrection. The Book of Mormon teaches in plain and unmistakable terms about the truth of all of those. It also provides the most complete explanation of the doctrine of the Atonement. Truly this divinely inspired book is a keystone in bearing witness to the world that Jesus is the Christ (see Book of Mormon Title Page).

The Book of Mormon is also the keystone of the doctrine of the Resurrection. As mentioned before, the Lord Himself has stated that the Book of Mormon contains the "fulness of the gospel of Jesus Christ" (D&C 20:9). That does not mean it contains every teaching, every doctrine ever revealed. Rather, it means that in the Book of Mormon we will find the fulness of those doctrines required for our salvation. And they are taught plainly and simply so that even children can learn the ways of salvation and exaltation. The Book of Mormon offers so much that broadens our understandings of the doctrines of salvation. Without it, much of what is taught in other scriptures would not be nearly so plain and precious. (CR October 1986, *Ensign* 16 [November 1986]: 5–6.)

A reason why the Book of Mormon is of such value to Latter-day Saints is given in the statement by the Prophet Joseph Smith. He said, "I told the brethren that the Book of Mormon was the most correct of any book on earth, and the keystone of our religion, and a man would get nearer to God by abiding by its precepts, than by any other book." (Book of Mormon Introduction.) It helps us draw nearer to God. Is there not something deep in our hearts that longs to draw nearer to God? If so, the Book of Mormon will help us do so more than any other book. It is not just that the Book of Mormon teaches us truth, though it indeed does that. It is not just that the Book of Mormon bears testimony of Christ, though it indeed does that too. But there is something more. There is a power in the book which will begin to flow into your lives the moment you begin a serious study of the book. You will find greater power to resist temptation. You will find the power to avoid deception. You will find the power to stay on the strait and narrow path. The scriptures are called "the words of life" (see D&C 84:85), and nowhere is that more true than it is of the Book of Mormon. When you begin to hunger and thirst after those words, you will find life in greater and greater abundance. These promises—increased love and harmony in the home, greater respect between parent and child, increased spirituality and righteousness—these are not idle promises, but exactly what the Prophet Joseph Smith meant when he said the Book of Mormon will help us draw nearer to God. (CR October 1986, *Ensign* 16 [November 1986]: 7.)

The Book of Mormon provides a second witness of the mission of Jesus Christ to the Bible. Book of Mormon prophets testified hundreds of years before the birth of Jesus that He would be born of a virgin named Mary and that His name would be Jesus Christ. Long before Jesus was born these prophets outlined His public ministry, that He would work mighty miracles, such as "healing the sick, raising the dead, causing the lame to walk, the blind to receive their sight . . . the deaf to hear, and curing all manner of diseases" (Mosiah 3:5).

Though He was God, and that by virtue of the fact that God our Heavenly Father was His literal Father, the Book of Mormon testifies that He was susceptible to mortal infirmities—temptation, pain, hunger, thirst, and fatigue.

The Book of Mormon tells us of the Messiah's great atoning sacrifice. It describes how Jesus willingly suffered the pains of all men and specifies the conditions by which His atonement may bring us to a remission of our sins, a peace of conscience, and great joy.

Many years before His first coming, Book of Mormon prophets foretold that He would be rejected by His nation, the Jews, that He would be scourged, crucified, and buried. But these same prophets also foretold that He would arise again from the dead, and because of His resurrection, all mankind will be resurrected—every mortal creature. These prophets testified that eventually Jesus will come again to judge the world.

The Book of Mormon is a second witness to Jesus Christ because it tells the account of His ministry to the people on this continent following His ascension in Jerusalem (see 3 Nephi 9–28). The Book of Mormon is a second witness to Jesus Christ because it contains the plain and precious truths of His gospel. Within this sacred record is the fulness of the gospel of Jesus Christ; in other words, the Lord's requirements for salvation. ("A Promised Lord—A Promised Land—A Promised People," Wichita, Kansas, 11 November 1976.)

The Book of Mormon is to be "a standard unto my people, which are of the house of Israel," said the Lord (2 Nephi 29:2). It is a standard we should heed and follow. (CR October 1984, *Ensign* 14 [November 1984]: 7.)

What is the major purpose of the Book of Mormon? To bring men to Christ and to be reconciled to Him, and then to join His Church—in that order. (See 2 Nephi 25:23; D&C 20:11–14, 35–37.) The title page of the Book of Mormon states the book is for "the convincing of the Jew and Gentile that Jesus is the Christ, the Eternal God." The Lord further instructed that the Book of Mormon proves that "God does inspire men and call them to his holy work in this age and generation, as in generations of old" (D&C 20:11). (CR October 1984, *Ensign* 14 [November 1984]: 6.)

The honest seeker after truth can gain the testimony that Jesus is the Christ as he prayerfully ponders the inspired words of the

Book of Mormon. Over one-half of all the verses in the Book of Mormon refer to our Lord. Some form of Christ's name is mentioned more frequently per verse in the Book of Mormon than even in the New Testament. He is given over one hundred different names in the Book of Mormon. Those names have a particular significance in describing His divine nature. (CR October 1987, *Ensign* 17 [November 1987]: 83.)

As far as preaching the gospel is concerned, the Book of Mormon contains the clearest, most concise, and complete explanation. There is no other record to compare with it. In what record do you get such a complete understanding of the nature of the Fall, the nature of physical and spiritual death, the doctrine of the Atonement, the doctrine of justice and mercy as it relates to the Atonement, and the principles and ordinances of the gospel? The Book of Mormon contains the most comprehensive account of these fundamental doctrines. (Salt Lake City, Utah, 2 October 1985.)

The Book of Mormon brings men to Christ through two basic means. First, it tells in a plain manner of Christ and His gospel. It testifies of His divinity and of the necessity for a Redeemer and the need of our putting trust in Him. It bears witness of the Fall and the Atonement and the first principles of the gospel, including our need of a broken heart and a contrite spirit and a spiritual rebirth. It proclaims we must endure to the end in righteousness and live the moral life of a Saint.

Second, the Book of Mormon exposes the enemies of Christ. It confounds false doctrines and lays down contention (see 1 Nephi 3:12). It fortifies the humble followers of Christ against the evil designs, strategies, and doctrines of the devil in our day. The type of apostates in the Book of Mormon are similar to the type we have today. God, with His infinite foreknowledge, so molded the Book of Mormon that we might see the error and know how to combat false educational, political, religious, and philosophical concepts of our time. ("The Book of Mormon Is the Word of God," Regional Representatives Seminar, Salt Lake City, Utah, 4 April 1986.)

We have an increasing number who have been convinced, through the Book of Mormon, that Jesus is the Christ. Now we need an increasing number who will use the Book of Mormon to become committed to Christ. We need to be convinced and committed.

Let us turn again to the Book of Mormon, to learn some principles about coming unto Christ, being committed to Him, centered in Him, and consumed in Him. (CR October 1987, *Ensign* 17 [November 1987]: 8.)

We urge you to study the Book of Mormon as individuals and families and then to do as the prophet Nephi counseled: liken the scriptures to yourselves so that it will be for your profit and learning (see 1 Nephi 19:23–24). (CR April 1984, *Ensign* 14 [May 1984]: 7.)

The Book of Mormon must be reenthroned in the minds and hearts of our people. We must honor it by reading it, by studying it, by taking its precepts into our lives and transforming them into lives required of the true followers of Christ. President Joseph Fielding Smith said: "It seems to me that any member of this Church would never be satisfied until he or she had read the Book of Mormon time and time again, and thoroughly considered it so that he or she could bear witness that it is in very deed a record with the inspiration of the Almighty upon it, and that its history is true. . . . No member of this Church can stand approved in the presence of God who has not seriously and carefully read the Book of Mormon." (In Conference Report, October 1961, p. 18.) (CR October 1986, *Ensign* 16 [November 1986]: 80.)

The Book of Mormon is a second witness along with the Bible that Jesus is the Christ. It testifies of Christ's appearance to the American inhabitants shortly after His resurrection in Jerusalem. It makes plain many of the precious truths of the gospel. The last chapter of the Book of Mormon contains the promise that if a person will read the book he may then ask God, the Eternal Father, in the name of Christ if the book is not true, and if he will ask with a sincere heart, with real intent, having faith in Christ, God will manifest the truth of it unto him by the power of the Holy Ghost

(Moroni 10:3–5). We invite all men to make this test. (*An Enemy Hath Done This*, p. 330.)

I promise you, if you are sincere, you will receive a confirmation of the truthfulness of the Book of Mormon by the Holy Ghost. Millions, with soberness and sincerity, testify they know it is from God. (CR October 1981, *Ensign* 11 [November 1981]: 61.)

I have a conviction: The more we teach and preach from the Book of Mormon, the more we shall please the Lord and the greater will be our power of speaking. By so doing, we shall greatly increase our converts, both within the Church and among those we proselyte. The Lord expects us to use this book, and we remain under His condemnation if we do not (see D&C 84:57). Our commission then is to teach the principles of the gospel which are in the Bible and the Book of Mormon. "These shall be their teachings, as they shall be directed by the Spirit" (D&C 42:13). (Salt Lake City, Utah, 2 October 1985.)

Written for Our Day. We must make the Book of Mormon a center focus of study because it was written for our day. The Nephites never had the book, neither did the Lamanites of ancient times. It was meant for us. Mormon wrote near the end of the Nephite civilization. Under the inspiration of God, who sees all things from the beginning, he abridged centuries of records, choosing the stories, speeches, and events that would be most helpful to us.

Each of the major writers of the Book of Mormon testified that they wrote for future generations. Nephi said: "The Lord God promised unto me that these things which I write shall be kept and preserved, and handed down unto my seed, from generation to generation" (2 Nephi 25:21). His brother Jacob, who succeeded him, wrote similar words: "For [Nephi] said that the history of his people should be engraven upon his other plates, and that I should preserve these plates and hand them down unto my seed, from generation to generation" (Jacob 1:30). Enos and Jarom both indicated that they too were writing not for their own peoples but for future generations (see Enos 1:15–16; Jarom 1:2).

Mormon himself said, "Yea, I speak unto you, ye remnant of the house of Israel" (Mormon 7:1). And Moroni, the last of the inspired writers, actually saw our day and time. "Behold," he said, "the Lord hath shown unto me great and marvelous things concerning that which must shortly come, at that day when these things shall come forth among you. Behold, I speak unto you as if ye were present, and yet ye are not. But behold, Jesus Christ hath shown you unto me, and I know your doing." (Mormon 8:34–35.)

If they saw our day, and chose those things which would be of greatest worth to us, is not that how we should study the Book of Mormon? We should constantly ask ourselves, "Why did the Lord inspire Mormon or Moroni or Alma to include that in their records? What lesson can I learn from that to help me live in this day and age?" And there is example after example of how that question will be answered. For example, in the Book of Mormon we find a pattern for preparing for the Second Coming. A major portion of the book centers on the few decades just prior to Christ's coming to America. By careful study of that time period we can determine why some were destroyed in the terrible judgments that preceded His coming and what brought others to stand at the temple in the land of Bountiful and thrust their hands into the wounds of His hands and feet.

From the Book of Mormon we learn how disciples of Christ live in times of war. From the Book of Mormon we see the evils of secret combinations portrayed in graphic and chilling reality. In the Book of Mormon we find lessons for dealing with persecution and apostasy. We learn much about how to do missionary work. And more than anywhere else, we see in the Book of Mormon the dangers of materialism and setting our hearts on the things of the world. Can anyone doubt that this book was meant for us and that in it we find great power, great comfort, and great protection? (CR October 1986, *Ensign* 16 [November 1986]: 6–7.)

How are we to use the book? We must first read it and gain a testimony for ourselves. Men may deceive each other, but God does not deceive men. Therefore, the Book of Mormon sets forth the best test for determining its truthfulness—namely, read it and then ask God if it is true (see Moroni 10:4).

This, then, is the supreme assurance for the honest in heart—to know by personal revelation from God that the Book of Mormon is true. Millions have put it to that test and know, and increasing millions will yet know. Now the spirit, as well as the body, is in need of constant nourishment. Yesterday's meal is not enough to sustain today's needs. So also an infrequent reading of "the most correct of any book on earth," as Joseph Smith called it (*History of the Church*, 4:461), is not enough. Not all truths are of equal value, nor are all scriptures of the same worth. What better way to nourish the spirit than to frequently feast from the book which the Prophet Joseph Smith said would get a man "nearer to God by abiding by its precepts than by any other book" (*History of the Church*, 4:461). (CR October 1984, *Ensign* 14 [November 1984]: 6–7.)

You know of my great love for the Book of Mormon. Sister Benson and I try to read it every morning, and we have a great love for that book. The Book of Mormon is the instrument that God has designed to "sweep the earth as with a flood, to gather out His elect unto the New Jerusalem." This sacred volume of scripture has not been, nor is it yet, central in our preaching, our teaching, and our missionary work. (Salt Lake City, Utah, 5 March 1987.)

Recently I have been reading again the marvelous account in the Book of Mormon of the visit of the resurrected Savior to the American continent. As Easter approaches, I have been deeply impressed with the beauty and power of this scriptural account in Third Nephi, and with its great value for our time and our generation.

It is clear that Third Nephi contains some of the most moving and powerful passages in all scripture. It testifies of Jesus Christ, His prophets, and the doctrines of salvation. At this Easter time, what a blessing it would be if every family would read together Third Nephi, discuss its sacred contents, and then determine how they can liken it unto themselves and apply its teachings in their lives. Third Nephi is a book that should be read and read again. Its testimony of the resurrected Christ in America is given in purity and beauty. (CR April 1987, *Ensign* 17 [May 1987]: 4, 6.)

We have not been using the Book of Mormon as we should. Our homes are not as strong unless we are using it to bring our children to Christ. Our families may be corrupted by worldly trends and teachings unless we know how to use the book to expose and combat the falsehoods in socialism, organic evolution, rationalism, humanism, and so forth. Our missionaries are not as effective unless they are "hissing forth" with it. Social, ethical, cultural, or educational converts will not survive under the heat of the day unless their taproots go down to the fulness of the gospel which the Book of Mormon contains. Our Church classes are not as spirit-filled unless we hold it up as a standard. And our nation will continue to degenerate unless we read and heed the words of the God of this land, Jesus Christ, and quit building up and upholding the secret combinations which the Book of Mormon tells us proved the downfall of both previous American civilizations. (*A Witness and a Warning*, p. 6.)

Not only should we know what history and faith-promoting stories it contains, but we should understand its teachings. If we really do our homework and approached the Book of Mormon doctrinally, we can expose the errors and find the truths to combat many of the current false theories and philosophies of men. I have noted within the Church a difference in discernment, insight, conviction, and spirit between those who know and love the Book of Mormon and those who do not. That book is a great sifter. ("Jesus Christ—Gifts and Expectations," Christmas Devotional, Salt Lake City, Utah, 7 December 1986.)

We are to use the Book of Mormon in handling objections to the Church. God the Father and His Son Jesus Christ revealed themselves to Joseph Smith in a marvelous vision. After that glorious event, Joseph Smith told a minister about it. Joseph was surprised to hear the minister say that there were no such things as visions or revelations in these days, that all such things had ceased. (See Joseph Smith—History 1:21.)

This remark symbolizes practically all of the objections that have ever been made against the Church by nonmembers and dissident members alike. Namely, they do not believe that God reveals His will today to the Church through prophets of God. All objections, whether they be on abortion, plural marriage, seventh-day worship, or other subjects, basically hinge on whether Joseph Smith and his successors were and are prophets of God receiving divine revelation.

Here, then, is a procedure to handle most objections through the use of the Book of Mormon. First, understand the objection. Second, give the answer from revelation. Third, show how the correctness of the answer really depends on whether or not we have modern revelation through modern prophets. Fourth, explain that whether or not we have modern prophets and revelation really depends on whether the Book of Mormon is true. Therefore, the only problem the objector has to resolve for himself is whether the Book of Mormon is true. For if the Book of Mormon is true, then Jesus is the Christ, Joseph Smith was His prophet, The Church of Jesus Christ of Latter-day Saints is true, and it is being led today by a prophet receiving revelation. ("The Book of Mormon Is the Word of God," Regional Representatives Seminar, Salt Lake City, Utah, 4 April 1986.)

If our children and grandchildren are taught and heed these same truths, will they fall away? We best instruct them in the Book of Mormon at our dinner table, by our firesides, at their bedsides, and in our letters and phone calls—in all of our goings and comings. Some spiritually alert parents hold early-morning devotionals with their families in their homes. They have a hymn, prayer, and then read and discuss the Book of Mormon. "The elders, priests and teachers of this church shall teach the principles of my gospel, which are in . . . the Book of Mormon," says the Lord (D&C 42:12). (CR October 1984, *Ensign* 14 [November 1984]: 7.)

The prophets, particularly of the Book of Mormon, saw our day. You will learn more from studying and reading the Book of Mormon (about our current problems) than you will by reading the daily paper or the slick magazines. (BYU Ten-Stake Fireside, Provo, Utah, 7 May 1972.)

May I suggest that you get a copy of the Book of Mormon that will fit in your purse and in your hip pocket, you brethren, and read it every day and become acquainted with it and gain a knowledge of how the adversary is organized and working, and what his designs are for this Church. (BYU Ten-Stake Fireside, Provo, Utah, 7 May 1972.)

I encourage you to become more familiar with the Book of Mormon, particularly. I remember an incident with my own son. He called me one day to ask if I wouldn't come up to his bedroom. When I got there, I found he had several books on the bed. He said to me, "You know, I have a job with my uncle herding turkeys this summer so I assume I am going to have time on my hands." Then he asked me to pick out the books I would recommend.

I picked up a little military edition of the Book of Mormon. I said, "This will fit in your hip pocket." He said, "You mean to tell me I am to take only one book?" I said, "Yes, and you will learn to love it, and you will learn to love missionary work"—and he did. (CR April 1984, *Ensign* 14 [May 1984]: 45.)

A young man who knows and loves the Book of Mormon, who has read it several times, who has an abiding testimony of its truthfulness, and who applies its teachings will be able to stand against the wiles of the devil and will be a mighty tool in the hands of the Lord. (CR April 1986, *Ensign* 16 [May 1986]: 43.)

There is a book we need to study daily, both as individuals and as families, namely the Book of Mormon. I love that book. President Romney recommended studying it half an hour each day. I commend that practice to you. I have always enjoyed reading the scriptures and do so on a daily basis individually and with my beloved wife. (CR April 1986, *Ensign* 16 [May 1986]: 78.)

We invite all men everywhere to read the Book of Mormon, another testament of Jesus Christ. The Bible sits on the pulpit of hundreds of different religious sects. The Book of Mormon, the record of Joseph, verifies and clarifies the Bible. It removes stumbling blocks, it restores many plain and precious things. We testify that when used together, the Bible and the Book of Mormon confound false doctrines, lay down contentions, and establish peace (see 2 Nephi 3:12).

We do not have to prove the Book of Mormon is true. The book is its own proof. All we need to do is read it and declare it! The Book of Mormon is not on trial—the people of the world, including the members of the Church, are on trial as to what they will do with this second witness for Christ. (CR October 1984, *Ensign* 14 [November 1984]: 8.)

Presently the Book of Mormon is studied in our Sunday School and seminary classes every fourth year. This four-year pattern, however, must not be followed by Church members in their personal study of the standard works. All scripture is not of equal value. The book that will get a man "nearer to God by abiding its precepts, than by any other book" needs to be studied constantly.

The Lord declares that the whole Church and all the children of Zion are under condemnation because of the way we have treated the Book of Mormon. This condemnation has not been lifted, nor will it be until we repent. (See D&C 84:51–81.)

The Lord states that we must not only say but we must do! We have neither said enough nor have we done enough with this divine instrument—the key to conversion. As a result, as individuals, as families, and as the Church, we sometimes have felt the scourge and judgment God said would be "poured out upon the children of Zion" because of our neglect of this book (D&C 84:58).

The Lord inspired His servant Lorenzo Snow to reemphasize the principle of tithing to redeem the Church from financial bondage. In those days the General Authorities took that message to the members of the Church. So too in our day the Lord has inspired His servant to reemphasize the Book of Mormon to get the Church out from under condemnation—the scourge and judgment. (Salt Lake City, Utah, 5 March 1987.)

Is the Book of Mormon the word of God? Yes. God has so testified. (See D&C 20:8–10.) So have its writers (see 2 Nephi 33:10; Moroni 7:35), so has its translator (see Article of Faith 8), so have its witnesses, and so do all those who have read it and received a personal revelation from God as to its truthfulness.

How important is the Book of Mormon? "Take away the Book of Mormon and the revelations," Joseph Smith said, "and where is our religion? We have none." (*History of the Church*, 2:52.) "This generation," said the Lord to Joseph Smith, the translator, "shall have my word through you" (D&C 5:10). And so it has. (CR October 1984, *Ensign* 14 [November 1984]: 6.)

Pay more attention to the Book of Mormon. My counsel would be to join me in this direction, which I know will pay dividends and which, if we accept, God will bless us as members of His priesthood and leaders in His kingdom. (Salt Lake City, Utah, 5 March 1987.)

During the past six months I have been deeply touched by the response of members of the Church who have heeded counsel to read and reread the word of the Lord as set forth in the Book of Mormon. This has resulted in increased spirituality and is helping to cleanse the inner vessel. Adults, youth, and children have borne powerful testimonies as to how the Book of Mormon has changed their lives. My life, too, continues to be changed by this sacred volume of scripture. ("The Savior's Visit to America," *Ensign* 17 [May 1987]: 4.)

I testify to you that I have read the Book of Mormon and that I have put it to the test; that God has revealed unto me the truthfulness of this added volume of scripture and revealed unto me that Joseph Smith is a prophet of God; and that His prophet and representative stands today as the earthly President of The Church of Jesus Christ of Latter-day Saints, the one man on the earth who holds the keys of God's kingdom, as did Peter anciently. (*God, Family, Country*, pp. 159–60.)

I bless you with increased discernment to judge between Christ and anti-Christ. I bless you with increased power to do good and to resist evil. I bless you with increased understanding of the Book of Mormon. I promise you that from this moment forward, if we will daily sup from its pages and abide by its precepts, God will pour out upon each child of Zion and the Church a blessing hitherto unknown—and we will plead to the Lord that He will begin to lift the condemnation—the scourge and judgment. Of this I bear solemn witness. (CR April 1986, *Ensign* 16 [May 1986]: 78.)

The First Principles of the Gospel

His law required all mankind, regardless of station in life, to repent and be baptized in His name and receive the Holy Ghost as the sanctifying power to cleanse themselves from sin. Compliance with these laws and ordinances will enable each individual to stand guiltless before Him at the day of judgment. Those who so comply are likened to one who builds his house on a firm foundation so that even "the gates of hell shall not prevail against them" (3 Nephi 11:39). (*Come unto Christ*, p. 129.)

Faith in the Lord Jesus Christ

The fundamental principle of our religion is faith in the Lord Jesus Christ. Why is it expedient to center confidence, hope, and trust in one solitary figure? Why is faith in Him so necessary to peace of mind in this life and hope in the world to come?

My answer to these questions is derived from a lifetime in His service and the confirmation of the Holy Spirit that only Jesus Christ is uniquely qualified to provide hope, confidence, and strength to overcome the world and rise above our human failings. This is the reason I place my faith and trust in Him and strive to abide by His laws and teachings. (*Come unto Christ*, pp. 127–28.)

Now let me describe to you what faith in Jesus Christ means. Faith in Him is more than mere acknowledgment that He lives. It is more than professing belief. Faith in Jesus Christ consists of complete reliance on Him. As God, He has infinite power, intelligence, and love. There is no human problem beyond His capacity to solve. Because He descended below all things, He knows how to help us rise above our daily difficulties.

Faith in Him means believing that even though we do not understand all things, He does. We, therefore, must look to Him "in every thought; doubt not, fear not" (D&C 6:36). Faith in Him means trusting that He has power over all men and all nations. There is no evil that He cannot arrest. All things are in His hands. This earth is His rightful dominion. Yet He permits evil so that we can make choices between good and evil.

His gospel is the perfect prescription for all human problems and social ills. But His gospel is effective only as it is applied in our lives. Therefore, we must "feast upon the words of Christ; for behold, the words of Christ will tell [us] all things that [we] should do" (2 Nephi 32:3). Unless we do His teachings, we do not demonstrate faith in Him. (*Come unto Christ*, p. 132.)

The first characteristic to which all the others are added is faith. Faith is the foundation upon which a godlike character is built. It is the prerequisite for all other virtues. (CR October 1986, *Ensign* 16 [November 1986]: 45.)

Every one of God's children from the savage to the head of state, "untouched by infidelity, has in his heart a belief in a supreme being—a deity." Inborn in every man is a strong instinct to worship—to look toward heaven. Man has a hereditary passion to worship. By nature man wants to find God and to worship Him in spirit and in truth. He cries out for contact with Him. ("Basic Doctrines of Church Explained to Youth Firesides," *Church News* [20 May 1961]: 13–14.)

It is the part of wisdom to acknowledge and experience that there is an unseen source of power and truth. Many have already come to the profound realization that man does not stand alone. They have learned that there are "hidden treasures of knowledge" for him who asks in faith, nothing wavering (see D&C 89:19). Such has been the fervent declaration of the world's truly great leaders in all ages of recorded history. (*The Red Carpet*, p. 294.)

The designs of peaceful people everywhere are always accomplished by those of great faith—faith in God; faith in what man can do through his God-given freedom; faith that, with God's blessing, justice will ultimately prevail; faith in the future of this choice land. (*The Red Carpet*, p. 288.)

We have so much faith within the Church. We are not only growing in numbers as never before, but we are also growing in faith. (Grantsville Utah Stake Conference, 1 September 1974.)

When faith lays hold of a man, it pervades all of life—all aspects of life, all functions, all activities, all that we say or even think. (Calvary Baptist Church, Washington D.C., 13 February 1959.)

Without faith in our Heavenly Father, we cannot be successful. Faith gives us vision of what may happen, hope for the future, and optimism in our present tasks. Where faith is, we do not doubt the ultimate success of the work.

We will all have disappointments and discouragements—that is part of life. But if we will have faith, our setbacks will be but a moment and success will come out of our seeming failures. Our Heavenly Father can accomplish miracles through each of us if we will but place our confidence and trust in Him. I have witnessed this on many occasions. ("Four Keys for Success," Churubusco Mexico Stake, 5 June 1982.)

There will be those little minds who, out of vanity for intellectual display, would attempt to destroy faith in the very foundations of life. Be assured, however, that no man worthy of the name, who has been humbled and awed before the inexplainable "wonders of this marvelous universe," will ever scoff at sacred things or try to rob you of your faith in the unseen. Our inability to explain a thing in terms of our materialism does not disprove its reality. By yielding obedience to your faith in God and the laws of the universe, both spiritual and physical, there will come a soul-satisfying security which is priceless. You will need this anchor as you face a doubting world. (*So Shall Ye Reap*, p. 149.)

Let not your faith waver. God still rules. He is at the helm. He has not forgotten you, nor will He do so, if you keep sacred your covenants as members of His Church. And if the clouds gather for a moment, be assured that behind every cloud for you there is a smiling providence. "What though the clouds seem dark today?/ Tomorrow's will be blue./When every cloud has cleared away,/ God's Providence shines through." (*So Shall Ye Reap*, p. 97.)

It is a great blessing to have an inner peace, to have an assurance, to have a spirit of serenity and inward calm during times of strife and struggle, during times of sorrow and reverses. It is soul-satisfying to know that God is at the helm, that He is mindful of His children, and that we can with full confidence place our trust in Him. I believe that all the truly great men of the earth have been men who trusted in God and who have striven to do that which is right as they understood the right. (CR April 1954, *Improvement Era* 57 [June 1954]: 406.)

The father must hunger and thirst and yearn to bless his family; he must go to the Lord, ponder the words of God, and live by the Spirit to know the mind and will of the Lord and what he must do to lead his family. It is soul-satisfying to know that God is mindful of us and ready to respond when we place our trust in Him and do that which is right. There is no place for fear among men and women who place their trust in the Almighty, who do not hesitate to humble themselves in seeking divine guidance through prayer. Though persecutions arise, though reverses come, in prayer we can find reassurance, for God will speak peace to the soul. That peace, that spirit of serenity, is a great blessing. (*Priesthood* [Salt Lake City: Deseret Book, 1981], pp. 142–43.)

Righteous concern about conditions is commendable when it leads to constructive action. But undue worry is debilitating. When we have done what we can do, then let us leave the rest to God. (CR April 1967, *Improvement Era* 70 [June 1967]: 59.)

Let us never be ashamed of the gospel of Jesus Christ (see Romans 1:16). Let us never be afraid to do what is right. Let us trust in God and keep His commandments, for this is the whole duty of man (Ecclesiates 12:13). I know, and so do you who have testimonies of the divinity of this work, that without God's help we cannot succeed, but with His help we can accomplish anything He asks us to do. And we can do it with a feeling of assurance, confidence, and with a spirit of serenity which can be a joy and blessing to all of us. (CR April 1954, *Improvement Era* 57 [June 1954]: 407.)

May we trust in God and keep His commandments. That is all the Lord expects of us. Joy and happiness will enter our hearts as we do so. It is the wicked who flee when no man pursueth. The righteous are bold as a lion (see Proverbs 28:1). People who live righteously have nothing to fear. In spite of the turmoil, anxiety, and insecurity which may seem to be everywhere, we will be able to stand erect and go forward with courage and faith. (*So Shall Ye Reap*, p. 62.)

Repentance

As I have sought direction from the Lord, I have had reaffirmed in my mind and heart the declaration of the Lord to "say nothing but repentance unto this generation" (D&C 6:9; 11:9).

This has been a theme of every latter-day prophet, along with his testimony that Jesus is the Christ and that Joseph Smith is a prophet of God.

Repentance was the cry of our late and great prophet, Spencer W. Kimball. This theme permeated his talks and the pages of his writings, such as his marvelous book *The Miracle of Forgiveness*. And it must be our cry today, both to member and to nonmember alike—repent. (CR April 1986, *Ensign* 16 [May 1986]: 4.)

Yes, one can repent of moral transgression. The miracle of forgiveness is real, and true repentance is accepted of the Lord. But it is not pleasing to the Lord to sow one's wild oats, to engage in sexual transgression of any nature and then expect that planned confession and quick repentance will satisfy the Lord. ("To the Young Women of the Church," *Ensign* 16 [November 1986]: 83.)

The Prophet Joseph Smith taught: "God does not look on sin with allowance, but when men have sinned, there must be allowance made for them" (*Teachings of the Prophet Joseph Smith*, pp. 240–41). That is another way of saying God loves the sinner, but condemns the sin. ("Keys to Successful Missionary Work," Texas San Antonio Mission, 2 March 1986.)

We all stand in need of change and reformation. We all need to rededicate ourselves to righteous, moral living. From this place, President Brigham Young urged such a reformation in the lives of the Latter-day Saints. Determine for yourselves if his words are not as applicable today as when they were given. "First reform in your moral character and conduct one towards another, so that every man and woman deal honestly, and walk uprightly with one another, and extend the arm of charity and benevolence to each other, as necessity requires. Be moral and strictly honest in every point, before you ask God to reform your spirit." (*Journal of Discourses*, 4:61.)

Is that not sound counsel? Is that not the need for Latter-day Saints today? Would there not be a great reformation if we all dealt honestly one with another? Certainly this is our need today! ("A Time for Rededication," Assembly Hall Rededication, Salt Lake City, Utah, 3 April 1983.)

If we wish to truly repent and come unto Him so that we can be called members of His Church, we must first and foremost come to realize this eternal truth—the gospel plan is the plan of happiness. Wickedness never did, never does, never will bring us happiness. Violation of the laws of God brings only misery, bondage, and darkness. ("A Mighty Change of Heart," address prepared [but not delivered] 1986.)

Lehi taught that "no flesh can dwell in the presence of God, save it be through the merits, and mercy and grace of the Holy Messiah" (2 Nephi 2:8). Even the most just and upright man cannot save himself solely on his own merits, for, as the Apostle Paul tells us, "all have sinned, and come short of the glory of God" (Romans 3:23). Therefore, repentance means more than simply a reformation of behavior. Many men and women in the world demonstrate great will-power and self-discipline in overcoming bad habits and the weaknesses of the flesh. Yet at the same time they give no thought to the Master, sometimes even openly rejecting Him. Such changes of behavior, even if in a positive direction, do not constitute true repentance. Repentance involves not just a change of actions, but a change of heart. ("A Mighty Change of Heart," address prepared [but not delivered] 1986.)

As we seek to qualify to be members of Christ's Church—members in the sense in which He uses the term, members who have repented and come unto Him—let us remember these principles. The gospel is the Lord's plan of happiness and repentance is designed to bring us joy. True repentance is based on and flows from faith in the Lord Jesus Christ. There is no other way. True repentance involves a change of heart and not just a change of behavior (see Alma 5:13). Part of this mighty change of heart is to feel godly sorrow for our sins. This is what is meant by a broken heart and a contrite spirit. God's gifts are sufficient to help us overcome every sin and weakness if we will but turn to Him for help. Most repentance does not involve sensational or dramatic changes, but rather is a step by step, steady and consistent movement toward godliness. ("A Mighty Change of Heart," address prepared [but not delivered] 1986.)

It is not uncommon to find men and women in the world who feel remorse for the things they do wrong. Sometimes this is because their actions cause them or loved ones great sorrow and misery. Sometimes their sorrow is caused because they are caught and punished for their actions. Such worldly feelings do not constitute "godly sorrow" (2 Corinthians 7:10).

Godly sorrow is a gift of the Spirit. It is a deep realization that our actions have offended our Father and our God. It is the sharp and keen awareness that our behavior caused the Savior, He who knew no sin, even the greatest of all, to endure agony and suffering. Our sins caused Him to bleed at every pore. This very real mental and spiritual anguish is what the scriptures refer to as having "a broken heart and a contrite spirit" (D&C 20:37). Such a spirit is the absolute prerequisite for true repentance.

We must take our sins to the Lord in humble and sorrowful repentance. We must plead with Him for power to overcome them. The promises are sure. He will come to our aid. We will find the power to change our lives. ("A Mighty Change of Heart," address prepared [but not delivered] 1986.)

We must be careful, as we seek to become more and more godlike, that we do not become discouraged and lose hope. Becoming Christlike is a lifetime pursuit and very often involves growth and change that is slow, almost imperceptible. The scriptures record remarkable accounts of men whose lives changed dramatically, in an instant as it were. Alma the Younger, Paul on the road to Damascus, Enos praying far into the night, King Lamoni. Such astonishing examples of the power to change even those steeped in sin give confidence that the Atonement can reach even those deepest in despair. ("A Mighty Change of Heart," address prepared [but not delivered] 1986.)

As we cleanse the inner vessel, there will have to be changes made in our own personal lives, in our families, and in the Church (see Alma 60:23). The proud do not change to improve, but defend their position by rationalizing. Repentance means change, and it takes a humble person to change. But we can do it. (CR April 1986, *Ensign* 16 [May 1986]: 7.)

It is fitting and proper that Christmas and the beginning of the new year should be a time for us to reexamine our lives and ideals, to humbly confess our shortcomings, and to determine to repent. But true repentance must do more than produce a sense of remorse or heartfelt sorrow—it must bring about a change in our way of thinking and acting. It is not easy. It demands the courage to face facts, admit the need to do better, and act accordingly. It demands a high resolve to adhere more closely to that course which is pleasing to the God of Heaven and of service to mankind and the cause of freedom. ("God and Country," Frankfurt am Main, Germany, 1964.)

To deny oneself of all ungodliness is to come to Christ by ordinances and covenants, to repent of any sins which prevent the Spirit of the Lord from taking precedence in our lives (see Moroni 10:32). To deny oneself of all ungodliness is to "offer a sacrifice unto the Lord thy God, even that of a broken heart and a contrite spirit" (D&C 59:8). (CR April 1979, *Ensign* 9 [May 1979]: 32.)

The nations of the earth continue in their sinful and unrighteous ways. Much of the unbounded knowledge with which men have been blessed has been used to destroy mankind instead of to bless the children of men as the Lord intended. Two great world wars, with fruitless efforts at lasting peace, are solemn evidence that peace has been taken from the earth because of the wickedness of the people. Nations cannot endure in sin. They will be broken up but the kingdom of God will endure forever.

Therefore, as humble servants of the Lord, we call upon the leaders of the nations to humble themselves before God, to seek His inspiration and guidance. We call upon rulers and people alike to repent of their evil ways. Turn unto the Lord, seek His forgiveness, and unite yourselves in humility with His kingdom. There is no other way. If you will do this, your sins will be blotted out, peace will come and remain, and you will become a part of the kingdom of God in preparation for Christ's second coming. But if you refuse to repent, to accept the testimony of His inspired messengers, or to unite yourselves with God's kingdom, then the terrible judgments and calamities promised the wicked will be yours.

The voice of warning is unto all people by the mouths of His servants (see D&C 1:4). If this voice is not heeded, the angels of destruction will increasingly go forth, and the chastening hand of Almighty God will be felt upon the nations, as decreed, until a full end thereof will be the result. Wars, devastation, and untold suffering will be your lot except you turn unto the Lord in humble repentance. Destruction even more terrible and far-reaching than attended the last great war will come with certainty unless rulers and people alike repent and cease their evil and godless ways. God will not be mocked (D&C 63:58). He will not permit the sins of sexual immorality, secret murderous combinations, the killing of the unborn, and disregard for all His holy commandments and the messages of His servants to go unheeded without grievous punishment for such wickedness. The nations of the world cannot endure in sin. The way of escape is clear. The immutable laws of God remain steadfastly in the heavens above. When men and nations refuse to abide by them, the penalty must follow. They will be wasted away. Sin demands punishment. (*This Nation Shall Endure*, p. 111.)

To those burdened and sorrowing with guilt, we offer hope. Your Redeemer loves you with a perfect love. He died to pay for the sins of all who truly repent and follow the course He prescribed. "Though your sins be as scarlet, they shall be as white as snow," He promised (Isaiah 1:18). Accept the healing of spirit that He alone can give. ("First Presidency—Christmas Message," *Church News* [15 December 1985]: 3.)

Each of us must surrender our sins if we are to really know Christ. We do not know Him until we become like Him. (*Come unto Christ*, pp. 51–52.)

Now, I would not have anyone believe that there is no hope if there are some who have made such a grievous mistake, because repentance and forgiveness are also a part of the gospel. Thank God for that! But it must be real repentance. Such repentance is a deep, heartfelt sorrow for sin that produces a reformation of life. It is not just a confession of guilt. Sometimes we regard all too lightly the principle of repentance, thinking that it only means confession, that it only means feeling sorry for ourselves. But it is more than that. It is a deep, burning, and heartfelt sorrow for sin that will drive us to our knees in humility and tears—a deep, heartfelt sorrow for sin that produces a reformation of life. That is the right test: a reformation of life. Only then may the God of Heaven in His mercy and His goodness see fit to forgive us.

He—not the priesthood on the earth—is the judge. Priesthood holders can only carry out certain requirements. They can require certain things set forth in the revelations, but forgiveness comes from above. (*God, Family, Country*, p. 196.)

Today I have in my heart a love for all of God's children. I have no ill feeling toward any human being. With you, I hate sin, but I love the sinner. We all have need to repent. (CR April 1955, *Improvement Era* 58 [June 1955]: 408.)

Baptism

As important as agreements are between individuals, more important are the agreements an individual makes with God. As members of the true Church of Jesus Christ, you made agreements with Him at baptism. That is why you are called the children of the covenant. As a part of that covenant, you agreed "to stand as witnesses of God at all times and in all things, and in all places that ye may be in, even until death" (Mosiah 18:9).

At the time of baptism you agreed to keep all God's commandments. He has not left you alone to flounder over what these are, or what is right or wrong. He is very specific and clear on how you should conduct your life as a member of His Church. ("Honor," *New Era* 14 [July 1984]: 4.)

Before investigators are baptized they should commit themselves to each of the principles of the gospel. An investigator who will not commit to praying, going to Church, or living the Word of Wisdom is certainly not prepared for the serious baptismal covenant. ("Success as a Mission President," Mission Presidents Seminar, Provo, Utah, 20 June 1978.)

As members of the Church we should live as our Heavenly Father expects us to live. Therefore we have a responsibility to encourage one another to be true to our covenants taken upon ourselves through baptism into the Church. ("The Church," Paris, France, 7 August 1960.)

Gift of the Holy Ghost

The world has the light of Christ to help guide it, but we are entitled to that great gift, the gift of the Holy Ghost. For the Holy Ghost to be fully operative we have to keep our channels clear of sin. The clearer our channels, the easier it is to receive God's message to us; and the more of His messages we receive and put into action, the greater will be our joy. If our channels are not clear of sin, then we may think we have gotten inspiration on a matter when it is really promptings from the devil. ("In His Steps," in *1979 Devotional Speeches of the Year* [Provo, Utah: BYU, 1980], p. 63.)

Spirituality—being in tune with the Spirit of the Lord—is a great need of Latter-day Saints. We should strive for the constant companionship of the Holy Ghost all the days of our lives. When we have the Spirit, we will love to serve, we will love the Lord, and we will love those whom we serve. (*Come unto Christ*, p. 22.)

One reason we are on this earth is to discern between truth and error. This discernment comes by the Holy Ghost, not just our intellectual faculties. (*Come unto Christ*, p. 22.)

Not all men will perceive the hand of God in this latter-day work. Jesus told Nicodemus, "Except a man be born again, he cannot see the kingdom of God" (John 3:3). Without the guidance and inspiration of the Holy Ghost, there will be some who will see nothing more to the progress of the Church than a social curiosity. (CR April 1978, *Ensign* 8 [May 1978]: 32.)

All those who have accepted this gospel and have the Holy Ghost in their lives possess an inner light that shows in their countenances. ("The Light of Christmas," Christmas Lighting Ceremony, Temple Square, Salt Lake City, Utah, 26 November 1982.)

We must always be responsive to the whisperings of the Spirit. These promptings most often come when we are not under the pressure of appointments and when we are not caught up in the worries of our day-to-day life. (Salt Lake City, Utah, 2 October 1985.)

We have been taught that the Spirit will not dwell in unclean tabernacles. Therefore, one of our first priorities is to make sure our own personal lives are in order. The Lord declared, "Be ye clean that bear the vessels of the Lord" (D&C 38:42). (*Come unto Christ*, p. 92.)

Inasmuch as all these warnings have come through the mouth-pieces of the Lord on earth today, there is one major question we should ask ourselves. Assuming we are living a life so we can know, then what does the Holy Ghost have to say about it? We are under obligation to answer this question. God will hold us responsible. Let us not be deceived in the sifting days ahead. Let us rally together on principle behind the prophet as guided by the promptings of the Spirit. (*God, Family, Country*, p. 342.)

We hear the words of the Lord most often by a feeling. If we are humble and sensitive, the Lord will prompt us through our feelings. That is why spiritual promptings move us on occasion to great joy, sometimes to tears. Many times my emotions have been made tender and my feelings very sensitive when touched by the Spirit. (*Come unto Christ*, p. 20.)

Born of God

When you choose to follow Christ, you choose to be changed. "No man," said President David O. McKay, "can sincerely resolve to apply to his daily life the teachings of Jesus of Nazareth without sensing a change in his own nature. The phrase 'born again' has a deeper significance than many people attach to it. This *changed feeling* may be indescribable, *but it is real*." (CR April 1962, p. 7.)

Can human hearts be changed? Why, of course! It happens every day in the great missionary work of the Church. It is one of the most widespread of Christ's modern miracles. If it hasn't happened to you—it should.

Our Lord told Nicodemus that "except a man be born again, he cannot see the kingdom of God" (John 3:3). Of these words President Spencer W. Kimball said, "This is the simple total answer to the weightiest of all questions. . . . To gain eternal life there must be a rebirth, a transformation." (CR April 1958, p. 14.)

President McKay said that Christ called for "an entire revolution" of Nicodemus's "inner man." "His manner of thinking, feeling, and acting with reference to spiritual things would have to undergo a fundamental and permanent change." (CR April 1960, p. 26.)

In addition to the physical ordinance of baptism and the laying on of hands, one must be spiritually born again to gain exaltation and eternal life.

Alma states: "And the Lord said unto me: Marvel not that all mankind, yea, men and women, all nations, kindreds, tongues, and people, must be born again; yea, born of God, changed from their carnal and fallen state, to a state of righteousness, being redeemed of God, becoming his sons and daughters;

"And thus they become new creatures; and unless they do this, they can in nowise inherit the kingdom of God." (Mosiah 27:25–26.)

The "change of heart" and "born again" processes are best described in the keystone of our religion, the Book of Mormon.

Those who had been born of God after hearing King Benjamin's address had a mighty change in their hearts. They had "no more disposition to do evil, but to do good continually." (See Mosiah 5:2, 7.)

The fourth chapter of Alma describes a period in Nephite history when "the church began to fail in its progress" (Alma 4:10). Alma met this challenge by resigning his seat as chief judge in government "and confined himself wholly to the high priesthood" responsibility which was his (Alma 4:20).

He "[bore] down in pure testimony" against the people (see Alma 4:19), and in the fifth chapter of Alma he asks over forty crucial questions. Speaking frankly to the members of the Church, he declared, "I ask of you, my brethren of the church, have ye spiritually been born of God? Have ye received his image in your countenances? Have ye experienced this mighty change in your hearts?" (Alma 5:14.)

He continued, "If ye have experienced a change of heart, and if ye have felt to sing the song of redeeming love, I would ask, can ye feel so now?" (Alma 5:26.)

Would not the progress of the Church increase dramatically today with an increasing number of those who are spiritually reborn? Can you imagine what would happen in our homes? Can you imagine what would happen with an increasing number of copies of the Book of Mormon in the hands of an increasing number of missionaries who know how to use it and who have been born of God? When this happens, we will get the bounteous harvest of souls that the Lord promised. It was the "born of God" Alma who as a missionary was so able to impart the word that many others were also born of God. (See Alma 36:23–26.)

The Lord works from the inside out. The world works from the outside in. The world would take people out of the slums. Christ takes the slums out of people, and then they take themselves out of the slums. The world would mold men by changing their environment. Christ changes men, who then change their environment. The world would shape human behavior, but Christ can change human nature.

"Human nature *can* be changed, here and now," said President McKay, and then he quoted the following:

"You can change human nature. No man who has felt in him the Spirit of Christ even for half a minute can deny this truth. . . . You do change human nature, your own human nature, if you surrender it to Christ. Human nature has been changed in the past. Human nature must be changed on an enormous scale in the future, unless the world is to be drowned in its own blood. And only Christ can change it. Twelve men did quite a lot to change the world [nineteen hundred] years ago. Twelve simple men." (Quoting Beverly Nichols, in *Stepping Stones to an Abundant Life*, pp. 23, 127.)

Yes, Christ changes men, and changed men can change the world. Men changed for Christ will be captained by Christ. Like Paul they will be asking, "Lord, what wilt thou have me to do?" (Acts 9:6.) Peter stated they will "follow his steps" (1 Peter 2:21). John said they will "walk, even as he walked" (1 John 2:6).

Finally, men captained by Christ will be consumed in Christ. To paraphrase President Harold B. Lee, they set fire in others because they are on fire (*Stand Ye in Holy Places*, p. 192).

Their will is swallowed up in His will (see John 5:30). They do always those things that please the Lord (see John 8:29). Not only would they die for the Lord, but more important they want to live for Him.

Enter their homes, and the pictures on their walls, the books on their shelves, the music in the air, their words and acts reveal them as Christians. They stand as witnesses of God at all times, and in all things, and in all places (see Mosiah 18:9). They have Christ on their minds, as they look unto Him in every thought (see D&C 6:36). They have Christ in their hearts as their affections are placed on Him forever (see Alma 37:36).

Almost every week they partake of the sacrament and witness anew to their Eternal Father that they are willing to take upon them the name of His Son, always remember Him, and keep His commandments (see Moroni 4:3).

In Book of Mormon language, they "feast upon the words of Christ" (2 Nephi 32:3), "talk of Christ" (2 Nephi 25:26), "rejoice in Christ" (2 Nephi 25:26), "are made alive in Christ" (2 Nephi 25:25), and "glory in [their] Jesus" (see 2 Nephi 33:6). In short, they lose themselves in the Lord, and find eternal life (see Luke 17:33). (*A Witness and a Warning*, pp. 61–65.)

Agency

The Church of Jesus Christ of Latter-day Saints proclaims that life is eternal, that it has purpose. We believe we lived as intelligent beings in a world of progress before this mortal life. Our life on this earth is a probation, a testing period (see Abraham 3:25), an opportunity for growth and experience in a physical world. It is all part of the plan of our Heavenly Father for the benefit and blessing of us, His children.

This is to be done through a great and all-wise plan—the gospel of Jesus Christ. This master plan, if lived, will build men of character, men of strength, men of deep spirituality, godlike men.

Basic to this all-important plan is our free agency, the right of choice. Free agency is an eternal principle. We enjoyed freedom of choice in the spirit world as spirit children. In fact, a counterplan to the gospel of our Lord was presented by Lucifer, a plan of force that would have robbed man of his freedom of choice. Lucifer's plan was rejected, and the scriptures tell us that he, with one-third of the hosts of heaven, was cast out; and they continue their opposition to God's plan, which is based on the freedom of the individual.

The scriptures make clear that there was a great war in heaven, a struggle over the principle of freedom, the right of choice (see Moses 4:1–4; D&C 29:36–38; 76:25–27; Revelation 12:7–9). History, both sacred and secular, clearly records that the struggle to preserve freedom has been a continuous one. Prophets of God, as watchmen on the towers, have proclaimed liberty. Holy men of God have led the fight against anarchy and tyranny. Moses was commanded to "proclaim liberty throughout all the land unto all the inhabitants thereof" (Leviticus 25:10).

Why have prophets of God been commanded to proclaim liberty and lead the battle to preserve freedom? Because freedom is basic to the great plan of the Lord. The gospel can prosper only in an atmosphere of freedom. This fact is confirmed by history, as well as by sacred scriptures. The right of choice—free agency—runs like a golden thread throughout the gospel plan of the Lord for the blessing of His children. To a modern-day prophet the Lord declared that "it is not right that any man should be in bondage one to another" (D&C 101:79). (*An Enemy Hath Done This*, pp. 323–24.)

The scriptures tell us about the War in Heaven over free agency —similar to the war we are going through now, where the devil's program was guaranteed security as opposed to the Lord's program of letting each choose for himself even if he makes the wrong choice.

The scriptures also tell about our inspired Constitution. If you accept these scriptures, you will automatically reject the counsel of men who depreciate our Constitution. If you use the scriptures as a guide, you know what the Book of Mormon has to say regarding murderous conspiracies in the last day and how we are to awake to our awful situation today (see Ether 8:18–25). I find certain elements in the Church do not like to read the Book of Mormon and Doctrine and Covenants so much—they have too much to say about freedom. (*Title of Liberty*, pp. 80–81.)

It was a struggle over free agency that divided us before we came here; it may well be the struggle over the same principle that will deceive and divide us again. (*God, Family, Country*, p. 338.)

Now, in this great struggle for free agency, just think what a power for good we could be in this world if we were united. (*God, Family, Country*, p. 341.)

You are a moral agent with freedom to choose between right and wrong. Man's free agency is an eternal principle embodied in the gospel and vouchsafed to us by our Creator. It is an inalienable right, but the preservation of its enjoyment will require eternal vigilance. Guard it with your life if need be. We all seek happiness. There cannot be true happiness without freedom. (*So Shall Ye Reap*, p. 150.)

Freedom of choice is a God-given eternal principle. The great plan of liberty is the plan of the gospel. There is no coercion about it; no force, no intimidation. A man is free to accept the gospel or reject it. He may accept it and then refuse to live it, or he may accept it and live it fully. But God will never force us to live the gospel. He will use persuasion through His servants. He will call us and He will direct us and He will persuade us and encourage us and He will bless us when we respond, but He will never force the human mind. (See *Hymns*, 1985, no. 240.) (Short Hills, New Jersey, 15 January 1961.)

Because God has given men their agency, there will always be those who will misuse it. The gospel net draws in the good and the bad, the best and the worst. The worst because the devil, before the final cleansing, will put some of his followers within the kingdom in order to try and destroy it. We have some of them within the kingdom today, and in due course their number shall be known. Time has a way of taking care of all things, of elevating the good and bringing down the bad. If we see things going on within the kingdom that disturb us, we might first resolve, if the matter falls within our stewardship, to go to the person or people involved. If it is of such a nature that we think it should be called to the attention of higher authority, then we can, in a kindly and quiet manner, take the necessary steps at the proper level. ("Jesus Christ—Gifts and Expectations," *New Era* 5 [May 1975]: 18.)

It has only been a short time since we were all preparing for our mortal existence, and while there we became acquainted with the principles which never change. The most important one is that of free agency. We had our choice—we had the opportunity to choose the gospel or oppose it. Satan opposed and was cast out. His plan proposed to save the lives of all, to take away free agency, and to force men to do right, but this ran contrary to the principles of God. (Czechoslovakia, 26 November 1946.)

Yes, we live in a wicked world, but we must not partake of the sins of the world. We are free agents. We have the right of choice, a God-given eternal principle, but the Lord has spoken. He has given us direction. He has inspired priesthood here, and He expects us to follow the counsel. (BYU Ten-Stake Fireside, Provo, Utah, 7 May 1972.)

Freedom and liberty are part of the gospel plan. Any program or philosophy that would destroy a person's free agency is not of God. Therefore, as citizens of this great land, as Latter-day Saints, I hope you will be good citizens, that you will support the laws of liberty and freedom and be guided in your activities by the basic principles of the gospel. I hope that you so live that you will eventually be exalted in the celestial kingdom, and I hope and pray that I will so live that I will be able to meet you there. (Tokyo, Japan, 27 October 1957.)

Yours is a great challenge. You are choice spirits. Forget not that each of you has been endowed with the priceless gift of free agency. You have been given the freedom to "choose liberty and eternal life, . . . or to choose captivity and death" (2 Nephi 2:27). You need not be the victims of circumstance, for unto you it is given to achieve and become "perfect, even as your Father which is in heaven is perfect" (Matthew 5:48). ("Your Charge: To Increase in Wisdom and Favor with God and Man," *New Era* 9 [September 1979]: 45.)

The fate of humanity and all civilization hinges on whether man will use his free agency to govern himself or ignore eternal laws at his own peril and reap the consequences. The real issues of today are, therefore, not economic nor political. They are spiritual —meaning that man must learn to conform to the laws which God has given to mankind. ("A Spiritual Approach to Manmade Problems," Brigham Young University—Hawaii, 11 February 1983.)

God has to work through mortals of varying degrees of spiritual progress. Sometimes He temporarily grants to men their unwise requests in order that they might learn from their own sad experiences. Some refer to this as the "Samuel principle." The children of Israel wanted a king like all the other nations. The prophet Samuel was displeased and prayed to the Lord about it. The Lord responded by saying, "Samuel . . . they have not rejected thee, but they have rejected me, that I should not reign over them" (1 Samuel 8:7). The Lord told Samuel to warn the people of the consequences if they had a king. Samuel gave them the warning. But they still insisted on their king. So God gave them a king and let them suffer. They learned the hard way. God wanted it to be otherwise, but within certain bounds He grants unto men according to their desires (see Alma 41:5). Bad experiences are an expensive school that only fools keep going to. (See 1 Samuel 8.) ("Jesus Christ—Gifts and Expectations," *New Era* 5 [May 1975]: 17–18.)

This life is a probation, a probation in which you and I prove our mettle, a probation that has eternal consequences for each of us. And now is our time and season—as every generation has had theirs—to learn our duties and to do them. That the Lord is displeased with wickedness is true; that He desires that it not occur is also true; that He will help those who oppose it is true. But that He allows wickedness to occur at all through His children here in mortality is proof of His having given them their freedom to choose, while reserving for Himself a basis for their final judgment. (*An Enemy Hath Done This*, pp. 53–54.)

Let me tell you why man will never solve his most basic problems without recognition of spiritual law and obedience thereto. It comes back to the truth of who man is. He is a son of God. As such he has within him an innate need to be responsible and accountable for his own actions. He can only be accountable if he is free to plan and make decisions. If he is not free to plan and make decisions, a spiritual law is violated. ("A Spiritual Approach to

Man-made Problems,'' Brigham Young University—Hawaii, 11 February 1983.)

When the God of Heaven said to one of His ancient prophets, "men are, that they might have joy" (2 Nephi 2:25), He also implied that men should have free agency. They might have joy if through their efforts and the wise exercise of their free agency they lived to merit that joy. (CR October 1954, *Improvement Era* 57 [December 1954]: 920.)

The Lord has so arranged things in this life that men are free agents unto themselves to do good or evil. The Lord allows men to go only so far, but the latitude is great enough that some men promote much wickedness and other men much righteousness. Clearly, there would be little trial of faith if we received our full reward immediately for every goodly deed, or immediate retribution for every sin. But that there will be an eventual reckoning for each, there is no question. (*God, Family, Country*, p. 326.)

Apostasy

Jesus said that the kingdom established in His time would be "given to a nation bringing forth the fruits thereof" (Matthew 21:43). In other words, Jesus knew, as did the Apostles, that an apostasy would take place before His kingdom would be finally established as a prelude to and preparation for His second coming.

The Apostle Paul wrote to members of the Church at Thessalonica that the second coming of Jesus Christ "shall not come, except there come a falling away first" (2 Thessalonians 2:3). And Peter likewise wrote: "There shall be false teachers among you, who privily shall bring in damnable heresies . . . and many shall follow their pernicious ways" (2 Peter 2:1—2).

So the world entered that long night of apostasy, the Dark Ages. The church, no longer sanctioned by God, exercised an oppressive tyranny on the minds of men and shackled them with chains of false traditions. Truth was turned to superstition, joy to despair, and worship to ritual. (*This Nation Shall Endure*, pp. 115—16.)

With the passing of the Apostles and the loss of the priesthood keys, corrupt doctrines were introduced into the Church. In the words of one eminent historian, "Christianity did not destroy paganism; it adopted it. The Greek mind, dying, came to a transmigrated [new] life in the theology and liturgy of the Church." (Will Durant, *The Story of Civilization*, 3:595.) By the second and third centuries, widespread changes had been made in the pure doctrines and ordinances given by the Savior. The Church that Jesus had established and sanctioned was no longer on this earth. (*This Nation Shall Endure*, p. 115.)

Not only by history, which is quite conclusive, but through prophecy also we have been informed definitely that there was and there would be a complete apostasy from the truth. Many of the early reformers recognized this fact as they struck out against the false teachings and practices of their day. John Wesley, the founder of Methodism, lamented that the "Christians had turned heathen again and had only a dead form left." Even in America, Roger Williams, head of the oldest Baptist congregation in the land, recognized, as he quit the ministry, that there was no divinely constituted authority or church upon the face of the earth, nor would there be such a church until one arose having Apostles and other officers as found in the Church established in the meridian of time. (*So Shall Ye Reap*, p. 51.)

It is an attested fact that as Joseph Smith, a humble boy, went into the woods to pray on that beautiful spring morning in 1820, the world—Christian and otherwise—was in a sad state of apostasy. The answer given to him is to me the greatest evidence we have in all the world that there had been an apostasy from the truth. When he beheld those two glorious beings, the one pointed to the other and said, "This is My Beloved Son. Hear Him." And after Joseph asked the question, "which of all the sects was right?" what was the answer that he received? These are his words: "I was answered that I must join none of them, for they were all wrong; . . . 'they teach for doctrines the commandments of men, having a form of godliness, but they deny the power thereof.' He again forbade me to join with any of them." (Joseph Smith—History 1:19–20.) (*So Shall Ye Reap*, p. 51.)

Joseph was to learn in the Sacred Grove that Christ established His Church in former days when He was here on earth. Being the Church of Jesus Christ, it was vitalized by revelation from heaven. Doctrinal disputes were settled on the basis of revelation. But persecution against the Church and disaffection from within caused the Apostles and prophets to be taken from the earth. This removed the appointed servants who were to receive revelation for the Church at large, to keep its membership in a unity of doctrine and faith. So revelation ceased and scripture ended. New doctrines and creeds of uninspired men were introduced into the Church. As predicted in the scriptures, there was an apostasy. ("A Promised Lord—A Promised Land—A Promised People," Wichita, Kansas, 11 November 1976.)

Do we realize to what extent the world has descended into spiritual darkness? It begins in a large measure with many of the clergy, some of whom now cast doubt on the existence of God, questioning the divinity of the Savior and denying the truthfulness of the Bible.

Into what darkness have people fallen when they regard religion as only a superstition, or as a mere listing of ethical teachings not even related to God? And what darkness comes when restraints upon sin are removed by a rejection of true religion, and men, women, and young men and women assume there are no moral laws, and therefore conclude that "anything goes"?

Into what depths have we fallen when government officials will announce publicly that morals do not count anymore, and that we should look upon deviations from chastity as the expected thing in this so-called enlightened age. How dark is the public mind which is lulled to sleep with such an evil philosophy when certain clergymen condone it! ("A Voice of Warning to the Nations of the World," New Zealand and Australia Area Conferences, 25 November 1979 and 2 December 1979.)

A man from down in the southern states—a publisher of some magazines—during his remarks at a New England Rally for God, Family, Country said, "Ladies and Gentlemen, I have been accused of leaving my church, but I want to say to you, 'I didn't leave my church; my church left me.' " He said, "My church no longer teaches the basic concepts that I was taught as a boy at my mother's knee, and in my Sunday School class. My church no longer teaches that Jesus is the Christ, the Redeemer of the world, the Savior of mankind, as I was taught as a boy. My church no longer teaches the basic concepts of Christianity, and the reality of the holy atonement, the resurrection, the final judgment.'' He said, ''I still believe these things; but the pulpit of my church has become a pipeline to collectivism, teaching the social gospel, and denying the basic concepts of Christianity.'' And then he repeated, ''I didn't leave my church; my church left me.'' (San Diego California South Stake Conference, 7 December 1969.)

The Apostle Paul saw our day. He described it as a time when such things as blasphemy, dishonesty, cruelty, unnatural affection, pride and pleasure seeking would abound (see 2 Timothy 3:1–7). He also warned that ''evil men and seducers would wax worse and worse, deceiving and being deceived'' (2 Timothy 3:12). Such grim predictions by prophets of old would be cause for great fear and discouragement if those same prophets had not, at the same time, offered the solution. In their inspired counsel we can find the answer to the spiritual crises of our age. (''The Power of the Word,'' address prepared [but not delivered] 1986.)

The Lord distinguishes between the Church and its members. He said He was well pleased with the restored Church, speaking collectively, but not individually (D&C 1:30). During His ministry on earth, the Lord spoke of the gospel net drawing in fish. The good fish, He said, were gathered into vessels, while the bad were cast away. (See Matthew 13:47–50.)

It is important to realize that while the Church is made up of mortals, no mortal is the Church. Judas, for a period of time, was a member of the Church—in fact, one of its Apostles—but the Church was not Judas.

Sometimes we hear someone refer to a division in the Church. In reality, the Church is not divided. It simply means that there are some who, for the time being at least, are members of the Church but not in harmony with it. These people have a temporary membership and influence in the Church; but unless they repent, they will be missing when the final membership records are recorded. (*God, Family, Country*, pp. 253–54.)

Six of the original Twelve Apostles selected by Joseph Smith were excommunicated. The Three Witnesses to the Book of Mormon left the Church. Three of Joseph Smith's counselors fell— one even helped plot his death. A natural question that might arise would be that if the Lord knew in advance that these men would fall, as He undoubtedly did, why did He have His prophet call them to such high office? The answer is: to fill the Lord's purposes. For even the Master followed the will of the Father by selecting Judas. (*Title of Liberty*, p. 217.)

The Lord strengthened the faith of the early Apostles by pointing out Judas as a traitor, even before this Apostle had completed his iniquitous work (see Matthew 26:23–25; Luke 13:21–26). So also in our day the Lord has told us of the tares within the wheat that will eventually be hewn down when they are fully ripe. But until they are hewn down, they will be with us, amongst us. (See D&C 86:6–7.) (CR April 1969, *Improvement Era* 72 [June 1969]: 42.)

Yes, within the Church today there are tares among the wheat and wolves within the flock. As President J. Reuben Clark, Jr., stated: "The ravening wolves are amongst us, from our own membership, and they, more than any others, are clothed in sheep's clothing because they wear the habiliments of the priesthood. We should be careful of them." (CR April 1949, p. 163.) The wolves amongst our flock are more numerous and devious today than when President Clark made this statement.

President David O. McKay said that "the Church is little, if at all, injured by persecution, and calumnies from ignorant, misinformed, or malicious enemies. A greater hindrance to its progress comes from faultfinders, shirkers, commandment-breakers, and apostate cliques within its own ecclesiastical and quorum groups." (CR October 1967, p. 9.)

Not only are there apostates within our midst, but there are also apostate doctrines that are sometimes taught in our classes and from our pulpits and that appear in our publications. And these apostate precepts of men cause our people to stumble. As the Book of Mormon, speaking of our day, states: "They have all gone astray save it be a few, who are the humble followers of Christ; nevertheless, they are led, that in many instances they do err because they are taught by the precepts of men" (2 Nephi 28:14). (*God, Family, Country*, p. 255.)

Certain individuals within the Church may go astray and even fall away. This may happen even to a person in the Church who is in a position of some influence and authority. It has happened in the past. It will happen in the future. If our faith is in Jesus Christ and not in the arm of flesh, then we will know that we are members of the Church of Jesus Christ and not the church of men. ("Jesus Christ—Gifts and Expectations," *New Era* 5 [May 1975]: 17.)

From time to time we receive reports that some of our members have become enamored and attracted to certain so-called faith healers. Some have been enticed away to a belief and acceptance of the works which they see performed. Some few have been enticed away from the Church and have apostatized. (Cardston, Alberta, Canada, 2 August 1975.)

To publish differences we may think we have with the leaders of the Church, to create strife and division, is a sure road to apostasy. Our task is to stick with the kingdom, to not let anything or anybody disaffect or sour us toward that great gift that Christ has given us—His Church. ("Jesus Christ—Gifts and Expectations," *New Era* 5 [May 1975]: 18.)

The Lord has stated that His Church will never again be taken from the earth because of apostasy (see D&C 138:44). But He has also stated that some members of His Church will fall away. There has been individual apostasy in the past; it is going on now, and there will be an ever-increasing amount in the future. While we cannot save all the flock from being deceived, we should, without compromising our doctrine, strive to save as many as we can. For, as President J. Reuben Clark, Jr., said, "We are in the midst of the greatest exhibition of propaganda that the world has ever seen." Do not believe all you hear. (*An Enemy Hath Done This*, p. 286.)

If there be any division among us, let us set aside anything of this kind and join ranks in the great responsibility to move forward the work of the Lord. If there be those who have become disaffected, we reach out to you in the pure love of Christ and stand ready to assist and welcome you back in full fellowship in the Church. (CR April 1986, *Ensign* 16 [May 1986]: 77.)

Gathering of Israel

In the scriptures there are set forth three phases of the gathering of Israel. One, the gathering of Israel to the land of Zion which is America, this land. That is under way and has been under way since the Church was established and our missions abroad were inaugurated. Then two, the return of the lost tribes, the ten lost tribes, from the land of the north (see D&C 133). And the third phase is the reestablishment of the Jews in Palestine as one of the events to precede the second coming of the Master. Isaiah said they will be gathered together, the dispersed of Judah, from the four corners of the earth and they will be set in their own land, they will build the old wastes and repair the waste cities (see Isaiah 11:11–12). Jeremiah, who predicted the dispersion and the scattering, said that in the last days the Lord would cause them to return to the land that He gave to their fathers and they shall possess it; and they shall build it up as at first (Jeremiah 30:3). ("The Jews Return to Palestine in Fulfillment of Prophecy," Washington D.C. Stake Conference, 3 March 1957.)

In the first visit of Moroni to the Prophet Joseph (see Joseph Smith—History 1:40) mention was made that the "dispersed of Judah would be gathered from the four corners of the earth" (Isaiah 11:12). Thirteen years later, when Moses delivered the keys for the gathering of Israel and the Kirtland Temple was dedicated, the Prophet Joseph made further reference to the promises made to Judah and appealed to the Lord that the time may soon come when the children of Judah would return to the land promised to their father, Abraham (D&C 109:61–65). (CR April 1950, *Improvement Era* 53 [May 1950]: 434.)

Historically, we must recognize that interest in the restoration of the Jews to their homeland is older than modern Zionism and the great work of Theodor Herzl and others. There were a number of Christian sects in the nineteenth century that held millennial views and saw the return of the Jews to their homeland as a "sign of the times" that would precede the second advent of Jesus Christ. The Mormon interest was and is more than this. Our concern and interest are a kinship to our Jewish brothers.

Our common heritage goes back to Abraham, Isaac, and Jacob. God reiterated to Jacob the same promise given to Abraham, and then gave Jacob the new name of Israel. His posterity—and those who descended through his twelve sons—were known by this designation. They were variously referred to as the "house of Israel" or the "children of Israel." Though all of his posterity received the family name designation through the twelve sons, today it has become common practice to identify only one of his twelve sons, Judah, with the family designation, Israelite, because they have maintained their separate identity. (*This Nation Shall Endure*, pp. 133–34.)

Gifts of the Spirit

What a privilege it is to serve in the kingdom of God. In this work it is the Spirit that counts—wherever we serve. I know I must rely on the Spirit. Let us obtain that Spirit and be faithful members of the Church, devoted children and parents, effective home teachers, edifying instructors, inspired ward and stake leaders. God bless you all for your noble labors in building the kingdom. (CR April 1986, *Ensign* 16 [May 1986]: 77.)

This latter-day work is spiritual. It takes spirituality to comprehend it, to love it, and to discern it. Therefore we should seek the Spirit in all we do. That is our challenge. (*Come unto Christ*, p. 23.)

Brethren—especially you priesthood leaders—would you counsel those under your watch-care to be prayerful and watchful, lest these deceptions take root in our midst. Counsel them to seek the gift of discernment which comes by prayer and living the commandments of God. (Logan, Utah, 6 December 1975.)

I have had the glorious pleasure of addressing the Saints in many languages—in Norwegian, Swedish, Finnish, and Danish. I have addressed the Saints in Holland, France, Germany, Poland, Austria, in at least eleven different languages, and on one or more occasions have spoken through three interpreters at the same time. When you do that it takes a long time to say much. But even in a meeting where there are several languages represented there is always the true spirit of the gospel. Someday we will all speak a common tongue, and perhaps that will be the pure Adamic language. Then it may be a little bit easier for us to convey our feelings. (Tokyo, Japan, 27 October 1957.)

The Hawaiian Temple has a special place in the hearts of our family. While my eternal companion, Flora Amussen, was on her mission in the Hawaiian Islands, she was called on during the first months to teach school in the Church's elementary school. There were seven different nationalities in her school room. While officiating in the temple in an evening session, and busying herself straightening things in the temple, she discovered that she was alone, that all the others had gone home.

It was necessary to get to the mission home by going over a fence by a stile and by a migrant workers' village. It was dark and she was concerned. She prayed to the Lord that she would be protected. As she left the temple door a circle of light surrounded her and moved with her all the way over the fence, past the village, and to the mission home. It didn't leave her until she entered the mission home door. She always felt this was an answer to prayer and that she was truly protected by her Heavenly Father. ("Temple Blessings and Covenants," Hawaii Temple Rededication, 13–15 June 1978.)

I hope you were listening carefully as the children were singing. Let me assure you that they were not alone. The angels were singing with them. And if the Lord would touch your spiritual eyes and understanding, you would see that many of your loved ones, whom you have lost during the war, are assembled with us today. As the children's chorus sang, I looked over toward them several times, for I heard more voices singing than those who are in the group. In truth their voices were mingled with voices from heaven.

We have truly had a taste of heaven today. (As quoted in Frederick W. Babbel, *On Wings of Faith* [Salt Lake City: Bookcraft, 1972], p. 116.)

I have never felt the Spirit of the Lord stronger than I do this morning. The veil between us and the world of spirits is very thin. I feel most strongly that there are others here besides those we can see—some of your loved ones are here, also some of the leaders of the Church who have passed on. Those in authority in the heavens above are pleased and willing that the spirits of our loved ones should be near us. (As quoted in Frederick W. Babbel, *On Wings of Faith* [Salt Lake City: Bookcraft, 1972], p. 116.)

Israel

The prophet Isaiah said that in the last days the Lord would proceed to do a marvelous work and a wonder; that the wisdom of their wise men should perish and the understanding of their prudent men should be hid (Isaiah 29:14; 2 Nephi 27:26). That prophecy, it seems to me, has been and is being fulfilled in what is transpiring over in Israel at the present time. ("The Jews Return to Palestine in Fulfillment of Prophecy," Washington D.C. Stake Conference, 3 March 1957.)

There is a great affinity for the Jews by the Mormons. The Jews have endured great persecution and suffering. This we understand, for our people have also undergone severe persecution and extermination. Indeed, the man we revere as a modern prophet, Joseph Smith, was martyred for his testimony in 1844. In 1846 our people had to leave the United States in exodus because of the threat of annihilation. We settled in a desert region similar to the topography around the Dead Sea and the Sea of Galilee. There we developed our "land of promise." Yes, we can empathize with the suffering of the Jews, for we have co-suffered with them. But our affinity toward modern Judah is not prompted out of mutual suffering; it is prompted out of a knowledge of our peculiar heritage. Jeremiah has prophesied that in the latter times, "the house of Judah shall walk with the house of Israel, and they shall come together" (Jeremiah 3:18). (*This Nation Shall Endure*, p. 131.)

From the very inception of this latter-day work, which claims to be a restoration of the covenants given by God to Abraham, Isaac, and Jacob, the Church has had a deep interest in the remnant of the house of Israel, the descendants of Judah.

In 1836, the Saints completed their first temple at Kirtland, Ohio. In the dedicatory prayer offered on that occasion, Joseph Smith petitioned the "Lord God of Israel":

> O Lord . . . thou knowest that thou hast a great love for the children of Jacob, who have been scattered upon the mountains for a long time. . . .
> We therefore ask thee to have mercy upon the children of Jacob, that Jerusalem, from this hour, may begin to be redeemed.
> And the yoke of bondage may begin to be broken off from the house of David.
> And the children of Judah may begin to return to the lands which thou didst give to Abraham, their father. (D&C 109:60–64.)

This was said during the Passover Season, 27 March 1836.

Before the Prophet was killed, he dispatched an Apostle by the name of Orson Hyde to dedicate the land of Palestine for the return of the Jews. This concern for a homeless people and the sending of this Apostle were done at a time when the Mormons themselves were virtually homeless, having been dispossessed of their lands and possessions in Missouri. Orson Hyde left on his assignment in the fall of 1840 and arrived in Palestine in October 1841. (*This Nation Shall Endure*, pp. 132–33.)

The Prophet Joseph and the leaders of the Church sent Orson Hyde and John E. Page to dedicate the land of Palestine for the return of the Jews. Elder Page did not complete the journey but Elder Hyde went on and in 1841 he went atop the Mount of Olives and dedicated that land for the return of the Jews. It had been predicted ten years before in a blessing upon his head that he would go. He was told that in due time he would go to Jerusalem the land of his fathers, because he was of Jewish extraction, and be a watchman on the tower in helping to bring about the gathering of dispersed Judah. The land was again dedicated by President George A. Smith in 1873. And so, we have been looking forward as Latter-day Saints for a hundred years, confidently expecting that in the Lord's own due time these prophecies made in the dedicatory prayers as well as in the scriptures would be fulfilled; and the promises made that this land would again become a fruitful land, that the sterility would be removed and the springs of living water would burst forth; that these too would be fulfilled. We knew that kings of the earth would be inspired to look with a friendly eye, as Brother Hyde prayed on that visit to the Holy Land, that the powers of the earth would look with a friendly eye upon the gathering of Judah. It was even mentioned that the nation of Great Britain would play a very important part in the gathering of Judah.

It was shortly after this dedication that the first organization sprang up, dedicated to the promotion of the return of the Jews to Palestine. And about this time also President Wilford Woodruff made his remarkable prophecy and statement regarding Judah when he said:

> The Lord has decreed that the Jews should be gathered from all the Gentile nations where they have been driven, into their own land . . . and this is the will of your great Elohim, O house of Judah, and whenever you shall be called upon to perform this work, the God of Israel will help you. You have a great future and destiny before you and you cannot avoid fulfilling it; you are the royal chosen seed, and the God of your father's house has kept you distinct as a nation for eighteen hundred years, under all the oppression of the whole Gentile world. You may not wait until you believe on Jesus of Nazareth but when you meet with Shiloh your king, you will know him; your destiny is marked out, you cannot avoid it.

Then he concludes by saying the time is not far distant when the rich men of the Jews will be called upon to use their abundant wealth to gather the dispersed of Judah and purchase the ancient dwelling places of their fathers in and about Jerusalem and rebuild the holy city and temple. ("The Jews Return to Palestine in Fulfillment of Prophecy," Washington D.C. Stake Conference, 3 March 1957.)

Ben-Gurion and I discussed the Old Testament prophecies. I told him about some of the references to the reestablishment of the Jews in our book of Doctrine and Covenants (see D&C 77:15; 109:61–64). I mentioned that many years ago in Elder Hyde's prayer of dedication on the Mount of Olives, he prayed that the barrenness and sterility of the land would be removed, that springs of water would burst forth, that the land would become fruitful again, that the Lord would subdue their unbelief and "incline them to gather in upon this land." He also prayed that God would inspire the kings of the earth to help bring about the promises made to Judah.

Ben-Gurion was most interested in this account; he knew something about it already. I left, convinced that he is a noble soul with a deep love for his people and a determination to give them faithful and courageous leadership.

In Israel I met hundreds of government officials, farmers, business and trade people and leaders in the professions. We drove by auto into rural and urban areas and flew in a small plane at low elevations over much of the country. We viewed such historic places (outside Jerusalem, which we covered thoroughly) as Nazareth, Jaffa, Cana, Mount Hermon, Mount Tabor, the Sea of Galilee, and Tiberias.

Obviously, great progress was being made in Israel—more than in any country of the Middle East. Capital was flowing in, the population was growing rapidly both from the influx of people and from natural increase. This nation, in spite of its political problems, was rapidly becoming the leading industrial center of this entire politically unstable area.

The greatest advancements of all were being made in agriculture. The deserts and hills were blossoming, becoming green and productive again. (See Isaiah 35:1.) Hills on either side of Galilee, for generations denuded and eroded, were being covered with forest trees and citrus and olive groves. Already, Israel was exporting millions of boxes of citrus to northern Europe. Swampy areas were being converted into fish farms as a principal source of protein. A wide variety of crops adapted to dry and irrigation farming were producing abundantly. Israel was on the move. (*Crossfire: The Eight Years with Eisenhower*, pp. 368–70.)

We need to know more about the Jews, and the Jews ought to know more about the Mormons. When we understand one another, perhaps we will understand why David Ben-Gurion said to me on one of my visits to Tel Aviv, "There are no people in the world who understand the Jews like the Mormons."

Among the kindred doctrines of the Mormons and the Jews is our mutual belief in Jehovah, a God of revelation. We share a common belief in prophets. We hold a common commitment to the return of the Jews to the "land of Jerusalem," in fulfillment of the words of the ancient prophets. There are many other doctrinal and social similarities. (*This Nation Shall Endure*, p. 131.)

The prophecies of so-called experts, of economists, of statesmen, of military people, have failed in the face of the prophecies which the Lord has made through His prophets regarding the future of the descendants of Judah and the future of that great nation, the great little country of Palestine. And a very interesting observation is the fact that these people, these Jewish people in Palestine, are virtually unanimous, I am told, in their feeling that the victory, the military victory of 1949, cannot be explained in any other terms except that it was a miracle.

May I refer to some of these prophecies briefly. There are many of them, not only regarding the dispersion of Judah and Israel but also the gathering. Jeremiah said: "Thus, saith the Lord of hosts; Behold, I will send upon them the sword, the famine, and the pestilence, and will make them like vile figs, that cannot be eaten, they are so evil." Then he tells how they will be persecuted and driven, how they will become a hiss and a reproach "among all the nations whither I have driven them: Because they have not hearkened to my words, saith the Lord, which I sent unto them by my servants, the prophets." (Jeremiah 29:17–19.) You remember the words recorded in Luke when the Lord predicted the fall of Jerusalem: "And they shall fall by the edge of the sword, and shall be led away captive into all nations: and Jerusalem shall be trodden down of the Gentiles, until the times of the Gentiles be fulfilled." (Luke 21:24.) This time of the Gentiles is being fulfilled and the prophecies regarding the reestablishment of Judah and Israel are likewise coming to pass. ("The Jews Return to Palestine in Fulfillment of Prophecy," Washington D.C. Stake Conference, 3 March 1957.)

There is great conflict yet to come before the millennial reign, before the Christ comes. If you want to get some indication of just what this conflict will be, you may wish to turn to the fourteenth chapter of Zechariah and the eleventh chapter of the book of Revelation, which make it very clear that nations will be pitted against Judah; that there will be great wars, great conflict; that at least two prophets will be raised up among them; that they will make predictions before Christ comes. I have no doubt but what these prophets will be assigned by the leadership of the priesthood, because the Lord's house is a house of order. The gospel will be carried to the Jews and many of them will accept it. ("The Jews Return to Palestine in Fulfillment of Prophecy," Washington D.C. Stake Conference, 3 March 1957.)

I was in Czechoslovakia just last Sunday (29 September 1946), meeting with a group of Saints. In speaking with President Wallace F. Toronto of that mission, he told me of some of the Jews leaving their former homelands. To some of them he said: "Why don't you stay here or stay in some other country? Why do you want to be moving to Palestine?" The answer he received was: "We don't know, except we have in our hearts an urge to go to the Holy Land." And they are going there by the thousands.

Elder Orson Hyde dedicated the land of Palestine for the return of the Jews and made great promises concerning their going there. The British nation is playing a great part in making these promises come true. General Allenby of the British forces, helped open that land for the return of the Jews in 1918. We know that the leaders of the nations do not fully realize why they are doing this, but we as Latter-day Saints know. It has been one of the missions that this great nation has had—the bringing about of the return of the Jews to Palestine in fulfillment of the Bible prophecies that are very clearly made concerning this event. We know they will gather there. They will become a strong nation. They will have their wars with outside nations. They will have their prophets (Revelation 11). Christ will appear to them and the Mount of Olives will cleave in twain (Zechariah 14:4–5). The enemies of the Jews will be overcome as Christ appears to them and then they will recognize for the first time that He is in very deed the long-looked-for King. Then they shall say, "What are these wounds in your hands and in your feet?" And He will answer: "These wounds are the wounds with which I was wounded in the house of my friends." Then, for the first time, they will realize that He is Jesus the Christ whom they crucified. That is all revealed to us. Read the forty-fifth section of the Doctrine and Covenants. ("I'll Go Where You Want Me to Go," *Church News* [23 September 1946]: 8.)

The great blessing to Judah is that it contemplated the coming of Shiloh who would gather His people to Him. This prophecy concerning Shiloh has been subject to several rabbinic and Christian interpretations and the object of considerable controversy. The interpretation given this passage by the Latter-day Saints is one based on revelation to modern prophets, not on scholarly commentary. It was revealed to Joseph Smith that Shiloh is the Messiah. (See Joseph Smith Translation, Genesis 50:24.) (*This Nation Shall Endure*, p. 139.)

We look forward to the day of fulfillment of God's promise when "the house of Judah shall walk with the house of Israel" (Jeremiah 3:18). As one who, by special assignment, has been given authority in the house of Israel, I ask the God of Abraham, Isaac, and Jacob to bless my brethren of Judah and have mercy on them; that the land to which Judah has returned after a long night of dispersion shall be fruitful, prosperous, and become the envy of her neighbors; that the nation Israel shall be delivered from all her oppressors and enemies; that Judah will "draw water out of the wells of salvation" and fulfill all those prophecies that God declared through His prophets Isaiah, Ezekiel, Jeremiah; and that "the Lord shall inherit Judah his portion in the holy land, and shall choose Jerusalem again." (Zechariah 2:12.) (*This Nation Shall Endure*, pp. 141–42.)

Joseph Smith

Joseph Smith, the latter-day Prophet, was an instrument in the hands of the Lord in opening a new gospel dispensation—the last and greatest of all gospel dispensations. He witnessed and participated in the greatest event that has transpired in this world since the resurrection of the Master. (CR October 1965, *Improvement Era* 68 [December 1965]: 1151.)

To get a vision of the magnitude of the Prophet's earthly mission we must view it in the light of eternity. He was among "the noble and great ones" whom Abraham described as follows:

> Now the Lord had shown unto me, Abraham, the intelligences that were organized before the world was; and among all these there were many of the noble and great ones;

> And God saw these souls that they were good, and he stood in the midst of them, and he said: These I will make my rulers; for he stood among those that were spirits, and he saw that they were good; and he said unto me: Abraham, thou art one of them; thou wast chosen before thou wast born. (Abraham 3:22–23.)

So it was with Joseph Smith. He too was there. He too sat in council with the noble and great ones. Occupying a prominent place of honor and distinction, he unquestionably helped in the planning and execution of the great work of the Lord to "bring to pass the immortality and eternal life of man," the salvation of all our Father's children (see Moses 1:39). His mission had, and was to have, impact on all who had come to earth, all who then dwelt on earth, and the millions yet unborn.

The Prophet Joseph Smith was not only "one of the noble and great ones," but he gave and continues to give attention to important matters here on the earth even today from the realms above. For in the eyes of the Lord, the God of this world under the Father, it is all one great eternal program in which the Prophet Joseph plays an important role, all through the eternal priesthood and authority of God. (*God, Family, Country*, pp. 30–31.)

The first vision of the Prophet Joseph Smith is bedrock theology to the Church. The adversary knows this and has attacked Joseph Smith's credibility from the day he announced the visitation of the Father and the Son. You should always bear testimony to the truth of the First Vision. Joseph Smith did see the Father and the Son. They conversed with him as he said they did. Any leader who, without reservation, cannot declare his testimony that God and Jesus Christ appeared to Joseph Smith can never be a true leader, a true shepherd. If we do not accept this truth—if we have not received a witness about this great revelation—we cannot inspire faith in those whom we lead.

Some of our own members have attempted to interpret the experiences of Joseph Smith and his revelations. They say that it really is not important whether or not Joseph Smith actually saw God the Father and His Son Jesus Christ. What matters, they claim, is that he thought he did. That is preposterous! (Salt Lake City, Utah, 20 May 1984.)

Joseph Smith received many revelations from Jesus Christ, as have the prophets who have succeeded him, which means that new scripture has been given. The Lord's mouthpiece and prophet on the face of the earth today received his authority through a line of prophets going back to Joseph Smith, who was ordained by Peter, James, and John, who were ordained by Christ, who was and is the head of the Church, the Creator of this earth, and the God before whom all men must stand accountable.

Now, this marvelous message that God has spoken to prophets in our day and reestablished His Church is for all the world. When Nathanael questioned Philip, who told him that he had found Jesus, Philip responded by saying, "Come and see" (John 1:46).

So do we respond, "Come and see." Men can deceive you, but God will not. If you sincerely desire to know of the truthfulness of this message, then make it a matter of fervent prayer, study it out, test it out, and God will let you know. (*God, Family, Country*, pp. 158−59.)

I remember an incident in the life of the Prophet Joseph. God bless his memory! He had been persecuted with his people, driven, and at this particular time he was in Liberty Jail, incarcerated upon trumped-up charges. Finally, when it seemed as though he could stand it no longer, he cried out in the anguish of his soul, "O God, where art thou? And where is the pavilion that covereth thy hiding place? How long shall thy hand be stayed, and thine eye, yea thy pure eye, behold from the eternal heavens the wrongs of thy people and of thy servants, and thine ear be penetrated with their cries?" (D&C 121:1−2.)

And you will recall, the word came back to him: "My son, peace be unto thy soul; thine adversity and thine afflictions shall be but a small moment; And then, if thou endure it well, God shall exalt thee on high; thou shalt triumph over all thy foes." (D&C 121:7−8.) Then the Lord pointed out to this great man, this prophet of God, that all these things had been given for the purpose of gaining experience, of helping to build him for the great responsibilities that lay ahead of him. How sweet and reassuring are the words of the Lord on that memorable occasion as He counseled: "Know thou, my son, that all these things shall give thee experience, and shall be for thy good . . . therefore, fear not what man can do, for God shall be with you forever and ever." (D&C 122:7, 9.) (CR April 1954, *Improvement Era* 57 [June 1954]: 407.)

Joseph Smith the Prophet went willingly to his death. He sealed his testimony with his life—his own blood. On that fateful day in Nauvoo, Illinois, as he looked back upon his city and people whom he loved, on his way to Carthage Jail and his martyrdom, he declared: "This is the loveliest place and the best people under the heavens; little do they know the trials that await them" (*History of the Church*, 6:554).

Later the Prophet said feelingly, but calmly and courageously: "I am going like a lamb to the slaughter, but I am as calm as a summer's morning. I have a conscience void of offense toward God and toward all men. If they take my life I shall die an innocent man, and my blood shall cry from the ground for vengeance, and it shall be said of me, 'He was murdered in cold blood!' " (*History of the Church*, 6:555.) (CR October 1965, *Improvement Era* 68 [December 1965]: 1151.)

Just as prophets of the past were without honor in their own countries and were persecuted and killed, Joseph Smith was maligned and martyred in his generation. Was Joseph Smith sent from God? We answer an emphatic "yes"! "He lived great, and he died great in the eyes of God and his people; and like most of the Lord's anointed in ancient times, has sealed his mission and his works with his own blood" (D&C 135:3). (CR October 1981, *Ensign* 11 [November 1981]: 63.)

As I have thumbed through more than a score of volumes on the Prophet in my own library, and recalled there are reported to be more than sixteen hundred separate volumes and more than twenty thousand books and pamphlets that refer to the Prophet in the library of the Church, I am prompted to ask, what except testimony and further witness can be added as we honor our greatest countryman around the world and acknowledge him as a prophet-representative of the Lord Jesus Christ without a peer? (*God, Family, Country*, p. 27.)

The world has generally revered the ancient dead prophets and rejected the living ones. It was so with Joseph Smith. Truth is often on the scaffold—error on the throne. But time is on the side of truth, for truth is eternal. (CR October 1965, *Improvement Era* 68 [December 1965]: 1151.)

The greatest activity in this world or in the world to come is directly related to the work and mission of Joseph Smith—man of destiny, prophet of God. That work is the salvation and eternal life of man. For that great purpose this earth was created, prophets of God are called, heavenly messengers are sent forth, and on sacred and important occasions even God, the Father of us all, condescends to come to earth and to introduce His Beloved Son. (*God, Family, Country*, p. 31.)

I know that Joseph Smith, although slain as a martyr to the truth, still lives and that as head of this dispensation—the greatest of all dispensations—he will continue so to stand throughout the eternities to come. He is a prophet of God, a seer, and a revelator, as are his successors. (*So Shall Ye Reap*, p. 100.)

God help us to live the gospel. I testify to you that God has again spoken from the heavens. The heavens are not sealed. The vision of God the Father and the Son to the boy prophet did in very deed occur. God lives. Jesus is the Christ, the Redeemer of the world, not just a great moral teacher, as much of the Christian world is claiming, but the Savior of mankind, the very Son of God.

Joseph Smith was a prophet of the Living God, one of the greatest prophets that has ever lived upon the earth. He was the instrument in God's hand in ushering in a great gospel dispensation, the greatest ever, and the last of all in preparation for the second coming of the Master.

I bear witness that these things are true, and that we have standing at the head of the Church today a prophet of the Living God, who holds all the keys and authority necessary to carry forward our Father's program for the blessing of His children. As God lives, I know these things to be true and bear this witness to you in the name of the Lord Jesus Christ, amen. (*Title of Liberty*, pp. 215–16.)

Last Days

For nearly six thousand years, God has held you in reserve to make your appearance in the final days before the second coming of the Lord. Some individuals will fall away; but the kingdom of God will remain intact to welcome the return of its head—even Jesus Christ. While our generation will be comparable in wickedness to the days of Noah, when the Lord cleansed the earth by flood, there is a major difference this time. It is that God has saved for the final inning some of His strongest children, who will help bear off the kingdom triumphantly. That is where you come in, for you are the generation that must be prepared to meet your God. ("In His Steps," Church Educational System Devotional, Anaheim, California, 8 February 1987.)

Many years before the coming of the Savior to this earth, the prophet Enoch saw the latter days. He observed the great wickedness that would prevail on the earth at this time and foretold the "great tribulations" that would result from such wickedness: but in the midst of what was otherwise a very gloomy prophecy, the Lord promised, "But my people will I preserve" (Moses 7:61). How would He do so? Note what the Lord Himself promised He would do to preserve His people. He said: "And righteousness will I send down out of heaven; and truth will I send forth out of the earth, to bear testimony of mine Only Begotten: and righteousness and truth will I cause to sweep the earth as with a flood, to gather out mine elect from the four quarters of the earth unto a place which I shall prepare" (Moses 7:62). (CR October 1986, *Ensign* 16 [November 1986]: 79.)

In all ages prophets have looked down through the corridors of time to our day. Billions of the deceased and those yet to be born have their eyes on us. Make no mistake about it—you are a marked generation. There has never been more expected of the faithful in such a short period of time than there is of us. Never before on the face of this earth have the forces of evil and the forces of good been as well organized. Now is the great day of the devil's power. But now is also the great day of the Lord's power, with the greatest number ever of priesthood holders on the earth. ("In His Steps," Church Educational System Devotional, Anaheim, California, 8 February 1987.)

We constantly hear or read of wars and rumors of wars. Atheism, agnosticism, immorality, and dishonesty are flaunted in our society. Desertion, cruelty, divorce, and infidelity have become commonplace, leading to a disintegration of the family. Truly we live in the times of which the Savior spoke, when "the love of men shall wax cold, and iniquity shall abound" (D&C 45:27).

The rejection of the testimony of the servants of God by the nations of the world will bring the consequence of greater calamities, for the Lord Himself declared:

> After your testimony cometh the testimony of earthquakes, that shall cause groanings in the midst of her, and men shall fall upon the ground and shall not be able to stand.
>
> And also cometh the testimony of the voice of thunderings, and the voice of lightnings, and the voice of tempests, and the voice of the waves of the sea heaving themselves beyond their bounds.
>
> And all things shall be in commotion; and surely, men's hearts shall fail them; for fear shall come upon all people. (D&C 88:89–91.)

(*Come unto Christ*, pp. 111–12.)

We live in difficult days—very difficult days. They are not improving. However, I do feel that there is some increase in the awakening to the dangers that face us. I am not sure that the awakening is going to be fast enough to avoid the disaster which could very seriously result in bloodshed, hardship, and much sorrow in this beloved country. (Salt Lake City, Utah, 8 April 1972.)

We will live in the midst of economic, political, and spiritual instability. When these signs are observed—unmistakable evidences that His coming is nigh—we need not be troubled, but "stand in holy places, and be not moved, until the day of the Lord come" (D&C 87:8). Holy men and women stand in holy places, and these holy places consist of our temples, our chapels, our homes, and stakes of Zion, which are, as the Lord declares, "for a defense, and for a refuge from the storm, and from wrath when it shall be poured out without mixture upon the whole earth" (D&C 115:6). We must heed the Lord's counsel to the Saints of this dispensation: "Prepare yourselves for the great day of the Lord" (D&C 133:10).

This preparation must consist of more than just casual membership in the Church. We must be guided by personal revelation and the counsel of the living prophet so we will not be deceived.

Our Lord has indicated who, among Church members, will stand when He appears: "At that day, when I shall come in my glory, shall the parable be fulfilled which I spake concerning the ten virgins" (D&C 45:56). (*Come unto Christ*, pp. 115–16.)

There is a real sifting going on in the Church, and it is going to become more pronounced with the passing of time. It will sift the wheat from the tares, because we face some difficult days, the like of which we have never experienced in our lives. And those days are going to require faith and testimony and family unity, the like of which we have never had. (Grantsville Utah Stake Conference, 1 September 1974.)

Now, we are assured that the Church will remain on the earth until the Lord comes again—but at what price? The Saints in the early days were assured that Zion would be established in Jackson County, but look at what their unfaithfulness cost them in bloodshed and delay.

President J. Reuben Clark warned us that "we stand in danger of losing our liberties, and that once lost, only blood will bring them back; and once lost, we of this church will, in order to keep the Church going forward, have more sacrifices to make and more persecutions to endure than we have yet known" (CR April 1944, p. 116). And he stated that if the conspiracy "comes here it will probably come in its full vigor and there will be a lot of vacant places among those who guide and direct, not only this government, but also this Church of ours" (CR April 1952). (CR April 1972, *Ensign* 2 [July 1972]: 61.)

The great destructive force which was to be turned loose on the earth and which the prophets for centuries have been calling the "abomination of desolation" is vividly described by those who saw it in vision (see Matthew 24:15; Joseph Smith—Matthew 1:12, 32). Ours is the first generation to realize how literally these prophecies can be fulfilled now that God, through science, has unlocked the secret to thermonuclear reaction.

In the light of these prophecies, there should be no doubt in the mind of any priesthood holder that the human family is headed for trouble. There are rugged days ahead. It is time for every man who wishes to do his duty to get himself prepared—physically, spiritually, and psychologically—for the task which may come at any time, as suddenly as the whirlwind. (*God, Family, Country*, pp. 345–46.)

In striving to prepare a people who are ready to meet the Lord for His impending second coming, we are faced with wickedness which has never been as well organized, extensive, and subtle. Our day is becoming comparable to the days of Noah, when the Lord had to cleanse the earth by flood—only in our day it will be cleansed by fire. ("Our Obligation and Challenge," Regional Representatives Seminar, Salt Lake City, Utah, 30 September 1977.)

Christ will come and will appear, according to the scriptures, on the Mount of Olives. The mountain will cleave in twain during this great last struggle in which Judah will participate and then no doubt will the prophecy be fulfilled in which the Master said to the Prophet Joseph: "And then shall Jews look upon me and say: What are these wounds in thine hands and in thy feet? Then shall they know that I am the Lord; for I will say unto them: These wounds are the wounds with which I was wounded in the house of my friends. I am he who was lifted up. I am Jesus that was crucified. I am the Son of God. And then shall they weep because of their iniquities; then shall they lament because they persecuted their king." (D&C 45:51–52.)

May God hasten the day when this great drama will be completed as one of the signs of the times in preparation for the second coming of the Master. And God bless us as Latter-day Saints who have been given the custody of the gospel of salvation, and who will have the responsibility of carrying it not only to Judah but to all the world. God bless us that we may discharge that obligation honorably and faithfully and do all those things which the Lord requires at our hands. ("The Jews Return to Palestine in Fulfillment of Prophecy," Washington D.C. Stake Conference, 3 March 1957.)

Restoration

Following the great apostasy from the principles and laws of Christ, the world became enslaved in a cloak of darkness. This long night of Christian apostasy placed an oppressive tyranny on the minds of men, which were shackled by chains of false priestly tradition. Before the gospel could shine forth its resplendent light, a flickering flame of religious and political freedom had to commence somewhere. Heaven determined that it begin in England. The stage had been set premortally. The characters in the drama had been held in reserve to come at appropriate times and intervals to influence the course of events in history. (*This Nation Shall Endure*, p. 1.)

It was historical documents such as the English Petition of Rights and the English Bill of Rights that first recognized the "immemorial rights of Englishmen." I believe these movements were inspired by the Lord. Later these God-given rights were to become guaranteed by New World documents, such as the Declaration of Independence and the American Bill of Rights. (*This Nation Shall Endure*, p. 3.)

Once a man's rights became guaranteed by the political institutions that would serve him, the time became propitious for the Prophet Joseph Smith to be sent on the world scene and for the kingdom of God to be restored by direct divine intervention. A light had burst forth among men again, and it was the fulness of the gospel! (See D&C 45:28.)

Yes, the freedom-loving men owe a debt of gratitude to Great Britain and those human instruments who provided that first flicker of "freedom's holy light" to future generations, and which made the restoration of the fulness of the gospel possible. (*This Nation Shall Endure*, p. 5.)

Before the gospel could again shine forth its resplendent light, religious and political freedom first had to be restored. This land had been preserved as a continent apart from the religious oppression, tyranny, and intolerance of Europe. In time, emigrants came to the new land and established colonies. By and large, they were a God-fearing people. A war was fought for their independence, and by God's intervention, victory was achieved. (See 1 Nephi 13:16–19.) By that same omnipotent power the Constitution was born (see D&C 101:80), which guaranteed religious and political liberty (see D&C 98:5–8). Only then was the time propitious for the kingdom of God—that "stone cut out without hands"—to be restored (see Daniel 2:34).

A prophet of God was sent to this new nation. This occurred in the year 1805, only sixteen years after the ratification of the Constitution. The prophet's name was Joseph Smith. In his fifteenth year, while troubled because of the "tumult of opinions" about which church was right, this young man sought an answer in prayer (see Joseph Smith—History 1:10). Secluding himself in a grove of trees near his father's farm in Palmyra, New York, he asked of God. His prayer was answered with a glorious manifestation in which he saw God the Father and His Son Jesus Christ. (*This Nation Shall Endure*, p. 116.)

This is the glorious message we desire to share with the world, that through God the Father and His Son Jesus Christ, the kingdom of God has been restored. It is the greatest message since the resurrection of Jesus Christ. Like the stone that Daniel saw, the kingdom is now rolling forward in the earth to fulfill its destiny to fill the whole earth (see Daniel 2:34, 44–45). We are under divine commandment to see that this is done (see D&C 65:2, 5–6). (*This Nation Shall Endure*, pp. 116–17.)

The Church of Jesus Christ of Latter-day Saints is, as Daniel prophesied, a spiritual kingdom "cut out of the mountain without hands" (Daniel 2:45), meaning that it was begun through the intervention of God. It is not just another human institution. What other organizations or churches ascribe their founding to the declaration that messengers have come to human beings from the God of Heaven with authority and power to restore ordinances and keys lost by apostasy? (CR April 1980, *Ensign* 10 [May 1980]: 32.)

On a spring day in the year 1820 in the state of New York, a young boy by the name of Joseph Smith went into a grove of trees on his father's farm to pray. He needed help. He wanted to join a church but he was confused as to which one. Seeking an answer he read one day these words from the Bible: "If any of you lack wisdom, let him ask of God, that giveth to all men liberally, and upbraideth not; and it shall be given him" (James 1:5).

This Joseph Smith did. In response to his prayer our Heavenly Father and His Son Jesus Christ appeared to him. Joseph was told to join none of the churches.

Joseph was to learn that Christ established the Church in former days when He was here on earth. Its members were called Saints, but because of the wickedness of men the prophets were taken away from the people and so revelation ceased, the scripture ended, and the doctrines and creeds of uninspired men prevailed. As predicted in the scriptures, there was an apostasy.

But, as had also been predicted, the Lord was planning to restore His Church in these latter days prior to His second coming, and like the former-day Church, His restored Church was to have Apostles and prophets and have new revelation and added scripture. And so through Joseph Smith the Lord established The Church of Jesus Christ of Latter-day Saints. (*An Enemy Hath Done This*, pp. 328–29.)

The Prophet Joseph Smith was the instrument in God's hands in restoring the gospel and establishing the true Church of Christ again upon the earth. In response to humble prayer Joseph relates: "I saw a pillar of light exactly over my head, above the brightness of the sun, which descended gradually until it fell upon me. When the light rested upon me I saw two Personages, whose brightness and glory defy all description, standing above me in the air. One of them spake unto me, calling me by name and said, pointing to the other—This is My Beloved Son. Hear Him!" (Joseph Smith—History 1:16–17.) To me this is the greatest event that has occurred in this world since the resurrection of the Master—and it happened in America. (*Title of Liberty*, p. 88.)

It was predicted in scripture that the Lord would restore His Church in these latter days prior to His second coming. Like the former-day Church, His restored Church was to have Apostles, prophets, and current revelation which added new scripture. We declare that this prophecy has come to pass. Through the Prophet Joseph Smith the Lord has established His Church again on earth. Within it you will find Apostles and prophets, revelation, and new scripture. One portion of the new scripture coming forth in our modern day is the Book of Mormon. ("A Promised Lord—A Promised Land—A Promised People," Wichita, Kansas, 11 November 1976.)

He lives today! Of that I bear solemn witness. This same Jesus has already come to earth in our day. The resurrected Christ—glorified, exalted, the God of this world under the Father—appeared to the boy Joseph Smith, Jr., in 1820. This same Jesus, who was the God of Abraham, Isaac, and Jacob, the God of Moses, the Creator of this earth, has come in our day.

There are some in our midst who sponsor the sophistry that this appearance of God the Father and His Son Jesus Christ was not literal, that it was probably a product of Joseph Smith's own imaginings. This is not true. This is an attempt to discredit the testimony of Joseph Smith. It is also an attempt to discredit the testimony of Jesus Himself, who came to Joseph as a witness of His own resurrection. As the restored Church of Jesus Christ, we humbly and gratefully bear this witness to all men. It is the truth, intended for all of our Father's children. (*Come unto Christ*, pp. 123–24.)

A recent effort to discredit the First Vision is the publication of several accounts of this vision. Some of these accounts, written during Joseph Smith's lifetime, vary in detail. Because of this variance, detractors charge that the vision was a product of Joseph Smith's imagination. How would you answer such a charge? Well, you must remember that each account understandably differs in some detail because he wrote or explained the First Vision under different circumstances to different audiences, including nonmembers.

At no time did Joseph reveal everything he learned in the First Vision. He admitted in the official account, "Many other things did he say unto me, which I cannot write at this time" (Joseph Smith—History 1:20).

The fact that every account that has come to light does not exactly agree in every minute detail does not discredit the essential truth of the First Vision. There are at least three recorded accounts of Paul's vision in the New Testament, each of which differs in details, with one account seemingly contradicting the other two. Each was presented to different audiences under different circumstances. Should we reject the testimony of Paul's vision because Luke's report appears contradictory in minor detail?

After the resurrection and ascension to heaven of the Savior, His disciples, by direction of the President of the Church, wrote accounts of Christ's ministry, crucifixion, and resurrection. These were recorded by Matthew, Mark, Luke, and John. There have been many critics of Christianity who have pointed out discrepancies and contradictions in the various accounts. But each was written for different audiences and at different times. Some of the details may not have been perfectly remembered, but responsible Bible scholars have shown that reconciliation of the four accounts is easily possible by those who desire truth. Rather than weakening the testimony of Joseph Smith, each account of the First Vision gives credence to his testimony. (Salt Lake City, Utah, 20 May 1984.)

One of the grand and glorious promises of the Lord when He restored His Church in the latter days was that His Church should never again be taken from the earth nor given to another people (see Daniel 2:44; D&C 138:44). From the very beginning of the Church in this dispensation, detractors, critics, and apostates have ridiculed our practices, misrepresented our doctrines, and slandered our leaders. But the Church has continued to prosper according to the destiny proclaimed by our Heavenly Father. Its detractors and their efforts have "come to naught." (See D&C 76:9.) And so it shall always be. (Salt Lake City, Utah, 20 May 1984.)

Christian denominations the world over have prayed for centuries for the kingdom of God to come (see Matthew 6:10). We earnestly and publicly declare: that day is now here! (CR April 1978, *Ensign* 8 [May 1978]: 34.)

God has again spoken from the heavens. The priesthood and authority to act in His name have been restored again to men on the earth, following centuries of darkness. The fulness of the everlasting gospel is here with all of its saving principles. (*God, Family, Country*, p. 395.)

Revelation

A distinctive teaching of Latter-day Saint theology is our belief in revelation from God to latter-day prophets. We testify that Joseph Smith was a prophet raised up by God to restore many great truths that had been lost because of the absence of revelation. Through him, God revealed the eternity of the marriage covenant and the timelessness of the family. The effect that this teaching has upon Church members is most pronounced. (*This Nation Shall Endure*, p. 102.)

By nature man wants to find God and to worship Him in spirit and in truth. He cries out for contact with Him. And this is as it should be—it is natural. (Youth Fireside Series for the Church, Washington, D.C., 27 September 1960.)

Revelation gives to man his fullest knowledge of God. No mortal man knew as much about God and the Godhead as did Joseph at the close of that glorious vision. He saw God the Father and His Son Jesus Christ. He heard their voices, for they spoke unto him. He felt of their glorious presence. (Youth Fireside Series for the Church, Washington, D.C., 27 September 1960.)

The veil is very thin, brothers and sisters. Impressions may and do come to us when we are in tune with the Spirit. (Washington D.C. Temple Workers, 5 January 1986.)

Worthy sons are entitled to receive from their Heavenly Father confirmation concerning the direction their mortal father gives them. It takes revelation to perceive revelation. (CR October 1985, *Ensign* 15 [November 1985]: 36.)

The Lord will increase our knowledge, wisdom, and capacity to obey when we obey His fundamental laws. This is what the Prophet Joseph Smith meant when he said we could have "sudden strokes of ideas" which come into our minds as "pure intelligence" (see *Teachings of the Prophet Joseph Smith*, p. 151). This is revelation. We must learn to rely on the Holy Ghost so we can use it to guide our lives and the lives of those for whom we have responsibility. (CR April 1983, *Ensign* 13 [May 1983]: 54.)

To the rulers and peoples of all nations, we solemnly declare again that the God of Heaven has established His latter-day kingdom upon the earth in fulfillment of prophecies. Holy angels have again communed with men on the earth. God has again revealed

Himself from the heavens and restored to the earth His holy priesthood with power to administer in all the sacred ordinances necessary for the exaltation of His children. His Church has been reestablished among men with all the spiritual gifts enjoyed anciently. All this is done in preparation for Christ's second coming. The great and dreadful day of the Lord is near at hand. In preparation for this great event and as a means of escaping the impending judgments, inspired messengers have gone, and are going forth to the nations of the earth carrying this testimony and warning. (*This Nation Shall Endure*, pp. 110–11.)

By virtue of the sacred priesthood in me vested, I invoke the blessings of the Lord upon the Latter-day Saints and upon good people everywhere. I bless you with added power to endure in righteousness amidst the growing onslaught of wickedness.

I promise you that as you more diligently study modern revelation on gospel subjects, your power to teach and preach will be magnified and you will so move the cause of Zion that added numbers will enter into the house of the Lord as well as the mission field.

I bless you with increased desire to flood the earth with the Book of Mormon, to gather out from the world the elect of God who are yearning for the truth but know not where to find it. I promise you that, with increased attendance in the temples of our God, you shall receive increased personal revelation to bless your life as you bless those who have died. (CR April 1987, *Ensign* 17 [May 1987]: 85.)

Truth

Truth is a glorious thing. We sing about it. "Oh say, what is truth?/'Tis the fairest gem/That the riches of worlds can produce." (*Hymns*, 1985, no. 272.) The Church and kingdom of God has no fear of the truth. (Seattle Washington LDS Institute Dedication, 29 October 1961.)

We are engaged in the greatest work in all the world—yes, the greatest in the whole universe: the saving and exaltation of our Father's children, our brothers and sisters. We are the custodians of the truth, the saving principles which, where applied, will build, save, and exalt men. (*God, Family, Country*, p. 129.)

While change is, and will continue to be, all about us in the physical world, we must ever know that there are certain heaven-sent verities, principles, and values which are eternal. These never change. It is well to remember with Robert Frost that "most of the change we think we see in life is due to truths being in and out of favor." ("Liberty Against Creeping Socialism," Brigham Young University, Provo, Utah, 26 August 1961.)

The Christian world—the real Christian world—knows that there are certain eternal verities, principles, that never change. Jesus Christ is in very deed "the way, the truth, and the life" (John 14:6). The Ten Commandments are verily true. They form a permanently binding code of conduct that man cannot violate without drastic damage to both his material and his spiritual welfare. (CR October 1969, *Improvement Era* 72 [December 1969]: 70.)

I declare to you in words of soberness, that while you enter a world seemingly filled with change, conflicts, strife, and misunderstandings, yet the purposes of God rule in the affairs of men and nations. Abraham Lincoln so declared. Other great men of the earth, ancient and modern, have given similar testimony. Eternal laws exist universally. They are present alike in the spiritual as well as in the physical world. These priceless, fundamental principles and values never change. Many of these are set forth in the Decalogue, Christ's Sermon on the Mount, and in the revelations of God to His prophets. It is therefore of the utmost importance that men and nations seek prayerfully to know these eternal laws that they may render obedience to them. (*So Shall Ye Reap*, p. 148.)

Time is on the side of truth—on the side of God's prophet. (*God, Family, Country*, p. 29.)

Our lives, to be successful, must constitute a constant pursuit of truth—all truth. The gospel encompasses all truth; it is consistent, without conflict, eternal. I have had the privilege of traveling to most parts of this world. I have known presidents and prime ministers—dictators and kings. Nothing I have seen or experienced has changed my resolve to stand with truth. (MIA Vanguard Program, Salt Lake City, Utah, 13 June 1960.)

As you perform your labors, it will be well for you to remember that man does not stand alone. There is no limit to truth. There are "hidden treasures" of knowledge—truths beyond the reach of reason alone (see D&C 89:19). Paul recognized this basic truth when writing to the Corinthians. He said: "For what man knoweth the things of man, save the spirit of man which is in him? even so the things of God knoweth no man, but the Spirit of God" (1 Corinthians 2:11). (*So Shall Ye Reap*, p. 153.)

We know beyond any question that the truths which we advocate, the truths of the gospel restored to the earth through the Prophet Joseph, are in very deed the truths of heaven. These truths will always be consistent with the discovery of any new truths. (CR April 1958, *Improvement Era* 61 [June 1958]: 434.)

While it is more difficult to live the truth, such as standing for free agency, some of us may in the not-too-distant future be required to die for the truth. But the best preparation for eternal life is to be prepared at all times to die—fully prepared by a valiant fight for right. (CR April 1964, *Improvement Era* 67 [June 1964]: 504.)

Religious and Secular Truth

There is an unseen source of power and truth. Eminent scientists recognize this glorious fact. There are "hidden treasures" of knowledge—truths beyond the reach of reason alone (see D&C 89:19). ("Concerning Values," Utah State University Baccalaureate Address, Logan, Utah, 28 May 1950.)

"Truth must be repeated again and again because error is constantly being preached round about" (Goethe). I realize that the bearer of bad news is always unpopular. As a people we love sweetness and light—especially sweetness. Ralph Waldo Emerson said that every mind must make a choice between truth and repose. Those who will learn nothing from history are condemned to repeat it. This we are doing in the Americas today. George Washington stated, "Truth will ultimately prevail where there are pains taken to bring it to light." To bring the truth to light is our challenge. (*Title of Liberty*, pp. 1–2.)

Religion and science have sometimes been in apparent conflict. Yet, the conflict can only be apparent, not real, for science seeks truth, and true religion is truth. There can never be conflict between true religion and scientific fact. That they have occupied different fields of truth is a mere detail. True religion accepts and embraces all truth; science is slowly expanding her arms and reaching into the invisible domain, in search of truth. The two are meeting daily; science as a child; true religion as the mother. Truth is truth, whether labeled science or religion. "Truth is knowledge of things as they are, as they were, and as they are to come" (D&C 93:24). Truth is always consistent. It can never be in conflict with itself.

This is a changing world beset with many perplexities. But while change is and will continue to be all about us in the physical world, we must recognize that there are certain heaven-sent verities, principles, and values which are eternal. These never change. Be sure you do not sacrifice these eternal values—for nothing will ever be found to take their place. Let us endeavor to recognize anew—all of us—that God truly rules the universe. (Annual Religion-in-Life Week, Ohio State University, Columbus, Ohio, 29 January 1957.)

"Ye shall know the truth and the truth shall make you free" (John 8:32). In these words the Master pointed out that the fundamental characteristic of truth is freedom. Every principle of truth, properly applied, will free man from doubts, fears, suspicions, prejudices, and those qualities which make for misunderstanding, pride, lust, and selfishness. Every principle of truth in its own domain can free man to achieve the greatest good, the most majestic nobility of which he is capable. Each new truth challenges man to greater achievement and service.

Using this simple standard we may examine each issue with confidence. It matters not whether the inquiry at hand be a consideration of politics, science, ethics, or religion. If it is a true principle, it will stimulate man to greater achievement of the kind which builds true character and real security. (*The Red Carpet*, p. 261.)

Opinions at variance with time-honored verities and principles, although receiving considerable current acceptance, may not always rest on truth. It is the truth that endures. It is truth that makes men courageous. It is the truth that makes men and nations free—and keeps them free. (*The Red Carpet*, p. 282.)

Blessed are you if you have a testimony that God has spoken from the heavens; that His priesthood is again among men; that the gospel in its purity and fulness is here to bless mankind; and that we will be judged by its principles. These truths will, if you are wise, take precedence in your lives "over all contrary theories, dogmas, hypotheses or relative-truths from whatever source or by whomsoever" advocated. Therefore, go forward intelligently and yield simple and loyal obedience to all the laws of the universe, remembering always that there are many phenomena in God's universe which cannot, to our present human understanding, be explained. Our inability to explain a thing in terms of our materialism does not disprove its reality. By yielding obedience to the laws of the universe, there will come a soul-satisfying security which is priceless. ("Concerning Principles and Standards," *Church News* [4 June 1947]: 5.)

Now, truth, if given as much time and emphasis as error, will invariably prove itself. And if our young students could have as much time studying the truth as they and some of their professors have had studying error, then there would be no question of the outcome. The problem arises when under the pressure of a heavy course of study and the necessity of parroting back what certain professors have said, the student does not have the time or take the time to learn the truth. If he does not learn the truth, someday he will suffer the consequences. Many an honest student, after graduation, has had to do some unlearning and then fresh learning of basic principles which never change and which he should have been taught initially. (*An Enemy Hath Done This*, p. 285.)

When men, in their energetic search for truth, make new discoveries, these will always be in harmony with all fundamental and eternal truths. Yes, truth is always consistent, whether it be revealed direct from God to man through His inspired prophets, or comes from the laboratory through the diligent searching of His children and the influence of the Spirit of the Lord upon them.

Continue to grow mentally—to grow in wisdom—to grow in truth. Desire it! Pray for it! Study it! Practice it! Do all this, and you will find truth; it cannot be denied you. Having found it, never forget its source, remembering always that "the glory of God is intelligence, or, in other words, light and truth" (D&C 93:36). (*So Shall Ye Reap*, pp. 170–71.)

Change whatever you wish to change within the limits of truth, lofty ideals, and eternal principles and we will praise your name through generations unborn. But be careful not to change those things which are eternal, for no satisfactory substitutes will ever be found to take their place. (*So Shall Ye Reap*, pp. 149–50.)

We must imitate Christ in our mental growth as we search for truth. Let us never fear truth, but only its misuse. On the contrary, let us love truth above all else, for God Himself is truth. ("Your Charge: To Increase in Wisdom and Favor with God and Man," *New Era* 9 [September 1979]: 40.)

Advance unafraid! Meet the challenge of a modern world! In doing so, beware of the philosophy which suggests that morality is out of date—that virtue, chastity, marriage, and honorable family life are throwbacks to a Victorian age. These are eternal principles —as eternal as life itself. Remember, it is truth that makes men courageous enough to become Christlike. It is the truth that makes men and nations free. Yes, be intelligent. Intelligence is the wise and judicious use of knowledge. ("Your Charge: To Increase in Wisdom and Favor with God and Man," *New Era* 9 [September 1979]: 42.)

As you resolve in your hearts to live the standards of the Church—and you cannot afford to do otherwise from a material standpoint, from a spiritual standpoint, from the standpoint of getting ahead in the world—I hope you will remember that your prescribed standards are a part of a great body of truth—the gospel of Jesus Christ—revealed truth from heaven. Please remember that no discovery of the future will ever be in conflict with the teachings of the gospel. The gospel encompasses all truth. When doubts come to your mind because of instructions you may receive in the classroom, I urge you to remember that time is always on the side of truth, and Mormonism is truth. (CR April 1959, *Improvement Era* 62 [June 1959]: 457.)

United Order and Consecration

We covenant to live the law of consecration. This law is that we consecrate our time, talents, strength, property, and money for the upbuilding of the kingdom of God on this earth and the establishment of Zion.

Until one abides by the laws of obedience, sacrifice, the gospel, and chastity, he cannot abide the law of consecration, which is the law pertaining to the celestial kingdom. "For if you will that I give you place in the celestial world, you must prepare yourselves by doing the things which I have commanded you and required of you" (D&C 78:7). ("Temple Blessings and Covenants," Temple Presidents Seminar, Salt Lake City, Utah, 28 September 1982.)

"Today," as the Lord has said, "is a day of sacrifice . . . of my people" (D&C 64:23). I am confident if we will properly teach the true purpose and underlying principles behind the present welfare plan, and encourage members to live according to these principles, we will not be far from living the united order. (Logan, Utah, 6 December 1975.)

"Zion cannot be built up unless it is by the principles of the law of the celestial kingdom" (D&C 105:5). Much has been written about this law and its attempted implementation in the early history of the Church; and much deception has taken root, even among some of our members, because of misinformed opinion or misguided interpretations. Some view it as merely an economic alternative to capitalism or the free enterprise system, others as an outgrowth of early communal experiments in America. Such a view is not only shortsighted but tends to diminish in importance a binding requirement for entrance into the celestial kingdom. The law of consecration is a celestial law, not an economic experiment. ("A Vision and a Hope for the Youth of Zion," in *1977 Devotional Speeches of the Year* [Provo, Utah: BYU, 1978], p. 74.)

Two separate groups of Saints have fully implemented this divine law. The first was the united order under Enoch, wherein the Lord designated this people Zion, "because they were of one heart and one mind, and dwelt in righteousness; and there was no poor among them" (Moses 7:18). A second instance was the Nephite civilization following the visit of the Savior to the Western Hemisphere after His resurrection (see 4 Nephi 3). The failure of the early Saints in this dispensation to live according to the fulness of the law is explained by the Lord in revelations recorded in the Doctrine and Covenants (see D&C 101; 105). ("A Vision and a Hope for the Youth of Zion," in *1977 Devotional Speeches of the Year* [Provo, Utah: BYU, 1978], p. 74.)

The vehicle for implementing the law of consecration is the united order. The basic principle underlying the united order is that everything we have belongs to the Lord; and, therefore, the Lord may call upon us for any and all of our property, because it belongs to Him. The united order was entered by "a covenant and a deed which cannot be broken" (D&C 42:30). Under the united order, idleness has no place, and greed, selfishness, and covetousness are condemned. The united order may therefore operate only with a righteous people. ("A Vision and a Hope for the Youth of Zion," in *1977 Devotional Speeches of the Year* [Provo, Utah: BYU, 1978], p. 74.)

It has been erroneously concluded by some that the united order is both communal and communistic in theory and practice because the revelations speak of equality. Equality under the united order is not economic and social leveling as advocated by some today. Equality, as described by the Lord, is "equal[ity] according to [a man's] family, according to his circumstances and his wants and needs" (D&C 51:3).

Is the united order a communal system? Emphatically not. It never has been and never will be. It is "intensely individualistic." Does the united order eliminate private ownership of property? No. "The fundamental principle of this system [is] the private ownership of property" (J. Reuben Clark, Jr., CR October 1942, p. 57). ("A Vision and a Hope for the Youth of Zion," in *1977 Devotional Speeches of the Year* [Provo, Utah: BYU, 1978], p. 74.)

We must not lose sight of the fact that all that we are doing now is but a prelude to the establishment of the united order, and living the law of consecration. The individual Saints must understand this. ("The Training Challenge," General Welfare Services Committee, Salt Lake City, Utah, 2 February 1977.)

When Zion is fully redeemed it will be "by the principles of the law of the celestial kingdom," or in other words the living of the united order (D&C 105:5). The principles which underlie the united order are consecration and stewardship and the contribution of one's surpluses into the bishop's storehouse. (Logan, Utah, 6 December 1975.)

The law of consecration is a law for an inheritance in the celestial kingdom. God, the Eternal Father, His Son Jesus Christ, and all holy beings abide by this law. It is an eternal law. It is a revelation by God to His Church in this dispensation. Though not in full operation today, it will be mandatory for all Saints to live the law in its fulness to receive celestial inheritance. You young people today abide a portion of this higher law as you tithe, pay a generous fast offering, go on missions, and make other contributions of money, service, and time. ("A Vision and a Hope for the Youth of Zion," in *1977 Devotional Speeches of the Year* [Provo, Utah: BYU, 1978], p. 75.)

Zion

In 1844, the Prophet Joseph Smith made this solemn proclamation: "The whole of America is Zion itself from north to south" (*Teachings*, p. 362). The Lord Himself decreed: "This is a land which is choice above all other lands" (Ether 2:10). This nation is part of the land of Zion. This is a land dedicated by God's servants. When a Book of Mormon prophet referred to the nations of the world, this hemisphere was designated as "good" (Jacob 5:25–26). (Puerto Rico Priesthood Leadership Meeting, 12–17 December 1980.)

The Book of Mormon talks about clearing away the branches "which bring forth bitter fruit, according to the strength of the good and the size thereof; and ye shall not clear away the bad thereof all at once, lest the roots thereof should be too strong for the graft, and the graft thereof shall perish . . . wherefore ye shall clear away the bad according as the good shall grow, that the root and the top may be equal in strength, until the good shall overcome the bad." (Jacob 5:65–66.) Only a Zion people can bring in a Zion society. And as the Zion people increase, so we will be able to incorporate more of the principles of Zion until we have a people prepared to receive the Lord. ("Jesus Christ—Gifts and Expectations," *New Era* 5 [May 1975]: 18.)

Never before has the land of Zion appeared so vulnerable as the Americas do at present. And our vulnerability is directly attributable to our loss of active faith in the God of this land, who has decreed that we must worship Him or be swept off. (CR October 1979, *Ensign* 9 [November 1979]: 33.)

PART 2

THE
CHURCH

THE CHURCH

Church History

We must see to it that all our publishing and writing, especially official and semiofficial Church publications, build faith and testimony. Our criteria must be, "Is it pleasing unto God?" As watchmen in Zion, we have the responsibility to see that all our writings are doctrinally sound and historically accurate, and that such writings build faith and testimony in the hearts of the Saints. (Salt Lake City, Utah, 6 June 1980.)

Some of our teachers have said, "I can see how the counsel to teach the gospel of Jesus Christ is applicable to gospel subjects, but what about subjects such as Church history that deal in facts?" I would answer this by saying that facts should be taught not only as facts; they should be taught to increase one's faith in the gospel, to build testimony. ("The Gospel Teacher and His Message," Religious Educators, Salt Lake City, Utah, 17 September 1976.)

From the time of Christ's heaven-heralded birth, heresies have crept into Christianity intended to dilute or undermine the pure doctrines of the gospel. These heresies, by and large, are sponsored by the philosophies of men and, in many instances, advocated by so-called Christian scholars. Their intent is to make Christianity more palatable, more reasonable, and so they attempt to humanize Jesus and give natural explanations to those things which are divine.

An example is Jesus' birth. The so-called scholars seek to convince us that the divine birth of Christ as proclaimed in the New Testament was not divine at all and that Mary was not a virgin at the time of Jesus' conception. They would have us believe that Joseph, the foster-father of Jesus, was His physical father, and that therefore Jesus was human in all attributes and characteristics. They appear generous in their praise of Him when they say that He was a great moral philosopher, perhaps even the greatest. But the import of their effort is to repudiate the divine sonship of Jesus, for on that doctrine rests all other claims of Christianity. (*Come unto Christ*, pp. 3–4.)

This humanistic emphasis on history is not confined only to secular history. There have been and continue to be attempts to bring this philosophy into our own Church history. Again the emphasis is to underplay revelation and God's intervention in significant events, and to inordinately humanize the prophets of God so that their human frailties become more apparent than their spiritual qualities. It is a state of mind and spirit characterized by one history buff who asked: "Do you believe the Church has arrived at a sufficient state of maturity where we can begin to tell our real story?" Inferred in that question is the accusation that the Church has not been telling the truth. Unfortunately, too many of those who have been intellectually gifted become so imbued with criticism that they become disaffected spiritually.

Some of these have attempted to reinterpret Joseph Smith and his revelations. They offer what they call a psychological interpretation of his motives and actions. This interpretation suggests that whether or not Joseph Smith actually saw God the Father and His Son, Jesus Christ, or other visions is really unimportant. What matters is that he thought he did. To those who have not sought after or received a testimony of Joseph Smith's divine calling, he will ever remain what one called "the enigma from Palmyra." (*This Nation Shall Endure*, pp. 20–21.)

We would warn you teachers of this trend, which seems to be an effort to reinterpret the history of the Church so that it is more rationally appealing to the world. We must never forget that ours is a prophetic history. Our students need to understand this prophetic history, but this can be done only by teachers who themselves possess the spirit of prophecy and revelation.

A few teachers (and I emphasize that word *few*) have delighted in digging up alleged facts about certain Church leaders to expose their frailties. In view of the covenants taken in holy places, I would not have such temerity. ("The Gospel Teacher and His Message," Religious Educators, Salt Lake City, Utah, 17 September 1976.)

Some want to expose the weaknesses of Church leaders in an effort to show that they too are subject to human frailties and error like unto themselves. The danger of this questionable philosophy is illustrated by the following experience.

President Brigham Young revealed that on one occasion he was tempted to be critical of the Prophet Joseph Smith regarding a certain financial matter. He said that the feeling did not last for more than perhaps thirty seconds. That feeling, he said, caused him great sorrow in his heart. The lesson he gave to members of the Church in his day may well be increased in significance today because the devil continues more active. He said:

> I clearly saw and understood, by the spirit of revelation manifested to me, that if I was to harbor a thought in my heart that Joseph could be wrong in anything, I would begin to lose confidence in him, and that feeling would grow from step to step, and from one degree to another, until at last I would have the same lack of confidence in his being the mouthpiece of the Almighty. . . .
>
> I repented of my unbelief, and that too, very suddenly; I repented about as quickly as I committed the error. It was not for me to question whether Joseph was dictated by the Lord at all times and under all circumstances. . . .
>
> It was not my prerogative to call him in question with regard to any act of his life. He was God's servant, and not mine. He did not belong to the people but to the Lord, and was doing the work of the Lord. (*Journal of Discourses*, 4:297.)

(*Come unto Christ*, pp. 15–16.)

Has it occurred to you that one may interpret doctrine when he or she undertakes to explain certain events in Church history? To suggest, for example, that the Word of Wisdom was an outgrowth of the temperance movement in America and that Joseph Smith selected certain prohibition and dietary features from that movement and presented them to the Lord for confirmation is also to pronounce an explanation contradictory to the one given by Brigham Young (see *Journal of Discourses*, 12:158). To suggest that Joseph Smith received the vision on the three degrees of glory (D&C 76) as he grappled for answers that contemporary philosophers were grappling for is to infer an interpretation contrary to the Prophet's own (see *History of the Church*, 1:252–53).

We would hope that if you feel you must write for the scholarly journals, you always defend the faith. Avoid expressions and terminology which offend the Brethren and Church members. I refer to such expressions as "he alleged" when a President of the Church described a revelation or manifestation; or other expressions such as "experimental systems" and "communal life" as they describe sacred revelations dealing with the united order and the law of consecration. A revelation of God is not an experiment. The Lord has already done His research. Revelations from God are not based on the theories or philosophies of men, regardless of their worldly learning. ("The Gospel Teacher and His Message," Religious Educators, Salt Lake City, Utah, 17 September 1976.)

Elder Mark E. Petersen and I were asked to review one of the manuscripts proposed as a new Church history publication. We both strongly recommended that much of the proposed volume be rewritten because what was contained therein did not increase faith or build testimony, and in some cases the manuscript actually detracted from building faith. In writing, we need to follow the example of Nephi when he said: "The things which are pleasing unto the world I do not write, but the things which are pleasing unto God and unto those who are not of the world" (1 Nephi 6:5). (Salt Lake City, Utah, 6 June 1980.)

It is a great honor to participate in the dedication of the Museum of Church History and Art. This building is dedicated to the conservation and preservation of historical artifacts and art work. As such it constitutes the most valid statement we as a Church can make to this generation and future generations about our Church history and artistic endeavors. This museum will be a place where individuals can be reminded of the past so they may better understand the vision of our forebears, which is the basis of our sacred heritage.

Years ago we had in the Quorum of the Twelve a great teacher by the name of Adam S. Bennion. On occasion when youth groups would come to Church headquarters, he would escort them over to Temple Square. He always took them to the southeast corner where the Osmyn Deuel log cabin stood. He would tell the young people that this was the kind of home many of their pioneer fore-fathers lived in — a one-room log hut with no bathroom, no indoor plumbing, no privacy.

He would then request the group to stand midway between the temple and the old log cabin. Then he taught: "On your right you see the circumstances of those early pioneers—how they lived—but on your left you see the temple—the vision they had of the future."

That is what we hope happens when individuals visit this museum — that they see what their forebears wrought and that this will give a perspective to the present that will inspire them to build a more glorious, a more righteous, future. Our past, after all, is our prologue to the future. (Museum of Church History and Art Dedication, Salt Lake City, Utah, 4 April 1984.)

With the evidence all about them that man's freedoms are ebbing away, faithful members of the Church ask, "What can be done? What can I do?" Of all people, leaders of the Church must not despair. As God has intervened in our past history, so He may in our present history. His purposes will not be thwarted. (Priesthood Leadership Meeting, Puerto Rico, 12–17 December, 1980.)

Church Officers

Prophet-President

God has in very deed revealed Himself from the heavens. He did raise up the boy prophet — the greatest prophet that has ever lived upon this earth, except Jesus Christ the Son of God.

Joseph Smith has done more for the salvation of men in this world than any man who ever lived in it, except the Master (see D&C 135:3). He stands at the head of this dispensation—the greatest gospel dispensation of all time—and all the world will someday come to realize that he is in very deed a prophet of the Living God. Those who have succeeded him have had the same power and authority and have been recognized by God as His mouthpieces upon the earth, even as President George Albert Smith. A sweeter, lovelier character than President Smith I have never met. This Church is not being directed by the wisdom of men. I know that. The power and influence of Almighty God are directing His Church. ("I'll Go Where You Want Me to Go," *Church News* [23 November 1946]: 8.)

Joseph Smith received many revelations from Jesus Christ, as have the prophets who have succeeded him, which means that new scripture has been given. The Lord's mouthpiece and prophet on the face of the earth today received his authority through a line of prophets going back to Joseph Smith, who was ordained by Peter, James, and John, who were ordained by Christ, who was and is the head of the Church, the Creator of this earth, and the God before whom all men must stand accountable.

There is no satisfactory substitute for the scriptures and words of the Lord's living oracle. These should be our sources, in addition to the power of the Holy Ghost which will give us "in the very hour that portion that shall be meted out to every man" (D&C 84:85). (Salt Lake City, Utah, 19 January 1977.)

The inspired words of prophets, when written down, have become scripture, and whenever God has His representatives on the earth, there is always new revelation and new scripture (see D&C 68:3–4). Only when men become so corrupt that the prophets are taken out of their midst do scriptures cease. And God has stated that only through His authorized representatives could men receive the ordinances essential for salvation and the commandments necessary for the perfection of His children.

Speaking to His prophets, the Lord said: "He that receiveth you receiveth me" (Matthew 10:40). Always the words of the living prophet have taken precedence, for it has been God's message to the people at that particular time. Had any man accepted the ancient scripture in the days of Noah but refused to follow the revelation that Noah received and failed to board the ark, he would have been drowned. Always the words of the living prophets are of the most vital concern to the people; and always, if a man would know of Christ and learn His commandments so that he can obey them, he must seek to find His authorized representatives. (*God, Family, Country*, p. 157.)

It seems to me that in spiritual matters mankind is inclined very much to ignore the present and to worship the past. We are inclined to revere prophets dead while rejecting the living oracles. We ignore to a very large extent current fulfillment of prophecies and refer back generations ago to prophecies that were then fulfilled. It was so in the meridian of time when the chosen people of our Lord kept referring to Abraham and Moses as their fathers and their prophets, and ignored the greatest prophet that ever walked the face of the earth, yea, the Redeemer of the world, the Savior of mankind. (See Luke 3:8.) In large measure that same spirit characterizes this generation. ("The Jews Return to Palestine in Fulfillment of Prophecy," Washington D.C. Stake Conference, 3 March 1957.)

The prophet will not necessarily be popular with the world or the worldly. As a prophet reveals the truth, it divides the people. The honest in heart heed his words, but the unrighteous either ignore the prophet or fight him. When the prophet points out the sins of the world, the worldly, rather than repent of their sins, either want to close the mouth of the prophet or else act as if the prophet didn't exist. Popularity is never a test of truth. Many a prophet has been killed or cast out. As we come closer to the Lord's second coming, you can expect that as the people of the world become more wicked, the prophet will be less popular with them.

The prophet and his counselors make up the First Presidency—the highest quorum in the Church. The Lord refers to the First Presidency as "the highest council of the Church" (D&C 107:80) and says, "Whosoever receiveth me, receiveth those, the First Presidency, whom I have sent" (D&C 112:20). ("Fourteen Fundamentals in Following the Prophet," in *1980 Devotional Speeches of the Year*, [Provo: BYU Press, 1981], p. 29.)

Sometimes, from behind the pulpit, in our classrooms, in our council meetings, and in our Church publications, we hear, read, or witness things that do not square with the truth. This is especially true where freedom is involved. Now, do not let this serve as an excuse for your own wrongdoing. The Lord is letting the wheat and the tares mature before He fully purges the Church. He is also testing you to see if you will be misled. The devil is trying to deceive the very elect.

Let me give you a crucial key to help you avoid being deceived. It is this—learn to keep your eye on the prophet. He is the Lord's mouthpiece and the only man who can speak for the Lord today. Let his inspired counsel take precedence. Let his inspired words be a basis for evaluating the counsel of all lesser authorities. Then live close to the Spirit so you may know the truth of all things. (*An Enemy Hath Done This*, p. 317.)

There is only one man on the earth today who speaks for the Church. That man is the President of the Church (see D&C 132:7; 21:4). Because he gives the word of the Lord for us today, his words have an even more immediate importance than those of the dead prophets. When speaking under the influence of the Holy Ghost, his words are scripture (D&C 68:4).

The President can speak on any subject he feels is needful for the Saints. As Brigham Young stated: "I defy any man on earth to point out the path a prophet of God should walk in, or point out his duty, and just how far he must go, in dictating temporal or spiritual things. Temporal and spiritual things are inseparably connected, and ever will be." (*Journal of Discourses*, 10:364.) Other officers in the kingdom have fallen, but never the Presidents. The words of a living prophet must and ever will take precedence. (*God, Family, Country*, pp. 339–40.)

The prophet is not limited by men's reasoning. There will be times when you will have to choose between the revelations of God and the reasoning of men—between the prophet and the politician or professor. Said the Prophet Joseph Smith, "Whatever God requires is right, no matter what it is, although we may not see the reason thereof until long after the events transpire." (*Scrapbook of Mormon Literature*, vol. 2, p. 173.)

Would it seem reasonable to an eye doctor to be told to heal a blind man by spitting in the dirt, making clay, and applying it to the man's eyes and then telling him to wash in a contaminated pool? Yet this is precisely the course that Jesus took with one man, and he was healed (see John 9:6–7). Does it seem reasonable to cure leprosy by telling a man to wash seven times in a particular river? Yet this is precisely what the prophet Elisha told a leper to do, and he was healed (see 2 Kings 5).

"For my thoughts are not your thoughts, neither are your ways my ways, saith the Lord. For as the heavens are higher than the earth, so are my ways higher than your ways, and my thoughts than your thoughts." (Isaiah 55:8–9.) ("Fourteen Fundamentals in Following the Prophet," in *1980 Devotional Speeches of the Year* [Provo: BYU Press, 1981], p. 28.)

In times past our Heavenly Father benevolently sent His servants, the prophets, to warn nations of their imminent ruin if they would not repent. These warnings were provided before destruction. ("A Voice of Warning to the Nations of the World," New Zealand and Australia Area Conferences, 25 November 1979 and 2 December 1979.)

What is a prophet of God? Let us consider what the scriptures say. I invite you if you wish to mark them.

> Son of man, I have made thee a watchman unto the house of Israel: therefore hear the word at my mouth, and give them warning from me.
> When I say unto the wicked, Thou shalt surely die; and thou givest him not warning, nor speakest to warn the wicked from his wicked way, to save his life; the same wicked man shall die in his iniquity; but his blood will I require at thine hand.
> Yet if thou warn the wicked, and he turn not from his wickedness, nor from his wicked way, he shall die in his iniquity; but thou hast delivered thy soul. (Ezekiel 3:17–19.)

This is the responsibility of a prophet, to give the message of warning to the wicked. When he does so, his skirts are clean. ("Apostles and Prophets," Missionary Home, Salt Lake City, Utah, 1 March 1977.)

A revealing characteristic of a true prophet is that he declares a message from God. He makes no apology for the message, nor does he fear for any social repercussions which may lead to derision and persecution. (CR October 1981, *Ensign* 11 [November 1981]: 61.)

The prophet does not have to say "Thus saith the Lord" to give us scripture. Sometimes there are those who haggle over words. They might say the prophet gave us counsel but that we are not obligated to follow it unless he says it is a commandment. But the Lord says of the Prophet Joseph, "Thou shalt give heed unto all his words and commandments which he shall give unto you" (D&C 21:4).

And speaking of taking counsel from the prophet, the Lord states: "Verily thus saith the Lord unto you, my servant Lyman: Your sins are forgiven you, because you have obeyed my voice in coming up hither this morning to receive counsel of him whom I have appointed" (D&C 108:1).

Said Brigham Young, "I have never yet preached a sermon and sent it out to the children of men, that they may not call scripture" (*Journal of Discourses*, 13:95). ("Fourteen Fundamentals in Following the Prophet," in *1980 Devotional Speeches of the Year* [Provo: BYU Press, 1981], pp. 27–28.)

The prophet can receive revelation on any matter—temporal or spiritual. Said Brigham Young:

> Some of the leading men in Kirtland were much opposed to Joseph the Prophet, meddling with temporal affairs. . . .
>
> In a public meeting of the Saints, I said, "Ye Elders of Israel, . . . will some of you draw the line of demarcation, between the spiritual and temporal in the Kingdom of God, so that I may understand it?" Not one of them could do it. (*Journal of Discourses*, 10:363–64.)

("Fourteen Fundamentals in Following the Prophet," in *1980 Devotional Speeches of the Year* [Provo: BYU Press, 1981], p. 28.)

Beware of those who would pit the dead prophets against the living prophets, for the living prophets always take precedence.

President Wilford Woodruff stated: "I say to Israel, The Lord will never permit me or any other man who stands as President of the Church to lead you astray. It is not in the program. It is not in the mind of God." (*The Discourses of Wilford Woodruff*, pp. 212–13.)

President Marion G. Romney tells of this incident which happened to him:

> I remember years ago when I was a Bishop I had President [Heber J.] Grant talk to our ward. After the meeting I drove him home. . . . Standing by me, he put his arm over my shoulder and said: "My boy, you always keep your eye on the President of the Church, and if he ever tells you to do anything, and it is wrong, and you do it, the Lord will bless you for it." Then with a twinkle in his eye, he said, "But you don't need to worry. The Lord will never let his mouthpiece lead the people astray." (CR October 1960, p. 78.)

("Fourteen Fundamentals in Following the Prophet," in *1980 Devotional Speeches of the Year* [Provo: BYU Press, 1981], p. 27.)

The prophet is not required to have any particular earthly training or credentials to speak on any subject or act on any matter at any time. Sometimes there are those who feel their earthly knowledge on a certain subject is superior to the heavenly knowledge which God gives to His prophet on the same subject. They feel the prophet must have the same earthly credentials or training which they have had before they will accept anything the prophet has to say that might contradict their earthly schooling. How much earthly schooling did Joseph Smith have? Yet he gave revelations on all kinds of subjects. We haven't yet had a prophet who earned a doctorate in any subject, but as someone said, "A prophet may not have his Ph.D. but he certainly has his LDS." We encourage earthly knowledge in many areas, but remember, if there is ever a conflict between earthly knowledge and the words of the prophet, you stand with the prophet, and you will be blessed and time will vindicate you. ("Fourteen Fundamentals in Following the Prophet," in *1980 Devotional Speeches of the Year* [Provo: BYU Press, 1981], p. 27.)

We are admonished to "seek out of the best books words of wisdom" (D&C 88:118). Surely these books must include the scriptures. Alongside them must be the words of the Presidents of the Church. The Lord said of the President of the Church, "His word ye shall receive, as if from mine own mouth" (D&C 21:5). These books make up what has been referred to as "the Lord's library"—namely the standard works and the various volumes that contain the words of the different Presidents of the Church. Of the latter volumes, that which would be of greatest importance to you would be the words of the current President of the Church, for his words are directed to our day and our needs. ("In His Steps," in *1979 Devotional Speeches of the Year* [Provo, Utah: BYU Press, 1980], p. 61.)

The prophet may be involved in civic matters. When a people are righteous they want the best to lead them in government. Alma was the head of the Church and of the government in the Book of Mormon, Joseph Smith was mayor of Nauvoo, and Brigham Young was territorial governor of Utah. Isaiah was deeply involved in giving counsel on political matters and of his words the Lord Himself said, "Great are the words of Isaiah" (3 Nephi 23:1). Those who would remove prophets from politics would take God out of government. ("Fourteen Fundamentals in Following the Prophet," in *1980 Devotional Speeches of the Year* [Provo: BYU Press, 1981], p. 29.)

The two groups who have the greatest difficulty in following the prophet are the proud who are learned and the proud who are rich. The learned may feel the prophet is only inspired when he agrees with them; otherwise, the prophet is just giving his opinion —speaking as a man. The rich may feel they have no need to take counsel of a lowly prophet.

In the Book of Mormon we read:

> O that cunning plan of the evil one! O the vainness, and the frailties, and the foolishness of men! When they are learned they think they are wise, and they hearken not unto the counsel of God, for they set it aside, supposing they know of themselves, wherefore, their wisdom is foolishness and it profiteth them not. And they shall perish.
>
> But to be learned is good if they hearken unto the counsels of God.
>
> And whoso knocketh, to him will he open; and the wise, and the learned, and they that are rich, who are puffed up because of their learning, and their wisdom, and their riches—yea, they are they whom he despiseth; and save they shall cast these things away, and consider themselves fools before God, and come down in the depths of humility, he will not open unto them. (2 Nephi 9:28–29, 42.)

("Fourteen Fundamentals in Following the Prophet," in *1980 Devotional Speeches of the Year* [Provo: BYU Press, 1981], p. 29.)

The prophets of a new gospel dispensation have counsel for us today—counsel on matters which concerned the Founding Fathers—freedom, liberty, righteousness which "exalteth a nation" (Proverbs 14:34). Do we believe and accept their counsel, or have we drifted away from those basic concepts and principles, without adherence to which no nation can be exalted? (*Title of Liberty*, p. 108.)

As members of the Church we have some close quarters to pass through if we are going to get home safely. We will be given a chance to choose between conflicting counsel given by some. That is why we must learn—and the sooner we learn, the better—to keep our eye on the prophet, the President of the Church. (*An Enemy Hath Done This*, p. 326.)

The prophet tells us what we *need* to know, not always what we *want* to know. "Thou hast declared unto us hard things, more than we are able to bear," complained Nephi's brethren. But Nephi answered by saying, "The guilty taketh the truth to be hard, for it cutteth them to the very center." (1 Nephi 16:1, 3.) Or, to put it in another prophet's, Joseph Smith's, words, "Hit pigeons flutter."

Said President Harold B. Lee: "You may not like what comes from the authority of the Church. It may contradict your political views. It may contradict your social views. It may interfere with some of your social life. . . . Your safety and ours depends upon whether or not we follow. . . . Let's keep our eye on the President of the Church." (CR October 1970, pp. 152–53.)

But it is the living prophet who really upsets the world. "Even in the Church," said President Spencer W. Kimball, "many are prone to garnish the sepulchres of yesterday's prophets and mentally stone the living ones" (*Instructor*, 95:257).

Why? Because the living prophet gets at what we need to know now, and the world prefers that prophets either be dead or mind their own business. Some so-called experts of political science want the prophet to keep still on politics. Some would-be authorities on evolution want the prophet to keep still on evolution. And so the list goes on and on.

How we respond to the words of a living prophet when he tells us what we need to know, but would rather not hear, is a test of our faithfulness. ("Fourteen Fundamentals in Following the Prophet," in *1980 Devotional Speeches of the Year* [Provo: BYU Press, 1981], p. 28.)

Christ has provided us the gift of a prophet. Of all mortal men, we should keep our eyes most firmly fixed on the captain—the prophet, seer, and revelator, and President of The Church of Jesus Christ of Latter-day Saints. This is the man who stands closest to the fountain of living waters (Jeremiah 2:13; 1 Nephi 11:25). There are some heavenly instructions for us that we can only receive through the prophet. A good way to measure your standing with the Lord is to see how you feel about, and act upon, the inspired words of His earthly representative, the prophet-president. The inspired words of the President are not to be trifled with. All men are entitled to inspiration, and various men are entitled to revelation for their particular assignment. But only one man stands as the Lord's spokesman to the Church and the world, and he is the President of the Church. The words of all other men should be weighed against his inspired words. Though His prophet is mortal, God will not let him lead His Church astray. (See *Discourses of Wilford Woodruff*, pp. 212–13.)

God knows all things, the end from the beginning, and no man becomes President of the Church of Jesus Christ by accident, or remains there by chance, or is called home by happenstance. Every generation has need of the ancient scripture, plus the current scripture from the living prophet. Therefore, the most crucial reading and pondering that you should do is of the latest inspired words from the Lord's mouthpiece. That is why it is essential that you have access to and carefully read his words in Church periodicals. Yes, We thank thee, O God, for a prophet to guide us in these latter days. (See *Hymns*, 1985, no. 19.) ("Jesus Christ—Gifts and Expectations," *New Era* 5 [May 1975]: 16–17.)

My feelings have been made tender, as have many thousands, through the passing of President Harold B. Lee. For fifty-five years in mortal life we have been associated, and prior to that, I feel sure, in premortal life. I have received the sweet assurance also and the comforting assurance that there is no untimely passing of a prophet of God. (CR April 1974, *Ensign* 4 [May 1974]: 104.)

You sustain the President of the Church as a prophet, seer, and revelator. Have you ever thought about the significance of those terms? Prophet: An inspired teacher of known truths. Seer: One who sees with spiritual eyes—one who foresees the future. Revelator: A revealer of new truth.

The first office and calling of the Church was that of a prophet, seer, and revelator. In a revelation on 6 April 1830, the day the Lord organized His Church again on earth, this instruction was given to members of the Church:

> Wherefore, meaning the church, thou shalt give heed unto all his words and commandments which he shall give unto you as he receiveth them, walking in all holiness before me;
>
> For his word ye shall receive, as if from mine own mouth, in all patience and faith.
>
> For by doing these things the gates of hell shall not prevail against you; yea, and the Lord God will disperse the powers of darkness from before you, and cause the heavens to shake for your good, and his name's glory.
>
> For thus saith the Lord God: Him have I inspired to move the cause of Zion in mighty power for good, and his diligence I know, and his prayers I have heard. (D&C 21:4–7.)

You will note the prophet's words are to be received as if from the mouth of the Lord Himself, and by so doing "the gates of hell shall not prevail against" us (3 Nephi 11:39; D&C 10:69). ("Apostles and Prophets," Missionary Home, Salt Lake City, Utah, 1 March 1977.)

There are some who would have us believe that the final test of the rightness of a course is whether everyone is united on it. But the Church does not seek unity simply for unity's sake. The unity for which the Lord prayed is the only unity which God honors— that is, "unity in righteousness," unity in principle (see John 17:11).

We cannot compromise good with evil in an attempt to have peace and unity in the Church, any more than the Lord could have compromised with Satan in order to avoid the War in Heaven. Think of the impact for good we could have if we all united behind the prophet in preserving our Constitution. Yet witness the sorry spectacle of those presently of our number who have repudiated the inspired counsel of our prophet when he has opposed federal aid to education and asked support for the right-to-work laws. (*An Enemy Hath Done This,* p. 311.)

All men are entitled to inspiration, but only one man is the Lord's mouthpiece. Some lesser men have in the past, and will in the future, use their office unrighteously. Some will use it to lead the unwary astray; some will use it to persuade us that all is well in Zion; some will use it to cover and excuse their ignorance. Keep your eye on the prophet—for the Lord will never permit His prophet to lead this Church astray. (*An Enemy Hath Done This*, p. 318.)

Each President has been uniquely selected for the time and situation which the world and Church needed. All were "men of the hour," as we have witnessed in President Spencer W. Kimball. Contemplate the miracle of that foreordination and preparation! Though called and given keys many years prior to the time that the mantle fell upon him, the President was always the right man in the right place for the times. This miracle alone is one of the marks of the divinity of the Church. (Salt Lake City, Utah, 19 January 1977.)

I have never felt the Spirit of the Lord stronger than when President George Albert Smith was set apart in the temple. Various rumors from enemies of the Church were being circulated that certain members of the Council of the Twelve were aspiring to be President.

In our meeting together, President Grant's two counselors took their places in the Council of the Twelve according to their seniority. President David O. McKay sat next to President George F. Richards, and President J. Reuben Clark, Jr., next to Elder Albert E. Bowen, being senior to him. President George Albert Smith, as President of the Council of the Twelve, was the presiding officer.

As the meeting progressed, I have never felt so powerfully the Spirit of the Lord. There was no feeling of selfishness or vain ambition present. The Spirit dictated to every man present whom the

Lord wanted and every man in that council was brought to tears. When the Spirit of the Lord is felt so powerfully that fourteen strong, mature men are all simultaneously brought to tears and the spirit of divine unity is manifest, as it was on that occasion, one cannot help but know that there is a greater power at the head of this Church than man. (As quoted in Frederick W. Babbel, *On Wings of Faith* [Salt Lake City: Bookcraft, 1972], p. 15.)

I have been aware of those who preceded me in this office as President of the Church. I have felt very keenly my dependence upon the Lord and the absolute necessity of relying upon Him for His direction in the conduct of the affairs of the Church as those in the past have done. (CR April 1986, *Ensign* 16 [May 1986]: 77.)

May we cherish God's revelations more than man's reasoning and choose to follow the prophets of the Lord rather than the precepts of men. (*God, Family, Country*, p. 263.)

Apostles

It is well to consider our responsibilities which have been delegated to us by none other than God Himself. The Twelve are designated, by revelation, as "special witnesses of the name of Christ in all the world." Our primary role is to "open the door by the proclamation of the gospel of Jesus Christ"—first to the Gentiles, then to the Jews (D&C 107:35). We hold the keys for that responsibility. (Salt Lake City, Utah, 6 June 1980.)

The foremost responsibility of the Twelve Apostles is to bear witness to the divinity of Jesus Christ and to the restoration of His gospel in these latter days to all the world. ("150th Year for the Twelve," *Church News* [27 January 1985]: 3.)

"The Twelve are under the direction of the Presidency of the Church . . . to build up the Church and regulate all the affairs of the same in all nations" (D&C 107:33). In Joseph Smith's time, *regulate* meant to "put in good order" (Webster's 1828 Dictionary). There are several ways that this is done within the Church today.

Under the direction of the First Presidency, individual members of the Twelve may put in order matters of the Church. This includes doctrine, priesthood procedures, administration of Church funds, and restoration of blessings. The Twelve take very seriously the following pronouncement made by a previous First Presidency:

> We do not wish incorrect and unsound doctrines to be handed down to posterity under the sanction of great names, to be received and valued by future generations as authentic and reliable. . . . The interests of posterity are, to a certain extent, in our hands. Errors in history and in doctrine, if left uncorrected by us who are conversant with the events, and who are in a position to judge of the truth or falsity of the doctrines, would go to our children as though we had sanctioned and endorsed them. (Brigham Young, Heber C. Kimball, Daniel H. Wells, *Messages of the First Presidency*, 2:232.)

("150th Year for the Twelve," *Church News* [27 January 1985]: 3.)

"It is the duty of the Twelve to ordain evangelical ministers" (D&C 107:39). As defined by revelation, an evangelical minister is a patriarch. The Twelve have responsibility of approving all patriarchs in the world. Stake presidents may recommend calls and ordain a patriarch when approved by the Quorum of the Twelve. Approval of the calls of all patriarchs rests with the Quorum of the Twelve. ("150th Year for the Twelve," *Church News* [27 January 1985]: 3, 11.)

The Lord has given a special mantle to the Apostles, and the significance of their words is pointed out in the Lord's preface to the Doctrine and Covenants, where He says that those who will not "give heed to the words of the prophets and apostles shall be cut off from among the people" (D&C 1:14). ("In His Steps," in *1979 Devotional Speeches of the Year* [Provo, Utah: BYU, 1980], p. 61.)

The Lord said in revelation that "every decision made by (the First Presidency and the Twelve) must be by unanimous voice" (D&C 107:27). This implies great love and unanimity among the First Presidency and the Twelve. Never, in my experience, has there been more love and unity than there is today. ("150th Year for the Twelve," *Church News* [27 January 1985]: 3.)

Now, this matter of unity is so very important. We know what it is in the Council of the Twelve. It is satisfying. It is strengthening. It is uplifting. It is sweet. I have said to my Brethren, and I mean it with all my heart, that I would be happy to serve under the leadership of any one of them. They know I mean it. It is a great blessing to work closely with one another in this glorious work. (Salt Lake City, Utah, 3 October 1978.)

General Authorities

We are His agents. An agent is one who sits for or in the place of another by authority from that person. In our case, we represent the Lord Jesus Christ. We are on the Lord's business. That business is to save souls. As His agents, we bind Him whom we represent, provided that all we do is within the scope and authority which has been delegated to us. In the language of the revelation, "Whatever ye do according to the will of the Lord is the Lord's business" (D&C 64:29). An effective agent neither promotes himself or his own private interpretations or gospel hobbies. Instead, he represents the views and the principles of Him whom he represents. To go beyond this constitutes a usurpation of his agency; to do less than this, a dereliction of his duty. (Salt Lake City, Utah, 2 October 1985.)

There is a great spirit of unity among the General Authorities of the Church. That unity is very real and most important, for the Lord has said, "If ye are not one ye are not mine" (D&C 38:27). We shall continue to work together as Brethren, united in one purpose—to move forward the work of the Lord. (CR April 1986, *Ensign* 16 [May 1986]: 77.)

I have witnessed the refining processes through which the Lord chips, buffs, and polishes those whom He has selected to hold the keys of His kingdom, that they become polished shafts in His hand. (Salt Lake City, Utah, 19 January 1977.)

May I relate an experience I had with Brother S. Dilworth Young. We used to travel in pairs to go to a stake conference. Some of you Brethren are old enough to remember those days. It was a sweet experience. We were going to East Sandy, if I remember correctly. He was driving his car and picked me up at my home. On Friday night, I had looked over the records of that stake. I always carefully review the records and statistics of a stake, sometimes more than once, before I leave for a stake conference. As I went over the records, I had a strong impression that the junior man on the high council (in fact he was an alternate member of the high council) should be the stake president.

Saturday morning I went over the roster again and got the same impression. As I got into Brother Young's car I thought, "Well, I should tell Brother Young." So I told him. I said, "I don't want this to influence you. Let us go ahead with the interviews and see how things turn out."

We interviewed the bishops, the high council, the stake presidency, and a few other officers. As I remember, every man but one recommended the junior member of the alternate high councilmen as the stake president. I know the Spirit operates. It is a great assurance that we can reorganize a stake presidency or divide a stake and have the witness of the Spirit. (Salt Lake City, Utah, 3 October 1978.)

Mention should be made of the almost reverent regard in which people hold us as we go out to conferences. It is not us as individuals—it is the office we hold that is important. We should never forget that. They reverence the office and what it represents. It represents authority, a sacred calling from the Lord. They reverence that office. (Salt Lake City, Utah, 3 October 1978.)

It is my conviction that these living oracles are not only authorized, but are obligated to give counsel to this people on any subject which is vital to the welfare of this people and the upbuilding of the kingdom of God. So, that measure should be applied. Is it right as measured by the counsel of the living oracles of God? (CR October 1954, *Improvement Era* 57 [December 1954]: 922.)

If you will follow the admonitions of the Lord and heed the counsel of His chosen servants in their callings as prophets, seers and revelators, I promise you that love at home and obedience to parents will increase; faith will be developed in the hearts of the youth of Israel and they will gain power and strength to combat the evil influences and temptations which beset them. Each of our homes may veritably become a little heaven on earth. ("Foundations for Family Solidarity," *Children's Friend* 56 [April 1957]: 26.)

My affections run deep for those whom God has called in times past to carry forth the work of His kingdom. I express the same feelings of love, loyalty, and affection for you, my Brethren. Your reciprocating affection shown to me over the years is among the choicest blessings of my life. (Salt Lake City, Utah, 19 January 1977.)

Stake Presidents and Bishops

Stake presidents and bishops need to be diligent in interviewing the Saints with the purpose of preparing them to receive higher covenants and to live according to these covenants. Are bishops interviewing those Church members who may not presently be worthy of a temple recommend, but who may become worthy through priesthood encouragement and counsel? We know, for example, that the time a leader spends in personal contact with members is more productive than time spent in meetings and administrative duties. Personal contact is the key to converting the inactive member. (Salt Lake City, Utah, 3 April 1981.)

Bishops, do you make sure new elders come under the care of their new shepherd, the quorum president? Do you provide significant Church-service opportunities for our returned missionaries so that these young men and women do not drift into inactivity because they do not have occasion to serve as they have been doing? (*Come unto Christ*, p. 67.)

The bishop's first and foremost responsibility is the Aaronic Priesthood and the young women of his ward. Bishops, stay close to both your young men and young women. Give as much attention to the young women's program in your ward as you do the young men's programs. Be as concerned about the young women's activities and classes, their camp-outs and socials, their firesides and conferences as you are the young men's.

Recognize with equal prominence the presentation of the Young Womanhood Recognition Award as you do the awarding of the Duty to God Award and Eagle Scout Badge. Spend the necessary time (and it takes time) in personal interviews with the young women of your ward. Talk with them regularly about their goals and aspirations, their challenges and their personal worthiness. Be a bishop who really cares about each of the young men and young women in his ward. ("To the Young Women of the Church," *Ensign* 16 [November 1986]: 85.)

Church Organizations and Programs

We are engaged in the greatest work in all the world: the building of men and women — men and women of strength, men and women of character, men and women of deep spirituality, godlike men and women. This is the greatest single activity in this whole world, yes in the whole universe, because it is an activity going on on both sides of the veil. It is the greatest work of all — helping to save and exalt our Father's children. We have, to assist us with this, the richest program to be found anywhere upon the face of the earth. I say this advisedly after meeting with so-called spiritual leaders of many faiths. Nowhere will you find a program that even approaches in effectiveness, in richness, the program which we have in the Church. It isn't perfect, of course, because it is operated by human beings, but it is the finest program to be found anywhere. (San Diego California South Stake Conference, 6 December 1969.)

The principles upon which the Church was established are divine and they have been clearly outlined, but the means of embracing and putting into operation those principles, the Lord has left very largely up to us to work out and plan. So we organize Primaries, Sunday Schools, and Mutual Improvement Associations. We adopted the Boy Scout program as a part of the program of the Church. We are constantly seeking to improve the program for the youth of the Church, and Scouting has been adopted because it helps to enrich and strengthen our youth program for young boys and men of the Church. (Eagle Recognition Banquet, Logan, Utah, 22 March 1974.)

These programs are not optional programs. They are the youth programs of the Church, approved by the leadership thereof. May God bless us that as leaders in Israel we may have the power and the inspiration to help our young people want to enjoy the full program of the Church offered through the Sunday School, the Primary, the Mutual Improvement Association, and the Aaronic Priesthood program, that they might eventually meet the expectations of their parents, their Church leaders, and our Heavenly Father. God bless us to this end. God bless the youth of Israel everywhere, that they may grow and develop into sterling characters, faithful and true to this great latter-day work. (CR April 1951, *Improvement Era* 54 [June 1951]: 423.)

Stakes and Wards

Nonmembers sometimes inquire, "What is a stake?" Members likewise inquire, "What is the significance of a stake? What does it mean to us as members?" To nonmembers, a stake is similar to a diocese in other churches. A stake is a geographical area comprising a number of wards (local congregations) and presided over by a presidency.

To members, the term *stake* is a symbolic expression. Picture in your mind a great tent held up by cords extended to many stakes that are firmly secured in the ground. The prophet Isaiah likened latter-day Zion to a great tent encompassing the earth. That tent was supported by cords fastened to stakes. (See 3 Nephi 22:2; Isaiah 54:2.) Those stakes, of course, are various geographical organizations spread out over the earth. Presently Israel is being gathered to the various stakes of Zion. (*Come unto Christ*, p. 101.)

In revelation the Lord states: "For Zion must increase in beauty and in holiness; her borders must be enlarged; her stakes must be strengthened; yea, verily I say unto you, Zion must arise and put on her beautiful garments" (D&C 82:14). Here the Lord declares a great purpose of a stake: to be a beautiful emblem for all the world to see. The phrase "put on her beautiful garments" refers, of course, to the inner sanctity that must be attained by every member who calls himself or herself a Saint. Zion is "the pure in heart" (D&C 97:21). (El Paso Texas Regional Conference, 25 January 1986.)

Stakes are organized to assist parents "who have children in Zion" to teach them the gospel of Jesus Christ and administer the ordinances of salvation (see D&C 68:25). Stakes are formed to perfect the Saints, and that development begins in the home with effective gospel instruction. (El Paso Texas Regional Conference, 25 January 1986.)

Each stake, presided over by three high priests and supported by twelve men known as a high council, becomes a miniature Church to the Saints in a specific geographic area. The purpose is to unify and perfect the members who live in those boundaries by extending to them the Church programs, ordinances, and gospel instruction.

Members of stakes are to be models or standards of righteousness. Stakes are to be a defense (see D&C 115:6). They do this as they unify under their local priesthood officers and dedicate themselves to do their duty and keep their covenants. Those covenants, if kept, become a protection from error, evil, or calamity. (El Paso Texas Regional Conference, 25 January 1986.)

Stakes are a defense for the Saints from enemies both seen and unseen. The defense is provided through priesthood channels that strengthen testimony and promote family solidarity and individual righteousness. (*Come unto Christ*, p. 103.)

The Lord gives this explanation of the purpose of stakes: "Verily I say unto you all: Arise and shine forth, that thy light may be a standard for the nations; And that the gathering together upon the land of Zion, and upon her stakes, may be for a defense, and for a refuge from the storm, and from wrath when it shall be poured out without mixture upon the whole earth." (D&C 115:5–6.)

In that revelation is a command to let your light shine so it becomes a standard for the nations. A standard is a rule of measure by which one determines exactness or perfection. The Saints are to be a standard of holiness for the world to see! That is the beauty of Zion. (El Paso Texas Regional Conference, 25 January 1986.)

Only after a stake is organized may full Church programs be authorized for the benefit of the members. This means priesthood quorums for young men and adult males (high priests, seventies, and elders) and the auxiliary programs of the Church. These exist to assist the home in building and strengthening testimonies of the gospel and preparing for spiritual growth during our probation on earth. (*Come unto Christ*, p. 102.)

As the Church grows, it is very important that we build solidly and well, and that our prospective stakes have the basic ingredients that are necessary for success and that existing stakes work tire-lessly for full stakehood in the sense of spiritual achievement. These stakes are to be the gathering spots for the Zion of today, and they need to be spiritual sanctuaries and to be self-sufficient in as many ways as is possible. (Regional Representatives Seminar, Salt Lake City, Utah, 4 April 1974.)

The Book of Mormon prophet Nephi foresaw the day when the Saints would be scattered in stakes all over the world. He saw the time when the Lord would extend His protection to them when menaced by a storm of destruction which threatened their exis-tence. Nephi prophesied: "And it came to pass that I, Nephi, be-held the power of the Lamb of God, that it descended upon the saints of the church of the Lamb, and upon the covenant people of the Lord, who were scattered upon all the face of the earth; and they were armed with righteousness and with the power of God in great glory." (1 Nephi 14:14.) (Geneva Switzerland Stake Cre-ation, 20 June 1982.)

Latter-day Saint chapels are more than just houses of worship. The stakes and districts of Zion are symbolic of the holy places spoken of by the Lord where His Saints are to gather in the last days as a refuge from the storm. You and your children will gather here to worship, to do sacred ordinances, to socialize, to learn, to perform in music, dance, drama, athletics, and to generally im-prove yourselves and one another. It is often thought significant that our chapels have on them a steeple, with spires toward the heavens symbolic of how our lives ought to be ever moving upward toward God. The Prophet Joseph Smith said, "If you wish to go where God is, you must be like God, or possess the principles, which God possesses" (*History of the Church*, 4:558). Then what kind of men and women are we to be? Jesus asked this question in His day, and then answered it by saying, even "as I am." (3 Nephi 27:27.) (Finglas Ireland Branch Dedication, 10 September 1980.)

This ward meetinghouse is first of all a place of worship, a place where we may prepare to fulfill the commandments of the Lord to go to the house of prayer and "to offer up thy sacraments upon my holy day, and to pay devotion unto the most high" (D&C 59:9). As a place of worship, as a house of prayer, may I commend you to keep it as a place of reverence. Your conversations and visiting should be confined to the foyer before and after worship service. If we desire this chapel to receive the presence of the Lord's Spirit, our conduct must merit that Spirit. This house is also a house of learning. In it we hold classes for all age groups. Our children have a place of instruction for Primary. Our youth have classrooms for Sunday School, Mutual, and seminary. Our adults have classes for priesthood quorum work, and for the adult gospel curriculum. And in this building we have a meetinghouse library. (Finglas Ireland Branch Dedication, 10 September 1980.)

We have the responsibility of building up the wards and stakes and branches of the Church and perfecting the Saints. This building will contribute to those great purposes and objectives. And so this is a good investment and the money has been provided by the people. (Seattle Washington LDS Institute Dedication, 29 October 1961.)

Since 1842 when the Prophet Joseph Smith organized the female Relief Society, the first national, world organization of women to be organized in my own country, the Church has encouraged all women, young and old, to improve their skills and broaden their understanding. In this meetinghouse is a Relief Society room for the sisters to meet on a weekly basis, to be instructed in areas of cultural refinement, spiritual living, homemaking, mother education and social relations. All this is an educational effort, and we believe it is in compliance with the Lord's instruction where He says to "obtain a knowledge of history and of countries and of kingdoms, [and] of laws of God and man . . . for the salvation of Zion" (D&C 93:53). (Finglas Ireland Branch Dedication, 10 September 1980.)

We attach to most of our chapels a cultural hall so that our youth may have a place to dance, to perform their talents in musicals and other uplifting entertainment, and we hope our youth leaders as trustees of the building will see to it that only wholesome, uplifting activities are performed in this building. Should you have any reservations whether or not an activity, a style of dancing or tempo of music is in accord with Church standards, may I suggest this guide: Does it uplift and inspire one to higher ideals? Does it develop wholesome relationships between young men and women, or appeal to and arouse their baser instincts? Will it cause one to be a better Latter-day Saint and lead one closer to the Savior? Avoid all activities and dances which bring the world's demoralizing standards into this sacred meeting place. If you adult leaders will counsel the youth, they can understand the inconsistency of opening our meetings with prayer asking that the Lord's Spirit be with us, and then engaging in an activity which repels His Spirit. We ask you to be very mindful of this. (Finglas Ireland Branch Dedication, 10 September 1980.)

I hope we never get the feeling that money for new buildings is coming from some bottomless treasury like we sometimes think of the federal government. All of these dollars have been contributed by faithful members of the Church who believe in the old law of the tithe in the Old Testament and who pay their tithes and their offerings—not wealthy people, so far as material things are concerned, but people of faith and devotion who love the Church, and who put the kingdom of God first. (Seattle LDS Institute Dedication, 29 October 1961.)

I know the Lord opens the windows of heaven for His people who contribute to the erection of buildings for the purpose of worshipping Him. Ofttimes contributions are made by people of the community who are not yet members of the Church. This we appreciate, and for this the Lord will add His blessings. And so, we are very happy that this building is completed, and we know those who have assisted in its erection will be greatly blessed, and the lives of others will benefit from this new building; children, nonmembers of the Church, and the community will be blessed. (Finglas Ireland Branch Dedication, 10 September 1980.)

To the Lord all things are spiritual. The material things of life such as this lovely building and the others like it all over the country, as well as the temples we construct, are but a means to an end, the end being the perfection of God's children, the building of real Latter-day Saints, men and women imbued with the principles and spirit of Christ. (Arlington Virginia Ward Chapel Dedication, 30 May 1949.)

Relief Society

When the Relief Society was organized by the Prophet Joseph Smith, he said, "The Church was never perfectly organized until the women were . . . organized" (Sarah M. Kimball, "The Story of the Organization of the Relief Society," *Relief Society Magazine* March 1919, p. 129). The Prophet gave the women of the Church this inspired counsel, which is as appropriate today as when it was given. Listen to how a woman is to use her attributes and nature to complement man:

> This is a charitable Society [the Prophet said] and according to your natures; it is natural for females to have feelings of charity and benevolence. You are now placed in a situation in which you can act according to those sympathies which God has planted in your bosoms. . . .
> You need not be teasing your husbands because of their deeds, but let the weight of your innocence, kindness and affection be felt, which is more mighty than a millstone hung about the neck; not war, not jangle, not contradiction, or dispute, but meekness, love, purity—these are the things that should magnify you in the eyes of all good men. . . .
> If this Society listens to the counsel of the Almighty, through the heads of the Church, they shall have power to command queens in their midst. . . .

Let this Society teach women how to behave towards their husbands, to treat them with mildness and affection. When a man is borne down with trouble, when he is perplexed with care and difficulty, if he can meet a smile instead of an argument or a murmur—if he can meet with mildness; it will calm down his soul and soothe his feelings; when the mind is going to despair, it needs a solace of affection and kindness. . . .

When you go home, never give a cross or unkind word to your husbands, but let kindness, charity and love crown your works henceforward; don't envy the finery and fleeting show of sinners, for they are in a miserable situation; but as far as you can, have mercy on them, for in a short time God will destroy them, if they will not repent and turn unto him.

The Prophet Joseph continued: "Let your labors be mostly confined to those around you in the circle of your own acquaintance, as far as knowledge is concerned, it may extend to all the world; but your administering should be confined to the circle of your immediate acquaintance, and more especially to the members of the Relief Society." (*History of the Church*, 4:605–7.) ("To the Elect Women of the Kingdom of God," Nauvoo Illinois Relief Society Monument Dedication, 30 June 1978.)

Mother was Relief Society president in the ward—a small, but solid, country ward. I remember how important Father considered her work in that assignment.

Father gave to me, as the oldest of seven at that time and eleven later, the responsibility of harnessing the horse and getting the buggy ready for Mother's two o'clock weekly Relief Society meetings. This had to be done before two o'clock so she could be there early. At that time I was not tall enough to buckle the collar or put the bridle on the horse without getting on the fence or a box.

In addition, I was to take a half-bushel of wheat from our granary and put it in the back of the buggy. In those days, the Relief Society sisters were building up a storage of wheat against a time of need. Following World War I the United States government called for that wheat to relieve hunger in Europe.

When Mother was called to visit the sick in the ward or to help mothers with new babies, it was always by horse and buggy. As the buggy rolled down the dirt road, the circling wheels left a track that stayed in my life and in the countless lives she blessed through compassionate service and example. How well she followed the admonition of the Prophet Joseph Smith to "let your labors be mostly confined to those around you, in the circle of your own acquaintances . . . and more especially to members of the Relief Society." ("To the Elect Women in the Kingdom of God," Nauvoo Illinois Relief Society Monument Dedication, 30 June 1978.)

Sunday School

It is one hundred years this winter since Brother Ballantyne, inspired with the thought "that the gospel was too precious to be withheld from the children," brought logs from Mill Creek Canyon, rock from the quarry in Red Butte Canyon, and adobes from a nearby yard for the construction of a home, the front part of which was to be dedicated to the Lord for the teaching of the gospel to children. From that humble structure, surrounded by a rude pole fence and cottonwood trees from City Creek Canyon, the Sunday School program has spread throughout the entire world wherever the restored gospel has been preached. ("The Sunday School Now and Then," *Instructor* 84 [November 1949]: 533–34.)

Attend your Sunday School classes every Sunday. Listen carefully to the lesson and participate in class discussions. Gospel scholarship and an increase in testimony will result. (CR April 1986, *Ensign* 16 [May 1986]: 44.)

Young Men and Young Women

To the Young Women leaders, may you truly love the young sisters with whom you are working. Get inside their lives. Be a true friend and counselor to them. Perform your stewardship well. With all the energy of your heart, help bring them back to our Father in Heaven clean and sweet and pure. ("To the Young Women of the Church," *Ensign* 16 [November 1986]: 85.)

The enemy of righteousness is supported by millions of people, and he has a most powerful and effective program to lead our youth astray. The big question of our time is, Who reaches youth today? Who communicates with them? Parents? Schoolteachers? Civil officials? Community leaders? Any adults? In too many cases, these people are having trouble talking to—as well as listening to—young people. Into this void steps the Mutual Improvement Associations, recognizing teens for what they are: growing individuals seeking to establish their identity, find themselves, and build upon sound intellectual and spiritual foundations. We have a program that should reach them. (*An Enemy Hath Done This,* p. 300.)

We have a well-rounded program for the youth of the Church. And we are not dealing with ordinary young people. We are working with choice spirits who need the full Church program. We want them to have the benefit of this program in its fulness, that they might develop into the kind of young men and young women which the Lord would have them become. Of course, these programs are not ends in themselves. They are tools. They are a means to an end. The end is the salvation and exaltation of God's children. (CR April 1951, *Improvement Era* 54 [June 1951]: 423.)

Primary

You are dealing with choice spirits among the many that have been created. I am persuaded that in the veins of these boys and girls in your Primary organizations flows some of the best blood that this world has ever known. These are choice spirits. Many of them, I feel confident, have been held back to come forth in this, the greatest of all gospel dispensations, in preparation for the second coming of the Master. (*So Shall Ye Reap,* p. 27.)

I am happy that in modern revelation, the Lord has referred to these little ones—the children. You have taken your theme from one of the very important revelations (D&C 68) which the Lord has given in which He tells about the responsibility of parents in Zion to teach their children faith, repentance, baptism, and the gift of the Holy Ghost. He tells of the condemnation that will follow if they fail, and then He also adds: "And they shall also teach their children to pray, and to walk uprightly before the Lord" (verse

28). That, I understand, is your theme, because you reach out to help and supplement the work of the parents in directing these precious souls along the paths of righteousness. ("Our First Obligation," Primary Conference, Salt Lake City, Utah, 5 April 1950.)

How many parents in the Church today owe their membership in the Church largely to the example of one of their own children, one of their children who first came in contact with the Church through the Primary, through a Scout troop or some other unit. When you teach them, often your lessons are carried into homes where parents may not be members of the Church, or may be inactive. The power of example in the life of a child is most potent indeed. ("Our First Obligation," Primary Conference, Salt Lake City, Utah, 5 April 1950.)

I thrilled as I read in your Primary literature this statement: "The joy of service cannot be equalled when the service is for a little child." Possibly I would have modified that just a little and said that "the joy of service cannot be surpassed"—I am sure it could not be surpassed. I have a feeling that the Lord has a way of equalizing the joy which comes to His children through service, whether they labor with the children of Zion, the small children; whether they work with the adult members of the Aaronic Priesthood; whether they serve in the Relief Society, or the Mutual Improvement Association, or wherever they serve. The Lord has the power to bring joy and happiness to our souls and to let us know the deep, soul-satisfying joy of unselfish service. ("Our First Obligation," Primary Conference, Salt Lake City, Utah, 5 April 1950.)

You have been charged with the responsibility of working with the souls of the children of men, the same as mission presidents. Oh, you do not go out on foreign missions. You stay home. You work with the Primary children close by, but, nevertheless, you are engaged in saving the souls of the children of men, in helping God's children to become the kind of men and women, sons and daughters, that our Heavenly Father would have them become. So your work is equally important, and I hope and pray that the brethren of the priesthood in your homes and in your wards sustain you wholeheartedly in the great calling which has come to you as handmaidens of our Heavenly Father, working with His children. The Lord has made it very clear in the revelations that the souls of men are precious in His sight. He tells us that He gave His very life in order to help save the souls of men and that if we labor all our days and bring save it be one soul unto him how great shall be our joy and rejoicing with that soul in the kingdom of our Father. (See D&C 18:11–15.) (*So Shall Ye Reap*, pp. 25–26.)

Important as the Primary organization is, it is but a means to an end, and not the end itself. The end is the perfection of God's children. You supplement the great responsibility of the home and of the father and mother, and your divine mission is of tremendous importance. (*So Shall Ye Reap*, p. 28.)

I would like to mention three things without which no Primary worker can be effective, three great essential requirements for officers and teachers in this great auxiliary of the Church, and any other auxiliary or part of the Church for that matter.

First of all, if you are going to be effective, you must have in your own hearts a testimony, a firm testimony and conviction of the divinity of this great latter-day work. If there are any within the sound of my voice who do not have that testimony, then I appeal to you. Through humble prayer, study, and meditation, seek for that testimony before you pursue your teaching and your leadership in the Primary of the Church.

Second is the matter of humility. "No one," says the Lord, "can assist with this work except he is humble and full of love" (D&C 12:8). That includes the sisters in the Primary also. Humility! That does not mean weakness; that does not mean lack of courage, lack of faith, lack of self-confidence; but it means the recognition of a higher power upon which we are dependent, that we must draw from that higher power if we would be effective as leaders in the Primary and teachers of the youth of the Church. We must know that without the Lord's help we cannot succeed, and with His help we cannot fail.

And third, it seems to me that we must have a love in our hearts for people; in your case, a love for children, if we are going to be effective in our leadership. With these requirements fully met, we will go forward, and under the blessings of heaven, we will succeed in helping the home and the parents to bring into the hearts of these children the most priceless thing in all the world—a testimony of the truth, a love of God and His great latter-day work.

As we go forward, I hope we will not become so completely involved in organization that we will forget our great and fundamental objectives, that we will not become so involved in the mechanics of our program that we will overlook the great responsibility and the great end to which we are striving as leaders and teachers in this wonderful organization. (*So Shall Ye Reap*, pp. 33–34.)

Correlation

The Lord has given us the broad organization outline, the purposes, and the objectives. But He leaves to us much of the working out of the methods. And this is where correlation and leadership training come in and why various segments of the program, such as wise delegation of responsibility, are under study. And as time passes we will come to appreciate and realize more fully the place and magnitude of this training and of the correlation program. (*God, Family, Country*, pp. 129–30.)

Just a word to you who work in the correlation review process. There is a principle given in the scriptures that applies to what you do. The principle is that "in the mouth of two and three witnesses shall every word be established" (D&C 6:28).

I have seen that principle work time and time again in the administrative councils of the Church. There is great safety in witnesses. This is also true of the review of our lesson materials and programs. It is through the eyes of two or three and many more that the curricula and programs are prepared, reviewed, and approved; and because of this process, we are, as a Church, more doctrinally sound and better correlated than ever before in our history. With recent refinements, and your continual cooperation, we will continue to improve. (Interdepartmental Meeting, Salt Lake City, Utah, 7 September 1982.)

Some of us remember the times when the organizations of the Church had their own programs and when there was often duplication of effort and curriculum. Over the past few years we have seen great strides made toward unity and oneness, with the priest-hood and auxiliaries working together for the good of the entire Church. All this has been a great blessing to families and individu-als throughout the Church. (Interdepartmental Meeting, Salt Lake City, Utah, 7 September 1982.)

When I think of correlation, I think of these words of the Savior: "I say unto you, be one; and if ye are not one ye are not mine" (D&C 38:27). We have seen a great evidence of that unity in the last few years, and we hope that you will all continue your cooperation in the effort to simplify and reduce the materials sent to the field. This is the desire of the First Presidency and the Twelve. (Interdepartmental Meeting, Salt Lake City, Utah, 7 Sep-tember 1982.)

Family History and Genealogy

The question may arise in one's mind, Why should I spend time in searching out my ancestors? How can they contribute anything to me? Why should I evidence more than passing interest in their welfare? We are largely a product of our progenitors, their strength sustains us, their weaknesses, if any, warn us of traits and tendencies to curb and avoid. Their love and devotion bring to fulfillment the Savior's great law of love with combined loved ones and families joyfully together in time and throughout eternity. We owe them much more than we can ever repay. A noble heritage has always been regarded as one of life's greatest treasures. ("Temple Memories," Ogden Utah Temple Dedication, 18 January 1972.)

Much more must be done in our personal genealogical research. We have an obligation to do temple work for our kin-dred dead. This means that we will do the necessary research in order for the names of our progenitors to be sent to the temples. We have an individual responsibility to see that we are linked to our progenitors. ("Our Duty as Latter-day Saints," Springfield-Burke Virginia Chapel Dedication, 15 October 1982.)

The work is progressing but I am afraid that *genealogy* remains just a word to be avoided or ignored by the average member of the

Church. Those of you who have worked at your genealogies, who realize the importance of the work and have felt the excitement that comes from tying families together and learning of your noble heritage, need to share that excitement with others. Help them to see the joy and fulfillment you see in the work. We need to prose-lyte more of our members into this work. There is much to be done, as you all know, and there are many, many members who could do the work and who would enjoy doing the work if some of us — all of you — would just ignite that spark in them through your enthusiasm, example, and devotion. ("Eternal Memories," Tenth Annual Priesthood Genealogical Research Seminar, BYU, Provo, Utah, 31 July 1975.)

Emphasize the necessity of genealogical work. Every region, stake, and ward leader should complete the four-generation program as stressed by the Church and encourage families and individuals to do likewise, and move on from there in their genealogical research. (Regional Representatives Seminar, Salt Lake City, Utah, 2 April 1982.)

Our responsibility to keep a journal and to write our own personal histories and those of our ancestors, particularly those who belong to the first four generations of our pedigree, has not changed. (CR October 1978, *Ensign* 8 [November 1978]: 30.)

More must be done to encourage our members to do their own genealogical research. Once they do their research, the spirit of Elijah will bless them so they, in turn, will inspire the Saints under their direction to do their own work. (Salt Lake City, Utah, 6 June 1980.)

Those who are acquainted with the Latter-day Saint scriptures and the process of genealogical research will recognize that the extraction program is but a first step in the overall program of preparing a Church book of remembrance "worthy of acceptation" (see D&C 128:24). The extraction program is primarily aimed at more efficient identification and processing of names for individual temple ordinance work. It solves the immediate need to provide many more names for the operation of the temples. (CR October 1978, *Ensign* 8 [November 1978]: 30–31.)

I believe the youth are not only willing and able to do genealogical research, but they are a good means of giving life to the whole program. How often have the youth actually been driven away by those who would close the door on genealogy to them, or at the best, insist that they must "drink milk" when they are ready for the "meat."

I am reminded of a little story told to me of a young girl who was assigned to give a two-and-a-half minute talk for Sunday School. She chose the subject of genealogy. She began her talk by saying, "Brothers and sisters, I have chosen to talk on genealogy." Then she stood silently at the pulpit, staring at the congregation, for two-and-one-half minutes. At the end of that time she said, "I guess you have been really concerned and worried waiting for me to talk about genealogy. How do you think our ancestors feel, waiting for us to do something about their genealogy?" Then she sat down. ("Eternal Memories," Tenth Annual Priesthood Genealogical Research Seminar, BYU, Provo, Utah, 31 July 1975.)

Perhaps the present inactive genealogist members of the Church would be more concerned about their dead if they began to fully realize that "salvation for the dead" is far from being something different, but is part of a two-way street upon which our mutual exaltation is dependent. ("Eternal Memories," Tenth Annual Priesthood Genealogical Research Seminar, BYU, Provo, Utah, 31 July 1975.)

Every person has choice memories of incidents and family stories to include in a book of remembrance. I have many precious memories of my family, before marriage and after, and countless memories of special incidents throughout my life which are priceless to me and will be to my posterity. ("Eternal Memories," Tenth Annual Priesthood Genealogical Research Seminar, BYU, Provo, Utah, 31 July 1975.)

In this work we cannot fail if we do our part. The Lord will not permit us to fail. This is His work. He will open the doors in our genealogical research. He will bless us as we come to the temple. No, we cannot fail. The Lord said to His little flock of Saints in the early days, "Therefore, fear not, little flock; do good; let earth and hell combine against you, for if ye are built upon my rock, they cannot prevail. Look unto me in every thought; doubt not, fear not." (D&C 6:34, 36.) (Mesa Arizona Temple Rededication, 16 April 1975.)

Remember always as we work in this glorious genealogical effort, that the veil may become very thin between this world and the spirit world. I know this is true. It is well also that we keep in mind that it is all one great program on both sides of the veil and sometimes I feel it is not too important whether we serve here or over there as long as we serve with all our heart, might, mind, and strength (see D&C 4:2). ("Eternal Memories," Tenth Annual Priesthood Genealogical Research Seminar, BYU, Provo, Utah, 31 July 1975.)

The Lord is in this work. He wants it to prosper. He wants us to be successful in our efforts. While living with my grandmother, Louise Ballif Benson, in Logan as a student, I knew she had been working very hard on her research. She kept referring to the fact that there was a gap that she couldn't fill and it worried her. She prayed about it fervently. One day she received a package addressed just "Benson Family, Utah." The package contained a printed book which had come from a man in Syracuse, New York, who had done research independently—not as a member of the Church. You can imagine the joy that filled my grandmother's heart when she found that this not only filled the gap, but did much more than that. Her prayers had been answered. Yes, there are many ways to help get the job done. ("Eternal Memories," Tenth Annual Priesthood Genealogical Research Seminar, BYU, Provo, Utah, 31 July 1975.)

When I think of genealogy, I see people—people I love who are waiting for our family, their posterity, to help them gain exaltation in the celestial kingdom. ("Eternal Memories," Tenth Annual Priesthood Genealogical Research Seminar, BYU, Provo, Utah, 31 July 1975.)

Growth of the Church

This is not just another Church. This is not just one of a family of Christian churches. This is the Church and kingdom of God, the only true Church upon the face of the earth, according to the Lord's own words (see D&C 1:30). His Church—it bears His name and it is directed under the authority of His priesthood. But it has always been true, to some extent, even among the Latter-day Saints, that we have taken our blessings for granted. And in the early days of the Church, the Lord kept urging the Saints to look up, to get a vision, to raise their sights that they might get the vision of the magnitude of this work, that this is a world organization. The gospel teaches a world message. This message is going to be carried to the entire world, to all of our Father's children, in spite of all opposition by the adversary and his lieutenants.

Even during the days while the Saints were being persecuted, driven from their homes, their property destroyed, their livestock stolen from them, many of them losing their lives—even during those dark days—the Lord kept pointing upward, helping them to realize that life is eternal and that the kingdom is going to prevail. (Star Valley Wyoming Stake Conference, 18 April 1971.)

Many years have come and gone since that first humble missionary set out to carry the message of salvation to a confused world. In fulfillment of the all-important God-given mandate, this great work has gone forward through the years unabated. It is a dramatic chapter in the history of a "peculiar people" (see 1 Peter 2:9). (*God, Family, Country*, p. 44.)

In the usual sense of the term *Church membership* means that a person has his or her name officially recorded on the membership records of the Church. By that definition, we have more than six million members of the Church.

But the Lord defines a member of His kingdom in quite a different way. In 1828, through the Prophet Joseph Smith, He said, "Behold, this is my doctrine—whosoever repenteth and cometh unto me, the same is my church" (D&C 10:67). To Him whose Church this is, membership involves far more than simply being a member of record. ("A Mighty Change of Heart," address prepared [but not delivered] 1986.)

It is pleasing to note the growth of the Church, the increased attendance at Church meetings, and the participation of our members in various Church activities. But the real measure of our faith is our private religious behavior—love and harmony in our homes, our personal prayers, private scripture study, temple attendance, magnifying Church callings, and offering love and service to our fellowmen. ("Lord, Increase Our Faith!" Provo Utah Tabernacle Rededication, 21 September 1986.)

During the past few years a number of resources have been set in place in the Church to help us. New editions of the scriptures have been published—are we taking advantage of them? More temples are located closer to our people—are we going to the house of the Lord more frequently? The consolidated meeting schedule was set up—are we taking advantage of the increased time with our families? A special home evening manual was provided—are we using it? A new hymnal has just been published —are we singing more songs of the heart? (See D&C 25:12.) And so the list goes on and on. We have received much help. We don't need changed programs now as much as we need changed people! (CR April 1986, *Ensign* 16 [May 1986]: 4.)

The Church has survived exile from four states, the harassment and persecution of its members, an extermination order from a governor, the execution of its prophet, disenfranchisement by the government, and continuous persecution of its leaders and people. That is what this Church endured and survived in the first sixty years of its history—and it was through such adversity, persecution, and impoverishment that the Church gained strength and matured. (CR April 1980, *Ensign* 10 [May 1980]: 32.)

Opposition has been and will be the lot of the Saints of the kingdom in any age. The finger of scorn has been pointed at us in the past, and we may expect it in the future. We also expect to see men in high places defend the Church; there will also be "pharaohs" who know neither Joseph nor his brethren (see Exodus 1:8). The seed planted and watered in 1830 has now matured to a fully grown tree for all to see. Some will seek the refuge of its shade in the heat of the day, but none will be neutral in their appraisal of its fruit. (CR April 1980, *Ensign* 10 [May 1980]: 33.)

The Church is going forward. We may drop by the wayside, or we may move forward with it. It is entirely up to us. (Bear Lake Idaho Stake Conference, 22 May 1971.)

The Church itself is God's great instrument to build and to save and to exalt men everywhere, through the application of the simple principles of the gospel. It is a way of life that will make men happy, and "men are, that they might have joy" (2 Nephi 2:25). This great instrument must withstand opposition and complacency. (CR April 1955, *Improvement Era* 58 [June 1955]: 407.)

As Latter-day Saints, we know the adversary will not succeed. The Church stands stronger today than ever before in its history. We are not only growing in numbers, we are also increasing in faith and testimony as measured by attendance at meetings, the payment of tithes and offerings, support of the great missionary program, the building program, temple work, and other phases of our program. Today we have the fullest and the richest program for the blessing of our Father's children to be found anywhere upon the face of the earth. (*God, Family, Country*, pp. 90–91.)

The Lord has prospered this work and He will continue to do so. He is close to His servants, even within whispering distance of heaven. You are engaged in the greatest and most important work in time and eternity—furthering the kingdom of God on the earth. (Salt Lake City, Utah, 20 May 1984.)

We are commanded by God to take this gospel to all the world. That is the cause that must unite us today. Only the gospel will save the world from the calamity of its own self-destruction. Only the gospel will unite men of all races and nationalities in peace. Only the gospel will bring joy, happiness, and salvation to the human family. Isaiah said that many in latter times would say: "Come . . . let us go up . . . to the house of the God of Jacob; and he will teach us of his ways, and we will walk in his paths" (Isaiah 2:3).

Is there any greater cause than to teach others the gospel so that they may be united in walking in the ways of the God of Israel? Will we so live His commandments that others will see that the ways of the God of Jacob are distinct from the world? That is our challenge. Let us then make His cause our cause. ("Zion Shall Flourish upon the Mountains," Days of '47 Committee Luncheon, Salt Lake City, Utah, 24 July 1982.)

The Kingdom Rolls Forth

In the Old Testament it is written that in the last days "the God of heaven [shall] set up a kingdom" (Daniel 2:44). Daniel likened the early beginnings of this kingdom to "a stone . . . cut out without hands," which would become "a great mountain" to fill the whole earth (see Daniel 2:34–35).

Our message to the world is that the kingdom of which Daniel prophesied is now on the earth. Its early beginnings were as inconspicuous as a small stone rolling down a mountain. Today, partly because of its accelerated growth, The Church of Jesus Christ of Latter-day Saints is no longer ignored. Prejudice has largely subsided as people have come in contact with Mormons and their message. (*This Nation Shall Endure*, p. 114.)

Today The Church of Jesus Christ of Latter-day Saints is extending the heralded message of the restoration of the gospel to every nation which permits us entrance through its borders. This is a fulfillment of the vision and revelation received by Daniel, the prophet (see Daniel 2:34–35, 44). (CR April 1978, *Ensign* 8 [May 1978]: 32.)

We should act without any fear when we feel impressed to go ahead as the Spirit prompts us. Don't hesitate to move. The Lord made that very clear to us when He said, "Fear not, little flock" (D&C 6:34). He was talking to a very small flock when the Church was in its infancy. You are now building on the foundation of a great work. (Salt Lake City, Utah, 3 October 1978.)

I have seen, at close range, the manner in which the Lord has turned disasters—war, occupation, and revolution—into blessings. Prophecies of the Lord are being fulfilled. The gospel is reaching peoples who a few years ago seemed unteachable. In spite of powerful traditions, religious dogmas, and ancient national policies, great changes have come over entire nations. Miracles are happening before our very eyes. The Lord is working great wonders, and His children are rejoicing as the blessings of the gospel touch their lives. It is marvelous to behold. (CR April 1970, *Improvement Era* 73 [June 1970]: 96.)

That the Church of Jesus Christ would have an inconspicuous beginning and then enjoy phenomenal growth was predicted. Jesus used the comparison of the small mustard seed to describe the early beginning of His Church. But eventually, He declared, that insignificant seed would become a great tree and many would find refuge in its branches. (See Matthew 13:31–32.)

As men have attempted to assess the Church at a given period of time, in many instances they have not been able to see its forward movement and potential. The growth of the Church, like the growth of grass or trees, has been almost imperceptible to the eye, but little by little, line by line, precept by precept, the Church has matured. (CR April 1980, *Ensign* 10 [May 1980]: 32.)

Simultaneous with the early development of the Church was a spirit of opposition and persecution. Wherever the tiny "mustard seed" was planted, attempts were made to frustrate its growth. But notwithstanding all the efforts to destroy the work—even the murder of the Prophet Joseph Smith and his brother—the Church prospered and grew (see Matthew 13:31–32). There were those who thought the Church would fail with the deaths of the martyrs Joseph and Hyrum, but they did not perceive that this latter-day kingdom should "never be destroyed" (see Daniel 2:44). (CR April 1980, *Ensign* 10 [May 1980]: 32.)

There has never been a time until now when the Church has had the strength and the means to reach out effectively to the Asian nations. In the timetable of the Lord, the door is now open, and this is apparently the time for the work in Asia. Each visit has been productive and inspirational. The work is expanding and further expansion is in the offing. In each of the countries the tremendous growth is an inspiration: this is where the people are—by the hundreds of millions—one-third of the population of the world. Of course, from the total standpoint of those many millions, we are just getting started. ("The Future of the Church in Asia," *Improvement Era* 73 [March 1970]: 14–15.)

After the restoration of His Church in modern times, Jesus Christ named His Church. With impeccable logic, He inquired of a former generation, "How be it my church save it be called in my name? . . . if it be called in the name of a man then it be the church of a man." (3 Nephi 27:8.) Thus by revelation in our day, He named His Church—even "The Church of Jesus Christ of Latter-day Saints" (see D&C 115:4). Since we accept His Church as the kingdom of God on earth, we are under obligation, as His disciples, to preach His gospel to all the world and to emulate the standards of His teachings to all men. (*Come unto Christ*, pp. viii–ix.)

The Church and kingdom of God are rolling forth in these latter days and are beginning to fill the earth with a knowledge of the Lord. (Texas San Antonio Mission, 2 March 1986.)

We live in a time when the devil is on the loose, and he is working amidst the Saints to thwart and tear down the work. But he will not succeed. Individuals may fall. We may have those who betray sacred covenants, but the kingdom of God will roll forward till it reaches its decreed destiny to fill the entire earth. (Salt Lake City, Utah, 20 May 1984.)

I feel the weight of this responsibility so great that were it not for the light which gives me hope I would not be able to bear it, but with that light I join with Peter and Paul, with Joseph Smith and Brigham Young, and with President Spencer W. Kimball and the others who have been charged with this work by the Lord. It is not too great to accomplish. The Lord is with us. This is His work. He will never fail us for He declared in that great revelation—designated as His preface to His "Book of Commandments" which He has given us to publish unto the "inhabitants of the earth"—this reassuring promise: "And they shall go forth and none shall stay them, for I the Lord have commanded them" (D&C 1:5–6). (Mission Presidents Seminar, Salt Lake City, Utah, 27–28 June 1974.)

We are people who love peace and who love freedom. We have endured much, it has cost some of the best blood of the world to establish this work, but it is here to stay. (Dedication of Bolivia, La Paz, Bolivia, 13 January 1979.)

The kingdom of God will not fail; it shall not be destroyed; it will not be left to other people; it will stand forever until "the kingdoms of this world [will] become the kingdoms of our Lord, and of his Christ" (Revelation 11:15; see D&C 138:44; Daniel 2:44). (CR April 1978, *Ensign* 8 [May 1978]: 33.)

Public Acceptance

This thing called Mormonism has not been done in a corner (see Acts 26:26). It has been before the world in a rather dramatic fashion from the very beginning until this present time. ("Dawn of a New Day for the Church," Washington D.C. Stake Conference, 7 December 1958.)

Never has the Church had the opportunity it has today. The Church is the most attractive religious body in the world. Its image has never been as good as it is today! We are known increasingly today for what we are and not for what our enemies have said about us. (Texas San Antonio Mission, 2 March 1986.)

Mormonism, as it is known to the world, has emerged as a worldwide church. The growth phenomenon alone has focused attention on the Church. Indeed, one of our major challenges is to cope with growth. But generally speaking, people are not attracted to an organization or a church simply because it is growing. There must be other reasons that explain the appeal. (*Come unto Christ*, p. 70.)

Opposition to the Church did not subside with the twentieth century, but gradually people came to see us for what we stood for, rather than what our enemies said about us. Our Mormon boys fought in two world wars and were recognized for their standards and principles. During the Great Depression of the thirties, the Church came to be known for independence, self-reliance, and taking care of its own. And over the century, Latter-day Saints distinguished themselves in the fields of science, education, medicine, business, and other endeavors. (CR April 1980, *Ensign* 10 [May 1980]: 32–33.)

The world has shrunk in size through modern means of transportation. Concurrently the Church has extended its missions and branches. Members of the Church in government service, private enterprise and missionary work have spread abroad until, as one foreign official said pleasantly, "The Mormons seem to be everywhere." ("We Saw the Church Around the World," *Instructor* 93 [March 1958]: 68.)

We must more effectively proclaim the gospel of Jesus Christ through the media. The restoration of the gospel is the most momentous message in the world. Our message is not that we are mainstream Christians; nor is it the Word of Wisdom; nor is it the family. Our message is that the gospel has been restored to earth, that the heavens have been opened again, that God has spoken in our day and currently reveals His mind and will. This is the message we must proclaim from the housetops. We must see to it that we more effectively utilize technology to help bring the gospel message to our people and the people of the world. (Salt Lake City, Utah, 6 June 1980.)

We must see to it that every enterprise, every project is so conducted as to strengthen and not weaken or damage the image of the Church. (Salt Lake City, Utah, 19 January 1977.)

Future Progress

This is the dispensation of the fulness of times. Every other gospel dispensation from the days of Adam through the ancient Apostles has drifted into apostasy. But our dispensation is different. We have been assured by the Lord that the kingdom of God, The Church of Jesus Christ of Latter-day Saints, will remain on earth to prepare the way and meet the kingdom of heaven when the Lord comes again. ("Our Obligation and Challenge," Regional Representatives Seminar, Salt Lake City, Utah, 30 September 1977.)

I hope that all of us can see in these developments the hand of the Lord moving His kingdom forward to accomplish on an accelerated basis what He designs to accomplish. I have often said that the Lord gives to us the broad blueprint of organization, purpose, and objectives, but leaves it to us to work out some of the organizational and other details. In that process is growth to the individual if we depend on the Lord for light and inspiration beyond our own natural talents.

The Lord is now revealing and will continue to do so through channels He has appointed everything necessary for the future development and perfection of His Church. ("The Role of the Church Planning and Coordinating Council," Interdepartmental Meeting, Salt Lake City, Utah, 16 March 1977.)

Many predictions have been made by the enemies of the Church regarding this work. I remember as a boy it was not uncommon to read predictions by some who professed to have made a study of Mormonism. They predicted that Mormonism would not endure beyond the third and fourth generation. I remember reading books written by critics of that time to this effect, and as a young boy, before I got a burning testimony, I used to wonder about it. There has never been any real doubt—just a little wonder during my early years. How wrong they have been! Mormonism would peter out after the third and fourth generation? Well, I am the fourth generation. I have two sons who are the fifth generation, and I am sure their faith is just as strong as their father's was at their age—possibly stronger. There are some of you here who probably represent the fifth and sixth generation. No, Mormonism is not going to peter out. (*So Shall Ye Reap*, p. 180.)

Every effort by evil and designing men has been used, without success, to stop the growth and progress of the restored gospel of Jesus Christ. I say unto you, that no power in earth or in hell can stop this work. It is God's truth. His power and authority are directing it. ("A Voice of Warning to the Nations of the World," New Zealand and Australia Area Conferences, 25 November 1979 and 2 December 1979.)

Now, do we see any signs of sleeping giants, lifeless homes, dead quorums, spiritless wards, stagnant stakes, and an apathetic citizenry? Then we must arise and awake, "for Zion must increase in beauty, and in holiness, her borders must be enlarged; her stakes must be strengthened; yea, verily I say unto you, Zion must arise and put on her beautiful garments" (D&C 84:14). Those are the words of the Lord. ("Our Obligation and Challenge," Regional Representatives Seminar, Salt Lake City, Utah, 30 September 1977.)

We now have the fulness of the everlasting gospel and the priesthood to act in God's name. We rejoice in this great opportunity and blessing. We rejoice in the growth of the Church—in numbers, in faith, in testimony. The outlook is most encouraging all over the world. We are operating in hundreds of countries and the end is not yet. The Lord will open the way. (Dedication of Bolivia, La Paz, Bolivia, 13 January 1979.)

With all my soul I testify that this work will go forward till every land and people have had opportunity to accept our message. Barriers will come down for us to accomplish this mission, and some of us will see this done. Our Heavenly Father will cause conditions in the world to change so that His gospel can penetrate every border. (Salt Lake City, Utah, 6 June 1980.)

May our family altars continue to ascend praises and honor to the Most High for His omnipotent guidance of modern Israel— and may we never forget that His hand guides the destiny of this Church today and will continue to do so in future years. ("Zion Shall Flourish upon the Mountains," Days of '47 Committee Luncheon, Salt Lake City, Utah, 24 July 1982.)

We should be willing to generously give of our time, talents, and means to the Church. No matter what happens to the world, the Church will grow in strength and will be intact when the Lord comes again. ("Jesus Christ—Gifts and Expectations," Christmas Devotional, Salt Lake City, Utah, 7 December 1986.)

Mission of the Church

The mission of the Church is to save souls by proclaiming the gospel, perfecting the Saints, and redeeming the dead. We urge you to do all within your talent and means to help build the kingdom of God on the earth. Always strive to sustain, support, and do what is best for the kingdom of God. (CR April 1984, *Ensign* 14 [May 1984]: 8.)

The aim of this organizing and concentration of resources is that the Church will be able to stand independent above all nations (which suggests that the Church will be self-governing, autonomous, and not reliant on human opinion or institutions for its temporal survival and support)—amidst a time when the wrath and judgments of God will be poured out on all nations (see D&C 78:13–14). ("The Energy Crisis," Salt Lake City, Utah, 18 August 1977.)

There are three great and important obligations, possibly overshadowing all others, which rest upon this people and upon this great Church of Jesus Christ of Latter-day Saints. The first of these, at least in the order of emphasis in this dispensation, is that of missionary work—the responsibility which rests upon this people to carry the message of the restored gospel to the people of the world. We have been engaged in that work ever since the Church was organized, yea, even before. Second, we have the responsibility of building up the stakes and wards and branches of Zion. This entails the providing of facilities—houses of worship, temples, seminary buildings—that are so necessary for us to carry on the spiritual part of the program. It entails taking care of our people—temporally, physically, culturally, and socially, as well as spiritually. And in the third place, we have the great responsibility of performing certain sacred ordinances in the temples of the Lord—a responsibility which rests upon every holder of the priesthood as well as upon the sisters of the Church. (*So Shall Ye Reap*, p. 37.)

Our mission as a Church is to preach the gospel to all the world. That means, in due time, every country, nationality, and people. In a letter to Mr. John Wentworth in March 1842, Joseph Smith prophesied: "No unhallowed hand can stop the work from progressing; . . . the truth of God will go forth boldly, nobly, and independent, till it has penetrated every continent, visited every clime, swept every country, and sounded in every ear, till the purposes of God shall be accomplished, and the Great Jehovah shall say the work is done." (*History of the Church*, 4:540.) (CR April 1985, *Ensign* 15 [May 1985]: 6.)

There is much to do before the work of God can be pronounced completed. Hearts of leaders must be softened, doors of nations opened, false ideologies overcome, and the gospel presented. (CR April 1985, *Ensign* 15 [May 1985]: 6.)

The Church will continue its opposition to error, falsehood, and immorality. The mission of the Church is to herald the message of salvation and make unmistakably clear the pathway to exaltation. Our mission is to prepare a people for the coming of the Lord. The power of God and the righteousness of the Saints will be the means by which the Church will be spared (see 1 Nephi 14:14–15). (CR April 1980, *Ensign* 10 [May 1980]: 33–34.)

We cannot stress enough the principles of welfare, genealogy, living within one's means, reactivation, and obedience to the laws and ordinances of the gospel. If we will live these principles consistently and repetitiously, the mission of the Church will be realized. (Salt Lake City, Utah, 2 June 1982.)

My heart lifts within me as I share the feeling of that first little group of six men as they sat in the Whitmer log house on 6 April 1830. They had just sustained Joseph and Oliver as the first and second elders of the newly organized Church of Jesus Christ. Some arose and prophesied that what had been done would expand until it filled the whole earth. They did not know how it would take place, but they knew that it would by the Spirit of truth within them. Then they went forth determined to start the process.

Many of those of that day believed they would live to see the fulfillment and the final coming of the Lord. We now know that truly no man knows when the Lord will come. We do know that the field is still white and the harvest goes on. In our eyes, this seems to be happening slowly, but in the eyes of the Holy One of Israel, it is more rapid than we think. "Not yet," He seems to say, "not yet." There is still wheat among the tares. We must realize, I suppose, that in each generation of men on earth is concealed the wheat which the Lord will harvest. Our generation must find its wheat. (See D&C 38:12.) With the Lord's help we shall not fail.

(Mission Presidents Seminar, Salt Lake City, Utah, 27–28 June 1974.)

In modern revelation, the Lord has said, "Behold, verily I say unto you, the angels are crying unto the Lord day and night, who are ready and waiting to be sent forth to reap down the fields" (D&C 86:5). He also said in this same revelation that He would "let the wheat and the tares grow together until the harvest is ripe; then ye shall first gather out the wheat from among the tares, and after the gathering of the wheat, behold and lo, the tares are bound in bundles, and the field remaineth to be burned" (verse 7). This is the time to "gather the wheat," the millions of righteous people. ("Safety in the Face of Wickedness," Tokyo Japan Area Conference, 8–10 August 1975.)

Keep in mind not only the importance of our message, but the promise that has been given that in this work we cannot fail if we do our part. This is not our work. It is the work of the Lord that we are called upon to help with, to carry this message to our Father's children. It is a message of salvation and exaltation. It is a message that will save and exalt the souls of the children of men. There is no other way, because this is the only true message and the only true church upon the face of the whole earth. Those are not my words; they are the words of the Lord Jesus Christ as found in the revelations. (D&C 1.) This gospel in its purity, now restored to the earth, is intended to reach all of our Father's children, and what a glorious thing it is to be permitted to participate in it! "This is my work and my glory—to bring to pass the immortality and eternal life of man" (Moses 1:39). That is the whole purpose of the Church, the whole purpose of the program, the whole purpose of missionary service, and we are called to help carry that out. (*God, Family, Country*, pp. 58–59.)

The Church exists to assist the father to get his family back into the presence of our Father in Heaven—the highest degree of glory in the celestial kingdom. (Regional Representatives Seminar, Salt Lake City, Utah, 28 June 1974.)

May we all go to our homes rededicated to the sacred mission of the Church as so beautifully set forth in the conference sessions—to "invite all to come unto Christ" (D&C 20:59), "yea, come unto Christ, and be perfected in him" (Moroni 10:32).

This grand mission of the Church is accomplished by proclaiming the gospel, perfecting the Saints, and redeeming the dead. In each of our homes, may we prayerfully consider specific ways we as families and individuals can accomplish this mission. Let us determine how each of us can be doers of the word and not hearers only (see James 1:22).

In proclaiming the gospel, would you prayerfully consider and ponder the following as it applies to you:

As a young man, are you earnestly preparing to serve a full-time mission? The Lord needs every young man between the ages of nineteen and twenty-six, worthy, prepared, and excited about serving in the mission field.

As a mature couple, having raised your children, have you prayerfully considered serving a full-time mission? The Lord needs many more couples in the mission field who can love and fellowship and lead people to Christ.

As a single sister, where marriage is not in your immediate future, have you prayed about serving a full-time mission and sought counsel from your parents and your bishop? Our single sisters are serving marvelous missions throughout the world.

Finally, as a member of the Church, do you realize that, as a member-missionary, you have a sacred responsibility to share the gospel with friends and family? The Lord needs every member of the Church having the faith and courage to set a date to have someone prepared to be taught by the missionaries. Would each member of the Church prayerfully consider this sacred challenge?

Another way we come unto Christ is by perfecting the Saints. How do we accomplish this? One way to help perfect ourselves and our families is by daily reading from the scriptures. Are we as families and individuals reading daily from the Book of Mormon and using its teachings to bless and perfect our lives and those of our children? I rejoice in the thousands of members who are responding to this invitation and who testify of the blessings they are receiving.

Communicating with our Father in Heaven through prayer also brings a spiritual power and strength found in no other way. Are we praying both morning and night as a family and as individuals?

Again, are we holding family home evenings each week? Your immediate results may seem far from ideal at times, but by holding weekly family home evenings, as we have been counseled, we help to perfect that eternal family unit.

And what about family preparedness? Family preparedness has always been an essential welfare principle in perfecting the Saints. Are each of us and our families following, where permitted, the long-standing counsel to have sufficient food, clothing, and, where possible, fuel on hand to last at least one year?

Finally, let us consider the divine charge to redeem the dead. As you ponder this responsibility, would you give serious consideration to the following:

Have we prepared ourselves to receive our own endowments, and have sealings for our families been performed in the holy temple? By precept and example, our posterity should understand the transcendent importance of marrying the right person in the right place and sealing families for time and eternity.

Also, have we identified and received the ordinances for at least one of our ancestors? All members of the Church should be actively engaged in working on their family histories and receiving the help they need from trained stake and ward temple and family history consultants.

Do we periodically participate in all of the temple ordinances and thus receive the full blessings of vicarious work for our ancestors?

Do we return to the temple often to receive the personal blessings that come from regular temple worship? Prayers are answered, revelation occurs, and instruction by the Spirit takes place in the holy temples of the Lord.

The mission of the Church is glorious—to invite all of us to come unto Christ through proclaiming the gospel, perfecting our lives, and redeeming the dead. As we come unto Christ, we bless our own lives, those of our families, and our Father in Heaven's children, both living and dead. (CR April 1988, *Ensign* 18 [May 1988]: 84–85.)

Missionary Work

Heavenly messengers came to restore the authority of the holy priesthood and important keys essential to the opening of the final gospel dispensation. The Church was organized in 1830. Immediately, in response to divine command, missionary-messengers began to carry the important message of salvation throughout the world. It is a world message intended for all of God's children. (*Title of Liberty*, p. 88.)

The early missionaries of the Church went forward, beginning with Samuel H. Smith, only a few days after the Church was organized. The number increased until the message was carried to all parts of the then known United States, into Canada, and, by 1837, missionaries were on the Eastern Hemisphere. Even during the dark days of Missouri and Illinois and in the pilgrimage across the plains, missionaries went forward with their work. At times it was interrupted slightly, but always there was that urge and desire on the part of the elders of the Church, who had burning within their souls the testimony of the truth—to carry the message of the restored gospel to the people of the world. After the Saints arrived in the valley, it was not an uncommon thing to have read long lists of names of men attending the general conference of the Church who were called to go into the mission field and carry the message of the restored gospel. In later years it became the custom to issue the calls by letter. (*So Shall Ye Reap*, p. 40.)

"That the fulness of my gospel might be proclaimed by the weak and the simple unto the ends of the world, and before kings and rulers" (D&C 1:23). As I reflect on the great contribution by the elders of this dispensation in bringing the gospel to their fellowmen, I think of their great fortitude, sacrifice, and boldness. Many of the early elders left their families without any support to go into the field of labor. I think of mission presidents who have sacrificed businesses to go. I think of the tremendous financial sacrifices of families today in sending their sons and daughters into the mission fields. Certainly the efforts of thousands in this dispensation who have served are without precedent. And yet, it is not enough. We need to do more in opening the doors of countries so the elders can enter with our message. (Salt Lake City, Utah, 6 June 1980.)

"Why does the Mormon Church continue to send missionaries out into the world, particularly to Christian countries?" May I read the words of the First Presidency of this Church, uttered from this very pulpit, in which they gave answer to this question.

"It is our duty, divinely imposed, to continue urgently and militantly to carry forward our missionary work. We must continue to call missionaries and send them out to preach the gospel, which was never more needed than now, which is the only remedy for the tragic ills that now afflict the world, and which alone can bring peace and brotherly love back amongst the peoples of the earth."

This is not a matter of our own choosing. It is not something that has been devised by man. The Lord has made it clear to us, my brethren, that the responsibility is ours, as holders of the priesthood, to carry this message of the restored gospel to the people of the world. (*So Shall Ye Reap*, p. 43.)

As Latter-day Saints everywhere, with personal testimonies of these great events, we accept humbly, gratefully, this major responsibility placed upon the Church. We are happy to be engaged in a partnership with our Heavenly Father in the great work of the salvation and exaltation of His children. Willingly we give of our time and the means with which He may bless us to the establishment of His kingdom in the earth. This we know is our first duty and our great opportunity. This spirit has characterized the missionary work of the Church of Jesus Christ in all ages. It has been an outstanding mark of the ushering in of the dispensation of the fulness of times—our time. Wherever faithful Latter-day Saints are to be found, this spirit of unselfish sacrifice for the greatest cause in all the earth exists. In a statement published to the world during the last world war, the First Presidency of the Church declared: "No act of ours or of the Church must interfere with this God-given mandate" (CR April 1942, p. 91). (*God, Family, Country*, pp. 49–50.)

Today the Church needs missionaries as never before! We are required to carry the gospel of Jesus Christ to every nation of the world. The Lord commanded it in these words: "Send forth the elders of my church unto the nations which are afar off; unto the islands of the sea; send forth unto foreign lands; call upon all nations, first upon the Gentiles, and then upon the Jews" (D&C 133:8).

This commission to take the gospel to every nation, kindred, tongue, and people is one of the signs by which believers will recognize the nearness of the Savior's return to earth. Concerning this sign of His second coming, Jesus prophesied: "And this gospel of the kingdom shall be preached in all the world for a witness unto all nations; and then shall the end come" (Matthew 24:14).

This task will require thousands of missionaries, many more than are presently engaged in worldwide missionary service today. You are needed in the service of the Lord today as never before. "The harvest truly is great, but the labourers are few" (Luke 10:2). Those who serve a faithful mission return from that experience with increased faith, devotion, and leadership. They learn by their sacrifice what only personal experience and devoted service to others can teach.

A missionary learns, for example, that God can use him as an instrument to accomplish His work. He can say, as did Ammon, a Book of Mormon missionary, "This is [a] blessing which hath been bestowed upon us, that we have been made instruments in the hands of God to bring about this great work" (Alma 26:3). A missionary learns that he must be humble and dependent on the Lord. He learns to pray with fervor and sincerity, not only for himself but for others, and to be led and directed by the Spirit. (CR April 1984, *Ensign* 14 [May 1984]: 43–44.)

A missionary learns that the priesthood conferred upon him is the power of God. Opportunities are presented for exercise of the priesthood through the ordinances of baptism, confirmation, and administrations to the sick. Almost without exception, our missionaries testify that God has not ceased to be a God of miracles! (See Mormon 9:15.)

A missionary learns that God, our Heavenly Father, can and does answer prayers. He learns to recognize the promptings of the Holy Spirit and to be directed by that Spirit. He prays for his own welfare—to be humble and susceptible to the influence of the Holy Ghost—as well as for the people with whom he is laboring. Through these experiences of prayer and service, he learns to love the Lord with all his heart and to more fully love his fellowmen. The question is frequently asked, Should every young man fill a mission? The answer to this inquiry has been given by the Lord. It is yes. Every young man should fill a mission.

While every young man should serve a mission, we realize that every young man is not physically, emotionally, nor morally prepared. As a consequence, some may be deprived of missionary opportunities. But all should prepare to go—to be worthy to serve the Lord. The Lord has said: "And . . . every man [notice the words *every man*] should take righteousness in his hands and faithfulness upon his loins, and lift a warning voice unto the inhabitants of the earth; and declare both by word and by flight that desolation shall come upon the wicked" (D&C 63:37).

Some young men, because of transgression, say they are not interested in serving a mission. The real reason, of course, is feelings of unworthiness. If such young men would go to their bishop, confide to him their problem, and sincerely repent, they may yet fill honorable missions. We, your Brethren, sincerely invite you to prepare. Prepare now to serve the Lord. Prepare yourself physically, morally, spiritually, and emotionally. Visit with your bishop. Tell him your desires. Confide your problems. Seek his counsel. Then pray to your Heavenly Father about this important decision in your life.

One of the Church's greatest missionaries, Elder LeGrand Richards, said, "I have had many people ask me what my greatest Church experience has been, and I unhesitatingly say, My first mission! That is where I began to really love the Lord and His Church and developed a desire to help build His kingdom." I hope that each of you young men has a savings account and is looking forward to a mission.

Recently, in Dallas, Texas, I had the pleasure of addressing nearly two hundred missionaries. Among them were several young sisters. As I spoke to them, I had the feeling that they are a good example of a group of young people who are living in this wicked world and yet are not partaking of the sins of the world.

I rejoice in our youth. I am proud of them and grateful for them and know that the Lord is blessing and magnifying them. It is my great joy to meet with them whenever we go to a mission headquarters. They are choice young people.

Now I want to say a few words to some of you older brethren. We have need for select missionary couples. Some of you who are grandparents can have more influence on your grandchildren by letters from the mission field than by any other means.

Two of my sisters, widows—one the mother of ten, and the other the mother of eight—after sending their children on missions, talked to their bishops about going on missions themselves. I well remember the day they called me on the telephone and said,

"Guess what? We have received our missionary calls." I said, "What missionary calls?" They replied, "Don't you know?" I said, "No, I hadn't heard." They responded, "Yes, we are both going to your old field of labor in England." The mission president assigned them to work as companions—twenty months without a transfer. I think that is some kind of record. (CR April 1984, *Ensign* 14 [May 1984]: 45.)

These ambassadors of the Lord Jesus Christ, as they firmly believe themselves to be, have trudged through mud and snow, swum rivers, and gone without the common necessities of food, shelter, and clothing in response to a call. Voluntarily, fathers and sons have left homes, families, and jobs to go to all parts of the world, enduring great physical hardship and unrelenting persecution. Families have been left behind, often in dire straits, willingly laboring the harder to provide means for their missionaries. And through it all there has been a joy and satisfaction that has caused families at home to express gratitude for special blessings received and the missionaries to refer to this period as "the happiest time of my life." (*God, Family, Country*, p. 44.)

The Lord made it plain to these humble ambassadors that they were "preparing the way of the Lord for his second coming" (D&C 34:6). They were promised that their words would be the will of the Lord and scripture unto the people, inasmuch as they were faithful (D&C 68:4). They were told in no uncertain terms that they were being sent "out to prove the world," that they should "not be weary in mind, neither darkened," and a hair of their head should "not fall to the ground unnoticed" (D&C 84:79–80).

Is it any wonder, then, that with their personal testimonies a new dispensation of the gospel was being opened; and coupled with these stirring promises of the Lord, they went forth in power and at great personal sacrifice, without monetary reward, even though their numbers were few and their circumstances poor? Add to this the fact that the heavenly pronouncements emphasized that this was the last time the gospel should be given to men as a witness, in preparation for Christ's second coming and the end of the world—the end of wickedness. Theirs was the responsibility of warning the world of impending judgments, as it is ours today. (*God, Family, Country*, pp. 47–48.)

We all have confidence that when we have fully prepared ourselves, the Lord will provide a way for us to take the gospel to those lands now closed to our missionaries. President Spencer W. Kimball has said, "Somehow, brethren, I feel that when we have done all in our power that the Lord will find a way to open doors. That is my faith." We all share this faith. (Mission Presidents Seminar, Salt Lake City, Utah, 27 June 1974.)

"The Twelve being sent out, holding the keys, to open the door by the proclamation of the gospel of Jesus Christ, . . . first unto the Gentiles and then unto the Jews" (D&C 107:35). Proselyting the gospel in nations of the world only occurs when a member of the First Presidency or the Twelve dedicates the land for that purpose. The Church works within the laws of each nation to ensure that Church practices do not conflict with the law or the customs of that nation. We do not proselyte where the laws of that country prohibit the practice. ("150th Year for the Twelve," *Church News* [27 January 1985]: 3.)

The Book of Mormon records one of the great lessons from the Nephite experience in these words: "The preaching of the word had a great tendency to lead people to do that which was just, yea, it had a more powerful effect upon the minds of the people than the sword or anything else which had happened to them." (Alma 31:5.) When this Book of Mormon prophet, Alma, wrote those words his people were sorely troubled, but his preaching brought about a great reformation which restored peace and happiness. It is so today. This is why we emphasize missionary work as we do. It is the real answer to the world's problems. ("A Voice of Warning to the Nations of the World," New Zealand and Australia Area Conferences, 25 November 1979 and 2 December 1979.)

Missionary work—the preaching of the gospel—has been the major activity of the true Church of Christ whenever the gospel has been upon the earth. Prophets of God and numerous other ambassadors of truth have preached the word "in season, out of season'' (2 Timothy 4:2). (CR April 1970, *Improvement Era* 73 [June 1970]: 95.)

There are at least twenty-seven sections of the Doctrine and Covenants that refer to missionary work. The first great responsibility placed upon this Church in our day was to carry this message to the world. It is still a major responsibility. It is going on here on earth and it is going on in greater volume on the other side, and whether you do it here or over there doesn't make very much difference, just so long as you are missionaries. If you are laboring as you should, if you love this work, you will be engaged in helping to save the souls of the children of man throughout eternity until they have all heard it. And so it is the greatest work in all the world. There isn't anything like it in magnitude, in importance, in size, in promise. (*God, Family, Country*, p. 66.)

I think the Lord expects us, as elders in Israel, to do much more than we have ever done in the past in order to help preserve and safeguard and save His base of operations for the continuation of His program, for His gospel to go to all the nations of the earth. I am sure that gospel is going to every nation under heaven. The message of the restored gospel which is intended for all our Father's children, whom He loves as we love our own children, even with a deeper love, is going to every nation, kindred, tongue, and people from this base of operations. That is why I am so concerned for this base to be safeguarded and protected and strengthened so that we can carry this message of salvation unto all men. (Salt Lake City, Utah, 8 April 1972.)

I testify to you of the truthfulness of these four great points of emphasis on missionary work. First, the sacredness of saving souls and the importance of greatly increasing the number of convert baptisms. Second, the necessity of increasing our own personal faith in order that convert baptisms will increase in a significant and dramatic way. Third, the importance of missionaries prayerfully and with the Spirit setting personal convert baptismal goals. Fourth, the urgency of being actively and productively engaged in member-missionary work in order that the Lord's harvest may be accomplished. ("President Kimball's Vision of Missionary Work," *Ensign* 15 [July 1985]: 11.)

Prophets of God, ancient and modern, have predicted that judgments would be poured out upon the world unless the people repented. Prophets and leaders of the Church from the days of the Prophet Joseph have spoken out clearly and courageously regarding the calamities, destructions, and plagues which would visit the earth unless the people repented of their evil ways. But now, before the greatest calamities come, is the time for all of us to unite, to "lengthen our stride," as President Spencer W. Kimball has indicated, to "raise our sights," and to get a vision of the magnitude and urgency of this great missionary work. ("Safety in the Face of Wickedness," Tokyo Japan Area Conference, 8–10 August 1975.)

No power on earth or in hell can stop this work or thwart the purposes of the Lord to have His soul-satisfying gospel message go to His children. It may take disasters in many forms to bring it about. But the purposes of God will be achieved. His children will hear the gospel of salvation in His own due time. (CR April 1970, *Improvement Era* 73 [June 1970]: 96.)

May God bless this great missionary program. May He bless each of us with the spirit of missionary work prompted out of love for our fellowman. I testify that this work is true and that the results of all our efforts today will one day fill the world with wards, stakes, and many millions of our Father's children whose souls are saved in His kingdom. (CR April 1985, *Ensign* 15 [May 1985]: 8.)

The appearance of God the Father and His Son Jesus Christ to the boy prophet is the greatest event that has occurred in this world since the resurrection of the Master. As the restored Church of Jesus Christ, we humbly and gratefully bear this witness to all men. This message is a world message. It is the truth, intended for all of our Father's children. Members of the Church throughout the world bear this solemn testimony.

Today thousands of faithful missionaries throughout the nations freely carry this all-important message to the world. Jesus is the Christ, the Savior of mankind, the Redeemer of the world, the very Son of God. He is the God of this world, our advocate with the Father. Today these missionary-messengers of truth and

members of The Church of Jesus Christ of Latter-day Saints—the
Mormon Church—bear witness that God has again spoken from
the heavens, that Jesus Christ has appeared again unto man, that
the Resurrection is a reality. (*God, Family, Country*, p. 26.)

The message of Mormonism, the restored gospel of Jesus
Christ, has now been before the world for many years. In June
1830, Samuel Harrison Smith trudged down a country road in
New York State on the first official missionary journey of the restored Church. He had been set apart by his brother, the Prophet
Joseph. This first missionary traveled twenty-five miles that first
day without disposing of a single copy of the new and strange
book that he carried on his back. Seeking lodging for the night,
faint and hungry, he was turned away, after briefly explaining his
mission, with the words: "You liar, get out of my house. You
shan't stay one minute with your books." Continuing his journey,
discouraged and with heavy heart, he slept that first night under an
apple tree. So began, in the most inauspicious way, the missionary
work of this dispensation through the restored Church, The
Church of Jesus Christ of Latter-day Saints. (*God, Family, Country*, pp. 43–44.)

We are commanded by God to take this gospel to all the world.
That is the cause that must unite us today. Only the gospel will
save the world from the calamity of its own self-destruction. Only
the gospel will unite men of all races and nationalities in peace.
Only the gospel will bring joy, happiness, and salvation to the
human family.
    Isaiah said that many in latter times would say: "Come . . . let
us go up . . . to the house of the God of Jacob; and he will teach
us of his ways, and we will walk in his paths" (Isaiah 2:3; 2 Nephi
12:3). Is there any greater cause than to teach others the gospel so
that they may be united in walking in the ways of the God of
Israel? Will we so live His commandments that others will see that
the ways of the God of Jacob are distinctive from the world? That
is our challenge. Let us then make His cause our cause. ("Zion
Shall Flourish upon the Mountains," Days of '47 Committee Luncheon, 24 July 1982.)

As members of the Lord's Church, we must take missionary
work more seriously. The Lord's commission to "preach the gos-

pel to every creature'' (Mark 16:15) will never change in our dispensation. We have been greatly blessed with the material means, the technology, and an inspired message to bring the gospel to all men. More is expected of us than any previous generation. Where "much is given much is required" (D&C 82:3). (CR April 1985, *Ensign* 15 [May 1985]: 6.)

Today we as a Church are sounding the voice of warning through our missionaries to the nations of all the earth. We send our missionaries to proclaim the gospel to those who will receive our message. We hope that every young man has plans to be a messenger for the Lord. ("A Voice of Warning," Hiram Ohio Branch Chapel Groundbreaking Service, 22 March 1986.)

Through the Prophet Joseph Smith the Lord proclaimed to John and Peter Whitmer, "The thing which will be of the most worth unto you will be to declare repentance unto this people that you may bring souls unto me" (D&C 15:6). Your greatest desire, as newly called mission presidents, should be to bring souls unto Him, converted souls taught by excellent missionaries in your field of labor. (Mission Presidents Seminar, Provo, Utah, 25 June 1986.)

The Lord has said, "This is my work and my glory—to bring to pass the immortality and eternal life of man" (Moses 1:39). The saving of souls is our major responsibility, and we cannot be saved or exalted unless we understand the gospel. The responsibility has been placed upon the priesthood of the Church to see that the message is carried to our Father's children. It is a tremendous obligation, but one we accept gratefully yet humbly. ("The Church," Paris, France, 7 August 1960.)

The sweetest work in all the world is the work in which we are engaged in helping to save and exalt the souls of the children of men. There isn't anything so important, so precious, so enjoyable, so soul-satisfying. (CR April 1953, *Improvement Era* 56 [June 1953]: 414.)

Missionaries are engaged in the greatest work in all the world —saving the souls of our Father in Heaven's children. They have been called by inspiration and revelation at this time for a sacred and holy purpose. They are serving exactly where the Lord wants them, for them they are in the best mission of the Church, they cannot fail in this work, they have been called to succeed, and succeed they will. (Mission Presidents Seminar, Provo, Utah, 25 June 1986.)

Preparation

May I now speak with you young women about missionary service in the kingdom. I feel very deeply about this. I pray that you will understand the yearnings of my heart. The Prophet Joseph Smith declared: "After all that has been said [our] greatest and most important duty is to preach the gospel." The Lord wants every young man to serve a full-time mission. Presently only a third of the eligible young men in the Church are serving missions. This is not pleasing to the Lord. We can do better. We must do better. Not only should a mission be regarded as a priesthood duty, but every young man should look forward to this experience with great joy and anticipation. A young man can do nothing more important. School can wait. Scholarships can be deferred. Occupational goals can be postponed. Yes, even temple marriage should wait until after a young man has served an honorable full-time mission for the Lord.

You can have a positive influence in motivating young men to serve full-time missions. Let the young men of your acquaintance know that you expect them to assume their missionary responsibilities, that you personally want them to serve in the mission field, because you know that is where the Lord wants them. Avoid steady dating with a young man prior to the time of his mission call. If your relationship with him is more casual, then he can make that decision to serve more easily and also can concentrate his full energies on his missionary work instead of the girlfriend back home. And after he returns honorably from his mission, he will be a better husband and father and priesthood holder, having first served a full-time mission. ("To the Young Women of the Church," *Ensign* 16 [November 1986]: 82–83.)

What is it that causes our young missionaries to want to go out and serve without any hope of material reward? I once interviewed one of them in a California stake, and we couldn't accept him because he wasn't old enough. He broke down and cried. He said, "Brother Benson, ever since I was a deacon, I have wanted to go on a mission." And he told how his parents had prayed that the time might come that he would be considered worthy to go out and represent the Church in the world. What is the impelling force back of it?

How did the Prophet Joseph know as a young man that men and women would respond to the call to fill missions, to go out into the world representing an unpopular cause, to carry this glorious message? How did he know that the Saints, when and if they accepted the gospel, would respond to the call of gathering and come to Zion? Yes, the spirit of this work is a precious and priceless thing. (*So Shall Ye Reap*, p. 58.)

Let me explain to you the challenge we face in the Church. Many of our worthy young men who desire to serve missions are in other countries of the world. Most of these elders and sisters do not have the resources to support themselves for two years on a mission and therefore must receive supplementary assistance. We have a general missionary fund in the Church to which we ask all members to contribute. Those who have received bounteously from the Lord can afford to give generously to support this program. Most adult members could contribute some each month and, by doing so, help prosper the missionary efforts throughout the world. (CR April 1985, *Ensign* 15 [May 1985]: 7–8.)

When missionaries are called to serve locally, great benefits accrue to the Church in the local areas. First, the missionaries can speak the language fluently so that no language training is necessary. Second, the acceptance by local people to the missionaries of their own nationality is superior to the reception received by non-nationals. Third, the great benefits which the missionaries themselves receive through their mission experience is not exported from the local area but serves to strengthen and build the kingdom in the homeland. Thus, there must be increased emphasis on the preparation of young men and women to step forward and carry the missionary responsibility in their own lands. (Language Training Mission Groundbreaking, Provo, Utah, 18 July 1974.)

God has a timetable—a sequence or season for good things. A mission, when its time has arrived, takes priority over marriage and education. And when one is mature enough and has found the right companion, marriage should not be delayed for education. While all three—mission, marriage, and education—are essential, there is a proper order to follow. ("In His Steps," Church Educational System Devotional, Anaheim, California, 8 February 1987.)

Reading the Book of Mormon is one of the greatest persuaders to get men on missions. We need more missionaries. But we also need better-prepared missionaries coming out of the wards and branches and homes where they know and love the Book of Mormon. A great challenge and day of preparation is at hand for missionaries to meet and teach with the Book of Mormon. We need missionaries to match our message. ("The Book of Mormon Is the Word of God," Regional Representatives Seminar, Provo, Utah, 4 April 1986.)

We love all of our missionaries who are serving the Lord full-time in the mission field. But there is a difference in missionaries. Some are better prepared to serve the Lord the first month in the mission field than some who are returning home after twenty-four months. We want young men entering the mission field who can enter the mission field "on the run," who have the faith, born of personal righteousness and clean living, that they can have a great and productive mission. (CR April 1986, *Ensign* 16 [May 1986]: 45.)

I pray, my young brethren, that our Heavenly Father will bless you with an understanding of how desperately you are needed in His service today. (CR April 1985, *Ensign* 15 [May 1985]: 37.)

Yes, young men, prepare now. Prepare yourselves physically, mentally, socially, and spiritually. Always be obedient to authority. Start a savings account for your mission if you haven't done so already. Pay your tithing, and seek a testimony of the gospel through study and prayer. (CR April 1985, *Ensign* 15 [May 1985]: 37.)

You must have a burning testimony of the divinity of this work if you are going to succeed. Your first obligation is to get that testimony through prayer, through fasting, through meditation, through study, through appealing to the Lord to give you the testimony, through responding to calls when they come to you. You must have a testimony of the divinity of this work. You must know that God lives; that Jesus is the Christ, the Redeemer of the world; that Joseph Smith is a prophet of God; that the priesthood and authority of our Heavenly Father is here; and that you bear that priesthood and have the authority to represent Him in the world. (*God, Family, Country*, pp. 60–61.)

A mission requires a great deal of mental preparation. You must memorize missionary discussions, memorize scriptures, and ofttimes learn a new language. The discipline to do this is learned in your early years. Establish now the daily practice of reading the scriptures ten to fifteen minutes each day. If you do so, by the time you reach the mission field, you will have read all four of the standard works. I urge you to read particularly the Book of Mormon so that you can testify of its truthfulness as the Lord has directed. (CR April 1985, *Ensign* 15 [May 1985]: 36.)

Too many of our young men have not yet decided to give two years of service to the Lord. I speak particularly to you young men who live in the United States and Canada, the host nations from which the gospel is to go to other nations. While you reap the benefits of prosperity unprecedented in the history of mankind, do you ever think that one of the reasons the Lord sent you to earth under such favorable circumstances is that you could use your talents, education, and money to bless others with the gospel? (CR April 1979, *Ensign* 9 [May 1979]: 33.)

Not only should a mission be regarded as a priesthood duty, but every young man should look forward to this experience with great joy and anticipation. What a privilege—what a sacred privilege—to serve the Lord full time for two years with all your heart, might, mind, and strength (D&C 4). Show your love and commitment to the Lord by responding to His call to serve. Know that the real purpose in going into the mission field is to bring souls unto Christ, to teach and baptize our Heavenly Father's children so that you may rejoice with them in the kingdom of our Father (see D&C 18:15). (CR April 1986, *Ensign* 16 [May 1986]: 44.)

Young men, this statement by President Spencer W. Kimball should be your personal motto: "Every LDS male who is worthy and able should fill a mission" (*Ensign*, May 1974, p. 87). We ask you to make the sacrifice. We call it that because of want for a better name for it. It is an investment. Enlist in this, the greatest service in the world. Do not evade the responsibility. Do not conscientiously object. We invite you to join the army that is swelling in numbers each day. Your job will be to proclaim the message of the Restoration to the world. Know that you have our confidence and love. We expect you to perform that mission. (CR April 1979, *Ensign* 9 [May 1979]: 33.)

Remember, young women, you may also have the opportunity to serve a full-time mission. I am grateful my own eternal companion served a mission in Hawaii before we were married in the Salt Lake Temple, and I am pleased that I have had three granddaughters serve full-time missions. Some of our finest missionaries are young sisters. ("To the Young Women of the Church," *Ensign* 16 [November 1986]: 83.)

If you want to get the spirit of the gospel in your home, support the missionary program. Prepare your sons and your daughters through your home evenings; through setting the proper example in your homes. Prepare to send them into the mission field. These young sons and daughters will bless your names forever if you help to make it possible through your training and your example and your willingness to sacrifice just a little, if you can call it sacrifice, to see them go into the mission field. (Glasgow Scotland Area Conference, 21 June 1976.)

From the Doctrine and Covenants I quote: "Again I say, hearken ye elders of my Church, whom I have appointed: Ye are not sent forth to be taught, but to teach the children of men the things which I have put into your hands by the power of my Spirit: And ye are to be taught from on high. Sanctify yourselves and ye shall be endowed with power, that ye may give even as I have spoken." (D&C 43:15–16.)

We want to send forth missionaries who have a testimony of the scriptures and who are spiritually prepared to be guided and instructed of the Spirit, that they in turn may teach by that same

Spirit. Is that too much to ask? Not if we commence early enough and prepare well enough. (Regional Representatives Seminar, Salt Lake City, Utah, 3 October 1974.)

At what age do we begin teaching our sons these gospel truths? Alma taught his son Helaman while he was in his youth (see Alma 36:3). Our youth ought not to wait until the mission field to get a grasp of the scriptures and a closeness to the Lord. Lehi said that his son Jacob beheld the glory of the Lord in his youth (see 2 Nephi 2:4). Imagine what would happen to missionary work if we sent out that kind of young men. (CR October 1985, *Ensign* 15 [November 1985]: 37.)

How do you build in boys a great desire to serve? You do not wait until they are nineteen years old to help them decide to serve a mission. You help them decide to go when they are nine, ten, or eleven! The home is the seedbed for the preparation of young men. And every young man should be prepared in his home to serve. Early preparation consists of teaching a young boy how to pray, reading him stories from the Book of Mormon and other scriptures, having home evenings and giving him a portion of the lesson, teaching him principles of moral cleanliness, starting a savings account for his future mission, teaching him how to work, and providing opportunities to serve others.

I know of families who always prayed in family prayer that their sons would be worthy to serve missions. This, they say, had a great effect on their sons. For our teenage young men and women, one of the best preparations for a mission is provided by the Church through seminary and institute of religion classes. We hope you will urge your children to take part in this inspired program. (CR April 1985, *Ensign* 15 [May 1985]: 7.)

Prepare young men to serve effective full-time missions. One of the great challenges in this Church is to help prepare teachers and priests to go on missions. The Lord revealed to the Prophet Joseph Smith that both teachers and priests had the duty of warning, expounding, exhorting, and teaching, inviting "all to come unto Christ" (see D&C 20:50, 59). I believe that when Aaronic Priesthood leadership provides opportunities to fulfill these specific duties, we are preparing our young men for missionary service. Quorum advisers/Scoutmasters must be examples as priesthood holders and must possess the vision to create these opportunities for Aaronic Priesthood youth to serve others. When we can offer a young man opportunities to serve others—to get outside of himself—we are well on our way to helping him get prepared for a mission. ("Challenges for Leaders of Aaronic Priesthood," Young Men's General Presidency and Board, 19 September 1979.)

Train up youth who, from boyhood, have had as a guiding goal and responsibility to accept and fulfill a mission in the service of the Lord. If we make it our clarion call so that it resounds in the ears of Church youth everywhere in the earth, we will indeed build the missionary force the Lord wants us to have. (Regional Representatives Seminar, Salt Lake City, Utah, 3 October 1974.)

The world needs the gospel, and we are charged by command of the Lord and through our Abrahamic lineage to spread it. Every young man in this Church should be qualified for a mission and then should go. Many sisters may also serve missions. I am grateful my wife went on a mission and that we have granddaughters and grandsons in the mission field. (CR April 1986, *Ensign* 16 [May 1986]: 77.)

A vital ingredient in preparation for your mission is to always live a clean life. We want morally clean young men in the mission field. We want you to live the clean life all of your life. We want the morally clean life to be your way of life. (CR April 1986, *Ensign* 16 [May 1986]: 44.)

You must live an exemplary life. Maintain the standards of the Church fully. Adhere to the counsel and the standards that have been set up for missionary service. Be true to every requirement and every regulation. They are all given for your benefit and blessing—not to bear you down, not to limit your freedom, but to make you more effective as missionaries. The eyes of the world are upon you. As you travel among the people, you may think that nobody knows you, but there is always someone watching you. Of course our Heavenly Father always has His eyes on us, but it is surprising how many people outside the Church know who you are and what you are doing and what the requirements are for missionary service. (*God, Family, Country*, p. 62.)

A two-year mission today requires good physical health. It requires that you keep your body clean. In your early teenage years, when temptations come to you to take things into your body which are unsuitable, have the courage to resist. Live the Word of Wisdom—no smoking, no drinking of any alcoholic beverages, and no drugs. Keep your body pure—a pure vessel for the Lord.

Stay morally clean. This means that you keep a clean mind. Your thoughts will determine your actions, and so they must be controlled. It is difficult to control those thoughts if you submit yourself to temptation. So you will have to carefully select your reading material, the movies you see, and the other forms of entertainment in order to have good thoughts rather than unwholesome desires. (CR April 1985, *Ensign* 15 [May 1985]: 36.)

Give me a young man who has kept himself morally clean and has faithfully attended his Church meetings. Give me a young man who has magnified his priesthood and has earned his Duty to God Award and is an Eagle Scout. Give me a young man who is a seminary graduate and has a burning testimony of the Book of Mormon. Give me such a young man and I will give you a young man who can perform miracles for the Lord in the mission field and throughout his life. (CR April 1986, *Ensign* 16 [May 1986]: 45.)

Couples

We can participate in missionary service by preparing for and serving a mission. One way couples can do this is to save and prepare to serve a mission together. Again I state, "We have need for select missionary couples" (CR April 1984, *Ensign* 14 [May 1984]: 45).

We urge you to seriously consider serving a full-time mission. Some of you younger couples have your sons already on missions. Perhaps now is the time for you to prepare financially and otherwise for missionary service. Many couples have provided distinguished service and stability to various missions in the Church. You can study the scriptures together, particularly the Book of Mormon. The Lord has said that we are condemned if we do not remember the new covenant, even the Book of Mormon (see D&C 84:56–57). (CR April 1985, *Ensign* 15 [May 1985]: 8.)

Missionary service requires great faith. I know how difficult it is for older couples to decide to serve missions. I have two widowed sisters who went on a mission to England together. A brother has just left for his third mission with his wife. Many couples can attest that their missionary service was among their happiest times together because they were completely dedicated to one purpose—missionary work. (CR April 1985, *Ensign* 15 [May 1985]: 8.)

Many older couples could serve missions. In so doing, they will find that a mission blesses their children, their grandchildren, and their great-grandchildren in a way that could not otherwise be done. It will set a great example for their posterity. (CR April 1986, *Ensign* 16 [May 1986]: 78.)

Keys to Success

We want missionaries who have the kind of faith that Wilford Woodruff and Heber C. Kimball had, each bringing hundreds and thousands of souls into the waters of baptism. (CR April 1986, *Ensign* 16 [May 1986]: 45.)

There are several areas that a missionary needs to be concerned with in order to be successful. First, he must develop a real deep spirituality. The Spirit is the most important matter in this glorious work. The Lord gives us a great law about teaching His gospel. He said, "And the Spirit shall be given you by the prayer of faith; and if ye receive not the Spirit ye shall not teach" (D&C 42:14).

To be a successful missionary one must have the Spirit of the Lord. We are also taught that the Spirit will not dwell in unclean tabernacles. Therefore, one of the first things a missionary must do to gain spirituality is to make sure his own personal life is in order. (Mission Presidents Seminar, Salt Lake City, Utah, 21 June 1975.)

You will never be effective as a missionary unless you are humble in your work. The Lord has made it very clear that no man can assist with this work unless he is humble and full of love (see D&C 12:8). But humility does not mean timidity. Humility does not mean fear. Humility does not mean weakness. You can be humble and still be courageous. You can be humble and still be vigorous and strong and fearless. In the early days of the Church the elders were human also, and the Lord was not always pleased with them, as He made very clear in some of the revelations. But great teacher that He is, He would often commend them for the work they had done and then correct them. That is good psychology. My wife uses it on our children and sometimes on her husband. The Lord used it with the early elders of the Church and one time was pretty severe on some of them, and I am sure it must have caused them to have very serious reflections. Speaking to the elders, those who are the men who were called to bear His name, He said: "But with some I am not well pleased, for they will not open their mouths, but they hide the talent which I have given unto them, because of the fear of men. Wo unto such, for mine anger is kindled against them." (D&C 60:2.)

That is pretty plain, isn't it? Sometimes we have among our missionaries those who are afraid because of the fear of man, and if you permit yourselves to get that spirit of fear, the adversary will back you up. He will support you. He will encourage you in it until you get to the point where you are afraid to exercise your authority and to bear testimony regarding this message. Remember the promise made: "And they shall go forth and none shall stay them, for I the Lord have commanded them" (D&C 1:5). There is no place for fear. There is no place for discouragement, because you can't fail in this work if you do your part. There is no place for timidity or hesitancy. Humility, yes, but you can be humble and courageous and fearless and effective. (*God, Family, Country*, pp. 61–62.)

Your greatest help will come from the Lord Himself as you supplicate and plead with Him in humble prayer. As you are driven to your knees again and again, asking Him for divine help in your mission, you will feel the Spirit, you will get your answer from above, your mission will prosper spiritually because of your dependence and your reliance on Him. (Mission Presidents Seminar, Provo, Utah, 25 June 1986.)

The modern-day challenging and testifying missionary prays every morning to "lead me this day to a family that I can fulfil my purpose." (Mission Presidents Seminar, Provo, Utah, 25 June 1986.)

Missionaries should have a standard of performance or excellence to which they ascribe and to which they commit. Missionaries should take pride in being in "the best mission in the Church" (for them), and being "missionaries of excellence." (Mission Presidents Seminar, Salt Lake City, Utah, 21 June 1975.)

The missionary is entitled to inspiration in choosing his personal goals; and when he has sought the Lord through prayer and meditation, he will be motivated best by those goals he selects himself and commits himself to attain. (Mission Presidents Seminar, Salt Lake City, Utah, 27 June 1974.)

It is vital that missionaries maintain the proper missionary image and have the reputation as great proselyting elders and not just "good guys." (Mission Presidents Seminar, Salt Lake City, Utah, 21 June 1975.)

I have often said one of the greatest secrets of missionary work is work! If a missionary works, he will get the Spirit; if he gets the Spirit, he will teach by the Spirit; and if he teaches by the Spirit, he will touch the hearts of the people and he will be happy. There will be no homesickness, no worrying about families, for all time and talents and interests are centered on the work of the ministry. Work, work, work—there is no satisfactory substitute, especially in missionary work. (Texas San Antonio Mission, 2 March 1986.)

If you want to keep the Spirit, to love your mission and not be homesick, you must work. But, remember the words of President Thomas S. Monson: "Work without vision is drudgery. Vision without work is dreaming. Work coupled with vision is destiny.'' There is no greater exhilaration or satisfaction than to know, after a hard day of missionary work, that you have done your best. (''Keys to Successful Missionary Work,'' Mission Presidents Seminar, Provo, Utah, 23 June 1987.)

Missionary work is not easy. It is the most demanding, the most compelling, the most exhausting, and yet, with it all, the most happy and most joyful work in all the world. (Mission Presidents Seminar, Provo, Utah, 25 June 1986.)

It is so important that you lose yourselves in this work, that you don't worry about ''what is it going to do for me.'' You are not out in the world with self-improvement as the major objective, but you can't help getting a maximum amount of self-improvement if you lose yourself in the work of the Lord. I don't know of any better preparation for life than two years of devoted, unselfish, dedicated service as a missionary. (*God, Family, Country*, pp. 59–60.)

We are to take the gospel to every person. Without exception, without excuse, without rationalization, we are to go ''unto all the world and preach the gospel to every creature'' (Mormon 9:22). (Regional Representatives Seminar, Salt Lake City, Utah, 5 April 1985.)

It is a time of harvest and not a time of gleaning, and if missionaries are true and faithful, they will literally be instruments in the hands of the Lord in bringing souls unto Him. The Apostle Paul's statement reminds them that in the conversion process some missionaries will plant, some will water, and some will baptize. You are not concerned with who gets the credit for the baptisms because ''God [gives] the increase'' (1 Corinthians 3:6). (Mission Presidents Seminar, Provo, Utah, 25 June 1986.)

Concentrate all of your time and effort and talent on your mission. The Apostle Paul declared: ''This one thing I do'' (Philippians 3:13), and you have just one marvelous thing to do and that is the most important work in all the world—missionary work. Give it all you have got and you will have true joy. As you come to the close of your mission, don't run out of steam. Sprint to the end. (Mission Presidents Seminar, Provo, Utah, 25 June 1986.)

President Harold B. Lee once instructed a group of new mission presidents to "save the missionaries and they will save the people." The key to saving anyone is to love them. It is still true that "a person doesn't care how much you know as long as he knows how much you care." (Mission Presidents Seminar, Provo, Utah, 25 June 1986.)

Teach correct principles to missionaries and you will bless their lives forever. (Mission Presidents Seminar, Provo, Utah, 25 June 1986.)

A missionary should never permit himself to see a movie or cheap literature, or hear music that tends to interfere with or which dampens the spirit of missionary work. There is ample evidence that rock music is offensive to the Spirit and affects adversely the spirituality of the missionaries and thus the success of the proselyting work. (Mission Presidents Seminar, Salt Lake City, Utah, 21 June 1975.)

The principle of not aspiring to positions in the mission field is taught well in Mark 9:34–35 and Matthew 23:11–12. Missionaries should be taught that it doesn't matter where they serve, but how. Position doesn't save anyone, but faithfulness does. Aspiring to positions of responsibility can destroy the spirit of the mission as well as the spirit of a missionary. (Mission Presidents Seminar, Provo, Utah, 25 June 1986.)

I hope you and your companion are true to each other. I hope you feel you have the best companion in the world. I hope you draw close to each other as companions, that you uphold and sustain each other before the Saints, before our friends, before the world. I have seen many examples of this, but one of the most impressive occurred in Philadelphia some years ago. I had been in a meeting of agricultural leaders all day, and in the evening I left my hotel to mail a couple of letters. As I walked into the post office, I heard the strains of a familiar Mormon hymn coming through the window from the opposite side. I dropped my letters in the box, walked over to the window, and looked out, and there were two young men in dark suits standing on the steps of the post office holding a street meeting. One of them was speaking and the other was holding in one hand two hats and in the other some copies of the Book of Mormon and some tracts. When they finished their meeting I went out and introduced myself. Then I said to the young man who was holding the hats and the copies of the Book of Mormon, "What were you doing while your companion was speaking?" His answer was most satisfying. He said, "Brother Benson, I was praying to the Lord that he would say the right thing that would touch the hearts of the people who were listening."

That is the kind of support I am referring to. When you reach the point where you can enjoy and rejoice in the success of your companion, even when that success exceeds your own, then you have got the real missionary spirit, the real unselfish spirit of love, the spirit of the gospel. When you can rejoice in the success of your companion, then you have a spirit that will make you effective as a missionary. Then you will really be truly, truly happy. Then you will have lost yourself in the service of this wonderful gospel, in service to our Father's children—the greatest work in all the world. (*God, Family, Country*, pp. 65–66.)

The Book of Mormon must be the heart of our missionary work in every mission of the Church if we are to come out from under this condemnation (see D&C 84:56–57). And what a marvelous missionary tool it is! Already we see an increase in baptisms, which testifies to the power of this sacred volume. (Mission Presidents Seminar, Provo, Utah, 25 June 1986.)

The Book of Mormon is the great standard we are to use in our missionary work. It shows that Joseph Smith was a prophet. It contains the words of Christ, and its great mission is to bring men to Christ. All other things are secondary. The golden question of the Book of Mormon is "Do you want to learn more of Christ?" The Book of Mormon is the great finder of the golden contact. It does not contain things which are "pleasing unto the world," and so the worldly are not interested in it. It is a great sieve. (See 1 Nephi 6:5.)

There is a difference between a convert who is built on the rock of Christ through the Book of Mormon and stays hold of the iron rod, and one who is not. I promise you that you will have more and better converts in every mission of the Church if you will teach and inspire missionaries to effectively use the Book of Mormon as the great converter. (Mission Presidents Seminar, Provo, Utah, 25 June 1986.)

We need missionaries to match our message. We need missionaries who really know and love the Book of Mormon, who have a burning testimony of its divinity, and who by the Spirit can challenge their investigators to read and ponder its pages, knowing with complete assurance that the Lord will manifest the truth of the Book of Mormon to them by the power of the Holy Ghost. (Mission Presidents Seminar, Provo, Utah, 25 June 1986.)

A missionary who is inspired by the Spirit of the Lord must be led by that Spirit to choose the proper approach to be effective. We must not forget that the Lord Himself provided the Book of Mormon as His chief witness. The Book of Mormon is still our most powerful missionary tool. Let us use it. (Mission Presidents Seminar, Provo, Utah, 24 June 1976.)

Anyone who has diligently sought to know the doctrines and teachings of the Book of Mormon and has used it conscientiously in missionary work knows within his soul that this is the instrument which God has given to the missionaries to convince the Jew and Gentile and Lamanite of the truthfulness of our message. ("The Book of Mormon Is the Word of God," Regional Representatives Seminar, Provo, Utah, 4 April 1986.)

As missionaries, you must learn to love the scriptures. Your purpose for being in the mission field is to save souls, to baptize converts, to bring converted families into the Lord's Church. I ask you to give particular attention to scriptures which explain your holy calling, such as Doctrine and Covenants sections, 4, 11, 15, 16, and 18, and the Book of Mormon. (Texas San Antonio Mission, 2 March 1986.)

The Book of Mormon is for both member and nonmember. Combined with the Spirit of the Lord, the Book of Mormon is the greatest single tool which God has given us to convert the world. If we are to have the harvest of souls, we must use the instrument which God has designed for that task — the Book of Mormon. (CR October 1984, *Ensign* 14 [November 1984]: 7.)

Be guided by the Spirit. I have said so many times to my Brethren that the Spirit is the most important single element in this work. With the Spirit, and by magnifying your call, you can do miracles for the Lord in the mission field. Without the Spirit you will never succeed regardless of your talent and ability. (Mission Presidents Seminar, Provo, Utah, 25 June 1986.)

The busy missionary is the happy missionary. I cannot recall a missionary who was really active and busy ever going astray. Occasionally we have missionaries who make mistakes. It usually starts when they become idle, when they stay in their lodgings when they ought to be out with the people. Occasionally you will find a missionary who is looking for excuses for not going out — who can look out the window and see a storm coming when there isn't any, who can see rain when it isn't raining. The important thing is to get out with the people, to keep active, to be devoted. Do not sleep longer than is needful. The same Lord who gave the Word of Wisdom in the 89th section also gave that instruction in the 88th section, and it is just as binding as the counsel that you are not to use tobacco or alcoholic beverages. So cease from all lightmindedness, cease to sleep longer than is needful, and retire to your bed early (see D&C 88:121, 124). You will be more effective, you will do more work, you will be happier, and you will have better health. (*God, Family, Country*, p. 60.)

I challenge you to enjoy your call and to magnify it completely. Be happy and joyful in the service of the Lord. Love missionary work with all your heart. I promise you that as you magnify your call this will be the sweetest and most glorious experience you have had in Church service to this time. (Mission Presidents Seminar, Provo, Utah, 25 June 1986.)

You must not allow yourselves to become discouraged. Missionary work brings joy, optimism, and happiness. Don't give Satan an opportunity to discourage you. Here again, work is the answer. The Lord has given us a key by which we can overcome discouragement: "Come unto me, all ye that labour and are heavy laden, and I will give you rest. Take my yoke upon you, and learn of me; for I am meek and lowly in heart; and ye shall find rest unto your souls. For my yoke is easy and my burden is light." (Matthew 11:28–30.) (Texas San Antonio Mission, 2 March 1986.)

You will not be an effective missionary until you learn to have sympathy for all of our Father's children—unless you learn to love them. People can feel when love is extended to them. Many yearn for it. When you sympathize with their feelings, they in turn will reciprocate goodwill to you. You will have made a friend. And as the Prophet Joseph Smith taught, "Whom can I preach to but my friends." Yes, love the people. ("Keys to Successful Missionary Work," Mission Presidents Seminar, Salt Lake City, Utah, 23 June 1987.)

Our main task is to declare the gospel and do it effectively. We are not obligated to answer every objection. Every man eventually is backed up to the wall of faith, and there he must make his stand. "And if they are not the words of Christ, judge ye," said Nephi, "for Christ will show unto you, with power and great glory, that they are his words, at the last day; and you and I shall stand face to face before his bar; and ye shall know that I have been commanded of him to write these things" (2 Nephi 33:11). Every man must judge for himself, knowing God will hold him accountable. ("The Book of Mormon Is the Word of God," Regional Representatives Seminar, Salt Lake City, Utah, 4 April 1986.)

One of the sweetest experiences that a person can have is to know they have been magnified under the influence of the Spirit. I hope some day every one of you will have that experience. I shall never forget when I first experienced it as a humble missionary on my first mission. I had been in the field only four months when it occurred. It was during the time of great opposition to the Church in Great Britain in the early twenties. The newspapers, the magazines, even anti-Mormon moving pictures were all over Great Britain; the opposition was so great we had to discontinue all street meetings, and many areas couldn't even tract. It seems almost fantastic because you can hardly get off the plane over there now but what they want to know the latest development in the Church. But in those days men of the caliber of Orson F. Whitney and David O. McKay couldn't even get one inch of space in the press to answer the lies that were printed against us.

But up in northern England where we were laboring, we had a group of people out at South Shields Branch who were very faithful and very devoted and very loyal, and they had invited my companion and me to come over and speak in their sacrament meeting. They said, "Many of our neighbors don't believe the lies that are being printed. If you will come, we will fill the little chapel."

And so we accepted the invitation and we started preparing and I started studying about the apostasy. It was a subject I liked, and I thought they needed it; and I worked and I studied, and I thought I could talk fifteen minutes on the subject.

We went over to the little chapel and it was filled. Everyone was happy. And after the opening exercises my companion spoke, then I spoke with a freedom I had never enjoyed in all my life. And when I sat down and looked at my watch, I had talked twenty-five minutes, and I hadn't mentioned the apostasy, I hadn't even thought of the apostasy. I had talked about Joseph Smith, and I had borne witness that he was a prophet of God and I knew it. I told about the coming forth of the Book of Mormon as a new witness for Christ, and I had borne testimony. When I realized what had happened, I couldn't hold back the tears.

At the end of the meeting, many of the Saints came forward and expressed their gratitude that something had been said about Joseph Smith. They said, "Several of our neighbors have said, 'We can accept everything about the Church except Joseph Smith.' " And then some of those same neighbors came up and said, "We are now ready. We are ready tonight. We have received the witness that Joseph Smith is a prophet of God."

Now, do you think that was a young missionary speaking out of his own wisdom? He was nothing but an instrument in the hands of the Lord in saying what the Lord wanted said to His children whom He loved that they might receive the witness that this work is true. In this work we are never alone. This is the Lord's work. These are His children we are working with. This is His great program; and He will not permit us to fail. He loves these children we are working with; they are His children—His sons and daughters. He loves them even as we love our own, even with a deeper love; and He will not permit us to fail if we will do our part. God bless us that we might measure up that we might receive joy and happiness in our service in our Father's kingdom. (San Diego California South Stake Conference, 6 December 1969.)

Member-Missionary Work

Our members need to understand their responsibility to do missionary work and then do it. I fully endorse the words of President Spencer W. Kimball: "Do we really believe in revelation? Then why cannot we accept fully as the revealed word of God the revelation of the Prophet-President David O. McKay, wherein he brought to the Church and to the world this valuable Church slogan, 'Every member a missionary'? How else could the Lord expect to perform His work except through the Saints who have covenanted to serve Him? You and I have made such a covenant. Will we honor our sacred covenant?" (Regional Representatives Seminar, Salt Lake City, Utah, 30 September 1977.)

Never have we had the opportunity which we have today to get our message before the world. Almost all over the world the Church is well-spoken of. Never has it been so easy to get a gospel conversation. Never has the Christian world been weaker than it is today. Never has there been a need, such a great need, for what we have. We must share the gospel with others. That is our responsibility—every member a missionary. That is the call of prophets of God. (Salt Lake Utah Emigration Stake Conference, 2 February 1975.)

No person can read section 1 of the Doctrine and Covenants, realizing that the Church accepts it as the word of the Lord, and ask why we send missionaries into all parts of the world. The responsibility, and a major one it is, falls squarely upon the membership of the Church, for "the voice of warning," says the Lord, "shall be unto all people by the mouths of my disciples, whom I have chosen in these last days" (D&C 1:4). (*God, Family, Country*, p. 48.)

We must emphasize the need for more member-missionary work. Experience has proven this is the most fruitful missionary work. Member-missionary work is one of the great keys to the individual growth of our members. It is my conviction that member-missionary work will raise the spirituality in any ward where applied. ("Strengthen the Stakes of Zion," El Paso Regional Conference, 25 January 1986.)

Open houses in stakes and wards should be held in every ward or branch chapel in the Church, as there is opportunity, and should have the full support of the full-time missionaries laboring in the area. It is a natural, effective, easy way for members to begin (or continue) to do their member-missionary work. In the days ahead there will be increasing opportunities as our stakes increase and our missions spread. (Mission Presidents Seminar, Salt Lake City, Utah, 21 June 1975.)

We desire all potential members to be friendshipped. Our youth should be involved in missionary work. Some of our finest converts come through the young people of the Church. We hope that home teachers are working closely with part-member families to see that the gospel is taught to the nonmembers in that household. (Regional Representatives Seminar, Salt Lake City, Utah, 5 April 1985.)

With a shepherd's care, many of our new members, those newly born into the gospel, should be nurtured by gospel knowledge and new standards. Such attention could ensure that there would be no returning to old habits and old friends. (*Come unto Christ*, p. 65.)

We held a service out at the base in Anchorage, Alaska, at the request of our wonderful Mormon servicemen. I know some of them make mistakes, but on the whole their record is something this Church can be proud of. We used to feel badly because our missionary work was disrupted during the war, but as I look back on it now, and as I keep hearing young men and women arise and bear their testimonies and say, "I first came in contact with the Church when I met a Mormon serviceman," I can't help but believe we did more missionary work during the war than during any comparable period in our history. ("The Greatest Leadership," BYU Student Leadership Conference, Sun Valley, Idaho, September 1959.)

One of our best missionary tools is the sterling examples of members who live the gospel. This is what the Lord meant when He said to the Church, "Zion must increase in beauty, and in holiness; . . . Zion must put on her beautiful garments" (D&C 82:14). (CR April 1985, *Ensign* 15 [May 1985]: 7.)

My experience is that most of our members do not question their missionary responsibility. Most want to know how it can be done effectively and without embarrassment to their friends. Our role as priesthood leaders is to show them how it may be done. (El Paso Texas Regional Conference, 25 January 1986.)

I encourage you not only to read the biblical account of Christ's resurrection, but to read and share with a nonmember acquaintance the Book of Mormon account of Christ's personal manifestation to those in America following His resurrection. Give them or lend them a copy of the Book of Mormon, even your own copy if necessary. It could bless them eternally. ("Joy in Christ," *Ensign* 16 [March 1986]: 5.)

How long has it been since you have invited a neighbor to sacrament meeting or to a stake conference, to come into your home for a home evening? How long has it been since you had a real gospel conversation? These are choice experiences. Members of the Church, stake missionaries, full-time missionaries working together is a thrilling experience. (Grantsville Utah Stake Conference, 1 September 1974.)

The Lord will sustain members in their missionary responsibility if they just have the faith to try. "Be not afraid, but speak, and hold not thy peace: For I am with thee, and no man shall set on thee to hurt thee: for I have much people in this city." (Acts 18:9–10.) Share with them the joy they will experience by finding and fellowshipping friends and neighbors. (Mission Presidents Seminar, Provo, Utah, 25 June 1986.)

As a Church, we have not yet caught that missionary vision. Members are not bringing several hundred thousand members into the Church each year. We have not yet met this challenge of a living prophet. We are still on some of the same plateaus. ("President Kimball's Vision of Missionary Work," *Ensign* 15 [July 1985]: 8.)

We shall continue to encourage all members to fulfill their missionary responsibilities. We shall do missionary work only in those nations that permit it. We urge our members everywhere to respect the laws of the lands in which they live. (Statement upon becoming President of the Church, 11 November 1985.)

It is time to raise our sights, to get a vision of the magnitude of this great work. The Lord expects it of us. It is not enough just to be members in the Church and go to sacrament meeting, pay our tithing, support the welfare program. That is all good — but that is not enough. The Lord expects us to be missionaries, to live the gospel — yes, wholly, and to help to build up His kingdom. (Grantsville Utah Stake Conference, 1 September 1974.)

I remember an experience I had with our second son, Mark. They were living in Dallas, Texas. It was about the time that President David O. McKay reiterated that great statement, "Every member a missionary." When they arrived at their new location in Dallas from Utah, they had their home evening. Their children never miss a home evening, all six of them. It was in that home evening where they taught missionary work. At one of their first ones with the family of six children together, they said, "Now the prophet of the Lord has asked that every member be a missionary. Let us set a goal as a family. We are surrounded by nonmembers here in Richardson, a suburb of Dallas. Let's set our goal." And so they talked about goals, and they set a goal to bring in one family, a complete family, every year as long as they lived in that area. All were to help, the little children in Primary and Sunday School, and the older ones as well.

I was coming through Dallas from Florida and I stopped overnight with them. I hadn't been in the home thirty minutes until the father said, "Dad, would you mind if we brought our families in to meet you?" They had been in Dallas four and one-half years. I am sure they had it all planned in advance, but in thirty minutes they had five families in their living room — five complete families. This was the work of one Latter-day Saint family.

I wish you could have been there with me. They didn't have enough chairs to seat these thirty people. I wish you could have heard the testimonies of those fathers and the comments of the teenagers. The teenage girls, speaking to me, said, "Brother Benson, why couldn't we have known of this fifteen years ago? We could have been reared in the Church." The fathers said, "Why couldn't we have known of it? There have been Mormons in this area a long time. Why couldn't we have known it? We could have reared our families in the Church." The comments from mothers, as tears rolled down their cheeks, "We have the pearl of great price. The message we have is priceless, absolutely priceless." (Glasgow Scotland Area Conference, 21 June 1976.)

Let us exhort each other to fulfill our missionary responsibility. Let us do it with love — not criticism. Let us do it with understanding — not berating. But let us do it, and do it with urgency. Let us catch the vision and the inspiration of President Spencer W. Kimball. We need to understand that member-missionary work is literally the key to the future growth of the Church and that we have covenanted with our Father in Heaven to do this work. ("President Kimball's Vision of Missionary Work," *Ensign* 15 [July 1985]: 11.)

We all share this great missionary responsibility. We cannot avoid it. Let no man or woman think that because of where we live, or because of our place in society, or because of our occupation or status, we are exempt from this responsibility. Membership in the Lord's Church is a gift and a blessing which the Lord has given us in mortality, and He expects us to share that blessing with those who do not have it.

We also have a great obligation to love our neighbors. It is the second of the two great commandments. Many of our neighbors are not yet members of the Church. We must be good neighbors. We must love all our Father's children and associate with them. How I pray that we will be filled with the love of God for our fellowman! (CR April 1985, *Ensign* 15 [May 1985]: 8.)

Joy in Your Labors

It was in the little country ward of three hundred people, where we had a bishop who was missionary-minded, who expected that every young man in that ward would qualify to fill a mission. He used to have the returned missionaries report their missions first in the Sunday School briefly, and then later in more detail in the sacrament meeting. I was one of the little boys sitting on the front bench, when my feet would hardly reach the floor, as I listened one Sunday morning to two of these returned missionaries report their missions. It wasn't uncommon to have two or three missionaries leave and return at one time from that little ward. So, as I sat there these missionaries told of their experiences. They had been out in the world; they had been persecuted; evil things had been spoken of them. They had had hardships, but they bore fervent testimonies, and when they came to the end of their testimonies they would say, "It was the happiest two years of my life." (Glasgow Scotland Area Conference, 21 June 1976.)

My beloved coworkers, you face the happiest years of your lives. I know whereof I speak. I have been there. I have tasted the joy of missionary work. There is no work in all the world that can bring an individual greater joy and happiness. I pray your joy will be full, and like Ammon of old, you will be able to say:

> I do not boast in my own strength, nor in my own wisdom; but behold, my joy is full, yea, my heart is brim with joy, and I will rejoice in my God. Yea, I know that I am nothing; as to my strength I am weak; therefore I will not boast of myself, but I will boast of my God, for in his strength I can do all things; yea, behold, many mighty miracles we have wrought in this land, for which we will praise his name forever. (Alma 26:11–12.)

(Texas San Antonio Mission, 2 March 1986.)

Patriarchal Blessings

The Council of the Twelve has the responsibility of directing patriarchs in the Church. This is one of the most difficult offices to fill in the Church because in order to serve effectively as a patriarch, a man must have the spirit of blessing, which means he must live so close to the Lord that the Lord can speak through him and he can utter the words of the Lord on the heads of those who come for blessings. (Star Valley Wyoming Stake Conference, 18 April 1971.)

Jesus knows that His kingdom will triumph, and He wants you to triumph with it. He knows in advance every strategy the enemy will use against you and the kingdom. He knows your weaknesses and He knows your strengths. By personal revelation you may discover some of your strengths through a careful and prayerful study of your patriarchal blessing. In prayer you can ask Him to reveal to you your weaknesses so that you can amend your life. ("In His Steps," Church Educational System Devotional, Anaheim, California, 8 February 1987.)

I would encourage you brethren of the Aaronic Priesthood to receive a patriarchal blessing. Study it carefully and regard it as personal scripture to you—for that is what it is. A patriarchal blessing is the inspired and prophetic statement of your life's mission together with blessings, cautions, and admonitions as the patriarch may be prompted to give. Young men, receive your patriarchal blessing under the influence of fasting and prayer, and then read it regularly that you may know God's will for you. (CR April 1986, *Ensign* 16 [May 1986]: 43–44.)

In a particularly stressful time, or in the anticipation of a critical event, one can seek for a blessing under the hands of the priesthood. Even the Prophet Joseph Smith sought and received a blessing under the hands of Brigham Young and received solace and direction for his soul. Fathers, so live that you can bless your own wives and children. To receive, and then consistently and prayerfully ponder one's patriarchal blessing can give helpful insight, particularly in an hour of need. (CR October 1974, *Ensign* 4 [November 1974]: 66.)

Priesthood

The privilege of holding the priesthood, which is the power and authority to act in God's name, is a great blessing, and one that carries with it equally great obligations and responsibilities. When I ponder what kind of men and boys we should be as priesthood holders, I cannot help but think of the Savior's questions to the Nephite twelve when He asked, "Therefore, what manner of men ought ye to be? Verily I say unto you, even as I am" (3 Nephi 27:27). (CR October 1986, *Ensign* 16 [November 1986]: 45.)

Priesthood transcends this mortal life. Its power and greatness have been referred to by prophets—modern and ancient. We may have the priesthood without the Church, but never the Church without the priesthood. (*So Shall Ye Reap*, p. 18.)

One of the distinguishing features and a very important feature of the true Church of Christ is its priesthood, the authority of God. It is widely distributed among the male membership of the Church—boys and men, fathers and sons—and its blessings are shared by our mothers, daughters, and wives. (*So Shall Ye Reap*, p. 17.)

Our boys twelve years of age, if worthy, receive the holy priesthood by the laying on of hands, and our young men are hardly more than boys when they receive the holy Melchizedek Priesthood, the authority to officiate in the most sacred ordinances known to man. This priesthood will, if they are worthy, entitle them eventually to a place in the celestial kingdom of God. (*So Shall Ye Reap*, pp. 18–19.)

Sometimes I wonder if we appreciate the priesthood, because it comes so easy to us. Boys, twelve years of age, receive it. Then they are advanced through the priesthood when they get older, and are ordained elders. I am confident in my own mind that there is no greater position that could come to any man than to receive the priesthood of God, coupled with the testimony of the divinity of this work; and those two should always go together. In other words, a man who does not have a testimony of the gospel should never be ordained to the Melchizedek Priesthood. The honors of men, the wealth of the world, are as nothing by comparison to the honor and the blessing which come to us when we were ordained to the priesthood. (Fresno California Priesthood Leadership Meeting, 13 September 1952.)

What is the obligation of the priesthood bearer? We have been referred to as the greatest body of men on the face of the earth. Of course, the fact that we possess the priesthood is no assurance of our exaltation. But certainly in terms of power, prerogative, and responsibility, no group of men in all the world has been blessed with such obligations and opportunities as has the body of men and boys in the Church who hold the priesthood.

I have been impressed that probably nowhere in all the world can we find a group of men who give so unselfishly of their time, their means, and their talents to the promotion of goodness and righteousness in the world as does this body of men. I marvel as I witness the great voluntary service which is carried forward by this body of priesthood, and always in the back of my head, as I give encouragement to greater activity, is the assurance that this is a choice group of men. (*So Shall Ye Reap*, p. 19.)

A priesthood holder is kind. One who is kind is sympathetic and gentle with others. He is considerate of others' feelings and courteous in his behavior. He has a helpful nature. Kindness pardons others' weaknesses and faults. Kindness is extended to all — to the aged and the young, to animals, to those low of station as well as the high. (CR October 1986, *Ensign* 16 [November 1986]: 47.)

As priesthood holders we are commanded to "be full of charity towards all men, and [especially] to the household of faith [that is, your fellow members in the Church, and members of your own family—your wife, your sons and daughters], and let virtue garnish thy thoughts unceasingly; then shall thy confidence wax strong in the presence of God; and the doctrine of the priesthood shall distill upon thy soul as the dews from heaven" (D&C 121:45). ("Three Imperative Responsibilities," London England Area Conference, 19–20 June 1976.)

An imperative responsibility, if you would lead more righteous lives, is to govern righteously in your priesthood stewardships. The revelation pertaining to this responsibility is in section 121 of the Doctrine and Covenants. Three phrases claim our attention: "the rights of the priesthood," "the powers of heaven," and "the principles of righteousness."

The rights of the priesthood are the keys or covenants pertaining to priesthood offices. The powers of heaven are the gifts of the

Spirit which the Lord God Omnipotent gives to righteous priesthood holders. The principles of righteousness are those godlike virtues—persuasion, long-suffering, gentleness, meekness, love unfeigned, kindness, and pure knowledge—which connect one with the powers of heaven.

To paraphrase, a man may have offices of the priesthood conferred upon him, but if he undertakes to cover his sins, gratify his pride, or his vain ambition, or exercise unrighteous dominion, the powers of heaven withdraw; the Spirit of the Lord is grieved, and when it is withdrawn, amen to the priesthood or the authority of that man (see D&C 121:37). When one departs from principles of righteousness, the rights of the priesthood and the powers of heaven are withdrawn; hence the statement, "many are called, but few are chosen" (D&C 121:40). ("Our Imperative Responsibilities," Houston Texas Area Conference, 23 June 1979.)

There are some among us in the Church who do not take their priesthood as seriously as they should. Too often there seems to be a desire to imitate the world's profane expressions, its extreme clothing fashions, and hair styles. Some of our brethren become so obsessed with material things that they neglect their priesthood responsibilities. Some even rationalize themselves into dishonesty and immorality. ("Three Imperative Responsibilities," London England Area Conference, 19–20 June 1976.)

Each member of the priesthood should set his own house in order. This should include holding regular family prayer, remembering especially our government leaders; getting out of debt; seeing that each member of the family understands the importance of keeping the commandments; seeing that the truth is shared with members of the family, with neighbors, and with associates; seeing that each member is performing his duties in the priesthood, in the auxiliary organizations, in the temple, and in the civic life of the community; seeing that every wage earner in the home is a full-tithe payer and fulfilling other obligations in financial support of the kingdom; providing a one-year supply of essentials. In doing these things a member of the Church is not only making himself an opponent of the adversary, but a proponent of the Lord. (*Title of Liberty*, pp. 192–93.)

In no other place, or any other dominion, does a priesthood holder have a greater opportunity than within the walls of his own home. There is found the true measure of his love, patience, forbearance, and consideration. ("Our Imperative Responsibilities," Houston Texas Area Conference, 23 June 1979.)

The quorum is organized to teach, inspire, and strengthen the father in his responsibility and help him to do his duty. This suggests involvement—involving each priesthood holder in the programs of the Church, giving him something to do, assuring him that he is needed and wanted in the Church. Concerning our duty, the Lord has said: "Now let every man learn his duty, and to act in the office in which he is appointed, in all diligence. He that is slothful shall not be counted worthy to stand, and he that learns not his duty and shows himself not approved shall not be counted worthy to stand." (D&C 107:99–100.) (*Priesthood* [Salt Lake City: Deseret Book, 1981], p. 140.)

The priesthood must be put in place if we are to achieve the Lord's blessing and maximum effectiveness. Priesthood quorums must be strengthened. We must do all we can to bring to pass the fulfillment of the vision of President Joseph F. Smith on the priesthood quorums assuming their rightful duties. (Salt Lake City, Utah, 6 June 1980.)

Now, to help to make this priesthood more effective in our lives and in the lives of those we serve, the Lord has provided quorums of the priesthood—service units, classes, brotherhood—through which we may operate and make our efforts more productive of good. (*So Shall Ye Reap*, p. 22.)

It is not enough to receive the priesthood and then sit back passively and wait until someone prods us into activity. When we receive the priesthood, we have the obligation of becoming actively and anxiously engaged in promoting righteousness in the earth, because the Lord says: "He that doeth not anything until he is commanded, and receiveth a commandment with doubtful heart, and keepeth it with slothfulness, the same is damned" (D&C 58:29). (*So Shall Ye Reap*, p. 21.)

If we could only get the vision of the importance of this priesthood, we wouldn't permit the honors of men, activities in various clubs, fraternal orders, and other organizations, to interfere with our performing our duties wholeheartedly as members of the Church and kingdom of God. The greatest power in this world is the power presented in this priesthood. That is the power that brought this earth into existence. No greater honor or blessing can come to man than the authority to act in the name of God. (Fresno California Priesthood Leadership Meeting, 13 September 1952.)

May we who hold the priesthood of God be unafraid to step forward and provide the righteous leadership which is necessary in our various fields of activity! This is a time for demonstration, my brethren of the priesthood, to let the world know something of the fruits of Mormonism, something of the testimonies which we bear, something of our faith and our determination to live the gospel. (CR October 1955, *Improvement Era* 58 [December 1955]: 952.)

Aaronic Priesthood

We have a great deal of work to do to strengthen the Aaronic Priesthood quorums of the Church. This must be done if we are to act preventively in a young man's life. President Spencer W. Kimball has told us: "The sad, simple truth is that when we do not act preventively in the early years, we must later on act redemptively, but with much less efficiency and fewer and more labored results" (Annual MIA Conference, 23 June 1974). ("Challenges for Leaders of Aaronic Priesthood," Young Men's General Presidency and Board, Salt Lake City, Utah, 19 September 1979.)

Who has the responsibility to prepare a young man for future leadership responsibilities in the Church? Those who have primary responsibility are fathers—ward bishoprics, quorum advisers, and quorum presidencies.

A father, of course, must be the example of priesthood leadership. If he is close to his son, he will be a positive influence when that boy comes to certain crossroads in his life.

Ward bishoprics, quorum advisers, and quorum presidencies are to create for the young man opportunities for spiritual experiences, friendship, and brotherhood, and while doing this the boy should have the benefits of Scouting, achievement, recreation, culture, the arts, and fun. But I stress that saving the souls of young men will take much more than fun and activities. It takes work, sacrifice, carefully planned spiritual experiences, character-building experiences, and work experiences. In addition, it takes leadership example by men committed to teach, train, and inspire young men to reach beyond where they are so they may realize greater achievement.

Every activity or experience for the quorum ought to be tailored to develop a young man's faith, talents, and abilities. Yes, the quorum can become the most important association, next to the family, when bishoprics, advisers, and Scoutmasters strive to provide young men with a balanced program of social, cultural, physical, service, and spiritual opportunities that will result in testimony and character-strengthening experiences.

Advisers must work closely with the quorum presidency so these young men will learn how to lead effectively. Presidencies of Aaronic Priesthood quorums were not intended to function without close adult supervision. They must have men as advisers who have had priesthood experience and who are examples for young men to look up to. ("Challenges for Leaders of Aaronic Priesthood," Young Men's General Presidency and Board, Salt Lake City, Utah, 19 September 1979.)

If we are to influence these young men, it has to begin early, before they arrive at Aaronic Priesthood age. But once they come into a quorum at age twelve, that quorum should become a young man's most important association next to his family. ("Challenges for Leaders of Aaronic Priesthood," Young Men's General Presidency and Board, Salt Lake City, Utah, 19 September 1979.)

Activate and strengthen all young men of Aaronic Priesthood age. We should all be mindful that the impact of the world on our young people today is not only greater than ever before, but it comes much sooner in their lives. Therefore, we have to do our work earlier and with much greater effectiveness. We must do all that is necessary through proper priesthood channels to train these young men—bearers of a preparatory priesthood—how to use their priesthood and receive the guidance of the Spirit, so they will be guided in paths of righteousness and be a strength in the affairs of the Church, the community, and the nation in which they live. ("Challenges for Leaders of Aaronic Priesthood," Young Men's General Presidency and Board, Salt Lake City, Utah, 19 September 1979.)

Young men need to understand that they are now participating in a priesthood apprenticeship. They need to understand that priesthood is the government of God on this earth; that in His wisdom He has given a preparatory priesthood before one receives the Melchizedek Priesthood. They need to have the oath and covenant of the Melchizedek Priesthood clearly explained to them so they have impressed on them the importance of keeping their covenants. (See D&C 84.) ("Challenges for Leaders of Aaronic Priesthood," Young Men's General Presidency and Board, Salt Lake City, Utah, 19 September 1979.)

We are now moving into an era when we need to have young men with strong spiritual strength who will stand up and teach with conviction the principles of the gospel. This will come about through a righteous home environment and activities in the quorum, including Scouting, which will build character. Boys should be engaged in service projects, work projects, and experiences where they may learn the principles of sacrifice and work. Also, they should understand the value and proper use of money. This will help prepare these young men for their foreordained responsibilities in the kingdom. ("Challenges for Leaders of Aaronic Priesthood," Young Men's General Presidency and Board, Salt Lake City, Utah, 19 September 1979.)

Young men of the Aaronic Priesthood, you have been born at this time for a sacred and glorious purpose. It is not by chance that you have been reserved to come to earth in this last dispensation of the fulness of times. Your birth at this particular time was foreordained in the eternities. You are to be the royal army of the Lord in the last days. You are "youth of the noble birthright" (*Hymns*, 1985, no. 255). (CR April 1986, *Ensign* 16 [May 1986]: 43.)

One of the great challenges in this Church is to help prepare teachers and priests to go on missions. The Lord revealed to the

Prophet Joseph Smith that both teachers and priests had the duty of warning, expounding, exhorting and teaching, inviting "all to come unto Christ" (see D&C 20:50, 59; Moroni 10:32). I believe that when Aaronic Priesthood leadership provides opportunities to fulfill these specific duties, we are preparing our young men for missionary service. Quorum advisers/Scoutmasters must be examples as priesthood holders and must possess the vision to create these opportunities for Aaronic Priesthood youth to serve others. When we can offer a young man opportunities to serve others—to get outside of himself—we are well on our way to helping him get prepared for a mission. ("Challenges for Leaders of Aaronic Priesthood," Young Men's General Presidency and Board, Salt Lake City, Utah, 19 September 1979.)

I say to you that it is not just programs or handbooks that will save boys. It is dedicated, inspired local leaders who take an interest in the individual boy. ("Challenges for Leaders of Aaronic Priesthood," Young Men's General Presidency and Board, Salt Lake City, Utah, 19 September 1979.)

Young men of the Aaronic Priesthood, remember the scriptural injunction "Be ye clean who bear the vessels of the Lord" (3 Nephi 20:41; D&C 38:42; see also Isaiah 52:11). Remember the story of Joseph in Egypt, who hearkened not to the wife of Potiphar and maintained his purity and virtue (see Genesis 39:6-20).

Consider carefully the words of the prophet Alma to his errant son, Corianton, "Forsake your sins, and go no more after the lusts of your eyes" (Alma 39:9). "The lusts of your eyes"—in our day what does that expression mean? Movies, television programs, and video recordings that are both suggestive and lewd. Magazines and books that are obscene and pornographic.

We counsel you, young men, not to pollute your minds with such degrading matter, for the mind through which this filth passes is never the same afterwards. Don't see R-rated movies or vulgar videos or participate in any entertainment that is immoral, suggestive, or pornographic. Don't listen to music that is degrading. (CR April 1986, *Ensign* 16 [May 1986]: 45.)

Live up to your godly potential. Remember who you are and the priesthood that you bear. Be modern-day sons of Helaman. Put on the whole armor of God. (CR April 1986, *Ensign* 16 [May 1986]: 46.)

The Aaronic Priesthood is to prepare you to serve—to serve our Heavenly Father all the days of your life. (CR April 1985, *Ensign* 15 [May 1985]: 36.)

Melchizedek Priesthood

No honor that will ever come to any of us conferred by men of the world, or any man-made honorable body, will ever approach in importance the great honor and blessing which came to us the day we were ordained to the holy Melchizedek Priesthood. This is a priceless blessing, an eternal blessing, and I hope and pray that we will honor it all the days of our lives. Wealth, power, position are as nothing, by comparison, to the honor and blessing which come through the priesthood of the Living God. (CR October 1952, *Improvement Era* 55 [December 1952]: 942.)

When a priesthood holder takes upon himself the Melchizedek Priesthood, he does so by oath and covenant. This is not so with the Aaronic Priesthood. The covenant of the Melchizedek Priesthood is that a priesthood holder will magnify his calling in the priesthood, will give diligent heed to the commandments of God, and will live by every word which proceeds "from the mouth of God" (see D&C 84:33–44). The oath of the Melchizedek Priesthood is an irrevocable promise by God to faithful priesthood holders. "All that my Father hath shall be given unto them" (see D&C 84:38). This oath by Deity, coupled with the covenant by faithful priesthood holders, is referred to as the oath and covenant of the priesthood. ("Three Imperative Responsibilities," London England Area Conference, 19–20 June 1976.)

There is a principle cited in the Doctrine and Covenants which, though directed specifically to the leading quorums of the Church, applies to all councils in Church government:

And every decision made by either of these quorums [and for our purposes we could substitute the word *council*] must be by the unanimous voice of the same; that is, every member in each quorum [council] must be agreed to its decisions.

The decisions of these quorums [or councils] . . . are to be made in all righteousness, in holiness, and lowliness of heart, meekness and long suffering, and in faith, and virtue, and knowledge, temperance, patience, godliness, brotherly kindness and charity;

Because the promise is, if these things abound in them they shall not be unfruitful in the knowledge of the Lord. (D&C 107:27, 30–31.)

This seems to me to be the pattern by which the Lord would have us operate through priesthood councils at all levels of Church government. We must be one in all aspects of this work—ecclesiastically and temporally—for all things are spiritual to Him whom we acknowledge as Master. You can see that this is a great step toward achieving greater unity in managing the affairs of the Church. We, as priesthood holders, need to act in the manner which the Lord instructs. (CR April 1979, *Ensign* 9 [May 1979]: 88.)

I can't conceive of a young man in this Church being fully happy without the Melchizedek Priesthood. I don't believe that the Lord blesses His children with full happiness, if they are members of the Church, unless they receive the priesthood, a priceless possession. So much of the joy of this life and of eternity is tied up in priesthood. (*God, Family, Country*, p. 192.)

Home Teaching

I feel impressed to speak to you now about a priesthood program that has been inspired from its inception—a program that touches hearts, that changes lives, and that saves souls; a program so vital that, if faithfully followed, it will help to spiritually renew the Church and exalt its individual members and families.

Home teaching is not just another program. It is the priesthood way of watching over the Saints and accomplishing the mission of the Church. Home teaching is not just an assignment. It is a sacred calling. Home teaching is not to be taken casually. A home teaching call is to be accepted as if extended to you personally by the Lord Jesus Christ Himself.

The Savior Himself was a teacher. The only perfect man to walk the face of the earth was a humble, dedicated, inspired teacher who brought to His followers salvation and exaltation. Oh, that all the brethren of the Church would catch that vision of home teaching! (CR April 1987, *Ensign* 17 [May 1987]: 48.)

My good brethren of the Melchizedek Priesthood and Aaronic Priesthood, home teaching is an inspired program. It is the heart of caring, of loving, of reaching out to the one—both the active and the less active. It is priesthood compassionate service. It is how we express our faith in practical works. It is one of the tests of true discipleship. It is the heart of the activation effort of the Church. It is a calling that helps to fulfill the scriptural injunction "Out of small things proceedeth that which is great" (D&C 64:33). There is no greater Church calling than that of a home teacher. There is no greater Church service rendered to our Father in Heaven's children than the service rendered by a humble, dedicated, committed home teacher. (CR April 1987, *Ensign* 17 [May 1987]: 49–50.)

Know well those you are to home teach. Really know them! You can't serve well those you don't know well. President Marion G. Romney emphasized this:

> Each pair of home teachers should become "personally" acquainted with every child, youth, and adult in the family to whom they are assigned.
>
> To perform fully our duty as a home teacher, we should be continually aware of the attitudes, the activities and interests, the problems, the employment, the health, the happiness, the plans and purposes, the physical, temporal, and spiritual needs and circumstances of everyone—of every child, every youth, and every adult in the homes and families who have been placed in our trust and care as a bearer of the priesthood, and as a representative of the bishop.

And the key to effectively working with the family is to be close to the father. And I would urge you to do the little things, the small things that mean so much to a family—for example, know the names of all the family members. Be aware of birthdays, blessings, baptisms, and marriages. On occasion write an appropriate note of commendation or make a phone call congratulating a member of the family on a special achievement or accomplishment. With your home teaching companion, regularly review pages eight and nine of the *Melchizedek Priesthood Handbook* for some excellent suggestions on how to be helpful to those you home teach.

Above all, be a genuine friend to the individuals and families you teach. As the Savior declared to us, "I will call you friends, for ye are my friends" (D&C 93:45). A friend makes more than a dutiful visit each month. A friend is more concerned about helping people than getting credit. A friend cares. A friend loves. A friend listens and a friend reaches out. Yes, know well those you are to home teach and be their friend.

We remember the story President Romney used to tell of the so-called home teacher who once called at the Romney home on a cold night. He kept his hat in his hand and shifted nervously when he was invited to sit down and give his message. "Well, I will tell you, Brother Romney," he responded, "it is cold outside and I left my car engine running so it wouldn't stop. I just stopped in so I could tell the bishop I made my calls." We can do better than that, brethren—much better. (CR April 1987, *Ensign* 17 [May 1987]: 50.)

A fundamental to effective home teaching is to know well the message you are to deliver in each home. And know that it is the particular message the Lord would have you give to the families and individuals you have been asked to serve. Home teachers should have a purpose or goal in mind and should plan each visit to help meet that purpose. Before making their home visits, home teaching partners should meet together to pray, to review instructions from their leaders, to go over the message they will take to the families, and to discuss any special needs.

Home teachers should present an important message that they have prepared or that they bring from priesthood leaders. We strongly recommend that the home teachers use the monthly message from the First Presidency printed in the *Ensign* and the Church's international magazines. The head of the family may also request a special message for family members.

And as a vital part of that message, whenever possible, read together the scriptures with the families you home teach. Make this a regular part of your visit. Especially read together verses from the Book of Mormon that will fortify your message, always remembering the words of the Prophet Joseph, that "a man [would] get nearer to God by abiding by its precepts than by any other book" (Book of Mormon Introduction). Your families need the continual strength of the Book of Mormon.

May our message be like Alma instructed the teachers of his day: "He commanded them that they should teach nothing save it were the things which he had taught, and which had been spoken by the mouth of the holy prophets" (Mosiah 18:19). As home teachers, live the kind of lives yourselves that will invite the Spirit. Live the gospel so you can effectively teach it.

Alma further instructs us, "Trust no one to be your teacher nor your minister, except he be a man of God, walking in his ways and keeping his commandments" (Mosiah 23:14). Therefore, Alma consecrated all the priests and all the teachers, "and none were consecrated except they were just men. Therefore they did watch over their people, and did nourish them with things pertaining to righteousness." (See Mosiah 23:17–18.)

Also remember that, whenever possible, praying in the home should be a part of every home teaching visit. As you may be called upon to pray, pray with the Spirit, pray with real intent, and invoke the Lord's blessings upon the individuals and families you are teaching. Yes, fundamental to effective home teaching is to know well your message, teach it by the Spirit, and make praying and reading of the scriptures an integral part of that message. (CR April 1987, *Ensign* 17 [May 1987]: 50–51.)

Home teaching should be so organized that priesthood strength is assigned to fellowship and teach family members who do not realize the importance of temple blessings and covenants. ("Our Duty as Latter-day Saints," Springfield-Burke Virginia Chapel Dedication, 15 October 1982.)

If the father fails in his responsibility, the home teacher must work with him to strengthen and help him to do his duty. This involves, of course, a lot of person-to-person work and informal contacts. It also involves love for our fellowman and concern for him. "Let every man esteem his brother as himself" (D&C 38:25). "By this shall all men know that ye are my disciples, if ye have love one to another" (John 13:35). (*Priesthood* [Salt Lake City: Deseret Book, 1981], p. 140.)

We appreciate that some married couples have not realized the importance of the temple ordinances. Some of these members are not engaged in Church activity. As brothers and sisters in full fellowship of the Church, home teachers have a responsibility to encourage them to full activity and then, by assignment of quorum leaders, to prepare them for the ordinances of the temple. ("Our Duty as Latter-day Saints," Springfield-Burke Virginia Chapel Dedication, 15 October 1982.)

Home teachers do not have to wait for a formal class to prepare members for the temple. Home teachers are home missionaries. They may teach those families just as our full-time missionaries teach investigators. ("Our Duty as Latter-day Saints," Springfield-Burke Virginia Chapel Dedication, 15 October 1982.)

Truly magnify your calling as a home teacher. Do not settle for mediocrity in this great priesthood program of home teaching. Be an excellent home teacher in every facet of the work. Be a real shepherd of your flock. Make your home teaching visit early in the month, allowing enough time for additional follow-up contacts as necessary. Whenever possible, make a definite appointment for each visit. Let your families know when you are coming and respect their time.

Melchizedek Priesthood bearers, when you have an Aaronic Priesthood young man as your companion, train him well. Use him effectively in working with your families and in teaching them. Have these young men feel of your love of home teaching, so that when they become senior companions they will love their calling and magnify it as you have.

Remember, both quality and quantity home teaching is essential in being an effective home teacher. You should have quality visits, but you should also make contact with each of your families each month. As shepherds to all of your families, both active and less active, you should not be content with only reaching the ninety and nine. Your goal should be 100 percent home teaching every month.

So that this can be quality home teaching, we urge priesthood leaders not to assign more than three to five families or individuals to a pair of home teachers. This may be a challenge in some cases, but we would invite you to give prayerful consideration to such assignments.

Keeping faithful track of each member you are called to home teach is essential. The Book of Mormon beautifully teaches this principle: "And after they had been received unto baptism, and were wrought upon and cleansed by the power of the Holy Ghost, they were numbered among the people of the church of Christ; and their names were taken, that they might be remembered and nourished by the good word of God, to keep them in the right way, to keep them continually watchful unto prayer, relying alone upon the merits of Christ, who was the author and the finisher of their faith" (Moroni 6:4).

Brethren, may we remember all of our individuals and families and "number" them each month and nourish them by the good word of God to keep them in the right way. We call upon quorum leaders to conduct spiritual monthly home teaching interviews, receive a report on the home teachers' activities, evaluate current needs, make assignments for the coming month, and teach, strengthen, and inspire the home teachers in their sacred callings. Such interviews with home teachers provide a setting for leaders to measure progress and better serve the individuals and members they have been called to serve. (CR April 1987, *Ensign* 17 [May 1987]: 51.)

The home teaching program of the Church offers a most excellent system for feedback. Home teachers will invite feedback from their families, priesthood leaders from the home teachers, the bishop from the priesthood leaders, and the stake president from the bishops. In this way the leader will not only receive many helpful ideas; he will also keep his finger on the pulse of those whom he leads. (*God, Family, Country*, p. 140.)

I can remember, as if it were yesterday, growing up as a boy in Whitney, Idaho. We were a farm family, and when we boys were out working in the field, I remember Father calling to us in a shrill voice from the barnyard, "Tie up your teams, boys, and come on

in. The ward teachers are here.'' Regardless of what we were doing, that was the signal to assemble in the sitting room to hear the
ward teachers. These two faithful priesthood bearers would come
each month either by foot or by horseback. We always knew they
would come. I can't remember one miss. And we would have a
great visit. They would stand behind a chair and talk to the family.
They would go around the circle and ask each child how he or she
was doing and if we were doing our duty. Sometimes Mother and
Father would prime us before they came so we would have the
right answers. But it was an important time for us as a family.
They always had a message and it was a good one.

We have refined home teaching a lot since those early days in
Whitney. But it is still basically the same, isn't it? The same principles are involved: caring, reaching out, teaching by the Spirit,
leaving an important message each month, and a concern and love
for each member of the family. God bless the home teachers of
this Church. You are in the front line of defense to watch over and
strengthen the individual and the family unit. Understand the sacredness of your calling and the divine nature of your responsibility.

Know well those you are to home teach. Know well your message and deliver it with the Spirit. And finally, truly magnify your
calling as a home teacher. As you do this, I promise you the blessings of heaven and the indescribable joy that comes from helping
to touch hearts, change lives, and save souls. (CR April 1987,
Ensign 17 [May 1987]: 51.)

Activation

I speak to you about our mission to perfect the Saints, particularly the challenge of activating those who have separated themselves from full activity in the Church. These members, who are
our brothers and sisters, presently live apart from the Church and
the influence of the gospel. In this group of less-active members
are many nonattenders who may be indifferent and noncaring.
Also included are those who are temporarily lost because we do
not know their whereabouts. Some of these are new converts who
apparently did not receive the nurturing attention and teachings
that would have caused them to be "fellow citizens with the
Saints" (Ephesians 2:19). Many are single adults.

To all such, we, as priesthood leaders, must extend and renew our love and heartfelt invitation to come back. "Come back. Come back and feast at the table of the Lord, and taste again the sweet and satisfying fruits of fellowship with the Saints." (*Church News*, 22 December 1985, p. 3.) The challenge before us is great. It will require us to put the Melchizedek Priesthood to work. We must exercise great faith, energy, and commitment if we are to reach these brothers and sisters. But we must do it. The Lord expects us to do it. And we will! ("Feed My Sheep," Regional Representatives Seminar, Salt Lake City, Utah, 3 April 1987.)

You have a lot of brethren, your brethren, who are not active in the Church. And whom do you suppose the Lord expects to go out and bring them in? He is not going to send angels from heaven to bring them in, when He has a whole group of men here who bear His priesthood, every one who has the authority to act in His name. He expects you to go out, and in a spirit of love and understanding and fellowship to put your arms around those brethren and to win them into activity. And I say to you that if you do your part, the Lord won't permit you to fail. (Fresno California Priesthood Leadership Meeting, 13 September 1952.)

The Good Shepherd gave His life for the sheep—for you and me—for us all (see John 10:17–18). The symbolism of the Good Shepherd is not without parallel in the Church today. The sheep need to be led by watchful shepherds. Too many are wandering. Some are being enticed away by momentary distractions. Others have become completely lost. We realize, as in times past, that some of the sheep will rebel and are "as a wild flock which fleeth from the shepherd" (Mosiah 8:21). But most of our problems stem from lack of loving and attentive shepherding, and more shepherds must be developed.

With a shepherd's care, our new members, those newly born into the gospel, must be nurtured by attentive fellowshipping as they increase in gospel knowledge and begin living new standards. Such attention will help to ensure that they will not return to old habits. With a shepherd's loving care, our young people, our young lambs, will not be as inclined to wander. And if they do, the crook of the shepherd's staff, a loving arm and an understanding heart, will help to retrieve them. With a shepherd's care, many of those who are now independent of the flock can still be reclaimed.

Many who have married outside the Church and have assumed the life-styles of the world may respond to an invitation to return to the fold.

There are no new solutions to this old problem. The charge Jesus gave to Peter, which He emphasized by repeating it three times, is the proven solution: "Feed my lambs. Feed my sheep. Feed my sheep." As in the glorious admonition of the Book of Mormon, those baptized into the Church of Christ must be constantly "remembered and nourished by the good word of God" (Moroni 6:4). The answer, then, is found in prayerfully shepherding and feeding the flock—in other words, priesthood watch-care. There must be real, heartfelt concern by a true and loving shepherd, not just the shallow concern that a hireling might show.

As we talk about the concept of a true shepherd, we recognize that the Lord has given this responsibility to priesthood holders. But sisters also have callings of "shepherding" in the charitable and loving service they render to one another, to youth, and to children.

Now, brethren, we must teach our local leaders to be true shepherds. They must manifest the same love that the Good Shepherd has for all of us. Each soul is precious to Him. His invitation beckons every member—every son and daughter of God. "Behold, he sendeth an invitation unto all men, for the arms of mercy are extended towards them, and he saith: Repent, and I will receive you. Come unto me and ye shall partake of the fruit of the tree of life; Yea, come unto me and bring forth works of righteousness." (Alma 5:33–35.) None are denied His invitation. All are welcome who will receive His gracious invitation to partake of His gospel. The sheep—some distracted, some indifferent, some preoccupied—must be found and loved back into activity. Every priesthood and auxiliary resource must be used to assist in this effort. This challenge will never be met until each stake, ward, and quorum leader exercises the will and the faith to bring the less-active back into full activity in the Church. ("Feed My Sheep," Regional Representatives Seminar, Salt Lake City, Utah, 3 April 1987.)

I wonder, brethren, why it was not you or why it was not I —why we are not among these less-active adult members. Maybe we came from better homes. Maybe our fathers were more devoted in taking us to priesthood meeting. Maybe we had better bishops.

Maybe we had better Aaronic Priesthood leaders. Maybe we had a Scoutmaster who inspired us to come to Church and to do our duty, to live clean, to keep the Word of Wisdom, to pay our tithing. We cannot tell. Only the God of Heaven can judge and judge accurately, but the fact remains that they are here among us and they are our brethren. They are choice spirits, many of them born under the covenant. The God of Heaven expects us to go out and win them into activity, and not only them, but you have a great amount of brethren who hold the Melchizedek Priesthood who are not fully active. We need to labor with them, through personal interviews, personal visits. There is no satisfactory substitute for personal contacts. You cannot use a shotgun method. You have to go to them directly, through personal contact. Maybe you will bring them in through a social. Maybe it will be done through softball. I wish you could have heard the testimonies, as I heard them, of men who took part in the softball program. I had the privilege of hearing some of them stand on their feet and bear their testimonies for the first time in their lives. I saw some of them go to the temple, men who had been smoking and drinking, who had never been active in the Church since they were boys, but because they went out on a diamond and played baseball with men who lived the gospel, they caught their spirit. (Fresno California Priesthood Leadership Meeting, 13 September 1952.)

No man in this Church who holds the holy priesthood and who has been active in this Church and then turns away into inactivity is ever really happy. They try to act happy, seek happiness, but I don't believe the God of Heaven blesses His sons with happiness when they refuse to honor their priesthood. I have heard the testimonies of as many of them as you have, men of promise, who have been out in the world and honored by the world, been inactive, then have come back into activity, and almost, so far as I know, without exception, they always have said that all during this period of inactivity there was something lacking inside. They didn't feel right. They weren't content. They weren't at peace with their own souls. And so you bring them happiness now and you open the door to the rich blessings of eternity. (Fresno California Priesthood Leadership Meeting, 3 September 1952.)

I call on all inactive priesthood holders—you who, for reasons best known to yourselves, are disassociated from your quorums and Church. You have formed new affiliations, and now some of you have become disinterested in the Church and no longer conform to its standards. Unhappily, many of your families tread in your paths and follow your examples. Brethren, when we fail to be true to our priesthood promises, the price we and our loved ones are forced to pay might well be entitled "the high cost for low living." What a blessing you would be to your wives and children if you would harmonize your lives with your covenants. Brethren of the priesthood, how we need your support, affiliation, and strength! Do not desert the cause of God at a time when the conflict is most imminent. Make President John Taylor's slogan your commitment: "The kingdom of God or nothing!" (*Journal of Discourses*, 6:26.) (CR April 1980, *Ensign* 10 [May 1980]: 34.)

The principles to activate souls do not change. The lost or less-active must be found and contacted. Loving concern must be demonstrated. They must feel of our love. They must be taught the gospel. They must feel the power of the Holy Ghost through the teachers. They must be included in our fellowship. They must have meaningful Church responsibilities. In the words of the Book of Mormon, we are to "continue to minister" (3 Nephi 18:32). We are particularly concerned that new converts be integrated into full fellowship in the Church. They must be welcomed with open arms. ("Feed My Sheep," Regional Representatives Seminar, Salt Lake City, Utah, 3 April 1987.)

When we bring fathers back into activity, we bring them and their families happiness in this life, to say nothing about the eternal blessings that are opened up to them. My heart goes out to those men, heads of families, who are inactive prospective elders. I don't believe we have a greater challenge in the Church today than to activate those men and bring them to the point where they can take their families to the house of the Lord and have opened to them the richest blessings known to men and women in this world and in the world to come.

Brethren, our hope and prayer is that you will see this activation effort as more than just a temporary program. We hope that when this period of our Church history is recorded, it will be said that this marked a time when many wandering and lost souls were reclaimed by the Church of God. (Regional Representatives Seminar, Salt Lake City, Utah, 6 April 1984.)

Scouting

I would to God that every boy of Boy Scout age in America could have the benefits and the blessings of the great Boy Scout program. It is truly a noble program; it is a builder of character, not only in the boys, but also in the men who provide the leadership. I have often said that Scouting is essentially a spiritual program, a builder of men. It is established, as is our government and its Constitution, upon a deeply spiritual foundation. (*So Shall Ye Reap*, p. 138.)

A Scout must be trustworthy, loyal, helpful, friendly, courteous, kind, obedient, cheerful, thrifty, brave, clean, reverent. To be a good Scout, he must be faithful in his religious duties. Scouting provides a program of training and experience. It is a program for character development. It is a supplementary educational program, a program of citizenship training and vocational exploration. Many boys have found their vocations through this program —through the merit badges which are concentrated courses in vocational guidance in fifteen different activity fields. Scouting teaches boys the crafts and the skills and to do something useful with their hands.

If we have the right kind of leadership through real boys' men, they will have it, enjoy it, and receive the blessings which come from the program. The responsibility rests with the priesthood —stake presidencies and bishoprics—to see that this leadership is provided and that every boy is reached. (CR April 1951, *Improvement Era* 54 [June 1951]: 423.)

In the first part of the Boy Scout oath we declare, "On my honor, I will do my best to do my duty to God and my country and to obey the Scout law." Scouting emphasizes duty to God, reverence for sacred things, observance of the Sabbath, maintenance of the standards of the church with which the boy is affiliated. As each boy repeats that pledge, usually at every Scout meeting or function, he says aloud in the presence of those whose friendship he values most highly, "On my honor, I will do my best to do my duty to God." It cannot help but make a deep and lasting impression upon him. It becomes the foundation upon which a noble character is built. The oath also pledges duty to country, and that, too, is basically spiritual. (*So Shall Ye Reap*, pp. 138–39.)

A Latter-day Saint boy who is living the Boy Scout oath would never break the Word of Wisdom, as we know it. He would keep himself morally clean. He would not take into his body those things that destroy and weaken it. The Scout motto is "Be prepared." Be prepared for any emergency. Be prepared to meet the temptations of evil in the world and resist them. Be prepared for any eventuality. That is emphasized in the Scout law, to say nothing of the other laws—glorious principles, religious, spiritual principles—all of them embodied in the gospel of the Master. (Eagle Recognition Banquet, Logan, Utah, 22 March 1974.)

Unselfish, willing service is emphasized in the Boy Scout program and is symbolized in the great motto—"Do a good turn daily." I dare say that the average Boy Scout does many good turns daily. It was because of a little incident in the life of a British Boy Scout who was doing his good turn to an American businessman visiting in London that Scouting was brought to America. (Eagle Recognition Banquet, Logan, Utah, 22 March 1974.)

Scouting is dedicated to a fourfold program: First, it teaches the boy his duty to God—reverence, observance of the Sabbath, and the maintenance of the spiritual standards and ideals of his church. Second, it teaches duty to country—true patriotism—a love for the Constitution, for our free institutions, and for our American way of life. Third, it teaches the value of service to others—willing, unselfish service, and that the greatest among them must be the servant of all—symbolized by the "good turn." Fourth, it teaches duty to self—that they must keep themselves physically strong, mentally awake, and morally straight. They must be prepared for any eventuality to serve themselves, their church, and their country. (CR April 1951, *Improvement Era* 54 [June 1951]: 423.)

As a movement, Scouting is a program or a method. It is a way of doing something. Its purpose is fivefold: character building—to help to fill the need for men of shining honor; citizenship training—to help young men to develop an uncompromising love for America and its great concepts and institutions; to develop a strong attitude and determination of self-reliance; leadership development—to help to answer the great need of leaders of capacity with high ideals; physical fitness—to help to beat down the tendency, if there is one, of physical deterioration; spiritual growth—American foundations and spiritual perpetuation of America are assured. ("Scouting: A Great American Partnership," *Improvement Era* 67 [February 1964]: 101.)

Religious emphasis is a part of Scouting. All would agree that the most important statement in Scouting is the Scout oath, and the first principle enunciated in it is "duty to God." To implement this great principle, the Boy Scouts of America has urged the churches of America to design awards and to establish requirements for their achievement, to recognize Scouts and Explorers when they have done their duty to God and have been faithful in their religious duties. This has been done by the churches and synagogues and has become a cornerstone among the great blessings of Scouting. ("Scouting: A Great American Partnership," *Improvement Era* 67 [February 1964]: 103.)

Why have we adopted Scouting? We were the first religious body to adopt Scouting as a part of the youth program of the Church. Some two and one-half years after Scouting came to America, it was made an official part of the program of the Church.

Someone has said that it isn't mentioned in the revelations given to the Prophet Joseph Smith, and of course that is true. Neither is the Primary nor the Sunday School, but one of our Articles of Faith clearly indicates that "if there is anything virtuous, lovely or of good report or praiseworthy, we seek after these things" (Article of Faith 13). Scouting is a help. It is a tool in achieving the objective of the building of real men. It helps to build character. It trains for citizenship. It helps to build leadership. It helps to prepare people to live in a wholesome manner, in a full and enjoyable manner here in this life, and prepares them for the life to come. (Eagle Recognition Banquet, Logan, Utah, 22 March 1974.)

Scouting helps prepare boys for Church responsibility. If this were not true, we would drop the program tomorrow, because we want these boys to become better men and boys and honor their priesthood and to be faithful members of the Church and kingdom of God. Scouting will help them do that and so it isn't any wonder that President Heber J. Grant at one time said, "It is my desire to see Scouting extended to every boy in the Church." President David O. McKay said, "Scouting is not an optional program. It is part of the official program for boys in the Church. We desire every Mormon boy to have the benefit and blessing of Scouting." (Eagle Recognition Banquet, Logan, Utah, 22 March 1974.)

It is one of the choicest experiences in my life to serve in and participate in Scouting, which I have done for almost seventy years. Scouting is a great program for leadership training, teaching patriotism, love of country, and the building of strong character. It is a builder of men, men of character and spirituality. As I have said many times, I would hope that every young man would become an Eagle Scout and not settle for mediocrity in the great Scouting program of the Church. ("When I Was Called as Scoutmaster," Boy Scout Satellite Broadcast, Salt Lake City, Utah, 14 February 1988.)

The Boy Scout program is very dear to my heart. I love it. I have had the pleasure of working in Scouting somewhat and I have great faith in it. I have been deeply impressed with the record that has been made by the Church in this field. We have many shortcomings—we have not reached perfection in any field of activity that I know of in the Church—but probably in no other field do we have a better reputation in the world than in the field of Scouting. It is true we have Scout troops in many nations, and I presume, in proportion to our population, have a higher proportion of Scout troops sponsored by the Church than any other church or civic organization in the world. Certainly, the records at national Scouting headquarters show that in proportion to the boys of Scout age we have the highest enrollment of boys in Scouting of any church on the earth. We have, through a combination of Scouting and Aaronic Priesthood work, the finest program for boyhood that this world knows anything about.

"Observing the Sabbath day according to Latter-day Saint standards and ideals plays its part in spiritualizing the program" (*Explorer Manual*). Explorers should plan on being at home on the Sabbath day and to attend Church services in the traditional Latter-day Saint way. The planning of hikes and mountain trips on the weekends does not conform to Latter-day Saint ideals.

("Scouting Serves the Church," *Improvement Era* 51 [September 1948]: 558, 560.)

Scouting stresses service to others. This has a spiritual base. The Scout pledges to help other people at all times. Was it not the Master who said, "Whosoever will be chief among you, let him be your servant"? (Matthew 20:27.) The slogan "Do a good turn daily" has become emblazoned upon American living beyond its place of origin in the Boy Scout movement. (*So Shall Ye Reap*, p. 139.)

There is a tendency to think of fitness solely in terms of physical, in terms of bodily strength. But to be truly fit, truly equal to the demands of life, requires much more than bodily strength. It involves the mind and the training of the mind, the emotions and their use and control. Yes, and it involves the soul and the spiritual growth, too. (*So Shall Ye Reap*, p. 140.)

The Scout's respect and love for learning is embodied in his being mentally awake. One who is hungering and thirsting after knowledge will not fail to gain a preeminent place of leadership among his fellowmen. And how the world needs sound, straight-thinking, wise leaders! ("Scouting—Builder of Men," Annual Meeting of the National Council, Boy Scouts of America, Washington, D.C., 29 May 1954.)

The genius of the program is to learn to do by doing. Almost limitless opportunities are provided to explore every field of worthy endeavor and to develop crafts and skills which will be a source of joy forever. Of such a program we may well say, "He who chops his own wood gets warm twice." Scouting encourages boys to chop their own wood. ("Scouting—Builder of Men," Annual Meeting of the National Council, Boy Scouts of America, Washington, D.C., 29 May 1954.)

A Scout is taught a love of the Constitution. He learns something of the basic concepts and principles upon which this nation has been established. He is taught to love our free institutions. That is why we have had, some years ago, our programs to "Strengthen Liberty" and "To Go Forward on Liberty's Team."

Some few years ago, one million posters were printed and circulated by the Boy Scouts throughout this country, emphasizing the principle of freedom and liberty. Thirty million doorknobs in the homes of America had little doorknob hangers placed on them by the Boy Scouts of America, calling attention to our heritage as American citizens and inviting all to renew their faith in these basic principles and their determination to help preserve them. (Eagle Recognition Banquet, Logan, Utah, 22 March 1974.)

Scouting is no longer on trial. It is past the experimental stage. It has ready acceptance. It is a definite part of American life, American lore, and American heritage. Scouts of today live the legendary lives of the great American pioneer scouts. The vision, perseverance, courage, determination, and self-reliance of the old scouts are inevitably a part of Scouting today and so are a part of America today. ("Scouting: A Great American Partnership," *Improvement Era* 67 [February 1964]: 100–101.)

Where Scouting is available, please understand that this is not an optional program. Make certain priesthood leaders in your regions understand this. It is an economically, socially, and spiritually sound program. It builds men of character and spirituality and trains them for citizen and leadership responsibility. Scouting teaches a boy to take care of himself and stand on his own two feet. It is an inspired program for a demanding time. This is that time! ("How to Be an Effective Regional Representative," Regional Representatives Seminar, Salt Lake City, Utah, 31 March 1978.)

Scout Leaders

Scouting is Church work. It is part of the Church program. Better Scouting makes better priesthood activities. I would like to say just this regarding the selection of men to serve in Scouting. Be sure that you select the best boys' man. All of us are not gifted in that direction. President Grant said, at one time, "If the best man in your ward for Scoutmaster is the bishop, then release the bishop and make him Scoutmaster." Now President Grant wasn't advocating the wholesale release of bishops, but he was emphasizing the fact that some men are gifted to lead boys. Sometimes I think there are fewer of that type of men than there are men qualified for some other positions in the Church. (Eagle Recognition Banquet, Logan, Utah, 22 March 1974.)

Scouting should not be a separate activity from quorum work. All activities should be carried out under the direction of the quorum presidency. The quorum presidency should meet with advisers and the bishopric and plan in advance quorum programs and activities to meet the needs of the young men. Just as athletics, service projects, or other programs are part of the quorum, so is Scouting. Yet, Scouting must not preempt the priesthood work of a quorum. The two should function together. ("Challenges for Leaders of Aaronic Priesthood," Young Men's General Presidency and Board, 19 September 1979.)

I shall ever be grateful that a good bishop in a little country town in southern Idaho came to me one day way back in 1917 or 1918 to ask me to be a Scoutmaster of that community. We had never had Scouting in that community. It was a community of only fifty families. There were twenty-four boys of Scout age and it was a great challenge for one who had never had Scouting himself to be asked to serve as a Scoutmaster. However, I went into that challenge with a good deal of satisfaction. ("Scouting and the Church," Washington, D.C., Boy Scout Court of Honor, 7 February 1954.)

One of the joys of working with boys is the fact that you do get your pay as you go along. You have an opportunity to observe the results of your leadership daily as you work with them through the years and watch them grow into stalwart manhood, accepting eagerly its challenges and responsibilities.

Such satisfaction cannot be purchased at any price; it must be earned through service and devotion. What a glorious thing it is to have even a small part in helping to build boys into men, real men. And that is the purpose of Scouting—to build men. (*So Shall Ye Reap*, p. 138.)

Scouting is a great program—a truly great program. I don't know of any program in America for boys that is more universally approved than is Scouting. Men of prominence in business, professional life, and in government and other activities are making contributions from time to time—big gifts of various kinds—because they want to make a contribution to the future of this country and there is no better way to do it than to invest something in boys. (Eagle Recognition Banquet, Logan, Utah, 22 March 1974.)

When you help a boy, a satisfied feeling takes hold of you. It never leaves and this is why—you have helped a boy on his way to manhood, honorable manhood, and you have enriched your own life in the process. (Eagle Recognition Banquet, Logan, Utah, 22 March 1974.)

Whether one studies the Scout oath, the Scout law, the Scout motto, or the Scout slogan, they all add up to America's finest character-building program. How fortunate are those who may participate in it and have their lives enriched thereby—boys and men alike. They with whom Scouting is concerned are made of eternal stuff; theirs is a divine destiny. Godlike men, men of character, men of truth, men of courage, men of goodwill—there, then, is our challenge.

Ours is not a boy problem; it is a man problem. Our boys want Scouting; we want them to have it. Our problem is leadership. Our great need is to provide the leadership to meet the demands of the boys. Through Scouting we can help them develop real character; we can teach them cooperation; we can help them develop qualities of leadership; we can teach them the value of staying power.

It is not for us to moan about juvenile delinquency and other problems of our youth. Let us rather use all possible time and energy in trying to help youth—through Scouting, 4-H Clubs, the Future Farmers of America, church, school, and community organizations. Youth need inspired leaders to help them to be honest with themselves; to guide youth safely along life's pathway.

We need to give them something wholesome to do. Only a warm heart can kindle warmth in another. Young people ask for a fair chance to succeed. Let us help provide wholesome challenges and opportunities, and they will complete the job of becoming well-adjusted, useful citizens. To awaken the youth of this land and to rekindle in the hearts of its leaders the high ideals of Scouting is to render one of the greatest services to our country. To guide right the millions of eager, yearning, active youth who are enrolled in Scouting and the many more who might be added is the mightiest of obligations. To win their confidence is one of the greatest responsibilities and privileges of life.

Let us mobilize men, hundreds of them, who love boys; who believe in them; who not only have the technical skills, but who will inspire them, because boys need inspiration even more than they need information.

Let us get men who are boys' men; who can appeal to them and inspire them to want to live right; who believe that it is best to be good—not goody-good, but happy, full of life, full of vigor—who want them to play and have a clean, wholesome time in life. It pays to live a good life. Scouting can help to emphasize and impress this fact upon the boys of today, the men of tomorrow, and us as men. Can we ignore such a challenge? Are you so busy and self-centered that you cannot take time out to help build a bridge for that boy? Scouting offers us that challenge. It is a tremendous test of leadership, devotion, and courage. Is that nobility within us going to rise up in majesty and answer the call?

I have faith in the manhood of America; we will not let our boys down. Upon the character of our boys depends America's future. They are our hope. Scouting, as a great spiritual character-building program, needs to grow as never before. America must be kept strong and free. May God bless us in this task of building men, real men. (*God, Family, Country*, pp. 214–15.)

Boy Scouts

Scouting helps to prepare a boy for honorable fatherhood. It helps to prepare a boy to head up a home. It helps to prepare him to take his place in life, in any profession or business or any occupation that is worthy. Yes, it does more than that. It brings to him personally a satisfaction, a feeling of confidence and assurance because he is basing his life on the fundamental principles of righteousness. It helps him to live the full life. So it isn't any wonder that men and women everywhere—good people everywhere—support the Boy Scout program. (Eagle Recognition Banquet, Logan, Utah, 22 March 1974.)

The Scouting program is not a substitute for the Aaronic Priesthood program. The most important possession that a boy can have is the Aaronic Priesthood. Scouting is a supplementary, a complementary program. It works hand in hand with the program of the Primary, Sunday School, and the Aaronic Priesthood, and is an important and vital part of our program for our boys. (CR April 1951, *Improvement Era* 54 [June 1951]: 423.)

The youth of this land, to me choice above all other lands, are the trustees of posterity; the future of our country will soon rest in their hands. Our common purpose in Scouting is to help prepare our boys to be worthy trustees, to help them fit themselves for the responsibilities of the future. (*So Shall Ye Reap*, pp. 135–36.)

Young men, take full advantage of the Church programs. Set your goals to attain excellence in the achievement programs of the Church. Earn the Duty to God Award—one of our most significant priesthood awards. Become an Eagle Scout—do not settle for mediocrity in the great Scouting program of the Church. (CR April 1986, *Ensign* 16 [May 1986]: 44.)

Give me a young man who has kept himself morally clean and has faithfully attended his Church meetings. Give me a young man who has magnified his priesthood and has earned the Duty to God Award and is an Eagle Scout. Give me a young man who is a seminary graduate and has a burning testimony of the Book of Mormon. Give me such a young man, and I will give you a young man who can perform miracles for the Lord in the mission field and throughout his life. (CR April 1986, *Ensign* 16 [May 1986]: 44.)

Temples and Temple Work

At a party at the Beverly Hills Hilton Hotel in Los Angeles, I had been asked by the President of the United States to greet the president of one of the newer republics, the president of 88 million people scattered on some three thousand islands a thousand miles long, a nation that had been in existence only a few years. As we sat there at this dinner, which was sponsored in large measure by the motion picture industry and at which many movie stars were present, I could look out a beautiful bay window. Down the avenue, on the elevation, I could see the soft floodlights around our glorious Los Angeles Temple, and I had the joy of pointing it out to my guests and to friends at our table and other tables. I thought, as we sat there, "Much of what goes on tonight is simply the froth of life. The things that endure, the things that are real, the things that are important are those things represented in the temple of God." (*God, Family, Country*, p. 85.)

The Prophet Joseph Smith declared that the heavenly messenger Moroni, "informed me of great judgments which were coming upon the earth, with great desolations by famine, sword, and pestilence; and that these grievous judgments would come on the earth in this generation" (Joseph Smith—History 1:45).

We live in a time when those days are imminent. Temples have been provided by a benevolent Father to protect us from these tribulations. Hear the promise given by President George Q. Cannon of the First Presidency: "When other temples are complete, there will be an increase of power bestowed on the people of God, and they will, thereby, be better fitted to go forth and cope with the powers of darkness and with the evils that exist in the world and to establish the Zion of God never more to be thrown down" (*Journal of Discourses*, 14:126).

The Saints in this temple district will be better able to meet any temporal tribulation because of this temple. Faith will increase as a result of the divine power associated with the ordinances of heaven and the assurance of eternal associations. (Jordan River Utah Temple Cornerstone Laying, 15 August 1981.)

Whenever land is dedicated for sacred work, it indeed becomes "holy ground." (From address prepared [but not delivered] 1982.)

Everything we learn in the holy places, the temples, is based on the scriptures. These teachings are what the scriptures refer to as the "mysteries of godliness" (see 1 Timothy 3:16; D&C 19:10). They are to be comprehended by the power of the Holy Ghost, for the Lord has given this promise to His faithful and obedient servants: "Thou mayest know the mysteries and peaceable things" (D&C 42:61). (*Come unto Christ*, p. 19.)

I am grateful to the Lord that my temple memories extend back —even to young boyhood. Thank God for the spirit of temple work. I remember so well, as a little boy, coming in from the field and approaching the old farm home in Whitney, Idaho. I could hear my mother singing, "Have I Done Any Good in the World Today?" (*Hymns*, 1985, no. 223.) I can still see her in my mind's eye bending over the ironing board with newspapers on the floor, ironing long strips of white cloth, with beads of perspiration on her forehead. I asked her what she was doing. She said, "These are temple robes, my son. Your father and I are going to the temple at Logan."

Then she put the old flatiron on the stove, drew a chair close to mine, and told me about temple work and how important it was to be able to go to the temple and participate in the sacred ordinances performed there. She also expressed her fervent hope that someday her children and grandchildren would have the opportunity to enjoy those priceless blessings. ("Temple Blessings and Covenants," Temple Presidents Seminar, Salt Lake City, Utah, 28 September 1982.)

We shall continue to emphasize temple work. The Lord has given us a great commission to perform vital ordinances for the living and the dead. (Statement upon becoming President of the Church, 11 November 1985.)

History

The first recorded revelation of this dispensation, section 2, given in 1823, described the great work for this dispensation: to seal living fathers to their families and progenitors. The Lord said that unless the sealing ordinances were performed, "the whole earth would be utterly wasted at his coming" (D&C 2:3). Steps have already been taken to expand the number of temples and to place them closer to the Saints. But we must do more. Wherever we have stakes, the ordinances of the temple should be available to our people without extensive travel or great financial sacrifice. (Salt Lake City, Utah, 6 June 1980.)

Seven hundred years before Christ, Isaiah prophesied that in the last days the Lord's house would be established in the tops of the mountains, and that the work of the Lord would proceed to the ends of the earth from the mountains (see Isaiah 2:2–3).

In the beginning of this dispensation, the Lord said "Zion shall flourish upon the hills and rejoice upon the mountains, and shall be assembled together unto the place which I have appointed" (D&C 49:25). Our assemblage today in these mountains beneath the shadow of the temple, hewn from the stone of these mountains, stands as a fulfillment of these prophecies. ("Zion Shall Flourish upon the Mountains," Days of '47 Committee Luncheon, Salt Lake City, Utah, 24 July 1982.)

We preside over the great redemptive work for the dead. Before the Savior can present this kingdom to His Father, all the descendants of Shem, Ham and Japheth who have not received the gospel in the flesh must have the opportunity to hear the gospel. That work is going forward on the other side of the veil with greater acceleration than it is here. Our work is to officiate in the temples of God for them. We don't build temples until the Church is well established in a country. Our predecessors have prophesied that temples will dot the landscape of North and South America, the isles of the Pacific, Europe, and elsewhere. If this redemptive work is to be done on the scale it must be, hundreds of temples will be needed. Our first step then is to see that nations are opened to receive the gospel so that stakes may be established. (Salt Lake City, Utah, 6 June 1980.)

The blessings and ordinances of the temple prepare one for exaltation. Of course, it is not possible for every stake to have a temple, but you are presently witnessing some remarkable, yes, miraculous developments in the building of temples in different parts of the world. Such a program permits members of the Church to receive the full blessings of the Lord. (Geneva Switzerland Stake Creation, 20 June 1982.)

I am very grateful to President McKay and the other members of the Presidency that Sister Benson and I were invited to attend that glorious dedication in Bern, Switzerland. I think I have never in all my life felt the veil quite so thin as it was three weeks ago this morning as we met in the opening session of that dedication service in that lovely spot in the house of the Lord and as we listened to the prayer offered by President McKay and the remarks which preceded that prayer. Surely he was inspired, and surely we were all uplifted and convinced beyond any shadow of a doubt that the action taken by the First Presidency in extending temples into Europe had the benediction and approval of our Heavenly Father. I shall never forget that glorious event! To me it was the most important event that has transpired in Europe since the gospel was first taken to those shores. I am grateful to the Lord that my official duties permitted me to attend that dedication, almost in a miraculous manner, because had it not been for the postponement of a week I probably would not have had the opportunity. I think, President McKay, that the postponement was in part an answer to my prayers. (CR October 1955, *Improvement Era* 58 [December 1955]: 950.)

Purpose

On the spire of this temple stands a bronze replica of an angelic messenger—Moroni—who came with a message from heaven. Quoting the Old Testament prophet Malachi, Moroni said:

> Behold I will reveal unto you the Priesthood, by the hand of Elijah the prophet, before the coming of the great and dreadful day of the Lord.
> And he shall plant in the hearts of the children the promises made to the fathers, and the hearts of the children shall turn to their fathers. If it were not so, the whole earth would be utterly wasted at his coming. (Joseph Smith—History 1:38–39.)

Temples are built and dedicated so that, through the priesthood, parents can be sealed to their children and children can be sealed to their parents. These sealing ordinances apply to both the living and the dead. If we fail to be sealed to our progenitors and our posterity, the purpose of this earth, man's exaltation, will be utterly wasted so far as we are concerned. (Jordan River Utah Temple Cornerstone Laying, 15 August 1981.)

It is not sufficient for a husband and wife to be sealed in the temple to guarantee their exaltation—if they are faithful—they must also be eternally linked with their progenitors and see that the work is done for those ancestors. "They without us," said the Apostle Paul, "cannot be made perfect—neither can we without our dead be made perfect" (D&C 128:15). Our members must therefore understand that they have an individual responsibility to see that they are linked to their progenitors—or, as sacred scripture designates, our "fathers." This is the meaning of section 2, verse 2, in the Doctrine and Covenants when Moroni declared that Elijah "shall plant in the hearts of the children the promises made to the fathers, and the hearts of the children shall turn to their fathers." (Salt Lake City, Utah, 6 May 1981.)

Ours is the privilege of opening the doors of salvation to those souls who may be imprisoned in darkness in the world of spirits, that they may receive the light of the gospel and be judged the same as we. Yes, "the works that I do"—proferring the saving ordinances of the gospel to others—"shall ye do also" (see John 14:12). How many thousands of our kindred yet await these sealing ordinances? It is well to ask, "Have I done all I can as an individual on this side of the veil? Will I be a savior to them—my own progenitors?" Without them, we cannot be made perfect! Exaltation is a family affair. (*Come unto Christ*, p. 126.)

Even though the Aaronic Priesthood and Melchizedek Priesthood had been restored to the earth, the Lord urged the Saints to build a temple to receive the keys by which this order of priesthood could be administered on the earth again, "for there [was] not a place found on earth that he may come to and restore again that which was lost . . . even the fulness of the priesthood" (D&C 124:28). Again the Prophet Joseph said: "If a man gets a fullness of the priesthood of God he has to get it in the same way that Jesus Christ obtained it, and that was by keeping all the commandments and obeying all the ordinances of the house of the Lord" (*Teachings of the Prophet Joseph Smith*, p. 308). ("What I Hope You Will Teach Your Children About the Temple," *Ensign* 15 [August 1985]: 10.)

We build temples because God has commanded us to do so. Early in the history of the Church in this dispensation, the Lord made known His displeasure toward the Saints for not building the temple at Kirtland in the time He allotted. (From address prepared [but not delivered] 1982.)

Today one more "holy place" is being prepared for dedication and for the sacred ordinances which will take place within its walls.

The Saints have been commanded to stand in holy places, such as this temple, in order to avoid the tribulations which are to come in the latter days. When the Savior walked this earth, He stated that there was no place to lay His head (see Matthew 8:20). He may have been referring to the fact that in His day there was no temple in the Holy Land which had not been desecrated. Today there are many dedicated temples, hallowed places where the Son of Man may come. (Jordan River Temple Cornerstone Laying, 15 August 1981.)

I think the temple is the most sacred spot on the earth. These are places to which the Savior will come. These are His houses. How do we know but what personages from the unseen world are here today? Perhaps prominent people who would have lived in this community in the past. President Harold B. Lee said to the missionaries in the Salt Lake Temple, "What more likely place is there for the Savior to come than to this temple?" ("Temple Memories," Ogden Utah Temple Dedication, 18 January 1972.)

We are a covenant-making people. The temple is one of the holy places in which the Savior commanded the faithful to stand. It is a holy place because it is a house of covenants. (Boise Idaho Temple Dedication, 25 May 1984.)

There are many Latter-day Saints who do not understand the nature of the obligations they are assuming in the temple. The late Elder George Q. Cannon said that young people go to the temple "with no particular desire, only to get married, without realizing the character of the obligations that they take upon themselves or the covenants that they make and the promises involved in the taking of these covenants. The result is that hundreds among us go to the house of the Lord and receive these blessings and come away without having any particular impression made upon them." (George Q. Cannon, *Gospel Truths*, 1:227–28.) What is said about the young people may be said today concerning some of the older ones as well. ("Temple Blessings and Covenants," Temple Presidents Seminar, Salt Lake City, Utah, 28 September 1982.)

The temple ceremony was given by a wise Heavenly Father to help us become more Christlike. The endowment was revealed by revelation and can be understood only by revelation. The instruction is given in symbolic language. The late Apostle John A. Widtsoe taught, "No man or woman can come out of the temple endowed as he should be, unless he has seen, beyond the symbol, the mighty realities for which the symbol stands" ("Temple Worship," address given in Salt Lake City, 12 October 1920). ("Lord, Increase Our Faith," Provo Utah Tabernacle Rededication, 21 September 1986.)

All the covenants we make in the temple are made before God. "With the taking of each covenant and the assuming of each obligation, a promised blessing is pronounced, contingent upon the faithful observance of the conditions" (Elder James E. Talmage, *The House of the Lord*, p. 84).

In the course of our visits to the temple, we are given insights into the meaning of the eternal journey of man. We see beautiful and impressive symbolisms of the most important events—past, present, and future—symbolizing man's mission in relationship to God. We are reminded of our obligations as we make solemn covenants pertaining to obedience, consecration, sacrifice, and dedicated service to our Heavenly Father. ("Temple Blessings and Covenants," Temple Presidents Seminar, Salt Lake City, Utah, 28 September 1982.)

In the peace of these lovely temples, sometimes we find solutions to the serious problems of life. Under the influence of the Spirit, sometimes pure knowledge flows to us there. Temples are places of personal revelation. When I have been weighed down by a problem or a difficulty, I have gone to the house of the Lord with a prayer in my heart for answers. These answers have come in clear and unmistakable ways.

I would like to direct my remarks to you parents and grandparents. I would like to share with you what I would hope you would teach your children about the temple. The temple is a sacred place, and the ordinances in the temple are of a sacred character. Because of its sacredness we are sometimes reluctant to say anything about the temple to our children and grandchildren. As a consequence, many do not develop a real desire to go to the temple, or when they go there, they do so without much background to prepare them for the obligations and covenants they enter into.

I believe a proper understanding or background will immeasurably help prepare our youth for the temple. This understanding, I believe, will foster within them a desire to seek their priesthood blessings just as Abraham sought his. ("What I Hope You Will Teach Your Children About the Temple," *Ensign* 15 [August 1985]: 8.)

Jesus described the temple as "a house of order" (D&C 132:8). Temples of God are houses of order, because only in this holy place may a man and a woman enter the new and everlasting covenant of marriage (D&C 131:2). After its dedication, this temple becomes our Heavenly Father's house—a house of order, a house of sacred ordinances, a house of prayer.

This temple will be a constant, visible symbol that God has not left man to grope in darkness. It is a place of revelation. Though we live in a fallen world—a wicked world—holy places are set apart and consecrated so that worthy men and women can learn the order of heaven and obey God's will.

We will not be able to dwell in the company of celestial beings unless we are pure and holy. The laws and ordinances which cause men and women to come out of the world and become sanctified are administered only in these holy places. They were given by revelation and are comprehended by revelation. It is for this reason that one of the Brethren has referred to the temple as the "university of the Lord." (Atlanta Georgia Temple Cornerstone Laying, 1 June 1983.)

If our children—and their children—are taught well by us, this temple will have special significance. It will be an ever-present reminder that God intends the family to be eternal. (Chicago Illinois Temple Cornerstone Laying, 9 August 1985.)

No member of the Church can be perfected without the ordinances of the temple. We have a mission to assist those who do not have these blessings to receive them. ("Our Duty as Latter-day Saints," Springfield-Burke Virginia Chapel Dedication, 15 October 1982.)

The work we are performing here has direct relationship to the work over there. Someday you will know that there are ordinances performed over there, too, in order to make the vicarious work which you do effective. It will all be done under the authority and power of the priesthood of God. (Sao Paulo Brazil Temple, 26 February 1979.)

The Lord has accepted your temple labors and has blessed you and will continue to bless you. You have made investments here that will never turn sour. You have laid up treasures in heaven where moth and rust will not corrupt and where thieves will not break through to steal; and where your treasure is, there will your heart be also (see Matthew 6:20). The Lord's great program moves forward on both sides of the wall. (Mesa Arizona Temple Rededication, 16 April 1975.)

The veil is very thin. We are living in eternity. All is as with one day with God. I imagine that to the Lord there is no veil. It is all one great program. I am sure there is rejoicing in heaven as we meet here today. Our progenitors are rejoicing, and my hope and prayer is that we will take advantage of the opportunities now afforded us to come regularly to the temple. ("Temple Memories," Ogden Utah Temple Dedication, 18 January 1972.)

Blessings

I love the temples of God. This is the closest place to heaven on earth—the house of the Lord. I have been blessed to be associated with temples from my boyhood. I hope and pray that all the rest of my life, short or long, I will have the privilege of going into the temple. My eternal companion feels the same way. Sister Benson is also in the temple each Thursday while we meet in the house of the Lord as the Council of the Twelve, from eight to ten o'clock, followed by a meeting with the First Presidency from ten until we get through (usually one to three o'clock). Our youngest daughter and her husband, both temple ordinance workers, have arranged their schedules so they can take Sister Benson and go in the temple to do endowment work while I am in the temple with the First Presidency and the Twelve. It has been a great blessing for all of us and I appreciate it deeply. (Sao Paulo Brazil Temple, 26 February 1979.)

With the coming of the temples, with the material restoration that has come to those European countries, and with what I hope is a deepened interest in spiritual matters—to which the temple will contribute in great measure—I hope too there will be a great increased interest in things spiritual, that those nations might be preserved in peace.

May God bless those wonderful people who will be recipients of the blessings of the temple, provided they prepare themselves for those blessings by living the gospel. And I sincerely hope and pray that not only they, but also all of us everywhere, will make that preparation that we may enjoy the richest blessings known to men and women in this world which are tied up with the sacred ordinances and blessings of the temples of God. While I recognize that there are many Saints who are still isolated and who will be unable, probably, to reach the temples, this movement in Europe which I am sure was made under inspiration will bring the temples closer to many thousands of our Father's children.

To those who are still isolated from temples may I say this: In my humble judgment if you continue to live the gospel and keep the commandments, and keep yourselves pure and unspotted from the world, the Lord will in some way make up to you that which your lives merit. (CR October 1955, *Improvement Era* 58 [December 1955]: 950, 952.)

Now let me say something to all who can worthily go to the house of the Lord. When you attend the temple and perform the ordinances that pertain to the house of the Lord, certain blessings will come to you: You will receive the spirit of Elijah, which will turn your hearts to your spouse, to your children, and to your forebears. You will love your family with a deeper love than you have loved before. You will be endowed with power from on high as the Lord has promised.

You will receive the key of the knowledge of God (see D&C 84:19). You will learn how you can be like Him. Even the power of godliness will be manifest to you (see D&C 84:20). You will be doing a great service to those who have passed to the other side of the veil in order that they might be "judged according to men in the flesh, but live according to God in the spirit" (D&C 138:34; 1 Peter 4:6). Such are the blessings of the temple and the blessings of frequently attending the temple. ("What I Hope You Will Teach Your Children About the Temple," *Ensign* 15 [August 1985]: 10.)

We should seek for the blessings and ordinances of the temple. This means that we are keeping the commandments of the Lord—honesty, integrity, personal chastity—and sustaining the Lord's priesthood leadership, and are worthy to be ordained to the Melchizedek Priesthood. ("Our Duty as Latter-day Saints," Springfield-Burke Virginia Chapel Dedication, 15 October 1982.)

We appreciate that some married couples have not realized the importance of the temple ordinances. Some of these members are not engaged in Church activity. As brothers and sisters in full fellowship of the Church, we have a responsibility to encourage them to full activity and then, by assignment of quorum leaders, to prepare them for the ordinances of the temple. ("Our Duty as Latter-day Saints," Springfield-Burke Virginia Chapel Dedication, 15 October 1982.)

I am grateful to see young adults go into the house of the Lord to be married for time and eternity; to see grandchildren born under the covenant. No richer blessings can come to us. The blessings of the house of the Lord are eternal. They are of the highest importance to us because it is in the temples that we obtain God's greatest blessings pertaining to eternal life. Temples are really the gateways to heaven. ("Temple Blessings and Covenants," Temple Presidents Seminar, Salt Lake City, Utah, 28 September 1982.)

I am grateful for the weekly temple sessions that Sister Benson and I enjoy together. The temple is the house of the Lord. Our attendance there blesses the dead and also blesses us, for it is a house of revelation. (CR April 1986, *Ensign* 16 [May 1986]: 78.)

I thank the Lord for the temples and for the sacred ordinances performed therein and the sweet spirit which is always prevalent in the house of the Lord. I love the temples of God and thank the Lord that we are building more and more of them. (Sao Paulo Brazil Temple, 26 February 1979.)

Is it not significant to you that today the Saints are scattered over the face of the world and, in their scattered situation, temples are being provided for them? By the ordinances that they receive in holy places, they will be armed with righteousness and endowed with the power of God in great measure. (From address prepared [but not delivered] 1982.)

Sometimes we live almost under the eaves, in the shade of the temple, and fail to take advantage of the priceless blessings that are available to us in the house of the Lord. The richest blessings of this life and of eternity are tied up with these sacred ordinances. (CR October 1952, *Improvement Era* 55 [December 1952]: 942.)

Let us make the temple a sacred home away from our eternal home. This temple will be a standing witness that the power of God can stay the powers of evil in our midst. Many parents, in and out of the Church, are concerned about protection against a cascading avalanche of wickedness which threatens to engulf Christian principles. I find myself in complete accord with a statement made by President Harold B. Lee during World War II. Said he: "We talk about security in this day, and yet we fail to understand that . . . we have standing the holy temple wherein we may find the symbols by which power might be generated that will save this nation from destruction" (CR April 1942, p. 87).

Yes, there is a power associated with the ordinances of heaven—even the power of godliness—which can and will thwart the forces of evil if we will be worthy of those sacred blessings. This community will be protected, our families will be protected, our children will be safeguarded as we live the gospel, visit the temple, and live close to the Lord. This temple will be a light to all in this area—a symbol of all we hold dear. It will be an inspiration not only to Latter-day Saints, but to many others as well. God bless us as Saints to live worthy of the covenants and ordinances made in this sacred place. May it be a constant reminder that life is eternal and that covenants made by us in mortality can be everlasting. (Atlanta Georgia Temple Cornerstone Laying, 1 June 1983.)

God bless Israel! God bless those of our forebears who constructed this holy edifice. God bless us to teach our children and our grandchildren what great blessings await them by going to the temple. God bless us to receive all the blessings revealed by Elijah the prophet so that our callings and election will be made sure. ("What I Hope You Will Teach Your Children About the Temple," *Ensign* 15 [August 1985]: 10.)

Sealings

How did Adam bring his descendants into the presence of the Lord? The answer: Adam and his descendants entered into the priesthood order of God. Today we would say they went to the house of the Lord and received their blessings. The order of priesthood spoken of in the scriptures is sometimes referred to as the patriarchal order because it came down from father to son. But this order is otherwise described in modern revelation as an order of family government wherein a man and woman enter into a covenant with God—just as did Adam and Eve—to be sealed for eternity, to have posterity, and to do the will and work of God throughout their mortality.

If a couple are true to their covenants, they are entitled to the blessing of the highest degree of the celestial kingdom. These covenants today can only be entered into by going to the house of the Lord. Adam followed this order and brought his posterity into the presence of God. He is the great example to follow. When our children obey the Lord and go to the temple to receive their blessings and enter into the marriage covenant, they enter into the same order of the priesthood that God instituted in the beginning with father Adam.

This order of priesthood can only be entered into when we comply with all the commandments of God and seek the blessings of the fathers as did Abraham by going to our Father's house. They are received in no other place on this earth! Our Father's house is a house of order. We go to His house to enter into that order of priesthood which will entitle us to all that the Father hath, if we are faithful. For as the Lord has revealed in modern times, Abraham's seed are "lawful heirs" to the priesthood (see D&C 86:8–11). ("What I Hope You Will Teach Your Children About the Temple," *Ensign* 15 [August 1985]: 9–10.)

The Kirtland Temple was completed at great sacrifice to the Saints. On 3 April 1836, the Lord Jesus Christ and three other heavenly beings appeared in this holy edifice (see D&C 110). One of these heavenly messengers was Elijah, to whom the Lord said He had "committed the keys of the power of turning the hearts of the fathers to the children, and the hearts of the children to the fathers, that the whole earth may not be smitten with a curse" (D&C 27:9).

Elijah brought the keys of sealing powers — that power which seals a man to a woman and seals their posterity to them endlessly, that which seals their forefathers to them all the way back to Adam. This is the power and order that Elijah revealed — that same order of priesthood which God gave to Adam and to all the ancient patriarchs which followed after him. ("What I Hope You Will Teach Your Children About the Temple," *Ensign* 15 [August 1985]: 10.)

The temple will be an ever-present reminder that God intended the family to be eternal. How fitting it will be for mothers and fathers to point to this temple and say, "That is the place where your mother (or father) and I were married for eternity." By so doing, they will instill within the minds and hearts of their children, while very young, the ideal of temple marriage. ("Latter-day Temples: Beacons to a Darkened World," Jordan River Utah Temple Groundbreaking, 9 June 1979.)

When your children ask why we marry in the temple, you should teach them that temples are the only places on the earth where certain ordinances may be performed. You should also share with your children your personal feelings as you knelt together before the sacred altar and took upon yourselves covenants which made it possible for them to be sealed to you forever. (Chicago Illinois Temple Cornerstone Laying, 9 August 1985.)

I make it a practice, whenever I perform a marriage, to suggest to the young couple that they return to the temple as soon as they can and go through the temple again as husband and wife. It isn't possible for them to understand fully the meaning of the holy endowment or the sealings with one trip through the temple, but as they repeat their visits to the temple, the beauty, the significance, and the importance of it all will be emphasized upon them. I have later had letters from some of these young couples expressing appreciation because that item was emphasized particularly. As they repeat their visits to the temple, their love for each other tends to increase and their marriage tends to be strengthened. (*God, Family, Country*, p. 183.)

I received a telephone call from a bishop in Ogden who said to me, "Elder Benson, do you think you could spend one night for our good ward?'' I told him I would like to. I told him that ''there are only some four thousand wards in the Church'' and that ''yours must be one of the best.'' He said, ''We have five wonderful men in our ward, and we have been working with them for about two years. They all have families and have just received the Melchizedek Priesthood and were ordained elders.'' He said, ''We want to bring them to Salt Lake and have you meet us in one of the sealing rooms of the temple and perform the sealings of wives to husbands and children to parents.'' I was happy to comply with his request and I spent one of the happiest evenings of my life in a sealing room in the Salt Lake Temple. All of these parents had children with them. One couple had nine children, all under eighteen years of age. I think I shall never forget that mother. She was so filled with emotion she could hardly control herself. Finally when the work was all done and the people were leaving the sealing room, she apologized to me and said, ''You will have to forgive me for the way I have acted tonight, but I have waited nineteen years for this moment.'' She further said, ''All during those nineteen years, I have prayed to God night and morning that the time would come when my husband would be counted worthy to receive the Melchizedek Priesthood and be worthy to bring me and the children to the house of the Lord.'' She said, ''Tonight my prayers have been answered.''

I do not suppose it is possible for us to realize her joy, but I daresay that in this temple district this very day, there are mothers and wives in a similar condition hoping and praying the time will soon come when their husbands will be able to receive the holy priesthood and bring them to the house of the Lord and there experience the richest blessings known to men and women in this world. (''Temple Memories,'' Ogden Utah Temple Dedication, 18 January 1972.)

The Lord's desire is for every adult man and woman in the Church to receive the ordinances of the temple. This means that they are to be endowed and that all married couples are to be sealed for eternity. These ordinances provide a protection and blessing to their marriage. Their children also are blessed to be born in the covenant. Birth in the covenant entitles those children to a birthright blessing which guarantees them eternal parentage regardless of what happens to the parents, so long as the children remain worthy of the blessings. (See *General Handbook of In-*

structions, p. 62.) ("Our Duty as Latter-day Saints," Springfield-Burke Virginia Chapel Dedication, 15 October 1982.)

Thank the Lord we have a temple in this land where our marriages may be sealed! All the young people should qualify and plan to be married in the house of God. Rich blessings will come as we make covenants and ponder eternal truths. The temple is the nearest place to heaven on mortal earth.

May the Lord bless us to understand the covenants we make in the temple. May He also instill these laws in the hearts of our posterity so they will live as covenant children of God. May we be a covenant-keeping people. May virtue and holiness abound in our lives, homes, and community. (Boise Idaho Temple Dedication, 25 May 1984.)

Welfare

The Lord is not unmindful of the temporal salvation of His Saints. Some of us saw the welfare program developed from its inception. The full purpose and intent of this inspired program has hardly been realized, and when we have passed through some of the tribulations that are in store for the world, we will see that this inspired plan was necessary to bring the Church to a condition of independence. The Church must become independent of the world — or, in other words, wholly self-sufficient. I quote from the revelation which established the united order in the early days of the Church, a revelation still awaiting fulfillment:

> For verily I say unto you, the time has come, and is now at hand; and behold, and lo, it must needs be that there be an organization of my people, in regulating and establishing the affairs of the storehouse of the poor of my people, both in this place and in the land of Zion —
> That through my providence, notwithstanding the tribulation which shall descend upon you, that the church may stand independent above all other creatures beneath the celestial world;
> That you may come up unto the crown prepared for you, and be made rulers over many kingdoms. (D&C 78:3, 14–15.)

Apparently, there will be certain tribulations that will disrupt the nations of the world to the extent that the Church will have to be self-reliant. (Salt Lake City, Utah, 6 June 1980.)

We must "dedicate our strength to serving the needs, rather than the fears, of the world," while realizing we can't possibly feed the world. I believe errands of mercy, such as the distribution of food, housing, and clothing to those in need, are rendered most effectively when handled by private individuals and organizations such as the Church. I was responsible for distributing thousands of tons of supplies from the Mormon welfare program to European refugees and war victims after the Second World War, and like my fellow Mormons I have fasted for twenty-four hours each month ever since I was a boy and given the money I would have spent for the food to assist any poor in the Church, thus benefiting the giver as well as the receiver. (*Crossfire: The Eight Years with Eisenhower*, pp. 579–80.)

The Church storehouse system is an organization of physical warehouses and transportation facilities, with operating and managing personnel. This system is set up to receive, store, transport, exchange, and distribute food and nonfood commodities to those in need. A fundamental unit of the Church storehouse system is the local bishops storehouse. Bishops storehouses are Church-owned facilities from which local bishops obtain food, clothing, and other commodities to care for the poor and needy who are unable to care for themselves. Deseret Industries are used as storehouses to provide nonfood commodities. Each bishop in the Church should have access to a local storehouse stocked with essential commodities produced in the program to meet the needs of his people.

The Lord, by revelation, has commanded that storehouses be established. The surpluses, or "residue," from the consecrated properties under the united order were to be kept in the storehouses "to administer to the poor and the needy" (D&C 42:34). Later, the Lord instructed the Presiding Bishop to "appoint a storehouse unto this church; and let all things both in money and in [food], which are more than is needful for the wants of this people, be kept in the hands of the bishop." (D&C 51:13.) (CR April 1977, *Ensign* 7 [May 1977]: 82.)

Unfortunately, there has been fostered in the minds of some an expectation that when we experience hard times, when we have been unwise and extravagant with our resources and have lived beyond our means, we should look to either the Church or government to bail us out. Forgotten by some of our members is an underlying principle of the Church welfare plan that "no true Latter-day Saint will, while physically able, voluntarily shift from himself the burden of his own support" (Marion G. Romney, in CR October 1973, p. 106). (CR October 1980, *Ensign* 10 [November 1980]: 32.)

A letter came to my office, accompanied by an article from the Brigham Young University *Daily Universe*, on the matter of BYU students taking food stamps. The query of the letter was: "What is the attitude of the Church on taking food stamps?" The Church's view on this is well known. We stand for independence, thrift, and abolition of the dole. "The aim of the Church is to help the people to help themselves. Work is to be re-enthroned as the ruling principle of the lives of our Church membership." (Heber J. Grant, CR October 1936, p. 3.)

When you accept food stamps, you accept an unearned handout that other working people are paying for. You do not earn food stamps or welfare payments. Every individual who accepts an unearned government gratuity is just as culpable as the individual who takes a handout from taxpayers' money to pay his heat, electricity, or rent. There is no difference in principle between them. You did not come to this university to become a welfare recipient. You came here to be a light to the world, a light to society—to save society and to help to save this nation, the Lord's base of operations in these last days—to ameliorate man's social conditions. You are not here to be a parasite or freeloader. The price you pay for "something for nothing" may be more than you can afford. Do not rationalize your acceptance of government gratuities by saying, "I am a contributing taxpayer too." By doing this you contribute to the problem which is leading this nation to financial insolvency. ("A Vision and a Hope for the Youth of Zion," in *1977 Devotional Speeches of the Year* [Provo, Utah: BYU, 1978], p. 78.)

I would respectfully urge you to live by the fundamental principles of work, thrift, and self-reliance, and to teach your children by your example. It was never intended in God's divine plan that man should live off the labor of someone else. Live within your own earnings. Put a portion of those earnings regularly into savings. Avoid unnecessary debt. Be wise by not trying to expand too rapidly. Learn to manage well what you have before you think of expanding further. This is the kind of advice I would give my own, and is, in my opinion, the key to sound home, business, and government management.

I would further counsel you to pay your honest tithes and contribute generously to the support of the poor and needy through the fast offerings. Then store at least a year's supply of basic food, clothing, and fuel. Then you will find these blessings will accrue: You will not be confronted with the danger of losing all you have because of inflation or depression. You will have security that no government can provide—savings and supplies for emergencies. ("The Ten Commandments," *New Era* 8 [July 1978]: 39.)

Americans have always been committed to taking care of the poor, aged, and unemployed. We have done this on the basis of Judaic-Christian beliefs and humanitarian principles. It has been fundamental to our way of life that charity must be voluntary if it is to be charity. Compulsory benevolence is not charity. Today's egalitarians are using the federal government to redistribute wealth in our society, not as a matter of voluntary charity, but as a matter of right. (*This Nation Shall Endure*, p. 91.)

The principles of self-help are economically, socially, and spiritually sound. The Lord will not do for us what we can and should do for ourselves. But it is the Lord's purpose to take care of His Saints (D&C 104:15). Everything that concerns the economic, social, and spiritual welfare of the human family is and ever will be the concern of The Church of Jesus Christ of Latter-day Saints. (*So Shall Ye Reap*, pp. 278–79.)

Preparedness

Not only should we have strong spiritual homes, but we should have strong temporal homes. We should avoid bondage by getting out of debt as soon as we can, pay as we go, and live within our incomes. There is wisdom in having on hand a year's supply of food, clothing, fuel (if possible), and in being prepared to defend our families and our possessions and to take care of ourselves. I believe a man should prepare for the worst while working for the best. Some people prepare and don't work, while others work but don't prepare. Both are needed if we would be of maximum service to our God, our family, and our country. (*God, Family, Country*, p. 405.)

We must do more to get our people prepared for the difficult days we face in the future. Our major concern should be their spiritual preparation so they will respond with faith and not fear. "If ye are prepared, ye shall not fear" (D&C 38:21). Our next concern should be for their temporal preparation. When the economies of nations fail, when famine and other disasters prevent people from buying food in stores, the Saints must be prepared to handle these emergencies. This is a matter of concern for area, region, and stake councils. (Salt Lake City, Utah, 6 June 1980.)

Now is the time to prepare. I am not talking only of physical commodities, important though those are. I am talking about faith, devotion, dedication, love of God, the willingness to heed the counsel of the leadership of this Church; men and women who are willing to put their all on the altar, who are doing their duty as fathers and mothers, husbands and wives, who have the strength to live in the world and not partake of the sins of the world. Sometimes there are emergencies, but there is no emergency that will take a mother away from little children if they are faithful members of this Church, because the Church stands back of every faithful mother and father and will come to their aid in time of need if they are living the gospel and participating in the great welfare program of the Church. The Lord does not give commandments except He prepares a way that we can keep those commandments (see 1 Nephi 3:7). (Grantsville Utah Stake Conference, 1 September 1974.)

A man should not only be prepared to protect himself physically, but he should also have on hand sufficient supplies to sustain himself and his family in an emergency. For many years the leaders of the Mormon Church have recommended, with instructions, that every family have on hand at least a year's supply of basic food, clothing, fuel (where possible), and provisions for shelter. This has been most helpful to families suffering temporary reverses. It can and will be useful in many circumstances in the days ahead. We also need to get out of financial bondage, to be debt-free. (*God, Family, Country*, p. 331.)

For years we have been counseled to have on hand a year's supply of food. Yet there are some today who will not start storing until the Church comes out with a detailed monthly home storage program. Now, suppose that never happens. We still cannot say we have not been warned.

Should the Lord decide at this time to cleanse the Church —and the need for that cleansing seems to be increasing—a famine in this land of one year's duration could wipe out a large percentage of slothful members, including some ward and stake officers. Yet we cannot say we have not been warned. (*God, Family, Country*, p. 383.)

You do not need to go into debt to obtain a year's supply. Plan to build up your food supply just as you would a savings account. Save a little for storage each paycheck. Can or bottle fruit and vegetables from your gardens and orchards. Learn how to preserve food through drying and possibly freezing. Make your storage a part of your budget. Store seeds and have sufficient tools on hand to do the job. If you are saving and planning for a second car or a television set or some item which merely adds to your comfort or pleasure, you may need to change your priorities. We urge you to do this prayerfully and do it now. I speak with a feeling of great urgency. (CR October 1980, *Ensign* 10 [November 1980]: 33.)

Some have rationalized that they have no time or space. May I suggest you do what others have done. Get together with others and seek permission to use a vacant lot for a garden, or rent a plot of ground and grow your gardens. Some elders quorums have done this as a quorum, and all who have participated have reaped the benefits of a vegetable and fruit harvest and the blessings of cooperation and family involvement. Many families have dug up lawn space for gardens. (CR October 1980, *Ensign* 10 [November 1980]: 32–33.)

An almost forgotten means of economic self-reliance is the home production of food. We are too accustomed to going to stores and purchasing what we need. By producing some of our food we reduce, to a great extent, the impact of inflation on our money. More importantly, we learn how to produce our own food and involve all family members in a beneficial project. (CR October 1980, *Ensign* 10 [November 1980]: 32.)

There are blessings in being close to the soil, in raising your own food, even if it is only a garden in your yard and a fruit tree or two. Those families will be fortunate who, in the last days, have an adequate supply of food because of their foresight and ability to produce their own. (CR October 1980, *Ensign* 10 [November 1980]: 33.)

"There is more salvation and security in wheat," said Orson Hyde years ago, "than in all the political schemes of the world" (*Journal of Discourses*, 2:207). The revelation to produce and store food may be as essential to our temporal welfare today as boarding the ark was to the people in the days of Noah. (CR October 1980, *Ensign* 10 [November 1980]: 33.)

As to the foodstuffs which should be stored, the Church has left that decision primarily to the individual members. Some excellent suggestions are available from the Church Welfare Committee. "All grain is good for the food of man" (D&C 89:16), the Lord states, but He particularly singles out wheat. Dry, whole, hard grains, when stored properly, can last indefinitely, and their nutritional value can be enhanced through sprouting, if desired. (*God, Family, Country*, p. 268.)

From the standpoint of food production, storage, handling, and the Lord's counsel, wheat should have high priority. Water, of course, is essential. Other basics could include honey or sugar, legumes, milk products or substitutes, and salt or its equivalent. (*God, Family, Country*, p. 269.)

Wood, coal, gas, oil, kerosene, and even candles are among those items which could be reserved as fuel for warmth, cooking, and light or power. Some may be used for all of these purposes and certain ones would have to be stored and handled cautiously. It would also be well to have on hand some basic medical supplies to last for at least a year. (*God, Family, Country*, p. 270.)

Food production is just one part of the repeated emphasis that you store a provision of food which will last for at least a year wherever it is legally permissible to do so. The Church has not told you what foods should be stored. This decision is left up to individual members. (CR October 1980, *Ensign* 10 [November 1980]: 33.)

Let us be in a position so we are able to not only feed ourselves through the home production and storage, but others as well. (CR October 1980, *Ensign* 10 [November 1980]: 34.)

Our bishops storehouses are not intended to stock enough commodities to care for all the members of the Church. Storehouses are only established to care for the poor and the needy. For this reason, members of the Church have been instructed to personally store a year's supply of food, clothing, and, where possible, fuel. By following this counsel, most members will be prepared and able to care for themselves and their family members, and be able to share with others as may be needed. (CR April 1977, *Ensign* 7 [May 1977]: 82.)

The times require that every officer of the Church be uniformly trained in principles of welfare, and that each one in turn train the rank and file until every individual is prepared for the calamities which are to come. I think it not extreme for me to say at this point that when all is written about the events to come, we may have hardly enough time to prepare, even if all our resources, spiritual and temporal, are taxed to the limit. ("The Training Challenge," General Welfare Services Committee, Salt Lake City, Utah, 2 February 1977.)

More than ever before, we need to learn and apply the principles of economic self-reliance. We do not know when a crisis involving sickness or unemployment may affect our own circumstances. We do know that the Lord has decreed global calamities for the future and has warned and forewarned us to be prepared. For this reason the Brethren have repeatedly stressed a "back to basics" program for temporal and spiritual welfare. (CR October 1980, *Ensign* 10 [November 1980]: 32.)

The Saints have been advised to pay their own way and maintain a cash reserve. Recent history has demonstrated that in difficult days it is reserves with intrinsic value that are of most worth, rather than reserves the value of which may be destroyed through inflation. It is well to remember that continued government deficits cause inflation; inflation is used as an excuse for ineffective price controls; price controls lead to shortages; artificial shortages inevitably are used as an excuse to implement rationing. When will we learn these basic economic principles?

"When we really get into hard times," said President J. Reuben Clark, Jr., "where food is scarce or there is none at all, and so with clothing and shelter, money may be no good for there may be nothing to buy, and you cannot eat money, you cannot get enough of it together to burn to keep warm, and you cannot wear it." (*Church News* [21 November 1953]: 4.)

The strength of the Church welfare program lies in every family following the inspired direction of the Church leaders to be self-sustaining through adequate preparation. God intends for His Saints to so prepare themselves "that the church may stand independent above all other creatures beneath the celestial world" (D&C 78:14). (*God, Family, Country*, pp. 270–71.)

PART 3

THE GOSPEL
IN OUR LIVES

THE GOSPEL
IN OUR LIVES

Brotherhood

There is a real spirit of brotherhood and fellowship in the Church. It is a very powerful thing, somewhat intangible but very real. I feel it, as do my associates, as we travel throughout the stakes and wards of Zion and throughout the missions of the earth. It matters not where we go. We may meet in a group with the priesthood in one of the stakes or out in one of the missions, but there is always that feeling of fellowship and brotherhood. It is one of the sweet things in connection with membership in the Church and kingdom of God. I have felt it way up in Alaska as I met with our brethren and sisters there. I felt it far up in East Prussia, throughout the missions of Europe, down in Mexico, in some of the islands of the sea, and throughout this land of Zion. It is very real. Oh, I know, my brethren and sisters, it isn't what it should be; it isn't what it could be; it isn't what the Lord would have it be, but nevertheless, there is nothing like it in all the world. It is one of the marks of the divinity of this great latter-day work, and I rejoice in it. (*So Shall Ye Reap*, p. 56.)

The basic goodness in man's nature stems from the spiritual truth that all men — every man, woman, and child on earth — share a common paternity. It is my belief that we are all literal brothers and sisters, not only by blood relationship from our mortal parentage, but as literal children of one Eternal Creator.

Believing as I do in this spiritual precept, my faith declares that the great religious leaders of the world such as Mohammed, Confucius, and the Reformers, as well as the philosophers — Socrates and others—received a portion of God's light. Moral truths were given to them by God to enlighten whole nations and to bring a higher level of understanding to individuals. ("A Spiritual Approach to Man-made Problems," Brigham Young University—Hawaii, 11 February 1983.)

From my extensive travels I am confident that the people of this world desire peace. They desire to live in a spirit of brotherhood. And we are all brothers and sisters, children of the same Father in spirit, and there is a spirit of brotherhood among the rank and file people. I find it everywhere I go—in the Christian world and outside.

People are much the same. They love their families, they love their homes, they love freedom, they desire freedom, they pray for freedom. They want to raise their standards of living, they want to enjoy the good things of life, and they want to live in peace with their neighbors regardless of race or creed or nationality. This longing for peace and for brotherhood is true throughout the world. And if the leaders of this world will respond to the will of the people, this world will be at peace. I know this as I know that I live. ("Free Agency," Washington D.C. Stake Conference, 22 May 1960.)

The gospel knows no national boundaries; it knows no race or color. The gospel is a great brotherhood, a brotherhood and a spirit of fellowship that is stronger than death, that reaches across borders, between nations. (*So Shall Ye Reap*, pp. 83–84.)

We are all brothers and sisters born of the same Father in the spirit. The scriptures tell us that God has made of one blood all nations and they dwell upon the face of the earth (see Acts 17:26). (Tokyo, Japan, 27 October 1957.)

Do we sometimes regard human brotherhood as a pretty theory rather than as a divine fact? Have we truly learned the lesson that man to man we must act not as enemies, not just as acquaintances, not even as mere friends—but as brothers? (*So Shall Ye Reap*, p. 7.)

Why is faith in God an imperative value to society? Because without it there is no validity to the concept of the brotherhood of man. Without faith in God and belief in divine immutable laws that enhance our relationships with one another, the values of honesty, integrity, and respect for life, property, and possessions of others would be meaningless; to love one's neighbor as oneself would be a mere platitude. ("The Values by Which to Live," *Leaders* [October 1984]: 152.)

Our role is to sustain each other. If you have a disagreement, go to the other brother and work it out or keep it to yourself. Do not discuss it with others first. (Salt Lake City, Utah, 2 October 1985.)

I am very grateful for the spirit of brotherhood and fellowship which we find in the Church. This spirit is a somewhat intangible thing. It is difficult to describe. But it is real—powerful—sweet. (CR April 1958, *Improvement Era* 61 [June 1958]: 433.)

Perhaps never in history has the need for cooperation, understanding, and goodwill among all people—nations and individuals alike—been so urgent as today. It is not only fitting—it is imperative—that we emphasize the ideal of brotherhood, and the reality of brotherhood, and the responsibility that the fact of human brotherhood confers upon us all. (*Title of Liberty*, p. 140.)

To those who are lonely, we extend the hand of friendship and fellowship. We invite you to become one with us in worship and in the service of the Master. ("First Presidency—Christmas Message" *Church News* [15 December 1985]: 3.)

Ideally, our family ought to be our closest friends. Most important, we should seek to become the friend of our Father in Heaven and our brother Jesus the Christ. What a boon to be in the company of those who edify us. To have friends, one should be friendly (see Proverbs 18:24). Friendship should begin at home and then be extended to encompass the home teacher, quorum leader, bishop, and other Church teachers and leaders. To meet often with the Saints and enjoy their companionship can buoy up the heart. ("Do Not Despair," *Ensign* 16 [October 1986]: 4.)

The fellowship of true friends who can hear you out, share your joys, help carry your burdens, and correctly counsel you is priceless. For one who has been in the prison of depression, the words of the Prophet Joseph Smith have special meaning: "How sweet the voice of a friend is; one token of friendship from any source whatever awakens and calls into action every sympathetic feeling" (*Teachings of the Prophet Joseph Smith*, p. 134). ("Do Not Despair," *Ensign* 16 [October 1986]: 4.)

We will never be effective until we learn to have sympathy for all our Father's children—until we learn to love them. People can feel when love is extended to them. Many yearn for it. When we sympathize with their feelings, they in turn will reciprocate good-will to us. We will have made a friend. As the Prophet Joseph Smith taught, "Whom can I preach to but my friends?" (*Come unto Christ*, p. 96.)

Character

The greatest work in all the world is the building of men and women of character. Without character there is not much that is worthwhile. The greatest activity of our Heavenly Father is the saving and exaltation of all His children. (*An Enemy Hath Done This*, p. 299.)

Youth of America, let us remember that character is today, as it always has been, the hope of our nation and of the world. It takes character to adhere to sound economic, social, and moral principles. (*The Red Carpet,* p. 280.)

We all recognize religion as the basis of true character-building, for which the world is starving. (*God, Family, Country*, p. 311.)

Throughout my life, it has been my privilege to associate with many of our Father's children, those of high and those of humble station. I have known men and women of great character. They were great because they were without compromise in their own life. I have also known men of great reputation who were without strong character. They were individuals of compromise in their private lives, and so they became expedient in their public trust.

Because our Heavenly Father foreknew that His children would have different degrees of character strength during their probationary state, He determined before the earth was formed that there would be degrees of reward. (See D&C 76; 88:22–24.) ("Be True to God, Country, and Self," Young Adult Fireside, Logan, Utah, 11 February 1979.)

We have here a priceless legacy—a legacy based on the solid truth that character is the one thing we develop in this world which we take with us into the next. This is a heritage that one cannot buy. It is a fountain of continuing strength for coping successfully with life's problems. (*So Shall Ye Reap*, p. 306.)

Thoughts lead to acts, acts lead to habits, habits lead to character—and our character will determine our eternal destiny. (*Come unto Christ*, p. 39.)

Charity and Love

The final and crowning virtue of the divine character is charity, or the pure love of Christ (see Moroni 7:47). If we would truly seek to be more like our Savior and Master, learning to love as He loves should be our highest goal. Mormon called charity "the greatest of all" (Moroni 7:46).

The world today speaks a great deal about love, and it is sought for by many. But the pure love of Christ differs greatly from what the world thinks of love. Charity never seeks selfish gratification. The pure love of Christ seeks only the eternal growth and joy of others. (CR October 1986, *Ensign* 16 [November 1986]: 47.)

The Lord Jesus Christ liberated man from the world by the pure gospel of love. He demonstrated that man, through the love of God and through kindness and charity to His fellows, could achieve His highest potential. He lived the plain and sure doctrine of service, of doing good to all men—friends and enemies alike. (CR April 1964, *Improvement Era* 67 [June 1964]: 504.)

I wish so much that I might speak to you in your own language, but I feel sure that we shall understand one another, because there is a language more powerful than the language of any nation; it is the language of the gospel of love. (As quoted in Frederick W. Babbel, *On Wings of Faith* [Salt Lake City: Bookcraft, 1972], p. 14.)

I think that if you are going to be successful, you must develop in your heart a love for people with whom you work. They need the gospel as they need no other thing. Develop in your hearts a love for them, a desire to lift them up, and a desire to help them and to bless them by teaching them the principles of the gospel. The gospel will absolutely revolutionize their lives, change their outlook. People are hungry for something that will give them an anchor, that will satisfy the questions of their souls, that will bring peace to their hearts and a feeling of security, inner satisfaction. (*God, Family, Country*, p. 62.)

We must develop a love for people. Our hearts must go out to them in the pure love of the gospel, in a desire to lift them, to build them up, to point them to a higher, finer life and eventually to exaltation in the celestial kingdom of God. We emphasize the fine qualities of the people with whom we associate, and love them as children of God whom the Lord loves. (*Come unto Christ*, p. 96.)

You will not be effective until you learn to have sympathy for all of our Father's children — unless you learn to love them. People can feel when love is extended to them. Many yearn for it. (Texas San Antonio Mission, 2 March 1986.)

There has been criticism of me, but I am frank and honest in saying that it has never bothered me very much, because in my heart I have been convinced I was doing the thing that seemed to me, at least, to be right. And I have nothing in my heart, nor have I had, except a love for the people. I have had no bitterness. I have no bitterness today. At times when the wonderful representatives of the press, who have been such a help, have said, "Surely, you must hate these people who criticize you," I have usually replied, "I do not hate any living soul. I love all of our Father's children. True, I love some more than others."

I have had no feeling of bitterness or hatred in my heart, for which I am deeply grateful because I have prayed — we have prayed as a family — that we could avoid any spirit of hatred or bitterness. I love our Father's children. I think the great rank and file of them are good. Oh, they have weaknesses—all of us do—but as I have visited them in forty-five nations, I found that they are very much the same. (*Title of Liberty*, p. 211.)

My heart has been filled with an overwhelming love and compassion for all members of the Church and our Heavenly Father's children everywhere. I love all our Father's children of every color, creed, and political persuasion. My only desire is to serve as the Lord would have me do. (Statement upon becoming President of the Church, 11 November 1985.)

Chastity and Virtue

The plaguing sin of this generation is sexual immorality. This, the Prophet Joseph said, would be the source of more temptations, more buffetings, and more difficulties for the elders of Israel than any other. (See *Journal of Discourses*, 8:55.)

President Joseph F. Smith said that sexual impurity would be one of the three dangers that would threaten the Church within— and so it does (see *Gospel Doctrine*, pp. 312–13). It permeates our society.

In the category of sins, the Book of Mormon places unchastity next to murder (see Alma 39:5). As Alma states, "Now . . . I would that ye should repent and forsake your sins, and go no more after the lusts of your eyes, . . . for except ye do this ye can in nowise inherit the kingdom of God" (Alma 39:9). If we are to cleanse the inner vessel, we must forsake immorality and be clean (see Alma 60:23). (CR April 1986, *Ensign* 16 [May 1986]: 4–5.)

"Thou shalt not commit adultery," and also, "Thou shalt not covet thy neighbor's wife" (Exodus 20:14, 17). Here God gives the great law of chastity that lies at the base of purity of family blood and the undefiled home. When the ancient prophets desired to excoriate Israel for her sins, they did it by comparing her to the prostitute. In the category of sins, unchastity stands next to murder, nor may we forget that growing crime of abortion, which often follows unchastity. Never in this generation of ours have morals been so loose as now. Sex is all but deified, and yet at the same time, it is put before youth in its lowest, coarsest, and most debasing forms. The curtain of modesty has been torn aside. In play, book, movie, and television; in magazine story, picture, and advertisement, immorality stands out in all its vulgarity and rottenness. (*This Nation Shall Endure*, p. 65.)

We covenant to live the law of chastity. The law of chastity is virtue and sexual purity. This law places us under covenant to live this commandment strictly. "Thou shalt love thy wife with all thy heart, and shalt cleave unto her and none else. And he that looketh upon a woman to lust after her shall deny the faith, and shall not have the Spirit; and if he repents not he shall be cast out. Thou shalt not commit adultery; and he that committeth adultery, and repenteth not, shall be cast out [excommunicated]." (D&C 42:22–24.) ("Temple Blessings and Covenants," Temple Presidents Seminar, Salt Lake City, Utah, 28 September 1982.)

A reason for virtue—which includes personal chastity, clean thoughts and practices, and integrity—is that we must have the Spirit and the power of God in our lives to do God's work. Without that power and influence we are no better off than individuals in other organizations. That virtue shines through and will influence others toward a better life and cause nonmembers to inquire of our faith. ("Four Keys for Success," Churubusco Mexico Stake, 5 June 1982.)

Parents should give their children specific instructions on chastity at an early age, both for their physical and moral protection. Years ago President David O. McKay, God bless him, read a statement written by Mrs. Wesley to her famous son John. I commend it to you as a basis for judgment pertaining to the matter of chastity. "Would you judge of the lawfulness or unlawfulness of pleasure? Take this rule: Now note, whatever weakens your reason, impairs the tenderness of your conscience, obscures your sense of God, takes off your relish for spiritual things, whatever increases the authority of the body over the mind, that thing is sin to you, however innocent it may seem in itself." (CR October 1964, *Improvement Era* 67 [December 1964]: 1069.)

One of the standards on which your happiness is based, now and in your future, is moral purity. The world would tell you that this standard is old-fashioned and out of date. The world would have you accept a so-called new morality, which is nothing more than immorality. ("To 'The Rising Generation,' " *New Era* 16 [June 1986]: 5.)

Sexual immorality is a viper that is striking not only in the world, but in the Church today. Not to admit it is to be dangerously complacent or is like putting one's head in the sand. In the category of crimes, only murder and denying the Holy Ghost come ahead of illicit sexual relations, which we call fornication when it involves an unmarried person, or the graver sin of adultery when it involves one who is married. I know the laws of the land do not consider unchastity as serious as God does, nor punish as severely as God does, but that does not change its abominableness. In the eyes of God, chastity will never be out of date.

The natural desire for men and women to be together is from God. But such association is bounded by His laws. Those things properly reserved for marriage, when taken within the bonds of marriage, are right and pleasing before God and fulfill the commandment to multiply and replenish the earth. But those same things when taken outside the bonds of marriage are a curse.

No sin is causing the loss of the Spirit of the Lord among our people more today than sexual promiscuity. It is causing our people to stumble, damning their growth, darkening their spiritual powers, and making them subject to other sins. (*God, Family, Country*, pp. 239–40.)

We know how important it is for our youth to possess clean minds in healthy clean bodies. Moral purity is an eternal principle. The Spirit of God "cannot dwell in an unclean tabernacle" (Mosiah 2:37). Purity is life-giving; impurity is deadly. God's holy laws cannot be broken with impunity. Great nations have fallen when they became morally corrupt, because the sins of immorality left their people scarred and misshapen creatures who were unable to face the challenge of their times. (*So Shall Ye Reap*, p. 196.)

The cause of so much social disease and the reason it has become a "killer-plague" is that so many, in their disregarding of God's truths, have abandoned the law of chastity. If we will live His law of virtue, we will destroy both immorality and its resultant diseases. ("A Voice of Warning to the Nations of the World,"

New Zealand and Australia Area Conferences, 25 November 1979
and 2 December 1979.)

The Church has no double standard of morality. The moral
code of heaven for both men and women is complete chastity
before marriage and full fidelity after marriage. ("To 'The Rising
Generation,' " *New Era* 16 [June 1986]: 5–6.)

The foundation of a happy home must be laid during premarital days. You young people should keep your associations on an
uplifting, spiritual level. Moral purity is an eternal principle. Its
violation destroys the noblest qualities and aspirations of man.

You should realize that there is a grave danger in building your
premarital associations on a physical basis of necking, petting, and
fornication. The harmful effects of such unlawful associations are
carried over into married life, bringing disappointment, heartache,
and the weakening of the structure of the home. Unchastity is one
of the most damning of all evils, while moral purity is one of the
greatest bulwarks of successful homemaking. Happy and successful homes — let alone individual lives — cannot be built on immorality. ("Your Charge: To Increase in Wisdom and Favor with
God and Man," *New Era* 9 [September 1979]: 43.)

God created sex, but not for self-indulgence. Men are not animals, left only to their instincts and self-indulgence. We are offspring of God. God Himself has set the boundaries of this sacred
act. Sex outside of marriage is wrong. Every form of homosexuality is wrong. Through His prophets He has declared and reiterated, "Thou shalt not commit adultery" (Exodus 20:14). (*This
Nation Shall Endure*, p. 96.)

To be successful, we must have the Spirit of the Lord. We have
been taught that the Spirit will not dwell in unclean tabernacles.
Therefore, one of our first priorities is to make sure our own personal lives are in order. The Lord declared, "Be ye clean that bear
the vessels of the Lord" (D&C 38:42). (*Come unto Christ*, p. 92.)

Solomon said that the price of a virtuous woman "is far above
rubies" (Proverbs 31:10). Young women, guard and protect your
virtue as you would your very life. We want you to live the morally

clean life all of your life. We want the morally clean life to be your way of life. ("To the Young Women of the Church," *Ensign* 16 [November 1986]: 83.)

Go to the marriage altar pure and clean. Reserve for the marriage relationship those sweet and intimate associations which the God of Heaven intended should be a part of marriage and not be indulged in outside of the marriage covenant. I care not what the world says, but these are the standards of the kingdom of God. (Scandinavia and Finland Area Conference Report, 16–18 August 1974.)

Some would justify their immorality with the argument that restrictions against it are merely religious rules, rules that are meaningless because in reality there is no God. This you will recognize is merely an untruthful rationalization designed to justify one's carnal appetite, lust, and passion. God's law is irrevocable. It applies to all, whether they believe in God or not. Everyone is subject to its penalties, no matter how one tries to rationalize or ignore them.

Immorality always brings with it attendant remorse. A person cannot indulge in promiscuous relations without suffering ill effects from it. He cannot do wrong and feel right—it is impossible. Anytime one breaks a law of God, he pays a penalty in heartache, in sadness, in remorse, in lack of self-respect, and he removes himself from contact with the Spirit of God. Is it any wonder that those who indulge in sex relations outside of marriage deny God? (*This Nation Shall Endure*, p. 97.)

So garbled in values have our morals become that some youth would not dare take a cigarette but freely engage in petting. Both are wrong, but one is infinitely more serious than the other. (CR October 1964, *Improvement Era* 67 [December 1964]: 1069.)

To you wonderful young girls and young women: keep yourselves clean. This is the safe way. Don't feel you have to throw yourself at every man that comes along in order to be popular. Reserve for your companion for time and all eternity those sweet relationships which God intended for marriage.

Young men, especially you who bear the priesthood of God, should be the protectors of women and not feel that you can take liberties, that you can rob them of that which is more priceless than life itself. You should treat that young girl whom you take out on a date as you would expect another young man to treat your sister. This is the way to live. This is God's way. This is the standard which He has provided in His Church. (San Diego California South Stake Conference, 7 December 1969.)

Some of the saddest letters that come to Church headquarters are from young people who have made serious mistakes. One came not so long ago which I am going to share with you without giving you any name. This lovely Mormon girl, for there is evidence that she was such, said, "I'm writing this from the depths of a broken heart, in the hope that it may be a warning to other girls never to have to partake of the bitterness that has come to me. I would give all that I have or ever hope to have if I could go back to those happy, carefree days before the first little taint of sin came upon my heart.

"I scarcely realized that I was slipping into something that could bring such sorrow and ruin into a person's life. I wish I could reveal to you the anguish and regret that fills my heart today, the loss of self-respect and the realization that life's most priceless gift has slipped away from me. I reached out too eagerly for the excitements and thrills of life, and they have turned to ashes in my hands."

Girls, learn to live simply, and enjoy to the fullest the sweet companionship of both girl friends, your mothers, and the association of your own family. If you keep yourselves sweet and lovely the joys and thrills of life will come to you in their own due time. Do not rush out too eagerly to find them or they will wither in your hands like a flower cut down by the frost before it has a chance to bloom. Oh, if girls could only see when parents try to warn them. (BYU Ten-Stake Fireside, Provo, Utah, 7 May 1972.)

Be modest. Modesty in dress and language and deportment is a true mark of refinement and a hallmark of a virtuous Latter-day Saint woman. Shun the low and vulgar and the suggestive. ("To the Young Women of the Church," *Ensign* 16 [November 1986]: 83.)

I am reminded of a story of a young girl who, with her date, was going to a place of questionable reputation, against the wise counsel of her parents. Her question was, "What harm is there in just going in to see what goes on there?" Her parents apparently gave in to her and suggested that she wear her lovely white dress for the occasion. Before her young man arrived, her father said, "Would you do me a favor before you go and go out to the smokehouse and bring in a side of bacon?"

The girl was aghast at this request and said, "In my best dress? I would never get rid of that awful smell." Her mother said, "That is right, you can't go into the smokehouse without absorbing some of the influence there. We think you are smart enough not to go into a place where you would come out any less beautiful and clean than when you went in." With that wise counsel, this young girl made the right decision to keep herself unspotted and clean from evil influences in the world. ("Stand Firm in the Faith," BYU Graduation, Provo, Utah, 17 August 1979.)

I would like to say to you sisters, you girls, that when a man who is a real man starts looking for his companion for eternity, he does not want shopworn and damaged goods. He wants a girl who is clean and pure and lovely. It is my hope and prayer that all of you will someday go to the marriage altar in the temple of God with a companion who is pure and clean, and that you will live so that you will be worthy of such a companion. ("A Fourfold Hope," Brigham Young University, Provo, Utah, 24 May 1961.)

Whenever a priesthood holder departs from the path of virtue in any form or expression, he loses the Spirit and comes under Satan's power. He then receives the wages of him whom he has chosen to serve. As a result, sometimes the Church must take disciplinary action, for we cannot condone or pardon unvirtuous and unrepented actions. All priesthood holders must be morally clean to be worthy to bear the authority of Jesus Christ. (CR October 1986, *Ensign* 16 [November 1986]: 46.)

A priesthood holder should be virtuous. Virtuous behavior implies that he has pure thoughts and clean actions. He will not lust in his heart, for to do so is to "deny the faith" and to lose the Spirit. (See D&C 42:23.)

He will not commit adultery "nor do anything like unto it" (D&C 59:6). This means fornication, homosexual behavior, self-abuse, child molestation, or any other sexual perversion. This means that a young man will honor young women and treat them with respect. He would never do anything that would deprive them of that, which in Mormon's words, is "most dear and precious above all things, which is virtue and chastity" (Moroni 9:9).

Virtue is akin to holiness, an attribute of godliness. A priesthood holder should actively seek for that which is virtuous and lovely and not that which is debasing or sordid. Virtue will "garnish [his] thoughts unceasingly" (D&C 121:45). How can any man indulge himself in the evils of pornography, profanity, or vulgarity and consider himself totally virtuous? (CR October 1986, *Ensign* 16 [November 1986]: 46.)

For those who are pure and chaste, may I give six steps that are steps of preparation and prevention, steps that will insure that you never fall into this transgression: Decide now to be chaste. Control your thoughts. Always pray for the power to resist temptation. If you are married, avoid flirtations of any kind. If you are married, avoid being alone with members of the opposite sex whenever possible. For those who are single and dating members of the opposite sex, carefully plan positive and constructive activities so that you are not left to yourselves with nothing to do but share physical affection.

There may be some for whom the counsel to prepare and prevent is too late. You may already be deeply entangled in serious sin. If this is the case, there is no choice now but to repair your lives and repent of your sins. To you I would suggest five important things you can do to come back to a state of moral purity. Flee immediately from any situation you are in that is either causing you to sin or that may cause you to sin. Plead with the Lord for the power to overcome. Let your priesthood leaders help you resolve the transgression and come back into full fellowship with the Lord. Drink from the divine fountain and fill your lives with positive sources of power. Remember that through proper repentance, you can become clean again.

For those who pay the price required by true repentance, the promise is sure. You can be clean again. The despair can be lifted. The sweet peace of forgiveness will flow into your lives. In this dispensation the Lord spoke with clarity when he said, "Behold, he who has repented of his sins, the same is forgiven, and I, the Lord, remember them no more" (D&C 58:42).

When it comes to the law of chastity, it is better to prepare and prevent than it is to repair and repent. ("The Law of Chastity," Brigham Young University Devotional, Provo, Utah, 13 October 1987.)

We must be *in* the amoral and immoral world, it is true, but not *of* it. We must be able to drop off to sleep at night without having to first sing lullabies to our conscience. (Softball Devotional, Salt Lake City, Utah, 21 August 1966.)

The writer of Proverbs says: "Whoso committeth adultery with a woman lacketh understanding: he that doeth it destroyeth his own soul" (Proverbs 6:32). Samuel the Lamanite taught the same thing when he said, "Ye have sought for happiness in doing iniquity, which thing is contrary to the nature of . . . righteousness" (Helaman 13:38).

Do not be misled by Satan's lies. There is no lasting happiness in immorality. There is no joy to be found in breaking the law of chastity. Just the opposite is true. There may be momentary pleasure. For a time it may seem like everything is wonderful. But quickly the relationship will sour. Guilt and shame set in. We become fearful that our sins will be discovered. We must sneak and hide, lie and cheat. Love begins to die. Bitterness, jealousy, anger, and even hate begin to grow. All of these are the natural results of sin and transgression. ("The Law of Chastity," Brigham Young University Devotional, Provo, Utah, 13 October 1987.)

Our counsel to you is this: Be clean. Be virtuous in your thoughts and actions. Read good books. Never let your minds be subjected to pornography in print or on film. In the words of the Lord, "Let virtue garnish thy thoughts unceasingly; then shall thy confidence wax strong in the presence of God. The Holy Ghost shall be thy constant companion." (D&C 121:45–46.) ("Four Keys for Success," Churubusco Mexico Stake, 5 June 1982.)

May I, as a member of a large family of children and a grateful father of six, say to the young men and women—keep the fountains of life pure. Guard your virtue as you would your lives. Reserve for the marriage relationship the sweet and soul-satisfying intimacies of life. The God of Heaven, who instituted the marriage covenant, so intended. He has commanded purity of life and a single standard for men and women. If you fail as young people properly to restrain yourselves, you will pay the penalty in heartache, disappointment, and loss of self-respect. Do not reach out too eagerly for the excitements and thrills of life or they will turn to ashes in your hands. They will come in their own due time in the sacred bonds of marriage. Youthful sweethearts, be true to God's holy laws. Remember, they cannot be broken with impunity. If you would be happy and successful in your early association, courtship, and home-building, conform your lives to the eternal laws of heaven. There is no other way. (*So Shall Ye Reap*, p. 106.)

Debt and Thrift

Our economic order is not perfect. It is operated by imperfect human beings, but it has given us more of the good things of life than any other system. The fundamental reason is that our economy is free. It must remain free. In that freedom ultimately lies our basic economic strength.

Let us admit the weaknesses that exist. Let us work aggressively to correct them. But never let us make the catastrophic blunder of putting chains on our basic economic freedom. (*An Enemy Hath Done This*, p. 24.)

The smaller the family income, the more important it is that every dollar be used wisely. Efficient spending and saving will give the family more security, more opportunities, more education, and a higher standard of living.

As I look back on the establishment of my own home, I am grateful for a companion who, although accustomed to many of the luxuries of life, was willing to start humbly. Vividly, I recall her doing the washing by hand until we could buy a secondhand washer. There was no overstuffed furniture, there was no carpeting on the floors. As a graduate student on a $70-a-month scholarship, I recall entertaining at dinner the head of the department at the college. He sat down at a card table (which was not used for cards) because there was no dining table. We gathered vegetables from the college experimental plots to cut down on the grocery bill and live within our means. Many have had similar experiences in a determination to make ends meet. ("Pay Thy Debt, and Live," *Ensign* 17 [June 1987]: 5.)

It is my humble judgment that economics and morals are both parts of one inseparable body of truth and these must be in harmony. We must square our actions and our policies with eternal principles if this nation is to be preserved and not go the way of Rome and other dead civilizations. In no other way may we enjoy the continuing blessings of peace, prosperity, and freedom. (*The Red Carpet*, p. 298.)

In the early revelations to this people, the Lord took occasion, many times, to give direction and commandment regarding temporal matters. He directed the Saints and the leaders of the Church in the purchase of land and other property; in the construction of temples; even in the establishment of a printing press and a store, and in the building of a boardinghouse for the "weary traveler" (D&C 124:23). In the great revelation known as the Word of Wisdom, he not only indicated what is good and what is not good for man, but he outlined a plan for the feeding of livestock which, through more than a hundred years, has gradually been sustained through scientific investigation of man (D&C 89). Whatever affects human welfare has always been and ever will be the concern of the Church. Our people have always been counseled in temporal affairs. (*So Shall Ye Reap*, pp. 273–74.)

Sound financial management is dependent upon careful and wise budgeting. To accomplish this it is necessary to assess what our goals and objectives are, and then determine what finances are required to attain those goals. The second aspect of effective budgeting is to live within the approved budget. If a careful analysis has been effected in the preparation of the budget, then it should not be difficult to confine expenditures within the budget as authorized. ("Budgets and Financial Discipline," Mission Presidents Seminar, Salt Lake City, Utah, 22 June 1971.)

The practice of setting aside a small portion of income during one's productive years in order to be self-sustaining in old age is not only commendable, but, in my opinion, it is an obligation to ourselves and to the younger generation that follows in our footsteps. Most people agree, but there are some who feel that the natural order of things calls for total investment in their children during productive years and reliance upon the family unit in old age. Others prefer to prepare for retirement through investments in property and securities which they feel will expand in value and keep pace with inflation-shrinking dollars. Still others prefer to build up a retirement fund with private insurance policies which provide such flexible features as a sizeable cash payment to surviving dependents in the event of premature death. (*An Enemy Hath Done This*, pp. 226–27.)

In the book of 2 Kings we read about a woman who came weeping to Elisha, the prophet. Her husband had died, and she owed a debt that she could not pay. The creditor was on his way to take her two sons and sell them as slaves.

By a miracle Elisha enabled her to acquire a goodly supply of oil. Then he said to her: "Go, sell the oil, and pay thy debt, and live thou and thy children of the rest." (See 2 Kings 4:1–7.)

"Pay thy debt, and live." How fruitful these words have ever been! What counsel they are for us today! ("Pay Thy Debt, and Live," *Ensign* 17 [June 1987]: 3.)

The Lord desires His Saints to be free and independent in the critical days ahead. But no man is truly free who is in financial bondage. "Think what you do when you run in debt," said Benjamin Franklin; "you give to another power over your liberty." "Pay thy debt, and live," said Elisha (2 Kings 4:7). And in the Doctrine and Covenants the Lord says, "It is my will that you shall pay all your debts" (D&C 104:78). (*God, Family, Country*, p. 268.)

Get out of debt if it is at all humanly possible. We have lived in an atmosphere of inflation for so long that many people now accept the benefits of permanent debt as a firm law of economics. But if inflation runs its full course and drops over into depression with little if any real income for millions of workers, the country may well have to start over with a brand new currency which will be in extremely short supply to pay off those existing debts. Even in times of economic stability it is sound practice to live within one's income and avoid unnecessary debt. Such practice is doubly sound in times like these.

Each of us should make every effort to become economically independent, at least within the family unit. Avoid looking to government for handouts or future security. Again, this is not only good practice in normal times, but especially important today. A government which is unable to pay its own bills can hardly be depended upon to pay yours. (*An Enemy Hath Done This*, p. 220.)

Inspired leaders have always urged us to get out of debt, to live within our means, and to pay as we go—and this is sound advice for governments as well as individuals. History teaches that when individuals have given up looking after their own economic needs and transferred a large share of that responsibility to the government, both they and the government have failed. (*The Red Carpet*, pp. 168–69.)

Thomas Jefferson counseled: "To preserve our independence, we must not let our rulers load us with perpetual debt. We must take our choice between economy and liberty, or profusion and servitude." Indeed, paying our debts or living within our means was always one of the sterling characteristics of Americans. We looked upon it as a duty to ourselves as individuals and as children of God. ("The American Free Enterprise System: Will It Survive?" *Contemporary Issues Forum*, Ogden, Utah, 18 January 1977.)

There is a tendency for all of us to want to keep up with our neighbors, even if our income is low. Sadly, in this respect, we have plenty of company. In the long run, it is easier to live within our incomes and resist borrowing from future reserves except in cases of necessity—never for luxuries. It is not fair to ourselves or our communities to be so improvident in our spending that the day our income stops we must turn to relief agencies or the Church for financial aid.

If you must incur debt to meet the reasonable necessities of life—such as buying a house and furniture—then I implore you, as you value your solvency and happiness, to buy within your means. Resist the temptation to plunge into property far more pretentious or spacious than you really need.

You can sometimes buy with little or no down payment, and on long terms. But these terms mean that a very large part of your total payments will go to pay interest charges, not to retire the principal of the debt. Remember, interest never sleeps or takes a holiday. Such payments of interest can easily become a tremendous burden, especially when you add to them taxes and cost of repairs. ("Pay Thy Debt, and Live," *Ensign* 17 [June 1987]: 4–5.)

We have mortgaged our future. We have done so because we live beyond our income. Now, I do not mean to say that all debt is bad. Of course not. Sound business debt is one of the elements of growth. Sound mortgage credit is a real help to a family that must borrow for a home. But is it not apparent that in the areas of both public and personal debt the limitations of soundness have been seriously strained? (*The Red Carpet*, p. 169.)

One reason for the increase in debt causes great concern. This is the rise of materialism as contrasted with spiritual values. Many a family, in order to make a "proper showing," will commit itself for a larger and more expensive house than is needed, in an expensive neighborhood. Almost everyone would, it seems, like to keep up with the Joneses. With the increasing standard of living, that temptation increases with each new gadget that comes on the market. The subtle and carefully planned techniques of modern advertising are aimed at the weakest points of consumer resistance. And there is a growing feeling, unfortunately, that material things should be had now, without waiting, without saving, without self-denial. ("Pay Thy Debt, and Live," *Ensign* 17 [June 1987]: 3–4.)

Credit is a willing servant but a cruel master. A large proportion of families with personal debt have no liquid assets whatsoever to fall back on. What troubles they invite if their income should be suddenly cut off or seriously reduced! We all know of families who have obligated themselves for more than they could pay.

Do not, I solemnly urge you, tie yourself to the payment of carrying charges that are often exorbitant. Save now and buy later, and you will be much further ahead. You will spare yourselves high interest and other payments, and the money you save may provide opportunity for you to buy later at substantial cash discounts. ("Good Mormons Don't Get into Debt," *Millennial Star* 124 [June 1962]: 142.)

Closely allied with the trend toward bigger and bigger government is the tendency toward loose fiscal policy, both public and private. This concerns us as free men. "The borrower is servant to the lender" (Proverbs 22:7). A nation can hang itself on the gallows of excessive public debt—and the United States is no exception. (*The Red Carpet*, p. 165.)

Often we are admonished not to worry about deficit spending and the national debt since, after all, we only owe it to ourselves. What utter nonsense! If that were the case, why don't we just cancel the debt to ourselves and stop paying all that interest? (*An Enemy Hath Done This*, p. 210.)

Use credit wisely. How much better off you will be, especially young families just starting out, if first you buy a small house which you can expect to pay for in a relatively short time. Do not leave yourself or your family unprotected against financial storms. Forgo luxuries, for the time being at least, to build up savings. How wise it is to provide for the future education of children and for old age. ("Good Mormons Don't Get into Debt," *Millennial Star* 124 [June 1962]: 142.)

When personal incomes are generally high is the time to pay off obligations. I doubt that there will soon be again a more favorable time for Latter-day Saints to get out of debt than now. Let us use the opportunity we have to speed up repayment of mortgages and to set aside provisions for education, possible periods of decreased earning power, and emergencies the future may hold. ("Pay Thy Debt, and Live," *Ensign* 17 [June 1987]: 5.)

Peace and contentment come into our hearts when we live within our means. God grant us wisdom and the faith to heed the inspired counsel of the priesthood to get out of debt, to live within our means, and to pay as we go. ("Pay Thy Debt, and Live," *Ensign* 17 [June 1987]: 5.)

A sterling virtue which builds manliness and independence is frugality of thrift. "Waste not, want not" has long been the clarion call. In more recent years, however, this maxim has given way to so-called "deficit spending." Many have been teaching that we must spend our way into prosperity. How do you regard this philosophy? Have you stopped to analyze its effect upon the independence, self-reliance, and character of the individual? And what of its possible effect upon the very existence of this nation as a haven for freedom-loving men and women?

No man in debt is truly free. He who has not learned thrift and economy is constantly beset with problems and misgivings about the future. His own freedom and peace of mind are endangered. Those dependent upon him are likewise jeopardized in their self-respect and freedom. (*So Shall Ye Reap*, p. 165.)

Economy is a prime requisite of a sound financial structure, whether in government, in business, or personal affairs. You cannot bring about prosperity by discouraging thrift and living beyond your means. Thrift and frugality are absolutely essential for the enjoyment of an abundant life.

Therefore, shrink not from your duty in these important matters. Be prayerful. Be frugal. Accept responsibility. Be grateful for work. Hesitate not to do your full share of it. Forget not that "he profits most who serves best." ("Concerning Values," University of Maine, Orono, Maine, 10 June 1956.)

Duty

We have many responsibilities, and a person cannot expect the full blessings of the kind Providence if he neglects any major duty. A man has duties to his church, to his home, to his country, and to his profession or job. But duty to church keeps man in communication with his God. He must determine the place and extent of the duty he owes to his church. The least any Christian can do is to daily study the word of the Lord and seek divine aid through daily prayer. (Softball Devotional, Salt Lake City, Utah, 21 August 1966.)

We are far removed from the days of our forefathers who were persecuted for their peculiar beliefs. Some of us seem to want to share their reward but are ofttimes afraid to stand up for principles that are controversial in our generation. We need not solicit persecution, but neither should we remain silent in the presence of overwhelming evils, for this makes cowards of men. We should not go out of the path of duty to pick up a cross there is no need to bear, but neither should we sidestep a cross that clearly lies within the path of duty. (CR October 1964, *Improvement Era* 67 [December 1964]: 1067.)

There should be no doubt what our task is today. If we truly cherish the heritage we have received, we must maintain the same virtues and the same character of our stalwart forebears—faith in God, courage, industry, frugality, self-reliance, and integrity. We have the obligation to maintain what those who pledged their lives, their fortunes, and their sacred honor gave to future generations (see Declaration of Independence). Our opportunity and obligation for doing so is clearly upon us. May we begin to repay this debt by preserving and strengthening this heritage in our own lives and in the lives of our children, their children, and generations yet unborn. (*This Nation Shall Endure*, p. 46.)

Remember, it is the individual who is of supreme worth. You cannot build character and courage by taking away man's initiative and independence. Our great benefactor, Brigham Young, understood the basic principle that you cannot help a man permanently by doing for him what he could do and should do for himself. Shrink not from duty as it is made known. Accept responsibility. Be grateful for work. Hesitate not to do your full share of it. ("Concerning Principles and Standards," *Church News* [4 June 1947]: 5.)

As we face the critical decisions just ahead, let us "do nothing through passion and ill temper" but let us "stand by our duty, fearlessly and effectively," making our own the words of Abraham Lincoln at Cooper Institute, "Let us have faith that right makes might, and in that faith, let us to the end, do our duty as we understand it." (*So Shall Ye Reap*, p. 331.)

Education

Knowledge is power, but the most vital and important knowledge is a knowledge of God—that He lives, that we are His children, that He loves us, that we are created in His image, that we can in faith pray to Him and receive strength and inspiration in time of need.

Such knowledge is priceless. True, "man is saved no faster than he gains knowledge" (*Teachings of the Prophet Joseph Smith*, p. 217). Knowledge of what? Knowledge of God! Knowledge of His purpose and plans for the welfare, blessing, and eternal exaltation of us, His children. All useful knowledge is of value. The seeking of such knowledge is, therefore, commendable and rewarding. But in all of our searching for truth, we must remember that the knowledge of God, our Father, and His plans for us, His children, is of supreme importance. (*God, Family, Country*, p. xi.)

Since Church Education's humble beginning in 1833, the Church has continued its emphasis on education. Today we sponsor education through a vast Church Educational System — seminaries, institutes, colleges, a university, and one of the largest adult education programs in the world. In the tradition of the School for the Elders, all elders and sisters who serve the Church as missionaries attend the Missionary Training Centers throughout the world. We maintain this worldwide educational program for the all-important purpose of preparing ourselves "as messengers of Jesus Christ, to be ready to do His will in carrying glad tidings to all that would open their eyes, ears, and hearts." (*History of the Church*, 2:176.) (Newel K. Whitney Store Dedication, Kirtland, Ohio, 25 August 1984.)

It is a joy to know that at Brigham Young University increased attention is being given to one of what I consider the three greatest objectives of this institution. The first objective is to help build real Latter-day Saints — men and women who live according to the standards of the Church and kingdom of God. Second, to train young men and women for honorable vocations and for life. And third, to teach the responsibilities of citizenship. This includes an understanding of the principles of Americanism, and a love for the Constitution of this land and the glorious concepts and principles embodied in that great document. It also means to teach something of the prophetic history of this great nation and of the fruits of our free enterprise system. ("Responsibilities of Citizenship," Brigham Young University Homecoming, Provo, Utah, 22 October 1954.)

I know what it is, as many of your faculty members do, to work my way through school, taking classes only during winter quarters. If you don't have the finances to complete your education, drop out a semester and go to work and save. You will be a better man or woman for so doing. You will have preserved your self-respect and initiative. Wisdom comes with experience and struggle, not just with going through a university matriculation. I hope you will not be deceived by current philosophies which will rob you of your godly dignity, self-respect, and initiative, those attributes that make a celestial inheritance possible. ("A Vision and a Hope for the Youth of Zion," in *1977 Devotional Speeches of the Year* [Provo, Utah: BYU, 1978], p. 78.)

Wisdom is the proper application of true knowledge. Not all knowledge has the same worth—nor are all truths equally valuable. The truths upon which our eternal salvation rests are the most crucial truths that we must learn. No man is truly educated unless he knows where he came from, why he is here, and where he can expect to go in the next life. He must be able to adequately answer the question which Jesus posed: "What think ye of Christ?" (Matthew 22:42.) The world cannot teach us these things. Therefore, the most essential knowledge for you to obtain is the saving knowledge of the gospel and its author—even Jesus Christ. Eternal life, the greatest gift that God can give and the life for which we all should be striving, comes from knowing our Father in Heaven and His Son, Jesus Christ. As the Savior said: "This is life eternal, that they might know thee the only true God, and Jesus Christ, whom thou hast sent" (John 17:3). We cannot know about God and Jesus without studying about them and then doing their will. This course leads to additional revealed knowledge which, if obeyed, will eventually lead us to further truths. If we follow this pattern, we will receive further light and joy, eventually leading into God's presence where we, with Him, will have a fulness. ("In His Steps," Church Educational System Devotional, Anaheim, California, 8 February 1987.)

Education in the Home

One of the great needs is more parental instruction in life's problems. I know there is a tendency for parents to shrink from this responsibility, the instructing of their own children in the problems of sex, the relationship with other young people, the problem of dating, and all of the many temptations that confront a growing boy and girl. These instructions should not be left to the school or to a class in sociology. The safest place, the best place, to give this vital counsel, these sacred instructions, in matters of moral purity should be in the home on a basis of confidence between parent and child. As parents, we should instruct our children. The sacred books of the ancient Persians say: "If you would be holy, instruct your children, because all the good acts they perform will be imputed unto you." (*So Shall Ye Reap*, pp. 120–21.)

Some fathers leave solely to the mother or to the school the responsibility of shaping a child's ideas and standards. Too often television and movie screens shape our children's values. We should not assume that public schools always reinforce teachings given in the home concerning ethical and moral conduct. We have seen introduced into many school systems false ideas about the theory of man's development from lower forms of life, teachings that there are no absolute values, attempts to repudiate beliefs regarded as supernatural, permissive attitudes toward sexual freedom that give sanction to immoral behavior and "alternative lifestyles," such as lesbianism, homosexuality, and other perverse practices.

Such teachings not only tend to undermine the faith and morals of our young people, they also deny the existence of God, who gave absolute laws, and the divinity of Jesus Christ. Surely we can see the moral contradiction of some who argue for the preservation of endangered species but who also sanction the abortion of unborn humans. The Lord expects great things from the fathers of Israel. Fathers must take time to find out what their children are being taught and then take steps to correct false information and teaching. (*Come unto Christ*, p. 59.)

What should we teach? The Lord has revealed the specific curriculum that parents should teach. Note His words: "Teach it unto your children, that all men, everywhere, must repent, or they can in nowise inherit the kingdom of God, for no unclean thing can dwell there, or dwell in his presence."

As further noted in this scripture, the fundamental doctrines consist of the doctrine of the Fall, the mission of Christ and His atonement, and the first principles and ordinances of the gospel, which include faith in Christ, repentance, baptism for a remission of sins, and the gift of the Holy Ghost as the means to a sanctified life. (Moses 6:57–59.) (*Come unto Christ*, p. 60.)

Education in the Nation

From the very beginning of recorded political thought, man has realized the importance of education as a tremendous potential for both good and evil. In a free and open society such as ours, a well-rounded education is an essential for the preservation of freedom against the chicanery and demagoguery of aspiring tyrants who would have us ignorantly vote ourselves into bondage. As the educational system falls into the hands of the in-power political faction or into the hands of an obscure but tightly knit group of professional social reformers, it is used not to educate but to indoctrinate. (*An Enemy Hath Done This*, p. 229.)

Let us never lose sight of the fact that education is a preparation for life—and that preparing for life is far more than knowing how to make a living or how to land on the moon. Preparing for life means building personal integrity, developing a sound sense of values, increasing the capacity and willingness to serve. Education must have its roots in moral principles. If we lose sight of that fact in our attempt to match our educational system against that of the materialists, we shall have lost far more than we could possibly gain. (*The Red Carpet*, p. 177.)

Could it be that through the proper training of youth we are helping to serve America? Can we not contribute to America's stamina and survival? We can teach reverence to God, unselfishness, love of country, and the fundamental principles of righteous living. We can try to train youth through men of character. We must urge a religious life; we must encourage good education; we must promote patriotism; we must emphasize honesty, trustworthiness, loyalty, and many other fine attributes of good character. The opportunity is ours, and the need is great. One of the tasks is to rediscover and reassert our faith in the spiritual, non-utilitarian values on which American life has rested from its beginning. ("Will America Be Destroyed by Americans?" Boy Scouts Banquet, Commerce, Texas, 13 May 1968.)

There is absolutely nothing in the Constitution which authorized the federal government to enter into the field of education. Futhermore, the Tenth Amendment says: "The powers not delegated to the United States by the Constitution, nor prohibited by it to the States, are reserved to the States respectively, or to the people." Nothing could be more clear. It is unconstitutional for the federal government to exercise any powers over education. (*An Enemy Hath Done This*, pp. 230–31.)

The phrase *federal aid to education* is deceptive and dishonest. What is really meant is "federal taxes for education." The federal government cannot "aid" education. All it can do is tax the people, shuffle the money from one state to another and skim off its administrative costs from the top. Only the people can aid education. They can do it safer, faster, and cheaper within their local communities than by going through the middleman in Washington. Federal taxes for education means federal control over education. No matter how piously the national planners tell us that they will not dictate policies to local school systems, it is inevitable that they will in the long run. In fact, they already are doing it. Whenever the federal government spends tax money for any purpose, it has an obligation to determine how and under what conditions that money is used. Any other course would be irresponsible. (*An Enemy Hath Done This*, p. 231.)

One recent development that gave new ammunition to the proponents of federal aid was the Russian successes in rocketry and space exploration. More and more critics were rising up to say our educational system was failing in the competition—and that this proved the need for federal aid.

That faults existed in our educational system no one could deny. In gearing the curricula to the middle of the class, our system too often had not provided sufficient challenge for the better student. Champions seldom become champions by competing only against mediocrity.

Some educators contended that even with courses geared to the average, our system in too many cases tended to accept inferior work as of passing grade. Surely there would be grave danger to our society if youth were allowed to grow up believing that a lick and a promise is all that is needed to get by. It is not generally true on the adult level that one reaps reward without effort, receives wages without work, or enjoys prestige without achievement. By the same token, neither could a nation nor a system of education maintain freedom and security without individual sacrifice. (*Crossfire: The Eight Years with Eisenhower*, pp. 425–26.)

We must guard against federal control of education, remembering that the Supreme Court said: "It is hardly lack of due process for the government to regulate that which it subsidizes." Federal control of education, the impairment of free inquiry, and the extinction of many independent and church-related colleges — these can be the consequence of an injudicious increase in federal aid to education. (*The Red Carpet*, pp. 178–79.)

The best way to prevent a political faction or any small group of people from capturing control of the nation's educational system is to keep it decentralized into small local units, each with its own board of education and superintendent. This may not be as efficient as one giant super educational system (although bigness is not necessarily efficient, either) but it is far more safe. There are other factors, too, in favor of local and independent school systems. First, they are more responsive to the needs and wishes of the parents and the community. The door to the school superintendent's office is usually open to any parent who wishes to make his views known. But the average citizen would be hard pressed to obtain more than a form letter reply from the national Commissioner of Education in Washington, D.C. (*An Enemy Hath Done This*, p. 230.)

We are rearing a generation which does not seem to understand the fundamentals of our American way of life, a generation which is no longer dedicated to its preservation. Our people, both before and after they arrive at the age of the ballot, should understand what it is that has made America great. We can only appreciate freedom if we understand the comparative fruits thereof. It is one thing to win freedom, but its preservation is equally important. If reference is made continually to weaknesses of the private enterprise system without any effort to point out its virtues and the comparative fruits of this and other systems, the tendency in this country will be, as it has been in other countries, to demand that the government take over more and more of the economic and social responsibilities and make more and more of the decisions for the people. This can result in but one thing, slavery of the individual to the state. This seems to be the trend of the world today. (*The Red Carpet*, p. 219.)

One of the tragedies of the Korean War was the fact that the enemy was able to brainwash some of our men. Those methods, highly refined and deviously developed, have been introduced on a broad scale into our own country by some behavioral scientists through a program commonly called sensitivity training. While claiming otherwise, the overall effect of this training has been to break down personal standards, encourage immorality, reduce respect for parents, and make well minds sick.

But some sensitivity training doesn't stop there. They usually want each person to tell the group about all of their innermost feelings, their personal secrets, their fears, their repressed desires. They have even conducted nudity sessions as a means of supposedly breaking down their inhibitions. They want the group to know each other's vulgar thoughts and lustful ideas, their hates, envies, jealousies. But this flies in the face of the counsel of a prophet, who has said, "All such evils you must overcome by suppression. That is where your control comes in. Suppress that anger! Suppress that jealousy, that envy! They are all injurious to the spirit." (President David O. McKay, *Gospel Ideals*, p. 356.)

In these sensitivity sessions one's standards, religion, family, and friends may be subjected to brutal and prolonged attack by the group. And when it is all over, if you have confessed all and had your values and ideals smashed, you may doubt if there is much worth believing or defending, and your loyalties may now have been realigned away from your family and church toward the group—for on them you may now feel very dependent, and you may be more anxious to get their consensus on a position and their approval than to find out what is right and do it. (CR April 1969, *Improvement Era* 72 [June 1969]: 44, 46.)

Results of Education

Let us be sure that our educational system turns out young men and women of character, who know the basic facts of economics, free enterprise, history, finance, and government, and who have a respect for law and an appreciation of the spiritual—otherwise that educational system will truly have been a failure. (*The Red Carpet*, pp. 279–80.)

In the first century of our nation's history, the university was the guardian and preserver of faith in God. In this present century, the university has become ethically neutral, by and large agnostic. Our country is now reaping the effects of this agnostic influence. It has cost us an inestimable price. ("God's Hand in Our Nation's History," Sons of Utah Pioneers, Salt Lake City, Utah, 23 August 1986.)

Across this great Christian nation—a nation with a spiritual foundation—we have schools without grades, schools without discipline, schools without prayers, schools without the pledge of allegiance, schools without Christmas programs commemorating the birth of Christ, without recognition of Easter and the great event of the Resurrection, schools without patriotism, schools without morals, schools without standards of speech, schools without standards of dress. As a result, we see the worst of their products, many of them almost intellectual gorillas as they leave some of these institutions. (BYU Ten-Stake Fireside, Provo, Utah, 7 May 1972.)

"My people are destroyed for lack of knowledge," said the prophet Hosea (see Hosea 4:6). Let us not let it happen to us. First, let us do our homework, because action without the proper education can lead to fanaticism. But after we have done our homework, let us take action, because education without action can only lead to frustration and failure. (*God, Family, Country*, p. 380.)

Learning

This quest for wisdom or intelligence, which the Lord defines as "light and truth" (D&C 93:36), is a glorious challenge. We have been assured by the Author of eternal life that "whatever principle of intelligence we attain unto in this life, it will rise with us in the resurrection. And if a person gains more knowledge and intelligence in this life through his diligence and obedience than another, he will have so much the advantage in the world to come." (D&C 130:18–19.)

Thus intelligence, or light and truth, becomes a vital force in our eternal journey. It is the one attribute above all others that links us to our divine parentage, for if "the glory of God is intelligence," intelligence is likewise the glory of His offspring—man (see D&C 93:36). (*So Shall Ye Reap*, p. 170.)

Today the world is full of alluring and attractive ideas that can lead even the best of our members into error and deception. Students at universities are sometimes so filled with the doctrines of the world they begin to question the doctrines of the gospel. How do you as a priesthood leader help fortify your membership against such deceptive teachings? The Savior gave the answer in His great discourse on the Mount of Olives when He promised, "And whoso treasureth up my word, shall not be deceived" (Joseph Smith—Matthew 1:37). ("The Power of the Word," Priesthood Leadership Meeting, Salt Lake City, Utah, 4 April 1986.)

We must be wise as serpents (see D&C 111:11); for as the Apostle Paul said, "We wrestle against the rulers of darkness . . . against spiritual wickedness in high places" (Ephesians 6:12). We are going through what J. Reuben Clark, Jr., once termed the greatest propaganda campaign of all time. We cannot believe all we read, and what we can believe is not all of the same value. We must sift. We must learn by study and prayer. (*An Enemy Hath Done This*, pp. 58–59.)

The most vital knowledge you can learn is the saving truths of the gospel—the truths that will make the difference in your eternal welfare. The most vital words that you can read are those of the

Presidents of the Church—particularly the living prophet—and those of the Apostles and prophets. God encourages learning in many areas, and vocational skills will have increasing importance. There is much reading material that is available which is either time-wasting or corrupting. The best yardstick to use in discerning the worth of true knowledge and learning is to go first and foremost to the words of the Lord's prophets. ("In His Steps," in *1979 Devotional Speeches of the Year* [Provo, Utah: BYU, 1980], p. 62.)

President Joseph F. Smith declared that some "read by the lamp of their own conceit; who interpret by rules of their own contriving; who have become a law unto themselves" (*Gospel Doctrine*, p. 373). Yes, it is intellectual pride that leads one to think he is self-sufficient in matters of mind and of spirit. Let us ever realize the difference that exists between a discoverer of the truth and the Lawgiver of all truth. The first is human; the other divine. ("Your Charge: To Increase in Wisdom and Favor with God and Man," *New Era* 9 [September 1979]: 40.)

President Joseph F. Smith said that one of the things that plagued the Church within was false educational ideas—and I am sure you will be introduced to some of these ideas somewhere along your path. Using the scriptures and the prophets and the Spirit as a guide, we can eliminate many of the deceptions and false philosophies and cure-alls of men, and discern between the wheat and the chaff. (*Title of Liberty*, p. 81.)

Under the guise of academic freedom—which some apparently feel is freedom to destroy freedom—some teachers reserve to themselves the privilege of teaching error, destroying faith in God, debunking morality, and depreciating our free economic system. (CR October 1964, *Improvement Era* 67 [December 1964]: 1068.)

If your children are required to put down on exams the falsehoods that have been taught, then perhaps they can follow President Joseph Fielding Smith's counsel of prefacing their answer with the words "teacher says," or they might say, "you taught" or "the textbook states." (*God, Family, Country*, p. 227.)

Students, study the writings of the prophets. Fortunately, a consistent position has been taken over the years by the prophets of the Church on vital issues facing this nation. Pray for inspiration and knowledge. Counsel with your parents. Let Sunday be the day to fill up your spiritual batteries for the week by reading good Church books, particularly the Book of Mormon. Take time to meditate. Don't let the philosophies and falsehoods of men throw you. Hold on to the iron rod. Learn to sift. Learn to discern error through the promptings of the Spirit and your study of the truth. (*God, Family, Country*, p. 239.)

Every Latter-day Saint should make the study of the Book of Mormon a lifetime pursuit. Otherwise he is placing his soul in jeopardy and neglecting that which could give spiritual and intellectual unity to his whole life. ("The Book of Mormon Is the Word of God," Regional Representatives Seminar, Provo, Utah, 4 April 1986.)

It was once thought, and still is in some places, that when a young man or woman set out upon a quest for academic knowledge, his faith in God would soon be destroyed. You yourselves are living proof to the contrary. It is not the search for knowledge—or knowledge itself—that costs a man his faith. It is rather the conceit of small minds proving anew that a little knowledge can be a dangerous thing. It is intellectual pride that leads one to think he is self-sufficient in matters of mind and of spirit. (*So Shall Ye Reap*, p. 93.)

With the abundance of books available, it is the mark of a truly educated man to know what not to read. "Of making many books there is no end" (Ecclesiastes 12:12). In your reading you would do well to follow the counsel of John Wesley's mother: Avoid "whatever weakens your reason, impairs the tenderness of your conscience, obscures your sense of God, takes off your relish for spiritual things, [and] increases the authority of the body over the mind."

The fact that a book or publication is popular does not necessarily make it of value. The fact that an author wrote one good work does not necessarily mean that all his books are worthy of your reading. Do not make your mind a dumping ground for other people's garbage. It is harder to purge the mind of rotten reading than to purge the body of rotten food, and it is more damaging to the soul. ("In His Steps," Church Educational System Devotional, Anaheim, California, 8 February 1987.)

People cannot think in a vacuum. Without facts, public discussion is but the pooling of ignorance. But without character — without faith in enduring verities — learning is the devil's tool. (American Association of School Administrators, Atlantic City, New Jersey, 14 February 1960.)

Repetition is a key to learning. Our sons need to hear the truth repeated, especially because there is so much falsehood abroad. (CR October 1985, *Ensign* 15 [November 1985]: 36.)

We should become informed about communism, about socialism, and about Americanism. What better way can one become informed than by first studying the inspired words of the prophets and using that as a foundation against which to test all other material? This is in keeping with the Prophet Joseph Smith's motto, "When the Lord commands, do it" (*History of the Church*, 2:170). (*God, Family, Country*, p. 354.)

While the gospel includes the more crucial saving truths contained within theology, it also embraces truth in other branches of learning. The Lord encouraged the early missionaries to be instructed more perfectly in "things both in heaven and in the earth, and under the earth; things which have been, things which are, things which must shortly come to pass; things which are at home, things which are abroad; the wars and the perplexities of the nations, and the judgments which are on the land; and a knowledge also of countries and of kingdoms" (D&C 88:79). ("In His Steps," Church Educational System Devotional, Anaheim, California, 8 February 1987.)

Study the scriptures and study the mortals who have been most consistently accurate about the most important things. When your freedom and your eternal welfare are at stake, your information best be accurate. (CR April 1967, *Improvement Era* 70 [June 1967]: 59.)

Teaching

We are to use the Book of Mormon as the basis for our teaching. The Lord states: "And again, the elders, priests and teachers of this church shall teach the principles of my gospel, which are . . . in the Book of Mormon, in the which is the fulness of the gospel." (D&C 42:12.) As we read and teach, we are to liken the Book of Mormon scriptures unto us "that it might be for our profit and learning" (1 Nephi 19:23). ("The Book of Mormon Is the Word of God," Regional Representatives Seminar, Salt Lake City, Utah, 4 April 1986.)

Fathers have the major responsibility for teaching their sons the gospel. As important as the organizations of the Church are for teaching our youth, fathers have a sacred calling to continually teach and instruct members of their families in the principles of the gospel of Jesus Christ. (CR April 1986, *Ensign* 16 [May 1986]: 46.)

I would hope that each morning before you leave your homes you kneel before the Lord in secret as well as family prayer. I also hope that before you go into the classroom you ask to be led by the Spirit. The most important part of your teaching preparation is that you are guided by the Spirit. ("The Gospel Teacher and His Message," Religious Educators, Salt Lake City, Utah, 17 September 1976.)

One of my old school friends approached me at the end of a stake conference. As we were visiting together I said to him: "Jack, what are you doing in the Church?" He said, "Oh, I am just a teacher." I replied, "Jack, don't ever say that again." "Just a teacher." Do you know of anything more important than being a teacher—touching the souls of the children of men? What did the Master spend His life doing? He was just a teacher, teaching human souls, inspiring them to live righteously. There is no higher calling than that. Whether it be done in the mission field or here at home with a group in a Primary class, they are all eternal souls that we work with. (*So Shall Ye Reap*, pp. 31–32.)

Powerful forces are at work to lead our young people into the weird and destructive world of drugs, moral decay, and revolution. To say it cannot happen here is to disregard all existing statistics. In this age of permissive parents and soft permissive educational leaders, it is happening to tens of thousands of our youth. Why? Because these choice young people have not been properly alerted and informed by parents and teachers who are recreant to the greatest God-given trust, and because many students do not seem to appreciate their priceless heritage and other rich blessings. ("Opportunity and Challenge," in *BYU Speeches of the Year* [Provo, Utah: BYU, 1970], p. 2.)

As a watchman on the tower, I feel to warn you that one of the chief means of misleading our youth and destroying the family unit is our educational institutions. There is more than one reason why the Church is advising our youth to attend colleges close to their homes where institutes of religion are available. It gives the parents the opportunity to stay close to their children, and if they become alerted and informed, these parents can help expose some of the deceptions of men like Sigmund Freud, Charles Darwin, John Dewey, John Keynes, and others.

Today there are much worse things that can happen to a child than not getting a full education. In fact, some of the worst things have happened to our children while attending colleges led by administrators who wink at subversion and amorality. Said Karl G. Maeser, "I would rather have my child exposed to smallpox, typhus fever, cholera, or other malignant and deadly diseases than to the degrading influence of a corrupt teacher. It is infinitely better to take chances with an ignorant but pure-minded teacher than with the greatest philosopher who is impure." (*God, Family, Country*, p. 225.)

Dr. A. A. Hodge pointed out:

It is capable of exact demonstration that if every party in the State has the right of excluding from public schools whatever he does not believe to be true, then he that believes most must give way to him that believes least, and then he that believes least must give way to him that believes absolutely nothing, no matter in how small a minority the atheists or agnostics may be. It is self-evident that on this scheme, if it is consistently and persistently carried out in all parts of the country, the United States system of national popular education will be the most efficient and widespread instrument for the propagation of atheism which the world has ever seen.

After the tragic prayer decision was made by the United States Supreme Court, President David O. McKay stated, "The Supreme Court of the United States severs the connecting cord between the public schools of the United States and the source of divine intelligence, the Creator Himself" (*Relief Society Magazine*, December 1962, p. 878). Does that make any difference to you? Can't you see why the demand of conscientious parents is increasing the number of private Christian and Americanist-oriented schools? (*God, Family, Country*, pp. 225–26.)

I hope there will never be any time when teachers in our own institutions will ever propose any theory or program, or present as fact anything that will tend to destroy the faith of our young people. ("The Greatest Leadership," BYU Student Leadership Conference, Sun Valley, Idaho, September 1959.)

When a teacher feels he must blend worldly sophistication and erudition to the simple principles of the gospel or to our Church history so that his message will have more appeal and respectability to the academically learned, he has compromised his message. We seldom impress people by this means and almost never convert them to the gospel. This also applies to our students. We encourage you to get your higher degrees and to further your education; but let us not forget that disaffection from the gospel and the Lord's Church was brought about in the past by the attempts to reconcile the pure gospel with the secular philosophies of men. Nominal Christianity outside the restored Church stands as an evidence that the blend between worldly philosophy and revealed truth leads to impotence. Likewise, you teachers will have no power if you attempt to do the same in your educational pursuits and classroom teaching. ("The Gospel Teacher and His Message," Religious Educators, Salt Lake City, Utah, 17 September 1976.)

Some teachers have felt that they have to expound some new slant on a doctrine, or reveal sensational or intimate and sacred personal experiences from their own lives, or allegedly from the lives of the Brethren in order to be popular with their students. You were not called to entertain students or unduly dramatize your message. ("The Gospel Teacher and His Message," Religious Educators, Salt Lake City, Utah, 17 September 1976.)

There are a few teachers within the Church who, while courting apostasy, still want to remain members of the Church, for being members makes them more effective in misleading the Saints. But their day of judgment is coming, and when it does come, for some of them it would have been better, as the Savior said, that a millstone had been put around their necks and they had been drowned in the depths of the sea than to have led away any of the youth of the Church (see Matthew 18:6; D&C 121:22). (*An Enemy Hath Done This*, p. 286.)

Your sole duty is to teach the gospel. You are not "to intrude into your work your own peculiar philosophy, no matter what its sources or how pleasing or rational it seems to you" (J. Reuben Clark, Jr., "Charted Course," p. 9). Your teaching should not be the "enticing words of man's wisdom, but in demonstration of the Spirit and of power: that your faith [and the faith of your students] should not stand in the wisdom of men, but in the power of God" (1 Corinthians 2:4, 5). ("The Gospel Teacher and His Message," Religious Educators, Salt Lake City, Utah, 17 September 1976.)

Before you can strengthen your students, it is essential that you study the doctrines of the kingdom and learn the gospel by both study and faith (see D&C 88:118). To study by faith is to seek understanding and the Spirit of the Lord through the prayer of faith. Then you will have the power to convince your students. This is not just good advice; it is a commandment of the Lord. ("The Gospel Teacher and His Message," Religious Educators, Salt Lake City, Utah, 17 September 1976.)

As you teach these children, remember this is our first obligation, to implant in their hearts a testimony of the divinity of this great work, in a period when the world, even the Christian world, is filled with doubt and insecurity, when it is groping, unable to see the future and to know where it is going. The youth of Israel must have in their hearts a firm conviction that God is directing this work, that His priesthood and power is here, and that this is His kingdom. They must have in their hearts a testimony that God lives, that He is watching over us as His children—that He loves us. (*So Shall Ye Reap*, pp. 35–36.)

Your purpose is to increase testimony and faith in your students. Should you wonder how this is done, carefully study the Book of Mormon to see how Mormon did it with his "and thus we see" passages. A careful study of Orson F. Whitney's *Life of Heber C. Kimball* or Matthias Cowley's *Life of Wilford Woodruff* will also demonstrate how one teaches facts and draws great lessons of faith therefrom. I would like to feel that all my grandchildren are edified, strengthened, and inspired as a result of your classes. ("The Gospel Teacher and His Message," Religious Educators, Salt Lake City, Utah, 17 September 1976.)

Let us teach the youth to love the prophets who have served as mouthpieces for God Almighty. Let us teach them a love for the pioneers. Teach them to be proud of their heritage, grateful for their foundations, for all the virtues and principles for which the Church stands. Teach them to love purity and virtue and the good life. Teach them to love all the commandments, and that they are given to them for their good by a kind Father who loves them. Teach them to love life, to love the Church and its programs, and to get in the full swing of it. (*Title of Liberty*, pp. 206–7.)

Teach our young people to love freedom, to know that it is God-given. Teach them that the Constitution of the United States was established by men whom God raised up for that very purpose, that it is not outmoded, that it is not an old-fashioned agrarian document, as some men in high places are calling it today. Teach them to love the scriptures, especially the Book of Mormon.

Teach them to form an acquaintance with Nephi, Alma, and Moroni. Teach them to know the power of prayer, that they can reach out and tap that unseen power, without which help no man can do his best. Teach them the need for spirituality, whether they are in the classroom or employed. But above all, teach them to know that God lives, that Jesus is the Christ, the Savior and Redeemer of the world, that these two heavenly beings, our Father and our Savior Jesus Christ, did in very deed appear to the boy prophet in the Sacred Grove. Teach them to know this, and it will be an anchor to them in all the days to come. (*An Enemy Hath Done This*, pp. 303–4.)

Teachers, because of your example and influence upon young people, they will come to you from time to time for counsel on personal problems. May I urge you to develop a close relationship with their ecclesiastical leaders, so that when they do come to you, you can guide them to their bishops. This permits the problems to be handled in the Lord's way. Never must you get between the student and his own bishop. ("The Gospel Teacher and His Message," Religious Educators, Salt Lake City, Utah, 17 September 1976.)

The Saints in all ages have come to be converted, or in the words of the Book of Mormon, "changed from their carnal and fallen state, to a state of righteousness, being redeemed of God, becoming his sons and daughters; and thus they become new creatures" (Mosiah 27:25–26). This is what is meant by partaking of the "power of God." You teachers—you who are to teach the power of this gospel—I would ask you, "Have [you] spiritually been born of God? Have [you] received his image in your countenances? Have [you] experienced this mighty change in your hearts?" (Alma 5:14.)

A measure of this change of heart is what happens to the motives and desires of the gospel teacher. Enos testified that he "began to feel a desire for the welfare of my brethren" (Enos 9). Alma, who also experienced this mighty change, said: "I have labored without ceasing, that I might bring souls unto repentance; that I might bring them to taste of the exceeding joy of which I did taste" (Alma 36:24). May your motives be likewise as pure. May the welfare of your students be the primary motive to your teaching. May you be converted so you can strengthen your students. ("The Gospel Teacher and His Message," Religious Educators, Salt Lake City, Utah, 17 September 1976.)

To paraphrase the Master Teacher, we would say to you, "Teacher, heal thyself!" (see Luke 4:23) or as He said on another occasion to His chief Apostle, "When thou art converted, strengthen thy brethren" (Luke 22:32). Conversion to Jesus Christ and His gospel is more than testimony; it is to be healed spiritually. In Paul's words, it is to partake of "the power of God" (Romans 1:16). A most commendable example of this process is found in the Book of Mormon in the story of Enos. You are all too familiar with the story for me to repeat the background. I only want to draw your attention to these verses. Enos testified: "I will tell you of the wrestle which I had before God, before I received a remission of my sins" (Enos 2).

Then Enos testified, "There came a voice unto me, saying: Enos, thy sins are forgiven thee, and thou shalt be blessed . . . wherefore, my guilt was swept away" (Enos 5–6). When he inquired of the Lord how this had been accomplished, the Lord answered him: "Because of thy faith in Christ . . . thy faith hath made thee whole" (Enos 8). Enos was spiritually healed. Through his mighty supplications to God, he experienced what the faithful of any dispensation can, do, and must experience if they are to see God. ("The Gospel Teacher and His Message," Religious Educators, Salt Lake City, Utah, 17 September 1976.)

In Lehi's vision of the tree of life, he saw a man dressed in a white robe who beckoned him to follow him through the dark and dreary waste, which represented the temptations of the world. With the help of prayer, Lehi was led to partake of the fruit of that tree, which provided him "with exceeding great joy." (See 1 Nephi 8:6–12.) We would hope that you teachers would be as men in white robes, leading our youth safely through the temptations of the world so that they too may partake of the tree of life and have exceeding great joy. ("The Gospel Teacher and His Message," Religious Educators, Salt Lake City, Utah, 17 September 1976.)

We who know of Him must teach others who are now in the dark. We Latter-day Saints are the custodians of a new revelation of God, the restored gospel of Christ. We, as members of His Church, are under covenant to preach it and live it. Our lives and our words can save the world. ("A Voice of Warning to the Nations of the World," New Zealand and Australia Area Conferences, 25 November 1979 and 2 December 1979.)

The teaching of the word then is the answer to the redemption of souls. This is what we are about today. (Regional Representatives Seminar, Salt Lake City, Utah, 6 April 1984.)

Preaching

I have a conviction: The more we teach and preach from the Book of Mormon, the more we shall please the Lord and the greater will be our power of speaking. By so doing, we shall greatly increase our converts, both within the Church and among those we proselyte. The Lord expects us to use this book, and we remain under His condemnation if we do not (see D&C 84:57). Our commission then is to teach the principles of the gospel which are in the Bible and the Book of Mormon. "These shall be their teachings, as they shall be directed by the Spirit" (D&C 42:13).

Our preaching and our teaching must be by the power of the Holy Ghost. There are so many passages that counsel us to teach by the power of the Holy Ghost. We must ever remember that in this glorious work, the most essential element is the Spirit. (Salt Lake City, Utah, 2 October 1985.)

"Seek not to declare my word, but first seek to obtain my word, and then shall your tongue be loosed; then, if you desire, you shall have my Spirit and my word, yea, the power of God unto the convincing of men" (D&C 11:21). His admonitions to us reveal a sequence to possessing the power of God in our message. First, it is to obtain the word, then we obtain understanding and the Spirit, and finally the power to convince. You can't fool the Spirit. Some have tried only to learn of their own folly. (Salt Lake City, Utah, 19 January 1977.)

I don't believe we ever lose anything by speaking out about the Church. I remember the Lord took some of the early elders to task because they were a bit hesitant to speak out. The Lord has a way all the time of driving points home. He is a wonderful teacher — the best of course — unequalled. Frequently in these early revelations He would praise the elders for the good things they had done, and then He would turn right around and chastise them for some of the things they hadn't done. Good parents do that with their children. Then He said that "with some I am not well pleased, for they will not open their mouths, but they hide the talent which I have given them, because of the fear of man. Wo unto such for mine anger is kindled against them." (D&C 60:2.) ("The Home and Family," BYU Religious Life Series, Provo, Utah, September 1960.)

As individuals and society depart more and more from the laws of God, we will need to regulate the affairs of the Church, teaching persuasively the laws of God and His pattern for happiness.

Alma bore testimony to this fact when he said, "And now, as the preaching of the word had a great tendency to lead the people to do that which was just—yea, it had had more powerful effect upon the minds of the people than the sword, or anything else, which had happened unto them—therefore Alma thought it was expedient that they should try the virtue of the word of God" (Alma 31:5). (Salt Lake City, Utah, 6 June 1980.)

The Lord speaks to us in this question: "Unto what were ye ordained?" (D&C 50:13.) He gives us the answer: "To preach my gospel by the Spirit, even the Comforter which was sent forth to teach the truth" (D&C 50:14). In the same manner He points out that if we speak in any other way than by the Spirit of truth, it will not be of God (D&C 50:17–18). He also tells us that if the listeners receive by any other spirit than the Spirit of truth, it is not of God (D&C 50:19–20). I am given comfort and hope that when both speaker and listener are given the power to speak and hear by the Spirit of truth, both are edified and rejoice together (D&C 50:21–22). They taste of the heavenly light (D&C 50:24). (Mission Presidents Seminar, Salt Lake City, Utah, 27–28 June 1974.)

I was down in southern Utah some years ago; it was in the summer and very hot. Their people were very faithful and the building was filled, and here again the stake president insisted that I take the last forty minutes or so, and at the end of the meeting, a lovely Primary teacher came up the aisle with her little group of boys so that I might shake hands with them, and as they went by I shook each boy's hand. Each one of them had something nice to say about the talk and I presume they had been properly coached, but as I came to the end of the line there was a little freckled-faced, red-headed fellow with a gleam in his eye and he looked me squarely in the face and he said, "Elder Benson, that was a good talk, but it sure was long." I have never forgotten it. (Star Valley Wyoming Stake Conference, 18 April 1971.)

Preaching the saving principles of the gospel has ever been a great responsibility of first importance. It is true in this gospel dispensation. Following the glorious appearance of God the Father and His Son Jesus Christ to Joseph Smith, it appears that the first great responsibility placed upon the restored Church was to carry the gospel to the world—to all our Father's children.

It has truly been a great drama of transcendent importance—a drama of sacrifice, joy, hardship, courage, and, above all, love of fellowmen. Nowhere upon the face of the earth will you find a human drama to equal it. Yes, it has cost blood, sweat, and tears to carry forth this labor of love. And why have we done it? Because the God of Heaven has commanded it; because He loves His children, and it is His will that the teeming millions of the earth shall have opportunity to hear and, of their own free will, accept and live the glorious saving and exalting principles of the gospel of Jesus Christ. (CR April 1970, *Improvement Era* 73 [June 1970]: 95.)

Seminary and Institute

Regularly attend seminary and be a seminary graduate. Seminary instruction is one of the most significant spiritual experiences a young woman or man can have. ("To the Young Women of the Church," *Ensign* 16 [November 1986]: 82.)

When we have asked mission presidents how we can more effectively prepare a young man for missionary service, they have responded that those young men who have availed themselves of the seminary and institute programs of the Church are much better prepared. Priesthood leaders must therefore give constant encouragement to these excellent programs. ("Challenges for Leaders of Aaronic Priesthood," Young Men's General Presidency and Board, Salt Lake City, Utah, 19 September 1979.)

There seems to be a decline in faith—faith in God as the Creator of heaven and earth, the Father of our spirits. There is a decrease in faith in Jesus the Christ as the Redeemer and Savior of mankind, not just a great teacher, our elder brother in the spirit, the Redeemer of the world. And this institution will be a place where men and women can come and learn the most essential knowledge available to men in this world. (Seattle Washington LDS Institute Dedication, 29 October 1961.)

Seminary and institute teachers, you represent the First Presidency in all you do and in the way you appear. We expect that you will be conservative and well groomed. The expression "follow the Brethren" has a broader meaning than some would apply to it. It means not only to agree with the counsel given to the Church by the Brethren, but also to follow their example in appearance and deportment. As teachers you need constantly to ask, "How would the Savior have me appear before others? How would He have me act?" You should not imitate worldly fashions in your dress or so-called modern expressions in your language. Your hair style should be in conformity with the standards of the Church. You are on the front line, so to speak, in impressing our young men to serve missions. Certainly you should provide them with an example of what we are asking future missionaries to conform to. ("The Gospel Teacher and His Message," Religious Educators, Salt Lake City, Utah, 17 September 1976.)

Your responsibility is to live as you teach. Be consistent in your life with the message you declare to your students. The majority of you have provided strong, commendable examples of what a Latter-day Saint life and home should be. How many students have been induced into righteous decisions because of the examples of their seminary and institute teachers! "I want to be just like them" is an often-heard expression referring to you as a husband and wife team We think those expressions are well deserved and we commend you for the examples you set. ("The Gospel Teacher and His Message," Religious Educators, Salt Lake City, Utah, 17 September 1976.)

It has come to our attention that some of our teachers, particularly in our university programs, are purchasing writings from known apostates, or from other liberal sources, in an effort to become informed about certain points of view or to glean from their research. You must realize that when you purchase their writings or subscribe to their periodicals, you help sustain their cause. We would hope that their writings not be on your seminary or institute or personal bookshelves. We are entrusting you to represent the Lord and the First Presidency to your students, not the views of the detractors of the Church. ("The Gospel Teacher and His Message," Religious Educators, Salt Lake City, Utah, 17 September 1976.)

Permit me to offer you a word of counsel about writing books or articles. Some of you have desired to write, and we do not discourage that. Because of problems with some writings from some of our teachers who have put themselves in print, it is well to give you some cautions. Doctrinal interpretation is the province of the First Presidency. The Lord has given that stewardship to them by revelation. No teacher has the right to interpret doctrine for the members of the Church. If Church members would remember that, we could do away with a number of books which have troubled some of our people. ("The Gospel Teacher and His Message," Religious Educators, Salt Lake City, Utah, 17 September 1976.)

Sometimes gospel principles are written with such erudition that the gospel is hardly recognizable in them. Worldly phraseology and authorities replace the scriptures and the prophets. You institute teachers need to be aware of this in teaching courses such as Courtship and Marriage, and in giving counsel on child rearing. Be careful of blending your worldly training with the gospel courses you teach lest you be guilty of diluting the pure gospel of Jesus Christ and end up teaching the philosophy of men mingled with a few scriptures. ("The Gospel Teacher and His Message," Religious Educators, Salt Lake City, Utah, 17 September 1976.)

We must balance our secular learning with spiritual learning. You young men should be as earnest in enrolling in seminary and learning the scriptures as you are in working toward high school graduation. Young adults enrolled in universities and colleges or other post-secondary training should avail themselves of the opportunity to take institute of religion courses or, if attending a Church school, take at least one religion course every term. Joining our spiritual education to our secular will help us keep focused on the things that matter most in this life. Though I am speaking to you priesthood holders, the same admonition applies to the women of the Church as well. (CR October 1986, *Ensign* 16 [November 1986]: 46.)

May God bless those who teach students, that they may be able to inspire and to plant faith in their hearts and give them that assurance and that confidence, that peace of mind which can be theirs with the proper balance between the spiritual and the secular. This is my prayer for all of the young people who will take part in the programs offered at the institute of religion. (Seattle Washington LDS Institute Dedication, 29 October 1961.)

Science

Be mindful that there are many phenomena in God's universe that cannot, to our present human understanding, be explained. There will always be those little minds who, out of vanity or intellectual display, will attempt to destroy faith in the very foundations of life. Be assured, however, that no man worthy of the name, who has been humbled and awed before the unexplainable wonders of this marvelous universe, will ever scoff at sacred things or try to rob you of your faith in the unseen. ("Your Charge: To Increase in Wisdom and Favor with God and Man," *New Era* 9 [September 1979]: 42.)

It is unscientific and unscholarly to waste time attempting to prove or disprove things that have already been established beyond question. The true scientist no longer attempts to disprove the pull of gravity, or the rotation of the earth, or the motion of heavenly bodies, or the sequence of the seasons, or man's need of food and water, or the function of the heart. These things are established, and for each individual to bring them into question and insist on going through all the experimentation whereby they have been established would be costly, wasteful, and unfeasible. ("Your Charge: To Increase in Wisdom and Favor with God and Man," *New Era* 9 [September 1979]: 41.)

Our educational system must be based on freedom—never force. But we can and should place special emphasis on developing in our youth constructive incentives—a love of science, engineering, and math, so that they will want to take advanced scientific courses and thereby help meet the needs of our times. Just as a musician has a love of music which drives him to become outstanding in that field, so we must inculcate in some of our qualified young people such an interest in science that they will turn to it of themselves. (*The Red Carpet*, p. 177.)

The people of the world generally know that this Church, this people, are intensely interested in education. I know of no people anywhere that have a deeper, more fundamental interest in education. It extends to all fields of education—agricultural science, yes, the science of crop production, the science of animal-livestock farming, the science of farm management, and the science of irrigation. Everything that has to do with man's life here on the earth and his eternal welfare is the concern of the Church and kingdom of God. (Welfare Meeting, General Conference, 5 April 1958.)

Humanism and Secularism

As a nation, we have become self-sufficient. This has given birth to a new religion in America which some have called secularism. This is a view of life with the idea that God is not in the picture and that He has nothing to do with the picture in the first place. ("God's Hand in Our Nation's History," Sons of Utah Pioneers, Salt Lake City, Utah, 23 August 1986.)

The world worships the learning of man. They trust in the arm of flesh (see D&C 1:19). To them, men's reasoning is greater than God's revelations. The precepts of man have gone so far in subverting our educational system that in many cases a higher degree today, in the so-called social sciences, can be tantamount to a major investment in error. Very few men build firmly enough on the rock of revelation to go through this kind of indoctrination and come out untainted. Unfortunately, of those who succumb, some use their higher degree to get teaching positions even in our Church Educational System, where they spread the falsehoods they have been taught. (See *Gospel Doctrine*, pp. 312–13.) (*God, Family, Country*, p. 258.)

It seems fashionable today for historians to "secularize" our history. Many modern scholars seem uncomfortable with the idea that a divine power had a hand in the beginning of our nation. They seek to explain away what the colonists themselves saw as divine intervention in their behalf. They credit even those remarkable events to "natural causes" or "rational" explanations. All events are explained from a "humanistic" frame of reference. This removes the need for faith in God or a belief that He is interested in the affairs of men. ("Righteousness Exalteth a Nation," Provo Utah Freedom Festival, 29 June 1986.)

A problem occurs on occasion when, in the pursuit of higher degrees, one becomes so imbued with the terminology and methodology of a secular discipline that, almost without realizing it, he compromises the gospel message. The simple principles of the gospel, not the disciplines of men, should always be our basis for truth. ("The Gospel Teacher and His Message," Religious Educators, Salt Lake City, Utah, 17 September 1976.)

Today, students are subjected in their textbooks and classroom lectures to a subtle propaganda that there is a "natural" or rational explanation to all causes and events. Such a position removes the need for faith in God, or belief in His interposition in the affairs of men. Events are only—and I stress that—only explained from a humanistic frame of reference.

Historians and educational writers who are responsible for this movement are classified as "revisionists." Their purpose has been and is to create a "new history." By their own admission they are more influenced by their own training and other humanistic and scientific disciplines than any religious conviction. This detachment provides them, they say, with an objectivity that the older historians did not have.

Many of the older historians, I should point out, were defenders of the patriots and their noble efforts. Feeling no obligation to perpetuate the ideals of the Founding Fathers, some of the "new historians" have recast a new body of beliefs for their secular faith. Their efforts, in some cases, have resulted in a new interpretation of our nation's history. ("God's Hand in Our Nation's History," Sons of Utah Pioneers, Salt Lake City, Utah, 23 August 1986.)

From the fifth grade through the fourth year of college, our young people are being indoctrinated with a Marxist philosophy, and I am fearful of the harvest. The younger generation is further to the left than most adults realize. The old concepts of our Founding Fathers are scoffed and jeered at by young moderns whose goals appear to be the destruction of integrity and virtue, and the glorification of pleasure, thrills, and self-indulgence. ("The Greatest Work in the World," *Improvement Era* 70 [January 1967]: 26.)

Youth of the world, as you strive to increase in favor with man, be ever on your guard that you do not unwittingly, in the name of tolerance, broadmindedness, and so-called liberalism, encourage foreign "isms" and unsound theories that strike at the very root of all we hold dear, including our faith in God. Proposals will be offered and programs will be sponsored that have wide, so-called "humanitarian" appeal. Attractive labels are usually attached to the most dangerous programs, often in the name of public welfare and personal security. Have the courage to apply this standard of truth. Determine what the effect of the various issues at stake is upon the character, the integrity, and the freedom of man. (*God, Family, Country*, p. 7.)

Entertainment

Successful parents have found that it is not easy to rear children in an environment polluted with evil. Therefore, they take deliberate steps to provide the best of wholesome influences. Moral principles are taught. Good books are made available and read. Television watching is controlled. Good and uplifting music is provided. But most important, the scriptures are read and discussed as a means to help develop spiritual mindedness. (CR April 1984, *Ensign* 14 [May 1984]: 6.)

Early in life, these two quotations regarding books greatly influenced me: "Be as careful of the book you read as of the company you keep, for your habits and character will be influenced by the former as by the latter"; and "Except a living man there is nothing so wonderful as good books." With all my heart, I urge young people to cultivate the reading habit. But in order that your reading be of maximum value choose it as carefully as you do your friends. I trust that we do so remembering that if we spend time reading a cheap book, we will be forced to pass by a choice one. (*So Shall Ye Reap*, p. 133.)

The leisure time of children must be constructively directed to wholesome, positive pursuits. Too much time viewing television can be destructive, and pornography in this medium should not be tolerated. (CR October 1982, *Ensign* 12 [November 1982]: 60.)

Now, what of the entertainment that is available to our young people today? Are you being undermined right in your homes through your television, radio, slick magazines, and rock music records? Much of the rock music is purposely designed to push immorality, narcotics, revolution, atheism, and nihilism through language that often carries a double meaning and with which many parents are not familiar. ("Strengthening the Family," Philippine Islands Area Conference, 12 August 1975.)

The devil-inspired destructive forces are present in our literature, in our art, in the movies, on the radio, in our dress, in our dances, on the television screen, and even in our modern so-called popular music. Satan uses many tools to weaken and destroy the home and the family, and especially our young people. Today, as never before, the devil's thrust is directed at you, our precious youth. (Scandinavia and Finland Area Conference, 16–18 August 1974.)

Most novels and pulp magazines are filled with a lot of rubbish, and most television and a lot of radio programs are a waste of time, if not corrupters of morals or distorters of truth. The less newspapers have to say of value and of truth, the more pages they seem to take to say it. Usually a few minutes is more than sufficient to read a paper. One must select wisely a source of news; otherwise it would be better to be uninformed than misinformed. The subscribers of some mass magazines and newspapers are ever reading but seldom able to come to a knowledge of the truth in the areas of most vital concern (see 2 Timothy 3:7). ("In His Steps," in *1979 Devotional Speeches of the Year* [Provo, Utah: BYU, 1980], pp. 61–62.)

Now, what kind of magazines come into your home? With perhaps one or two exceptions, I would not have any of the major national slick magazines in my home. As President J. Reuben Clark, Jr., so well put it, "Take up any national magazine, look at the ads and, if you can stand the filth, read some of the stories—they are, in their expressed and suggestive standards of life, destructive of the very foundations of our society" (CR April 1951, p. 79). (CR April 1969, *Improvement Era* 72 [June 1969]: 47.)

Youth leaders, are you holding aloft our standards, or have you compromised them for the lowest common denominator in order to appease the deceived or vile within the Church? Are the dances and music in your cultural halls virtuous, lovely, praiseworthy, and of good report (Article of Faith 13), or do they represent a modern Sodom with short skirts, loud beat, strobe lights, and darkness? (*God, Family, Country*, p. 229.)

Our young people must lead clean lives—clean in their actions, clean in their thoughts. This means that they cannot indulge promiscuously in so-called petting and necking. My advice to them would be not to engage in these promiscuous relationships, these close and intimate contacts including cheek-to-cheek dancing on the ballroom floor, whether it be at a Church dance, a public dance, or wherever it might be. I urge that they never do anything, on the dance floor or off the dance floor, that they would be ashamed to have their own fathers and mothers witness.

In all your relationships, when in doubt, do not enter into the act or practice. In fact, our young people should not enter into any activity if there is any doubt as to its propriety. If you are living right, you will have the prompting of the Spirit which will tell you whether it is right or wrong. Do not fail to heed that prompting, as I hope you will heed the counsel of your own parents and your leaders. (CR April 1959, *Improvement Era* 62 [June 1959]: 457.)

Promote only good literature and music in the home. Introduce your children to the best in art, music, literature, and entertainment. (CR October 1981, *Ensign* 11 [November 1981]: 107.)

The Book of Mormon declares that "every thing which inviteth and enticeth to do good, and to love God, and to serve him, is inspired of God." And "whatsoever thing persuadeth men to do evil, and believe not in Christ, and deny him, and serve not God, then ye may know with a perfect knowledge it is of the devil." (Moroni 7:13, 17.) Let us use that standard to judge what we read, the music we hear, the entertainment we watch, the thoughts we think. Let us be more Christlike. (CR April 1986, *Ensign* 16 [May 1986]: 78.)

Music

I enjoy music. I am grateful for good music. I think it is the finest of the fine arts. I am grateful to our Heavenly Father that He has blessed some of His children with a fine musical talent and that He has blessed others with an appreciation of good music. (Czechoslovakia, 26 November 1946.)

Inspiring music may fill the soul with heavenly thoughts, move one to righteous action, or speak peace to the soul. When Saul was troubled with an evil spirit, David played for him with his harp and Saul was refreshed and the evil spirit departed (see 1 Samuel 16:23). "Memorize some of the inspiring songs of Zion and then, when the mind is afflicted with temptations, sing aloud, keep before your mind the inspiring words and thus crowd out the evil thoughts." This could also be done to crowd out debilitating, depressive thoughts. ("Do Not Despair," *Ensign* 16 [October 1986]: 5.)

Encourage our people to have music that contributes to spirituality and worship, whether it be prelude music or the songs that are selected. That doesn't mean it wouldn't be appropriate to have a patriotic song, such as "The Battle Hymn of the Republic" (*Hymns*, 1985, no. 60). "America" is also a hymn (*Hymns*, 1985, no. 339). Music is such an important part of our service. (Salt Lake City, Utah, 3 October 1978.)

One of our fine musicians has suggested a top ten for great music. May I just mention them—at least three or four of them. Bach's "Jesu, Joy of Man's Desiring," known to you as the pop tune, "Joy"; Handel's *Messiah*—start by listening to single numbers and then expand as they become familiar, (the "Hallelujah Chorus" may be a good starting point); Mozart's "Symphony No. 40 in G minor" (you will recognize this also from the pops version); Beethoven's "Symphony No. 5 in C Minor;" and so on. (BYU Ten-Stake Fireside, Provo, Utah, 7 May 1972.)

Have you been listening to the music that many young folks are hearing today? Some of it is nerve-jamming in nature and much of it has been deliberately designed to promote revolution, dope, immorality, and a gap between parent and child. And some of this music has invaded our Church cultural halls.

Have you noticed some of our Church dances lately? Have they been praiseworthy, lovely, and of good report? (Article of Faith 13.) "I doubt, " said President David O. McKay, "whether it is possible to dance most of the prevalent fad dances in a manner to meet LDS standards." (CR April 1969, *Improvement Era* 72 [June 1969]: 46–47.)

The Spirit of the Lord blesses that which edifies and leads men to Christ. Would His Spirit bless with its presence these festering rock festivals of human degradation? Its music, crushing the sensibilities in a din of primitive idolatry, is in glorification of the physical to the debasement of the spirit. In the long panorama of man's history, these rock music festivals are among Satan's greatest successes. The legendary orgies of Greece and Rome cannot compare to the monumental obscenities found in these cesspools of drugs, immorality, rebellion, and pornophonic sound. The famed Woodstock festival was a gigantic manifestation of a sick nation. Yet the lurid movie and rock recordings of its unprecedented filth were big business in our own mountain home.

The Lord said, "For my soul delighteth in the song of the heart; yea, the song of the righteous is a prayer unto me" (D&C 25:12). It was pleasing unto the Lord where in the Book of Mormon we read that "they did break forth, all as one, in singing, and praising their God" (3 Nephi 4:31). It was pleasing unto Satan when Lehi's children and the "sons of Ishmael and also their wives began to make themselves merry, insomuch that they began to dance, and to sing, and to speak with much rudeness" (1 Nephi 18:9). (*God, Family, Country*, pp. 248–49.)

The magnetism of television and radio is in the accessibility of their mediocrity. *Lovely* is not an adjective to describe most of their products. The inventors of these wonders were inspired by the Lord. But once their good works were introduced to the world, the powers of darkness began to employ them for our destruction.

May I quote from Richard Nibley, a musician who for many years has observed the influence of music on behavior:

> Satan knows that music hath charms to sooth or stir the savage beast. That music has power to create atmosphere has been known before the beginning of Hollywood. Atmosphere creates environment, and environment influences behavior—the behavior of Babylon or of Enoch.
>
> Parents who retch at the radio and records reverberating in psychedelic revolt would do well to inventory their own record collection before complaining. If it is small, undiversified, and unused, the complaint must rest on the parent. Seeds of culture are best sown in the fertile ground of infant imitation. No amount of criticizing in the teen years can substitute for the young years of example that are lost.

(*God, Family, Country*, p. 250.)

Rock music, with its instant physical appeal, is an ideal door-crasher, for the devil knows that music has the power to ennoble or corrupt, to purify or pollute. He will not forget to use its subtle power against you. His sounds come from the dark world of drugs, immorality, obscenity, and anarchy. His sounds are flooding the earth. It is his day—a day that is to become as the days of Noah before the Second Coming, for the prophets have so predicted. The signs are clear. The signs are here in this blessed land. You cannot escape this mass media environment which is controlled by financial censorship. Records, radio, television, movies, magazines—all are monopolized by the money managers who are guided by one ethic, the words *wealth* and *power*. (BYU Ten-Stake Fireside, Provo, Utah, 7 May 1972.)

Don't listen to music that is degrading. "Music can, by its tempo, by its beat, by its intensity (and I would add by its lyrics) dull the spiritual sensitivity of men (and women). Young people, you cannot afford to fill your minds with this unworthy, hard music of our day." ("Inspiring Music—Worthy Thoughts," *Ensign* 4 [January 1974]: 25.)

Instead, we encourage you to listen to uplifting music, both popular and classical, that builds the spirit. Learn some favorite

Example 327

hymns from our new hymnbook that build faith and spirituality. Attend dances where the music and the lighting and the dance movements are conducive to the Spirit. ("To the Young Women of the Church," *Ensign* 16 [November 1986]: 84.)

Give more than lip service to the thirteenth article of faith, and actually seek after that "which is lovely and of good report." Enlist your parents in a project to replace your record library with music of the masters, of your heritage. Peter pictured the times so evident today when in the last days he saw "scoffers walking after their own lusts" (2 Peter 3:3). The scoffers are "in" and your will must be strong to stay a "square." (BYU Ten-Stake Fireside, Provo, Utah, 7 May 1972.)

Example

Christ, the Great Exemplar

A man can ask no more important question in his life than that which Paul asked: "Lord, what wilt thou have me to do?" (See Acts 9:6.) A man can take no greater action than to pursue a course that will bring to him the answer to that question and then to carry out that answer. What would the Lord Jesus Christ have us do? He has answered that question by saying, "Be ye therefore perfect, even as your Father which is in heaven is perfect" (Matthew 5:48), and, "Therefore, what manner of men ought ye to be? Verily, I say unto you, even as I am" (3 Nephi 27:27).

Christ, then, has set us the example of what we should be like and what we should do. While many men have admirable qualities, there is only one man who ever walked the earth who was without sin, whose father of His physical body was God the Father, and who had the power to resurrect His own body. This Jesus is our exemplar and has commanded us to follow in His steps. (*God, Family, Country,* pp. 155–56.)

The only measure of true greatness is how close a man can become like Jesus. That man is greatest who is most like Christ, and those who love Him most will be most like Him. How, then, does a man imitate God, follow His steps, and walk as He walked, which we are commanded to do? (See 3 Nephi 27:27; 1 Peter 2:21; 1 John 2:6.) We must study the life of Christ, learn His commandments, and do them. God has promised that to follow this course will lead a man to an abundant life, a fulness of joy, and the peace and rest for which those who are heavy burdened long. (*God, Family, Country*, p. 156.)

He gave us the perfect model—Himself—after which we are to pattern our lives. He said, "Greater love hath no man than this, that a man lay down his life for his friends" (John 15:13). Not only did He set for us the perfect example of earthly living, but for our sake He willingly gave up His life. He went through agony both in body and spirit, which we cannot comprehend, to give to us the glorious blessing of the Atonement and the Resurrection. (See D&C 19:15–19.)

Some men are willing to die for their faith, but they are not willing to fully live for it. Christ both lived and died for us. By walking in His steps and through His atonement, we can gain the greatest gift of all—eternal life—which is that kind of life lived by the great Eternal One—our Father in Heaven. ("Jesus Christ—Gifts and Expectations," Christmas Devotional, Salt Lake City, Utah, 7 December 1986.)

The Lord said, "Look unto me in every thought" (D&C 6:36). Looking unto the Lord in every thought is the only possible way we can be the manner of men and women we ought to be. (*Come unto Christ*, p. 41.)

Let our actions be Christlike so that by our diligence and with God's grace we may add to our character faith, virtue, knowledge, temperance, patience, brotherly kindness, godliness, charity, humility, and diligence. Our objective is to attain such a "divine nature." (See 2 Peter 1:5–7.)

Let us therefore strive to have, as Alma admonished, "the image of God engraven on [our] countenances" (Alma 5:19). Let our personal lives, our homes, and our work performance reflect our Christlike character. So live that others will say about you, "There is a true Christian!"

Yes, we believe in Jesus Christ, but more—we look to Him, we trust Him and strive to emulate His attributes because there has not been nor will there ever be "any other name given nor any

Example 329

other way nor means whereby salvation can come unto the children of men, only in and through the name of Christ, the Lord Omnipotent" (Mosiah 3:17). ("After All We Can Do," Christmas Devotional, Salt Lake City, Utah, 9 December 1982.)

Men changed for Christ will be captained by Christ. Peter stated, they will "follow his steps" (1 Peter 2:21). John said they will "walk, even as he walked" (1 John 2:6).

Finally, men captained by Christ will be consumed in Christ. To paraphrase President Harold B. Lee, they set fire in others because they are on fire (see *Stand Ye in Holy Places*, p. 192). Their will is swallowed up in His will (see John 5:30). They do always those things that please the Lord (see John 8:29). Not only would they die for the Lord, but more important they want to live for Him. (CR October 1985, *Ensign* 15 [November 1985]: 6.)

Personal Example

Lehi, Nephi's father, lived an exemplary life. He had a vision in which he "beheld a tree, whose fruit was desirable to make one happy" (1 Nephi 8:10). This tree represented the love of God (see 1 Nephi 11:25). Lehi partook of its fruit, which "filled [his] soul with exceeding great joy" (verse 12). After he had a personal testimony of its goodness, he took the next step of inviting his family to also partake.

Fathers, here is a divine pattern: As the leader of the family, Lehi first taught by example. He led out in righteousness—in conversion to Christ. Then he taught by word, saying, "Believe as I believe." (CR October 1985, *Ensign* 15 [November 1985]: 35.)

The Lord has admonished us to "arise and shine" and be a "standard to the nations" (see D&C 115:5). He said, "Let your light so shine before men, that they may see your good works, and glorify your Father which is in heaven" (Matthew 5:16). Yes, the Lord intends that we be a light to the world. ("Youth—Promise for the Future," BYU Graduation, Provo, Utah, 19 April 1986.)

We are in the world, and I fear some of us are getting too much like the world. Rather than continue a peculiar people, some are priding themselves on how much they are like everybody else, when the world is getting more wicked. The Lord, as He prayed for His Apostles, said, "The world hath hated them, because they are not of the world, even as I am not of the world" (John 17:14). As Latter-day Saints, we too have been called out of the world. (CR October 1964, *Improvement Era* 67 [December 1964]: 1067.)

I wish that a record were available of the number of people who have been attracted to the Church because of the example they have seen in missionaries. I heard two wonderful women in a meeting one night bear testimony that they were first attracted to the Church by seeing a couple of Mormon elders go by their window day after day. One said that she would see them go out in the morning, come back about noon, go out shortly after lunch, and come back in the evening. She said, "Sometimes we would be working in the garden, but mostly we would be sitting in the front room and we would see them go by. They made such an impression upon us that we asked the police officer in our neighborhood who they were and what they were doing." And she said, "It was that example that first compelled us to go to one of their meetings. Now we are members of the Church." (*God, Family Country*, p. 64.)

The gospel of Jesus Christ has always been essentially a plan for living more abundantly. To do so requires righteous, worthwhile effort and application. If we are to pattern our lives in accordance with the divine example set for us by the Savior, we must attain to that stature by releasing and developing our capacities to the fullest through devoted service. Only in this way may we become worthy examples of the kingdom of God on earth and merit consideration for membership in the kingdom of God in heaven. ("Power Through Service," *Millennial Star* 118 [9 October 1956]: 298.)

The proper example is all-important. Let us be what we profess to be. There is no satisfactory substitute. Who was it said, "What you are rings so loud in my ears I cannot hear what you say?" It was said of one of the great Chinese philosophers and teachers that he did not have to teach, all he had to do was to be. ("Leadership and the Needs of Youth," *Improvement Era* 51 [August 1948]: 494.)

We do stand as witnesses before God "at all times and in all things, and in all places" by our actions (see Mosiah 18:9). When our actions are honorable, we bring credit to His Church and kingdom; when they are not, it reflects on the entire Church. ("Honor," *New Era* 14 [July 1984]: 6.)

God bless and keep you. Be true to every principle, standard, and ideal of the gospel of Jesus Christ. Only in one way can you pay the debt you owe to these who proudly watch you. You must be what you profess to be, worthy descendants of noble progenitors who have vouchsafed to you a glorious heritage and who loved truth and virtue more than life itself. Can you live worthy of your heritage and of meeting them in those eternal worlds? It is up to you. ("Concerning Values," Utah State University Baccalaureate Address, Logan, Utah, 28 May 1950.)

Fasting

Periodic fasting can help clear up the mind and strengthen the body and the spirit. The usual fast, the one we are asked to participate in for fast Sunday, is for twenty-four hours without food or drink. Some people, feeling the need, have gone on longer fasts of abstaining from food but have taken the needed liquids. Wisdom should be used, and the fast should be broken with light eating. To make a fast most fruitful, it should be coupled with prayer and meditation; physical work should be held to a minimum, and it is a blessing if one can ponder on the scriptures and the reason for the fast. (CR October 1974, *Ensign* 4 [November 1974]: 66–67.)

Prayer can be combined with other gospel principles to accomplish marvelous things. Combined with fasting, it can cast out devils (see Matthew 17:21). (*God, Family, Country*, p. 119.)

I am confident that as leaders we do not do enough fasting and praying. If you want to get the spirit of your office and calling as a new president of a quorum, a new high councilman, a new bishop —try fasting for a period. I don't mean just missing one meal, then eating twice as much the next meal. I mean really fasting, and praying during that period. It will do more to give you the real spirit of your office and calling and permit the Spirit to operate through you than anything I know. (Fresno California Priesthood Leadership Meeting, 13 September 1952.)

Following the Brethren

There is no more crucial question that a man should be constantly asking than that which Paul asked: "Lord, what wilt thou have me to do?" (Acts 9:6.) There is no more essential answer than that which he received: to go to those who are authorized by the Lord to give directions. (*God, Family, Country*, p. 162.)

Latter-day Saints should not become bewildered. They should not become worried. They should not become confused in this great and modern world in which we live, with the great changes which are taking place, because we can have an anchor in these eternal principles and verities which should always bring to us the answer to the problems which face us from day to day. This is true whether it be a problem involving government, whether it be a problem involving us in business, whether it be some moral issue or some economic issue, we have the guide for the answer to these problems in the eternal principles that have been revealed and are set forth in holy writ and are given to us by the priesthood of God from the lips of those who preside in the earth in the day in which we live. (Washington D.C. Stake Conference, 8 March 1959.)

A lesson to be learned from the Kirtland, Ohio, experience is that those who complain and murmur against the leaders of the Church lose their faith. A testimony of the gospel is contingent on one's possessing the Spirit of the Lord. If we complain against the Lord's servants, the heavens are offended, the Spirit is withdrawn, and amen to that individual's faith. President David O. McKay once wrote: "Murmuring against priesthood and auxiliary leadership is one of the most poisonous things that can be introduced into the home of a Latter-day Saint" (*Improvement Era*, March 1969, p. 3). ("The Significance of Kirtland," Kirtland Ohio Ward Chapel Dedication, 17 October 1982.)

We should learn to accept counsel. All of us need counsel. Sometimes there is need for reprimanding. I do not suppose that any of us who served for any length of time have not been on the receiving end of some pointed counsel that was for our benefit. "Whom the Lord loveth he chasteneth" (Hebrews 12:6).

Brethren, if you can receive counsel, and will seek it, you will prosper in the work; if you cannot, you will not be magnified. I have seen a few over the years who were determined to pursue their own course, their own program. I have come to see that receiving counsel is a test of obedience by which the Lord magnifies His servants. (Salt Lake City, Utah, 2 October 1985.)

When one understands that God reveals His work only through chosen witnesses, we should not think it extraordinary that He has chosen witnesses today to establish His truths. ("Martin Harris—A Special Witness," Martin Harris Memorial Amphitheater Dedication, Clarkston, Utah, 6 August 1983.)

The Lord spoke frequently regarding the obligations of the elders of the Church and ofttimes commended them for their faithfulness and devotion, even to the extent of indicating that whatever they spoke when moved upon by the Holy Ghost would be the will of the Lord, the word of the Lord, and would be scripture to the people (see D&C 68:4). (*So Shall Ye Reap*, p. 39.)

I commend my Brethren of the General Authorities for the excellent addresses they have given. My humble prayer is that all of us will follow the counsel and instruction we have received.

As we have felt the Spirit and made new and sacred resolves, may we now have the courage and fortitude to carry out those resolves.

For the next six months your conference edition of the *Ensign* should stand next to your standard works and be referred to frequently. As my dear friend and brother Harold B. Lee said, we should let these conference addresses "be the guide to [our] walk and talk during the next six months. These are the important matters the Lord sees fit to reveal to this people in this day." (CR April 1946, p. 68.) (CR April 1988, *Ensign* 18 [May 1988]: 84.)

All the words of the Lord will be fulfilled, whether He gives the words Himself or through inspiration and revelation to His servants to declare those words, and the Holy Spirit bears testimony to all who seek to know the truth of the revelations and commandments (see D&C 1:38). ("A Voice of Warning," Hiram Ohio Branch Chapel Groundbreaking Service, 22 March 1986.)

Suppose a leader of the Church were to tell you that you were supporting the wrong side of a particular issue. Some might immediately resist this leader and his counsel or ignore it, but I would suggest that you first apply a great civic standard for the faithful Saints. That standard is to live for, to get, and then to follow the promptings of the Holy Spirit. (*God, Family, Country*, p. 323.)

I am reminded how Moses up on the hill raised his arms for the victory of the armies of Israel. As long as his arms were raised, Israel prevailed, but when they dropped from weariness, the enemy prevailed. And so Aaron and Hur "stayed up his hands, the one on the one side, and the other on the other side," and Israel was victorious (Exodus 17:12). So will we be victorious as we hold up the arms of the Lord's anointed servants. (CR April 1986, *Ensign* 16 [May 1986]: 77.)

If you want to be close to the Lord, if you want to have His favor and Spirit to be with you, follow the counsel of those who have been called to preside over you. ("Three Imperative Responsibilities, " London England Area Conference, 19–20 June 1976.)

The prophet and the presidency—the living prophet and the First Presidency—follow them and be blessed; reject them and suffer. President Harold B. Lee relates this incident from Church history:

> The story is told in the early days of the Church—particularly, I think, at Kirtland—where some of the leading brethren in the presiding councils of the Church met secretly and tried to scheme as to how they could get rid of the Prophet Joseph's leadership. They made the mistake of inviting Brigham Young to one of these secret meetings. He rebuked them, after he had heard the purpose of their meeting. This is part of what he said: "You cannot destroy the appointment of a prophet of God, but you can cut the thread that binds you to the prophet of God and sink yourselves to hell." (CR April 1963, p. 81.)

In a general conference of the Church, President N. Eldon Tanner stated:

A man said to me, "You know, there are people in our state who believe in following the Prophet in everything they think is right, but when it is something they think isn't right, and it doesn't appeal to them, then that's different." He said, "Then they become their own prophet. They decide what the Lord wants and what the Lord doesn't want."

I thought, how true! We will be led astray, because we are false prophets to ourselves when we do not follow the prophet of God. No, we should never discriminate between these commandments, as to those we should and should not keep. (CR October 1966, p. 98.)

"Look to the Presidency and receive instruction," said the Prophet Joseph Smith (*Teachings of the Prophet Joseph Smith*, p. 161). But Almon Babbitt didn't, and the Lord stated: "And with my servant Almon Babbitt, there are many things with which I am not pleased; behold, he aspireth to establish his counsel instead of the counsel which I have ordained, even that of the Presidency of my Church" (D&C 124:84). ("Fourteen Fundamentals in Following the Prophet," in *1980 Devotional Speeches of the Year*, [Provo: BYU Press, 1981], pp. 29–30.)

The living prophet is more important to us than a dead prophet. The living prophet has the power of TNT. By that I mean "Today's News Today." God's revelations to Adam did not instruct Noah how to build the ark. Noah needed his own revelation. Therefore, the most important prophet, so far as you and I are concerned, is the one living in our day and age to whom the Lord is currently revealing His will for us. Therefore, the most important reading we can do is any of the words of the prophet contained each week in the Church section of the *Deseret News* and any words of the prophet contained each month in our Church magazines. Our marching orders for each six months are found in the general conference addresses, which are printed in the *Ensign* magazine. ("Fourteen Fundamentals in Following the Prophet," in *1980 Devotional Speeches of the Year* [Provo: BYU Press, 1981], p. 27.)

It is too much to suppose that all the priesthood at this juncture will unite behind the prophet in the fight for freedom. Yet we can pray for that day, and in the meantime the faithful should strive to be in harmony with the inspired counsel given by the Lord's mouthpiece—the prophet—and thus in unity with the Lord—and hence receive peace to their souls. The more we are united with the Lord and His prophet, the greater will be our chances to preserve our families and to live in freedom. (*An Enemy Hath Done This*, p. 311.)

We don't need a prophet—we have one; we need a listening ear. And if we do not listen and heed, then "the day cometh that they who will not hear the voice of the Lord, neither the voice of his servants, neither give heed to the words of the prophets and apostles, shall be cut off from among the people" (D&C 1:14). (*God, Family, Country*, pp. 348–49.)

What we need is a listening ear, a humble heart, and a soul that is pure enough to follow the prophet's inspired guidance. (*An Enemy Hath Done This*, p. 307.)

If we want to know how well we stand with the Lord, let us ask ourselves how well we stand with His mortal captain. How closely do our lives harmonize with the words of the Lord's anointed—the living prophet, the President of the Church, and with the Quorum of the First Presidency? May God bless us all to look to the prophet and the presidency in the critical and crucial days ahead is my prayer. ("Fourteen Fundamentals in Following the Prophet," in *1980 Devotional Speeches of the Year* [Provo: BYU Press, 1981], p. 30.)

I know not what course others may take, but as for me and my house, we will strive to walk with the prophet. (*An Enemy Hath Done This*, p. 322.)

Gospel Living

Theology is not religion, although the terms are used loosely and often as if they were completely interchangeable in meaning. Both are important. Theology is a science—religion is an art. The sciences stress the acquisition of knowledge while the concern of the arts is mainly the development of specific skills. "The difference between theology and religion is much like the difference between knowing and doing.'' Theology represents what we know and say regarding God—our beliefs. Religion is what we do about it—the way we live our beliefs.

Religion might be defined as a mode of life which is the result of a belief in a superior being. Theological discussion alone is not in itself evidence that a person is living his religion. Not until we thoroughly and persistently apply the theological principles learned, can it be said that we are living our religion. (Annual Religion-in-Life Week, Ohio State University, Columbus, Ohio, 29 January 1957.)

We covenant to live the law of the gospel. The law of the gospel embraces all laws, principles, and ordinances necessary for our exaltation. We agree to exercise faith in Jesus Christ and sincere repentance borne out of a broken heart and a contrite spirit. As we comply with the ordinances of baptism and confirmation, and continue in faith and prayer, the power of the Savior's atoning sacrifice covers our sins and we are cleansed from all unrighteousness.

Now, this is the commandment: ''Repent, all ye ends of the earth, and come unto me and be baptized in my name, that ye may be sanctified by the reception of the Holy Ghost, that ye may stand spotless before me at the last day. Verily, verily, I say unto you, this is my gospel.'' (3 Nephi 27:20–21.)

The law of the gospel is more than understanding the plan of salvation. It consists of partaking of the ordinances and the sealing powers culminating in a man being sealed up unto eternal life. ''Being born again,'' said the Prophet Joseph Smith, ''comes by the spirit of God through ordinances'' (*Teachings*, p. 162). (''Temple Blessings and Covenants,'' Temple Presidents Seminar, Salt Lake City, Utah, 28 September 1982.)

It is not going to be enough just to accept the teachings, standards, and ideals of the Church passively. It will require real activity, real dedication to the principles of righteousness if we are to face the future unafraid. But if we have the courage, sound judgment, and the faith so to do, then no matter what happens we will be able to face any situation with courage and with faith and with the assurance that God will sustain us. I know that now is the time probably more than any other time in our lives to live the gospel.

We should not be lulled away into false security as Nephi said many would be in the last days. We should not be pacified and feel in our hearts that we can sin a little, that we can attend to our meetings part of the time, that we can pay a token tithing, that we can live the gospel when it is convenient, and all will be well. We must not be "at ease in Zion" and say "Zion prospers, all is well" (2 Nephi 28:21, 24). But we must live the gospel plan in its fulness every day of our lives. Therein is safety. Therein will come a satisfaction which comes from righteous living which will enter our hearts, give us the courage and the strength that we need. There is no security in unrighteousness. The sinful always live in despair (see Moroni 10:22). (*So Shall Ye Reap*, pp. 59–60.)

I believe that you gain more respect and more admiration and more love from people by being what you profess to be. We profess to be Latter-day Saints! I can't think of any finer profession for us to make than to be a Latter-day Saint and then live up to it. ("The Greatest Leadership," BYU Student Leadership Conference, Sun Valley, Idaho, September 1959.)

You can participate in this glorious endeavor to bring the gospel to all mankind. You can live the principles of the gospel. The Lord expects this of us. The Apostle Paul commended, "Be thou an example of the believers, in word, in conversation, in charity, in spirit, in faith, in purity" (1 Timothy 4:12). We are grateful that members of the Church for the most part are striving to live the gospel and dealing justly with their fellowmen. But are we not all saddened and disappointed when Church members are found guilty of taking advantage of others through business transactions or are judged guilty of breaking the laws of God and man? As Church members, blessed with the truths of the gospel, the Lord expects us to be honest, morally clean, chaste, free from profanity and vulgarity, trustworthy, and exemplary in all our conduct.

The Lord said to Church members of this dispensation: "But inasmuch as they keep not my commandments, and hearken not to observe all my words, the kingdoms of the world shall prevail against them. For they were set to be a light unto the world, and to be the saviors of men; And inasmuch as they are not the saviors of men, they are as salt that has lost its savor, and is thenceforth good for nothing but to be cast out and trodden under foot of men.'' (D&C 103:8–10.) (CR April 1985, *Ensign* 15 [May 1985]: 6–7.)

Happiness

The Lord wants us to be happy. He will do His part if we will do our part. The Christlike life is the life that brings true happiness. There is no true happiness without God. Sin brings sorrow, disappointment, and heartaches. Only the good life brings a happy new year. It pays to live the gospel of Jesus Christ. It pays to accept the teachings of the Master, to apply them in our lives, to be true to the standards of the Church, to be true to our covenants— to live the gospel. And if we do this we will be bigger and can be bigger than anything that can possibly happen to us. I am sure that is the desire of all of us because those who have this faith, and have a testimony of the divinity of this work, can endure anything and keep their spirits sweet. (''New Year 1961,'' Washington D.C. Ward, 31 December 1960.)

Be cheerful in all that you do. Live joyfully. Live happily. Live enthusiastically, knowing that God does not dwell in gloom and melancholy, but in light and love. (''Your Charge: To Increase in Wisdom and Favor with God and Man,'' *New Era* 9 [September 1979]: 42.)

Do we realize that happiness here and now consists in freely, lovingly, joyfully acknowledging God's will for us—and doing it in all ways and all affairs big and small? To live perfectly is to live happily. To live happily is to grow in spiritual strength toward perfection. Every action performed in accord with God's will is part of that growth. Let us not partition our lives. Let us unify our lives, being contemptuous of fictitious honors and glories that do not come with God's approval. Let us remember that the real source of our strength and happiness is beyond the reach of men and circumstances. (*So Shall Ye Reap*, p. 318.)

We have the responsibility of living this gospel. It is impossible for one who has received a testimony of this work and holds membership in the Church to be truly happy and not live the gospel. I have seen people who have drifted away from the Church, who have become inactive, and I have seen them brought back into activity, and the testimony of all of them is to the effect that during periods of inactivity there is something lacking—they are not happy inside, they are not satisfied. Men are that they might have joy (see 2 Nephi 25), but joy and happiness come only through living the principles of the gospel. There is no happiness in wickedness, no happiness in sin, no happiness in inactivity (see Alma 41:10; Helaman 13:38). And there is no safety in inactivity. If we want to be happy, if we want to be secure in our testimonies and in our faith and in our membership in the Church, we must live the gospel, we must try to build up the kingdom, we must shoulder our part of the responsibility in helping to carry this message to the nations of the earth. (Washington D.C. Stake Conference, 4 December 1960.)

We have some divorces in the Church, entirely too many, especially of those who have been married in the temple. I interview some of these couples who are having these problems and I find, almost without exception, they have not been living the gospel. They haven't had family prayer. They haven't had family home evening. They haven't been going to sacrament meeting and Sunday School with their families together. They haven't been living the gospel. (Grantsville Utah Stake Conference, 1 September 1974.)

Of course we have our free agency. We are not bound to have family prayers. We will not be excommunicated if we ignore the counsel that is given. But if we want to be happy, if we want to have a good feeling inside, and if we want to be of maximum influence among our fellowmen who are not members of the Church, we will live the gospel, we will keep the commandments, we will maintain the standards which have been prescribed by the priesthood of the Church, by the First Presidency. ("The Home and Family," BYU Religious Life Series, Provo, Utah, September 1960.)

With the assurance that the Church shall remain intact with God directing it through the troubled times ahead, it then becomes our individual responsibility to see that each of us remains faithful to the Church and its teachings. "He that remaineth steadfast and is not overcome, the same shall be saved" (Joseph Smith—Matthew 1:11). To help us from being overcome by the devil's designs of despair, discouragement, depression, and despondency, the Lord has provided ways which, if followed, will lift our spirits and send us on our way rejoicing. (CR October 1974, *Ensign* 4 [November 1974]: 65.)

We have a responsibility of bearing off His kingdom, building up His Church, being a light to the world, and getting organized in a way that we will be a refuge from the storm. I don't mean rain or thunder. I mean the storm of sin that will be destructive of human life and government: "For a defense, and for a refuge from the storm, and from wrath when it shall be poured out without mixture upon the whole earth" (D&C 115:6). And some of that wrath is going to be poured out upon the heads of the Latter-day Saints who have the gospel, but who refuse to live it and to maintain the standards which the Lord has provided us. I hope the number will be few. (Grantsville Utah Stake Conference, 1 September 1974.)

The gospel of Jesus Christ certainly offers incentives to achieve and accomplish challenges which develop a person's inner powers. Only by daily applying its principles and teachings in our lives may the power which is inherent within us be released and made manifest among men. Thus may we achieve the ideal spoken of by Paul when he explained to the Corinthian Saints that "the kingdom of God is not in word, but in power" (1 Corinthians 4:20). ("Power Through Service," *Millennial Star* 118 [9 October 1956]: 298.)

As Latter-day Saints, we have great hope for the future. As we live the commandments of God, we can look forward with joyful anticipation to the second coming of the Lord Jesus Christ and know that through our efforts we are worthy, with our loved ones, to dwell in His presence for all eternity. Surely nothing is too hard to gain this great goal. We cannot let down for a moment. We must prove, every day of our lives, that we are willing to do the will of the Lord—to spread the restored gospel, to bear testimony to the world, to share the gospel with others. All of this is required if we would be exalted in the celestial kingdom. ("Safety in the Face of Wickedness," Tokyo Japan Area Conference, 8–10 August 1975.)

There aren't any better people in all the world than the Latter-day Saints, and you are a good representation of the Latter-day Saints. I would rather live among them than in any other place on this earth, and it matters little whether I live among them in England, in Germany, in the Scandinavian countries, in Washington, D.C., in Boise, Idaho, or in Salt Lake City. It is not where we live that matters so much: it is how we live. I could be very happy to remain here with you for the rest of my days—I say that sincerely—so long as I could live among Latter-day Saints. Of course, I would like to have my family with me. We all have that desire. ("I'll Go Where You Want Me to Go," *Church News* [23 November 1946]: 8.)

God help us to live the gospel, to be real Latter-day Saints—not Jack-Mormons—and to live the gospel, to go forward with our heads up high, to raise our sights and get a vision of this, the greatest work in all the world. (Grantsville Utah Stake Conference, 1 September 1974.)

The door is open. The plan is here. The authority and power is here. It is up to you. If you live according to that plan, you will be happy; you will be successful; you will be exalted in the celestial kingdom with all your worthy loved ones. (Scandinavia and Finland Area Conference, 16–18 August 1974.)

We have no cause to really worry. Live the gospel, keep the commandments. Attend to your prayers night and morning in your home. Maintain the standards of the Church. Try and live calmly and cheerfully. The Lord has said, "Ask and ye shall receive," but He has never said you will receive without asking. You cannot reach the celestial kingdom on the record of your progenitors. We must each work out our salvation individually. The Lord has also said, "Seek and ye shall find" (3 Nephi 14:7). It is not easy to be a good Latter-day Saint. Happiness must be earned from day to day. But it is worth the effort. ("The Church," Paris, France, 7 August 1960.)

Obedience

One principle of the gospel that all young people of the Church should understand is this: God, our Heavenly Father, governs His children by law. He has instituted laws for our perfection. If we obey His laws, we receive the blessings pertaining to those laws. If we do not obey, we receive the consequences. (CR April 1983, *Ensign* 13 [May 1983]: 53.)

A spiritual person obeys all the Lord's commandments. He prays to our Heavenly Father and he gives service to others. You are learning now to keep all the commandments of the Lord. As you do so, you will have His Spirit to be with you. You will feel good about yourselves. You can't do wrong and feel right. It is impossible! One of the great lessons I learned on my first mission was the principle of total obedience. (CR April 1985, *Ensign* 15 [May 1985]: 36.)

What increases our favor with God? One of the purposes of life is to be proved to see if we "will do all things whatsoever the Lord [our] God shall command [us]" (Abraham 3:25). In short, we are to learn the will of the Lord and do it. We are to follow the model of Jesus Christ and be like Him. God's will for you can be determined from three sources: (1) The scriptures—particularly the Book of Mormon. (2) Inspired words from the Lord's anointed—counsel from prophets, seers, and revelators. Local Church leaders likewise are also entitled to give inspired direction for those over whom they preside. (3) The Spirit of the Lord. The people of the world have the Light of Christ to help guide them, but we are entitled to the gift of the Holy Ghost. For the Holy Ghost to be fully operative in our lives, we must keep our channels clear of sin. The clearer our channels, the easier it is for us to receive God's message. And the more of His promptings we receive and follow, the greater will be our joy. ("In His Steps," Church Educational System Devotional, Anaheim, California, 8 February 1987.)

As a nation we need the refining and sustaining influences which come from obedience to divine law. Without such blessings the future of the nation is insecure. How can we expect divine acceptance when as a nation we are drunken through the staggeringly increased uses of intoxicating liquors, narcotics, and tobacco. The increase in these vices weakens the moral fiber of our nation and brings disappointment and sadness followed by greater sins. All these evidences are but the fruits of disobedience to divine injunction. (*The Red Carpet*, pp. 297–98.)

Men receive blessings by obedience to God's law. And without obedience there is no blessing. Before the final triumphal return of the Lord, the question as to whether we may save our constitutional republic is simply based on two factors — the number of patriots and the extent of their obedience.

That the Lord desires to save this nation which He raised up there is no doubt. But that He leaves it up to us, with His help, is the awful reality. There is a time and season for all righteous things, and many of life's failures arise when men neither take the time nor find the season to perform their eternal duties. (*An Enemy Hath Done This*, p. 55.)

I wish that every Latter-day Saint could say and mean it with all his heart: "I'll go where you want me to go. I'll say what you want me to say. I'll be what you want me to be." (*Hymns*, 1985, no. 270.) If we could all do that, we would be assured of the maximum of happiness here and exaltation in the celestial kingdom of God hereafter. ("I'll Go Where You Want Me to Go," *Church News* [23 November 1946]: 8.)

May we stay on the Lord's side of the line in all matters. And may our report to our Heavenly Father when we return to His celestial home be as follows: "Father, we are all here—father, mother, all of our posterity. Each chair is filled. We are all back home!" (Cardston, Alberta, Canada, 2 August 1975.)

Righteousness

We represent Jesus Christ. How that thought ought to prompt us toward more righteousness and a desire to be more like Him! ("Three Imperative Responsibilities," London England Area Conference, 19–20 June 1976.)

Christ, who was born in the meridian of time, pointed the way for men and nations to achieve true and lasting peace. He taught that peace comes from within—peace must come to the hearts of men. Now as then the price of peace is righteousness, not alone frowning battlements, not bristling seacoasts, not weapons capable of indescribable destruction.

With the passing years we have come to recognize more clearly that people do not like to be forced to do anything, even if it is for their own good. But people do respond to effective leadership, whatever its nature. The power of example is still our most effective weapon. Wholesome, righteous leadership is our greatest need.

The power of Christ's leadership grew from the challenge of His example. His clarion call was, "Come, follow me!" (See *Hymns*, 1985, no. 116.) His conquest for the loyalty and devotion of men to principles of righteousness depends upon love as the great motivating factor. He helped us realize that the godlike qualities in each of us clamoring for expression can become glorious living realities. His example continues as the greatest hope and strength of mankind.

Somehow it seems difficult to live nobly and unselfishly; yet the price of our failure to do so breeds greater misery, sorrow, misunderstanding, and wars. Such vestiges of freedom and liberty as still remain in this troubled world cannot survive unless there is a resurgence of righteousness. There is no other way. (*The Red Carpet*, pp. 285–86.)

The Lord promised that righteousness would come from heaven and truth out of the earth (see Psalm 85:11). We have seen the marvelous fulfillment of that prophecy in our generation. The Book of Mormon has come forth out of the earth, filled with truth, serving as the very "keystone of our religion" (see Book of Mormon Introduction). God has also sent down righteousness from heaven. The Father Himself appeared with His Son to the Prophet Joseph Smith. The angel Moroni, John the Baptist, Peter, James, and numerous other angels were directed by heaven to restore the necessary powers to the kingdom. (CR October 1986, *Ensign* 16 [November 1986]: 79–80.)

With the evidence all about them that tyranny is on the increase and that man's freedoms are ebbing, faithful members of the

Church are asking, "What can be done? What can I do?" Of all people, members of the Church must not despair. As God has intervened in our past history, so He may in our present history. His purposes will not be thwarted.

To come under the protective and preserving hand of God, it is vital that we keep before us the conditions for such protection. "Righteousness exalteth a nation; but sin is a reproach to any people" (Proverbs 14:34). (*This Nation Shall Endure*, p. 9.)

The early leaders and the people generally of this great nation recognized the necessity for spiritual support if the nation was to endure. They gave humble expression to this conviction in the inscription "In God We Trust" found on the coins of the land. To them the Sabbath day was a day of rest and worship. Religious devotion in the home was a common practice. Family prayer, reading of the holy scriptures, and the singing of hymns were everyday occurrences. There is every evidence that "our fathers looked to God for their direction." (*The Red Carpet*, p. 284.)

It seems clear that as a people we have become indifferent, irreverent seekers after passing pleasures which have no permanent value. We have turned away from the eternal principles of righteousness. In our rush for material things we have forgotten the God of this land. We claim to be a Christian nation, but we ignore the teachings of Christ. Religion seems to be a declining influence in the lives of our people. (*The Red Carpet*, p. 297.)

Many Americans have lost sight of the truth that righteousness is the one indispensable ingredient to liberty. Perhaps as never before in our history is our nation collectively deserving of the indictment pronounced by Abraham Lincoln in these words:

> We have been the recipients of the choicest bounties of heaven. We have been preserved, these many years, in peace and prosperity. We have grown in numbers, wealth, and power as no other nation has ever grown; but we have forgotten God. We have forgotten the gracious hand which preserved us in peace, and multiplied and enriched and strengthened us; and we have vainly imagined, in the deceitfulness of our hearts, that all these blessings were produced by some superior wisdom and virtue of our own. Intoxicated with unbroken success, we have become too self-sufficient to feel the necessity of redeeming and preserving grace, too proud to pray to the God that made us:

It behooves us, then, to humble ourselves before the offended Power, to confess our national sins, and to pray for clemency and forgiveness. ("A Proclamation by the President of the United States of America," 30 March 1863, as cited in *Complete Works of Abraham Lincoln*, 1905, p. 236.)

Unless we as citizens of this nation forsake our sins, political and otherwise, and return to the fundamental principles of Christianity and of constitutional government, we will lose our political liberties, our free institutions, and will stand in jeopardy before God of losing our exaltation. (*This Nation Shall Endure*, pp. 34–35.)

While man continues to proclaim peace and yearn for it, he must realize that the price of peace is righteousness. Peace cannot be imposed or enforced. It must come from the hearts and minds of people. There is no other way. ("The Abundant Life for All," Sixteenth Interfaith Day, Washington, D.C., 26 September 1954.)

Man is an eternal child of Deity. Millions of men and women throughout the nations of the earth have come to this profound realization. Challenged by the glorious opportunity this affords and by the tremendous responsibility this places upon man, they stand as a bulwark for human decency and righteousness. ("The Abundant Life for All," Sixteenth Interfaith Day, Washington, D.C., 26 September 1954.)

The Lord has made it very clear in the revelations. "Verily I say unto you all, " He said, back in 1838, "Arise and shine forth, that thy light may be a standard for the nations" (D&C 115:5). And six years earlier, He said to a then struggling Church, small in numbers, inflicted with persecutions: "For Zion must increase in beauty, and in holiness; her borders must be enlarged; her stakes must be strengthened; yea, verily I say unto you, Zion must arise and put on her beautiful garments" (D&C 82:14). What are those garments? Those garments are the garments of righteousness, the garments of devotion to the truth—the gospel in action. (CR April 1955, *Improvement Era* 58 [June 1955]: 407.)

May I remind you that no person who has ever accepted the gospel and taken upon himself the responsibilities and obligations of membership can ever be fully happy unless he lives the gospel.

The person who accepts membership and refuses to live it is not happy. So the path of righteousness is the road to happiness. (Tokyo, Japan, 27 October 1957.)

It has been said that the death of a righteous man is never untimely because our Father sets the time. I believe that with all my soul. ("Spencer W. Kimball: A Star of the First Magnitude," *Ensign* 15 [December 1985]: 33.)

We must become pure and holy as Jesus Christ and His Father are pure and holy—for Man of Holiness is the name of God. We become pure only as we subscribe to the laws and ordinances the Savior has prescribed in His gospel. This means we acknowledge the name of Christ as the only name under heaven by which salvation may come to us. It means we fully repent and forsake all that has been evil in our past lives. It means we receive the ordinances of baptism and the gift of the Holy Ghost so that we are cleansed from sin "every whit," as the scriptures teach. It means thereafter a life committed to practicing His teachings. Then we truly are His disciples. ("After All We Can Do," Christmas Devotional, Salt Lake City, Utah, 9 December 1982.)

The Great Commandment

The *great test of life* is obedience to God. "We will prove them herewith," said the Lord, "to see if they will do all things whatsoever the Lord their God shall command them" (Abraham 3:25).

The *great task of life* is to learn the will of the Lord and then do it.

The *great commandment of life* is to love the Lord.

"Come unto Christ," exhorts Moroni in his closing testimony, " . . . and love God with all your might, mind and strength" (Moroni 10:32).

This, then, is the first and great commandment. "Thou shalt love the Lord thy God with all thy heart, and with all thy soul, and with all thy mind, and with all thy strength" (Mark 12:30; see also Matthew 22:37; Deuteronomy 6:5; Luke 10:27; Moroni 10:32; D&C 59:5).

It is the pure love of Christ, called charity, that the Book of Mormon testifies is the greatest of all—that never faileth, that endureth forever, that all men should have, and that without which they are nothing (see Moroni 7:44–47; 2 Nephi 26:30).

"Wherefore, my beloved brethren," pleads Moroni, "pray unto the Father with all the energy of [your] heart, that ye may be filled with this love, which he hath bestowed upon all who are true followers of his Son, Jesus Christ; that ye may become the sons of God; that when he shall appear we shall be like him" (Moroni 7:48).

In the closing accounts of both the Jaredites and the Nephites, Moroni records that except men shall have this pure love of Christ, called charity, they cannot inherit that place which Christ has prepared in the mansions of His Father, nor can they be saved in the kingdom of God (see Ether 12:34; Moroni 10:21).

The fruit that Lehi partook of in his vision and that filled his soul with exceeding great joy and that was most desirable above all things was the love of God. (CR April 1988, *Ensign* 18 [May 1988]: 4.)

To love God with all your heart, soul, mind, and strength is all-consuming and all-encompassing. It is no lukewarm endeavor. It is total commitment of our very being—physically, mentally, emotionally, and spiritually—to a love of the Lord.

The breadth, depth, and height of this love of God extend into every facet of one's life. Our desires, be they spiritual or temporal, should be rooted in a love of the Lord. Our thoughts and affections should be centered on the Lord. "Let all thy thoughts be directed unto the Lord forever" (Alma 37:36).

Why did God put the first commandment first? Because He knew that if we truly loved Him we would want to keep all of His other commandments. "For this is the love of God," says John, "that we keep his commandments" (1 John 5:3; see 2 John 1:6).

We must put God in the forefront of everything else in our lives. He must come first, just as He declares in the first of His Ten Commandments: "Thou shalt have no other gods before me" (Exodus 20:3).

When we put God first, all other things fall into their proper place or drop out of our lives. Our love of the Lord will govern the claims of our affection, the demands on our time, the interests we pursue, and the order of our priorities. (CR April 1988, *Ensign* 18 [May 1988]: 4.)

We should put God ahead of everyone else in our lives. When Joseph was in Egypt, what came first in his life—God, his job, or Potiphar's wife? When she tried to seduce him, he responded by saying, "How then can I do this great wickedness, and sin against God?" (Genesis 39:9.)

Joseph was put in prison because he put God first. If we were faced with a similar choice, where would we place our first loyalty? Can we put God ahead of security, peace, passions, wealth, and the honors of men?

When Joseph was forced to choose, he was more anxious to please God than to please his employer's wife. When we are required to choose, are we more anxious to please God than our boss, our teacher, our neighbor, or our date?

The Lord said, "He that loveth father or mother more than me is not worthy of me: and he that loveth son or daughter more than me is not worthy of me" (Matthew 10:37). One of the most difficult tests of all is when you have to choose between pleasing God or pleasing someone you love or respect—particularly a family member.

Nephi faced that test and handled it well when his good father temporarily murmured against the Lord (see 1 Nephi 16:18–25). Job maintained his integrity with the Lord even though his wife told him to curse God and die (see Job 2:9–10).

The scripture says, "Honor thy father and thy mother" (Exodus 20:12; see also Mosiah 13:20). Sometimes one must choose to honor a Heavenly Father over a mortal father.

We should give God, the Father of our spirits, an exclusive preeminence in our lives. He has a prior parental claim on our eternal welfare ahead of all other things that may bind us here or hereafter. Should we not love Him for it and honor Him first?

There are faithful members who joined the Church in spite of the objections of their mortal relatives. By putting God first, many later became the instruments to lead those loved ones into the kingdom of God. (CR April 1988, *Ensign* 18 [May 1988]: 4–5.)

Jesus said, "I do always those things that please [God]" (John 8:29). What is the condition in our homes? Are we striving to put the Lord first and to please Him?

Fathers, would it please the Lord if there were daily family prayer and scripture reading in your home? And what about the holding of weekly home evenings and periodically having individual time with your wife and each child? And if your child went temporarily astray, do you think it would please the Lord and He would honor your efforts if you continued to live an exemplary life, consistently prayed and frequently fasted for that child, and kept the name of that son or daughter on the temple prayer roll?

You mothers who are especially charged with the righteous rearing of the youth of Zion, are you not putting God first when you honor your divine calling by not leaving the home front to follow the ways of the world? Our mothers put God first when they fill their highest mission within the walls of their own homes.

Children, do you pray for your parents? Do you try to support them in their noble endeavors? They, like you, will make mistakes but they have a divine mission to accomplish in your life. Will you help them do so? Will you add honor to their name and bring comfort and support to them in their older years?

If someone wants to marry you outside the temple, whom will you strive to please—God or a mortal? If you insist on a temple marriage, you will be pleasing the Lord and blessing the other party. Why? Because that person will either become worthy to go to the temple—which would be a blessing—or will leave—which could also be a blessing—because neither of you should want to be unequally yoked (see 2 Corinthians 6:14).

You should qualify for the temple. Then you will know that there is no one good enough for you to marry outside the temple. If such individuals are that good, they will get themselves in a condition so that they too can be married in the temple. (CR April 1988, *Ensign* 18 [May 1988]: 5–6.)

We bless our fellowmen the most when we put the first commandment first. "Whatever God requires is right," said the Prophet Joseph Smith (*Teachings of the Prophet Joseph Smith*, p. 256)—and so Nephi slew Laban. And God asked Abraham to sacrifice Isaac.

Had Abraham loved Isaac more than God, would he have consented? As the Lord indicates in the Doctrine and Covenants, both Abraham and Isaac now sit as gods (D&C 132:37). They were willing to offer or to be offered up as God required. They have a deeper love and respect for each other because both were willing to put God first. (CR April 1988, *Ensign* 18 [May 1988]: 6.)

One of the trials of life is that we do not usually receive immediately the full blessing for righteousness or the full cursing for wickedness. That it will come is certain, but ofttimes there is a waiting period that occurs, as was the case with Job and Joseph.

In the meantime, the wicked think they are getting away with something. The Book of Mormon teaches that the wicked "have joy in their works for a season, [but] by and by the end cometh, and they are hewn down and cast into the fire, from whence there is no return" (3 Nephi 27:11).

The righteous must continue to love God, trust in His promises, be patient, and be assured, as the poet said, that—

> Who does God's work will get God's pay,
> However long may seem the day,
> However weary be the way.
> No mortal hand God's hand can stay,
> He may not pay as others pay,
> In gold, or lands, or raiment gay,
> In goods that perish and decay;
> But God's high wisdom knows a way,
> And this is sure, let come what may—
> Who does God's work will get God's pay.
>   (Author unknown)

I testify to you that God's pay is the best pay that this world or any other world knows anything about. And it comes in full abundance only to those who love the Lord and put Him first.

God bless us to put the first commandment first and, as a result, reap peace in this life and eternal life with a fulness of joy in the life to come. (CR April 1988, *Ensign* 18 [May 1988]: 6.)

Only those who know and love God can best love and serve His children. For only God fully understands His children and knows what is best for their welfare. Therefore, one needs to be in tune with God to best help His children.

Therefore, if you desire to help your fellowmen the most, then you must put the first commandment first (see Matthew 22:37–38). When we fail to put the love of God first, we are easily deceived by crafty men, who profess a great love of humanity, while advocating programs that are not of the Lord. (*An Enemy Hath Done This*, p. 191.)

Keeping the Commandments

I would urge you to heed strictly the commandments of God, particularly the Ten Commandments. As long as we regard God as our Sovereign and uphold His laws, we shall be free from bondage and be protected from external danger. ("The Ten Commandments," *New Era* 8 [July 1978]: 38.)

God has not left us alone to flounder over right and wrong in the area of personal ethics and morality. His laws are circumscribed in the Decalogue—the Ten Commandments. These laws embody our relationships with God, family, and fellowmen. Yes, the Ten Commandments and the Sermon on the Mount are the foundation principles upon which our personal happiness is predicated. To disregard them will lead to inevitable personal character loss and ruin. ("Be True to God, Country, and Self," Young Adult Fireside, Logan, Utah, 11 February 1979.)

As a Church, we are in accord with Nephi, who said, "it is by grace that we are saved, after all we can do" (2 Nephi 25:23). Grace consists of God's gift to His children wherein He gave His Only Begotten Son that whosoever would believe in Him and comply with His laws and ordinances would have everlasting life.

By grace, the Savior accomplished His atoning sacrifice so that all mankind will attain immortality. By His grace, and by our faith in His atonement and repentance of our sins, we receive the strength to do the works necessary that we otherwise could not do by our own power. By His grace we receive an endowment of blessing and spiritual strength that may eventually lead us to eternal life if we endure to the end. By His grace we become more like

His divine personality. Yes, it is "by grace that we are saved, after all we can do" (2 Nephi 25:23).

What is meant by "after all we can do"? "After all we can do" includes extending our best effort. "After all we can do" includes living His commandments. "After all we can do" includes loving our fellowmen and praying for those who regard us as their adversary. "After all we can do" means clothing the naked, feeding the hungry, visiting the sick and giving "succor [to] those who stand in need of [our] succor" (Mosiah 4:15)—remembering that what we do unto one of the least of God's children, we do unto Him (see Matthew 25:34–40; D&C 42:38). "After all we can do" means leading chaste, clean, pure lives, being scrupulously honest in all our dealings and treating others the way we would want to be treated. ("After All We Can Do," Christmas Devotional, Salt Lake City, Utah, 9 December 1982.)

In the Book of Mormon the prophet Nephi exclaims: "O Lord, I have trusted in thee, and I will trust in thee forever. I will not put my trust in the arm of flesh; for I know that cursed is he that putteth his trust in man or maketh flesh his arm." (2 Nephi 4:34.) Prophesying of our day, Nephi said, "They have all gone astray save it be a few, who are the humble followers of Christ; nevertheless, they are led, that in many instances they do err because they are taught by the precepts of men." (2 Nephi 28:14.) Yes, it is the precepts of men versus the revealed word of God. The more we follow the word of God the less we are deceived, while those who follow the wisdom of men are deceived the most.

Increasingly, the Latter-day Saints must choose between the reasoning of men and the revelations of God. This is a crucial choice, for we have those within the Church today who, with their worldly wisdom, are leading some of the members astray. President J. Reuben Clark warned: "The ravening wolves are amongst us, from our own membership, and they, more than any others, are clothed in sheep's clothing, because they wear the habiliments of the Priesthood. . . . We should be careful of them." (CR April 1949, p. 163.)

The Lord does not always give reasons for each commandment. Sometimes faithful members, like Adam of old, are called upon to obey an injunction of the Lord even though they do not know the reason why it was given (see Moses 5:6). Those who trust in God will obey Him, knowing full well that time will provide the reasons and vindicate their obedience. (*An Enemy Hath Done This*, pp. 189–90.)

How do you learn the commandments? You learn the commandments through the words of the Lord in the scriptures, through the revelations received by His authorized servants, through the Light of Christ, like a conscience that comes to every man, and through personal revelation. (*God, Family, Country*, p. 156.)

"Thou shalt not take the name of the Lord thy God in vain" (Exodus 20:7). The stage, the screen, the novel, casual conversation, the street discussion, and too often the fireside intimacies are punctuated with blasphemy, to which may be added, as of the same nature, coarse, ribald jokes, foul stories, and low small talk. Some would have us believe that profanity is a sign of masculinity and emotional maturity. ("The Ten Commandments," *New Era* 8 [July 1978]: 36–37.)

One of the cardinal sins in our country is profanity—the taking of the name of the Lord in vain. Reverence for the name of Deity is enjoined in holy writ. Jesus made this clear when teaching His disciples to pray. He said, addressing the Father, "Hallowed be thy name" (see Matthew 6:9). Blaspheming the name of God separates man from his Creator. ("America—What of the Future?" Radio Address—WRVA, Richmond, Virginia, 8 October 1950.)

"Thou shalt not kill" (Exodus 20:13). Need we be reminded in what small esteem life is now held? Men are to live, else they could not work out their destiny. This mandate was given to Israel and to each child thereof. It is the command not to commit the sin of Cain. It is binding upon every one of God's children. It speaks to them as individuals; it commands them as associated together in nations. It covers the single case of another, Abel; it embraces the mass slaughter of war. It is the law higher than the law of punishment: "Eye for eye, tooth for tooth, hand for hand, foot for foot" (Exodus 21:24). It forecast the Master's law of love and forgiveness: "Love your enemies, bless them that curse you, do good to them that hate you, and pray for them which despitefully use you, and persecute you" (Matthew 5:44). (*This Nation Shall Endure*, p. 52.)

"Thou shalt not steal" (Exodus 20:14). What do our criminal court records disclose on this—records that are filled with accounts of juvenile delinquencies in numbers never before equaled in this country? When God commanded, "Thou shalt not steal," He thereby recognized the fundamental right of property. How much we pay for this in increased costs of merchandise because of employee pilfering and shoplifting, higher insurance rates, courts of law, and penal institutions! ("The Ten Commandments," *New Era* 8 [July 1978]: 37.)

Covetousness is one of the besetting sins of this generation, and our covetousness reaches every item forbidden in the commandments—our neighbor's house, his wife, his help, his worldly goods, and everything that is our neighbor's. Covetousness, plus love of idleness, lies at the root of our violation of the law of work, with all the ills that has brought. Covetousness has invaded our homes, our communities, the nations of the world. It has brought with it greed, avarice, ambition, and love of power. Men scheme, plan, overreach, cheat, and lie to get their neighbor's heritage. Covetousness threatens the peace of the world today more than any other one element. God said, "Thou shalt not covet" (Exodus 20:17). (*This Nation Shall Endure*, p. 53.)

For a year, right after the war, I spent my time with the suffering Saints of Europe and many of their friends and neighbors. I was there. My wife was at home with our little children. I saw people who had lost every member of their family, their homes destroyed, and yet I saw them stand up and bear their testimonies and thank God for the knowledge which they had and for their testimonies of the gospel; for the assurance there would be a happy reunion for their families in the eternities to come, where there is no war or death or separation. It can't be done without the gospel.

I saw people bewildered, frustrated, sick at heart, some of them taking their own lives because they had no anchor, nothing to hold to. They didn't have that inner peace, that assurance that comes with the gospel of Jesus Christ and a burning testimony. In the days ahead we are going to need that kind of strength; we are going to need an anchor. We are going to need something to hold to. It is going to take more than dollars and cents, stocks and bonds, cattle on the hills. It is going to take faith and testimony and the living of the commandments of God. (Grantsville Utah Stake Conference, 1 September 1974.)

If we keep the commandments, we will refrain from joining secret orders. Our first allegiance will be to the Church and the priesthood quorums. We will attend our meetings. We will take our families with us to the sacrament meeting and sit with them and worship with them. If we keep the commandments, we will pay our tithes and offerings, our fast offerings, and our welfare contributions. We will respond to the calls in the Church, and we will not resign from office when called under the authority of the holy priesthood. We will follow the counsel of the leadership of the Church and call our families together periodically in home evenings in order that the home might be safeguarded and the solidarity of the family increased. We will read the scriptures in our homes as the Lord has admonished us. We will not violate the sacred covenants we have taken upon ourselves in the waters of baptism and in the temples of the Lord, nor will we desecrate or cast to one side the garments of the holy priesthood. We will attend to our temple work. We will become saviors on Mount Zion in very deed. (*So Shall Ye Reap*, p. 61.)

One of Satan's most frequently used deceptions is the notion that the commandments of God are meant to restrict freedom and limit happiness. Young people especially sometimes feel that the standards of the Lord are like fences and chains, blocking them from those activities that seem most enjoyable in life. But exactly the opposite is true. The gospel plan is the plan by which men are brought to a fulness of joy. The gospel principles are the steps and guidelines which will help us find true happiness and joy.

The understanding of this concept caused the Psalmist to exclaim, "O how love I thy law! . . . Thou through thy commandments hast made me wiser than mine enemies. . . . Thy word is a lamp unto my feet, and a light unto my path. . . . Thy testimonies have I taken as an heritage for ever: for they are the rejoicing of my heart.'' (Psalm 119:97–98, 105, 111.) (''A Mighty Change of Heart,'' address prepared [but not delivered] 1986.)

Because of His infinite love, God has seen fit from the very beginning of this earth to give men commandments. These commandments were designed to exalt man from his fallen state to a state of righteousness and joy. They were also designed to bring about accord in homes, communities, and nations. History has shown that when individuals and nations have kept the commandments of God they have been happy, prosperous, and most blessed. When they have departed from those commandments, pride, strife, contention, and warfare have resulted. There have been times in the history of mankind when nations have brought down upon them the judgments of God, and this because they deliberately chose a course contrary to God's purposes and their own happiness. Famine, disease, and war—that terrifying triad of human tragedy—have led many great civilizations to ruin and oblivion. The history of mankind is a testament of this fact. (''A Promised Lord—A Promised Land—A Promised People,'' Wichita, Kansas, 11 November 1976.)

God's laws are not to be trifled with. One cannot cancel out what God Himself has decreed. He will not tolerate it. (*This Nation Shall Endure*, p. 97.)

Be true to every standard and teaching of the Church. Support loyally your mission, district, and branch presidents and other officers. Cease from all evil speaking and faultfinding. Be united. Keep the Sabbath day holy. Pay your tithes and offerings. Attend to your family and secret prayers daily. Give freely of your time, means, and talents for the building up of the kingdom of God on earth. Be kind to your families. Be pure in mind and body. Keep the Spirit of God in your homes and in your hearts. Be wise and prudent as you go forward with energy and determination to fill the full measure of your creation in the earth. Perform with soberness, but with happy and joyous hearts, the work at hand, knowing that all is well if we live righteously. Do all this, and eventually you will be exalted on high and triumph over all your enemies. There, I trust, in that eternal world we shall meet in sweet reunion, where war and sin are no more, in the sweet fellowship which we have but tasted here. If we are worthy, it shall be so. (*So Shall Ye Reap*, p. 97.)

Blessings of the Gospel

The Lord has declared: "I am the light which shineth in darkness. . . . I am the true light that lighteth every man that cometh into the world." (D&C 6:21; 93:2.) Who has not seen the light in the face of a loving mother with her child, or a noble father with his wife and children? Or the light in the eyes of one who is loved—as son or daughter, husband or wife?

There is an inner light manifested in the countenances of those who have sought and found truth, who have set standards and principles in their lives and have been enlightened by the light of the gospel—hence, the brightness and spiritual illumination of those who have learned of and accepted the gospel of Jesus Christ. ("The Light of Christmas," Christmas Lighting Ceremony, Temple Square, Salt Lake City, Utah, 26 November 1982.)

Try as you may, you cannot put the Lord in your debt. For every time you try to do His will, He simply pours out more blessings upon you. Sometimes the blessings may seem to you to be a little slow in coming—perhaps this tests your faith—but come they will and abundantly. It has been said, "Cast your bread upon the waters and after a while it shall come back to you toasted and buttered." ("Jesus Christ—Gifts and Expectations," Christmas Devotional, Salt Lake City, Utah, 7 December 1986.)

Success in righteousness, the power to avoid deception and resist temptation, guidance in our daily lives, healing of the soul—these are but a few of the promises the Lord has given to those who will come to His word. Does the Lord promise and not fulfill? Surely if He tells us that these things will come to us if we lay hold upon His word, the blessings can be ours. And if we do not, then the blessings may be lost. However diligent we may be in other areas, certain blessings are to be found only in the scriptures, only in coming to the word of the Lord and holding fast to it as we make our way through the mists of darkness to the tree of life (see

1 Nephi 8:19–23). ("The Power of the Word," *Ensign* 16 [May 1986]: 81.)

Mormonism is a nickname for the gospel of Jesus Christ in its fulness. It answers our questions. It gives us a feeling of security. It provides an anchor, gives us something to hold to. It gives us peace of mind. It answers the questions: where did I come from, why am I here, what is the purpose of life, and where am I going? These are the problems that worry many people, including many Christian people, because there is much doubt and lack of faith even among leaders of Christianity. But with a Latter-day Saint who has received a testimony of this work, there is no question or doubt. We know the purpose of life. We know why we are here. We know where we are going and we know where we came from. It is a great satisfaction to hold membership in the Church. To me my most priceless possessions are my testimony of the gospel and my membership in the Church. These are priceless blessings. The honors of men and the wealth of the world are as nothing by comparison with these blessings. ("The Church," Paris, France, 7 August 1960.)

Spiritual strength promotes positive thinking, positive ideals, positive habits, positive attitudes, and positive efforts. These are the qualities that promote wisdom, physical and mental well-being, and enthusiastic acceptance and response from others. Favor with God gives necessary incentive and perspective to life. It gives man real purpose for living and achieving. ("Your Charge: To Increase in Wisdom and Favor with God and Man," *New Era* 9 [September 1979]: 45.)

We must learn and learn again that only through accepting and living the gospel of love as taught by the Master and only through doing His will can we break the bonds of ignorance and doubt that bind us. We must learn this simple, glorious truth so that we can experience the sweet joys of the Spirit now and eternally. We must lose ourselves in doing His will. We must place Him first in our lives. Yes, our blessings multiply as we share His love with our neighbor. (*God, Family, Country*, p. 24.)

It is our hope and prayer that people throughout the world will incorporate into their daily thoughts and actions the principles espoused by Jesus. To do so would most assuredly lead to less war and more peace, less turmoil and more serenity, less unrest and more stability, less crime and sin and more self-respect and happiness. ("First Presidency—Easter Message," *Church News* [23 March 1986]: 1.)

I hope that we will keep ever burning in our hearts the spirit of this great work which we represent. As we do so, we will have no anxiety. We will have no fear. We will not worry about the future because the Lord has given us the assurance that if we live righteously, if we keep His commandments, if we humble ourselves before Him, all will be well. (*So Shall Ye Reap*, pp. 58–59.)

"Men are that they might have joy" (2 Nephi 2:25). Our Heavenly Father wants us to be happy. He expects us to be happy. But there is no happiness in a letting down of standards. There is no happiness when you fail to live according to your convictions, according to that which you know to be right. It is so easy to form the habit of taking it just a little easy on certain things. It is so easy to form the habit of faultfinding, or criticizing, of carrying in our hearts reservations regarding certain things in the Church. It is so easy for us to become a bit bitter, and then dwell on that, to become sad and carry a sad face with us. A sad face never won a battle in war or love. ("The Home and Family," BYU Religious Life Series, Provo, Utah, September 1960.)

Men and women who turn their lives over to God will discover that He can make a lot more out of their lives than they can. He will deepen their joys, expand their vision, quicken their minds, strengthen their muscles, lift their spirits, multiply their blessings, increase their opportunities, comfort their souls, raise up friends, and pour out peace. Whoever will lose his life in the service of God will find eternal life (see Matthew 10:39). ("Jesus Christ—Gifts and Expectations," Christmas Devotional, Salt Lake City, Utah, 7 December 1986.)

We encourage those who recognize the Lord's blessings and great mercy in their lives to reach out and bless the lives of others. By so doing, you can go beyond the mere custom and ritual of the season. You can become instruments through which the Lord blesses the poor, the lonely, the despairing. You will have a greater sense of the reality of the Savior's existence. And your celebration of His birth will indeed be joyous. ("First Presidency—Christmas Message," *Church News* [15 December 1985]: 3.)

It pays to live a good life. Oh, I don't mean you have to be "goody-good." Enjoy yourselves, have a good time, but keep it on a high plane. Have it in a way you will have no regrets, no heartaches; so that you can look back on your life with satisfaction. So, whoever you meet in the future you can look them squarely in the eye without embarrassment. (Munich Germany High School Graduates, April 1964.)

God judges us not only by what we do, but by what we would do and desire to do if we had the opportunity. He will not withhold any blessing from us of which we are truly worthy. (As quoted in Frederick W. Babbel, *On Wings of Faith* [Salt Lake City: Bookcraft, 1972], p. 20.)

I shall never forget my feelings when I read in the press the announcement by the First Presidency regarding our call to Europe following World War II. The magnitude of it seemed overwhelming. They gave us a four-point charge: First, to attend to the spiritual affairs of the Church in Europe; second, to work to make available food, clothing, and bedding to our suffering Saints in all parts of Europe; third, to direct the reorganization of the various missions of Europe; and, fourth, to prepare for the return of missionaries to those countries.

Our great desire was to live so that the Lord would bless us in carrying out those directions, and I testify to you that the Lord has in very deed blessed us on every turn. He has gone before us. Barriers have melted away. Problems that seemed impossible to solve have been solved, and the work in large measure has been accomplished through the blessings of the Lord. (CR April 1947, *Improvement Era* 50 [May 1947]: 293.)

Don't worry too much about the laurels, or the credit. The credit will come and the laurels will come, and you will get your share. After all, the real credit comes from above. And you will never lose out on credit up there. You will get all you earn. ("The Greatest Leadership," BYU Student Leadership Conference, Sun Valley, Idaho, September 1959.)

Gratitude

The Prophet Joseph is reported to have said at one time that one of the greatest sins for which the Latter-day Saints would be guilty would be the sin of ingratitude. I presume most of us have not thought of that as a serious sin. There is a great tendency for us in our prayers—in our pleadings with the Lord—to ask for additional blessings. Sometimes I feel we need to devote more of our prayers to expressions of gratitude and thanksgiving for blessings already received. Of course we need the daily blessings of the Lord. But if we sin in the matter of prayer, I think it is in our lack of the expressions of thanksgiving for daily blessings.

President Brigham Young uttered very much the same warning as the Prophet Joseph—that this would be one of our great sins as Latter-day Saints. I do not think this is because we are less grateful than other people—but we have so much more to be grateful for. This was driven home to me as a young man when I heard of a visit made to the home of my grandfather, George Taft Benson, who was then bishop of a little country ward at Whitney, Idaho. Elder Joseph F. Smith was visiting the old Oneida Stake of Zion. He had arranged to honor my grandfather and to take a meal at his home. The table was laden with good things to eat. The family was gathered around—I don't know how many (there were thirteen children in that wonderful family and I presume some of them were away on missions as they usually were).

Just before they were ready to start the meal, President Smith stretched his long arms over the table and turned to my grandfather and said, "Brother Benson, all this and the gospel too?" What did President Smith mean? All this and the gospel too? The food represented the good things of life—food, clothing, and all the rest—the material blessings of life. This family of children —home, family, loved ones—all that the world has and the gospel too. I think that is what the Prophet Joseph had in mind. ("Receive All Things with Thankfulness," *New Era* 6 [November 1976]: 5.)

The Lord said to the Prophet Joseph, "And if thou shouldst be cast into the pit, or into the hands of murderers, and the sentence of death passed upon thee; if thou be cast into the deep; if the billowing surge conspire against thee; if fierce winds become thine

enemy; if the heavens gather blackness, and all the elements combine to hedge up the way; and above all, if the very jaws of hell
shall gape open the mouth wide after thee, know thou, my son,
that all these things shall give thee experience, and shall be for thy
good. The Son of Man hath descended below them all. Art thou
greater than he?'' (D&C 122:7–8.) How do you measure your re-
versals or problems against those of the Prophet Joseph Smith, or
more particularly the Lord Jesus Christ, when they were on the
earth? How much we have to be grateful for! Our prayers and the
prayers of our children should ascend to heaven full of gratitude
and love for the mercies of the Lord unto us.

God help us to be grateful for our blessings, never to be guilty
of the sin of ingratitude, and to instill this same gratitude into the
lives of our children. Someone has said that an ungrateful man is
like a hog under a tree eating apples and never looking up to see
where they come from. And the Lord has said, ''And he who receiveth all things with thankfulness shall be made glorious; and the
things of this earth shall be added unto him, even an hundred fold,
yea, more'' (D&C 78:19). This great principle of gratitude, made a
daily part of our lives and our prayers, can lift and bless us as individuals, as members of the Church, and as parents and families.
(''Strengthening the Family,'' Philippine Islands Area Conference, 12 August 1975.)

What better time and place can proper prayers of gratitude to
the Lord be taught than in our weekly home evenings? What a
great opportunity for parents to teach their children the principles
of the gospel. (''Strengthening the Family,'' Philippine Islands
Area Conference, 12 August 1975.)

As we travel through this topsy-turvy, sinful world, filled with
temptations and problems, we are humbled by the expectancy of
death, the uncertainty of life, and the power and love of God. Sadness comes to all of us in the loss of loved ones. But there is gratitude also. Gratitude for the assurance we have that life is eternal.
Gratitude for the great gospel plan, given freely to all of us. Gratitude for the life, teachings, and sacrifice of the Lord Jesus Christ.
(*God, Family, Country,* p. 20.)

We need to be more grateful. I think there is no true character
without gratitude. It is one of the marks of a real strong character

to have a feeling of thanksgiving and gratitude for blessings. We need more of that spirit in our homes, in our daily associations, in the Church, everywhere. It doesn't cost anything, and it is so easy to cultivate. (*God, Family, Country,* p. 202.)

We are so inclined to take our blessings for granted. Most of us haven't known anything else. I haven't. I was born into the Church, under the covenant. I received the priesthood as a boy twelve years of age. It came so easy to me. I don't believe I fully appreciated it. We live in this wonderful land where we have enjoyed freedom and a high standard of living. Most of us have never seen the suffering and the stress and the shortage of everything necessary for civilized living. ("Receive All Things with Thankfulness," *New Era* 6 [November 1976]: 5.)

As I contemplate leaving the shores of Europe, I can truthfully say that never in all my experience have I appreciated more deeply a period of service in the Church. I have met Latter-day Saints in practically every country in Europe, under the most unusual conditions, in fact under almost every conceivable circumstance. I have met them in rags, huddled together, suffering with the cold, in bombed-out buildings, some of them in the last stages of starvation. I have been in their homes where they had no food, no furniture to speak of, none of the comforts of life, and yet they have been happy. I have heard them bear testimony to the divinity of this work, with tears streaming down their cheeks as they expressed their gratitude for their blessings, yet practically every material thing had been swept away from them—homes, all the comforts of life, and in some cases every member of their family through death. That is what a testimony will do. That is a most priceless possession—your testimony of the divinity of this work. ("I'll Go Where You Want Me to Go," *Church News* [23 November 1946]: 8.)

I well remember our first meeting at Karlsruhe, Germany. After we had made visits through Belgium, Holland, and the Scandinavian countries, we went into occupied Germany. We finally found our way to the meeting place, a partially bombed-out building located in the interior of a block. The Saints had been in session for some two hours waiting for us, hoping that we would come because the word had reached them that we might be there for the conference. And then for the first time in my life I saw almost an entire audience in tears as we walked up onto the platform, and they realized that at last, after six or seven long years, representatives from Zion, as they put it, had finally come back to them. Then as the meeting closed, prolonged at their request, they insisted we go to the door and shake hands with each one of them as they left the bombed-out building. And we noted that many of them, after they had passed through the line went back and came through the second and third time, so happy were they to grasp our hands. As I looked into their upturned faces, pale, thin— many of these Saints dressed in rags, some of them barefooted—I could see the light of faith in their eyes as they bore testimony to the divinity of this great latter-day work, and expressed their gratitude for the blessings of the Lord. (*Improvement Era* 50 [May 1947]: 293.)

I never travel across this great nation without experiencing a feeling of gratitude and thanksgiving for all that we have and are. As I see its broad fruitful farms, its humming factories, its gleaming cities, certainly it is easy to realize that we have achieved unequalled material progress in this great country. (*The Red Carpet*, p. 120.)

We are recipients of God's choicest blessings. We enjoy an abundance of material things beyond that enjoyed by any other nation in the history of the world; but unless we keep alive a realization that all these blessings come from God and are a part of our great spiritual heritage, they may crumble as ashes in our hands. "In nothing doth man offend God, or against none is his wrath kindled, save those who confess not his hand in all things and obey not his commandments" (D&C 59:21). (*The Red Carpet,* p. 292.)

Someone has said it is better to appreciate the things you don't own than to own things you don't appreciate. I hope we will have with us a spirit of appreciation for all of the good things we enjoy, all the blessings that we have, many of which have come so easy to us, with very little effort on our part, and yet they are very real and very choice and are truly rich blessings. ("New Year 1961," Washington D.C. Ward, 31 December 1960.)

I hope we can be happy where we are, be grateful for our blessings — now — here, accept the challenge that is ours and make the most of it, and don't be envious of others. God help us to be grateful. ("Receive All Things with Thankfulness," *New Era* 6 [November 1976): 7.)

Honesty

"Thou shalt not bear false witness" (Exodus 20:16). When we speak of morality, we imply that a man is true to his word — true to his signature on a contract. The violations of God's laws are evidence that lying and misrepresentation are not absent from us. ("The Spiritual Foundation of America," Utah Bankers Association, Sun Valley, Idaho, 15 June 1981.)

Have you ever asked yourself why one person is honorable and another dishonorable; why one is honest, another dishonest; why one is moral, another immoral? Most individuals do not intend to be dishonest, dishonorable, or immoral. They seem to allow their characters to erode by a series of rationalizations, lies, and compromises. Then when grave temptation presents itself, they haven't the strength of character to do what they know to be right. ("Be True to God, Country, and Self," Young Adult Fireside, Logan, Utah, 11 February 1979.)

One day in the middle of an important examination in high school, the point of my lead pencil broke. In those days we used pocketknives to sharpen our pencils. I had forgotten my penknife, and turned to ask a neighbor for his. The teacher saw this; he accused me of cheating. When I tried to explain, he gave me a tongue-lashing for lying; worse, he forbade me to play on the basketball team in the upcoming game.

I could see that the more I protested the angrier he seemed to become. But again and again I stubbornly told what had happened. Even when the coach pleaded my cause, the teacher refused to budge. The disgrace was almost more than I could bear. Then, just minutes before the game, he had a change of heart and I was permitted to play. But there was no joy in it. We lost the game;

and though that hurt, by far the deeper pain was being branded a cheat and a liar.

Looking back, I know that lesson was God-sent. Character is shaped in just such crucibles. My parents believed me; they were understanding and encouraging. Supported by them and a clear conscience, I began to realize that when you are at peace with your Maker you can, if not ignore human criticism, at least rise above it. And I learned something else—the importance of avoiding even the appearance of evil. Though I was innocent, circumstance made me look guilty. Since this could so easily be true in many of life's situations, I made a resolution to keep even the appearance of my actions above question, as far as possible. And it struck me, too, that if this injustice happened to me, it could happen to others, and I must not judge their actions simply on appearances. (*Crossfire: The Eight Years with Eisenhower*, p. 17.)

Honor

If there is one word that describes the meaning of character, it is the word *honor*. Without honor, civilization would not long exist. Without honor, there could be no dependable contracts, no lasting marriages, no trust or happiness. What does the word *honor* mean to you? To me, honor is summarized in this expression by the poet Tennyson, "Man's word [of honor] is God in man" (*Idylls of the King*, "The Coming of Arthur," line 132). An honorable man or woman is one who is truthful; free from deceit; above cheating, lying, stealing, or any form of deception. An honorable man or woman is one who learns early that one cannot do wrong and feel right. A man's character is judged on how he keeps his word and his agreements. ("Honor," *New Era* 14 [July 1984]: 4.)

"On my honor"—what an ennobling phrase! Three short words, nine letters, but the summation of all we call character. ("On My Honor," Explorer Presidents Conference, Ogden, Utah, 4 March 1978.)

I speak of honor—your honor to God—your honor to country—your honor to self. I sincerely believe it to be the cure to most of our ills, both on a national or individual basis. ("On My Honor," Explorer Presidents Conference, Ogden, Utah, 4 March 1978.)

You must keep your honor! You can't speak for the country; you can do little about the national economy or actions of moral weaklings who excuse themselves with the expression, "That is politics"; nor can you be responsible for deception in others. But you are responsible for yourself! There are no collective panaceas —only individual ones. ("On My Honor," Explorer Presidents Conference, Ogden, Utah, 4 March 1978.)

As Latter-day Saints, we have been driven, mobbed, misunderstood, and maligned. We have been a peculiar people. Now we are faced with world applause. It has been a welcome change, but can we stand acceptance? Can we meet the danger of applause? In the hour of man's success, applause can be his greatest danger.

There is, of course, nothing wrong with being honored by men, if one is being honored for a good thing, if one comes to these honors through righteous living, and if, while holding these honors, one lives honorably. One should strive to have wide influence for good. (*An Enemy Hath Done This*, p. 281.)

Humility

A word about humility. I think of what the Lord has said to us: "And no one can assist in this work unless he shall be humble and full of love" (D&C 12:8). I hope we carry that spirit of humility and love with us. It is so easy to love the Latter-day Saints. I think of Brother LeGrand Richards. When he would return home and see his wife, who was left at home alone, he would say, "Oh, the Saints are so wonderful." And she would usually reply, "Yes, and they really spoil you." Well, we all love the Saints and it is easy to love them and to let them know of our love and our appreciation. Humility, of course, is not a sign of weakness. Humility does not mean timidity. A person can be humble, powerful, and courageous. The Prophet Joseph is a good example. Humility is an acknowledged recognition of our dependence on a higher power. In this work, we will never be successful unless we have that spirit of humility. (Salt Lake City, Utah, 3 October 1978.)

With humility, there come many blessings. For example, "Be thou humble; and the Lord thy God shall lead thee by the hand, and give thee answer to thy prayers" (D&C 112:10). The humble will "be made strong, and blessed from on high, and receive knowledge" (D&C 1:28). The Lord is "merciful unto those who confess their sins with humble hearts" (D&C 61:2). Humility can turn away God's anger (see Helaman 11:11). (CR April 1986, *Ensign* 16 [May 1986]: 7.)

Probably the Lord puts into our hearts a certain amount of fear and trembling in order that His Spirit might more effectively operate through us as His humble instrument. ("Free Agency," Washington D.C. Stake Conference, 22 May 1960.)

Acquire humility. There is no true success without it. (Texas San Antonio Mission, 2 March 1986.)

Leadership

You can become courageous leaders! Who can better fulfill this need of our times than you who have been so favored by heritage, home, and Church? You must not fail. Forget not that each of you has been endowed with the priceless gift of free agency. You need not be the "victims of circumstance," for unto you it is given to achieve and become "perfect, even as your father which is in heaven is perfect" (Matthew 5:48). (*So Shall Ye Reap*, p. 177.)

A love of people is essential to effective leadership. Do you love those whom you work with? Do you realize the worth of souls is great in the sight of God (see D&C 18:10)? Do you have faith in youth? Do you find yourself praising their virtues, commending them for their accomplishments? Or do you have a critical attitude toward them because of their mistakes? ("Leadership and the Needs of Youth," *Improvement Era* 51 [August 1948]: 494.)

One of the marks of great leadership always has been and ever will be the humble spirit. ("Leadership and the Needs of Youth," *Improvement Era* 51 [August 1948]: 494.)

A good leader expects loyalty. He in turn gives his loyalty. He backs up those to whom he has given a job. The loyalty extends to matters beyond the call of duty. He is loyal when honors come to those with whom he serves. He takes pride in their successes. He does not overrule unless he first confers with him whose decision he overrules. He does not embarrass an associate before others. He is frank and open with him. (*God, Family, Country,* p. 138.)

No wise leader believes that all good ideas originate with himself. He invites suggestions from those he leads. He lets them feel that they are an important part of decision making. He lets them feel that they are carrying out their policies, not just his. (*God, Family, Country,* p. 139.)

Even harder to bear than criticism, oftentimes, is no word from our leader on the work to which we have been assigned. Little comments or notes, which are sincere and specific, are great boosters along the way. (*God, Family, Country*, p. 140.)

Spiritual strength promotes positive thinking, positive ideals, positive habits, positive attitudes, and positive efforts. These are the qualities which promote wisdom, physical and mental well-being, and enthusiastic acceptance and response by others. (*So Shall Ye Reap*, p. 175.)

Ecclesiastical Leadership

The Church of Jesus Christ builds leaders. When Christ was on earth, He called twelve Apostles to assist Him in administering the Church. He also called the seventy. He delegated to others. There were to be no spectators in His Church. All were to be involved in helping build the kingdom. And as they built the kingdom, they built themselves. (*God, Family, Country,* p. 135.)

In the Church today a leader generally gets in performance what he truly expects. He needs to think tall. He should assure those to whom he gives assignments that in the service of the Lord they have even greater powers than in ordinary responsibilities. There can be no failure in the work of the Lord when men do their best. We are but instruments; this is the Lord's work. This is His Church, His gospel plan. These are His children we are working with. He will not permit us to fail if we do our part. He will magnify us even beyond our own talents and abilities when necessary. This I know. I am sure many of you have experienced it as I have. It is one of the sweetest experiences that can come to a human being. (*God, Family, Country,* pp. 138–39.)

If you are to provide future leadership for the Church, our country, and your own homes, you must stand firm in the faith, unwavering in the face of evil, and as Paul said, "Put on the whole armour of God, that ye may be able to stand against the wiles of the devil. For we wrestle not against flesh and blood, but against principalities, against powers, against the rulers of the darkness of this world, against spiritual wickedness in high places." (Ephesians 6:11–12.) Satan is especially anxious to gain victory over this group because of the profound influence you will have in the growth of the Church. ("Be True to God, Country, and Self," Young Adult Fireside, Logan, Utah, 11 February 1979.)

There is a "union required by the law of the celestial kingdom; And Zion cannot be built up unless it is by the principles of the law of the celestial kingdom." (D&C 105:4–5.) Among the required principles and attributes is a unity of mind and heart. "I say unto you, be one; and if ye are not one ye are not mine," is the Savior's injunction to His modern Church (D&C 38:27; John 17:20–23). Nowhere is this requirement more essential than among those whom He has called to preside throughout His kingdom. (Salt Lake City, Utah, 19 January 1977.)

We must remember that though the Church is engaged in business, it is not the business world. Its success is measured in terms of souls saved, not in profit and loss. We need, of course, to be efficient and productive, but we also need to keep our focus on eternal objectives. Be cautious about imposing secular methods and terminology on sacred priesthood functions. Remember that rational problem-solving procedures, though helpful, will not be solely sufficient in the work of the kingdom. God's work must be done by faith, prayer, and by the Spirit, "and if it be by some other way it is not of God" (D&C 50:18). (Salt Lake City, Utah, 19 January 1977.)

The greatest leadership to be found anywhere in the world is the leadership under which you serve—the leadership in the Church and kingdom of God. There isn't anything like it anywhere. There are no greater men anywhere than the men who serve as leaders in our own Church. I think there does not live upon the earth today a greater leader than the man who stands at the head of this Church as prophet, seer, and revelator, under whose direction you serve as leaders. I say this in terms of the standards which our Father has set up for the measurement of real leadership.

Why is that leadership great? First of all because it is leadership imbued with the authority and power of God, the priesthood. Because it is leadership of prophets, seers, and revelators, because it is leadership that expresses character, manhood, and the building of real men and women. Character is the one thing we make in this world and take with us into the next. There isn't anything more important. And any leadership or any system or any philosophy which tends to weaken character is not worth the effort.

The whole purpose of the Church is to build men and women who will be godlike in their attitudes and in their attributes and in their ideals. "Men are blind until they see that in the human plan/ Nothing is worth the building if it does not build the man./Why build these cities glorious if man, unbuilded goes./In vain we build the world unless the builder also grows." ("The Greatest Leadership," BYU Student Leadership Conference, Sun Valley, Idaho, September 1959.)

Here are some effective suggestions our leaders can use to assist them in correctly deciding what actions should be taken. Is the problem clearly understood? All too often our leaders haven't defined what is to be decided. The problem must be expressed clearly on paper.

Is the stated problem the real one? Is our leader treating the symptoms or the causes? For example, a stake president was concerned with home teaching in his stake and wanted to make some decisions in order to improve it. The records established that fewer families were being visited each month. The stake president was upset with the home teachers without realizing that he wasn't properly communicating on a continuing basis with the bishops and quorum leaders about home teaching and its importance. The real problem wasn't low home teaching activity; the difficulty was inadequate communication between the stake president and his subordinates. Once the stake president realized the difficulty and corrected it, the home teaching improved greatly in his stake.

Does the problem "feel" right? We in the Church are open to inspiration and should seek it, and our Father in Heaven will let us know if the problem we are concerned about is one demanding a decision. Inspiration is an important aspect of decision making.

Diagnose the problem. The problem must be analyzed and divided into its parts. Common sense dictates that the items to be decided should be written down and each facet be listed. Assess the whole situation, looking to the experience of the past and present as much as possible. Keep an open mind.

Evaluate the available alternatives. The selected facts must be carefully evaluated and listed in their order of importance as we best see them. How the Saints are affected must be of primary concern.

Pray and fast for inspiration. "Counsel with the Lord in all thy doings, and he will direct thee for good" (Alma 37:37). After an adequate evaluation of the situation, prayer and fasting must then be brought in as the final step before the decision. Listen for an answer. Too often we pray without listening.

Make the decision. "Decision making is a lonely business," said my good friend Clarence B. Randall, former head of Inland Steel Company, "and the greater the degree of responsibility, the more intense the loneliness." After following the six steps previously mentioned, however, most decisions our priesthood brethren make will be for the best. Determine how to accomplish the decision. Action must follow the decision. The procedures of accomplishment must be listed and assignments made.

Follow up and reevaluate. One good brother said, "If a decision has come from inspiration, then why evaluate?" Circumstances change and with change comes time to review and, at least some of the time, to begin the decision-making process all over again. In any event, a follow-up to see if the job is being done must be part of the procedure. (*God, Family, Country,* pp. 149–51.)

Leaders are counseled to study the doctrines of the Church so as to be able to adequately represent our doctrines to others. To use the Apostle Paul's phraseology, we expect you to be a "workman that needeth not to be ashamed" (2 Timothy 2:15).

Because of the efforts of our enemies and critics, you may expect to have members of the Church come to you seeking to know the Church's position in relation to certain doctrines and practices. Are you able to counsel them and keep them on course?

You will not be able to intelligently discuss such matters with members unless you have set an example of personal gospel scholarship and study. You should know our Church history. Further, you should ensure that the scriptures are used to teach correct doctrines in priesthood, auxiliary, and sacrament meetings. In a word, we call upon you to encourage members to read and study the scriptures in an effort to strengthen their testimonies of this great latter-day work. (Salt Lake City, Utah, 20 May 1984.)

There is no satisfactory substitute for the Spirit. I know of no more impressive scripture than the inspiring words of the Lord to the Prophet Joseph in Liberty Jail (D&C 121:34–44). Read them today. Sublime in spirit, ever timely for instruction, and ever profound in deep meaning for the priesthood of God are these words, which every leader in the Church should follow. (*God, Family, Country,* pp. 140–41.)

One of the best ways for leaders to understand correct principles is to have a thorough knowledge and understanding of the scriptures and the appropriate handbook. Most situations have already arisen before, perhaps many times, and policy and procedure have already been determined to handle the problem. It is always wise, therefore, to refer to and be familiar with existing written instructions and Church policy on questions as they arise. (*God, Family, Country,* p. 147.)

Our young people need fewer critics and more models. You are the models to which they will look for a pattern in life to which they can follow and adhere. They will need the inspiration which can come from you as you square your lives fully with the teachings of the gospel. ("The Greatest Leadership," BYU Student Leadership Conference, Sun Valley, Idaho, September 1959.)

To officer a ward it will take approximately one-third of you in active leadership positions; think of it. What a glorious organization the Lord has provided, a Church of organized workers, for everyone has an opportunity to develop in leadership capacity. (Finglas Ireland Branch Dedication, 10 September 1980.)

To priesthood leaders we say, look to the prophetic counsel of Lehi and Paul and others like them. In that counsel you will find the solution to the challenges you face in keeping your flocks safe from the "ravening wolves" that surround them. (See Matthew 7:15.) We know that you too have great anxiety for the members of your wards and stakes and expend great time and effort in their behalf. There is much that we ask of you who have been chosen for leadership. We place many loads upon your shoulders. You are asked to run the programs of the Church, interview and counsel with the membership, see that the financial affairs of the stakes and wards are properly handled, manage welfare projects, build buildings, and a host of other time-consuming activities. ("The Power of the Word," *Ensign* 17 [May 1987]: 81.)

President John Taylor said: "If a thing is well done, no one will ask how long it took to do it, but who did it." There is no room for shoddy performance in the Church. An able leader will expect quality, and he will let those whom he assigns know that he expects quality. (*God, Family, Country,* p. 139.)

In the Church especially, asking produces better results than ordering—better feeling, too. Remember to tell why. Follow up to see how things are going. Show appreciation when people carry out instructions well. Express confidence when it can be done honestly. When something gets fouled up, it is well to check back and find out where you slipped up—and don't be afraid to admit that you did. Remember, our people are voluntary, free-will workers. They also love the Lord and His work. Love them. Appreciate them. When you are tempted to reprimand a fellow worker, don't. Try an interesting challenge and a pat on the back instead. Our Father's children throughout the world are essentially good. He loves them. We should also. (*God, Family, Country,* p. 132.)

Leaders of youth, we want our young people on the field. We want them sweating it out. We want them to have responsibility, because they grow under responsibility. We are not a Church of organized sitters. We are a Church of organized workers, and we want our young people to get into it, with all their enthusiasm and power. (*Title of Liberty*, p. 200.)

You are now called on to act. And as you lengthen your stride, we hope you will leave large footprints so others will tread in your tracks. (Regional Representatives Seminar, Salt Lake City, Utah, 5 April 1985.)

National Leadership

Leaders of America have a basic responsibility which embraces all the others and which is fundamental to sound federal-state relationships: That is, to do everything they possibly can to foster in the minds and hearts of our people the spirit of self-reliance and self-help which has made this nation great and which this nation must have if it is to continue great. (*The Red Carpet,* p. 150.)

Leadership must not be expected merely from those who serve in high offices. This is the kind of leadership we should be cultivating at every level, among parents, teachers, students, judges, the various professions, businessmen, laborers, technicians, ministers —all of us need to join a crusade to develop men and women who talk straight, tell the truth, and who are willing to take a course deserving of God's blessings.

A genuine leader tries to stay well informed. He is a person who acts on principle rather than expediency. He tries to learn from all human experience measured against revealed principles of divine wisdom. As a rule, a good leader is not easily deceived. (*Title of Liberty,* p. 162.)

Delegation of Leadership

The term *delegation* is widely used and generally understood. But the delegation we speak of is so different — so much more important — so far-reaching. It is Church delegation through and by the authority of the holy priesthood of God. And as the Church grows in total membership and regional distribution, wise delegation becomes more and more important — in fact, imperative for continued success. The character of our Church membership distribution is changing and will continue to change. This emphasizes the increasing need for leadership training and the wise delegation of responsibility. (*God, Family, Country,* p. 129.)

The very foundations of the world were laid by delegated authority. Many times Jesus reminded people that His mission on earth was one through delegated authority. The restoration of His Church had its very beginning with delegated authority.

In speaking to the Jews in the synagogue, Jesus told them that He had been delegated by His Father: "For I came down from heaven, not to do mine own will, but the will of him that sent me" (John 6:38).

In the opening lines of his gospel book, the Apostle John noted that, at the very beginning of the foundations of the earth, Jesus acted as a divine son delegated by the Father: "In the beginning was the Word, and the Word was with God, and the Word was God. The same was in the beginning with God. All things were made by him; and without him was not anything made that was made." (John 1:1–3.) (*God, Family, Country,* pp. 133–34.)

Jesus gives us the master example of good administration through proper delegating. His leadership was perfect. Rugged, able men whom He called to be His Apostles gave up prosperous business careers to follow Him. Many of His delegated missionaries traveled without purse or scrip. Men suffered great hardships in carrying out His instructions. Some of them died cruel deaths in His service. But His delegated disciples went forth into the world bold as lions through His charge. They accomplished things they had never dreamed of. No leader ever motivated men and women as did He. (*God, Family, Country,* p. 135.)

This is the Lord's organization through which we operate. We are dealing with voluntary workers—our Father's children whom He loves, regardless of their mistakes and weaknesses. There must be no force, coercion, or intimidation in our delegation. To be effective, we must seek and obtain the Spirit if we are to delegate wisely. Without the Spirit we flounder, unsure of our decisions and counsel. Wise delegation requires the same Spirit required to preach the gospel. (*God, Family, Country,* p. 130.)

We may seek help from the good and wise men of the earth. There has been much done in this field of managing the services of men, delegation of responsibility, outside Church organizations that may be helpful—tried and tested procedures, approaches, and principles. Many of these when used in company with the Spirit can be helpful.

Here are a few examples: Good management means delegating authority. Delegating part of the workload helps you and your organization. Effective management is the art of multiplying yourself through others. The jobs to delegate are the ones you do best.

The number of subordinates who can report directly to one supervisor is limited because of time, distance, human limitations, and type of work. Authority and responsibility may be delegated. Accountability may not be delegated. The most eligible candidate for a bigger job is the man who has already trained his own replacement.

Why delegation goes wrong: failing to delegate enough, delegating by formula, failing to keep communication lines open, failing to define the assignment, failing to make the assignment stick, failing to delegate enough authority to do the job, being too narrow in your delegation, and failing to allow for mistakes. (*God, Family, Country,* pp. 131–32.)

A wise administrator in the Church today will not try to do the job himself, giving the impression that no one else is quite qualified. And as he delegates, he will give an assurance that he who has been delegated has his full backing. (*God, Family, Country,* p. 137.)

Wise delegation requires prayerful preparation, as does effective teaching or preaching. The Lord makes this clear in these words: "And the Spirit shall be given unto you by the prayer of faith; and if ye receive not the Spirit ye shall not teach" (D&C 42:14). And we might add, ye shall not delegate without the Spirit. (*God, Family, Country,* p. 131.)

At the time of delegation there is usually excellent opportunity to get close to people, to build them up and give them needed counsel and direction. Theodore Roosevelt said, "The best executive is the one who has sense enough to pick good men to do what he wants done, and self-restraint enough to keep from meddling with them while they do it." (*God, Family, Country,* p. 133.)

Remember that you are the coach, not the quarterback on this great team. When you get a man to assume his duties, you have not only blessed his family and done the world a favor, but you have helped him to develop and grow. (Regional Representatives Seminar, Salt Lake City, Utah, 3 April 1975.)

Jesus aimed to make of every man a king, to build him in leadership into eternity. On that memorable night after the last supper, He said to the eleven (after Judas had slunk out into the night to go about his dark mission), "Verily, verily, I say unto you, he that believeth in me, the works that I do shall he do also; and greater works than these shall he do; because I go unto my Father" (John 14:12). Through delegating, Jesus desired to lift, rather than suppress the individual. And all through the Church today, men and women are growing in stature through positions delegated to them. (*God, Family, Country,* p. 136.)

Stewardship

Stewardship is a framework of responsibility wherein the fulfillment of your duties must be accomplished. Put another way (and this from an agriculturist), it is that each cow stays in its own pasture. When one leaves the realm of his own responsibility (stewardship), he not only frustrates his personal growth, but he becomes guilty of ignoring the priorities of his own responsibility.

No stewardship can be fully filled without divine direction. This involves study of the scriptures, the words of living prophets, and calling upon the Lord for intelligence beyond your own. It also involves knowing people and being sincerely concerned about their interests and needs. (Salt Lake City, Utah, October 1961.)

Under true stewardship, there is no room for vain ambition, pettiness, or status seeking. One's ambition is to serve the Lord and His kingdom first. Carelessness, mediocrity, feigned effort, or inconsistent performance have no place where true stewardship is manifest. Love is the motivating force—love for God and love for others. (Salt Lake City, Utah, October 1961.)

We must not be cast down or discouraged in this work. There is no basis for discouragement. We are not alone. We will not, we cannot fail if we will do our duty. The Lord will magnify us even beyond our present talents and abilities. (Salt Lake City, Utah, 19 January 1977.)

As members of the Church, we have some close quarters to pass through if we are to save our souls. As the Church gets larger, some men have increasing responsibility and more and more duties must be delegated. We all have stewardships for which we must account to the Lord.

Unfortunately some men who do not honor their stewardship may have an adverse effect on many people. Often the greater the man's responsibility the more good or evil he can accomplish. There are some regrettable things being said and done by some people in the Church today. (*An Enemy Hath Done This,* p. 317.)

When individual actions of some Church members disturb you, here is another principle to consider. And this is the principle of stewardship. As the kingdom grows larger, more and more responsibilities have to be delegated and stewardships handed out. Men respond in different degrees of valiancy to their stewardships. God is very patient and long-suffering as He waits for some of us to rise to our responsibilities. He usually gives a man a long enough rope and a long enough time to either pull himself up to the presence of God or drop off somewhere below. But while God is patient, no puny arm of man in His stewardship can long impede or pervert the work of the Lord. The mills of God grind slowly, but they grind ever so finely. ("Jesus Christ—Gifts and Expectations," *New Era* 5 [May 1975]: 18.)

Being called of God makes us stewards in His house with definite responsibilities. We are, in very deed, custodians of the truth. (Regional Representatives Seminar, Salt Lake City, Utah, 3 April 1975.)

Management

The mind has been likened to a stage on which only one act at a time can be performed. From one side of the wings the Lord, who loves us, is trying to put on the stage of our minds that which will bless us. From the other side of the wings the devil, who hates us, is trying to put on the stage of our minds that which will curse us.

We are the stage managers; we are the ones who decide which thought will occupy the stage. Remember, the Lord wants us to have a fulness of joy like His, while the devil wants all men to be miserable like unto himself (see 2 Nephi 2:18, 27). We are the ones who must decide whose thought will prevail. We are free to choose, but we are not free to alter the consequences of those choices. We will be what we think about—what we consistently allow to occupy the stage of our minds (see Proverbs 23:7).

Sometimes we may have difficulty driving off the stage of our minds a certain evil thought. To drive it off, Elder Boyd K. Packer suggested that we sing an inspirational song of Zion or think on its words. Elder Bruce R. McConkie has recommended that after the opening song, we might preach a sermon to ourselves.

We should not invite the devil to give us a stage presentation. Usually without our realizing it, he slips into our thoughts. Our accountability begins with how we handle the evil thought immediately after it is presented. Like Jesus, we should positively and promptly terminate the temptation. We should dismiss the evil one without further argument.

It is our privilege to store our memories with good and great thoughts and bring them out on the stage of our minds at will. When the Lord faced His three great temptations in the wilderness, He immediately rebuked the devil with appropriate scripture that He had memorized. (*Come unto Christ*, pp. 40–41.)

We must not allow our Church activity to come between us and our families. Let us keep in mind that we can budget our time to take care of both. We must not neglect our families. (Salt Lake City, Utah, 6 April 1983.)

I believe that to tell a man what is expected of him is more important than to prescribe exactly how he is to get the job done. (CR April 1981, *Ensign* 11 [May 1981]: 34.)

The overall objective to be accomplished in missionary work, temple work, providing for the needy, and bringing up our children in righteousness has always been the same; only our methods to accomplish these objectives have varied. Any faithful member in this dispensation, no matter when he lived, could have found righteous methods to have carried out these objectives without having to wait for the latest, specific Churchwide program. (*God, Family, Country,* p. 382.)

We hold leadership meetings, seminars, and organize committees. As we proceed so to do, we must never depart from the Lord's plan of organization. And of equal or even greater importance, we must ever be guided by the purposes, objectives, and the great divine plan of the Lord as set forth in holy writ. (Salt Lake City, Utah, 19 January 1977.)

We know that time is eternal. We will probably use it in different ways. Benjamin Franklin said: "Dost thou love life? Then do not squander time for time is the stuff life is made of." ("New Year 1961," Washington D.C. Ward, 31 December 1960.)

Goal Setting

Every accountable child of God needs to set goals, short- and long-range goals. A man who is pressing forward to accomplish worthy goals can soon put despondency under his feet, and once a goal is accomplished, others can be set up. Some will be continuing goals. Each week when we partake of the sacrament we commit ourselves to the goals of taking upon ourselves the name of Christ, of always remembering Him and keeping His commandments (see Moroni 4:3; D&C 20:27). Of Jesus' preparation for His mission, the scripture states that He "increased in wisdom and stature, and in favour with God and man'' (Luke 2:52). This encompasses four main areas for goals: spiritual, mental, physical, and social. "Therefore, what manner of men ought ye to be?" asked the Master, and He answered, "Verily I say unto you, even as I am" (3 Nephi 27:27). Now, there is a lifetime goal—to walk in His steps, to perfect ourselves in every virtue as He has done, to seek His face (see D&C 101:38), and to work to make our calling and election sure (see 2 Peter 1:10). ("Do Not Despair," *Ensign* 16 [October 1986]: 5.)

When we set goals we are in command. If we know where we are going, we can judge more accurately where we are now and make effective plans to reach our destination. If we keep a goal firmly in mind, we will know when we have reached it. This gives us a sense of accomplishment and the challenge of establishing fresh, new goals—always keeping the long-range objective in mind. If we can state our goals clearly, we will gain a purpose and meaning in all our actions. Clearly understood goals bring our lives into focus just as a magnifying glass focuses a beam of light into one burning point. Without goals our efforts may be scattered and unproductive. Without knowing it, we may be torn by conflicting impulses or desires. (Mission Presidents Seminar, Salt Lake City, Utah, 27 June 1974.)

If we are to achieve long-range goals, we must learn to set up and accomplish short-range goals that will move us along the way. If we do not consciously select our goals, we may be controlled by goals not of our own choosing—goals imposed by outside pressures (such as the expectations of others) or by our habits (such as procrastination) or by our desire for the approval of the world. (Mission Presidents Seminar, Salt Lake City, Utah, 27 June 1974.)

We cannot do everything at once, but we can do a great deal if we choose our goals well and work diligently to attain them. (Mission Presidents Seminar, Salt Lake City, Utah, 27 June 1974.)

In the work of the Lord there should be no serious mistakes. The most important point of your planning should be on your knees. (CR April 1977, *Ensign* 7 [May 1977]: 83.)

Usually the Lord gives us the overall objectives to be accomplished and some guidelines to follow, but He expects us to work out most of the details and methods. The methods and procedures are usually developed through study and prayer and by living so that we can obtain and follow the promptings of the Spirit. Less spiritually advanced people, such as those in the days of Moses, had to be commanded in many things. Today those spiritually alert look at the objectives, check the guidelines laid down by the Lord and His prophets, and then prayerfully act—without having to be commanded "in all things" (D&C 58:26). This attitude prepares men for godhood. (*An Enemy Hath Done This,* pp. 271–72.)

Let your minds be filled with the goal of being like the Lord, and you will crowd out depressing thoughts as you anxiously seek to know Him and do His will. "Let this mind be in you," said Paul (Philippians 2:5). "Look unto me in every thought," said Jesus (D&C 6:36). And what will follow if we do? "Thou wilt keep him in perfect peace, whose mind is stayed on thee" (Isaiah 26:3). ("Do Not Despair," *Ensign* 16 [October 1986]: 5.)

We will never be alone if we live as we should, because our Father will always be with us to bless us. He wants us to be successful. He wants us to be happy. He wants us to achieve the good goals we set. He will do His part if we do our part. ("New Year 1961," Washington D.C. Ward, 31 December 1960.)

Decision Making

The biggest business of any life is making decisions. While one of the greatest gifts of God to man is free agency or the right of choice, He has also given man responsibility for these choices. We may choose between good and evil. We put our own lives in the direction of success or failure. We may not only choose our ultimate goals, but we may also determine and decide for ourselves, in many cases, the means by which we will arrive at those goals, and by our industry or lack of it determine the speed by which they may be reached. This takes individual effort and energy and will not be without opposition or conflict. (*God, Family, Country*, p. 145.)

Making decisions is probably the most important thing people ever do. Nothing happens until someone makes a decision. Even the world itself circled into being as the result of God's decisions. God said, "In the beginning I created the heaven, and the earth," "Let there be light; and there was light," "Let there be a firmament in the midst of the water, and it was so." (Moses 2:1, 3, 6.)

Fortunately the ability and judgment necessary to make decisions can be acquired. Certain methods and practices can bring to us all greater skill in everyday, every-week, every-month opportunities to make decisions. There are some basic principles recommended and used by specialists in the field. It is generally recognized that there are fundamental steps in decision making.

Defining the problem, its scope and significance: What kind of problem is it? What is its critical factor? When do we have to solve it? Why solve it? What will it take to solve it? What is the value or gain in solving it?

Collect facts and analyze and use them. Develop and weigh possible solutions to arrive at conclusions. Carry a decision into action with plans and controls. Follow up on the results of the decisions and action. (*God, Family, Country*, pp. 145–46.)

Decisions should be based on correct principles and facts. A thorough knowledge of the principles and facts surrounding any particular problem usually leads to an easy and correct decision. A thorough knowledge of the facts surrounding a welfare problem, for example, will, when considered in connection with fundamental welfare principles, bring the bishop to the right answer in that particular case. One of the most basic elements of decision making, therefore, is to have possession of the facts and to understand and be familiar with the basic and underlying principles. (*God, Family, Country*, p. 146.)

Decisions should be timely. Sometimes a lack of decision on a point is actually a decision in the opposite direction. We need to make up our minds. Elijah said to ancient Israel: "How long halt ye between two opinions? if the Lord be God, follow him: but if

Baal, then follow him. And the people answered him not a word."
(1 Kings 18:21.) (*God, Family, Country,* p. 147.)

One of our most serious problems is the inferiority complex
which people feel when they are not informed and organized. They
dare not make a decision on these vital issues. They let other people
think for them. They stumble around in the middle of the road trying to avoid being "controversial," and get hit by traffic going
both ways. In this mighty struggle each of you has a part. Every
person on the earth today chose the right side during the War in
Heaven. Be on the right side now. Stand up and be counted. (*Title
of Liberty,* p. 41.)

I hope we will not live in the past. People who live in the past
don't have very much future. There is a great tendency for us to lament about our losses, about decisions that we have made that we
think in retrospect were probably wrong decisions. There is a great
tendency for us to feel badly about the circumstances with which
we are surrounded, thinking they might have been better had we
made different decisions. We can profit by the experience of the
past. But let us not spend our time worrying about decisions that
have been made, mistakes that have been made. Let us live in the
present and in the future. ("New Year 1961," Washington D.C.
Ward, 31 December 1960.)

Wise decisions are the stepping-stones of progress. They are
the building blocks of life. Decisions are the ingredients of success.
For individuals and institutions, they mark the way of progress.
The mind of an individual or the collective mind of the council,
committee, or board of directors decides what the present state
and the future direction of the individual or institution will be.
(*God, Family, Country,* p. 143.)

The world is gradually beating a path to our door to see how
we do things. Stick by your righteous guns and you will bless your
fellowmen. Be right and then be easy to live with, if possible, but
in that order. ("In His Steps," *1979 Devotional Speeches of the
Year* [Provo, Utah: BYU, 1980], p. 65.)

Earnestly seeking our Father in Heaven, having faith that He will answer our prayers, is a comforting base on which to begin deciding. Joseph Smith said the Lord will not take water from a dry well, so we must do our part. Sometimes attempting to find a correct decision takes great amounts of energy, study, and long-suffering. (*God, Family, Country,* p. 149.)

In The Church of Jesus Christ of Latter-day Saints we face momentous decisions. Our people—heads of families, parents, children—must make important decisions. Help is needed and help is available. (*God, Family, Country,* p. 143.)

A man should always be sure that he consults the Spirit in his decision making. In other words, he should keep the door ajar in case the Spirit wants to dictate a course other than the one he might have naturally followed. Brigham Young at one time said that he wanted to do a certain thing, but that the Spirit dictated otherwise. (*God, Family, Country,* p. 153.)

Wise decisions are usually arrived at following work, struggle, and prayerful effort. The Lord's response to Oliver Cowdery's ineffective effort makes this clear: "But, behold, I say unto you, that you must study it out in your mind; then you must ask me if it be right, and if it is right I will cause that your bosom shall burn within you; therefore, you shall feel that it is right" (D&C 9:8). (*God, Family, Country,* p. 149.)

Sometimes it requires a man to submit himself in spiritual struggle before the Lord before he can feel good about a decision. Some of us have had to do this after a season of pondering and prayer. It is one thing to agree to a decision; it is another thing to · know the decision is inspired from God. (Salt Lake City, Utah, 19 January 1977.)

In decisions of crucial importance, fasting combined with prayer can bring great spiritual insight. (*God, Family, Country,* p. 152.)

Some decisions are simply a matter of making good judgment, and simply coming to a decision. For instance, in the Doctrine and Covenants, the Lord tells the brethren He is not concerned whether they go by land or by sea, as long as they get going (see D&C 61:22). (*God, Family, Country,* p. 152.)

There are a few cases where a decision cannot be made immediately, because the Lord wants to bring other factors to the attention of the decision maker. In that case, a man must learn to wait on the Lord or, as the Lord would say, "Be still, and know that I am God" (Psalm 46:10). (*God, Family, Country,* p. 152.)

While it is usually advisable to try to see the long-range view of the decision you make, sometimes the Lord will inspire you to make only temporary decisions that will lead to an end that only He knows about. A man should never hesitate to make such decisions. Wilford Woodruff had to make a number of those decisions that required him to say, "I know not, save the Lord commanded me" (Moses 5:6). Nephi returned to Jerusalem without knowing exactly what his plan of action was going to be (see 1 Nephi 4:6). (*God, Family, Country,* pp. 152–53.)

Some people intend to make a decision and then never get around to it. They intend to paint the barn, to fix the fence, to haul away that old machinery or remove that old shed, but the time of decision just never arrives. Some of us face a similar situation in our personal lives. We intend to pay a full tithing, to begin keeping the Word of Wisdom, to make our initial home teaching visits early in the month. However, without actual decision followed by implementation, the weeks and months go by and nothing is accomplished. We could drift into eternity on these kinds of good intentions. The Lord apparently sensed this weakness in His children, for He said: "Wherefore, if ye believe me, ye will labor while it is called today" (D&C 64:25).

Get the facts—then decide promptly. As an excuse for postponing decisions, do not rely on the old cliches some people use, such as "I want to sleep on it." We don't make decisions in our sleep. However, don't jump to conclusions or make snap judgments. Get the facts, be sure of the basic principles, and weigh the consequences. Then decide! (*God, Family, Country,* p. 148.)

Our decisions have made us what we are. Our eternal destiny will be determined by the decisions we yet will make. (*God, Family, Country,* p. 143.)

We must take advantage of our opportunities. Our progenitors cannot save us. They have provided a wonderful inheritance for us, but the decision is ours. We will have to do the job. It is a tremendous challenge. It is a great opportunity. ("The Greatest Leadership," BYU Student Leadership Conference, Sun Valley, Idaho, September 1959.)

God will be the judge and His judgments will be just because He sees not only the results of our decisions, but judges us by the intent of our hearts as well. (As quoted in Frederick W. Babbel, *On Wings of Faith* [Salt Lake City: Bookcraft, 1972], p. 37.)

Meditation

Man must take time to meditate, to sweep the cobwebs from his mind, so that he might get a more firm grip on the truth and spend less time chasing phantoms and dallying in projects of lesser worth. (CR April 1967, *Improvement Era* 70 [June 1967]: 59.)

Take time to meditate. Ponder the meaning of the work in which you are engaged. The Lord has counseled, "Let the solemnities of eternity rest upon your minds" (D&C 43:34). You cannot do that when your minds are preoccupied with the worries and cares of the world. (Salt Lake City, Utah, 2 October 1985.)

Opposition and Adversity

I would like to raise this warning: In this period of apparent goodwill—good feeling toward the Church—when it seems as if we have no great obstacles anymore as we once had, there should be deep concern. In my judgment, the hour of our success is our greatest danger. And apparently this is the hour of great success. No more persecution—persecution which once tended to drive us together and make us united! Now we seem to be accepted by the world. Will it mean disunity? Will it mean that we will rest on our laurels and sit back, as it were, and think that all is well in Zion (see 2 Nephi 28:21)? I think there is real danger in this period of praise and commendation. I am happy for it, provided we be careful, that we be on our guard. The praise of the world will not save us. It will not exalt us in the celestial kingdom. Only the living of the principles of the gospel will bring us salvation and exaltation. And so I hope that our performance in living the gospel will be equal to the commendation and the praise we are receiving, that our performance will at least equal our reputation, and we have a good reputation. God grant that we may merit all the good things that have been said about us, and that more good things might be accurately said about us in the future. (CR October 1955, *Improvement Era* 58 [December 1955]: 952.)

Sometimes I think we are so inclined to be complacent and to more or less take things as they are. The prophets in the Book of Mormon saw our day, and, oh, how I wish every American would read the Book of Mormon. To practically every problem that faces us as a nation today and as a people, you can find the answer in the Book of Mormon. And yet we have people going up and down the land crying, "All is well in Zion; yea, Zion prospereth, all is well" (2 Nephi 28:21). The early prophets saw our day and they used almost those exact words. As they were permitted to look down through the stream of time, they saw the evils and the wickedness of our day and how people would tend to lower their standards and to speak out against that which is good. Today, more than any other time in my memory, certainly we see evidence of that trend. (Star Valley Wyoming Stake Conference, 18 April 1971.)

Individually the enemy is ourselves. Are we not our own worst enemy with our declining moral standards, our increasing selfishness, the constant search for pleasure, the piling on of luxury upon luxury for the sake of softer and softer living and the possession of a hollow, vacillating national purpose? The battleground is in our hearts, in our intellects, in our homes and our communities—and the war goes relentlessly on. (*The Red Carpet,* p. 300.)

Christ taught that we should be in the world but not of it. Yet there are some in our midst who are not so much concerned about taking the gospel into the world as they are about bringing worldliness into the gospel. They want us to be in the world and of it.

They want us to be popular with the worldly even though a prophet has said that this is impossible, for all hell would then want to join us. (CR April 1969, *Improvement Era* 72 [June 1969]: 43.)

Of course there will be opposition. There will be conflicts. There will be misrepresentation. We must stand firm, however, for that which we believe to be right as measured by these standards, for those things which we know to be good and true, and the God of Heaven will sustain us. (CR October 1954, *Improvement Era* 57 [December 1954]: 922.)

We tend to associate with those of like ideals. Only the wholesome have the capacity to lift and encourage one another to greater service, to greater achievement, to greater strength. Those who follow an opposite course serve only to intensify those unwholesome actions and desires which are the breeding ground for regrets and disillusionment. ("Purposeful Living," *Listen, A Journal of Better Living* [January–March 1955]: 19.)

You, as our great youth, are surrounded and bombarded from all sides by the atrocious, destructive evils of the devil, which are revealed in modern music, in modern art, in sex perversion, in so-called sex education in the schools, in destructive sensitivity training—a powerful form of Pavlovian brainwashing. These evils are prominent in the promotion of drugs (LSD, marijuana, and a host of others), in leading magazines and underground publications for youth, in television, in movies and radio programs, in pornographic literature, in morally destructive paperback books available to all on newsstands. (Scandinavia and Finland Area Conference, 16–18 August 1974.)

Concerning those who will receive the terrestrial, or lesser, kingdom, the Lord said, "These are they who are not valiant in the testimony of Jesus; wherefore, they obtain not the crown over the kingdom of our God" (D&C 76:79). Not to be valiant in one's testimony is a tragedy of eternal consequence. These are members who know that this latter-day work is true but who fail to endure to the end. Some may even hold temple recommends, but they do not magnify their callings in the Church. Without valor, they do not take an affirmative stand for the kingdom of God. Some seek the praise, adulation, and honors of men; others attempt to conceal their sins; and a few criticize those who preside over them. (*Come unto Christ,* p. 13.)

Some of our members have become disturbed because of derogatory things said about the Church and its leaders, or because of misrepresentations about our doctrines or our practices. But opposition is not new to the Church. We have had opposition in the past, and we shall continue to have opposition in the future. Do not become discouraged by what others say or do. Stay on the strait and narrow path. You do this by holding fast to the iron rod —the words of God as contained in the scriptures and as given by His living servants on this earth (see 1 Nephi 8:19). (CR April 1984, *Ensign* 14 [May 1984]: 8.)

The prophet Lehi saw our day in his great visionary dream of the tree of life. He saw that many people would wander blindly in the mists of darkness, which symbolized the temptations of the devil (see 1 Nephi 12:17). He saw some fall "away in forbidden paths" (1 Nephi 8:28), others who drowned in rivers of filthiness and still others wandering in "strange roads" (1 Nephi 8:32). When we read of the spreading curse of drugs in the land, or read of the pernicious flood of pornography and immorality, does anyone doubt that these are the forbidden paths and rivers of filthiness Lehi described? Not all of those Lehi saw perishing were of the world. Some had come to the tree and partaken of the fruit. In other words, some members of the Church today are among those souls Lehi saw which were lost. ("The Power of the Word," *Ensign* 17 [May 1986]: 81.)

We want our children to be happy. It is possible, even in a wicked world. We don't wish them a life of ease. Everyone will have problems, disappointments, heartaches. It isn't on the pinnacle of success and ease where men and women grow into strong characters. But God intended that this life be essentially a satisfying and joyous life. This joy and satisfaction will come as you look to the standards of the Church for guidance and direction, and teach your children to do the same. (London England Area Conference, 19–20 June 1976.)

Some of the most prominent targets now under withering fire in this war against us are the Ten Commandments, the Sermon on the Mount, the Constitution of the United States, the institution of private property, and the basic concepts of the gospel of Jesus Christ. Surely this is a time when consideration might well be given by the people of America, and the entire free world, to the important matter of citizenship responsibility and, more importantly, membership in the churches of the free world. (CR October 1969, *Improvement Era* 72 [December 1969]: 69.)

As nations tend to enjoy higher and higher standards of living, greater and greater comforts, greater and greater material blessings, there seems to be a tendency for them to become more and more interested in preserving their luxuries and their comforts than in preserving and safeguarding the ideals and principles that have made them great. In other words, there is a tendency for them to become infected with the germs of decadent morality. (*The Red Carpet,* p. 296.)

Today you cannot effectively fight for freedom and moral principles and not be attacked, and those who think they can are deceiving themselves. While I do not believe in stepping out of the path of duty to pick up a cross I don't need, a man is a coward who refuses to pick up a cross that clearly lies within his path. No cross, no crown. No gall, no glory. No thorns, no throne. (Taipei Taiwan Area Conference, 13–14 August 1975.)

This work will prevail in spite of all the opposition which might be mustered against it. This work will prevail! It will never be thrown down or given to another people (Daniel 2:44; D&C 138:44). God's kingdom has been established upon the earth for the last time in preparation for the second coming of the Master. We have the word of Jesus Christ whose name this Church bears to that effect. (Washington D.C. Stake Conference, 4 December 1960.)

Trials and Temptations

We are fortunate indeed as Latter-day Saints, to have all the knowledge which we possess, the assurance that has been given in the revelations, the dangers that have been pointed out by prophets of God that no people in this world will have the knowledge that we have. Who should be better prepared for the difficult days ahead than the Latter-day Saints? (Bear Lake Idaho Stake Conference, 22 May 1971.)

Years ago a ball player started his prayer like this, "Dear God: Help me to be a [good] sport in this game of life. I don't ask for an easy place in the lineup, play me anywhere you need me. . . . If all the hard drives seem to come my way, I thank you for the compliment. Help me to remember that you won't ever let anything come my way that You and I can't handle." (George Brimhall, *Long and Short Range Arrows*.) That is a good thing to remember in the game of life. A man must not only stand for the right principles, but he must fight for them. Those who fight for principles can be proud of the friends they have gained and the enemies they have earned. (Softball Devotional, Salt Lake City, Utah, 21 August 1966.)

I was thrilled the other day as I heard of the philosophy of one good woman. She said when things go well we give God the credit, and when things go wrong it is a test of our faith. I think that is a wonderful philosophy. When things go well, we give God the credit. No room there for egotism or pride or self-righteousness. And when things go wrong it is a test of our faith. No room for discouragement or depression because it is all going to be for her benefit and blessing if it is a test of her faith. ("New Year 1961," Washington D.C. Ward, 31 December 1960.)

As I look into your tear-stained eyes and see many of you German Saints at the end of World War II virtually in rags and at death's door, yet with a smile upon your cracked lips and the light of love and understanding shining in your eyes, I know that you have been true to your covenants, that you have been clean, that you have not permitted hatred and bitterness to fill you hearts. You — many of you — are some of the Lord's choicest witnesses of the fruits of the gospel of Jesus Christ. (As quoted in Frederick W. Babbel, *On Wings of Faith* [Salt Lake City: Bookcraft, 1972], p. 38.)

When George A. Smith was very ill, he was visited by his cousin, the Prophet Joseph Smith. The afflicted man reported:

"He told me I should never get discouraged, whatever difficulties might surround me. If I were sunk into the lowest pit of Nova Scotia and all the Rocky Mountains piled on top of me, I ought not to be discouraged, but hang on, exercise faith, and keep up good courage, and I should come out on the top of the heap." (*George A. Smith Family,* comp. Zora Smith Jarvis, p. 54.)

There are times when you simply have to righteously hang on and outlast the devil until his depressive spirit leaves you. As the Lord told the Prophet Joseph Smith: "Thine adversity and thine afflictions shall be but a small moment; And then, if thou endure it well, God shall exalt thee on high" (D&C 121:7–8).

To press on in noble endeavors, even while surrounded by a cloud of depression, will eventually bring you out on top into the sunshine. Even our Master, Jesus the Christ, while facing that supreme test of being temporarily left alone by our Father during the Crucifixion, continued performing His labors for the children of men, and then shortly thereafter He was glorified and received a fulness of joy. While you are going through your trials, you can recall your past victories and count the blessings that you do have with a sure hope of greater ones to follow if you are faithful. And you can have that certain knowledge that in due time God will wipe away all tears (Revelation 7:17) and that "eye hath not seen, nor ear heard, neither have entered into the heart of man, the things which God hath prepared for them that love him" (1 Corinthians 2:9). (CR October 1974, *Ensign* 4 [November 1974]: 67.)

We are far removed from the days of our forefathers who were persecuted for their peculiar beliefs. Some of us seem to want to share their reward, but are ofttimes afraid to stand up for principles that are controversial in our generation. We need not solicit persecution, but neither should we remain silent in the presence of overwhelming evils, for this makes cowards of men.

We are in the world, and I fear some of us are getting too much like the world. Rather than continue a peculiar people, some are priding themselves on how much they are like everybody else, when the world is getting more wicked. The Lord, as He prayed for His Apostles, said, "the world hath hated them, because they are not of the world, even as I am not of the world" (John 17:14). As Latter-day Saints, we too have been called out of the world. (*An Enemy Hath Done This*, p. 282.)

Today the Christian constitutionalist mourns for his country. He sees the spiritual and political faith of his fathers betrayed by wolves in sheep's clothing. He sees the forces of evil increasing in strength and momentum under the leadership of Satan, the archenemy of freedom. He sees the wicked honored and the valiant abused. He senses that his own generation faces Gethsemanes and Valley Forges that may yet rival or surpass the trials of the early Apostles and the men of '76. And this gives him cause to reflect on the most basic of fundamentals—the reason for our existence. Once we understand that fundamental, the purpose for mortality, we may more easily chart a correct course in the perilous seas that are engulfing our nation. (*An Enemy Hath Done This,* p. 53.)

There will be trials and disappointments to our young people, but I am convinced that any person who has real faith in God and a testimony of this work can endure anything and still keep his spirit sweet. We want our young people prepared so they can endure anything. (*Title of Liberty,* p. 205.)

Clearly, there would be little trial of faith if we received our full reward immediately for every goodly deed, or immediate retribution for every sin. But that there will be an eventual reckoning for each, there is no question. (CR April 1967, *Improvement Era* 70 [June 1967]: 57.)

What is the Lord's way to help us prepare for calamities? The answer is found in section 1 of the Doctrine and Covenants, wherein He says: "Wherefore, I the Lord, knowing the calamity which should come upon the inhabitants of the earth, called upon my servant Joseph Smith, Jr., and spake unto him from heaven, and gave him commandments; and also gave commandments to others." (D&C 1:17–18.) He has also said: "Search these commandments, for they are true and faithful, and the prophecies and promises which are in them shall all be fulfilled" (D&C 1:37).

Here then is the key—look to the prophets for the words of God, which will show us how to prepare for the calamities that are to come. For the Lord, in that same section, states: "What I the Lord have spoken, I have spoken, and I excuse not myself; and though the heavens and the earth pass away, my word shall not pass away, but shall all be fulfilled, whether by mine own voice or by the voice of my servants, it is the same" (D&C 1:38). (*God, Family, Country,* p. 266.)

There may come persecution; there may come opposition; there may come reverses; there may come criticism and misrepresentation. Your motives may be questioned. You may be attacked. But if we place our trust in the Almighty and do that which is right, there will come an inner assurance, an inner calm, a peace that will bring joy and happiness to our souls. (CR April 1954, *Improvement Era* 57 [June 1954]: 407.)

We must not lose hope. Hope is an anchor to the souls of men. Satan would have us cast away that anchor. In this way he can bring discouragement and surrender. But we must not lose hope. The Lord is pleased with every effort, even the tiny, daily ones in which we strive to be more like Him. Though we may see that we have far to go on the road to perfection, we must not give up hope. ("A Mighty Change of Heart," address prepared [but not delivered] 1986.)

To those who mourn we speak comfort. Know that your Savior is well acquainted with grief. He who notes the sparrow's fall is aware of you and desires to comfort and bless you. Turn to Him and lay your burden at His feet. ("First Presidency—Christmas Message," *Church News* [15 December 1985]: 3.)

"Salvation," said the Prophet Joseph Smith, "is nothing more nor less than to triumph over all our enemies and put them under our feet" (*Teachings of the Prophet Joseph Smith,* p. 297). We can rise above the enemies of despair, depression, discouragement, and despondency by remembering that God provides righteous alternatives. As it states in the Bible, "There hath no temptation taken you but such as is common to man: but God is faithful, who will not suffer you to be tempted above that ye are able; but will with the temptation also make a way to escape, that ye may be able to bear it" (1 Corinthians 10:13).

Some of you will recall that in that great book *Pilgrim's Progress* by John Bunyan the main character, known as Christian, was trying to press forward to gain entrance to the celestial city. He made it to his goal, but in order to do so, he had to overcome many obstacles, one of which was to escape from the Giant Despair. To lift our spirits and send us on our way rejoicing, the devil's designs of despair, discouragement, depression, and despondency can be defeated in a dozen ways, namely: repentance, prayer, service, work, health, reading, blessings, fasting, friends, music, endurance, and goals. ("Do Not Despair," *Ensign* 16 [October 1986]: 5.)

God is at the helm. I know it, and you know it. Surely no group of people in all the world has greater evidence of that fact than do the Latter-day Saints. Even during the days of persecution and hardship, the Lord has continually encouraged us to trust in Him, to keep His commandments, to do that which is right, and then to be unafraid.

We live in a world of fear today. Fear seems to be almost everywhere present. But there is no place for fear among the Latter-day Saints, among men and women who keep the commandments, who place their trust in the Almighty, who are not afraid to get down on their knees and pray to our Heavenly Father. (CR April 1954, *Improvement Era* 57 [June 1954]: 407.)

Satan

In the War in Heaven the devil advocated absolute eternal security at the sacrifice of our freedom. Although there is nothing more desirable than eternal security in God's presence, and although God knew, as did we, that some of us would not achieve this security if we were allowed our freedom—yet the very God of Heaven, who has more mercy than us all, still decreed no guaranteed security except by a man's own freedom of choice and individual initiative. (*The Red Carpet*, p. 111.)

We live in that time of which the Lord spoke when He said that "peace shall be taken from the earth, and the devil shall have power over his own dominion" (D&C 1:35). We live in that day which John the Revelator foresaw when "the dragon was wroth with the woman, and went to make war with the remnant of her seed, which keep the commandments of God and have the testimony of Jesus Christ" (Revelation 12:17). The dragon is Satan;

the woman represents the Church of Jesus Christ. Satan is waging war against the members of the Church who have testimonies and are trying to keep the commandments. And while many of our members are remaining faithful and strong, some are wavering. Some are falling. Some are fulfilling John's prophecy that in the war with Satan, some Saints would be "overcome" (Revelation 13:7). ("The Power of the Word," *Ensign* 16 [May 1986]: 81.)

Satan would have you believe that he wants only your freedom and happiness, but his motive in enticing you is that you "might be miserable like unto himself" and that "he may reign over you in his own kingdom" (2 Nephi 2:27, 29). How different from our Father in Heaven, who seeks your eternal joy and exaltation. ("Be True to God, Country, and Self," Young Adult Fireside, Logan, Utah, 11 February 1979.)

Why is the Lord angry with the wicked? Because they have rejected the Author of salvation. When you reject the gospel, when you reject the Author of our salvation, what have you to rely on? Nothing! Nothing but the devil's plan. What is the devil's plan? To force men; to take away from them their agency; to compel them to do the bidding of somebody else, whether they like it or not. That is the feeling that has spread over the world. ("Safety in the Face of Wickedness," Tokyo Japan Area Conference, 8–10 August 1975.)

Whenever the God of Heaven establishes by revelation His design, Satan always comes among men to pervert the doctrine, saying, "Believe it not" (Moses 5:13). He often establishes a counterfeit system, designed to deceive the children of men. His aim, as it was before the foundation of this earth was laid, is to thwart the agency of man and to subjugate him. Throughout all ages of mankind, the adversary has used human agents and despotic governments to establish his purpose. Satan is determined to destroy all that is dear, all that will ennoble and exalt man to a celestial kingdom. ("A Vision and a Hope for the Youth of Zion," in *1977 Devotional Speeches of the Year* [Provo, Utah: BYU, 1978], p. 75.)

Great battles can make great heroes, but great heroes will make great battles. You will never have a better opportunity to be a greater hero in a more crucial battle than in the battle you will face today and in the immediate future. Be warned that some of the greatest battles you will face will be fought within the silent chambers of your own soul. David's battles in the field against the foe were not as critical as David's battles in the palace against a lustful eye. We will each find our own battlefield. The tactics that the enemy will use against us will vary from time to time; he will feel after our weak spots. We must be alert to the devil's devious designs, to the subtle sins and clever compromises as well as the obvious offenses. ("In His Steps," Church Educational System Devotional, Anaheim, California, 8 February 1987.)

We live in an age when, as the Lord foretold, men's hearts are failing them, not only physically but in spirit (see D&C 45:26). Many are giving up heart for the battle of life. Suicide ranks as a major cause of death among college students. As the showdown between good and evil approaches, with its accompanying trials and tribulations, Satan is increasingly striving to overcome the Saints with despair, discouragement, despondency, and depression.

Yet, of all people, we as Latter-day Saints should be the most optimistic and the least pessimistic. For while we know that "peace shall be taken from the earth, and the devil shall have power over his own dominion," we are also assured that "the Lord shall have power over his saints, and shall reign in their midst" (D&C 1:35–36). (CR October 1974, *Ensign* 4 [November 1974]: 65.)

Throughout this great Christian nation there seems to be a desperate effort on the part of the adversary—through the great conspiracy, yes—and through other means also, to try to downgrade and depreciate and cheapen everything that's good and holy and pure and uplifting. You see evidence of it in every phase of our economic, social, and even spiritual life. It is a challenge to all of our ideals and traditions of the past. And it is all planned.

The adversary knows. He is smart. He knows this Church, and he knows where to strike, and today he is striking in two places particularly—at the home and the family—because he knows that no Church will ever be stronger than its families, and he knows that this nation will never rise above its homes. He knows that in large measure the home is where children are reared and trained and become good or bad. And so he is striking at the home and the family, trying to weaken that great, basic institution of the home.

He is emphasizing abortion, playing down the seriousness of divorce, playing up permissiveness, telling you to do what you feel like doing, regardless of the principle involved. He is promoting a permissive generation of parents—trying to get them to feel that they have no particular responsibility towards guiding their children, and that they should let the children have their own way, with no counseling. He doesn't like the home evening. He doesn't like family prayer. So he is trying to get us to concentrate our attention on the material things of the world, the styles of the world, the habits of the world, the cheapness of the world—anything to weaken our families and our homes. (Bear Lake Idaho Stake Conference, 22 May 1971.)

I realize that the devil is alert. He is the enemy of the work. He is the enemy of all righteousness, and I know that he is clever, that he never takes a holiday. He works overtime. He is ingenious. I am confident he will devise new ways to fight this work. We may not know just what form those schemes will take, but we must be vigilant. (CR October 1955, *Improvement Era* 58 [December 1955]: 952.)

Satan would tell you that these commandments restrict your freedom, that they are oppressive and unpleasant, that they prevent you from finding happiness, but his whisperings are lies. (London England Area Conference, 19–20 June 1976.)

Years of happiness can be lost in the foolish gratification of a momentary thrill. Satan would have you believe that true joy comes only as you surrender to his enticements, but one only needs to look at the twisted and shattered lives of those who violate God's laws to know why Satan is called the "father of lies." (London England Area Conference, 19–20 June 1976.)

There are boundaries beyond which Satan cannot go. Within those bounds, he is presently being permitted to offer an unrighteous alternative to God's righteous principles, thus allowing men to choose between good and evil and thereby determine the station they shall occupy in the next life. (*God, Family, Country,* p. 402.)

The gospel is being extended to all nations that permit our missionaries to penetrate their countries. The Church is prospering and growing. Yet in undiminished fury, and with an anxiety that his time is short (and it is), Satan, that great adversary to all men, is attempting to destroy all that we hold dear. (*Come unto Christ,* p. 111.)

I am sure you know of the insidious efforts that are being made to weaken our youth, to tear them down, to cheapen them, to vulgarize them. You see evidence of it in drugs, in deportment. Yes, we have drugs, and we have other things. Never have the young people of the Church been faced with such temptations as they are today—temptations that their parents or their grandparents never dreamed about—insidious, devious, devastating.

I would like to express to the wonderful young people we have in this Church the hope which I have for them, which the leadership of this Church has for them. They are our future. Our greatest assets are not our lands and our herds and our stocks and bonds or our business blocks, but our young people. Only a matter of years and they will be in positions of leadership in the kingdom. The adversary knows this, and he knows that the place to strike is at the young people. (Star Valley Wyoming Stake Conference, 18 April 1971.)

The Lord has on the earth some potential spiritual giants whom He saved for some six thousand years to help bear off the kingdom triumphantly and the devil is trying to put them to sleep. The devil knows that he probably won't be too successful in getting them to commit many great and malignant sins of commission. So he puts them into a deep sleep, like Gulliver, while he strands them with little sins of omission. And what good is a sleepy, neutralized, lukewarm giant as a leader?

We have too many potential spiritual giants who should be more vigorously lifting their homes, the kingdom, and the country. We have many who feel they are good men, but they need to be good for something—stronger patriarchs, courageous missionaries, valiant genealogists and temple workers, dedicated patriots, devoted quorum members. In short, we must be shakened and awakened from a spiritual snooze. ("Our Obligation and Challenge," Regional Representatives Seminar, Salt Lake City, Utah, 30 September 1977.)

We are meeting the adversary every day. The challenges of this era will rival any of the past, and these challenges will increase both spiritually and temporally. We must be close to Christ, we must daily remember Him and keep His commandments. (CR October 1987, *Ensign* 17 [November 1987]: 85.)

Amid the encircling gloom, the kindly light of the Lord can lead us on (*Hymns*, 1985, no. 97)—can help expose and stop evil in some places, slow it down in others, give the forces of freedom the chance to become better entrenched, provide righteous alternatives, and develop faith and hope to keep on keeping on in the divine assurance that in the brightness of the Lord's coming, the darkness of Satan's conspiracy will eventually be fully exposed and destroyed. (*God, Family, Country,* p. 404.)

Deception

There is a conspiracy of evil. The source of it all is Satan and his hosts. He has a great power over men to "lead them captive at his will, even as many as would not hearken" to the voice of the Lord (Moses 4:4). His evil influence may be manifest through governments; through false educational, political, economic, religious, and social philosophies; through secret societies and organizations; and through myriads of other forms. His power and influence are so great that, if possible, he would deceive the very elect (see Matthew 24:24). As the second coming of the Lord approaches, Satan's work will intensify through numerous insidious deceptions. (CR April 1978, *Ensign* 8 [May 1978]: 33.)

We know that Satan has great power to deceive, and because of this, we must be aware. The safeguard against his sophistry and deception has been specified by revelation. We are to give heed to the words of eternal life. In other words, we must understand and live by the revelations the Lord has granted to His prophets. These are contained in the four standard works and the written and public declarations of our current prophet. ("Three Imperative Responsibilities," London England Area Conference, 19–20 June 1976.)

We live in a time when the values of the world are distorted and changed and challenged. Some people are not sure what is right, and their lives prove it. Many have lost their way and are dragging others down with them, away from the teachings of the Lord Jesus Christ, to be enchained by the adversary. They are swearing allegiance to the wrong side. ("Strengthening the Family," Philippine Islands Area Conference, 12 August 1975.)

The only way to avoid being deceived is to get the facts. There are people who would try to hide the facts from us and replace the truth with a falsehood. They want us to believe that America is a failure, that her system of capitalistic free enterprise is doomed, that she must remedy her failures by adopting theories of collectivized control. I recognize these voices. I heard them in forty-three nations which I visited in the past. I heard them often during my eight years in Washington. None of them came to me in the name of communism or even socialism, but they came. And while many of us fought them and resisted them on every front, nevertheless, it was alarming to discover how many others were willing to believe and follow. Why do otherwise loyal Americans believe and follow? Because these voices came from masters of deception. (*Title of Liberty*, pp. 166–67.)

May I suggest three short tests to avoid being deceived, both pertaining to the freedom struggle and all other matters.

First, what do the standard works have to say about it? "To the law and to the testimony: If they speak not according to this word, it is because there is no light in them," said Isaiah (Isaiah 8:20; 2 Nephi 18:20). And Hosea said, "My people are destroyed for lack of knowledge" (Hosea 4:6). We must diligently study the scriptures. Of special importance to us are the Book of Mormon and the Doctrine and Covenants.

The second guide is this: What do the latter-day Presidents of the Church have to say on the subject—particularly the living

President? The President can speak on any subject he feels is needful for the Saints.

The third and final test is the Holy Ghost—the test of the Spirit. By the Spirit we "may know the truth of all things" (Moroni 10:5). This test can only be fully effective if one's channels of communication with God are clean and virtuous and uncluttered with sin. Will this Spirit be needed to check actions in other situations? Yes, and it could be used as a guide and a protector for the faithful. (*Title of Liberty,* pp. 220–23.)

As people grow older, they seem to accumulate two kinds of moral and spiritual supplies or values. One is a pile of doubts, suspicions, questionings, and mysteries; the other is usually a much smaller accumulation of positive conclusions. There is often a great temptation to expatiate upon the doubts and questionings, for negative and critical statements have a seductive appearance of depth and somewhat more of a flavor of wisdom than clear and succinct declarations of conviction. ("Concerning Values," Utah State University Baccalaureate, Logan, Utah, 28 May 1950.)

In a real Latter-day Saint home there is no such thing as a generation gap. We never heard of it until a few years ago, and where did it start? It started with some of these so-called social reformers, these do-gooders who are used as tools of the adversary to try to drive young people away from their parents and to get parents to let down in their responsibility to give guidance and direction to their own children. (Bear Lake Idaho Stake Conference, 22 May 1971.)

President George Q. Cannon states: "Perhaps it is His own design that faults and weaknesses should appear in high places in order that His Saints may learn to trust in Him and not in any man or men" (*Millennial Star,* 53:658–59).

And this would parallel Nephi's warning: Put not your "trust in the arm of flesh" (2 Nephi 4:34).

It is from within the Church that the greatest hindrance comes. And so, it seems, it has been. Now the question arises, will we stick with the kingdom and can we avoid being deceived? Certainly this is an important question, for the Lord has said that in the last days the "devil will rage in the hearts of men" (2 Nephi 28:20), and if it were possible he "shall deceive the very elect" (see Joseph Smith—Matthew 1:22). (*Title of Liberty,* p. 218.)

Wickedness

Why is the Lord angry with the wicked? Because they have rejected the gospel. They have rejected Jesus Christ as the God of this world. They have rejected the Author of salvation. (*God, Family, Country,* p. 93.)

The warnings of the prophets, ancient and modern, shall in very deed be fulfilled. The Lord is "angry with the wicked." He is "holding [His] Spirit from the inhabitants of the earth." (D&C 63:32.) The one hope for this wicked world is to accept and live the gospel, to keep the commandments, to heed the warnings of the prophets, ancient and modern. (*God, Family, Country,* p. 95.)

As the world becomes more wicked, a possible way to attain worldly success may be to join the wicked. The time is fast approaching when it will require great courage for Latter-day Saints to stand up for their peculiar standards and doctrine—all of their doctrine, including the more weighty principles such as the principle of freedom. Opposition to this weighty principle of freedom caused many of our brothers and sisters in the premortal existence to lose their first estate in the War in Heaven. (*An Enemy Hath Done This,* pp. 281–82.)

The Lord is displeased with wickedness, and He will help those who oppose it. But He has given all of us freedom to choose, while reserving for Himself our final judgment. (CR April 1967, *Improvement Era* 70 [June 1967]: 57.)

We live in the day of the smooth and subtle sins, the fashionable immoralities, the clever compromises, the routine treason, with evil on the rampage. ("Our Obligation and Challenge," Regional Representatives Seminar, Salt Lake City, Utah, 30 September 1977.)

Every physical or moral force which impairs or destroys man's ability to think clearly, to act nobly, to serve zealously and purposefully, is destructive of man's character and is an enemy of peace. The fruits of such indulgence are indolence, lust, greed, suspicion, hatred, and all their attendant companions. ("Purposeful Living," *Listen, A Journal of Better Living* [January–March 1955]: 19.)

Our problems for the most part are directly traceable to the transgression of those sacred laws given to Moses on Mount Sinai over three thousand years ago. These eternal laws were honored by our Founding Fathers. But today worship and service to God have noticeably declined. In the midst of all our prosperity, we may say with Abraham Lincoln, "We have forgotten God." Blasphemy, foul stories, and questionable humor characterize films, television programs, and the daily conversations of many Americans. The Sabbath has become a desecrated day of amusement. Idleness, greed, covetousness, cheating, lying, stealing, shoplifting, and immorality are commonplace in our society. ("The Faith of Our Founding Fathers," in *Faith* [Salt Lake City: Deseret Book, 1983], p. 26.)

Society may rationalize immorality, but God cannot condone it. Society sponsors Sabbath-breaking, but the Church counsels otherwise. Society profanes the name of Deity, but Latter-day Saints cannot countenance it. ("A Vision and a Hope for the Youth of Zion," in *1977 Devotional Speeches of the Year* [Provo, Utah: BYU, 1978], p. 78.)

War, famine, pestilences, earthquakes—these are conditions for which we must prepare our people. They are judgments to be poured out on the nations of the world because of the rejection of the gospel. "And thus, with sword and by bloodshed the inhabitants of the earth shall mourn; and with famine, and plague, and earthquake, and the thunder of heaven, and the fierce and vivid lightning also, shall the inhabitants of the earth be made to feel the wrath, indignation, and chastening hand of an Almighty God, until the consumption decreed hath made a full end of all nations" (D&C 87:6).

We, of all men, should not be surprised to see wickedness increase—though we deplore it. Nor should we be surprised to see a rising increase in divorces, family break-ups, moral problems, infidelity, unchastity, and every conceivable evil. The Savior said that iniquity would abound, and because of it the love of many will wax cold in the latter days (see D&C 45:27; Joseph Smith—Matthew 1:10). (Salt Lake City, Utah, 6 June 1980.)

Never have the forces of evil been so insidious, widespread, and enticing. Everywhere there seems to be a cheapening, weakening, downgrading of all that is fine, good, and uplifting—all aimed at our youth, while many of their parents are lulled away into a false security as they enjoy their comfortable complacency. (*God, Family, Country,* p. 245.)

When I think of the increase of sex sin—and I have had the opportunity to look into this question of obscene literature, and the relationship between filthy literature and sex crime—when I look into it I can't help but believe that in this respect this nation is becoming more sinful rather than less sinful. I can't help but be convinced that Satan is using this powerful tool, this God-given impulse in men and women, to try and destroy God's children. It is very, very real, and it is almost rampant. You find it almost everywhere, at times even among people whom you have looked upon as respectable.

Satan recognizes that this is one of his most powerful tools. He tries to promote it, to promulgate it. He tries to sell immodesty. And usually, he starts with immodesty. He tries to emphasize that the body, this physical body, is a beautiful thing; therefore, it should be admired and appreciated. And then the next step is to persuade us that it is to be handled. It is a terrible thing, the evils that are coming from this emphasis upon sex. Sex was created and established by our Heavenly Father for sacred, holy, and high purposes. ("The Greatest Leadership," BYU Student Leadership Conference, Sun Valley, Idaho, September 1959.)

Recently, a young man commented that if he quit reading books, watching television, seeing movies, reading newspapers and magazines, and going to school, there was a chance he might live a clean life. This explains, in large part, the extent to which the insidious evil of sexual promiscuity has spread, for the world treats this sin flippantly. These evil forces build up your lust and then fail to tell of the tragic consequences. In so many movies the hero is permitted to get away with crime so long as he can joke about it, or explain he was powerless to do anything, or else at the close of the movie show forth one minimal virtue that is supposed to cover over the grossest of sin. Many of our prominent national magazines pander to the baser side, but then try to cover themselves by including other articles, too. (CR October 1964, *Improvement Era* 67 [December 1964]: 1068–69.)

It is unscientific, unscholarly, and costly for each individual to insist upon personally conducting the experiments that have proven that sin brings sorrow, that disbelief brings emptiness and unrest, that things forbidden of God are not good for man, that the use of liquor and tobacco are enslaving habits, that unchastity brings unhappiness. ("Concerning Values," Utah State University Baccalaureate, Logan, Utah, 28 May 1950.)

The world is already beginning to reap the consequences of their abandonment of any standards of morality. As just one example, the Secretary of the Department of Health and Human Services in the United States warned that if a cure for AIDS is not quickly found, it could become a worldwide epidemic that "will dwarf such earlier medical disasters as the black plague, smallpox, and typhoid" (*Salt Lake Tribune*, 30 January 1987, p. A-1).

As the world seeks solutions for this disease, which began primarily through widespread homosexuality, they look everywhere but to the law of the Lord. There are numerous agencies, both public and private, trying to combat AIDS. They seek increased funding for research. They sponsor programs of education and information. They write bills aimed at protecting the innocent from infection. They set up treatment programs for those who have already become infected. These are important and necessary programs and we commend those efforts. But why is it we rarely hear anyone calling for a return to chastity, for a commitment to virtue and fidelity? ("The Law of Chastity," Brigham Young University Devotional, Provo, Utah, 13 October 1987.)

Many parents, in and out of the Church, are concerned about security against a cascading avalanche of wickedness which threatens to engulf Christian principles. I refer to bold and stark "best sellers" that exploit adulterous confessions, open declarations of atheism, so-called "gay rights," and other vulgar displays of debauchery. When decent people resist such encroachments into their community, accusations are made that civil liberties authorized by the Constitution are being curbed. And sometimes these fallacious arguments are upheld by the courts. Concerned people rightfully ask, "Is there no protection?" ("Latter-day Temples: Beacons to a Darkened World," Jordan River Utah Temple Groundbreaking, 9 June 1979.)

I have known good men, decent men, both in and out of the Church who, because of some bad habit, prevented greater happiness and progress from occurring in their lives. One of these good men who saw the great merits of the Church, though he never joined, said to me on one occasion, with cigar in hand, "Ezra, what is your redeeming vice?" It was the first time I had ever heard such an expression. From the Lord's view, there are no redeeming vices — only redeeming virtues! (CR April 1979, *Ensign* 9 [May 1979]: 32.)

More and more the honors of this world are being promoted by the wicked for the wicked. We see this in publicity and awards that are given to movies, literature, art, journalism. We see in our own newspapers widely read columnists carried who advocate one-world socialism, who have been consistently caught in falsehoods, and who continually parrot the Communist line. Less and less we see the virtuous rewarded by the world, and when they are, ofttimes it almost seems to be done insidiously in order to get us to swallow the many evils for which the wicked are even more profusely honored. (*An Enemy Hath Done This,* p. 283.)

The nations of the earth continue in their sinful and unrighteous ways. Much of the unbounded knowledge with which men have been blessed has been used to destroy mankind instead of to bless the children of men as the Lord intended. Two great world wars, with fruitless efforts at lasting peace, are solemn evidence that peace has been taken from the earth because of the wickedness of the people. Nations cannot endure in sin. They will be broken up, but the kingdom of God will endure forever. (*This Nation Shall Endure,* p. 111.)

We must defend our youth, in the interests of this nation which God has blessed above all others. We must rise to this task, stand up and be counted on the side of decency. We must show by our lives and actions that we possess the virtues that made America great.

There will be those who will cry "censorship" and "suppressing of freedom of information." To these people there does not seem to be any difference between liberty and license — but there is a real difference. It is not a denial of liberty to forbid the sale of narcotics or alcohol to children, and neither is it a denial of liberty to ban the distribution of filthy, obscene, character-destroying materials.

There has developed in this country, I am sorry to say, a species of so-called "broadmindedness" which tolerates anything and everything. It is high time right-thinking citizens showed they are fed up with such false broadmindedness. I for one fail to see where this so-called "tolerance" of evil has made society any better or individuals any happier. We cannot steer a safe course without a compass. We cannot build an enduring society except on principles of righteousness. (*So Shall Ye Reap*, pp. 202–3.)

The voice of warning is unto all people by the mouths of His servants. If this voice is not heeded, the angels of destruction will increasingly go forth, and the chastening hand of Almighty God will be felt upon the nations, as decreed, until a full end thereof will be the result. Wars, devastation, and untold suffering will be your lot except you turn unto the Lord in humble repentance. Destruction, even more terrible and far-reaching than attended the last great war, will come with certainty unless rulers and people alike repent and cease their evil and godless ways. God will not be mocked. He will not permit the sins of sexual immorality, secret murderous combinations, the killing of the unborn, and disregard for all His holy commandments and the messages of His servants to go unheeded without grievous punishment for such wickedness. The nations of the world cannot endure in sin. The way of escape is clear. The immutable laws of God remain steadfastly in the heavens above. When men and nations refuse to abide by them, the penalty must follow. They will be wasted away. Sin demands punishment. (*This Nation Shall Endure,* p. 111.)

We live today in a wicked world. Never in our memory have the forces of evil been arrayed in such a deadly formation. The devil is well organized and has many emissaries working for him. His satanic majesty has proclaimed his intention to destroy our young people, to weaken the home and family, and to defeat the purposes of the Lord Jesus Christ through His great Church. (*God, Family, Country,* p. 90.)

Certainly spirituality is the foundation upon which any battle against tyranny must be waged. And because this is basically the struggle of the forces of Christ versus anti-Christ, it is imperative that our people be in tune with the supreme leader of freedom — the Lord our God. And men only stay in tune when their lives are in harmony with God. For apart from God we cannot succeed, but as a partner with God we cannot fail. (*An Enemy Hath Done This,* p. 56.)

Pioneering

Our forefathers gloried in hard work, but at the same time they drew liberally upon their prodigious spiritual reserves. They did not place their trust "in the arm of flesh" (D&C 1:19; 2 Nephi 4:34). They were strong and courageous in the Lord, knowing that He was their defense, their refuge, their salvation. Strengthened by this faith, they relied on their cherished independence, their frugality, and honest toil. And history records that even the climate was tempered for their sakes, and their humble untiring efforts made "the desert to blossom as the rose" (Isaiah 35:1). (*This Nation Shall Endure,* p. 42.)

We have been blessed with the most glorious pioneer heritage ever known because of their faith, their devotion, their courage. And those who follow us will likewise reap the harvest, or the whirlwind, which springs from our attitudes, our ideals, our ac-

tions, and our decisions. We must not falter or hesitate. The pioneers' spirit must continue to move our action. (*So Shall Ye Reap*,
p. 313.)

If these indomitable pioneers were to express in words their
fundamental beliefs, so manifest in their acts, what would they say
to us? They would counsel us to believe in the dignity of work; to
believe that the world owes no man a living but that it owes every
man an opportunity to make a living.

They would counsel us to believe in the supreme worth of the
individual and in his right to life, liberty, and property—that these
are inalienable rights, guaranteed by our Constitution and sacredly
upheld by the Church so "that every man may be accountable for
his own sins in the day of judgment" (D&C 101:78). Their counsel
would be that we cannot strengthen the weak by weakening the
strong, and that truth and justice are fundamental to an enduring
social order.

They would counsel us to believe in the sacredness of a promise; to believe that a man's word should be his bond; that character
—not wealth, power, or position—is of supreme worth to individuals and nations; that we cannot build character and courage by
taking away man's initiative and independence.

Yes, every right implies a responsibility; every opportunity an
obligation; every possession a duty. They would counsel us that
the law was made for man and not man for the law; government is
the servant of the people, not their master.

They would advise us that we cannot produce prosperity by
discouraging thrift; thrift is essential to well-ordered living, and
economy is a prime requisite of a sound financial structure,
whether in government, business, or personal affairs.

They would counsel that you cannot help men permanently by
doing for them what they could do and should do for themselves;
the rendering of useful service is the common duty of mankind,
and only in the purifying fire of sacrifice is the dross of selfishness
consumed and the greatness of the human soul set free.

Yes, they would urge us to believe that love is the greatest force
in the world; in love there is no fear; love alone can overcome hate;
right can and will triumph over might; there is an all-wise and all-
loving Heavenly Father, and the individual's highest fulfillment,

greatest happiness, and widest usefulness are to be found in living in harmony with His divine will.

However outmoded some of these standards may be considered today, they are nonetheless enduring truths without which no character worthy of the name can be built. We have respectfully called them "pioneers," because they prepared the way for us to follow. May we possess courage to direct our lives in accordance with the enduring values so represented by their lives. ("A Tribute to Pioneer Ideals," Sandy Utah Park Historical Marker Dedication, 14 September 1977.)

Opportunities for pioneering are not past. There are many fields in which individuals are challenged and for which they must be prepared (as were our pioneers) to meet their challenges.

We can pioneer in maintaining and continuing to strengthen our systems of education. We can pioneer in maintaining and strengthening our systems of cooperation. Our pioneering can be in the avenues of keeping ourselves informed, thinking straight, and giving wise counsel to our leaders of government — for in our free system it is what we as individuals believe that will determine the course of our government. Our great pioneering challenge today is to maintain and expand that state of freedom in which man can best grow — a state of freedom in which man is the master of his own destiny, and in which government is his servant.

If we, now or in the future, shrink from facing up to this basic challenge, there will always be others willing to find answers for us. But their answers may not be the answers we seek. They might cost us not only peace but freedom, too. Instead of growing, mankind all over the world would then decline. The new pioneering is difficult. It calls for the utmost self-discipline — a discipline based on truth. It demands that we seek wisdom, act with integrity and courage, and accept individual responsibility. It demands that we be fully awake, fully aware, and fully alert to the dangerous trend today of socialism and the loss of more and more of our freedoms, and act with the courage and resourcefulness of our pioneers. (*The Red Carpet*, pp. 313–14.)

These noble founders and pioneers — our benefactors — would counsel us to preserve the freedoms granted to us by God. They knew that the foundation of this nation was spiritual, that the source of all our blessings was God. They knew that this nation can only prosper in an atmosphere of freedom. Those intrepid forebears knew that their righteousness was the indispensable ingredient to liberty, that this was the greatest legacy they could pass on to future generations. They would counsel us to preserve this liberty by alert righteousness. Righteousness is always measured by a nation or an individual keeping the commandments of God. (*This Nation Shall Endure,* p. 45.)

Mormon Pioneers

In the early days of this country, a special breed of men and women came from all over the world, seeking not only opportunity, but freedom. They were strong, proud, and fiercely independent. They believed that the surest helping hand was at the end of their own sleeves. They shared one thing in common—an unshakable faith in God and in themselves.

As the nation developed, out of this same mold came a special group, who, in a dramatic exodus, pushed the frontier of America from the banks of the Mississippi to the valleys of these magnificent mountains. They were the Mormon pioneers and we, who today enjoy the good life here in the Intermountain West, are the beneficiaries of their noble efforts. The world knows that the Mormon pioneers were led here by Brigham Young; but the Mormon pioneers knew that they were led here by the hand of Almighty God. They came here as a religious group—as a persecuted people—and they came here as American citizens.

They were a unique people, for they had been expelled from what was then the borders of the United States, by citizens and government leaders of their own America, and yet they continued firm in their allegiance to the United States and its great, inspired Constitution. ("The Mormon Pioneers as American Citizens," Idaho Falls, Idaho, 24 July 1975.)

I deeply desire to pay reverent tribute to the heroes of the past —to their faithful deeds, their noble lives, and their lasting lessons of courage, faith, self-reliance, stamina, industry, and integrity. All generations have need of these virtues.

We stand today as beneficiaries of their priceless legacy to us, a legacy based on the solid truth that character is the one thing we develop in this world that we take with us into the next. And what is that legacy? The pioneers came to the Salt Lake Valley with credentials that spanned the centuries, a bloodline coursing through their veins from illustrious parentage: Abraham and Sarah, Isaac and Rebekah, Jacob and Rachel. Theirs was a bloodline preserved through four centuries of Egyptian captivity; an exile and exodus from the land of their captivity that lasted forty years—a time necessary for a new, less-enslaved generation to develop; and then a settlement in a promised land, which lasted over seven centuries. Theirs was a bloodline that endured a long dispersion and centuries of migrations that brought their sifted lineage into northern Europe and Great Britain. (*This Nation Shall Endure*, p. 37.)

As I look back on the generations who preceded us and who provided us our lineage in Israel, I am impressed by the fact that the pioneer stock came not out of the ruling families of Europe. By and large, they came from the poor and common people—those who had been oppressed for centuries by the ruling classes.

Some emigrated to America to better their conditions and then received the gospel here; others received the gospel in Europe and then emigrated to Zion. Their conversion to the gospel united them together in a common cause and, though in many instances they came out of different nations and spoke diverse tongues, they learned to think alike, speak alike, and share the mutual aim of building Zion.

The hand of God was behind the coming of the pioneers to this valley. The hand of God has been in the prosperity of the commonwealth of Israel—and His hand prospers the work of His Church today. We honor the pioneers because they were honored by God to lay the foundation of Zion (see D&C 58:7).

We honor them because they were obedient to a prophet and had the faith to make the trek West. We honor them because they came here to serve God, to worship Him, to keep all His commandments according to the dictates of their religion—and to do so without interference. ("Zion Shall Flourish upon the Mountains," Days of '47 Committee Luncheon, 24 July 1982.)

The exodus from Nauvoo commenced in February 1846, in the midst of severe winter weather. There were many hardships and privations; there was sickness and there was death. But the spirit of mutual service and cooperation prevailed. Temporary settlements were constructed along the way and a few families were left at each one to care for crops to be harvested by the companies that followed.

May I give you here an interesting sidelight. Just before the expulsion of the Saints from Nauvoo, my great-grandfather, Ezra T. Benson, whose name I proudly bear as his oldest great-grandson, met Brigham Young on the street. President Young said, in substance, "Brother Benson, there is no peace here—no peace for us. We must move again. I would like you to go in the first company." Great-grandfather responded, "President Young, I will be glad to follow you anywhere. However, I have no conveyance of any kind. All I own is a new brick home and a lot, neither one of which I have been able to sell. Do you have any suggestions?" Brigham Young said, "Yes—go down the street and ask every man you meet to give you some help until you get a conveyance."

Great-grandfather met the first man, who loaned him a horse. The second man loaned him a horse. A third one loaned him a wagon. Then he said he sold his wife's shawls to buy canvas for a wagon cover. Then, putting some cornmeal, sugar, and a few other food items in the back of the wagon, they left Nauvoo, leaving the furniture standing in their home and looking back on the beautiful temple where Great-grandfather and his two wives had been officiating night and day, giving blessings to the Saints. Both women were expecting babies.

The first gave birth to her child a few days later at Sugar Creek in wintry February. A rude shelter was held over the mother at the time of the delivery. The baby passed away a few days later. The second wife gave birth to her baby in a wagon box on the trail at Garden Grove, Iowa. This baby was my grandfather, George T. Benson.

Typical of the spirit of the women, my great-grandfather, after they had reached Winter Quarters, near Omaha, where he was ordained a member of the Twelve, commenting on his wives, said, "Never at any time did I hear a murmur from their lips." ("The Mormon Pioneers as American Citizens," Idaho Falls, Idaho, 24 July 1975.)

The pioneer diaries contain many accounts of heart-breaking hardships. But the hardships are not viewed as unbearable, nor is there complaint against the providence of the God in whom these pioneers trusted. There is a spirit of optimism, encouragement, and gratitude for blessings received. How much we need a rebirth of these virtues today! How much we need to realize that hardships, deprivation, even suffering, need not necessarily cause unhappiness.

In 1848, a year after my progenitors arrived in Salt Lake Valley, wide fields of green grain gave promise of a bounteous first harvest. Looking out over the valley they felt well rewarded for their fall, winter, and spring labors. Then one day the crickets came. Day by day the insects increased and multiplied until they, too, seemed almost to cover the face of the earth. The pioneers fought them with fire, with water, with shovels, with brooms. Finally, desperate, and utterly exhausted, they turned to God, pleading in prayer for help. Then, to their amazement, they saw flocks of sea gulls fly over from the lake to the West and settle on the fields, eating the crickets, flying away, then returning for more. The crops were saved. Their prayers had been answered.

Critical circumstances did not discourage our progenitors. Confidently they relied upon resourcefulness born of courage, trial, determination, herculean effort, faith, and prayer. All generations have equal need of these virtues. (Annual Religion-in-Life Week, Ohio State University, Columbus, Ohio, 29 January 1957.)

The Mormon pioneers were the Lord's people. They endured many tests and they endured them well. Throughout their sufferings they remained loyal to God and to their country. They tried to live the laws given to them by God, for they understood that men are incapable of governing themselves without the help of God. This effort brought accusations of Mormon disloyalty to the United States, to which Brigham Young gave the clear answer: "To accuse us of being unfriendly to the Government, is to accuse us of hostility to our religion, for no item of inspiration is held more sacred with us than the Constitution under which she acts. . . . It is held as a shield to protect the dearest boon of which man is susceptible—his religious views and sentiments." (*Journal of Discourses,* 2:174.) ("The Mormon Pioneers as American Citizens," Idaho Falls, Idaho, 24 July 1975.)

It is ironic that in the course of their exodus, this same government that stood by while they were forcibly expelled from Illinois should now come to them with a request for five hundred able-bodied men to fight in the war with Mexico. So disproportionate, inequitable, and unjust in terms of their numbers and their situation was the request for manpower that President Brigham Young commented later:

> Look . . . at the proportion of the number required of us, compared with that of any other portion of the Republic. A requisition of only thirty thousand from a population of more than twenty million was all that was wanted, amounting to only one person and a half to a thousand inhabitants. If all other circumstances had been equal . . . our quota of an equitable requisition would not have exceeded four persons. Instead of this, five hundred must go, thirteen thousand percent above an equal ratio. (*Journal of Discourses*, 2:174.)

But they did comply with the request—an extraordinary example of loyalty to their nation. (*This Nation Shall Endure*, pp. 40–41.)

It is difficult for us to imagine now that there was not a settlement except a trapper's camp or an outpost for a thousand miles eastward and seven hundred miles westward when that first company came here; that their only means of transportation was by ox team and wagon, and yet in spite of their difficulties, their hardships, their struggles, the record clearly indicates that they were a happy people. They were not downhearted, they were not depressed, they did not feel insecure. (Daughters of Utah Pioneers Building Dedication, Salt Lake City, Utah, 23 July 1950.)

Our pioneers came, with faith and industry, and carved an Eden out of a desert. Their promised land has become a prosperous valley. (*This Nation Shall Endure,* pp. 41–42.)

The greatest contribution of the Mormon pioneers was their testimony. Their testimony stands against their persecutors who attacked them and against the government officials who failed them or conspired to expel them. But, above all, their testimony stands as a witness for the Lord—that He lives and reigns over the earth and that He ordained the Constitution and its principles to be honored among men. ("The Mormon Pioneers as American Citizens," Idaho Falls, Idaho, 24 July 1975.)

Our heritage will not save us; the deeds of the pioneers were *their* deeds. We, as their descendants, must stand on our own feet and, as President J. Reuben Clark, Jr. so aptly stated, "not only on our own feet but in our own shoes." We must carve out our own course. No, there is no aristocracy of birth in the commonwealth which they established, but there are opportunities unlimited. It is for us, their descendants, to adhere strictly to their ideals, to exhibit their courage and their faith and their determination, to work out our own salvation as we follow their examples. We must never forget why the pioneers came to this valley—they came here by the design of Almighty God.

Some casual observers of history may conclude that their coming was strictly a matter of necessity. And, true, the precipitating cause of their coming to these valleys was the intense hatred, persecution, and opposition to their religion. Had it not been for that opposition, it is doubtful that many would have been willing to leave their comfortable homes and prosperous communities. But that religious persecution served as the means to accomplish the Lord's purposes. ("Zion Shall Flourish upon the Mountains," Days of '47 Committee Luncheon, Salt Lake City, Utah, 24 July 1982.)

May we walk in the footsteps of our great forebears—that our children and our children's children following in our footsteps will safely walk the way of truth and right. Should we ignore those enduring guideposts to follow forbidden paths of our own making, the keen displeasure of an all-wise and just Father will surely be visited upon us. (*So Shall Ye Reap,* p. 313.)

Prayer

Prayer is man's means of communicating with his Heavenly Father, the Almighty, Creator of heaven and earth. Only the deceived and the fool refuse to pray. An urgent need today is for more prayer—secret, individual prayer; family prayer; prayer in organizations, associations, and meetings generally, and in schools, and in government bodies. People of all nations need more prayer. We need to be on our knees. (*God, Family, Country,* p. 114.)

Prayer has literally changed the development of man. It has brought him out of the morass of indecision and discouragement into the sunlight born of faith through works and love and trust. Fervent prayer on the part of a young fourteen-year-old boy in New York State in 1820 started a chain of events which is literally changing the lives of millions of people today. The direct result of this prayer has brought a positive understanding of the being of God the Father and His Son, Jesus Christ. It has caused the uncovering of ancient histories which contain divine truths that if obeyed will lead directly to the eventual exaltation of man and to a situation of happiness and joy that words cannot describe.

Prayer will bring solace and comfort. It has healed sickness, comforted those distressed, and has continued the faithful in paths of righteousness. The value of a man is evidenced in part by the dust on his knees. His willingness to believe in and accept a being greater than himself as evidenced by his prayer has increased his moral stature, refined his understanding, and has brought him along the road of his eternal development. Our great example in prayer is our Lord and Master Jesus Christ who knew that only through constant supplication and obedience would God the Father manifest His will and release the power for its attainment through man. Truly there is power in prayer. ("There Is Power in Prayer," in *We Believe in Prayer* [Minneapolis, Minnesota: T. S. Denison, 1958], p. 219.)

We should live to have the Spirit of the Lord, which will teach us to pray (2 Nephi 32:8). We should cultivate such a strong testimony that when we pray, we follow the example of Joseph Smith and have faith with "nothing wavering" (James 1:5–6; Moroni 10:4–5).

We should develop a feeling that we are talking directly with our Father in Heaven. "He that cometh to God must believe that he is, and that he is a rewarder of them that diligently seek him" (Hebrews 11:6). "You cannot imagine an effective prayer without visualizing and feeling a personal God" (David O. McKay, *Treasures of Life*, p. 308). (*God, Family, Country*, p. 121.)

We should pray about our work, against the power of enemies and the devil, for our welfare and the welfare of those around us (Alma 34:20, 22–25, 27). We should counsel with the Lord pertaining to all our activities (Alma 37:36–37). Some of us are afraid to ask the Lord about certain matters for fear He will give us an answer we don't want to hear. We should be polite and grateful enough to give thanks for all we have (Psalm 107:17–21; Philemon 4:6; D&C 78:19; 59:21). As the Son directs, we should count our many blessings and give thanks for our calls in the Church. Ingratitude is one of our great sins. We should make known our needs (Philemon 4:6; Alma 7:23), so long as it is not because of pride or for selfish reasons (James 4:3). Sometimes we have not, because we ask not (James 4:2). Think of all the revelations that came to the Prophet Joseph Smith because he was willing to ask the Lord about certain matters and needs. We should ask for strength to overcome (Alma 31:31–33). We should pray for the inspiration and well-being of the President of the Church, the General Authorities, our stake president, our bishop, our quorum president, our home teachers, and so forth. Our exaltation depends to an extent upon the inspiration of our leaders. We should pray for mercy (Alma 34:18). Many other suggestions could be made; but with the spirit of prayer, we will know what to pray (Romans 8:26). (*God, Family, Country,* pp. 122–23.)

He is interested in us and invites us to counsel with Him — pray to Him. In our homes, at work on the job, in our Church assignments, in our studies at school — at home or abroad — it is possible to reach out and tap that unseen power — our Father in Heaven. ("Basic Doctrines of Church Explained to Youth Firesides," *Church News* [20 May 1961]: 14.)

If the great men of America — past and present — turned as if by instinct to God in prayer, surely we, too, should give prayer — daily prayer, secret prayer — a foremost place in our lives. It is true, as Alfred Tennyson wrote: "More things are wrought by prayer than this world dreams of." (Vaughn Bible Class Anniversary Banquet, Calvary Baptist Church, Washington, D.C., 13 February 1959.)

To the extent that we stray from the path marked out for us by the Man of Galilee, to that extent we are failing in our individual battles to overcome our worlds. But we are not without His help. Again and again He told His disciples, and all of us, "Let not your heart be troubled. . . . If ye shall ask any thing in my name, I will do it. I will not leave you comfortless. . . . Peace I leave with you, my peace I give unto you." (John 14:1, 14, 18, 27.)

We feel His comforting Spirit in the sweet prayer of a child and the quiet abiding faith of all who have let His gospel permeate their lives. What a priceless gift it is that we can know Him through our own prayers and through the sacred and solemn testimonies of those who have seen Him, known Him, felt His presence. (*God, Family, Country,* p. 25.)

Will you value and take advantage of the opportunity to tap these unseen but very real spiritual powers? Will you be able to affirm the solemn declaration of an illustrious past president of one of America's leading universities, who has counseled: "Men who search out truth are prayerful. They stand with uncovered heads before the unknown. They know their own insignificance before the eternal fount of knowledge. . . . Manly men who really love truth are proud to pray to God for help and guidance. They get down on their knees. . . . To win knowledge of the unseen, to obtain a testimony of truth, one must pray without ceasing. It must be the first and the last act of the day."

Prayer will help you understand the apparent conflicts in life — to know that God lives, that life is eternal. He who is able to avail himself of this blessing in life is free as the boundless universe. He unlocks the doors to the storehouse of all knowledge and power. He who does not, dwarfs his own potential and enshrouds himself in a mantle of obscurity. He effectively shuts the door on the greatest source of knowledge, power, and joy that is available to man. Prayer with all its promise is meaningless, however, unless we live as we pray and work diligently to make our prayers come true. ("Concerning Values," University of Maine, Orono, Maine, 10 June 1956.)

Never before in this gospel dispensation has there been a greater need for prayer, and never in history has there been a greater threat to our God-given right to pray when, how, or where we wish. How timely and appropriate for the true Church of Christ to emphasize this basic right and all-important need! (*God, Family, Country,* pp. 126–27.)

I think there would be great safety in a nation on its knees. What assurance it would give of the blessings of the Almighty if the American people could all be found daily—night and morning—on their knees expressing gratitude for blessings already received, acknowledging dependence upon Him, and seeking for His divine guidance.

I hope we may encourage that practice in our service clubs, schools, in our meetings of farmers, businessmen, and professional men. I have been pleased to see what I think was a turn toward an increase of interest in prayer and religion. I was very pleased to find an increasing number of prayer groups in the Congress of the United States, where members of that body, of opposite political faiths, could come together weekly and unite in humble prayer and petition to the Almighty.

I was pleased to find the increasing evidence of the practice of prayer in the executive branch of the government. I testify to the blessings which prayer brought to the cabinet meetings of the President and to my own staff meetings. I think there is need for it throughout government.

I am convinced in my heart that the spectacle of a nation praying is more awe-inspiring, more powerful, than the explosion of an atomic bomb. The force of prayer is greater than any possible combination of man-controlled powers because, "prayer is man's greatest means of tapping the resources of God." I would like to see this nation on its knees in humble prayer. (*The Red Carpet,* p. 295.)

We should pray frequently. We should be alone with our Heavenly Father at least two or three times each day: "morning, midday, and evening" (Alma 34:21). Someone has said that when you wake up in the morning, the first thing to hit the floor should be your knees. In addition, we are told to pray always (Luke 21:34–36; 2 Nephi 32:9; D&C 61:39; 88:126; 93:49). This not only shows we should pray frequently but also continually have a prayer in our heart (Alma 34:27). Even when the Lord's time was most in demand, He was not too busy to pray (Luke 5:15–16). (*God, Family, Country,* p. 120.)

Our prayers should be meaningful and pertinent. We should avoid using the same phrases in each prayer. Any of us would become offended if a friend said the same few words to us each day, treated the conversation as a chore, and could hardly wait to finish in order to turn on the television set and forget us. (*Come unto Christ,* p. 26.)

For whom do we speak? As the prayer is in behalf of a group, the prayer should, in general, express the thinking, the needs, and the desires of the group—not so much those of the individual. Prior to praying, some thought should be given to the nature of the group and its needs and desires. Prayer should be loud enough for the entire congregation to hear. All in the audience should audibly say "amen" after the prayer. This shows we agree with the prayer and are a part of it.

The language of prayer: our language should be meek, yet it should edify (D&C 52:16). Since the prayer is in behalf of a group, it should be phrased in terms of "our" and "we", instead of "my" and "I". As with any prayer, it should be addressed to our Heavenly Father. The Lord set the proper example in saying, "Our Father which art in heaven" (Luke 11:2). There is no need for flowery descriptions. We are just reverently calling Him by name before we begin talking to Him. "Thy", "thou", and "thine" should be used so proper reverence can be shown. We should always end by asking in the name of Jesus Christ, but not "thy name". (John 16:24–26.) (*God, Family, Country,* pp. 123–24.)

Of whom should we think when we pray? Too frequently we may think of how we sound to the audience rather than concentrating on communicating with our Father in Heaven. It then becomes merely another talk to the audience. It lacks sincerity. It may not even be considered by our Father in Heaven (James 4:3). We do not feel the spirit of prayer. As said in Shakespeare's *Hamlet,* "My words fly up; my thoughts remain below./Words without thoughts never to heaven go." Sometimes the so-called "good-prayers" are called upon to the exclusion of the humble but less articulate members. But the Lord expects all to qualify to pray in meetings (D&C 19:28). We must consciously tune ourselves spiritually to our Heavenly Father so we actually feel we are talking to Him.

Our public prayers need not be everlasting to be immortal. We are advised not to multiply many words (3 Nephi 19:24) and to avoid vain repetitions (Matthew 6:7). An invocation should set the spiritual tone of the meeting, and the benediction should leave the people on a high spiritual plane, because they have been present when one has talked with God. It is the feeling rather than the length which determines a good public prayer.

We should assist others in preparing for public prayer. We should teach them to pray privately. Offering frequent vocal prayers gives experience in forming phrases and adds to confidence. We should provide experience in small groups where they will be more comfortable—family prayer, group meetings, quorum meetings, and home teachers prior to visits. We should teach that an effective public prayer depends more on the feeling of the individual than the words he uses. Therefore, developing a spirit of prayer through a proper life can best qualify a person to give a meaningful public prayer. Without this, the prayer becomes hollow and does not inspire. (*God, Family, Country,* pp. 124–25.)

After making a request through prayer, we have a responsibility to assist in its being granted. We should listen. Maybe while we are on our knees, the Lord wants to counsel us. In addition to asking and thanking the Lord for things, we might well stay on our knees long enough to report for duty and ask Him if He has any marching orders for us. "Sincere praying implies that when we ask for any virtue or blessing, we should work for the blessing and cultivate the virtue" (David O. McKay, *True to the Faith,* p. 208). (*God, Family, Country,* p. 123.)

Personal Prayer

If we would advance in holiness—increase in favor with God—nothing can take the place of prayer. And so I adjure you to give prayer—daily prayer, secret prayer—a foremost place in your lives. Let no day pass without it. Communion with the Almighty has been a source of strength, inspiration, and enlightenment through the world's history to men and women who have shaped the destinies of individuals and nations for good.

Will you value and take advantage of the opportunity to tap these unseen but very real spiritual powers? Will you, with Abraham Lincoln before Gettysburg and George Washington at Valley Forge, humble yourselves before Almighty God in fervent prayer? (*God, Family, Country*, p. 8.)

When you pray—when you talk to your Heavenly Father—do you really talk out your problems with Him? Do you let Him know your feelings, your doubts, your insecurities, your joys, your deepest desires? Or is prayer merely a habitual expression with the same words and phrases? Do you ponder what you really mean to say? Do you take time to listen to the promptings of the Spirit? Answers to prayer come most often by a still voice and are discerned by our deepest, innermost feelings. I tell you that you can know the will of God concerning yourselves if you will take the time to pray and to listen. ("To 'The Rising Generation,' " *New Era* 16 [June 1986]: 8.)

We should find an appropriate place where we can meditate and pray. We are admonished that this should be "in [our] closets, and [our] secret places, and in [our] wilderness" (Alma 34:26). That is, it should be free from distraction, in secret (3 Nephi 13:5–6). We should prepare ourselves for prayer. If we do not feel like praying, then we should pray until we do feel like praying. We should be humble (D&C 112:10). We should pray for forgiveness and mercy (Alma 34:17–18). We must forgive anyone against whom we have bad feelings (Mark 11:25). Yet the scriptures warn that our prayers will be vain if we "turn away the needy, and the naked, and visit not the sick and afflicted, and impart [not] of [our] substance" (Alma 34:28). (*Come unto Christ*, pp. 25–26.)

I don't believe it is possible for a man to be happy who doesn't pray every day—and not just once. I think you need the strength that comes from prayer. ("The Home and Family," BYU Religious Life Series, Provo, Utah, September 1960.)

Great men pray. Washington at Valley Forge, Lincoln before Gettysburg, Eisenhower on D-Day, Jesus at Gethsemane and at Golgotha—all these have prayed. Be honest with yourself. Pray. Follow the example of the great and good and wise men of all ages. Ask and receive. "In all thy ways acknowledge him and he shall direct thy paths" (Proverbs 3:6). Yes, be honest with yourself. Pray. (*So Shall Ye Reap,* p. 94.)

The least any Christian can do is to study daily the word of the Lord and seek divine aid through daily prayer. We invite all men to examine prayerfully The Church of Jesus Christ of Latter-day Saints—the Mormon Church—which I testify is the Church of Christ, restored to the earth and led today by a prophet of God. (CR April 1967, *Improvement Era* 70 [June 1967]: 58.)

All through my life the counsel to depend on prayer has been prized above any other advice I have ever received. It has become an integral part of me, an anchor, a constant source of strength. ("The Best Advice I Ever Had," *Reader's Digest* [November 1954]: 97.)

Family Prayer

Prayer has been and is the ever-present anchor for strength and a source of direction in our family activities. I remember kneeling at the bedside of our young children, helping them with prayers in their younger years, and later seeing the older brothers and sisters helping the younger ones. We had family prayer night and morning, with children given the opportunity to lead, and had special prayers to meet particular problems. Mention was made in family prayer, for instance, of children with assignments such as a two-and-a-half-minute talk in Sunday School or a new teaching assignment in the MIA. We asked for help when one of the children faced a difficult examination in high school. Special mention was made of members of the family away at girls' camp, Scout camp, school, or working. This special mention of particular concerns in our family prayers gave confidence, assurance, and strength to members of the family facing difficult problems and assignments. ("Family Joy," *New Era* 3 [January 1973]: 4–5.)

Resorting to prayer in time of crisis was not born of desperation. It was merely the outgrowth of the cherished custom of family prayer with which I had been surrounded since earliest childhood. How well I remember that while the family was small we frequently knelt together in the kitchen. As we grew in numbers and size we moved into the dining room which had been added. As children we all took our turns in offering simple, heartfelt prayers. How grateful I am that we have continued that practice in my own home, and that my devoted wife and children look upon it as a never-failing source of strength and contentment. ("The Best Advice I Ever Had," *Reader's Digest* [November 1954]: 98.)

A father has the responsibility to lead his family by loving God and looking to Him for daily counsel and direction. That means he must have family prayer as well as personal prayer. I often wish there were some way to measure accurately the value of family prayer. What it would mean to little Mary, who is giving her first talk in Sunday School or perhaps her first little talk in Primary, to have the family go onto their knees that morning and make special mention of her that she will do her best and not be too frightened. What it would mean to a special teenage son who is facing a stiff examination in high school to have him specially mentioned in family prayer. Family prayer can greatly increase the unity and solidarity in the family. (*Priesthood* [Salt Lake City: Deseret Book, 1981], p. 141.)

Family prayer night and morning and special prayers in between are a unifying, strengthening anchor in Latter-day Saint homes. Just before mealtime in the morning and the evening is usually the best time for getting all of the family together for family prayers. This practice, so very important, was once widely practiced. The journals of the early pioneers, not only in the West but in the Midwest and East also, reveal the widespread practice of daily devotion in the home. The scriptures were read and a hymn was often sung. The practice of daily family devotion has almost left much of the world, and in our busy lives of getting and spending, Latter-day Saints also are often neglectful of this important matter. (*God, Family, Country*, p. 116.)

In exemplary Latter-day Saint homes, parents teach their children to understand faith in God, repentance, baptism, and the gift of the Holy Ghost (see D&C 68:25). Family prayer is a consistent practice in these families. Prayer is the means to acknowledge appreciation for blessings and to humbly recognize dependence on Almighty God for strength, sustenance, and support. It is a wise and true maxim that families that kneel together stand upright before the Lord! (CR April 1984, *Ensign* 14 [May 1984]: 6–7.)

Pray in your homes morning and evening. Pray for the leaders of the Church. Pray, as you have been counseled, that the doors of nations of the world will be opened to the preaching of the gospel. (CR April 1978, *Ensign* 8 [May 1978]: 34.)

The homes of America need the blessings which come from daily communication with God. In such homes secret prayers are said night and morning by members of the household. Individual and family problems are approached with confidence after invoking the favor of heaven. Young people participating in such a family devotional have hearts freed from evil intent as they leave for an evening of entertainment. These will be the restraining influences in the group when gilded temptations arise. Parents who surround their children with the refining influence of daily devotion are making their contribution to the safeguarding of the American home. (Chevy Chase Presbyterian Church, Washington, D.C., 18 March 1956.)

Power and Blessing

Prayer is direct communication with God who hears and answers, though not always at the time or in the manner that we might suppose. To hear the sweet, simple prayer of a child is to know that prayer is real. Prayer not only keeps us closer to God, but in so doing it strengthens our daily actions for righteousness because of our willingness to acknowledge Him and to bring Him into partnership with us. It helps keep our thinking straight and positive. It teaches faith and helps bring understanding. It develops an attitude in which joy and love know no bounds. ("There Is Power in Prayer," in *We Believe in Prayer*, p. 219.)

The holy scriptures are replete with convincing admonitions regarding the importance of prayer, impressive examples of the power of prayer. Even prophets of God have been chastised for failing to call on the Lord. Consider the hours-long interview of the brother of Jared with the Lord and the serious warning given: "And it came to pass at the end of four years that the Lord came again unto the brother of Jared, and stood in a cloud and talked with him. And for the space of three hours did the Lord talk with the brother of Jared, and chastened him because he remembered not to call upon the name of the Lord." (Ether 2:14–15.) (*God, Family, Country,* p. 117.)

It is soul-satisfying to know that God is mindful of us and ready to respond when we place our trust in Him and do that which is right. There is no place for fear among men and women who place their trust in the Almighty, who do not hesitate to humble themselves in seeking divine guidance through prayer. Though persecutions arise, though reverses come, in prayer we can find assurance, for God will speak peace to the soul. That peace, that spirit of serenity, is a great blessing.

If I could wish for anyone a priceless gift, it would not be wealth, profound wisdom, or the honors of men. I would rather pass on the key to inner strength and security which my father gave to me when he advised, "Receive His aid through prayer." ("The Best Advice I Ever Had," *Reader's Digest* [November 1954]: 98–99.)

Prayer in the hour of need is a great boon. From simple trials to our Gethsemanes, prayer can put us in touch with God, our greatest source of comfort and counsel. "Pray always, that you may come off conqueror" (D&C 10:5) — persistent prayer. "Exerting all my powers to call upon God to deliver me" is how the young Joseph Smith describes the method which he used in the Sacred Grove to keep the adversary from destroying him (Joseph Smith — History 1:16). This is also a key to use in keeping depression from destroying us. (CR October 1974, *Ensign* 4 [November 1974]: 66.)

Enos was spiritually healed. Through his mighty supplications to God, he experienced what the faithful of any dispensation can, do, and must experience if they are to see God and be filled with His Spirit. (Texas San Antonio Mission, 2 March 1986.)

It is the part of wisdom to acknowledge and experience that there is an unseen source of power and truth. I testify to you with all the fervor of my soul that this is true. Many of you have doubtless already come to the profound realization that man does not stand alone. You have learned that there are "hidden treasures of knowledge" for him who asks in faith, nothing wavering. Such has been the fervent declaration of the world's truly great leaders in all ages of recorded history. Prayer has always been an unfailing source of strength and inspiration. (*So Shall Ye Reap*, p. 164.)

What a grievous error it would be if we should become so filled with self-sufficiency as to no longer feel the need of prayer. How much protection will our missiles and nuclear weapons prove to be if we do not take at face value the Lord's injunction, "Thou shalt love the Lord thy God with all thy heart and with all thy soul, and with all thy strength and with all thy mind; and thy neighbor as thyself" (Luke 10:27). ("He Is Risen," Hollywood, California, 29 March 1959.)

Inspiration comes from prayer (D&C 63:64). Inspiration is essential to properly lead (D&C 50:13–14). We must have the spirit of inspiration whether we are teaching (D&C 50:13–14) or administering the affairs of the kingdom (D&C 46:2). If we do our part in preparation and work and have the Spirit of the Lord, we can be led, though we do not know beforehand what needs to be done (1 Nephi 4:6; Alma 17:3). Therefore, we should always pray, especially prior to commencing the work of the Lord (2 Nephi 32:9). (*God, Family, Country,* p. 126.)

Pray. There is no temptation placed before you which you cannot shun. Do not allow yourself to get in positions where it is easy to fall. Listen to the promptings of the Spirit. If you are engaged in things where you do not feel you can pray and ask the Lord's blessings on what you are doing, then you are engaged in the wrong kind of activity. (CR October 1964, *Improvement Era* 67 [December 1964]: 1069.)

Is there a man or woman in this Church who, in his or her most private, intimate moments, does not feel a deficiency in faith and spirituality? The Lord has appealed to us: "Draw near unto me and I will draw near unto you; seek me diligently and ye shall find me; ask and ye shall receive; knock, and it shall be opened unto you" (D&C 88:63).

To hunger and thirst for more faith and more righteousness creates a humble dependency on the Lord for help and strength. There is no greater example of this humble spirit than that of Nephi's prayer in the Book of Mormon:

> O Lord, I have trusted in thee, and I will trust in thee forever. I will not put my trust in the arm of flesh; for I know that cursed is he that putteth his trust in the arm of flesh. . . .
>
> Yea, I know that God will give liberally to him that asketh. Yea, my God will give me, if I ask not amiss; therefore I will lift up my voice unto thee; yea, I will cry unto thee, my God, the rock of my righteousness. (2 Nephi 4:33–35.)

President George Q. Cannon said: "Every defect in human character can be corrected through the exercise of faith and pleading with the Lord for the gifts that He has said He will give unto those who believe and obey the commandments" (*Gospel Truths,* 1:196). Having experienced some weighty matters of life in my time, when human judgment was so inadequate, I know the Lord sustains and supports those who call on Him. ("Lord, Increase our Faith," Provo Utah Tabernacle Rededication, 21 September 1986.)

God does hear and answer prayers. I have never doubted that fact. From childhood, at my mother's knee where I first learned to pray; as a young man in my teens; as a missionary in foreign lands; as a father; as a Church leader; as a government official, I know without any question that it is possible for men and women to reach out in humility and prayer and tap that Unseen Power; to have prayers answered. Man does not stand alone, or, at least, he need not stand alone. Prayer will open doors; prayer will remove barriers; prayer will ease pressures; prayer will give inner peace and comfort during times of strain and stress and difficulty. Thank God for prayer. (CR October 1956, *Improvement Era* 59 [December 1956]: 953.)

May prayer increase your faith in God—and your trust and love—so that whatever trials and desolation life may hold for you, you may say with Job: "I know that my redeemer liveth" (Job 19:25). (*So Shall Ye Reap,* p. 176.)

I counsel you, in the words of Jesus Christ, to "watch and pray always lest ye enter into temptation; for Satan desireth to have you, that he may sift you as wheat" (3 Nephi 18:18). If you will earnestly seek guidance from your Heavenly Father, morning and evening, you will be given the strength to shun any temptation. ("To 'The Rising Generation,' " *New Era* 16 [June 1986]: 8.)

Pride

One of Satan's greatest tools is pride: to cause a man or a woman to center so much attention on self that he or she becomes insensitive to his Creator or fellow beings. It is a cause for discontent, divorce, teenage rebellion, family indebtedness, and most other problems we face. (CR April 1979, *Ensign* 9 [May 1979]: 34.)

In the scriptures there is no such thing as righteous pride. It is always considered as a sin. We are not speaking of a wholesome view of self-worth, which is best established by a close relationship with God. But we are speaking of pride as the universal sin, as someone has described it. Mormon writes that "the pride of this nation, or the people of the Nephites, hath proven their destruction" (Moroni 8:27). The Lord says in the Doctrine and Covenants, "Beware of pride, lest ye become as the Nephites of old" (D&C 38:39). Essentially, pride is a "my will" rather than "thy will" approach to life. The opposite of pride is humbleness, meekness, submissiveness, or teachableness (see Alma 13:28). (CR April 1986, *Ensign* 16 [May 1986]: 6.)

Pride does not look up to God and care about what is right. It looks sideways to man and argues who is right. Pride is manifest in the spirit of contention. Was it not through pride that the devil became the devil? Christ wanted to serve. The devil wanted to rule. Christ wanted to bring men to where He was. The devil wanted to be above men. Christ removed self as the force in His perfect life. It was not my will, but thine be done (see Mark 14:36; Luke 22:42).

Pride is characterized by "What do I want out of life?" rather than by "What would God have me do with my life?" It is self-will as opposed to God's will. It is the fear of man over the fear of God. (CR April 1986, *Ensign* 16 [May 1986]: 6–7.)

Many of us have a tendency to forget the Gracious Hand which has preserved our nation, enriched it, strengthened it. Many of us imagine in the foolishness of pride, that our manifold blessings are due not to God's goodness, but to our own wisdom and virtue. Too many of us have been so drunk with self-sufficiency as no longer to feel the need of prayer. (*Title of Liberty*, p. 156.)

Humility responds to God's will—to the fear of His judgments and to the needs of those around us. To the proud, the applause of the world rings in their ears; to the humble, the applause of heaven warms their hearts. Someone has said, "Pride gets no pleasure out of having something, only out of having more of it than the next man." Of one brother, the Lord said, "I, the Lord, am not well pleased with him, for he seeketh to excel, and he is not sufficiently meek before me" (D&C 58:41). (CR April 1986, *Ensign* 16 [May 1986]: 7.)

As we cleanse the inner vessel, there will have to be changes made in our own personal lives, in our families, and in the Church. The proud do not change to improve, but defend their position by rationalizing. Repentance means change, and it takes a humble person to change. But we can do it. (CR April 1986, *Ensign* 16 [May 1986]: 7.)

Recreation and Sports

We are not interested in our brethren becoming expert softball players. We do not care about that. Yes, of course, we want to enjoy ourselves in recreational and cultural activities, but we are interested in building men, we are interested in saving men, exalting them, getting them to hold the priesthood and to magnify it; that is why we organize softball in the Church. Ofttimes you can get less-active men to take part in the softball games or to take part on a welfare project when you could not get them into a priesthood meeting or get them to offer a prayer, but if you can warm them up on a welfare project, on a new building, on a softball diamond, gradually they will come into full activity.

Our business is to build men, to exalt them, to save them, and all this machinery, all this program of the Church, is simply a means to an end. That is why we meet so much, why we study, have our classes, why we have our activities. (Fresno California Priesthood Leadership Meeting, 13 September 1952.)

Athletics are explosive, as any of us know who have participated in them. Young men make every effort to win. They should be trying their best to win or they shouldn't be playing. The problem therefore, is to do everything that is fair and honorable to win, and also to know the line where sportsmanship stops and mockery starts. How do you teach boys to exert every energy to win, but also stop short of winning if integrity is to be impaired.

It is a real test of character. We believe the conduct as a whole is excellent. Of course, there are always a few who raise doubt, protests, and complaints. There are too many still who play by the letter of the rules instead of by the spirit of the rules. This is our challenge. It is one of the difficult challenges in the Church, athletics being of an explosive nature as they are. (Softball Devotional, Salt Lake City, Utah, 21 August 1966.)

This athletic program entices boys to Church who haven't the slightest interest in Church. They come to be eligible but in the process they find the things that lead to a happy life and a happy future.

It can be safely said that no Church has the athletic program or the activity program that we have. You know it is important to the Church particularly today. It is a part of the great program to build men. (Softball Devotional, Salt Lake City, Utah, 21 August 1966.)

Sportsmanship is the spirituality in athletics, and we believe that the Church athletic program is a spiritual program. If it wasn't we wouldn't continue it, because our purpose is to build men and women of character and spirituality. We have dozens of stories of conversion, of boys finding the secret of what is most important in life by starting out just for physical activities. We believe that one of the best ways to bring inactive boys into the chapel is through the gym. We know this works. (Softball Devotional, Salt Lake City, Utah, 21 August 1966.)

I hope we will keep in mind and remember always the big ball game of life. We are all engaged in that game. Life is eternal. We are eternal beings. Softball is not the end. It is a means to the end.

The end is the perfection of our Father's sons. The building of men of strength, men of character, and to do it joyfully, joyously, because He said that men are that they might have joy. (Softball Devotional, Salt Lake City, Utah, 21 August 1966.)

It pays to live the good life. True, this is not a life of ease. We have tests, we have reverses, and we will have some of them on the diamond as we play in this great tournament. Yes, we must prepare for the battle of life—economic battles, social battles, moral battles, spiritual battles. (Softball Devotional, Salt Lake City, Utah, 21 August 1966.)

Sabbath Day

The purpose of the Sabbath is for spiritual uplift, for a renewal of our covenants, for worship, for rest, for prayer. It is for the purpose of feeding the spirit, that we may keep ourselves unspotted from the world by obeying God's command. (D&C 59:9.) (*God, Family, Country,* pp. 103–4.)

Few, if any, subjects in the great, eternal gospel plan of the Lord have been spoken of more frequently than that of the Sabbath. Ancient prophets of God have proclaimed it, Presidents of the Church and other General Authorities have repeatedly emphasized it, lay Christians and men of goodwill throughout Christendom have spoken approvingly of its place and value in the lives of men, women, and children of all races and climes. (*God, Family, Country,* p. 97.)

Many—too many—have almost ceased to observe the Sabbath. Not only is it a workday now, but it is supremely a day of amusement and recreation: golf, skiing, skating, hunting, fishing, picnicking, racing, movies, theaters, ball playing, dancing, and other forms of fun-making—all are coming largely to be the rule among too many so-called Christians. Some churches are said to encourage all these, if properly conducted. But God's law says keep the Sabbath day holy. "Six days shalt thou labour, and do all thy work" (Exodus 20:9). (*This Nation Shall Endure,* p. 51.)

What fits the purpose of the Sabbath? Here are a few suggestions: Activities that contribute to greater spirituality; essential Church meetings in the house of prayer; acquisition of spiritual knowledge—reading the scriptures, Church history and biographies, and the inspired words of the Brethren; resting physically, getting acquainted with the family, relating scriptural stories to children, bearing testimonies, building family unity; visiting the sick and aged shut-ins; singing the songs of Zion and listening to inspired music; paying devotions to the Most High—personal and family prayer; fasting, administrations, father's blessings; preparing food with singleness of heart—simple meals prepared largely on Saturday. (*God, Family, Country,* p. 104.)

I don't believe that it is possible to keep our spirituality on a high plane by spending our Sabbaths on the beach, on the golf course, in the mountains, or in our own homes reading newspapers and looking at television. When the Lord said, "And that thou mayest more fully keep thyself unspotted from the world, thou shalt go to the house of prayer" (D&C 59:9), that is exactly what He meant. We must have spiritual food.

Of course you can live a pretty good life out on the golf course on Sunday. But you don't build your spirituality. Probably you could worship the Lord out there, but the fact is you don't do it as you don't worship Him down on the beach. But if you go to the house of the Lord you will worship Him. If you attend to your prayers in your home with your family you will worship Him. And your spirituality will be raised. The spiritual food which your body requires will be provided and you are much more apt to have this joy. ("The Home and Family," BYU Religious Life Series, Provo, Utah, September 1960.)

Men from time immemorial have recognized the need for blessed rest—time for physical and spiritual refreshment. The human body and the spirit of man require it for happy, purposeful living. (*God, Family, Country,* p. 98.)

Yes, Sunday is wonderful, but how much more wonderful it might be if honored as a sacred Sabbath. Man has tried on several occasions to change God's law of the Sabbath. Each attempt has resulted in failure. (*God, Family, Country,* p. 99.)

The new consolidated meeting schedule is a marvelous step toward achieving our expectations. Think on this! Every Latter-day Saint father gathering his family together on the Sabbath and instructing them in gospel principles, gospel responsibilities, missionary service, and genealogy work. Will this not cause every man, woman, and child to move toward the ideal to speak in the name of the Lord? Will not faith increase in the hearts of many? Will there not be more covenants made with sincerity, and more covenants kept? And will there not come from these faithful homes those who can proclaim the gospel message to others? As the families of the Church follow the counsel of their leaders and instruct their families in the gospel principles and obligations, we will see results far beyond that which we initially contemplated. (Salt Lake City, Utah, 6 June 1980.)

We have requested priesthood leaders to minimize administrative meetings on the Sabbath so that families may engage in worship and family time. Our hope is that you will use this time to attend your meetings, render Christian service, visit family members, hold family home evenings, and study the scriptures. (CR April 1984, *Ensign* 14 [May 1984]: 7.)

Remember, Sunday is the Lord's day—a day to do His work. (*God, Family, Country,* p. 104.)

I believe in honoring the Sabbath day. I love a sacred Sabbath. I am grateful that as a boy I had a constant example and sound parental counsel as to the importance of keeping the Sabbath day a holy day. My memories of the Sabbath from infancy have been joyful, uplifting, and spiritually profitable, for which I am deeply grateful. (*God, Family, Country,* p. 9.)

I am grateful for the Sabbath day. I sometimes wonder what I would do without it. I mean that literally. A day of rest, but more than a day of rest—a day of prayer, a day of worship, a day of devotion, a day to be spiritually fed, a day to reflect on the purpose of life and the privileges, opportunities, and obligations which are ours as members of the Church.

The Lord has said that we should come to the house of prayer upon His holy day. He has made it very clear that if we would keep ourselves unspotted from the world we shall go to the house of prayer and offer up our sacraments upon His holy day. For verily this is a day appointed unto us to rest from our labours and to pay our devotion to the Most High. (See D&C 59:9–10.) So we come to the house of the Lord, if we would keep the Sabbath day holy. It is not possible to keep the Sabbath day holy just by resting from our labors. I am happy for the Sabbath day and all that it brings to us. ("Free Agency," Washington D.C. Stake Conference, 22 May 1960.)

A recommendation for perfecting the Saints is to see that the gospel of Jesus Christ is being taught in the various meetings of the Church. Sacrament meetings should be occasions where the gospel is taught by testimony. This is not now occurring on a regular, consistent basis. Within our ward meetings, members should be edified—built up in their faith and, to use Peter's phrase, given "a reason [for] the hope that is in [them]" (1 Peter 3:15). (Salt Lake City, Utah, 3 April 1981.)

Attend all of your Church meetings. Faithful attendance at Church meetings brings blessings you can receive in no other way. Attend your Young Women meetings every Sunday and your weekly activities. Learn well your responsibilities in the gospel and then perform them with diligence. ("To the Young Women of the Church," *Ensign* 16 [November 1986]: 82.)

Attend your Sunday School classes every Sunday. Listen carefully to the lesson and participate in class discussions. Gospel scholarship and an increase in testimony will result. Attend your priesthood quorum meetings every Sunday and your quorum activities held on weeknights. Learn well your priesthood responsibilities and then perform them with diligence and reverence. (CR April 1986, *Ensign* 16 [May 1986]: 44.)

You should participate in the programs and activities of the Church—keep the Sabbath as a holy day; attend your meetings; accept callings extended to you, and magnify those callings. Give service willingly and I promise you will have great joy. (Geneva Switzerland Stake Creation, 20 June 1982.)

I feel confident in my own heart that one of the reasons—probably the principal reason—why the Lord has provided such a full program with meetings, priesthood quorums, group meetings, sacrament meetings, stake conferences, general conferences, and all the rest is to help us as His children, whom He loves and wants to save and exalt, to endure to the end. (Fresno California Priesthood Leadership Meeting, 13 September 1952.)

The gospel of Jesus Christ is to be taught, particularly during our sacrament services. The purpose of that meeting is twofold: first, it is to partake of the sacrament and renew our covenants; and second, it is to teach the gospel and testify of Jesus Christ.

I recall as a young boy hearing the gospel from the older members who had been through "the fire." I can still see their fervent faces and hear their inspired testimonies. We need to get back to that. ("Our Duty as Latter-day Saints," Springfield-Burke Virginia Chapel Dedication, 15 October 1982.)

We go to our chapels each week to worship the Lord and renew our covenants by partaking of the sacrament. We thereby promise to take His name upon us, to always remember Him, and keep all His commandments. Our agreement to keep all the commandments is our covenant with God. Only as we do this may we deserve His blessings and merit His mercy. (*Come unto Christ*, p. 36.)

Attend your sacrament meeting every Sunday. Listen carefully to the messages. Pray for the spirit of understanding and testimony. Be worthy to prepare and bless and pass the sacrament. Come to the sacrament table with clean hands and a pure heart (2 Nephi 25:16). (CR April 1986, *Ensign* 16 [May 1986]: 44.)

Whenever you are called on to speak at a sacrament meeting, would you teach the gospel! Teach from the scriptures. Bear your testimony. ("Our Duty as Latter-day Saints," Springfield-Burke Virginia Chapel Dedication, 15 October 1982.)

The sacrament will bless the souls of all those who worthily partake of it, and as such it should be taken often, even by the bedfast (see D&C 20:77, 79). (CR October 1974, *Ensign* 4 [November 1974]: 66.)

Sacrifice

Joseph Smith said this about sacrifice:

> For a man to lay down his all, his character and reputation, his honor and applause, his good name among men, his houses, his lands, his brothers and sisters, his wife and children, and even his own life also—counting all things but filth and dross for the excellency of the knowledge of Jesus Christ—requires more than mere belief or supposition that he is doing the will of God; but actual knowledge, realizing that, when these sufferings are ended he will enter into eternal rest, and be a partaker of the glory of God. ... A religion that does not require the sacrifice of all things never has power sufficient to produce the faith necessary unto life and salvation; for, from the first existence of man, the faith necessary unto the enjoyment of life and salvation never could be obtained without the sacrifice of all earthly things. It was through this sacrifice, and this only, that God has ordained that men should enjoy eternal life. (*Lectures on Faith,* p. 58.)

Elder Bruce R. McConkie said, "Sacrifice pertains to mortality; in the eternal sense there is none. Sacrifice involves giving up the things of this world because of the promises of blessings to be gained in a better world. In the eternal perspective there is no sacrifice in giving up all things—even including the laying down of one's life—if eternal life is gained through such a course." (See D&C 98:13–15.) But, just as when one loses his life to God, he really finds the abundant life, so also when one sacrifices all to God then God in return shares all that He has with him. (Salt Lake City, Utah, October 1961.)

Solemnize your marriage in the house of the Lord. While in South America, I was touched by the sacrifices made by many of our Saints to have their families sealed to them for eternity. I shed tears of gratitude as I heard some of the experiences recounted.

One of our stake presidents brought his family to the Sao Paulo Temple from Lima, Peru, normally a nine-day bus ride, but, because of bus strikes and other problems, the journey took them fourteen days of travel. Upon their arrival at Sao Paulo, the family went to the first session they could, and the sealing ceremony was performed. Then they immediately prepared to leave. The temple president asked them if they were staying the night. The father replied that the family had to leave immediately since they did not have sufficient money for lodging and food. He said they would have to travel several days without food as it was. The family was then persuaded to stay the night and have breakfast before their departure. That represents the spirit of sacrifice of many of our Saints worldwide. (CR April 1979, *Ensign* 9 [May 1979]: 33.)

Do you know one reason why righteous mothers love their children so much? It is because they sacrifice so much for them. We love what we sacrifice for and we sacrifice for what we love.

She was a young girl. She had sacrificed her worldly plans to spend long, tedious hours at work in order to provide for and raise her younger orphan brother, but now she lay on her bed dying of a sickness. She called her bishop, and as she talked to him in her last moments, he held her rough, hard, work-calloused hands in his. Then she asked the question, "How will God know that I am His?" Gently he raised her wrist and answered, "Show Him your hands."

Someday we may see that pair of hands that sacrificed so much for us. Are our hands clean and do they show the signs of being in His service? Are our hearts pure and filled with His thoughts? ("Jesus Christ—Gifts and Expectations," Christmas Devotional, Salt Lake City, Utah, 7 December 1986.)

To sacrifice, serve with your time and means to build the kingdom of God on earth. The great law for spiritual happiness and progress was stated by the Master in these words: "If any man will come after me, let him deny himself, and take up my cross, and follow me. For whosoever will save his life shall lose it: and whosoever will lose his life for my sake shall find it." (Matthew 16:24–25.) (CR April 1979, *Ensign* 9 [May 1979]: 34.)

One great measure of increased faith among members of the Church is their willingness to succor those who stand in need of succor. King Benjamin truly taught: "And now, . . . for the sake of retaining a remission of your sins from day to day, that ye may walk guiltless before God—I would that ye should impart of your substance to the poor, every man according to that which he hath, such as feeding the hungry, clothing the naked, visiting the sick and administering to their relief, both spiritually and temporally, according to their wants" (Mosiah 4:26). No better example of imparting our substance to our neighbor was demonstrated than the generous offerings of Church members to relieve the suffering of starving people throughout the world. ("Lord, Increase Our Faith," Provo Utah Tabernacle Rededication, 21 September 1986.)

What can we possibly give to the Lord? Considering all that He has done and is doing for us, there is something that we might give Him in return. Christ's great gift to us was His life and sacrifice. Should that not then be our small gift to Him — our lives and sacrifices, not only now, but in the future? ("Jesus Christ — Gifts and Expectations," Christmas Devotional, Salt Lake City, Utah, 7 December 1986.)

Self-Control

A purpose of this probationary state is that man learns to control all of his bodily appetites, desires, and passions. For as the Apostle Paul instructed the members of the Church at Corinth: "Know ye not that ye are the temple of God, and that the Spirit of God dwelleth in you? If any man defile the temple of God, him shall God destroy, for the temple of God is holy, which temple ye are." (1 Corinthians 3:16–17.) The phrase "temple of God" refers, of course, to man's mortal body. Our aim should be to become fully masters of our bodies. ("Man — The Temple of God," Miami, Florida, 19 March 1976.)

There is something higher than intellect. There is something higher than excellence. It is dedication to principle. It is self-mastery, self-control. It is living what one really believes in his heart. ("New Year 1961," Washington D.C. Ward, 31 December 1960.)

Think clean thoughts. Those who think clean thoughts do not do filthy deeds. You are responsible before God not only for your acts but also for controlling your thoughts. So live that you would not blush with shame if your thoughts and acts should be flashed on a screen in your chapel. The old adage is still true that you sow thoughts and you reap acts, you sow acts and you reap habits, you sow habits and you reap a character, and your character determines your eternal destiny. "As [a man] thinketh in his heart, so is he" (Proverbs 23:7). (London England Area Conference, 19–20 June 1976.)

An attribute described by Peter as being part of the divine nature is temperance. A priesthood holder is temperate. This means he is restrained in his emotions and verbal expressions. He does things in moderation and is not given to overindulgence. In a word, he has self-control. He is the master of his emotions, not the other way around.

A priesthood holder who would curse his wife, abuse her with words or actions, or do the same to one of his own children is guilty of grievous sin. "Can ye be angry, and not sin?" asked the Apostle Paul (Joseph Smith Translation, Ephesians 4:26).

If a man does not control his temper, it is a sad admission that he is not in control of his thoughts. He then becomes a victim of his own passions and emotions, which leads him to actions that are totally unfit for civilized behavior, let alone behavior for a priesthood holder.

To our temperance we are to add patience. A priesthood holder is to be patient. Patience is another form of self-control. It is the ability to postpone gratification and to bridle one's passions. In his relationships with loved ones, a patient man does not engage in impetuous behavior that he will later regret. Patience is composure under stress. A patient man is understanding of others' faults.

A patient man also waits on the Lord. We sometimes read or hear of people who seek a blessing from the Lord, then grow impatient when it does not come swiftly. Part of the divine nature is to trust in the Lord enough to "be still, and know that [he] is God" (D&C 101:16). A priesthood holder who is patient will be tolerant of the mistakes and failings of his loved ones. Because he loves them, he will not find fault nor criticize nor blame. (CR October 1986, *Ensign* 16 [November 1986]: 47.)

Ours must be a crusade for clean, purposeful living. Only those who steadfastly pursue such a course ever experience real peace, real freedom. Those fettered by insatiable appetites for things destructive of man's noblest qualities never know either real freedom or the sweet fruits of inward peace. (*So Shall Ye Reap,* p. 54.)

Service

In a revelation given through the Prophet Joseph a year before the Church was organized to his own father Joseph Smith, Senior, the Lord makes it very clear what He expects of us. In that revelation, the Lord says this: "Now behold, a marvelous work is about to come forth among the children of men. Therefore, O ye who embark in the service of God, see that ye serve him with all your heart, might, mind and strength, that ye may stand blameless before God at the last day." (D&C 4:1–2.) Not one word about office, but that we serve Him with all our heart, might, mind, and strength. Not "where we serve" but "how we serve." And the Lord has a way of blessing His children, magnifying them, and bringing them joy and happiness wherever they serve in His kingdom so long as they serve Him with all their heart, might, mind, and strength. (San Diego California South Stake Conference, 6 December 1969.)

The formula for successful relationships with others boils down to that divine code known as the Golden Rule. "Therefore, all things whatsoever ye would that men should do to you, do ye even so to them" (Matthew 7:12). It was the Master who said: "And whosoever will be chief among you, let him be your servant" (Matthew 20:27). Unselfish, willing service to others was the keynote of His relationship with men. "For even the Son of man came not to be ministered unto, but to minister, and to give his life a ransom for many" (Mark 10:45). To serve others willingly and unselfishly should be one of our greatest virtues. It is not even a matter of choice. It is an obligation, a sacred command. ("Your Charge: To Increase in Wisdom and Favor with God and Man," *New Era* 9 [September 1979]: 43–44.)

In spite of the evils, almost daily we see in action men and women and youth responding in unselfish, devoted service. All are ready to serve faithfully, courageously, in the world but not of the world. There is nothing to equal this voluntary service anywhere in the world outside The Church of Jesus Christ of Latter-day Saints. In one sense, we do "live in the worst of times." Evil in new and enticing forms is almost everywhere. But, more important for us to keep in mind is the fact that "we live in the very best of times."

The gospel is here in its fulness. We have the richest program ever in the Church, and we have an ever-increasing army of loyal, devoted workers throughout the world. We know where we are going and we are on our way. We know we are going to win, with the Lord's help. God help us to be worthy of it. (Regional Representatives Seminar, Salt Lake City, Utah, 28 June 1974.)

Do we find it a burden to give of our time to others? Did Christ not heal all those who were brought to Him, even though many a day and a night it seemed the whole city was gathered around Him? Are we sometimes asked to do for others what may seem to be beneath us, or what is tiresome and monotonous? Was not the Son of God born in a stable? Did He not make Himself a servant, even to washing the feet of His disciples, saying to them, "The servant is not greater than his Lord?" (John 13:16.) Love one another. Serve your fellowman. The example has been given you. ("Your Charge: To Increase in Wisdom and Favor with God and Man," *New Era* 9 [September 1979]: 44.)

We are all familiar with the divine injunction of our Savior to "seek ye first the kingdom of God and his righteousness" (Matthew 6:33). Nothing in this world is more important than putting first the kingdom of God in our lives. I wonder whether some of us have become too occupied with the pursuit of worldly things that we place our own interests first. ("Lord, Increase Our Faith," Provo Utah Tabernacle Rededication, 21 September 1986.)

Paul wrote that we are "every one members one of another" (Romans 12:5). Therefore, let us serve one another with brotherly love, never tiring of the demands upon us, being patient and persevering and generous, living in harmony and, if possible, at peace with all men. If we would serve God through service to our brethren, we shall have need of a love for work. (*So Shall Ye Reap,* pp. 173–74.)

Opportunities to lose oneself for the good of others present themselves daily: the mother who serves her children's needs; the father who gives his time for their instruction; parents who give up worldly pleasure for quality home life; children who care for their aged parents; home teaching service; visiting teaching; time for compassionate service; giving comfort to those who need strength; serving with diligence in Church callings; community and public service in the interest of preserving our freedoms; financial donations for tithes, fast offerings, support of missionaries, welfare, building, and temple projects. Truly, the day of sacrifice is not past. (CR April 1979, *Ensign* 9 [May 1979]: 34.)

If you would find yourself, learn to deny yourself for the blessing of others. Forget yourself and find someone who needs your service, and you will discover the secret to the happy, fulfilled life. (CR April 1979, *Ensign* 9 [May 1979]: 34.)

You can get an individual to do selfless service. Such service is its own reward. Help him to have that experience, then he will know the joy that comes from serving the Lord. (Regional Representatives Seminar, Salt Lake City, Utah, 3 April 1975.)

We urge you, particularly priesthood brethren and Relief Society sisters, to be sensitive to the needs of the poor, the sick, and the needy. We have a Christian responsibility to see that the widows and fatherless are assisted. "Pure religion and undefiled before God and the Father is this, to visit the fatherless and widows in their affliction, and to keep himself unspotted from the world" (James 1:27). (CR April 1984, *Ensign* 14 [May 1984]: 7.)

To lose yourself in righteous service to others can lift your sights and get your mind off personal problems, or at least put them in proper focus. "When you find yourselves a little gloomy," said President Lorenzo Snow, "look around you and find somebody that is in a worse plight than yourself; go to him and find out what the trouble is, then try to remove it with the wisdom which the Lord bestows upon you; and the first thing you know, your gloom is gone, you feel light, the Spirit of the Lord is upon you, and everything seems illuminated." (CR April 6, 1899, pp. 2–3.) (CR October 1974, *Ensign* 4 [November 1974]: 66.)

I hope that our young people are learning to serve mankind. Here is happiness. Here is opportunity for personal growth. We can't help others without helping ourselves. The sweetest joys of all come from serving our Heavenly Father in His work. To be a partner in His employ, to feel the warmth and peace of His Spirit, to learn His will, to feel His presence in humble prayer—these things make us realize that our great purpose in life is to overcome adversity and worldly consideration as we strive for things of the Spirit. By such service, we can achieve a measure of faithfulness and worthiness that will enable us, when our time comes, to stride ahead into the eternities to come. (MIA Vanguard Program, Salt Lake City, Utah, 13 June 1960.)

Today we see missionaries going into the world to take the restored gospel to others. Numbered among these missionaries are thousands of young men who have interrupted schooling or careers to give service, young women who have volunteered, and many couples who serve in their retirement years.

I reflect on the innumerable hours of service freely given by priesthood and auxiliary leaders, teachers, and other Church members. I think of those who devote hours to genealogical research and temple workers and members who work in the temples throughout the world—all in a glorious effort to provide opportunities for salvation to those who have passed through mortality without the blessings of the gospel.

I think of conscientious parents throughout the world who gather their families together by hearthsides to sing, to pray, to read the scriptures, and to learn the truths of the gospel of Jesus Christ. All of this service, dedication, and devotion are indications that faith has indeed increased in the earth. Surely the Lord is pleased with the consecrated efforts, time, love, and generous support of so many of His Saints throughout the world.

As His appointed servants, our hearts are filled with overwhelming gratitude to you for all you do to contribute to the onrolling of His work in the earth. The efforts of few result in the blessing of many! ("Lord, Increase Our Faith," Provo Utah Tabernacle Rededication, 21 September 1986.)

May you gain the deep and abiding satisfaction that comes from rendering the maximum service of which you are capable. May your life be enriched to overflowing as you realize the fulfillment of your fondest hopes and noblest aspirations. ("Your Charge: To Increase in Wisdom and Favor with God and Man," *New Era* 9 [September 1979]: 45.)

Accepting and Magnifying Callings

I think of the words of the Apostle Paul, as he stood before King Agrippa making his defense—Paul, a persecutor of the Saints, converted to Christianity through a glorious manifestation. And there as he stood before King Agrippa in chains, the king permitted him to make his own defense.

I remember that as he made his defense, outlining the mission of Christ, referring to this thing called Christianity, he said in substance, to the king, "Surely, King, you must have heard of this new movement, for this thing [has not been] done in a corner" (see Acts 26:26). How well that applies to Mormonism today. Yes, persecutions have come in the past. Our people have endured much. I think of the Prophet in Liberty Jail. I think of the brethren who were shot down by mobs. I think of the missionaries and the persecutions that met them.

No, this thing has not been "done in a corner." The hand of God has been directing His Church and His people. And so it will be in the future. While honors may come to us conferred by men, and those honors are important, of course, no honor will ever come to a member of this Church in the political world that will equal or even approach the honor which comes to a man when he has conferred upon him the holy priesthood, that which is eternal, that which is most priceless. (*So Shall Ye Reap,* p. 240.)

The Lord said, "Knock and it shall be opened unto you" (3 Nephi 14:7; Matthew 7:7). In other words, it requires effort on our part. In a revelation given to the Prophet Joseph we are told that men should be anxiously engaged in a good cause (see D&C 58:27). That suggests effort, initiative. Now, we don't seek office in the Church and we don't resist release when it comes, and neither do we resign from office in the Church. I sometimes wonder what would happen to this Church if we ran for office. We do not seek office, we do not resist calls to service, we accept releases willingly when they come, and we serve until we are honorably released. ("The Church," Paris, France, 7 August 1960.)

Some of our bishops and stake presidents report that members are turning down calls to serve claiming they are "too busy" or they "haven't got time." Others, they say, accept such callings, but refuse to magnify those callings. I am concerned when I hear reports about this kind of attitude.

The Lord expects each of us to have a calling in His Church so that others may be blessed by our talents and influence. He expects us to magnify those callings. The way we do that is to do the work which goes with the calling or the office we accept.

Is there a priesthood holder who has not time to visit three, four, five families at least once each month? Is there a sister who is so busy she cannot visit teach? If we are "too busy" to hold a Church calling, we had better look at our priorities. ("Lord, Increase Our Faith," Provo Utah Tabernacle Rededication, 21 September 1986.)

I know we cannot fail in this work, no matter to what office we are called, if we do our best. (Salt Lake City, Utah, 31 March 1974.)

Lead your members to participate in the programs and activities of the Church—to keep the Sabbath as a holy day; to attend their meetings; to accept callings extended to them and magnify those callings. Teach them to give service willingly and I promise you will have great joy. (El Paso Texas Regional Conference, 25 January 1986.)

We have a great program and we have the privilege of playing a part in this great and important program of saving, exalting, and building our Father's children. The Lord has made it very clear what He expects of every one of us. He has made it very clear that it is not so much where we serve, but how we serve. (San Diego California South Stake Conference, 6 December 1969.)

John saw the end from the beginning: he saw the Creation, he saw the gospel dispensations, he saw the establishment of the Church in the meridian of time, he saw the great apostasy, the falling away, and he saw the angel flying through the midst of heaven having the everlasting gospel to preach to men who dwell on the earth, he saw the Restoration, and he saw the final winding-up scene. (See Revelation 14:6.)

And do you remember what he said? He said, "I saw the dead,

small and great, stand before God; and the books were opened: and another book was opened, which is the book of life: and the dead were judged out of those things which were written in the books'' (Revelation 20:12).

And so it will be with us—each and everyone of us. We, too, will be expected to stand before the judgment bar of God; and when that time comes, I have the conviction in my heart that the question will not be, "What office did you hold?" but, "Did you serve me with all your heart, might, mind, and strength?" That will be the real test!

And so, how important it is as leaders in the Church, as teachers—wherever we serve—as a Primary teacher, as a home teacher, as a head of an elders quorum, as a secretary—how important it is that we serve Him with all our heart, might, mind, and strength, that we too may stand blameless before God at the last day (see D&C 4:2). (San Diego California South Stake Conference, 6 December 1969.)

Since all men who will be ordained to the Melchizedek Priesthood do so by covenant, may I have you consider the covenant we take upon ourselves when we are ordained to the higher priesthood. We promise or agree to our Father in Heaven that we will magnify our callings which come to us (see D&C 84:39–44). What does that mean? To magnify our callings in the priesthood means to build it up in dignity and importance, to strengthen it, and to cause others to respect and honor the office because of the virtue and righteousness of the man who fills the office. ("Three Imperative Responsibilities," London England Area Conference, 19–20 June 1976.)

In the Church and kingdom of God there is no unimportant office or calling or service (see 1 Corinthians 12:12–25). We are all in it together; and the Lord has a way of magnifying us. (San Diego California South Stake Conference, 6 December 1969.)

It is essential to all we do in our ministry that it be done with "an eye single to the glory of God" (D&C 4:5). That should be our primary motive. We have not been called to build up ourselves, but to build the kingdom of God. We shall be instrumental in achieving this momentous goal as we magnify our callings and honor the Lord. (Salt Lake City, Utah, 19 January 1977.)

Now is the time to live the standards of the Church, to magnify our priesthood, to live worthy of the rich promises made to us as bearers of the priesthood. Let us, therefore, be anxiously engaged in a good cause (see D&C 58:27). Let us exercise the priesthood upon the principles of righteousness (see D&C 121:36). And let us learn our duty and act in the office in which we have been appointed in all diligence (see D&C 107:99). (*So Shall Ye Reap*, p. 24.)

"Those who are just and true" (D&C 76:53). What an apt expression for those valiant in the testimony of Jesus! These are members of the Church who magnify their callings in the Church (see D&C 84:33), pay their tithes and offerings, live morally clean lives, sustain their Church leaders by word and action, keep the Sabbath as a holy day, and obey all the commandments of God. They are courageous in defending truth and righteousness. To these the Lord has promised that "all thrones and dominions, principalities and powers, shall be revealed and set forth upon all who have endured valiantly for the gospel of Jesus Christ" (D&C 121:29). (*Come unto Christ,* p. 13.)

This is the work of the Lord. This work is destined to fill the earth. If we, His current leaders, will not do the work, He will raise up others who will. (Regional Representatives Seminar, Salt Lake City, Utah, 5 April 1985.)

We counsel you to accept callings in the Church and to serve faithfully in the positions to which you are called. Serve one another. Magnify your callings. As you do so, you will be the means of blessing others and you will increase in spirituality. (CR April 1984, *Ensign* 14 [May 1984]: 7.)

God bless us that we may serve so that we will never have any serious regrets, that we will know we have been magnified even beyond our natural talents. (Texas San Antonio Mission, 2 March 1986.)

Standards

A standard is a rule of measure by which one determines exactness or perfection. The Saints are to be a standard of holiness for the world to see. That is the beauty of Zion. (*Come unto Christ*, p. 103.)

We must establish a standard of measurement for determining which principles and ideals may be accepted as being eternally sound. Such a standard should enable us to differentiate clearly between that which is good for man and that which is not.

This then should be the standard: If a principle promotes well-being and initiative and strengthens the morale and character of a person, it is good for man. If it increases self-reliance, moral courage, service, and integrity, it is a principle of truth which will contribute to inward strength and true security. If the course tends toward perfection, as charted by Jesus Christ, it is indeed desirable and will ultimately free mankind. (*The Red Carpet*, p. 261.)

Certain principles and truths are shared in common by the majority of mankind. These principles, which are termed values, transcend culture, race, nationality, or religion. They represent something more than mere preference or belief. Values are those truths we all know we should seek after, whether we do or not, because they are good for us and will result in greater moral and spiritual development. ("The Values by Which to Live," *Leaders* [October 1984]: 953.)

It takes courage to trust in God and do the right. No other course, however, leads to a fulness of joy and achievement. Successful happy living must be builded each day with care. Essential foundation stones are clean thoughts, clean speech, and clean actions. Sometimes those who follow such a course are branded as being "different." To be different may be embarrassing if one is wrong—but it is an enviable distinction to be different if one is right.

We tend to associate with those of like ideals. Only the wholesome have the capacity to lift and encourage one another to greater service, to greater achievement, to greater strength. Those who follow an opposite course serve only to intensify those unwholesome actions and desires which are the breeding ground for regrets, sorrow, confusion, and disillusionment. (*So Shall Ye Reap,* p. 54.)

There is an all-too-prevalent spirit of experimenting with things that have already been proved beyond doubt. It finds expression in such phrases as "I'll try anything once," "You're only young once," "Be a good sport," "You only go around once in life," and "Times are different."

Times are different, but fundamentals remain unchanged. Honesty is still honesty. Virtue is still virtue. Truth is still truth. Honest effort is still rewarded. Gravity still pulls all things to earth. Disregard for law still brings punishment. Two and two still make four. The Ten Commandments are still in force, as are all the other laws of life, nature, and the universe. Cecil B. DeMille once said that men and nations cannot break the Ten Commandments; they can only break themselves upon them. ("Your Charge: To Increase in Wisdom and Favor with God and Man," *New Era* 9 [September 1979]: 40.)

Youth, be true to God's holy laws. Remember, they cannot be broken with impunity. If you would be happy and successful in your earthly association, courtship, and home building, conform your lives to the eternal laws of heaven. There is no other way. ("Your Charge: To Increase in Wisdom and Favor with God and Man," *New Era* 9 [September 1979]: 43.)

There is a lot of sentiment in this country, outside the Church, in support of our ideals and standards as Latter-day Saints. Let us not fail the Church. Let us not fail ourselves by being so unwise as to feel we have to let down our standards in order to be accepted by the world. It is not true. The world may not live by our standards, but they have respect and appreciation for those of us who have the wisdom and the courage to maintain those standards. (*God, Family, Country,* pp. 86–87.)

We seek that which is praiseworthy, lovely, virtuous, and of good report, and we salute Beethoven, Shakespeare, Rembrandt, and Michelangelo (Article of Faith 13). In due time, we will also have more of our own giants—particularly great father-patriarchs and noble companions and mothers of men. There is certain music heard, feminine-like hair styles seen on men, art displayed, and clothes worn among our youth and some adults also that must pass away—not because the styles change, but because our standards will be improved. (Salt Lake City, Utah, October 1961.)

All happiness, all success, all glorious achievement rest with the individual. He can make a heaven or a hell upon the earth. No person who knowingly compromises principles or standards of eternal truth is being fair to himself or mankind. If he is not true to himself, he cannot be relied upon by his fellowmen. (*So Shall Ye Reap,* p. 166.)

Standards of the World

While the world may not maintain our standards, the world is willing to pay for the services of young men who do. ("Strengthen Your Families," Star Valley Wyoming Stake Conference, 18 April 1971.)

Are we too much bound up in the affairs of the world—obsessed with secular measuring sticks—gauging our deeds by whether or not they have brought us praise, honor, esteem, profits? Do we seek wealth, honor, and esteem as though they were ends in themselves, thus putting us at cross purposes with God because we become more attached to the material than to the spiritual? ("For Security—Look Beyond Materialism," *Instructor* 92 [January 1957]: 9.)

The fact that we live in a fast-changing world makes it doubly important that we cling fast to sound principles. True principles are eternal and do not change. Their application and specific circumstances may change, but the truth itself is constant and unvarying. (*The Red Carpet,* p. 130.)

Hear this test proposed by President George Q. Cannon: "If the breach is daily widening between ourselves and the world . . . we may be assured that our progress is certain, however slow. On the opposite hand, if our feeling and affections, our appetites and desires, are in unison with the world around us and we freely fraternize with them . . . we should do well to examine ourselves." (*Millennial Star* 23 [5 October]: 645–46.) (*God, Family, Country,* pp. 262–63.)

Relatively few, it seems, turn their attention to those standards and principles which strengthen moral fiber and which develop spiritual and personal security from within. Yet the history of mankind testifies abundantly that lasting security comes only to a people who are spiritually and morally strong. (*The Red Carpet*, p. 260.)

Standards of the Gospel

In the Church we have certain standards — of living, of morality, of character — which are coming to be well known to the world. These standards are admired. People with such standards are sought after. These standards are based upon true, eternal principles. They are eternal verities. (CR April 1958, *Improvement Era* 61 [June 1958]: 434.)

What of your standards? Do you have a deep reverence and respect for the commandments of God? Those who have are the people in this world who are happiest and prosper most. Those who ignore God's holy laws will always live in despair. "Be not deceived: God is not mocked: for whatsoever a man soweth, that shall he also reap. For he that soweth to his flesh shall of the flesh reap corruption; but he that soweth to the Spirit shall of the Spirit reap life everlasting." (Galatians 6:7–8.) Your chance of material success in your chosen field will be increased by maintaining every standard of decency and righteousness. The experience of the race proclaims the blessings which follow righteous living. Try it and see. ("Concerning Principles and Standards," *Church News* [4 June 1947]: 5.)

Today we have an opportunity the like of which we have never had in the Church. All over the world the Church is well spoken of. Today we are known for what we are and not for what our enemies have said about us in the past. What an opportunity to "arise and shine forth" as the Lord has commanded! (See D&C 115:5;

82:14.) Now is the time to wield our influence for good in this world, which is sick. Now is the time for us as leaders of youth to prepare these young men and women for the difficult days ahead.

How are we going to do it? First of all, we must look to ourselves. We must set our own lives in order. We must set our homes in order. We must be modest. We must be humble. We must be clean—morally clean—in our own hearts and in our own minds. We must be what we want our followers to be. We cannot be effective if, while we teach them the Word of Wisdom, we are serving tea and coffee and cocktails in our homes.

We cannot be effective if we are going out to card parties when we ought to be home reading the scriptures, tending our families, or spending more time with the youth of the Church. We cannot be effective if we neglect our family prayers. We cannot be effective if we are not honorable in our dealings with our fellowmen. We cannot be effective if we let down our standards. (*Title of Liberty*, pp. 205–6.)

You cannot let down your standards. Anytime you break a law of God you pay the penalty in heartache, in sadness, in remorse, in lack of self-respect, and you remove yourselves from contact with the Spirit of God. ("Stand Firm in the Faith," BYU Graduation, Provo, Utah, 17 August 1979.)

Are you holding aloft our standards or have you compromised them for the lowest common denominator in order to appease and deceive? Are you doing that which will help the home and strengthen our young people? Have we, as Moroni warned, "polluted the holy church of God" (Mormon 8:38)? ("Strengthening the Family," Philippine Islands Area Conference, 12 August 1975.)

Sometimes in our attempts to mimic the world, and contrary to the prophet's counsel, we run after the world's false educational, political, musical, and dress ideas. New worldly standards take over, a gradual breakdown occurs, and, finally, after much suffering, a humble people are ready to be taught once again a higher law.

Now, during all this gradual lowering of standards, the righteous should be living up to the highest personal standards they can, not forcing those standards on others, but preparing for and awaiting a better day, which surely must come. ("Jesus Christ — Gifts and Expectations," *New Era* 5 [May 1975]: 18.)

It was a stake conference day and between meetings these two members went out to get their lunch. They ordered their lunch and then the waiter said, "What'll you have to drink?" One said, "I'll have milk." The other said, "I'll have milk." He brought the milk and as he gave it to them, he stood there shaking his head, and said, "I don't understand. When you come alone, you order coffee. But when you come together you order milk." Well, I don't believe that happened, but there is a real lesson to it. Let us be what we profess to be. Let us maintain the standards fully. ("A Fourfold Hope," Brigham Young University, Provo, Utah, 24 May 1961.)

We must stand as a leaven among the nations, true to the principles of righteousness. We need to be humble. We need to be grateful. We need as families to kneel in family prayer, night and morning. Just a few words added to the blessing on the food, as is becoming the custom in some parts, is not enough. We need to get onto our knees in prayer and gratitude as Alma admonished (Alma 34:17–27). We need the spirit of reverence in our houses of worship. We need to keep the Sabbath day holy. We need to close our businesses on Sunday and as Latter-day Saints refrain from making purchases on the Sabbath. We need to refrain from going to moving pictures on the Sabbath, and if we are operating show houses, we should close them on Sunday. We should not seek pleasure in any form on the Sabbath day. We should stand firm in opposition to Sunday baseball and other amusements regardless of what much of the Christian world may do. We should oppose gambling in all of its forms, including the parimutuel betting at horse races. We should refrain from card playing, against which we have been counseled by the leaders of the Church. We should stand united in opposition to the wider distribution of alcohol and other things declared by the Lord to be harmful. (*So Shall Ye Reap,* pp. 60–61.)

We do not compromise principle. We do not surrender our standards regardless of current trends or pressures. As a Church, our allegiance to truth is unwavering. Speaking out against immoral or unjust actions has been the burden of prophets and disciples of God from time immemorial. It was for this very reason that many of them were persecuted. Nevertheless, it was their God-given task, as watchmen on the tower, to warn the people. (*God, Family, Country,* p. 359.)

Hold fast to the iron rod (1 Nephi 11:25), that we may be true to the faith, that we may maintain the standards which the Lord has set in His Church, that we might follow a course that is safe so that we may be exalted. ("Youth—Promise for the Future," BYU Graduation, Provo, Utah, 19 April 1986.)

Never has the Church had the opportunity and the challenge which it faces today. Now is the time for us to arise and shine as a people (D&C 115:5), to put on our beautiful garments (2 Nephi 8:24), to demonstrate to the world the fruits of the gospel, and to proclaim the standards which the Lord has revealed for the blessings of His children. ("Opportunity and Challenge," in *BYU Speeches of the Year* 1969 [Provo, Utah: BYU, 1970], p. 5.)

Remember, my young brethren and sisters, you will never have an occasion to be embarrassed—among people of character, people who count, real men and women—because you live according to the standards, the teachings, and ideals of the Church. (Scandinavia and Finland Area Conference, 16–18 August 1974.)

Success

In order to be successful in the eyes of the Lord, we have at least a fourfold duty to perform. First: We must do our duty to our homes and our families. I believe we are doing a fairly good job of that. At least we are getting a lot of favorable publicity. Second: We have a duty as Latter-day Saints to the Church to help spread the gospel, to carry the message, to live the gospel, to keep the commandments, to be an example to the world, to "arise and shine" (D&C 115:5). Third: We have a responsibility to our occupation, our profession, our employment, to provide for our own families. The scriptures tell us that he who will not provide for his own is worse than an infidel (see 1 Timothy 5:8). Fourth: We have a citizenship responsibility. I believe the person who is truly successful, in the eyes of the Lord, must do his duty in all four areas. (Salt Lake Utah Emigration Stake Conference, 5 November 1978.)

We believe that students will be better students if they go onto their knees night and morning. We want them to excel in their chosen fields, that they might become leaders among men all over this great nation and wield an influence for good that will help to preserve our God-inspired Constitution and our American way of life that has given us more of the good things of life than any other system in operation in the world today, the highest standard of living. Yes, we want them to succeed. (Seattle Washington LDS Institute Dedication, 29 October 1961.)

While the world may not live our standards, I know that the world is willing to pay for the services of young men who do. As one who has sat on the boards of big corporations, some of them international in character, I know the kind of men they are looking for for leadership. They are looking for young men who, if married, are good family men, and who, if unmarried, are keeping themselves clean and not chasing cheap and lewd women around, but looking for the time when they can establish homes of their own. (BYU Ten-Stake Fireside, Provo, Utah, 7 May 1972.)

I believe that we should all strive to be as self-reliant as possible —that we should help each other when this becomes necessary. I believe that we will individually and collectively achieve our greatest potential through personal effort and achievement. The sum total of the success of each of us has and will continue to make this country great. (*The Red Carpet,* p. 127.)

Remember this: there is no one great thing that you can do which will determine your happiness or success in life. Life is a series of little things—how you do your work from day to day, personal honesty in your everyday contacts, a smile and a handshake, courtesy and kindness—these are the "little things" that become the sum of your character. (4-H Club Show, Modesto, California, 10 May 1980.)

We need more men and women of Christ who will always remember Him, who will keep His commandments which He has given them. The greatest yardstick of success is to see how closely you can walk each moment in His steps. ("In His Steps," Church Educational System Devotional, Anaheim, California, 8 February 1987.)

The Lord wants us to be successful. Oh, I know He doesn't worry too much about material things. All material things are but a means to an end. The end is spiritual, yet if we'll read the revelations, we will discover that many of them have to do with material things.

I am sure the Lord wants each young man and woman of His Church to excel in his or her chosen field, whatever it may be, whether it be in the home, in business, in professions, in teaching, medicine, dentistry, government, or agriculture. I am sure it is pleasing to the Lord to see His sons and daughters who have taken upon themselves the covenants of membership in His Church—and particularly young men who bear the priesthood—to be more than just average. He wants them to succeed, to be outstanding. He will open the way before them if they will just live worthy of it.

By that I don't mean that all a person has to do is go to church in order to succeed in his chosen field, but I do mean that if we put forth an effort equal to our associates outside the Church, and live the gospel at the same time, the Lord will bless us with added success. If we keep the Sabbath day holy and devote ourselves to spiritual things, in the long run I am convinced the Lord will add His blessings. He will bless us with hidden treasures of knowledge, as the Word of Wisdom so clearly indicates. He will give us the power to tap that unseen source of knowledge and strength that is beyond the knowledge of the men of the world. He will make us pillars of strength and power among our associates.

The world is seeking for the services of young men and women who are trained according to Mormon standards, who have the technical training, plus that training in character, in spirituality, and in faith, that gives them confidence, assurance, a feeling of security, and makes them a safe risk for the employer. (*God, Family, Country,* pp. 193–94.)

The honors of men, more often than not, are fleeting. Anxious to run after the honors of office or succumb to the pressures of public glamour and worldly acclaim, some of us are no longer willing to stand up for all the principles of the gospel. We seek to justify our unrighteousness by claiming that if only we can get title or position, think of the good we can do. Hence we lose our salvation en route to those honors. We sometimes look among our numbers to find one to whom we can point who agrees with us, so we can have company to justify our apostasy. We rationalize by saying that some day the Church doctrine will catch up with our way of thinking. (*An Enemy Hath Done This*, p. 282.)

To you young men—we hope you will be successful in your chosen fields, whatever they might be, so long as they are honorable. Live so you can reach out and tap that unseen power without which no man can do his best. Do not be afraid to go out in the world. Sink your roots down. Become part of the community life, and wield an influence for good. Remain true to the faith. Live the standards of the Church. You have everything to gain and nothing to lose by so doing. (BYU Ten-Stake Fireside, Provo, Utah, 7 May 1972.)

Personal revelation, consecration of performance, attention to detail, and dependency on God—with these qualities you cannot fail; without them you may not succeed. (Salt Lake City, Utah, October 1961.)

Don't ever apologize for the standards of the kingdom of God. They are divine. They are true. They will build men and women. They will bless them with success. ("What We Desire for Our Youth," MIA Conference, Salt Lake City, Utah, 16 June 1963.)

We hope you will be happy. There is no happiness in wickedness. We hope you will be successful. The Lord wants you to be successful. You bear His priesthood. We hope you will be true to the best within you to be good men, honorable citizens, and respected home and nation builders. We hope you will keep yourself morally worthy in every respect so that you may be called on for leadership and service. We hope you marry well, live together in love, rear a family in righteousness, and know that joy which comes from a righteous posterity. We hope you will be better than the generations which preceded you. I have confidence that you will. ("On My Honor," Explorer Presidents Conference, Ogden, Utah, 4 March 1978.)

May God bless us to be grateful, even in times of trouble and reverses. We all have our reverses: "Whom the Lord loveth, he chasteneth" (Hebrews 12:6). It is in the depths where men and women learn the lessons which help them gain strength—not at the pinnacle of success. The hour of man's success is his greatest danger. It sometimes takes reverses to make us appreciate our blessings and to develop us into strong, courageous characters. We can meet every reverse that can possibly come with the help of the Lord. The Lord taught the Prophet Joseph Smith that every reverse can be turned to our benefit and blessing and can make us stronger, more courageous, more godlike (see D&C 122). ("Strengthen Your Families," Preston Idaho North Stake, 10 June 1984.)

God loves us. He is watching us. He wants us to succeed. We will know someday that He has not left one thing undone for the eternal welfare of each of us. If we only knew it, heavenly hosts are pulling for us—friends in heaven we cannot now remember, who yearn for our victory. This is our day to show what we can do— what life and sacrifice we can daily, hourly, instantly, make for God. If we give our all, we will get His all from the greatest of all. ("Jesus Christ—Gifts and Expectations," Christmas Devotional, Salt Lake City, Utah, 7 December 1986.)

Testimony and Conversion

A most priceless blessing available to every member of the Church is a testimony of the divinity of Jesus Christ and His Church. A testimony is one of the few possessions we may take with us when we leave this life. (*Come unto Christ*, p. 11.)

To have a testimony of Jesus is to possess knowledge through the Holy Ghost of the divine mission of Jesus Christ. A testimony of Jesus is to know the divine nature of our Lord's birth—that He is indeed the Only Begotten Son in the flesh.

A testimony of Jesus is to know that He was the promised Messiah and that while He sojourned among men He accomplished many mighty miracles. A testimony of Jesus is to know that the laws which He prescribed as His doctrine are true and then to abide by these laws and ordinances. To possess a testimony of Jesus is to know that He voluntarily took upon Himself the sins of all mankind in the Garden of Gethsemane, which caused Him to suffer in both body and spirit and to bleed from every pore. All this He did so that we would not have to suffer if we would repent. (See D&C 19:16, 18.)

To possess a testimony of Jesus is to know that He came forth triumphantly from the grave with a physical, resurrected body. And because He lives, so shall all mankind. To possess a testimony of Jesus is to know that God the Father and Jesus Christ did indeed appear to the Prophet Joseph Smith to establish a new dispensation of His gospel so that salvation may be preached to all nations before He comes. To possess a testimony of Jesus is to know that the Church, which He established in the meridian of time and restored in modern times is, as the Lord has declared, "the only true and living church upon the face of the whole earth" (D&C 1:30). Having such a testimony is vital. ("Valiant in the Testimony of Jesus," *Ensign* 17 [February 1987]: 2.)

Today in Christ's restored Church, The Church of Jesus Christ of Latter-day Saints, He is revealing Himself and His will—from the first prophet of the Restoration, even Joseph Smith, to the present. "And now," said the Prophet Joseph, "after the many testimonies which have been given of him, this is the testimony, last of all, which we give of him: That he lives! For we saw him, even on the right hand of God; and we heard the voice bearing record that he is the Only Begotten of the Father." (D&C 76:22–23.) ("Joy in Christ," *Ensign* 16 [March 1986]: 4.)

Any true Latter-day Saint parents would rather have a son or daughter of theirs grow up with a firm testimony of the divinity of this work, and be active in and devoted to the Church, than anything else in the world. The wealth of the world, the honors of men, are as nothing compared with a testimony of the divinity of this work and a love for God and His holy priesthood. I know that to be true, and I am sure that my words echo in your hearts today. (*So Shall Ye Reap,* p. 35.)

Missionaries are in the field to testify of the greatest event which has transpired in this world since the resurrection of the

Master—the coming of God the Father and His Son Jesus Christ to the boy prophet. You are sent out to testify of a new volume of scripture—a new witness for Christ. May God bless you to testify effectively, to bear a strong testimony to the truthfulness of this glorious message. No one can compete against a strong testimony. (Texas San Antonio Mission, 2 March 1986.)

Our missionaries go out into the world to proclaim that there has been an apostasy from the truth, but that through the goodness of God the heavens have again been opened and the gospel revealed unto man through Joseph Smith, the Prophet. I am grateful for this knowledge. To me it is the most precious thing in all the world. I would to God that all within the sound of my voice, and all God's children everywhere, could know of the sweetness of the gospel and what it means to hold the priesthood and to feel the fellowship and brotherhood which we have in the Church—yes, to know of the security that comes to the heart of man as a testimony of the truth is borne in upon his soul. (*So Shall Ye Reap,* pp. 52–53.)

Not to be valiant in one's testimony is a tragedy of eternal consequences. There are members who know this latter-day work is true, but who fail to endure to the end. One who rationalizes that he or she has a testimony of Jesus Christ but cannot accept direction and counsel from the leadership of His Church is in a fundamentally unsound position and is in jeopardy of losing exaltation. ("Valiant in the Testimony of Jesus," *Ensign* 17 [February 1987]: 2.)

You can't live the full life without that anchor which comes from a testimony. Oh, it is glorious to have a testimony of the truth! I have seen so much evidence of the strength of testimony under the most adverse economic and social conditions, that I have reached this conclusion in my own mind: that a man and woman can endure anything and keep their spirits sweet and wholesome, provided they have a testimony of the divinity of this work. And so, if you are going to live a full, purposeful, and joyful life, you must have a testimony of the truth and the divinity of this work. You must seek for it, pray for it, live for it. Assuredly it will come, because the God of Heaven wants every one of His children to know that He lives, that Jesus is the Christ, and that Joseph Smith is a prophet. You may each know that as you live for it. (*So Shall Ye Reap,* p. 183.)

Not only was Jesus born in a humble setting in Bethlehem and crucified on a cross on Golgotha, but on the third day He arose from the grave. Today He lives! Of that I personally testify. I know it. He is close to His Church and to His servants. The knowledge that He lives is the most priceless knowledge in the world.

Our belief in Jesus Christ does not stem from historical tradition alone, although we fully accept the historical records of both the Old and New Worlds that constitute witnesses of His divinity. Our belief in Jesus Christ stems also from His direct visitation, in company with our Heavenly Father, to the boy-prophet Joseph Smith. ("After All We Can Do," Christmas Devotional, Salt Lake City, Utah, 9 December 1982.)

Thank God for faith, for testimony. Thank God for the Church of Jesus Christ. It has not left us — it will never leave us. Thank God for the eternal truths of the gospel of peace and salvation. Thank God for the anchor, the feeling of security, the inner calm that the everlasting truths of the gospel bring to every faithful child of God. (*God, Family, Country*, p. 12.)

I do not believe that a member of the Church can have an active, vibrant testimony of the gospel without keeping the commandments. A testimony is to have current inspiration to know the work is true, not something we receive only once. The Holy Ghost abides with those who honor, respect, and obey God's laws. And it is that Spirit which gives inspiration to the individual. (CR April 1983, *Ensign* 13 [May 1983]: 53.)

Those who are not members of the Church, may I ask you to study these principles and on bended knees to ask God the Eternal Father if they are not true. If you will do this with a sincere heart, with real faith in Christ, He will manifest the truth of it unto you by His Holy Spirit (see Moroni 10:4). This I testify to you in the name of Jesus Christ. ("The Church," Paris, France, 7 August 1960.)

I know that God is a personal being, the Father of our spirits, and that He loves His children and hears and answers their righteous prayers. I know that it is His will that His children be happy. It is His desire to bless us all. I know that Jesus Christ is the Son of God, our Elder Brother, the very Creator and Redeemer of the world. I know that God has again established His kingdom on the earth in fulfillment of prophecy and that it will never be overcome, but it shall ultimately hold universal dominion in the earth and Jesus Christ shall reign as its King forever.

I know that God in His goodness has again revealed Himself from the heavens and that Joseph Smith was called of God to reestablish that kingdom—The Church of Jesus Christ of Latter-day Saints. I testify that he accomplished this work, that he laid the foundations, and that he committed to the Church the keys and powers to continue the great latter-day work, which he began under the direction of Almighty God.

I know that Joseph Smith, although slain as a martyr to the truth, still lives, and that, as head of his dispensation—the greatest of all gospel dispensations—he will continue so to stand throughout the eternities to come. He is a prophet of God, a seer and a revelator, as are his successors. I know that the inspiration of the Lord is directing the Church today because I have felt of its power. I know that the First Presidency and other General Authorities of the Church have as their object and purpose the glory of God and the exaltation of His children. And finally, I know that no person who does not receive this work can be saved in the celestial kingdom of God and escape the condemnation of the Judge of us all. (*This Nation Shall Endure*, pp. 112–13.)

The personal conversion of every man, woman, and child must be our sovereign purpose. We must see that our people are properly and effectively instructed in the fundamental doctrines of the gospel of Jesus Christ. It is vital that sacrament meetings be occasions when the gospel is taught by testimony. Too frequently they are not. Our primary responsibility is to be special witnesses of Him whom we represent. In all our assignments we must be certain to bear testimony of Jesus Christ and this grand and glorious work. When difficulties and calamities befall the Saints, this need will be even greater. (Salt Lake City, Utah, 6 June 1980.)

You have heard me tell of my father who went to the mission field, and left Mother and seven children at home. That sacrifice brought into our home a spirit of love of missionary work that never left it, and a willingness to put the Lord first in our lives.

It was a custom in those days for missionaries to stay in the homes of the Saints as they labored in a city. When Father and his companion moved to a new city, they stayed at a home where elders had lived before. During their stay, Father found, to his surprise, that the family where they were staying had not joined the Church. Father asked the head of the home, "How long have you known the missionaries?" "Ten years," was the reply.

"Ten years! Why, you have an obligation! You have heard the truth for ten years and you are not in the Church? Have you prayed about it? Have you read the Book of Mormon?" "Yes, but only part of it." They taught the family the gospel. Father was called on to pray and he prayed for each member of that family. All joined the Church. (Salt Lake City, Utah, 2 October 1985.)

When King Benjamin finished his remarkable address in the land of Zarahemla, the people all cried with one voice that they believed his words. They knew of a surety that his promises of redemption were true, because, said they, "the Spirit of the Lord Omnipotent . . . has wrought a mighty change in us, or in our hearts, [and note this] that we have no more disposition to do evil, but to do good continually" (Mosiah 5:2).

When we have undergone this mighty change, which is brought about only through faith in Jesus Christ and through the operation of the Spirit upon us, it is as though we have become a new person. Thus the change is likened to a new birth. Thousands of you within the sound of my voice have experienced this change. You have forsaken lives of sin, sometimes deep and offensive sin, and through applying the blood of Christ in your lives, have become clean. You have no more disposition to return to your old ways. You are in reality a new person. This is what is meant by a change of heart. ("A Mighty Change of Heart," address prepared [but not delivered] 1986.)

Tithes and Offerings

Tithes and offerings are the Lord's way to finance His kingdom. He expects us to follow that program. His promise to open the windows of heaven is contingent on following His counsel. "Will a man rob God? Yet ye have robbed me. But ye say, Wherein have we robbed thee? In tithes and offerings." (3 Nephi 24:8–12; Malachi 3:8–12.) In this statement we see that God may be robbed in both tithes and offerings. (Salt Lake City, Utah, 6 May 1981.)

Tithing is not a donation. It is not optional for members. It is a commandment from God, with great blessings and promises given to those who obey.

Hear the words of the Lord:

> Bring ye all the tithes into the storehouse, that there may be meat in mine house, and prove me now herewith, saith the Lord of hosts, if I will not open you the windows of heaven, and pour you out a blessing, that there shall not be room enough to receive it.
>
> And I will rebuke the devourer for your sakes, and he shall not destroy the fruits of your ground; neither shall your vine cast her fruit before the time in the field, saith the Lord of hosts.
>
> And all nations shall call you blessed: for ye shall be a delightsome land, saith the Lord of hosts. (Malachi 3:10–12; 3 Nephi 24:10–12.)

The Lord's promises to those who faithfully comply with this commandment are that spiritual and temporal blessings will be poured out on them; bounteous harvest (that is, hunger will not stalk the door of that home); and a blessing to an entire nation. (El Paso Texas Regional Conference, 25 January 1986.)

Father and Mother taught their family complete devotion to the Church and full integrity in the payment of their tithes and offerings. On one occasion when I was a teenager, I overheard Father and Mother talking about their finances in preparation for tithing settlement the following day. Father had a note for twenty-five dollars at the bank, which was due during the week. In figuring their tithing, he owed twenty-five dollars more. He also had a hay derrick, which he had built. He got the timbers out of the canyon and was trying to sell it, but had met with no success.

What were they to do—clear the note at the bank, pay their tithing later, or pay their tithing and hope that they could meet the note when it was due in just a few days? After discussing the matter, and I am sure praying together before they retired, Father decided next day to go to tithing settlement and pay the twenty-five dollars, which would make him a full-tithe payer. As he rode home by horseback, one of his neighbors stopped him and said, "George, I understand you have a derrick for sale. How much are you asking for it?"

Father said, "Twenty-five dollars." The neighbor said, "I haven't seen it, but knowing the way you build, I am sure it is worth twenty-five dollars. Just a minute and I will go in the house and make out a check for it. I need it." This is a lesson that I have not forgotten. (Regional Representatives Seminar, Salt Lake City, Utah, 2 April 1982.)

There are those whose names are on the records of the Church who have forgotten Malachi's question and answer: "Will a man rob God? . . . But ye say, Wherein have we robbed thee? In tithes and offerings." (Malachi 3:8.) Some may protest: "But we cannot afford to tithe." To them, perhaps the gentle but forceful reminder from President Spencer W. Kimball is needed: "What? Cannot afford integrity? Cannot afford to return to the Great Provider's program that which was already His? . . . God promised He would open heaven's windows and pour you out rich gifts beyond your comprehension, premised on your faithfulness. Do you not need those blessings? For that one-tenth, He will compensate with blessings little dreamed of." (*Faith Precedes the Miracle,* p. 288.)

Some may be inclined to feel generous when they pay a full tithing. Again President Kimball asks: "Do you feel generous when you pay your tithes? Boastful when the amount is large? Has the child been generous to his parents when he washes his car, makes the bed? Are you liberal when you pay your rent, or pay off notes at the bank? You are not generous or liberal but merely honest when you pay your tithes." (*Faith Precedes the Miracle,* p. 289.) (Logan, Utah, 6 December 1975.)

One is blessed temporally for obedience to the law of tithing. But the greatest blessings of the Lord are, after all, spiritual in nature. Perhaps that is the deeper meaning to the expression, "I will open you the windows of heaven and pour you out a blessing, that there shall not be room enough to receive it" (Malachi 3:10). The late Elder Melvin J. Ballard, an Apostle, said that "the Lord has promised that the man and woman who pay their honest tithing shall be provided for, [but] He doesn't promise to make them rich, not in material things. The greatest blessings of the Lord are spiritual, and not material." (*Crusader for Righteousness*, p. 124.) (Logan, Utah, 6 December 1975.)

When the Church was faced with financial bondage during the administration of President Lorenzo Snow, the Lord reaffirmed by revelation this counsel to the Saints: "The word of the Lord is: The time has now come for every Latter-day Saint, who calculates to be prepared for the future and to hold his feet strong upon a proper foundation, to do the will of the Lord and to pay his tithing in full. That is the word of the Lord to every settlement throughout the land of Zion." (In LeRoi C. Snow, "The Lord's Way Out of Bondage," *Improvement Era* 41 [July 1938]: 439.)

That admonition is just as true today—if not more so—than when it was given. And it needs to be emphasized and reemphasized. If the Latter-day Saints want to be prepared for the future and to hold their feet on a proper foundation, they must be full-tithe payers. (Logan, Utah, 6 December 1975.)

We will depend on tithing more than ever to finance the programs of the Church. That will be possible only as all our leaders and more of our membership are full-tithe payers. (Regional Representatives Seminar, Salt Lake City, Utah, 2 April 1982.)

Where would we be if every member of the Church understood the principle of tithing, believed and practiced it? Imagine the power that would come into the lives of individual members, not to mention fulfillment of the scriptural promise that the heavens would be opened and all of our stakes and homes would be blessed beyond our expectations. (Regional Representatives Seminar, Salt Lake City, Utah, 2 April 1982.)

A word about fast offerings. There are inquiries from time to time regarding the amount of the fast offering contribution. The Brethren have counseled that the fast offering should be a generous contribution, and as a minimum should be the "equivalent of the value of two meals" (*General Handbook of Instructions*, No. 21, 1976). (Logan, Utah, 6 December 1975.)

Let us pay first our obligations to our Heavenly Father. Then we will more easily pay our debts to our fellowmen. (*So Shall Ye Reap,* p. 219.)

Wealth

One of the first principles revealed to father Adam when he was driven out of the Garden of Eden was this: "In the sweat of thy face shalt thou eat bread, till thou return unto the ground" (Genesis 3:19). All we obtain in life of a material nature comes as a product of labor and the providence of God. Work produces life's necessities. (CR October 1980, *Ensign* 10 [November 1980]: 32.)

Your chance of material success in your chosen field will be increased by maintaining every standard of decency and righteousness. The experience of the race proclaims the blessings which follow righteous living. Try it and see. Jesus said, "If any man will do his will, he shall know of the doctrine, whether it be of God, or whether I speak of myself" (John 7:17). The moral order exists and is just as exacting as the physical order. The blessings received in each realm come through obedience to the respective laws. ("Concerning Values," Utah State University Baccalaureate, Logan, Utah, 28 May 1950.)

We must come to the realization that it is people—not things —that are all-important. Material things may contribute much to our comforts, our opportunities, our safety. Qualities which make for sterling character and true leadership, however, can be and have been developed in all ages regardless of the physical things with which men have been surrounded. (*So Shall Ye Reap,* p. 158.)

There are blessings in being close to the soil, in raising your own food, even if it is only a garden in your yard and a fruit tree or two. Man's material wealth basically springs from the land and other natural resources. Combined with his human energy and multiplied by his tools, this wealth is assured and expanded through freedom and righteousness. Those families will be fortunate who, in the last days, have an adequate supply of each of these particulars. (*God, Family, Country,* p. 269.)

If you are thinking only of getting ahead in this world financially, it pays to maintain the standards of the Church. I could tell you of experience after experience in my own life—in my own observations. If you want to be successful, it will help you to maintain the standards of the Church and you will never be embarrassed by men and women of real character because of your standards. You will be praised, you will be honored, you will be esteemed because you have had the courage and the good common sense to be true to your ideals and standards. ("Strengthen Your Families," Preston Idaho North Stake, 10 June 1984.)

Our affections are often too highly placed upon the paltry, perishable objects. Material treasures of earth are merely to provide us, as it were, room and board while we are here at school. It is for us to place gold, silver, houses, stocks, lands, cattle, and other earthly possessions in their proper places. Yes, this is but a place of temporary duration. We are here to learn the first lesson toward exaltation—obedience to the Lord's gospel plan. (*God, Family, Country,* p. 21.)

More and more the world is coming to recognize the great achievements of The Church of Jesus Christ of Latter-day Saints —the fact that we have a program that works, that it not only brings joy and happiness spiritually but that it also brings material comfort and safeguards which provide for all of the needful things of life. (Welfare Session, General Conference, 5 April 1958.)

Freedom, a willingness to work, and the desire to serve your God through service to your fellowmen—these are the sources of true wealth. Cling fast to these truths, and you must inevitably increase in favor with man. (*So Shall Ye Reap,* p. 175.)

Word of Wisdom

The condition of the physical body can affect the spirit. That is why the Lord gave us the Word of Wisdom. He also said that we should retire to our beds early and arise early (see D&C 88:124), that we should not run faster than we have strength (see D&C 10:4; Mosiah 4:27), and that we should use moderation in all good things. In general, the more food we eat in its natural state and the less it is refined without additives, the healthier it will be for us. Food can affect the mind, and deficiencies in certain elements in the body can promote mental depression. A good physical examination periodically is a safeguard and may spot problems that can be remedied. Rest and physical exercise are essential, and a walk in the fresh air can refresh the spirit. (CR October 1974, *Ensign* 4 [November 1974]: 66.)

We can be grateful for the Word of Wisdom. Healthful foods, proper rest, adequate exercise, and a clear conscience can prepare us to tackle the trials that lie ahead. (*God, Family, Country,* pp. 269–70.)

The Word of Wisdom leads to clean habits, thoughts, and actions. It will make you more receptive to the Spirit of God which cannot dwell in an unclean tabernacle (see Helaman 4:24). Follow the gospel plan. It provides for solid work, clean entertainment, and activity to promote growth of stature. (*So Shall Ye Reap,* p. 172.)

In the Word of Wisdom are announced the eternal, basic principles which never change, and we must always remember that time is on the side of truth and the Word of Wisdom is the truth. ("Our Obligation as Leaders of Youth," MIA Conference, Salt Lake City, Utah, 14 June 1959.)

To a great extent we are physically what we eat. Most of us are acquainted with some of the prohibitions, such as no tea, coffee, tobacco, or alcohol. What needs additional emphasis are the positive aspects—the need for vegetables, fruits, and grains, particularly wheat. In most cases, the closer these can be, when eaten, to their natural state—without overrefinement and processing—the healthier we will be. To a significant degree, we are an overfed and undernourished nation digging an early grave with our teeth, and lacking the energy that could be ours because we overindulge in junk foods. I am grateful to know that on the Brigham Young University campus you can get apples from vending machines, that you have in your student center a fine salad bar, and that you produce an excellent loaf of natural whole-grain bread. Keep it up and keep progressing in that direction. We need a generation of young people who, as Daniel, eat in a more healthy manner than to fare on the "king's meat"—and whose countenances show it (see Daniel 1). ("In His Steps," in *1979 Devotional Speeches of the Year* [Provo, Utah: BYU, 1980], p. 62.)

As a nation we need the refining and sustaining influences which come from obedience to divine law. Without such blessings the future of the nation is insecure. How can we expect divine acceptance when as a nation we are drunken through the staggeringly increased uses of intoxicating liquors, narcotics and tobacco. The human body is the tabernacle of the spirit and God expects that it be kept clean and unimpaired. The increase in these vices weakens the moral fiber of our nation and brings disappointment and sadness followed by greater sins. ("America—What of the Future?" Radio Address—WRVA, Richmond, Virginia, 8 October 1950.)

There is real danger we may let down our guard, as it were; that we may be tempted to join with the world and adopt some of their standards against which we have been warned by the Lord. Only recently there came to my attention the fact that a group of young wives (some of whose husbands are employed in the government of the United States, men who had attained a certain amount of prominence in their respective fields) had more or less concluded that in order to be accepted by the world, in order that their husbands might get ahead in the world, they would have to let down just a little in their standards. They had concluded they would have to serve cocktails and coffee in their homes when friends came. I want to testify to you, and particularly to the young married couples of this Church, that such a conclusion is not only unwise and unjustified, but it is also dangerous and can lead only to heartache and disappointment and a loss of faith. (CR October 1955, *Improvement Era* 58 [December 1955]: 952.)

In relation to our law of health, some complain about the Word of Wisdom as though it is some policy or merely a rule of conduct imposed on us by the Church authorities, and as a rule, it may be changed by Church authorities. I recall the answer given by President J. Reuben Clark, Jr.:

The word of wisdom is not a rule of conduct; it is a law—the Lord's law—of health. It was promulgated by Him. The law existed before He told it to us; it would exist if the revelation were blotted out from the book. The Church authorities have nothing to do with the law. God, speaking through the forces of the physical world, has prescribed it, and so long as those forces exist the law will remain.

It is therefore the foolish ignorance of a child to assume that the First Presidency can issue a rule that will permit the use of any of these injurious things without their harmful effects. It would be an easy and, in one sense, a pleasing gesture, as satisfying Church members who wish to use these harmful substances, to declare the Word of Wisdom no longer existent. But such a declaration would be no more efficacious than a declaration that the law of gravitation no longer operates. (*Improvement Era* 36 [November 1933]: 806.)

There are some who feel that the Word of Wisdom is only a code of health, and a social drink or two, or serving drinks or permitting smoking in their homes is not a violation of the commandment since it does no physical harm. The words of President Stephen L Richards give effective rebuttal to this rationalization: "The Word of Wisdom is spiritual. It is true that it prohibits the use of deleterious substances and makes provision for the health of the body. But the largest measure of good derived from its observance is in increased faith and the development of more spiritual power and wisdom. Likewise, the most regrettable and damaging effects of its infractions are spiritual, also. Injury to the body may be comparatively trivial to the damage to the soul in the destruction of faith and the retardation of spiritual growth." (CR April 1949, p. 141.) One is reminded of President George Albert Smith's counsel—"Don't step over in the devil's territory." That counsel is as appropriate today as when it was given. (Cardston, Alberta, Canada, 2 August 1975.)

The Lord foresaw the situation of today when motives for money would cause men to conspire to entice others to take noxious substances into their bodies. Advertisements which promote beer, wine, liquors, coffee, tobacco, and other harmful substances are examples of what the Lord foresaw. But the most pernicious example of an evil conspiracy in our time is those who induce young people into the use of drugs.

In all love, we give you warning that Satan and his emissaries will strive to entice you to use harmful substances, because they well know if you partake, your spiritual powers will be inhibited and you will be in their evil power. Stay away from those places or people which would influence you to break the commandments of God. Keep the commandments of God and you will have the wisdom to know and discern that which is evil. (CR April 1983, *Ensign* 13 [May 1983]: 54–55.)

Physical Well-Being

Our common purpose is to help our young men and women fit themselves for the responsibilities of the future. Physical well-being is not only a priceless asset to oneself—it is a heritage to be passed on. With good health, all other activities of life are greatly enhanced. A clean mind in a healthy body enables one to render far more effective service to others. It helps one provide more vigorous leadership. It gives our every experience in life more zest and more meaning. Robust health is a noble and worthwhile attainment. (*God, Family, Country,* p. 217.)

Take care of yourselves physically. Guard your health carefully. It is one of our greatest blessings. I especially encourage some type of exercise program so you can stay physically fit and physically capable in proportion to the demands on your body. (Salt Lake City, Utah, 2 June 1982.)

The body needs the rejuvenation that comes from exercise. Walking in the fresh air can be exhilarating and refreshing. Properly directed, running can have some beneficial effects. Simple situps or sporting activity can be helpful. ("In His Steps," Church Educational System Devotional, Anaheim, California, 8 February 1987.)

Have a good physical outlet of some sport or exercise. Overcome evil with good. You can overcome many evil inclinations through good physical exertion and healthful activities. A healthy soul, free of the body- and spirit-dulling influences of alcohol and tobacco, is in better condition to overthrow the devil. (CR October 1964, *Improvement Era* 67 [December 1964]: 1069.)

There is a tendency to think of fitness solely in terms of the physical, in terms of bodily strength. It involves the mind and the training of the mind, the emotions and their use and control — yes, and it involves the soul and spiritual growth, too. (*God, Family, Country,* p. 218.)

Sin debilitates. It affects not only the soul but the body. The scriptures are replete with examples of the physical power that can attend the righteous. On the other hand, unrepented sin can diffuse energy and lead to both mental and physical sickness. Jesus healed a man of physical malady and then told him to "sin no more, lest a worse thing come unto thee" (John 5:14). Galahad said that his strength was as the strength of ten because his heart was pure. ("In His Steps," Church Educational System Devotional, Anaheim, California, 8 February 1987.)

To meet and beat the enemy will take clear heads and strong bodies. Hearts and hands grow strong based on what they are fed. Let us take into our bodies or souls only those things that would make us more effective instruments. We need all the physical, mental, and moral power we can get. Righteous concern about conditions is commendable when it leads to constructive action. But undue worry is debilitating. When we have done what we can, then let us leave the rest to God — including the worrying.

Man needs beneficial recreation, a change of pace that refreshes him for heavy tasks ahead. Man also must take time to meditate, to sweep the cobwebs from his mind so that he might get a more firm grip on the truth and spend less time chasing phantoms and dallying in projects of lesser worth.

Clean hearts and healthful food, exercise, early sleep and fresh air, wholesome recreation, and meditation, combined with optimism that comes from fighting for the right and knowing you will eventually win for keeps — this is the tonic every patriot needs and deserves. (*An Enemy Hath Done This,* p. 59.)

We have a duty to survive, not only spiritually but also physically. Not survival at the cost of principles, for this is the surest way to defeat, but a survival that comes from intelligent preparation. We face days ahead that will test the moral and physical sinews of all of us. (*God, Family, Country,* p. 331.)

Work

Energetic, purposeful work leads to vigorous health, praiseworthy achievement, a clear conscience, and refreshing sleep. Work has always been a boon to man. May you have a wholesome respect for labor whether with head, heart, or hand. May you ever enjoy the satisfaction of honest toil. The decree that "in the sweat of thy face shalt thou eat bread" (Genesis 3:19) is still basic. You will never wish or dream yourself into heaven. You must pay the price in toil, in sacrifice, and righteous living. ("Your Charge: To Increase in Wisdom and Favor with God and Man," *New Era* 9 [September 1979]: 44.)

"Six days shalt thou labour, and do all thy work" (Exodus 20:9). We are becoming an idle people. We more and more expect to live with little or no work. It takes so many man-hours to raise the necessary foods to sustain a man's life and to provide the other necessities of clothing, shelter, and fuel. ("The Ten Commandments," *New Era* 8 [July 1978]: 37.)

Man is commanded by God to live by the sweat of his own brow, not someone else's. In his first inaugural address, Thomas Jefferson counseled us toward a wise and frugal government, one that "shall not take from the mouth of labor the bread it had earned." (*This Nation Shall Endure*, p. 45.)

Every man should provide the necessities of food, clothing, and shelter for his family. As Paul wrote to Timothy: "But if any provide not for his own, and specially for those of his own house, he hath denied the faith, and is worse than an infidel" (1 Timothy 5:8).

Indolence invites the benevolent straightjacket of the character-destroying welfare state. But a man pays too high a price for worldly success if in his climb to prominence he sacrifices his spiritual, home, and civic responsibilities. How a person should apportion his time among his several duties requires good judgment and is a matter over which each should invite divine assistance. (CR April 1967, *Improvement Era* 70 [June 1967]: 58.)

Remember, it is the individual who is of supreme worth. His morals and character must be safeguarded if America is to continue as a great nation. You cannot build character and courage by taking away man's initiative and independence. It is a basic principle that you cannot help a man permanently by doing for him what he could do and should do for himself. Dependence upon the state for sustenance means the eventual surrender of political freedom. Therefore, shrink not from your duty in these important matters as your responsibility as an American is made clear to you. Accept responsibility. Be grateful for work. Hesitate not to do your full share of it. (*So Shall Ye Reap,* p. 153.)

Every young person requires the spur of economic insecurity to force him to do his best. We must have the courage to stand against undue governmental paternalism and the cowardly cry that "the world owes me a living." Nobody owes us anything for goods we do not produce, or work we do not do! ("Liberty Against Creeping Socialism," Brigham Young University, Provo, Utah, 26 August 1961.)

Today we are witnessing a trend in all countries — a trend away from the work ethic to the welfare ethic. To put it another way, you young people, no doubt, have heard some express that it is their right to be supported by another man's labors. That philosophy is wrong. It has proved the ruination of character in individuals, and the downfall of nations. (4-H Club Show, Modesto, California, 10 May 1980.)

Faith, courage, and freedom represent the life elements of growth—either in man or a nation. Spiritual faith and courage were the bone and sinew of the first freedom our people enjoyed on this continent. Then, as free, hard-working Americans, our growth to abundance was only a matter of time. It is most significant that during this uphill struggle by Americans to create a civilization with an abundance for all, they gave no thought to the word *ease* as it might apply to their own way of life. People who are imbued with a strong spiritual faith which, in turn, endows them with the courage to fight and win their battles for freedom and abundance, would view with contempt any person seeking an easy way through life. (*An Enemy Hath Done This*, p. 118.)

It seems highly significant that our forefathers gloried in hard work while drawing liberally upon their prodigious spiritual reserves. They were not content to place their trust "in the arm of flesh" alone (see 2 Nephi 4:34). They sought to rely upon their cherished independence, their frugality and honest toil, nurtured and fortified by a kind Providence to whose service they were dedicated. History records that even the climate was tempered for their sakes and their humble untiring efforts made "the desert to blossom as the rose" (see Isaiah 35:1).

Today we need to rededicate and reconsecrate our lives. Unless the efforts of our hearts and hands are blessed by the God of this land, in vain do they labor who attempt to achieve sound and lasting prosperity and freedom. (*The Red Carpet,* p. 287.)

Studies affirm the fact that while prospective employers look for and expect technical skills, their primary consideration is, "How does he get along with people?" Perhaps it is also well to realize that 80 percent of the people who lose their jobs, lose them not from lack of ability to do the job, but from lack of ability to get along with coworkers, bosses, and customers. These facts point out the significant impact that growing in favor with man has upon our ultimate success. I used to have on my desk a catchy slogan that read, "People do not care how much we know, if they do not know how much we care." ("Your Charge: To Increase in Wisdom and Favor with God and Man," *New Era* 9 [September 1979]: 43.)

"Show me a man who cannot do the little things well and I will show you a man who cannot perform great things well." Great things are but the composite of little things done well. This means day by day attention to little things — to details and relationships. (Salt Lake City, Utah, October 1961.)

If we want to keep the Spirit, we must work. There is no greater exhilaration or satisfaction than to know, after a hard day of work, that we have done our best. (*Come unto Christ*, p. 96.)

Ours is a gospel of work—purposeful, unselfish and rendered in the spirit of the true love of Christ. Only thus may we grow in godly attributes. Only thus may we become worthy instruments in the hands of the Lord for blessing others through that power which can lead to changing the lives of men and women for the better.

We should be humbly grateful for this challenge, this heritage, this opportunity for service and its abundant rewards. How fortunate are those who may follow the Lord's plan to develop this power and use it for the blessing of others. That is what the Christ did. That is what we are privileged to do. ("Power Through Service," *Millennial Star* 118 [9 October 1956]: 299.)

The earth was cursed for Adam's sake (see Genesis 3:17). Work is our blessing, not our doom. God has a work to do, and so should we (Moses 1:39). Retirement from work has depressed many a man and hastened his death. It has been said that even the very fiends weave ropes of sand rather than to face the pure hell of idleness. We should work at taking care of the spiritual, mental, social, and physical needs of ourselves and those whom we are charged to help. In the Church of Jesus Christ there is plenty of work to do to move forward the kingdom of God. Every member a missionary, family genealogy and temple work, home evenings, receiving a Church assignment and magnifying it are but a few of our required labors. (CR October 1974, *Ensign* 4 [November 1974]: 66.)

Brethren, it is your role to be the leader in the home. While the wife may be considered the heart of the home, you are the head. You are the provider. What will you choose for a career? What will your work be? It has been said that no one is born into this world whose work is not born with him or her. We bring from our premortal state various talents and abilities. We strive to find the right wife, and it is our responsibility to strive to find where we can make a contribution to our fellowman—an area where we have some interest and abilities and where we can, at the same time, provide for our own.

I am glad Beethoven found his way into music, Rembrandt into art, Michelangelo into sculpturing, and President David O. McKay into teaching. To find your proper niche and do well at it can bless you, yours, and your fellowmen. If you need help in finding your career, it is available: Ponder and pray about it; study closely your patriarchal blessing; consider what you do well; take some vocational and interest tests; and get acquainted with various professions to see what is available. ("In His Steps," in *1979 Devotional Speeches of the Year* [Provo, Utah: BYU, 1980], pp. 64–65.)

We should ask the Lord's blessings on all our doings and should never do anything upon which we cannot ask His blessings. We should not expect the Lord to do for us what we can do for ourselves. I believe in faith and works, and that the Lord will bless more fully the man who works for what he prays for than He will the man who only prays. (*God, Family, Country,* p. 329.)

The constant and most recurring question in our minds, touching every thought and deed of our lives, should be, "Lord, what wilt thou have me to do?" (Acts 9:6.) The answer to that question comes only through the light of Christ and the Holy Ghost. We have a work to do—to follow Him. I testify to you that His pay for His work is the best pay that you can receive in this world or any other. ("Jesus Christ—Gifts and Expectations," Christmas Devotional, Salt Lake City, Utah, 7 December 1986.)

The Church of Jesus Christ of Latter-day Saints is not a body of organized listeners but a group of organized workers, and we grow best by taking responsibilities and entering into activity. So every person in the Church who is willing and faithful and worthy is given the opportunity of taking responsibility and taking positions of leadership, and by so doing they grow toward perfection. (Tokyo, Japan, 27 October 1957.)

In the final letter recorded in the Book of Mormon from Mormon to his son Moroni, he gave counsel that applies to our day. Both father and son were seeing a whole Christian civilization fall because they would not serve the God of the land, even Jesus Christ. Mormon wrote:

> And now, my beloved son, notwithstanding their hardness, let us labor diligently; for if we should cease to labor, we should be brought under condemnation; for we have a labor to perform

whilst in this tabernacle of clay, that we may conquer the enemy of all righteousness, and rest our souls in the kingdom of God (Moroni 9:6).

You and I have a similar labor to perform now—to conquer the enemy and rest our souls in the kingdom.

Then that great soul Mormon closes his letter to his beloved son, Moroni, with these words:

> My son, be faithful in Christ; and may not the things which I have written grieve thee, to weigh thee down unto death; but may Christ lift thee up, and may his sufferings and death, and the showing his body unto our fathers, and his mercy and long suffering, and the hope of his glory and of eternal life, rest in your mind forever. And may the grace of God the Father, whose throne is high in the heavens, and our Lord Jesus Christ, who sitteth on the right hand of his power, until all things shall become subject unto him, be, and abide with you forever." (Moroni 9:25–26.)

(CR October 1987, *Ensign* 17 [November 1987]: 85.)

PART 4

FAMILY
AND HOME

FAMILY AND HOME

Family

The Church of Jesus Christ of Latter-day Saints views the family as the most important organization in time and all eternity. The Church teaches that everything should center in and around the family. It stresses that the preservation of family life in time and eternity takes precedence above all other interests; it venerates parental and filial love and duty. ("Strengthen Your Families," Preston Idaho North Stake, 10 June 1984.)

There is no theme I would rather speak to than home and family, for they are at the very heart of the gospel of Jesus Christ. The Church, in large part, exists for the salvation and exaltation of the family. ("To the Mothers in Zion," Parents' Fireside, 22 February 1987.)

Some of the sweetest, most soul-satisfying impressions and experiences of our lives are those associated with home, family, children, brothers, and sisters. My heart fills with gratitude as I recall the joys of our rich family life when all six children were at home. We set our goal for twelve. My wife laments, "If we could just have had twins each time we would have made it." ("America's Strength — The Family," Seattle Washington National Family Night Program, 23 November 1976.)

I was at a reunion some years ago, and after the reunion, someone sent me a definition of family, titled "What Is a Family?"

This is what it said: "A family is the greatest security and the dearest possession. A family is living together and praying together; understanding one another; sharing tears, toothpaste, and small change; swapping sweaters, chores, jokes; borrowing records, talents, wisdom; keeping snapshots, letters, homemade gifts, and memories; giving first aid, parties, and lots of advice; and taking part in everything and in every member of the family. A family is living together and loving one another, and being loyal to each other. (*God, Family, Country,* pp. 182–83.)

Successful families have love and respect for each family member. Family members know they are loved and appreciated. Children feel they are loved by their parents. Thus, they are secure and self-assured. Strong families cultivate an attribute of effective communication. They talk out their problems, make plans together, and cooperate toward common objectives. Family home evening and family councils are practiced and used as effective tools toward this end.

Fathers and mothers in strong families stay close to their children. They talk. Some fathers formally interview each child, others do so informally, and others take occasion to regularly spend time alone with each child.

Every family has problems and challenges. But successful families try to work together toward solutions instead of resorting to criticism and contention. They pray for each other, discuss, and give encouragement. Occasionally these families fast together in support of one of the family members. Strong families support each other. Successful families do things together: family projects, work, vacations, recreation, and reunions. (CR April 1984, *Ensign* 14 [May 1984]: 6.)

It was through Joseph Smith that the God of Heaven revealed the truth that the family may endure beyond the grave—that our sympathies, affections, and love for each other may exist forever. (*Come unto Christ,* p. 124.)

Marriage, home, and family are established by God as part of His divine plan for the blessing of His children. The richest blessings and deepest joys of this life and the life to come are tied up with the performance of these sacred duties. In fact, our very exaltation in the celestial kingdom is directly related to the family and the eternity of the marriage covenant. (*So Shall Ye Reap,* p. 110.)

The Church was created in large measure to help the family, and long after the Church has performed its mission, the celestial patriarchal order will still be functioning. This is why President Joseph F. Smith said: "To be a successful father or a successful mother is greater than to be a successful general or a successful statesman," and President David O. McKay added: "When one puts business or pleasure above his home, he, that moment, starts on the downgrade to soul weakness." And this is why President Harold B. Lee said, "The Church must do more to help the home carry out its divine mission." (*God, Family, Country,* p. 223.)

Let us strengthen the family. Family and individual prayers morning and evening can invite the blessings of the Lord on our households. Mealtime provides a wonderful time to review the activities of the day and to not only feed the body but to feed the spirit as well, with members of the family taking turns reading the scriptures, particularly the Book of Mormon. Nighttime is a great time for the busy father to go to the bedside of each of his children, to talk with them, answer their questions, and tell them how much they are loved. In such homes there is no generation gap. This deceptive phrase is another tool of the devil to weaken the home and family. Children who honor their parents and parents who love their children can make a home a haven of safety and a little bit of heaven. (*God, Family, Country,* pp. 231–32.)

The family is the most effective place to instill lasting values in its members. Where family life is strong and based on principles and practices of the gospel of Jesus Christ, problems do not as readily appear. (CR October 1982, *Ensign* 12 [November 1982]: 59.)

Home and family. What sweet memories surge up in our breasts at the mere mention of these cherished words! May I wish for you prayerfully, and with all the fervor of my soul, that you may know the unspeakable joy and satisfaction of honorable parenthood. You will miss one of the deepest joys of this life and eternity if you wilfully avoid the responsibilities of parenthood and home-building. As revealed through the Prophet Joseph Smith, the glorious concept of home and the enduring family relationship lies at the very basis of our happiness here and hereafter. I trust you will make your happiness secure. ("Concerning Principles and Standards," *Church News* [4 June 1947]: 5.)

Much of the growth of the Church during the past few years has been a result of families being converted and baptized. We need to continue this emphasis because families are the foundation of solidarity in the Church. (El Paso Texas Regional Conference, 25 January 1986.)

I wish we could have more family reunions. It seems to me they used to be more common than they are today. It is a great opportunity to warm up inactive members of the Church, inactive heads of families, to get them into a reunion. (Regional Representatives Seminar, Salt Lake City, Utah, 28 June 1974.)

Remember, the family is one of God's greatest fortresses against the evils of our day. Help keep your family strong and close and worthy of our Father in Heaven's blessings. As you do, you will receive faith and strength which will bless your lives forever. (CR April 1986, *Ensign* 16 [May 1986]: 43.)

The love we know here is not a fleeting shadow, but the very substance that binds families together for time and eternity. (Asenath S. Conklin Funeral Service, 7 August 1982.)

Because of our confidence in the perpetuity of the home and family into the eternities, we build our most elaborate and expensive structures—temples of God—so that man, woman, and their children may be bound together by covenant in an everlasting union that will transcend all the limitations of this mortal sphere. It is because of this belief that the Church decries divorce, and that we are actively engaged in teaching fathers that their most important duty is within the walls of their own homes, and mothers that they should be full-time mothers in the home. It is why we encourage parents to teach their children fundamental spiritual principles that will instill faith in God, faith in the family, and faith in their country. There is no other institution that can take the place of the family or fulfill its essential function.

Yes, families are intended to have joy. David O. McKay once said, "In the well-ordered home we may experience on earth a taste of heaven" (in CR April 1969, p. 5). My plea to all who read these words is that we strengthen our families so that our memories of home may be happy ones, that our home life may be a foretaste of heaven. (*This Nation Shall Endure,* p. 129.)

Does this poem describe your family gatherings?

> We are all here:
>   Father, mother
>   Sister, brother,
> All who hold each other dear.
> Each chair is filled, we are all at home.
> Tonight, let no cold stranger come;
> It must be often thus around
> Our old familiar hearth we're found.
> Bless, then, the meeting and the spot,
> For once be every care forgot;
> Let gentle peace assert her power,
> And kind affection rule the hour,
> We're all—all here.
> (Adapted from a poem by Charles Sprague)

God intended the family to be eternal. With all my soul, I testify to the truth of that declaration. May He bless us to strengthen our homes and the lives of each family member so that in due time we can report to our Heavenly Father in His celestial home that we are all there—father, mother, sister, brother, all who hold each other dear. Each chair is filled. We are all back home. ("America's Strength—The Family," Seattle Washington National Family Night Program, 23 November 1976.)

The family is under attack today as never before, at least in my memory, and it is very real. Yet the family is the rock foundation, the cornerstone, of civilization. The Church will never be stronger than its families, and this nation will never rise above its homes and its families. (*God, Family, Country,* p. 186.)

Thank God for the joys of family life. I have often said there can be no genuine happiness separate and apart from a good home. The sweetest influences and associations of life are there. Life cannot be fully successful, no matter what goals we attain in the material world, no matter what honors of men come to us in our lives, if we fail as fathers, mothers, and children. (*God, Family, Country,* p. 178.)

Responsibilities of Family Members

The family is the basis for the righteous life. Divinely pre-scribed roles for father, mother, and children were given from the very beginning. God established that fathers were to preside in the home. Fathers are to procreate, provide, love, teach, and direct. A mother's role is also God-ordained. Mothers are to conceive, bear, nourish, love, and train. They are the helpmates and counselors to their husbands.

Children are likewise counseled in holy writ in their duty to parents (see Ephesians 6:1–3). When parents, in companionship, love, and unity, fulfill their heaven-imposed responsibility, and children respond with love and obedience, great joy is the result. (*This Nation Shall Endure,* p. 101.)

For young people to be in the world but not of the world has never been more difficult than today. But this burden must be shared by the parents. The family home evening is an important barrier to the works of Satan. Our Church youth program must protect our youth against every evil influence and should fill a vacuum left by rejecting worldly enticements. And, of course, a great panacea for all problems and personal doubts is prayer — pri-vate and family prayer, night and morning.

The critical and complaining adult will be less effective than the interested and understanding. Love and understanding are only ef-fective when they are genuine. We must love our young people, whether they are in righteousness or in error. In this way we can give them a chance to discern and to learn. But we must also give them a fair choice. (*God, Family, Country,* p. 251.)

Setting your home in order is keeping the commandments of God. This brings harmony and love in the home between you and your companion and between you and your children. It is daily family prayer. It is teaching your family to understand the gospel of Jesus Christ. It is each family member keeping the command-ments of God. It is you and your companion being worthy to receive a temple recommend, all family members receiving the ordinances of exaltation, and your family being sealed together for eternity. It is being free from excessive debt, with family members paying honest tithes and offerings. (CR April 1981, *Ensign* 11 [May 1981]: 36.)

Fathers, you cannot delegate your duty as the head of the home. Mothers, train up your children in righteousness; do not attempt to save the world and thus let your own fireside fall apart. The duty of parents is to be of help to each other and to their children; then comes their duty to their neighbors, community, nation, and world, in that order. (*God, Family, Country*, pp. 328–29.)

There is no inequality between the sexes in God's plan. It is a matter of division of responsibility. (CR April 1984, *Ensign* 14 [May 1984]: 6.)

Our wives are our most precious eternal helpmates, our companions. They are to be cherished and loved. (*Come unto Christ*, p. 52.)

Above all else, children need to know and feel they are loved, wanted, and appreciated. They need to be assured of that often. Obviously, this is a role parents should fill, and most often the mother can do it best. Rearing happy, peaceful children is no easy challenge in today's world, but it can be done, and it is being done. Responsible parenthood is the key. (CR October 1982, *Ensign* 12 [November 1982]: 60.)

I know that the Lord is sending to the earth some of His very choicest spirits in this day when wickedness is most intense, when the temptations are the greatest that we have ever known, when the gospel is upon the earth in all its fulness. I am sure He is sending to earth some of His very choicest spirits to help build up the kingdom to prove to those in the world that they should live the gospel, keep the commandments of God, and to be in the world and not partake of the sins of the world. Those kinds of young men and women are coming into our homes. Many of them are our children, our grandchildren, and our great-grandchildren. It is a great time to be alive — the greatest age in all the world. It is a joy to be a part of it. (Sao Paulo Brazil Temple Workers, 26 February 1979.)

Responsibilities of Parents

The family is a divine institution established by our Heavenly Father. It is basic to civilization and particularly to Christian civilization. The establishment of a home is not only a privilege, but marriage and the bearing, rearing, and proper training of children is a duty of the highest order.

It is a glorious thing to have a family where there is unity and love. I hope you seek for it; I hope you pray for it. I hope you have family prayer. You need it so much. I hope you have your secret prayers. ("Foundations for Family Solidarity," *Children's Friend* 56 [April 1957]: 26.)

For a man, there is no calling as high as that of a righteous patriarch, married in the house of the Lord, presiding over His children. Even the very Elohim has us address Him as "our Father who art in heaven" (Matthew 6:9; 3 Nephi 13:9). For a woman there is no calling as high as that of a righteous mother, married in the house of the Lord, rearing a posterity. ("In His Steps," in *1979 Devotional Speeches of the Year* [Provo, Utah: BYU, 1980], p. 64.)

It is an obligation of parents to see that sacred ordinances are performed after the children have been properly taught. It is not the prerogative of parents to permit their children to grow up and choose for themselves. It is their duty and obligation to train them when they are yet young, and to see that these important ordinances are performed in their behalf (see D&C 68:25–28). (*So Shall Ye Reap,* p. 111.)

Knowing in part the hopes and aspirations of my earthly as well as my divine parents, I am dedicated to passing on, if possible, as noble a heritage as I have received, and a name as unsullied and honorable as it was when it was given to me. To do so is to bequeath to my children and my children's children a legacy most precious above all earthly possessions. It is to give them an eternal heritage which leads to eternal life. ("Temple Memories," Ogden Utah Temple Dedication, 18 January 1972.)

I call your attention to the revelations given by the Lord with reference to the responsibility of parents to train their children, to teach them the fundamental principles of the gospel, to teach them to pray, and that parents who fail to accept and discharge this obligation will have the sin rest upon them (see D&C 68:25–28). In the very early days of the Church, the Lord saw fit to chastise some of the leading brethren of the Church for their failure to train their children, to teach them correct principles, to teach them to pray, and they were admonished to put their own houses in order. (See D&C 93:40–50.) (CR April 1944, *Improvement Era* 47 [May 1944]: 287, 324.)

We encourage parents to teach their children fundamental spiritual principles that will instill faith in God, faith in their family, and faith in their country. We plead with parents to spend time with their children, both in teaching them and in building positive relationships. These are the things that create and foster strong family units and a stable society. ("Righteousness Exalteth a Nation," Provo Utah Freedom Festival, 29 June 1986.)

It seems easier for many mothers and fathers to express and show their love to their children when they are young, but more difficult when they are older. Work at this prayerfully. There need be no generation gap. And the key is love. Our young people need love and attention, not indulgence. They need empathy and understanding, not indifference, from mothers and fathers. They need the parents' time. A mother's kindly teachings and her love for and confidence in a teenage son or daughter can literally save them from a wicked world. ("To the Mothers in Zion," Parents' Fireside, Salt Lake City, Utah, 22 February 1987.)

Every boy and girl needs the safeguard which an intimate association with mother or father will provide. The failure of parents and children to understand each other weakens the framework of the home. This relationship must be built upon love and mutual confidence. Then when the problems of life arise, father and mother will be the first sought for counsel. Herein is safety.

Parents in this close association have no difficulty teaching virtue, honesty, industry, the principles basic to our American way of life, and the dangers of foreign philosophies and ideologies. Effective parental guidance—the greatest need of the home—is here provided to the profit of the individual, the home, the community, and the nation. (*So Shall Ye Reap,* p. 108.)

The Lord pointed out that He had commanded parents to bring up their children in light and truth (D&C 93:30). Then He said, "You have not taught your children light and truth" (verse 42). This is, of course, our first great obligation, to teach these children light and truth, the gospel, the plan of salvation. As you teach them, I am sure you are impressed with the fact that you not only teach the child, but that child—through the lessons you carry to him—reflects through his own example your teachings which are extended into the lives of others. (*So Shall Ye Reap,* p. 29.)

Children must be taught to pray, to rely on the Lord for guidance, and to express appreciation for the blessings that are theirs. I recall kneeling at the bedsides of our young children, helping them with their prayers. Children must be taught right from wrong. They can and must learn the commandments of God. They must be taught that it is wrong to steal, lie, cheat, or covet what others have. Children must be taught to work at home. They should learn there that honest labor develops dignity and self-respect. They should learn the pleasure of work, of doing a job well. (CR October 1982, *Ensign* 12 [November 1982]: 60.)

Regarding the divinely appointed responsibility of parents, the sobering counsel is given that they shall "teach their children to pray, and to walk uprightly before the Lord," and inasmuch as parents "teach them not to understand the doctrine of repentance, faith in Christ, the Son of the Living God, and of baptism and the gift of the Holy Ghost by the laying on of hands, when eight years old, the sin be upon the heads of the parents" (see D&C 68:25–28).

These and other similar scriptures make crystal clear the divine origin of marriage, the home and family, the heaven-imposed responsibilities resting upon parents, and the penalties imposed when laws governing these hallowed institutions are disregarded. (Chevy Chase Presbyterian Church, Washington, D.C., 18 March 1956.)

The obligation to teach the principles of the gospel to the youth of Zion rests squarely upon the parents of the Church. Not only is there an obligation to teach these principles, but the Lord says: "And their children shall be baptized for the remission of their sins when eight years old, and receive the laying on of the hands" (D&C 68:27). (*So Shall Ye Reap,* p. 111.)

Praise your children more than you correct them. Praise them for even their smallest achievement. Encourage your children to come to you for counsel with their problems and questions by listening to them every day. Discuss with them such important matters as dating, sex, and other matters affecting their growth and development, and do it early enough so they will not obtain information from questionable sources. (CR October 1981, *Ensign* 11 [November 1981]: 107.)

Treat your children with respect and kindness—just as you would when guests are present. They are, after all, more meaningful to you than guests. Teach your children never to speak unkindly to others regarding members of the family. Be loyal to one another. Implant within children a desire to serve others. Teach them to be thoughtful to the aged, the sick, and the lonely. Help them to plan early for a mission so they can bless others who do not have the gospel. (CR October 1981, *Ensign* 11 [November 1981]: 107.)

Parents are directly responsible for the righteous rearing of their children, and this responsibility cannot be safely delegated to relatives, friends, neighbors, the school, the church, or the state.

"I appeal to you parents, take nothing for granted about your children," said President J. Reuben Clark, Jr. "The great bulk of them, of course, are good, but some of us do not know when they begin to go away from the path of truth and righteousness. Be watchful every day and hour. Never relax your care, your solicitude. Rule kindly in the spirit of the gospel and the spirit of the priesthood, but rule, if you wish your children to follow the right path." Permissive parents are part of the problem. (*God, Family, Country,* pp. 224–25.)

Parents, stay close to your children; you cannot delegate your responsibility to the educators, no matter how competent they may be. Parents have a duty to train their children, to talk over their problems with them, to discuss what they are learning at school. And it is neither wise nor safe to leave the determination of our educational system and policies exclusively to the professional educators. (*God, Family, Country,* pp. 238–39.)

Today, because some parents have refused to become informed and then stand up and inform their children, they are witnessing the gradual physical and spiritual destruction of their posterity. If we would become like God, knowing good and evil, then we had best find out what is undermining us, how to avoid it, and what we can do about it. (See Alma 12:31; Genesis 3:22.) (*God, Family, Country,* pp. 229–30.)

Parents need to take a stand for all that is honest, virtuous, and praiseworthy. It is the responsibility of heads of families to support wholesome influences for their children in government, schools, in the home, in the neighborhoods, in stores, in local theaters. Parents have responsibility to see that freedom is preserved for their children, and that the present generation does not burden future generations with debt and wasteful extravagance. (CR April 1978, *Ensign* 8 [May 1978]: 33.)

Because parents have departed from the principles the Lord gave for happiness and success, families throughout the world are undergoing great stress and trauma. Many parents have been enticed to abandon their responsibilities in the home to seek after an elusive "self-fulfillment." Some have abdicated parental responsibilities for pursuit of material things, unwilling to postpone personal gratification in the interest of their children's welfare. (CR October 1982, *Ensign* 12 [November 1982]: 59.)

There are many people today in the Christian world, and possibly even among Latter-day Saints, who feel that they have done their duty when they have provided food, shelter, clothing, secular education, and accumulated wealth which their children will inherit later. However, this is not enough. According to the revelations which the Lord has given, it is not sufficient to provide all of these and even to send our children to Sunday School, to Primary, and to the Mutual Improvement Association. There is still much to be done. (*So Shall Ye Reap,* pp. 110–11.)

One of the greatest needs is more time of parents in the home. Youth of the Church and of the nation need more than physical comforts. We will need to leave them more than lands and stocks. They need more than a modern automobile and a lovely modern building to live in. (*God, Family, and Country,* pp. 169–70.)

When parents themselves have complied with the ordinances of salvation, when they have set the example of a temple marriage, not only is their own marriage more likely to succeed, but their children are far more likely to follow their example. (CR October 1982, *Ensign* 12 [November 1982]: 61.)

Husbands and wives who love each other will find that love and loyalty are reciprocated. This love will provide a nurturing atmosphere for the emotional growth of children. Family life should be a time of happiness and joy that children can look back on with fond memories and associations. (CR October 1982, *Ensign* 12 [November 1982]: 59.)

The most important teachings in the home are spiritual. Parents are commanded to prepare their sons and daughters for the ordinances of the gospel: baptism, confirmation, priesthood ordinations, and temple marriage. They are to teach them to respect and honor the Sabbath day, to keep it holy. Most important, parents are to instill within their children a desire for eternal life and to earnestly seek that goal above all else. (CR October 1982, *Ensign* 12 [November 1982]: 60–61.)

We shall continue to stress the importance of strong Christian homes and family life. We feel the increasing necessity for parents to teach their children to live the principles of the gospel as revealed in the Bible, the Book of Mormon, and other sacred scripture. (Statement upon becoming President of the Church, 11 November 1985.)

Live close to your children, that you have their love and confidence, that you are not harsh, that you are not cross, that you are understanding. Be firm in the right—yes, in a kindly, sweet way. I pray that the time will never come when your children will go to others for counsel and advice which you should be giving them. If you have a kindly spirit in your homes it is not going to be difficult for you to live the gospel, and it is not going to be difficult for your children to grow up to be true Latter-day Saints as you would have them become. ("I'll Go Where You Want Me to Go," *Church News* [23 November 1946]: 8.)

In an eternal sense, salvation is a family affair. God holds parents responsible for their stewardship in rearing their family. It is a most sacred responsibility. (CR October 1982, *Ensign* 12 [November 1982]: 59.)

For the ultimate in happiness, we need to experience the glorious blessings of honorable parenthood—at least we need to be worthy of it. I realize that some of the choicest spirits of our Heavenly Father go through mortality without that glorious privilege, but in the Lord's own due time they will realize that blessing—if not in this life, in the life to come. (*God, Family, Country,* p. 193.)

May we be faithful to this great obligation of parenthood, this sacred obligation, that we may build our homes solidly upon eternal principles, that we may have no regrets. May we never be recreant to the great trust that has been imposed in us. May we always keep in mind that these spirits that have entered our homes are choice spirits. Many of them have been born under the covenant. As we look into their faces and contemplate their needs, we might well consider that some of them were probably choicer spirits up there than we were. It is a grave responsibility. May we not shirk it. (*God, Family, Country,* p. 172.)

Our Heavenly Father loves all of His children of all nations everywhere. Because He loves us so much, He has given us loving parents who care for us and teach us. Our mothers and fathers are our first and best teachers, and what they teach us can help us to grow up to be good and useful men and women. The tremendous influence for good of responsible parents throughout history is impossible to measure. ("The Teachings of Parents," *Friend* 5 [July 1975]: 6.)

Responsibilities of Fathers

The sacred title of "father" is shared with the Almighty. In the Church men are called and released. Did you ever hear of a mortal father being released? (CR April 1981, *Ensign* 11 [May 1981]: 36.)

Each father in the Church is establishing, or should be establishing, his patriarchal order—an order that will extend into the eternities. (*Priesthood* [Salt Lake City: Deseret Book, 1981], p. 138.)

Only through sin can a father be relieved of his obligations to that family, and that is a terrifying thing to contemplate. (Regional Representatives Seminar, Salt Lake City, Utah, 4 October 1973.)

Our pattern, or model, for fatherhood is our Heavenly Father. How does He work with His children? Well, in order to know that, of course, this head of the family will need to know something about the gospel, the great plan of the Lord. (Regional Representatives Seminar, Salt Lake City, Utah, 28 June 1974.)

The worthy priesthood holder who magnifies both his priesthood and his fatherhood, who is a true patriarch in his family, may inherit great blessings, for the Lord has said:

> Ye shall come forth in the first resurrection; and if it be after the first resurrection, in the next resurrection; and shall inherit thrones, kingdoms, principalities, and powers, dominions, all heights and depths . . . and if ye abide in my covenant . . . it shall be done unto them in all things whatsoever my servant hath put upon them, in time, and through all eternity; and shall be of full force when they are out of the world; and they shall pass by the

angels, and the gods, which are set there, to their exaltation and glory in all things, as hath been sealed upon their heads, which glory shall be a fulness and a continuation of the seeds forever and ever. (D&C 132:19.)

(*Priesthood* [Salt Lake City: Deseret Book, 1981], p. 139.)

Fatherhood is a supreme opportunity in life. (*Come unto Christ,* p. 58.)

What did the righteous fathers of the Book of Mormon teach their sons? They taught them many things, but the overreaching message was "the great plan of the Eternal God"—the Fall, rebirth, Atonement, Resurrection, judgment, and eternal life (see Alma 34:9). Enos said he knew his father was a just man, "for he taught me in his language, and also in the nurture and admonition of the Lord—and blessed be the name of my God for it" (Enos 1:1).

Those in the Book of Mormon who were taught nothing concerning the Lord but only concerning worldly knowledge became a cunning and wicked people (see Mosiah 24:5, 7). All truths are not of the same value. The saving truths of salvation are of greatest worth. These truths the fathers taught plainly, frequently, and fervently. Are we fathers doing likewise? (CR October 1985, *Ensign* 15 [November 1985]: 36.)

Devoted Book of Mormon fathers constantly reminded their sons of saving truths. "O remember, remember, my sons, the words which king Benjamin spake unto his people," said Helaman. "Yea, remember that there is no other way nor means whereby man can be saved, only through the atoning blood of Jesus Christ." (Helaman 5:9.) "My sons, remember, remember," Helaman continued, "that it is upon the rock of our Redeemer, who is Christ, the son of God, that ye must build your foundation" (Helaman 5:12).

In the Book of Mormon, loving fathers commended their sons when they deserved it. Alma complimented Shiblon, saying, "You have commenced in your youth to look to the Lord" (Alma 38:2). Mormon told his son Moroni, "I recommend thee unto God" (Moroni 9:22). Our sons need to be encouraged in their righteous endeavors. (CR October 1985, *Ensign* 15 [November 1985]: 36.)

May we fathers teach our sons as the exemplary Book of Mormon fathers taught their sons. And may our sons, like Nephi, listen and obey, knowing that because of those teachings they too were born of goodly parents. (CR October 1985, *Ensign* 15 [November 1985]: 37.)

In a revelation to the Prophet Joseph, the Lord directed fathers to bring up their children in light and truth. He rebuked several because of their failure to do so. Each of us would do well to review those principles given to Joseph Smith, Jr., Frederick G. Williams, Sidney Rigdon, and Newel K. Whitney. (See D&C 93.) In this revelation the Lord states that Satan "cometh and taketh away light and truth, through disobedience, from the children of men, and because of the tradition of their fathers" (D&C 93:39). The "tradition of their fathers" refers, of course, to the bad examples and teachings of fathers. (CR April 1981, *Ensign* 11 [May 1981]: 35.)

We are to teach the fundamental doctrines of the Church in such a way that our children may understand. Some fathers teach, but their children do not understand. This places responsibility on fathers to study and learn the gospel. (CR April 1981, *Ensign* 11 [May 1981]: 36.)

One of the greatest things a man can do for his children is to love his wife and let them know he loves her. A father has the responsibility to lead his family by desiring to have children, loving them, and by letting virtue garnish his thoughts unceasingly (see D&C 121:45). This is one of the great needs today. (*God, Family, Country,* p. 185.)

May I suggest two basic responsibilities of every father in Israel. First, you have a sacred responsibility to provide for the material needs of your family. The Lord clearly defined the roles of providing for and rearing a righteous posterity. In the beginning, Adam, not Eve, was instructed to earn the bread by the sweat of his brow.

The Apostle Paul counsels husbands and fathers, "But if any provide not for his own, and specially for those of his own house, he hath denied the faith, and is worse than an infidel" (1 Timothy 5:8).

Early in the history of the restored Church, the Lord specifically charged men with the obligation to provide for their wives and family. In January of 1832 He said, "Verily I say unto you, that every man who is obliged to provide for his own family, let him provide, and he shall in nowise lose his crown" (D&C 75:28). Three months later the Lord said again, "Women have claim on their husbands for their maintenance, until their husbands are taken" (D&C 83:2). This is the divine right of a wife and mother. While she cares for and nourishes her children at home, her husband earns the living for the family, which makes this nourishing possible.

In a home where there is an able-bodied husband, he is expected to be the breadwinner. Sometimes we hear of husbands who, because of economic conditions, have lost their jobs and expect the wives to go out of the home and work, even though the husband is capable of providing for his family. In these cases, we urge the husband to do all in his power to allow his wife to remain in the home caring for the children while he continues to provide for his family the best he can, even though the job he is able to secure may not be ideal and family budgeting may have to be tighter.

Also, the need for education or material things does not justify the postponing of children in order to keep the wife working as the breadwinner in the family. I remember the counsel of our beloved prophet Spencer W. Kimball to married students. He said: "I have told tens of thousands of young folks that when they marry they should not wait for children until they have finished their schooling and financial desires . . . they should live together normally and let children come . . . I know of no scripture where an authorization is given to young wives to withhold their families and go to work to put their husbands through school. There are thousands of husbands who have worked their own way through school and have reared families at the same time." ("Marriage Is Honorable," in *1973 Speeches of the Year* [Provo, Utah: BYU, 1974], p. 263.)

Sometimes the mother works outside of the home at the encouragement, or even insistence, of her husband. It is he who wants the items or conveniences that the extra income can buy. Not only will the family suffer in such instances, brethren, but your own spiritual growth and progression will be hampered. I say to all of you, the Lord has charged men with the responsibility to provide for their families in such a way that the wife is allowed to fulfill her role as mother in the home.

Fathers, another vital aspect of providing for the material needs of your family is the provision you should be making for your family in case of an emergency. Family preparedness has been a long-established welfare principle. It is even more urgent today.

I ask you earnestly, have you provided for your family a year's supply of food, clothing, and where possible, fuel? The revelation to produce and store food may be as essential to our temporal welfare today as boarding the ark was to the people in the days of Noah.

Also, are you living within your income and saving a little? Are you honest with the Lord in the payment of your tithes? Living this divine law will bring both spiritual and material blessings. Yes, brethren, as a father in Israel you have a great responsibility to provide for the material needs of your family and to have the necessary provisions in case of emergency.

Second, you have a sacred responsibility to provide spiritual leadership in your family. In a pamphlet published some years ago by the Council of Twelve, we said the following: "Fatherhood is leadership, the most important kind of leadership. It has always been so . . . it will always be so. Father, with the assistance and counsel and encouragement of your eternal companion, you preside in the home."

However, along with that presiding position, comes important obligations. We sometimes hear accounts of men, even in the Church, who think that being head of the home somehow puts them in a superior role and allows them to dictate and make demands upon their family.

The Apostle Paul points out that the husband is the head of the wife even as Christ is the head of the Church (see Eph. 5:23). That is the model we are to follow in our role of presiding in the home. We do not find the Savior leading the Church with a harsh or unkind hand. We do not find the Savior treating His Church with disrespect or neglect. We do not find the Savior using force or coercion to accomplish His purposes. Nowhere do we find anything but that which edifies, uplifts, comforts, and exalts the Church. Brethren, I say to you with all soberness, His is the model we must follow as we take the spiritual lead in our families.

Particularly is this true in your relationship with your wife. Here again the counsel from the Apostle Paul is most beautiful and to the point. He said simply, "Husbands, love your wives, even as Christ also loved the Church."

In latter-day revelation the Lord speaks again of this obligation. He said, "Thou shalt love thy wife with all thy heart, and shalt cleave unto her and none else." To my knowledge there is only one other thing in all scripture that we are commanded to love with all our hearts, and that is God Himself. Think what that means!

This kind of love can be shown for your wives in so many ways. First and foremost, nothing except God Himself takes priority over your wife in your life—not work, not recreation, not hobbies. Your wife is your most precious eternal helpmate—your companion.

What does it mean to love someone with all your heart? It means with all our emotional feelings and with all our devotion. Surely when you love your wife with all your heart, you cannot demean her, criticize her, find fault with her, nor abuse her by words, sullen behavior, or actions.

What does it mean to "cleave unto her"? It means to stay close to her, to be loyal and faithful to her, to communicate with her, and to express your love for her.

Love means being sensitive to her feelings and needs. She wants to be noticed and treasured. She wants to be told that you view her as lovely and attractive and important to you. Love means putting her welfare and self-esteem as a high priority in your life.

You should be grateful that she is the mother of your children and the queen of your home—grateful that she has chosen homemaking and motherhood—to bear, to nourish, to love, and to train your children—as the noblest calling of all.

Husbands, recognize your wife's intelligence and her ability to counsel with you as a real partner regarding family plans, family activities, and family budgeting. Don't be stingy with your time or with your means. Give her the opportunity to grow intellectually, emotionally, and socially as well as spiritually.

Remember, brethren, love can be nurtured and nourished by little tokens. Flowers on special occasions are wonderful, but so is your willingness to help with the dishes, change diapers, get up with a crying child in the night, leave the television or the newspaper to help with dinner. Those are the quiet ways we say "I love you" with our actions. They bring rich dividends for such little effort. This kind of loving priesthood leadership applies to your children as well as your wives.

Mothers play an important role as the heart of the home, but this in no way lessens the equally important role fathers should play in nurturing, training, and loving their children as head of the home.

As the patriarch in your home, you have a serious responsibility to assume leadership in working with your children. You must help create a home where the Spirit of the Lord can abide. Your place is to give direction to all family life. You should take an active part in establishing family rules and discipline.

Our homes should be havens of peace and joy for our families. Surely no child should fear his own father—especially a priesthood father. A father's duty is to make his home a place of happiness and joy. He cannot do this when there is bickering, quarreling, contention, or unrighteous behavior. The powerful effect of righteous fathers in setting an example, disciplining and training, nurturing and loving is vital to the spiritual welfare of his children. (CR October 1987, *Ensign* 17 [November 1987]: 48–49.)

Once you determine that a high priority in your life is to see that your wife and your children are happy, you will do all in your power to do so. I am not just speaking of satisfying material desires, but of filling other vital needs such as appreciation, compliments, comforting, encouraging, listening, and giving love and affection. (CR April 1981, *Ensign* 11 [May 1981]: 34.)

The question is sometimes asked by younger priesthood holders, "Where do I place my greatest priorities—to the Church, to my family, or to my profession?" I have answered that question by emphasizing that heads of families have four major responsibilities. Certainly the first is to the home and family. There should be no question about this. A man may succeed in business or his Church calling, but if he fails in his home he will face eternity in disappointment. One of the great areas of emphasis in President

Spencer W. Kimball's administration was that fathers spend more time at home. This includes priesthood officers! Home is the place where the Lord intended a father's greatest influence to be felt.

> But behold, I say unto you, that little children are redeemed from the foundation of the world through mine Only Begotten;
> Wherefore, they cannot sin, for power is not given unto Satan to tempt little children, until they begin to become accountable before me;
> For it is given unto them even as I will, according to mine own pleasure, that great things may be required at the hand of their fathers. (D&C 29:46–48.)

Fathers—do you see the significance of that statement? The Lord expects great things from you during those impressionable years before a child becomes accountable for his own sins. It is the father's duty to teach and influence the child in righteousness. Fathers, the Lord expects your greatest priority to be your own household. Your second priority is your Church responsibility: exercising your priesthood in righteousness, responding to calls, paying tithing and fast offerings, and supporting the missionary program, the welfare program, the building funds—the entire program of the Church.

Third, you have a priority to your job, your employment, so you can support those who are dependent on you. And fourth, you have a citizenship responsibility, a special responsibility to help maintain a free government. You should always keep before you the principle that the gospel can only prosper in an atmosphere of freedom. ("Our Imperative Responsibilities," Houston Texas Area Conference, 23 June 1979.)

Every man should provide the necessities of food, clothing, and shelter for his family. As Paul wrote to Timothy: "But if any provide not for his own, and specially for those of his own house, he hath denied the faith, and is worse than an infidel" (1 Timothy 5:8).

A man pays too high a price for worldly success if in his climb to prominence he sacrifices his spiritual, home, and civic responsibilities. How a person should apportion his time among his several duties requires good judgment and is a matter over which each should invite divine assistance. (*God, Family, Country,* p. 329.)

The father must hunger and thirst and yearn to bless his family, go to the Lord, ponder the words of God, and live by the Spirit to know the mind and will of the Lord and what he must do to lead his family. (Regional Representatives Seminar, Salt Lake City, Utah, 28 June 1974.)

Fathers, stay close to your sons. Earn and deserve their love and respect. Be united with their mother in the rearing of your children. Do nothing in your life to cause your sons to stumble because of your example. Guide your sons. Teach them. (CR April 1986, *Ensign* 16 [May 1986]: 45–46.)

With love in my heart for the fathers in Israel, may I suggest ten specific ways that fathers can give spiritual leadership to their children:

1. Give father's blessings to your children. Baptize and confirm your children. Ordain your sons to the priesthood. These will become spiritual highlights in the lives of your children.

2. Personally direct family prayers, daily scripture reading, and weekly family home evenings. Your personal involvement will show your children how important these activities really are.

3. Whenever possible, attend Church meetings together as a family. Family worship under your leadership is vital to your children's spiritual welfare.

4. Go on daddy-daughter dates and fathers and sons outings with your children. As a family, go on campouts and picnics, to ball games and recitals, and to school programs. Having Dad there makes all the difference.

5. Build traditions of family vacations and trips and outings. These memories will never be forgotten by your children.

6. Have regular one-on-one visits with your children. Let them talk about what they would like to. Teach them gospel principles. Teach them true values. Tell them you love them. Personal time with your children tells them where Dad puts his priorities.

7. Teach your children to work and show them the value of working toward a worthy goal. Establishing mission funds and education funds for your children shows them what Dad considers important.

8. Encourage good music and art and literature in your homes. Homes that have a spirit of refinement and beauty will bless the lives of children forever.

9. As distances allow, regularly attend the temple with your wife. Your children will then better understand the importance of temple marriage and temple vows and the eternal family unit.

10. Have your children see your joy and satisfaction in service to the Church. This can become contagious to them, so they too will want to serve in the Church and love the kingdom.

Oh, husbands and fathers in Israel, you can do so much for the salvation and exaltation of your families. Your responsibilities are so important. Remember your sacred calling as a father in Israel—your most important calling in time and eternity—a calling from which you are never released.

May you always provide for the material needs of your family and with your eternal companion at your side, may you fulfill your sacred responsibility to provide the spiritual leadership in your home. (CR October 1987, *Ensign* 17 [November 1987]: 50.)

We must be more Christlike in our attitude and behavior than what we see in the world. We should be as charitable and considerate with our loved ones as Christ is with us. He is kind, loving, and patient with each of us. Should we not reciprocate the same love to our wives and children? (*Come unto Christ*, p. 53.)

Fathers and husbands, we look to you to give righteous leadership in your home and families and, with your companions and the mothers of your children, to lead your families back to our Eternal Father. ("To the Mothers in Zion," Parents' Fireside, Salt Lake City, Utah, 22 February 1987.)

Fatherhood is not a matter of station or wealth; it is a matter of desire, diligence, and determination to see one's family exalted in the celestial kingdom. If that prize is lost, nothing else really matters. God bless all the fathers in Israel to do well the work within the walls of our own homes. With the Lord's help we shall succeed in this, our most important responsibility. (CR April 1981, *Ensign* 11 [May 1981]: 36.)

Responsibilities of Mothers

Mothers are, or should be, the very heart and soul of the family. No more sacred word exists in secular or holy writ than *mother.*

President David O. McKay declared: "Motherhood is the greatest potential influence either for good or ill in human life. The mother's image is the first that stamps itself on the unwritten page of the young child's mind. It is her caress that first awakens a sense of security; her kiss, the first realization of affection; her sympathy and tenderness, the first assurance that there is love in the world." (*Gospel Ideals,* p. 452.)

President McKay continues: "Motherhood consists of three principal attributes or qualities: namely, (1) the power to bear, (2) the ability to rear, (3) the gift to love. . . . This ability and willingness properly to rear children, the gift of love, and eagerness, yes, longing to express it in soul development, makes motherhood the noblest office or calling in the world. She who can paint a masterpiece or write a book that will influence millions deserves the admiration and the plaudits of mankind; but she who rears successfully a family of healthy, beautiful sons and daughters, whose influence will be felt through generations to come, . . . deserves the highest honor that man can give, and the choicest blessings of God." (*Gospel Ideals,* pp. 453–54.) With all my heart I endorse the words of President McKay. ("To the Mothers in Zion," Parents' Fireside, Salt Lake City, Utah, 22 February 1987.)

The Lord states that the opportunity and responsibility of wives is "to multiply and replenish the earth, according to my commandment, and to fulfil the promise which was given by my Father before the foundation of the world, and for their exaltation in the eternal worlds, that they may bear the souls of men; for herein is the work of my Father continued, that he may be glorified" (D&C 132:62). With this divine injunction, husbands and wives, as co-creators, should eagerly and prayerfully invite children into their homes.

Then, as each child joins their family circle, they can gratefully exclaim, as did Hannah, "For this child I prayed, and the Lord hath given me my petition which I asked of him; therefore also I have lent him to the Lord: as long as he liveth he shall be lent to the Lord" (1 Samuel 1:27–28). Isn't that beautiful? A mother praying to bear a child and then giving him to the Lord. ("To the Mothers in Zion," Parents' Fireside, Salt Lake City, Utah, 22 February 1987.)

Our beloved prophet, Spencer W. Kimball, had much to say about the role of mothers in the home and their callings and responsibilities. I am impressed to share with you some of his inspired pronouncements. I fear that much of his counsel has gone unheeded, and families have suffered because of it. But I stand as a second witness to the truthfulness of what President Spencer W. Kimball said. He spoke as a true prophet of God.

President Kimball declared: "Women are to take care of the family—the Lord has so stated—to be an assistant to the husband, to work with him, but not to earn the living, except in unusual circumstances. Men ought to be men indeed and earn the living under normal circumstances." (*Teachings of Spencer W. Kimball*, p. 318.)

Remember the counsel of President Kimball to John and Mary: "Mary, you are to become a career woman in the greatest career on earth—that of homemaker, wife, and mother. It was never intended by the Lord that married women should compete with men in employment. They have a far greater and more important service to render."

Again President Kimball speaks: "The husband is expected to support his family and only in an emergency should a wife secure outside employment. Her place is in the home, to build the home into a haven of delight.

"Numerous divorces can be traced directly to the day when the wife left the home and went out into the world into employment. Two incomes raise the standard of living beyond its norm. Two spouses working prevents the complete and proper home life, breaks into the family prayers, creates an independence which is not cooperative, causes distortion, limits the family, and frustrates the children already born." (Spencer W. Kimball, San Antonio Fireside, 3 December 1977, pp. 9–10.)

Finally, President Kimball counsels: "I beg of you, you who could and should be bearing and rearing a family: Wives, come home from the typewriter, the laundry, the nursing, come home from the factory, the cafe. No career approaches in importance that of wife, homemaker, mother—cooking meals, washing dishes, making beds for one's precious husband and children. Come home, wives, to your husbands. Make home a heaven for them. Come home, wives, to your children, born and unborn. Wrap the motherly cloak about you and, unembarrassed, help in a major role to create the bodies for the immortal souls who anxiously await.

"When you have fully complemented your husband in home life and borne the children, growing up full of faith, integrity, responsibility, and goodness, then you have achieved your accomplishment supreme, without peer, and you will be the envy [of all] through time and eternity." (Spencer W. Kimball, San Antonio Fireside, 3 December 1977, pp. 11–12.) President Kimball spoke the truth. His words are prophetic. ("To the Mothers in Zion," Parents' Fireside, Salt Lake City, Utah, 22 February 1987.)

It is a fundamental truth that the responsibilities of motherhood cannot be successfully delegated. No, not to day-care centers, not to schools, not to nurseries, not to baby-sitters. We become enamored with men's theories such as the idea of preschool training outside the home for young children. Not only does this put added pressure on the budget, but it places young children in an environment away from mother's influence. Too often the pressure for popularity, on children and teens, places an economic burden on the income of the father, so mother feels she must go to work to satisfy her children's needs. That decision can be most shortsighted. (CR October 1981, *Ensign* 11 [November 1981]: 105.)

Mothers in Zion, your God-given roles are so vital to your own exaltation and to the salvation and exaltation of your family. A child needs a mother more than all the things money can buy. Spending time with your children is the greatest gift of all.

With love in my heart for the mothers in Zion, I would like to suggest ten specific ways our mothers may spend effective time with their children.

First, take time to always be at the crossroads when your children are either coming or going—when they leave and return from dates—when they bring friends home. Be there at the crossroads whether your children are six or sixteen. In Proverbs we read: "A child left to himself bringeth his mother to shame" (Proverbs 29:15). Among the greatest concerns in our society are the millions of latchkey children who come home daily to empty houses unsupervised by working parents.

Second, mothers, take time to be a real friend to your children. Listen to your children, really listen. Talk with them, laugh and joke with them, sing with them, play with them, cry with them, hug them, honestly praise them. Yes, regularly spend unrushed one-on-one time with each child. Be a real friend to your children.

Third, mothers, take time to read to your children. Starting from the cradle, read to your sons and daughters. Remember what the poet said, "You may have tangible wealth untold;/Caskets of jewels and coffers of gold./Richer than I you can never be—/I had a mother who read to me." (Strickland Gillilan, "The Reading Mother.") You will plant a love for good literature and a real love for the scriptures if you will read to your children regularly.

Fourth, take time to pray with your children. Family prayers, under the direction of the father, should be held morning and night. Have your children feel of your faith as you call down the blessings of heaven upon them. Paraphrasing the word of James: "The . . . fervent prayer of a righteous [mother] availeth much" (James 5:16). Have your children participate in family and personal prayers and rejoice in their sweet utterances to their Father in Heaven.

Fifth, take time to have a meaningful weekly home evening. With your husband presiding, participate in a spiritual and an uplifting home evening each week. Have your children actively involved. Teach them correct principles. Make this one of your great family traditions. Remember the marvelous promise made by President Joseph F. Smith when home evenings were first introduced to the Church: "If the Saints obey this counsel, we promise that great blessings will result. Love at home and obedience to parents will increase. Faith will be developed in the hearts of the youth of Israel, and they will gain power to combat the evil influences and temptations which beset them." This wonderful promise is still in effect today.

Sixth, take time to be together at mealtimes as often as possible. This is a challenge as the children get older and lives get busier. But happy conversation, sharing of the day's plans and activities, and special teaching moments occur at mealtime because mothers and fathers and children work at it.

Seventh, take time daily to read the scriptures together as a family. Individual scripture reading is important, but family scripture reading is vital. Reading the Book of Mormon together as a family will especially bring increased spirituality into your home and will give both parents and children the power to resist temptation and to have the Holy Ghost as their constant companion. I promise you that the Book of Mormon will change the lives of your family.

Eighth, take time to do things as a family. Make family outings and picnics and birthday celebrations and trips special times and memory builders. Whenever possible attend as a family events where one of the family members is involved, such as a school play, a ball game, a talk, a recital. Attend Church meetings together and sit together as a family when you can. Mothers who help families pray and play together will stay together and will bless children's lives forever.

Ninth, mothers, take time to teach your children. Catch the teaching moments. This can be done anytime during the day—at mealtime, in casual settings or at special sit-down times together, at the foot of the bed at the end of the day, or during an early-morning walk together. Mothers, you are your children's best teacher. Don't shift this precious responsibility to day-care centers or baby-sitters. A mother's love and prayerful concern for her children are her most important ingredients in teaching her own.

Teach children gospel principles. Teach them it pays to be good. Teach them there is no safety in sin. Teach them a love for the gospel of Jesus Christ and a testimony of its divinity. Teach your sons and daughters modesty and teach them to respect manhood and womanhood. Teach your children sexual purity, proper dating standards, temple marriage, missionary service, and the importance of accepting and magnifying Church callings. Teach them a love for work and the value of a good education. Teach them the importance of the right kind of entertainment, including appropriate movies, videos, music, books, and magazines. Discuss the evils of pornography and drugs and teach them the value of living the clean life.

Yes, mothers, teach your children the gospel in your home, at your own fireside. This is the most effective teaching that your children will ever receive. This is the Lord's way of teaching. The Church cannot teach like you can. The school cannot. The day-care center cannot. But you can, and the Lord will sustain you. Your children will remember your teachings forever, and when they are old, they will not depart from them. They will call you blessed—their truly angel mother. Mothers, this kind of heavenly, motherly teaching takes time—lots of time. It cannot be done effectively part-time. It must be done all the time in order to save and exalt your children. This is your divine calling.

Tenth, and finally, mothers, take the time to truly love your children. A mother's unqualified love approaches Christlike love. ("To the Mothers in Zion," Parents' Fireside, Salt Lake City, Utah, 22 February 1987.)

There is no satisfactory substitute for mother, and no one can take care of her children as she can. No so-called social obligations, social enticements, or outside interests should impel any mother to neglect the sacred charge that is hers of caring for her own flesh and blood. I feel confident that while civic and social activities may be rewarding, a mother will serve her community and her nation best if she first devotes herself to the needs of her own children. ("Strengthen Your Families," Preston Idaho North Stake, 10 June 1984.)

As mothers and future mothers, you will influence the course of the Church in this great country, and the destiny of its coming leaders. If you are to provide the training for these future generations, you must stand firm in the faith, unwavering in the face of evil, and as Paul said, "Put on the whole armour of God, that ye may be able to stand against the wiles of the devil" (Ephesians 6:11). (London England Area Conference, 19–20 June 1976.)

Mothers, stay close to your daughters. Earn and deserve their love and respect. Be united with their father in the rearing of your children. Do nothing in your life to cause your daughters to stumble because of your example.

Teach your daughters to prepare for life's greatest career—that of homemaker, wife, and mother. Teach them to love home because you love home. Teach them the importance of being a full-time mother in the home.

My eternal companion has wisely counseled mothers: "Radiate a spirit of contentment and joy with homemaking. You teach by example your attitude toward homemaking. Your attitude will say to your daughters, 'I am only a housewife.' Or it will convey, 'Homemaking is the highest, most noble profession to which a woman might aspire.' " ("To the Young Women of the Church," *Ensign* 16 [November 1986]: 84–85.)

God bless our wonderful mothers. We pray for you. We sustain you. We honor you as you bear, nourish, train, teach, and love for eternity. I promise you the blessings of heaven and "all that [the] Father hath" (see D&C 84:38) as you magnify the noblest calling of all—a mother in Zion. ("To the Mothers in Zion," Parents' Fireside, Salt Lake City, Utah, 22 February 1987.)

Responsibilities of Children

Children need to know who they are in the eternal sense of their identity. They need to know that they have an eternal Heavenly Father on whom they can rely, to whom they can pray, and from whom they can receive guidance. They need to know from whence they came so that their lives will have meaning and purpose. (CR October 1982, *Ensign* 12 [November 1982]: 60.)

Children are born innocent, not evil. They are not sent to earth, however, to neutral environments. They are sent to homes that, for good or evil, influence their ideas, emotions, thoughts, and standards, by which future choices will be made. (CR April 1981, *Ensign* 11 [May 1981]: 34.)

Children are counseled in holy writ in their duty to parents. Paul the Apostle wrote: "Children, obey your parents in the Lord: for this is right. Honor thy father and mother (which is the first commandment with promise;) That it may be well with thee, and thou mayest live long on the earth." (Ephesians 6:1–3; see Colossians 3:20.) When parents, in companionship, love, and unity, fulfill their heaven-imposed responsibility, and children respond with love and obedience, great joy is the result. ("America's

Strength—The Family," Seattle Washington National Family Night Program, 23 November 1976.)

We need a closer parent-child relationship. One of the greatest needs of our young people is a closer, more frequent companionship with father and mother. There is no satisfactory substitute. (*God, Family, Country,* p. 171.)

Your most important friendships should be with your own brothers and sisters and with your father and mother. Love your family. Be loyal to them. Have a genuine concern for your brothers and sisters. Help carry their load so you can say, like the lyrics of that song, "He ain't heavy, he's my brother." (CR April 1986, *Ensign* 16 [May 1986]: 43.)

My young sisters, I am happy to see so many of you with your mothers. I counsel each of you to draw close to your own mother. Love her. Respect her. Honor her. Receive your mother's counsel as she loves and instructs you in righteousness. Honor and obey your father as he stands as the head of the home by emulating his spiritual qualities. ("To the Young Women of the Church," *Ensign* 16 [November 1986]: 81.)

In the spiritual battles you are waging, I see you as today's sons of Helaman. Remember well the Book of Mormon account of Helaman's two thousand stripling warriors and how the teachings of their mothers gave them strength and faith. These marvelous mothers taught them to put on the whole armor of God, to place their trust in the Lord, and to doubt not. By so doing not one of these young men was lost. (See Alma 53:10–23; 56:41–56.) My young brethren, I counsel each of you to draw close to your own mother. Respect her. Honor her. Receive your mother's counsel as she loves and instructs you in righteousness. And honor and obey your father as he stands as the head of the home, emulating his manly qualities. (CR April 1986, *Ensign* 16 [May 1986]: 43.)

Now, there are some things that come only with age, and one of those is wisdom. Father and mother may be bent over, in part because of the responsibility of bearing you and caring for you. Just remember you need them, you need their counsel. ("A Fourfold Hope," Brigham Young University, Provo, Utah, 24 May 1961.)

Home

Our most basic institution is the home, because, after all, it is still our greatest and most primary educational institution. It is, in very deed, the center of our economic, social, and cultural interest. (*God, Family, Country,* p. 167.)

Our homes need the blessings which come from daily communion with God. Devotion in the home, which has been such an anchor to youth and parents alike, has all but vanished. A few generations ago it was a common practice. Then families knelt together in prayer; the scriptures were read aloud; and households joined in the singing of Church hymns. This practice, if revived, would contribute much to the strength of the home and the nation. The differences and irritations of the day melt away as families approach the throne of heaven together. Unity increases. The ties of love and affection are reinforced and the peace of heaven enters.

Such an atmosphere can be created as parents plan for recreation and diversion together with their children. An evening at home in wholesome activity; a picnic in the mountains or nearby park; or a fathers and sons' and mothers and daughters' project— these all tend to increase filial affection and love in the home and strengthen parent-children relations. Time thus spent yields big dividends. Love at home and obedience to parents increases as the bonds of home are made secure. (*So Shall Ye Reap,* pp. 107–8.)

Some people ask me as a Church leader why we place so much emphasis on the home and family when there are such larger problems around us? The answer is, of course, that the larger problems are merely a reflection of individual and family problems. For example, decaying cities and slums are merely a delayed reflection of individuals suffering under a decadent attitude. To paraphrase Goethe, if everyone swept in front of his own door, the whole world would be clean! ("The Values by Which to Live," *Leaders* 7 [October–December 1984]: 153.)

All is not well with this basic institution, the American home. In fact, it is in grave danger, if not in deadly peril. There is convincing evidence that a creeping rot of moral disintegration is eating into the very vitals of this temple of civilization. It gives cause for great concern. (*This Nation Shall Endure*, p. 99.)

The home is the rock foundation, the cornerstone of civilization. No nation will rise above its homes, and no nation will long endure when the family unit is weakened or destroyed. I need not remind you of the great threat to the family in all nations of the world today. Divorce is epidemic. The father's place at the head of the home is being challenged, and mothers have, in many instances, left the hearth to join the work force, thus weakening the stability of the home. Children, not growing up with strong parental guidance and spiritual influence, are allowed to roam freely. Not only does this lack of training and permissiveness sponsor indolence, but many of these youth, out of boredom, have also turned to drugs, juvenile delinquency, or crime. (*This Nation Shall Endure,* p. 70.)

As conditions in the world get progressively worse, it is crucial that the family draw closer together in righteousness and that family solidarity be established. As Richard L. Evans said, "There are too many pulls away from the home today. We should seriously consider whether or not too many activities and other interests take too much time and attention from our families, from our children, from those whom the Lord God gave us to love, to nourish, to teach, and to help through life." (*God, Family, Country*, p. 230.)

Far-reaching changes, resulting from industrialization, concentration of populations, commercialization of recreation, and other activities once performed in the home, all tend to lead away from home association.

Accompanying these changes, and in some measure resulting from them, has been a marked increase in pleasure seeking; the mad rush for money and other material things; the unwarranted indulgence of personal gratification; the insidious inroads of tobacco, liquor, gambling, and many other tendencies in our complex modern civilization. All these have exerted a pulling power away from the home and have weakened its structure.

There seems to be a tendency for many married people to become soft and seek a life filled with ease and the pleasure of the moment. They invite the pleasure of conjugality but often refuse to shoulder the responsibility of parenthood. (*This Nation Shall Endure,* p. 99.)

It is mother's influence during the crucial formative years that forms a child's basic character. Home is the place where a child learns faith, feels love, and thereby learns from mother's loving example to choose righteousness.

How vital are mother's influence and teaching in the home—and how apparent when neglected! I do not wish to wound any feelings, but all of us are aware of instances of active Latter-day Saint families who are experiencing difficulties with their children because mother is not where she ought to be—in the home. (CR October 1981, *Ensign* 11 [November 1981]: 105.)

As society draws women out of the home unnecessarily, as we tax ourselves to then make up for failures in the home, we substitute some programs that are really self-defeating and counterproductive. We err spiritually in doing so. If we are really concerned about alienation, we must do everything we can to spare the family, since it is the basic source of love, discipline, and values. Love at home is one of the basic needs in life, a spiritual law which, if violated, brings harsh, irrevocable consequences. One writer has said, "For when we emit from our families unloved, undisciplined individuals into the stream of humanity, this is more dangerous than emitting raw sewage." It is clear that we cannot have peace in the world without harmony in the home. (*This Nation Shall Endure,* p. 58.)

Can you see why Satan wants to destroy the home through having the mother leave the care of her children to others? And he is succeeding in too many homes. Protect your family from this danger just as you would instinctively protect them from physical harm. (CR October 1981, *Ensign* 11 [November 1981]: 107.)

One great thing the Lord requires of each of us is to provide a home where a happy, positive influence for good exists. In future years the costliness of home furnishings or the number of bathrooms will not matter much, but what will matter significantly is whether our children felt love and acceptance in the home. It will greatly matter whether there was happiness and laughter, or bickering and contention. (CR April 1981, *Ensign* 11 [May 1981]: 34.)

Give regular jobs to your children. Let them share in family projects, gardening, lawn care, and cleanup. (CR October 1981, *Ensign* 11 [November 1981]: 107.)

The future homes of America will be fortified as parents uphold the Christian virtues before their children. If parents love and respect each other, and if in their sacred partnership there is full support and unquestioned fidelity, these essentials will be translated into the homes of tomorrow. Conversely, if there is bickering, quarreling, and lack of harmony at home and participation in the dangerous practice of flirtations with others when away, the homes of tomorrow will be weakened thereby. (*So Shall Ye Reap,* p. 107.)

Fathers cannot delegate their duty as head of the home. They must train up their children in righteousness. Do not attempt to save the world and let your own fireside fall apart. (Softball Devotional, Salt Lake City, Utah, 21 August 1966.)

Some of our patriots are losing their children. In our attempt to save our country, we must not let our own homes crumble. Don't neglect your own. You can't delegate that divine duty or neglect it without tragic consequences. Be careful in sending them away from your hearth for additional education. There are worse things that can happen to a young person today than not getting a liberal college degree. (*God, Family, Country,* pp. 404–5.)

There has never been and there never will be a satisfactory substitute for the home established by the God of Heaven. If this nation is to endure, the home must be safeguarded, strengthened, and restored to its rightful importance. (*God, Family, Country,* p. 169.)

Possibly the best measure of the stature of a man or woman is in their home, at their own fireside. As you look hopefully forward, what conclusions have you reached about marriage, the home, and family? What value do you place on "the old-fashioned American home with its goodly number of children, its religious atmosphere, its prayer, its blessings and its rather Puritanical ideas about duties and obligations, including deference and respect for parents and older folk?" ("Your Charge: To Increase in Wisdom and Favor with God and Man," *New Era* 9 [September 1979]: 42–43.)

It is in the home and family that the bases for wise decisions and fruitful actions are established. There is no other place of such challenge and such opportunity. Thank God for the heritage of a good home and family, and the challenge and opportunity to build such.

Our homes are divinely ordained. Americans, from the very inception of our nation, have been lovers of home. It has been true of nations generally. (*God, Family, Country,* p. 173.)

Our homes must become bulwarks of strength through enthroning righteousness and bringing into them the peace, unity, and unselfishness engendered by personal purity, unquestioned fidelity, and simple family devotion. Parents must accept marriage as a divine institution and honor parenthood. Children must be inspired by precept and example in preparation for marriage, to guard against unchastity as against a loathsome disease, and to practice the other fundamental virtues. Love and mutual confidence must be safeguarded to strengthen parent-children relationships. Home must become the abiding place of the Spirit of God because the pure in heart dwell therein. (*So Shall Ye Reap,* p. 108.)

I am grateful for my home and my family. I am grateful for my companion and for her inspiration, strength, and help. I know that I could not have accomplished the little that I have achieved without her great faith, devotion, and support. I am grateful that I have come from a good Latter-day Saint home. (CR April 1955, *Improvement Era* 58 [June 1955]: 407.)

Parents who provide a home where gospel principles are lived will have, as the Lord has said, "a house of prayer, a house of fasting, a house of faith, a house of learning, . . . a house of order, a house of God" (D&C 88:119). Regardless of how modest or humble that home may be, it will have love, happiness, peace, and joy. Children will grow up in righteousness and truth, and will desire to serve the Lord. (CR October 1982, *Ensign* 12 [November 1982]: 61.)

Home is love, understanding, trust, welcome, and a sense of belonging. If you, as wives, mothers, and daughters take proper care of yourselves, your families, and your homes, and keep close to each other as sisters in the Relief Society, many of the problems of the day troubling youth and parents will pass you by. (CR October 1981, *Ensign* 11 [November 1981]: 107.)

The adversary knows "that the home is the first and most effective place for children to learn the lessons of life: truth, honor, virtue, self-control, the value of education, honest work, and the purpose and privilege of life. Nothing can take the place of home in rearing and teaching children, and no other success can compensate for failure in the home." (Letter of President David O. McKay, *Family Home Evening Manual,* 1968–69, p. iii.) (*God, Family, Country,* p. 224.)

It is time that the hearts of the fathers are turned to their children to a greater extent, and the hearts of the children are turned to their fathers (see Malachi 4:6). The seeds of divorce are often sown and the blessings of children delayed by wives working outside the home. Working mothers should remember that their children usually need more of mother than of money. ("Strengthening the Family," Philippine Islands Area Conference, 12 August 1975.)

We are actively engaged in teaching fathers to be compassionate fathers, and mothers to be full-time mothers in the home. Fathers are commanded to take the lead in all spiritual matters. ("Righteousness Exalteth a Nation," Provo Utah Freedom Festival, 29 June 1986.)

We need to arise and shine and to get the vision of this great work and to incorporate it into our lives and homes and our families. If we do so the Lord will bless us because He loves us. We are His people. We have accepted His gospel. You have taken upon yourselves sacred covenants and He wants to bless you. He wants to pour out His blessings, the blessings of heaven, upon you and your families. In those homes where you live the gospel, where mother and father and children are skimping just a little more to make ends meet, He will bless you even more, much more than He will in those homes where we find so many mothers unnecessarily working outside the home in order to get better clothes, a new living room suite, a new rug on the floor. Working mothers contribute to increased divorce, to infidelity, to the weakening of homes.

Brothers and sisters, it isn't worth it. The Lord help us, on bended knees, to seek the inspiration of heaven, that we may be guided to live the gospel, to do our duties as parents and as young people also, that we may grow up together as families with family solidarity and unity in our homes. (Grantsville Utah Stake Conference, 1 September 1974.)

Let your home radiate what you are, and that quiet influence will have a lasting impression on all who come to it. That influence is the greatest contribution to our missionary work. We only teach what we really are! ("Keys to Successful Missionary Work," Mission Presidents Seminar, Provo, Utah, 20 June 1979.)

If our homes are to be seedbeds of faith, a prerequisite condition to increasing faith is to have love and harmony in the home. Husbands and wives must love and cherish one another. Unselfish attitudes must be overcome. Faults must be overlooked. Contention must cease. Husbands and wives must be true and loyal to each other and the sacred covenant of marriage. Expressions of love must be tendered one to another. "Clothe yourselves with the bond of charity," said the Lord, "as with a mantle, which is the bond of perfectness and peace" (D&C 88:125). Yes, love at home is a prerequisite condition to increasing your faith. ("Lord, Increase Our Faith," Provo Utah Tabernacle Rededication, 21 September 1986.)

The Lord has implanted in every breast a desire for mating and home-building. The intimate associations of husband and wife, parents and children are among the sweetest and most soul-satisfying experienced in this life. The desire for home and family is a strong and natural impulse. What sweet memories surge up in our hearts at the mere mention of mother, father, brothers and sisters, home and family. The Lord has designed it so. The establishment of a home is not only a privilege, but marriage and the bearing, rearing, and proper training of children is a duty of the highest order. (*So Shall Ye Reap,* p. 110.)

Family Home Evening

In 1915, the First Presidency of the Church inaugurated the home evening program by a letter. I recall when my own father read that letter to the family at the supper table on the farm. When he concluded the letter, he said, "The Presidency has spoken, and this is the word of the Lord to us!" From that time forward, we diligently held family home evenings in my boyhood home. I testify out of this experience and the experience of family nights in my own home that great spiritual blessings can result. ("America's Strength—The Family," Seattle Washington National Family Night Program, 23 November 1976.)

Designed to strengthen and safeguard the family, the Church's home evening program establishes one night each week that is to be set apart for fathers and mothers to gather their sons and daughters around them in the home. Prayer is offered, hymns and other songs are sung, scriptures are read, family topics are discussed, talent is displayed, principles of the gospel are taught, and often games are played and homemade refreshments served.

Games should be played which develop the mental, physical, and spiritual qualities of family members. Singing songs and hymns can be a means of bringing inspiring music into the home and of helping each child to build his own musical vocabulary. Many parents have simply turned the musical education of their children over to the local rock radio station, with increasingly unpleasant results. Most children are delighted to discover music of genuine merit when their parents help to make it available to them. Bringing great music into the home can be an enriching and exciting experience not only for children but for parents as well. The main value of a talent time is the manner in which it can help children overcome shyness and reticence when performing before an audience.

What could be more richly rewarding than compassionate service in which the whole family can take part? Such activities can help instill in young people the desire to be personally helpful to others in times of need. ("Strengthening the Family," Philippine Islands Area Conference, 12 August 1975.)

Monday night has been set aside as an evening for the family together. No Church activity or social appointments may be sponsored on this night. ("America's Strength—The Family," Seattle Washington National Family Night Program, 23 November 1976.)

An evening at home once a week, which I call "Home Evening," where parents and children can all be together to discuss matters, exhibit their talents, enjoy inspiring reading, and have some recreation, is a good protector against the breakdown of the family. For many years now our Church has encouraged parents to hold weekly family home evenings. To this end the Church has published a home evening manual with helpful suggestions for each week's activities that include family recreation and character-building lessons. (*An Enemy Hath Done This,* pp. 56–57.)

There are some today who complain that the home evening manual should have been issued years ago. If this is true, the Lord will hold His servants accountable; but no one can say that from the inception of the Church up to the present day the Lord, through His Spirit to the individual members and through His spokesmen, the prophets, has not given us the objectives and plenty of guidelines and counsel. The fact that some of us have not done much about it even when it is spelled out in detail is not the Lord's fault. (*God, Family, Country,* p. 383.)

The Lord knew that in the last days Satan would try to destroy the family unit. Never in the history of the world have we witnessed such a bombardment of propaganda against the basic institution in the Lord's kingdom—the family. How grateful we should be that God inspired His prophet over half a century ago to institute the weekly home evening program. This is the vanguard for getting parents to assume the responsibility of instructing their children. An increasing number of faithful Saints are holding more than one home evening a week and are adding to or deleting from the home evening manual as the Spirit dictates. (Logan, Utah, 6 December 1975.)

A major responsibility of family heads is to help prepare youth for the future. Gospel principles may be instilled through effective family home evenings where youth will be fortified so that they have no need to fear for their future. Such teaching must be done in faith, testimony, and optimism. (CR April 1978, *Ensign* 8 [May 1978]: 33.)

The inspired home evening and family council program has provided many happy hours and great joy together. It has built faith, strengthened testimonies, and created a family solidarity and unity that will endure throughout the eternity. ("America's Strength—The Family," Seattle Washington National Family Night Program, 23 November 1976.)

Sometimes the Lord hopefully waits on His children to act on their own, and when they do not, they lose the greater prize, and the Lord will either drop the entire matter and let them suffer the consequences or else He will have to spell it out in greater detail. Usually, I fear, the more He has to spell it out, the smaller is our reward.

Often, because of circumstances, the Lord, through revelation to His prophets or through inspired programs designed by faithful members which later become adopted on a Churchwide basis, will give to all the membership a righteous means to help accomplish the objective. For instance, any member of the Church a century ago who studied Church doctrine would have known that he had the prime responsibility to see that his children had spiritualized family recreation and were taught in the home lessons in character building and gospel principles. But some did not do it. Then, in 1915 President Joseph F. Smith introduced Churchwide "the weekly home evening program," with promised blessings to all who faithfully adopted it. Many refused and lost the promised blessings. (At the October Conference, 1947, I referred to that promise in a talk on family home evenings.) Today we have the home evening manual and other helps. Yet some still refuse to bring up their children in righteousness. (*An Enemy Hath Done This*, p. 272.)

Here are the promised blessings for those who will hold a weekly home evening: "If the Saints obey this counsel, we promise that great blessings will result. Love at home and obedience to parents will increase. Faith will be developed in the hearts of the youth of Israel, and they will gain power to combat the evil influences and temptations which beset them." (First Presidency, April 27, 1915, in *Improvement Era* 18:733–34.) (*God, Family, Country*, p. 228.)

There is a great need for family recreation and cultural activities together. We should do things together as a family. It may mean a reduction in participation in women's clubs, in men's clubs, but if families could only seek their recreation and cultural activities more as a family unit, I am sure that untold benefits and blessings would accrue. Let us take more of our vacations together as families. Can we have a weekly evening at home, as has been admonished and counseled for years by the First Presidency of the Church? More wholesome activities together is a great need of families. ("The Home and Family," BYU Religious Life Series, Provo, Utah, September 1960.)

May I heartily commend to all—whether or not you are a Latter-day Saint—to gather your family about you on a once-a-week basis for a family home evening night. Such evenings where scriptures are read, skits acted out, songs sung around the piano, games played, special refreshments enjoyed, and family prayers offered, like links in an iron chain, bind a family together with love, tradition, strength, and loyalty to each other. ("America's Strength—The Family," Seattle Washington National Family Night Program, 23 November 1976.)

Having come out of a home where home evenings were practiced, having continued such a practice with our own children, and now seeing them carry on this same happy tradition, I testify to its blessings and benefits and commend the practice to you. ("The Ten Commandments," *New Era* 8 [July 1978]: 38–39.)

Marriage

You will need to find your wife or husband. This will require careful and prayerful consideration. It would be well to mingle with many good people to have a better understanding of others. If you desire a fine companion, you should be that kind of fine person for whom that companion would be looking. Your dating should be on a high and wholesome level. One of the best yardsticks for knowing whether a certain person may be best for you is to ask yourself what kind of an influence this person has on you. In their presence do you wish you were better than you are? Do you think some of your noblest thoughts? Are you encouraged to goodly deeds? If this is so, that person could be worthy of greater consideration. But if being in their company makes you tend in the opposite direction, you had best leave them.

Young women, you are not required to lower your standards to get a husband. Keep yourselves attractive, maintain high standards, place yourselves in a position to meet worthy men, and be engaged in constructive work. Then, if you are married later than sooner—if you even have to wait until the next life to get a choice man—God will make up the difference to you. Time is numbered only to man. God has your eternal perspective in mind. ("In His Steps," in *1979 Devotional Speeches of the Year* [Provo, Utah: BYU, 1980], p. 64.)

A married couple have an obligation not only to each other, but to God. He has promised blessings to those who honor that covenant. Fidelity to one's marriage vows is absolutely essential for love, trust, and peace. Adultery is unequivocally condemned by the Lord. (CR October 1982, *Ensign* 12 [November 1982]: 59.)

I would like to say to all young married couples: Work together. Don't be afraid to set your sights high and don't settle for less than you are capable of—in service to God, your home, your nation, and your career. Do today's job, whatever it is, as best you can. This is the best possible preparation for tomorrow's opportunities. (*Crossfire: The Eight Years with Eisenhower,* p. 330.)

Restraint and self-control must be ruling principles in the marriage relationship. Couples must learn to bridle their tongues as well as their passions. (CR October 1982, *Ensign* 12 [November 1982]: 60.)

The family has serious problems. Divorce is epidemic. The incidence of delinquency is on the rise. The answer is not more marriage counselors or social workers. The answer lies in a husband and wife taking their marriage covenant seriously, realizing that they both have a responsibility to make their marriage a happy one. ("The Ten Commandments," *New Era* 8 [July 1978]: 38.)

We teach and emphasize that the key to family stability is happy marriage based on family worship. ("Righteousness Exalteth a Nation," Provo Utah Freedom Festival, 29 June 1986.)

Prayer in the home and prayer with each other will strengthen your union. Gradually thoughts, aspirations, and ideas will merge into a oneness until you are seeking the same purposes and goals. Rely on the Lord, the teachings of the prophets, and the scriptures for guidance and help, particularly when there may be disagreements and problems.

Spiritual growth comes by solving problems together—not by running from them. Today's inordinate emphasis on individualism brings egotism and separation. Two individuals becoming "one flesh" is still the Lord's standard.

The secret of a happy marriage is to serve God and each other. The goal of marriage is unity and oneness, as well as self-development. Paradoxically, the more we serve one another, the greater is our spiritual and emotional growth. (CR October 1982, *Ensign* 12 [November 1982]: 60.)

The advocates of complete materialism would do away with marriage. Yet marriage, designed to be an eternal covenant, is the most glorious and most exalting principle ordained for the mature development of man. It has the greatest capacity to develop to the fullest the positive virtues of life—unselfishness, tenderness, compassion, love, devotion, integrity, honesty, service, purity, nobility, and a host of others. No ordinance is of more importance and none more sacred and more necessary to the eternal joy of man. (*The Red Carpet*, p. 276.)

Eternal Marriage

Marriage, designed to be an eternal covenant, is the most glorious and most exalting principle of the gospel of Jesus Christ. Faithfulness to the marriage covenant brings the fullest joy here and glorious rewards hereafter. The abuse of this sacred ordinance despoils the lives of individuals, wrecks the basic institution of the home, and causes the downfall of nations. (*So Shall Ye Reap,* p. 106.)

Marriage, the home, and family are more than mere social institutions. They are divine, not man-made. God ordained marriage from the very beginning. In the record of that first marriage recorded in Genesis, the Lord makes four significant pronouncements: first, that it is not good for man to be alone; second, that woman was created to be a helpmeet for man; third, that they twain should be one flesh; and fourth, that man should leave father and mother and cleave unto his wife. (See Genesis 2:18, 24.)

Later, as though to reinforce the earlier statement, the Lord said: "What therefore God hath joined together, let not man put asunder" (Matthew 19:6). He also said, "Thou shalt love thy wife with all thy heart, and shalt cleave unto her and none else" (D&C 42:22).

This first marriage, instituted by God, was between two immortal beings. Marriage was thus intended to be eternal. Following the consummation of this marriage, God gave Adam and Eve important instruction about the perpetuation of the family, instruction that has never been rescinded: "Be fruitful, and multiply, and replenish the earth" (Genesis 1:28). (*This Nation Shall Endure,* p. 100.)

The scriptures tell us: "Adam began to till the earth . . . as I the Lord had commanded him. And Eve also, his wife, did labor with him . . . they began to multiply and to replenish the earth. And Adam and Eve, his wife, called upon the name of the Lord. . . . And Adam and Eve blessed the name of God, and they made all things known unto their sons and their daughters. And Adam and Eve, his wife, ceased not to call upon God." (Moses 5:1–2, 4, 12, 16.)

From this inspired record we see that Adam and Eve provided us with an ideal example of a covenant marriage relationship. They labored together; they had children together; they prayed together; and they taught their children the gospel—together. This is the pattern God would have all righteous men and women imitate. ("To the Elect Women of the Kingdom of God," Beneficial Life Convention, Oahu, Hawaii, 12 May 1986.)

I would like to express the hope which we all have for you, which is so real, that you will be exalted in the highest degree of glory in the celestial kingdom. What does that mean? That means you will enter into the new and everlasting covenant of marriage for time and for all eternity—an absolute requirement to attain to the highest degree of glory in the celestial kingdom. That means you will marry in the Church. That means you will marry in one of the temples of God. (BYU Ten-Stake Fireside, Provo, Utah, 7 May 1972.)

The record clearly shows that your chances of success in marriage are much greater if you marry someone of your own faith, and infinitely greater if you marry in the temple of God. And I don't say this critically of those who are here who may have married out of the Church, and who are hoping and praying for the time when they will have spiritual unity in their home and family; but I am saying to you, marry in the Church. Marry in the temple of God that you may start out right and have a successful married life. (San Diego, California South Stake Conference, 7 December 1969.)

If you are going to be fully happy, you need to be married in the temple of God. Marriage can never mean the same outside the temple as it does inside. It is God's way. You can afford to sacrifice almost anything for that blessing, in order to complete your plans and realize your dreams of being married right, in the house of the Lord. Ofttimes feeble excuses are given. Temples are far away. Of course, they are far away. Yet it is no farther from Washington, D.C., to Salt Lake today than it was from Salt Lake to St. George when President Heber J. Grant was married. It isn't as far in point of time. President Grant made it in a wagon. Devote at least as much planning to marriage as you do to your vacation plans. However, you can't rightly draw a comparison between the two. Yes, marriage in the temple is absolutely essential if we would be truly happy. (*So Shall Ye Reap,* pp. 183–84.)

As stake president, I had been meeting with a group of seventies and stake missionaries north of Washington, D.C. I was ready to return home when one of the seventies, a stake missionary, came to me and said, "President Benson, how are you going back to Washington?"

I told him I was driving and he said he would like to have a personal visit with me. I invited him to return to Washington with me, some ninety miles. In the course of our travel, he said, "I presume you have noted that Jane and I are keeping company."

I said, "Yes."

"And that we have announced our engagement?" he responded. He then said, "We would like you, as our stake president, to perform our marriage."

I replied, "No, you don't want me to perform your marriage. Aren't you a returned missionary?"

"Yes," he said.

Then I said, "Don't you want to be married in the temple?"

"Yes, of course," he replied, "but Jane wants a marriage in the chapel like her sister had."

I recalled that rather elaborate marriage in the chapel. It was the first social function we attended after coming to the Washington area—a bit shocking to a former stake president of Boise, Idaho.

On arrival at our destination, I asked the young man to leave the matter with me and I would see if I could help. I called the girl's father—a faithful high priest—and told him of my conversation with his future son-in-law. I asked him if he would like to see his daughter married in the temple.

He said, "There isn't anything I wouldn't do that's right to see her go to the temple. When her sister was married, they said that as soon as the husband got a vacation they would go to the temple and be sealed. But now he has a new job and has to wait a year before he is eligible for a vacation. Also, a baby is now on the way and they seem to have lost interest in temple marriage."

I had only recently learned about another young couple who were debating whether they should be married in the temple. They were from Arizona. The young man's mother was coming out to visit him—no doubt to try and persuade them to go to the temple.

We arranged for those two young couples to travel together by automobile, with the one young man's mother as chaperone, to be married in the Mesa Temple (the Washington D.C. Temple had not yet been built). On their return, we had a joint reception for them in the cultural hall. The young woman who wanted a marriage like her sister asked her stake president to stand in the line with her. As young people went through the line, this lovely girl repeated over and over again to them, "Don't ever be satisfied with anything less than a temple marriage."

Now, if that can be done under their circumstances, what of those who live in the shadow of the temple? I wonder if we as parents are doing all we can to teach, encourage, and impress on our youth the importance of temple marriage. ("Temple Blessings and Covenants," Washington D.C. Temple, 21 January 1981.)

May I tell you about something most sacred? Picture in your mind a small room beautifully adorned—something akin to a lovely living room. In the center is an altar covered with velvet and lace. Chairs line the walls of the room, where just family and closest friends may observe. With family observing, and a priesthood man of God officiating, you will be asked to kneel at the altar opposite your companion. You will be given instructions, and a benediction will be pronounced upon you. Then you will be sealed together as husband and wife for time and all eternity. You are given the same promise that Adam, Abraham, Isaac, and Jacob received.

Temple marriage is a gospel ordinance for exaltation. (CR April 1979, *Ensign* 9 [May 1979]: 33.)

If our children—and their children—are taught well by us, this temple will have special significance. When your children ask why we marry in the temple, you should teach them that temples are the only places on the earth where certain ordinances may be performed. You should also share with your children your personal feelings as you knelt together before the sacred altar and took upon yourselves covenants which made it possible for them to be sealed to you forever. Yes, this temple is the place where families may become an eternal unit. (Atlanta Georgia Temple Cornerstone Laying, 1 June 1983.)

Because of confidence in the perpetuity of the home and family into the eternities, we build our most elaborate and expensive structures—temples of God—so that men, women, and their children may be bound together by covenant in an everlasting union which will transcend all the limitations of this mortal sphere.

("Strengthen Your Families," Preston Idaho North Stake, 10 June 1984.)

I want to speak frankly to you young men and young women of the Church. When you marry, your decision not only affects you, but your future children and generations after you. Every child born to Latter-day Saint parents deserves to be born in the covenant of temple blessings. (CR April 1979, *Ensign* 9 [May 1979]: 33.)

The temple is an ever-present reminder that God intends the family to be eternal. How fitting it is for mothers and fathers to point to the temple and say to their children, "That is the place where we were married for eternity." By so doing, the ideal of temple marriage can be instilled within the minds and hearts of your children while they are very young. ("What I Hope You Will Teach Your Children about the Temple," *Ensign* 15 [August 1985]: 6–7.)

Don't trifle away your happiness by an involvement with someone who cannot take you worthily to the temple. Make a decision now that this is the place where you will marry. To leave that decision until a romantic involvement develops is to take a risk, the importance of which you can't calculate now.

I would urge you further to pray about this matter. Obtain the testimony of the truth of these things before a romantic involvement can take root. Covenant with your Heavenly Father that you will do His will. Live a clean, moral life, and be worthy of His Spirit to bless you.

No sacrifice is too great to have the blessings of an eternal marriage. To most of us, a temple is easily accessible, perhaps so conveniently that the blessing is taken too casually. As with other matters of faithfulness in gospel living, being married the Lord's way takes a willingness to deny yourself ungodliness — worldliness — and a determination to do our Father's will. By this act of faith, we show our love to God and our regard for a posterity yet unborn. As our family is our greatest source of joy in this life, so it may well be in the eternity. (CR April 1979, *Ensign* 9 [May 1979]: 33–34.)

Multiply and Replenish

Man enters into a lawful marriage covenant and propagates his own posterity. To fulfill this purpose, God ordained marriage. The Lord declared that: "Marriage is ordained of God . . . that the earth might answer the end of its creation; And that it might be filled with the measure of man, according to his creation before the world was made." (D&C 49:15–17.)

A law of procreation was decreed by God to the lawfully married. "Be fruitful, and multiply, and replenish the earth" (Genesis 1:28). This law permits others of our Heavenly Father's children to be legitimately born into good families where these spirits can also grow to maturity and work out their salvation. The law of procreation has never been rescinded. (Miami, Florida, 19 March 1976.)

In The Church of Jesus Christ of Latter-day Saints chastity will never be out of date. We have one standard for men and women, and that standard is moral purity. We oppose and abhor the damnable practice of wholesale abortion and every other unholy and impure act which strikes at the very foundation of the home and family, our most basic institutions. (*God, Family, Country*, p. 364.)

As parents, what is our attitude regarding the sacred obligations of parenthood? One of the major purposes of marriage is children. Nations which refuse to accept this God-given obligation sink into oblivion. Will our sons and daughters want children because of our attitude and example? (*So Shall Ye Reap*, p. 106.)

We can't build a happy home, we can't build a happy married life, on the foundation of immorality. It can't be done. So I would beseech our young people to reserve for the marriage relationship those sweet and lovely and intimate associations. Not only that, but when those associations come, let them be primarily for the purpose of procreation, for the having of a family, because it is not pleasing in the sight of God to enjoy the pleasures of those associations and refuse to accept the responsibility of parenthood. (*God, Family, Country*, pp. 196–97.)

Do not postpone the blessings of honorable parenthood following marriage. When God said it was our responsibility to multiply and replenish the earth, that marriage was primarily for that purpose, He didn't insert any provisions. (London Area Conference, 19–20 June 1976.)

A modern trend is to rationalize the commandment to procreate, saying that the earth cannot support this great number of unrestricted births, or that it is not financially possible to support a great number of children today. The Lord said to the Prophet Joseph, referring to the productive capacity of the earth, "For the earth is full and there is enough and to spare" (D&C 104:17). (Miami, Florida, 19 March 1976.)

A major reason why there is famine in some parts of the world is because evil men have used the vehicle of government to abridge the freedom that men need to produce abundantly. True to form, many of the people who desire to frustrate God's purposes of giving mortal tabernacles to His spirit children through worldwide birth control are the very same people who support the kinds of government that perpetuate famine. They advocate an evil to cure the results of the wickedness they support. (CR April 1969, *Improvement Era* 72 [June 1969]: 44.)

Brigham Young emphasized: "There are multitudes of pure and holy spirits waiting to take tabernacles, now what is our duty? —to prepare tabernacles for them; to take a course that will not tend to drive those spirits into the families of the wicked, where they will be trained in wickedness, debauchery, and every species of crime. It is the duty of every righteous man and woman to prepare tabernacles for all the spirits they can." (*Discourses of Brigham Young,* p. 197.)

Yes, blessed is the husband and wife who have a family of children. The deepest joys and blessings in life are associated with family, parenthood, and sacrifice. ("To the Mothers in Zion," Parents' Fireside, Salt Lake City, Utah, 22 February 1987.)

The undue postponement of parenthood is bound to bring disappointment and is not pleasing in the sight of God. Yes, of course, one can always find excuses. The young husband is going through school. I know how difficult it is. I remember our first year of married life on seventy dollars a month for both of us. I thank the Lord for my noble companion and her fervent determination to put first things first.

It thrills me to witness young couples where the husband is struggling through medical school or dental school or some other school and they have the courage and strength and the faith to know that in some way the God of Heaven will assist them if they do their duty and have their families.

So, I would ask our young people to think seriously about these things, pray about them, fast about them. The Lord will give them the answers, because He wants them to have the blessings of a righteous posterity. Sometimes marriage may be postponed to the point where, for physical and other reasons, parenthood is denied. Oh, what a loss when the time comes! It is worth practically any sacrifice to have those sweet spirits come into the home and to have them come early, that the parents might enjoy them for a longer period, that they might enjoy their parents for a longer period, and that the children might enjoy their grandparents for a longer period. (*God, Family, Country,* pp. 197–98.)

Today the undermining of the home and family is on the increase, with the devil anxiously working to displace the father as the head of the home and create rebellion among the children. The Book of Mormon describes this condition when it states, "As for my people, children are their oppressors, and women rule over them." And then these words follow—and consider these words seriously when you think of those political leaders who are promoting birth control and abortion: "O my people, they which lead thee cause thee to err, and destroy the way of thy paths" (Isaiah 3:12; 2 Nephi 13:12). Let me warn the sisters in all seriousness that you who submit yourselves to an abortion or to an operation that precludes you from safely having additional healthy children are jeopardizing your exaltation and your future membership in the kingdom of God. (*God, Family, Country,* p. 224.)

We realize that some women, through no fault of their own, are not able to bear children. To these lovely sisters, every prophet of God has promised that they will be blessed with children in the eternities and that posterity will not be denied them. Through pure faith, pleading prayers, fasting, and special priesthood blessings, many of these same lovely sisters, with their noble companions at their sides, have had miracles take place in their lives and have been blessed with children. Others have prayerfully chosen to adopt children, and to these wonderful couples we salute you for the sacrifices and love you have given to those children you have chosen to be your own. ("To the Mothers in Zion," Parents' Fireside, Salt Lake City, Utah, 22 February 1987.)

Some well-known persons advocate drastic steps by government action to limit population growth. They contend that the world must stabilize its population or many must starve. In short, the only course that can save mankind from disaster lurking just around the corner is the worldwide adoption by government of population restriction policies.

This, I firmly believe, is an unrealistic and dangerous oversimplification. It is inconceivable to me that the problem of food and people either will, or can, be solved in this way. For one thing, the right to marry and have a family, and to determine the size of one's family in accordance with one's conscience and legitimate desires is so fundamental that I just can't visualize people permitting government to tamper with it. The whole thing smacks of government interference at its totalitarian worst. It is not the business of government to enter this area.

Moreover, the available facts do not support the notion that mankind must become increasingly sterile or starve. Those who are fond of projecting population trends into the future never seem willing to do the same for food production trends. They concentrate their gaze on the people side of the equation and blind themselves to the food side. It is true that there has been a population explosion of sorts in recent decades. But there has been an even greater agricultural technological explosion—not only in the United States but also in the world in general. The population explosion is running substantially behind the agricultural explosion —and the agricultural explosion is just beginning except where hampered by government interference. (*Title of Liberty,* pp. 127–28.)

We know that every spirit assigned to this earth will come, whether through us or someone else. There are couples in the

Church who think they are getting along just fine with their limited families but who will someday suffer the pains of remorse when they meet the spirits that might have been part of their posterity. The first commandment given to man was to multiply and replenish the earth with children (Genesis 1:28). That commandment has never been altered, modified, or cancelled. The Lord did not say to multiply and replenish the earth if it is convenient, or if you are wealthy, or after you have gotten your schooling, or when there is peace on earth, or until you have four children. The Bible says, "Lo, children are an heritage of the Lord and . . . Happy is the man that hath his quiver full of them" (Psalm 127:3, 5). We believe God is glorified by having numerous children and a program of perfection for them. So also will God glorify that husband and wife who have a large posterity and who try to raise them up in righteousness. (*God, Family, Country,* pp. 257–58.)

I know the special blessings of a large and happy family, for my dear parents had a quiver full of children (Psalm 127:5). Being the oldest of eleven children, I saw the principles of unselfishness, mutual cooperation, loyalty to each other, and a host of other virtues developed in a large and wonderful family with my noble mother as the queen of that home.

Young mothers and fathers, with all my heart I counsel you not to postpone having your children, being co-creators with our Father in Heaven. Do not use the reasoning of the world, such as, "We will wait until we can better afford having children, until we are more secure, until John has completed his education, until he has a better paying job, until we have a larger home, until we have obtained a few of the material conveniences," and on and on. This is the reasoning of the world and is not pleasing in the sight of God. Mothers who enjoy good health, have your children and have them early. And, husbands, always be considerate of your wives in the bearing of children.

Do not curtail the number of children for personal or selfish reasons. Material possessions, social convenience, and so-called professional advantages are nothing compared to a righteous posterity. In the eternal perspective, children—not possessions, not position, not prestige—are our greatest jewels. ("To the Mothers in Zion," Parents' Fireside, Salt Lake City, Utah, 22 February 1987.)

Single Adults

To you single adult brethren, I want you to know of my great love for each of you. I have great expectations for you and a great hope in you. You have so much to contribute to the Lord and to the kingdom of God now and in the future. You may be twenty-seven years of age, or thirty, or possibly even older.

Just what are your priorities at this time in your life?

Remember the counsel of Elder Bruce R. McConkie that "the most important single thing that any Latter-day Saint ever does in this world is to marry the *right* person in the *right* place by the *right* authority." ("Choose an Eternal Companion," *BYU Speeches of the Year*, [Provo, Utah: BYU, 1986], p. 2.)

Just a few weeks ago, I received a letter from two devoted parents, part of which reads as follows:

> Dear President Benson: We are concerned about what seems to be a growing problem—at least in this part of the Church familiar to us—that is, so many choice young men in the Church over the age of thirty who are still unmarried.
>
> We have sons thirty, thirty-one, and thirty-three in this situation. Many of our friends also are experiencing this same concern for unmarried sons and daughters.
>
> In our experience these are usually young men who have been on missions, are well educated, and are living the commandments (except this most important one). There does not appear to be a lack of choice young ladies in the same age bracket who could make suitable companions. It is most frustrating to us, as their parents, who sometimes feel we have failed in our parental teachings and guiding responsibilities.

My dear single adult brethren, we are also concerned. We want you to know that the position of the Church has never changed regarding the importance of celestial marriage. It is a commandment of God. The Lord's declaration in Genesis is still true: "And the Lord God said, It is not good that the man should be alone" (Genesis 2:18).

To obtain a fulness of glory and exaltation in the celestial kingdom, one must enter into this holiest of ordinances.

Without marriage, the purposes of the Lord would be frustrated. Choice spirits would be withheld from the experience of mortality. And postponing marriage unduly often means limiting your posterity, and the time will come, brethren, when you will feel and know that loss.

I can assure you that the greatest responsibility and the greatest joys in life are centered in the family, honorable marriage, and rearing a righteous posterity. And the older you become, the less likely you are to marry, and then you may lose these eternal blessings altogether.

President Spencer W. Kimball recounted an experience he once had:

> Recently I met a young returned missionary who is thirty-five years old. He had been home from his mission for fourteen years and yet he was little concerned about his bachelorhood, and laughed about it.
>
> I shall feel sorry for this young man when the day comes that he faces the Great Judge at the throne and when the Lord asks this boy: "Where is your wife?" All of his excuses which he gave to his fellows on earth will seem very light and senseless when he answers the Judge, "I was very busy," or "I felt I should get my education first," or "I did not find the right girl"—such answers will be hollow and of little avail. He knew he was commanded to find a wife and marry her and make her happy. He knew it was his duty to become the father of children and provide a rich, full life for them as they grew up. He knew all this, yet postponed his responsibility. (*Ensign*, February 1975, p. 2.)

I realize that some of you brethren may have genuine fears regarding the real responsibilities that will be yours if you do marry. You are concerned about being able to support a wife and family and provide them with the necessities in these uncertain economic times. Those fears must be replaced with faith.

I assure you, brethren, that if you will be industrious, faithfully pay your tithes and offerings, and conscientiously keep the commandments, the Lord will sustain you. Yes, there will be sacrifices required, but you will grow from these and will be a better man for having met them.

Work hard educationally and in your vocation. Put your trust in the Lord, have faith, and it will work out. The Lord never gives a commandment without providing the means to accomplish it (see 1 Nephi 3:7).

Also, do not be caught up in materialism, one of the real plagues of our generation—that is, acquiring things, fast-paced living, and securing career success in the single state.

Honorable marriage is more important than wealth, position, and status. As husband and wife, you can achieve your life's goals together. As you sacrifice for each other and your children, the Lord will bless you, and your commitment to the Lord and your service in His kingdom will be enhanced.

Now, brethren, do not expect perfection in your choice of a mate. Do not be so particular that you overlook her most important qualities of having a strong testimony, living the principles of the gospel, loving home, wanting to be a mother in Zion, and supporting you in your priesthood responsibilities.

Of course, she should be attractive to you, but do not just date one girl after another for the sole pleasure of dating without seeking the Lord's confirmation in your choice of your eternal companion.

And one good yardstick as to whether a person might be the right one for you is this: in her presence, do you think your noblest thoughts, do you aspire to your finest deeds, do you wish you were better than you are?

Know, my good brethren, that I have spoken from my heart and by His Spirit because of my love and concern for you. It is what the Lord would have you hear today. With all my heart I echo the words of the prophet Lehi from the Book of Mormon, "Arise from the dust, my sons, and be men" (2 Nephi 1:21). (CR April 1988, *Ensign* 18 [May 1988]: 51–53.)

Women

Before the world was created, in heavenly councils the pattern and role of women were prescribed. You were elected by God to be wives and mothers in Zion. Exaltation in the celestial kingdom is predicated on faithfulness to that calling.

Since the beginning, a woman's first and most important role has been ushering into mortality spirit sons and daughters of our Father in Heaven. Since the beginning, her role has been to teach her children eternal gospel principles. She is to provide for her children a haven of security and love—regardless of how modest her circumstances might be. (CR October 1981, *Ensign* 11 [November 1981]: 105.)

The Lord designated Emma Smith as "the elect lady" (D&C 25:3). To you, the faithful sisters, I address you as the "elect women" of the kingdom of God.

Commenting on the phrase "the elect lady," the Prophet Joseph Smith said that elect means "to be elected to a certain work" (*History of the Church*, 4:552). I address you today as elect women, for you have been elected by God to perform a unique and sacred work in our Heavenly Father's eternal plan.

The Gods counseled and said that "it was not good that man should be alone; wherefore, I will make an help meet for him" (Genesis 2:18; Moses 3:18). Why was it not good for man to be alone? If it was only man's loneliness with which God was concerned, He may have provided other companionship. But He provided woman, for she was to be man's helpmeet.

It is not good for man to be alone because a righteous woman complements what may be lacking in man's natural personality and disposition. Paul said: "Neither is the man without the woman, neither the woman without the man, in the Lord" (1 Corinthians 11:11). Nowhere is this complementary association more ideally portrayed than in the eternal marriage of our first parents —Adam and Eve. ("To the Elect Women of the Kingdom of God," Beneficial Life Convention, Oahu, Hawaii, 12 May 1986.)

In the beginning, Adam—not Eve—was instructed to earn the bread by the sweat of his brow. Contrary to conventional wisdom, a mother's calling is in the home, not in the marketplace.

"Women have claim on their husbands for their maintenance, until their husbands are taken" (D&C 83:2). This is the divine right of a wife and mother. She cares for and nourishes her children at home. Her husband earns the living for the family, which makes this nourishing possible. With that claim on their husbands for their financial support, the counsel of the Church has always been for mothers to spend their full time in the home in rearing and caring for their children. ("To the Mothers in Zion," Parents' Fireside, Salt Lake City, Utah, 22 February 1987.)

You were not created to be the same as men. Your natural attributes, affections, and personalities are entirely different from a man's. They consist of faithfulness, benevolence, kindness, and charity. They give you the personality of a woman. They also balance the more aggressive and competitive nature of a man.

The business world is competitive and sometimes ruthless. We do not doubt that women have both the brainpower and skills — and in some instances superior abilities — to compete with men. But by competing they must, of necessity, become aggressive and competitive. Thus their godly attributes are diminished and they acquire a quality of sameness with man.

I received a letter from a sister who has spent most of her life in the work force — providing a second income to the home. Her marriage finally ended in divorce. Her greatest concern was that she felt robbed from not having the time to teach her own children the lasting spiritual values, a woman's godly prerogative.

The conventional wisdom of the day would have you be equal with men. We say, we would not have you descend to that level. More often than not the demand for equality means the destruction of the inspired arrangement that God has decreed for man, woman, and the family. Equality should not be confused with equivalence. It is well to remember this inspired counsel of President David O. McKay: "Woe to that home where the mother abandons her holy mission or neglects the divine instruction, influence, and example — while she bows, a devotee, at the shrine of social pleasure; or neglects the essential duties of her own household, in her enthusiasm to promote public reform" (*Gospel Ideals,* p. 481). ("To the Elect Women of the Kingdom," Nauvoo Illinois Relief Society Monument Dedication, 30 June 1978.)

One apparent impact of the women's movement has been the feelings of discontent it has created among young women who have chosen the role of wife and mother. They are often made to feel that there are more exciting and self-fulfilling roles for women than housework, diaper changing, and children calling for mother. This view loses sight of the eternal perspective that God elected women to the noble role of mother and that exaltation is eternal fatherhood and eternal motherhood. ("To the Elect Women of the Kingdom of God," Nauvoo Illinois Relief Society Dedication, 30 June 1978.)

It is divinely ordained what a woman should do, but a man must seek out his work. The divine work of women involves companionship, homemaking, and motherhood. It is well if skills in these three areas can first be learned in the parents' home and then be supplemented at school if the need presents itself. The first priority for a woman is to prepare herself for her divine and eternal mission, whether she is married soon or late. It is folly to neglect that preparation for education in unrelated fields just to prepare temporarily to earn money. Women, when you are married it is the husband's role to provide, not yours. Do not sacrifice your preparation for an eternally ordained mission for the temporary expediency of money-making skills which you may or may not use. ("In His Steps," in *1979 Devotional Speeches of the Year* [Provo, Utah: BYU, 1980], p. 84.)

There are voices in our midst which would attempt to convince you that these home-centered truths are not applicable to our present-day conditions. If you listen and heed, you will be lured away from your principal obligations. Beguiling voices in the world cry out for "alternative life-styles" for women. They maintain that some women are better suited for careers than for marriage and motherhood. These individuals spread their discontent by the propaganda that there are more exciting and self-fulfilling roles for women than homemaking. Some even have been bold to suggest that the Church move away from the "Mormon woman stereotype" of homemaking and rearing children. They also say it is wise to limit your family so you can have more time for personal goals and self-fulfillment. (CR October 1981, *Ensign* 11 [November 1981]: 105.)

A woman whose life is involved in the righteous rearing of her children has a better chance of keeping up her spirits than the woman whose total concern is centered in her own personal problems. (CR October 1974, *Ensign* 4 [November 1974]: 66.)

Some sisters are widowed or divorced. My heart is drawn to you who are in these circumstances. The Brethren pray for you, and we feel a great obligation to see that your needs are met. Trust in the Lord. Be assured He loves you and we love you. Resist bitterness and cynicism. (CR October 1981, *Ensign* 11 [November 1981]: 105.)

We realize that some of our choice sisters are widowed and divorced and that others find themselves in unusual circumstances where, out of necessity, they are required to work for a period of time. But these instances are the exception, not the rule.

In a home where there is an able-bodied husband, he is expected to be the breadwinner. Sometimes we hear of husbands who, because of economic conditions, have lost their jobs and expect their wives to go out of the home and work even though the husband is still capable of providing for his family. In these cases, we urge the husband to do all in his power to allow his wife to remain in the home caring for the children while he continues to provide for his family the best he can, even though the job he is able to secure may not be ideal and family budgeting will have to be tighter. ("To the Mothers in Zion," Parents' Fireside, Salt Lake City, Utah, 22 February 1987.)

Not all women in the Church will have an opportunity for marriage and motherhood in mortality. But if you in this situation are worthy and endure faithfully, you can be assured of all blessings from a kind and loving Heavenly Father—and I emphasize *all* blessings.

Solutions for you who are in a minority are not the same as for the majority of women in the Church who can and should be fulfilling their roles as wives and mothers. It is a misguided idea that a woman should leave the home, where there is a husband and children, to prepare educationally and financially for an unforeseen eventuality. Too often, I fear, even women in the Church use the world as their standard for success and basis for self-worth.

Some are deluded into believing that more and better circumstances will improve their self-image. A positive self-image has little relationship to our material circumstances. Mary, the mother of our Savior, was of most modest circumstances, yet she knew well her responsibility and took joy in it. Remember her humble exclamation to her cousin Elisabeth: "He hath regarded the low estate of his hand-maiden: for, behold, from henceforth all generations shall call me blessed" (Luke 1:48). Her strength was inward, not from outward material things. (CR October 1981, *Ensign* 11 [November 1981]: 105.)

Young women, we hope you will keep yourselves clean. We hope you will look forward to the time when you can become honorable mothers—homemakers. There is no higher calling for woman. We hope you will prepare for it, look forward to it, and that you will enjoy it. (Salt Lake Utah Seminary Fireside, 1974.)

There is no question that faithful Latter-day Saint young women can have a great impact for good in helping young men to magnify their priesthood and to motivate them to good works and to be their best selves. ("To the Young Women of the Church," *Ensign* 16 [November 1986]: 83.)

Often a woman shapes the career of her husband, or brother, or son. "A man succeeds and reaps the honors of public applause, when in truth," a steadfast and courageous woman has in large measure "made it all possible—has by her tact and encouragement held him to his best, has had faith in him when his own faith has languished, has cheered him with the unfailing assurance, 'You can, you must, you will.' " (David O. McKay, *Treasures of Life,* pp. 53–54.) ("To the Elect Women of the Kingdom of God," Beneficial Life Convention, Oahu, Hawaii, 12 May 1986.)

Support, encourage, and strengthen your husband in his responsibility as patriarch in the home. You are partners with him. A woman's role is to lift him, to help him uphold lofty standards, and to prepare through righteous living to be his queen for all eternity. (CR October 1981, *Ensign* 11 [November 1981]: 107.)

You, my sisters, set the example through your lives and through your teachings that influence children to set proper examples for others. "A little child shall lead them" (Isaiah 11:6). No one is too young to exert influence. We begin to lead others, appreciably, as soon as we have character of our own. There is a certain innocence of heart, purity of soul, and refinement of feeling peculiar to children, to youth, which affects other people, ofttimes more vitally and potently than we are accustomed to think. These are mature spirits in infant bodies, in child bodies—precious, eternal souls. Let us ever consider them as such. So, as you teach these children, remember this is our first obligation, to implant in their hearts a testimony of the divinity of this great work. ("Our First Obligation," Annual Conference of the Primary Association, Salt Lake City, Utah, 5 April 1950.)

Youth

Young people are the key to success in any movement, good or bad, for they are idealistic, bold, and vigorous. ("The Greatest Work in the World," *Improvement Era* 70 [January 1967]: 26.)

Too often we have a tendency to overlook the youth. They have great minds, retentive minds. They are choice spirits. ("Eternal Memories," Tenth Annual Priesthood Genealogical Research Seminar, BYU, Provo, Utah, 31 July 1975.)

Youth have a duty to themselves. They need to develop in themselves the finest characteristics of mankind: Inward peace, faith, humility, integrity, charity, courage, thrift, cooperation, and an ability for good hard work—all ingredients for a good character. (*The Red Carpet*, p. 282.)

It seems to me that the best way to get ready for tomorrow is by being sure that we are living up to the opportunities of today. The way to prepare for the responsibilities of manhood and womanhood is by living up to the responsibilities of youth. The way to build a solid basis for meeting big problems in the future is by carefully and soberly meeting smaller problems in the present.

It has been said that our young people are becoming soft—that they are demanding harder and harder butter on softer and softer bread. I for one do not believe it. (*The Red Carpet,* pp. 280–81.)

Each generation faces issues and problems different from any other generation. Yet running throughout are difficulties, temptations, and trends very closely related and common to each period. The same principles are involved, the same unchangeable, eternal verities, and the same enduring standards of right and wrong are being tested.

Today as in generations past, there are powers and influences at work which strike at the very foundations of all that youth has been taught from their mother's knee as a heritage of righteousness from generations gone before. (Foreword to *Youth and the Church* [Salt Lake City: Deseret Book, 1970], p. vii.)

Youth should realize their duty to our country. They should love and honor the Constitution of the United States, the basic concepts and principles upon which this nation has been established. Yes, they need to develop a love for our free institutions.

They should realize their duty to serve others. To serve others willingly and unselfishly is one of the greatest virtues. They should learn cooperation. Not everybody can lead, but everybody can cooperate. We need in the world today the ability to work together and serve one another in peace and harmony. (*God, Family, Country,* p. 219.)

We can never survive unless our young people understand and appreciate our American system which has given more of the good things of life than any other system in the world—unless they have a dedication that exceeds the dedication of the enemy. Character must become important in this country again. The old essentials of honesty, self-respect, loyalty, and support for law and order must be taught the younger generation. (*An Enemy Hath Done This,* p. 11.)

I often think of what the jailer said to General Dean as he and some other American servicemen were finally released from jail at the end of the Korean War. Some of the North Korean jailers turned to General Dean and said, "General, don't feel bad about leaving us; we will see you again." When General Dean said, "What do you mean?" they said, "We are going to destroy the character of one whole generation of American youth. And when we have finished, you will have nothing with which to defend yourselves."

I would like to say to you that there is every evidence that that effort is underway. It is organized. It is directed by evil forces—evil forces that are smart in their way, and the thrust and the aim is at the youth of this great country. It comes at a time when the churches of the Christian world have probably never been weaker than they are today. (BYU Ten-Stake Fireside, Provo, Utah, 7 May 1972.)

We must make sure that freedom means more to our youth than just peace. We must make sure that freedom means more to our youth than just security. We must make sure that freedom means more to our youth than just selfish gain. We must emphasize the need of character in the citizens of America.

The power of America lies in every boy and girl back in the hinterlands of this great nation. The strength of America will be no greater than these young people as they grow in character and prepare themselves to step across the threshold of citizenship. As citizens of our community, let us make sure we do our best in building the utmost in character and faith and judgment in these young people who, someday, will take our places. (*An Enemy Hath Done This,* pp. 121–22.)

Could it be that through the proper training of youth we are helping to serve America? Can we not contribute to America's stamina and survival? We can teach reverence to God, unselfishness, love of country, and the fundamental principles of righteous living. We can try to train youth through means of character. We must urge a religious life; we must encourage good education; we must promote patriotism; we must emphasize honesty, trustworthiness, loyalty, and many other fine attributes of good character. The opportunity is ours, and the need is great. One of the tasks is to rediscover and reassert our faith in the spiritual values on which American life has rested from its beginning.

We might survive a nuclear attack—but we cannot survive (any better than Athens and Rome) moral degeneration and the abandonment of fundamental principles. (*An Enemy Hath Done This,* p. 121.)

Latter-day Saint Youth

It is my conviction that the finest group of young people that this world has ever known anything about has been born under the covenant into the homes of Latter-day Saint parents. I have a feeling that in many cases at least, these choice spirits have been held back to come forth in this day and age when the gospel is upon the earth in its fulness, and that they have great responsibilities in establishing the kingdom. (CR April 1951, *Improvement Era* 54 [June 1951]: 422.)

Our young people are not just ordinary people. They are not just run-of-the-mill. They are choice spirits. President Wilford Woodruff said this: "The Lord has chosen a small number of choice spirits of sons and daughters out of all the creations of God, who are to inherit this earth; and this company of choice spirits have been kept in the spirit world for six thousand years to come forth in the last days to stand in the flesh in this last dispensation of the fulness of times, to organize the kingdom of God upon the earth, to build it up and to defend it and to receive the eternal and everlasting priesthood [of God]." (*Title of Liberty,* p. 197.)

Your heritage is one of the very greatest in all the world. You need never envy one born heir to millions in worldly wealth, nor even one whose birth entitles him to rule an empire. Your birthright surpasses all these, and blessed are you because of your lineage.

Your life has come down from generation to generation through the patriarchs and the prophets of ancient Israel, through the noblest and most faithful of the descendants of the dark days of their dispersion, from kings and rulers, great nobles and warriors and law-givers of many nations, from many God-fearing men and women of honest lives—some of them outstanding leaders in service to their race and age. You need never apologize for your earthly fathers and mothers, for in your veins runs the best blood in the land.

You are now on your mission. As someone has said, "Your days of preparation and expectancy are over." You looked forward to this time in the spirit world when you could come here, receive bodies through noble parentage, where you could face a sinful world and prove yourselves worthy of the rich blessings which are in store for the faithful. ("The Greatest Leadership," BYU Student Leadership Conference, Sun Valley, Idaho, September 1959.)

The most successful program of complete youth fitness ever known to man was described in fourteen words. They are the words of the beloved disciple Luke in the New Testament. He uses just one sentence to cover a period of eighteen years—the eighteen years in which the Savior of the world, after returning to Nazareth from Jerusalem, prepared Himself for His public life: "And Jesus increased in wisdom and stature, and in favour with God and man" (Luke 2:52). There is the ideal of any program of youth fitness, to help our youth increase in wisdom and stature and in favor with God and man. It covers everything—physical fitness, mental fitness, social fitness, emotional fitness, and spiritual fitness. (*So Shall Ye Reap*, p. 140.)

You are part of a great Church organization, a worldwide organization. The movement now is out from Church headquarters. I hope our young people will continue to spread out and take their places in the communities, in the states, and in the countries of the world; that they will maintain the standards of the Church; that they will excel in their chosen fields; that they will have God as their companion, and the companionship of His Spirit; and that they will be ready, when the time comes, to defend and to support this free system under which we live. ("A Fourfold Hope," Brigham Young University, Provo, Utah, 24 May 1961.)

I am very anxious that the young people of the Church measure up in every way to that which the Lord expects of them. They are a choice group. They are a peculiar group also. Peter, in writing to the Saints anciently, said, "Ye are a chosen generation, a royal priesthood, an holy nation, a peculiar people" (1 Peter 2:9). And our young people today are peculiar in many ways. Certainly they are peculiar in their standards if they are living the gospel. (*God, Family, Country,* p. 189.)

Our youth in action have been an inspiration to people everywhere. The eyes of the world are focused on The Church of Jesus Christ of Latter-day Saints and its young people as never before in its history. ("Opportunity and Challenge," in *Speeches of the Year* [Provo, Utah: BYU, 1970], p. 6.)

You, my young brothers and sisters, were sent to earth through royal lineage. You were provided with a fulness of truth so you would not be blinded by the sophistries of men or of devils. You young men were given the priesthood which empowers you to be a representative of Jesus Christ. You young sisters will be blessed to bear sons and daughters and bring them through the veil to mortality. You were chosen to come here when the gospel is on the earth, and during a time when events are building toward the return of Jesus Christ. What a challenging day we live in—and what a responsibility is ours! ("Be True to God, Country, and Self," Young Adult Fireside, Logan, Utah, 11 February 1979.)

Satan knows that youth is the springtime of life when all things are new and young people are most vulnerable. Youth is the spirit of adventure and awakening. It is a time of physical emerging when the body attains the vigor and good health that may ignore the caution of temperance. Youth is a period of timelessness when the horizons of age seem too distant to be noticed. Thus, the now generation forgets that the present will soon be the past, which one will look back upon either with sorrow and regret or joy and remembrance of cherished experiences. Satan's program is "play now and pay later." He seeks for all to be miserable like unto himself (see 2 Nephi 2:27). The Lord's program is happiness now and joy forever through gospel living. ("To 'The Rising Generation,' " *New Era* 16 [June 1986]: 5.)

May I admonish you to participate in a program of daily reading and pondering of the scriptures. We remember the experience of our beloved prophet President Spencer W. Kimball. As a fourteen-year-old boy he accepted the challenge of reading the Bible from cover to cover. Most of his reading was done by coal oil light in his attic bedroom. He read every night until he completed the 1,519 pages, which took him approximately a year; but he attained his goal.

Of the four great standard works of the Church—the Bible, the Book of Mormon, the Doctrine and Covenants, and the Pearl of Great Price—I would particularly urge you to read again and again the Book of Mormon and ponder and apply its teachings.

The Book of Mormon will change your life. It will fortify you against the evils of our day. It will bring a spirituality into your life that no other book will. It will be the most important book you will read in preparation for a mission and for life. A young man who knows and loves the Book of Mormon, who has read it several times, who has an abiding testimony of its truthfulness, and who applies its teachings will be able to stand against the wiles of the devil and will be a mighty tool in the hands of the Lord. (CR April 1986, *Ensign* 16 [May 1986]: 43.)

Our young generation, as a group, is even more faithful than the older generation. God has reserved you for the eleventh hour —the great and dreadful day of the Lord. It will be your responsibility not only to help bear off the kingdom of God triumphantly but to save your own soul and strive to save those of your family. ("Fourteen Fundamentals in Following the Prophet," in *1980 Devotional Speeches of the Year* [Provo, Utah: BYU, 1981], p. 26.)

We need youth of faith, youth of courage, youth of patriotism, youth of wisdom, youth of vision, youth who are prepared. Someone has said that today's youth needs truth. I remember one of your own professors at this institution, Brother Hugh Nibley, said, "There comes a time when the general defilement of society becomes so great that the rising generation is put under undue pressure and cannot be said to have a choice between the way of light and the way of darkness." Thank God, we are not in that position in this Church. (BYU Ten-Stake Fireside, Provo, Utah, 7 May 1972.)

Give me a young woman who loves home and family, who reads and ponders the scriptures daily, who has a burning testimony of the Book of Mormon. Give me a young woman who faithfully attends her Church meetings, who is a seminary graduate, who has earned her Young Womanhood Recognition Award, and wears it with pride! Give me a young woman who is virtuous and who has maintained her personal purity, who will not settle for less than a temple marriage, and I will give you a young woman who will perform miracles for the Lord now and throughout eternity. ("To the Young Women of the Church," *Ensign* 16 [November 1986]: 84.)

We hope that you will draw close to your homes, unto your families, unto your parents—to Mom and Dad. I know, sometimes the relationship becomes somewhat strained. We sometimes think our parents don't understand us and sometimes we think they are old-fashioned. Young people today need the wisdom of age as never before, and the older people need the enthusiasm of youth. Fortunately the home is where you can find that, both of them in the family circle. Build up a strength in your own home that will stand you in good stead in the days ahead. ("Strengthen Your Families," Star Valley Wyoming Stake Conference, 18 April 1971.)

Beloved youth, you will have your trials and temptations through which you must pass, but there are great moments of eternity which lie ahead. You have our love and our confidence. We pray that you will be prepared for the reins of leadership. We say to you, "Arise and shine forth" (D&C 115:5) and be a light unto the world, a standard to others. You can live in the world and not partake of the sins of the world. You can live joyously, beautifully, unmarred by the ugliness of sin. This is our confidence in you. ("To 'The Rising Generation,' " *New Era* 16 [June 1986]: 8.)

I would hope that you young men and women would have the spiritual maturity (and I have confidence you do) to see that our Heavenly Father gave His commandments to bless your life. They are given so you will know how to achieve joy. God is mindful of you. His work and glory is to bring about your immortality and eternal life (see Moses 1:39). He has given you commandments to discipline you. He has also given you your agency so that you could be proved "to see if [you] will do all things whatsoever [He] shall command" (Abraham 3:25). His kingdom is well organized, and your leaders are dedicated to help you. May you know that you have our love, our concern, and our constant prayers. ("Be True to God, Country, and Self," Young Adult Fireside, Logan, Utah, 11 February 1979.)

If youth are going to inherit the highest degree of glory in the celestial kingdom, this means marriage for time and all eternity in the temples of God. That is the only plan that has been provided by our Heavenly Father. We want them to keep their covenants after they have been in those sacred places. We want them to marry in the Church and to marry in the temple of God. ("What We Desire for Our Youth," Annual MIA Conference, Salt Lake City, Utah, 16 June 1963.)

You are a royal generation. The heavenly grandstands are cheering you on. We are fast coming to the close of this game. The opposition is real and is scoring. But we have scored, we are scoring, and we will score in the future. The Lord is our coach and manager. His team will win and we can be a valiant part of it if we so desire. Rise up, O youth of Zion! You hardly realize the great divine potential that lies within you. May you all follow your leader, Jesus Christ, and increase mentally, physically, spiritually, and socially. ("In His Steps," in *1979 Devotional Speeches of the Year* [Provo, Utah: BYU, 1980], p. 59.)

I think that our Heavenly Father expects the youth of our Church to become exalted in the celestial kingdom. I guess all the rest is encompassed in that. We are not striving for the lower kingdoms. We are not candidates for the telestial or terrestrial kingdoms. The young people of this Church are candidates for the celestial kingdom and the highest degree of glory in that kingdom. That requires a great deal, a great deal that has to do with our day-to-day standards. This means not just going to Church, not just holding the priesthood, not just being married in the temple, not just being a good citizen, not just being happy, as measured by the world. It means living every standard of the Church fully.

To you young people it means keeping yourselves clean—clean in body and in mind. It means that you go to the marriage altar pure and clean. It means that you will reserve for the marriage relationship those sweet and intimate associations which the God of Heaven intended should be a part of marriage and not be indulged in outside the marriage covenant. The curse of this age is unchastity—next to murder in the category of crimes.

No, my young brothers and sisters, you cannot let down your standards. You cannot indulge in promiscuous relations outside the marriage covenant without suffering ill effects from it. (*So Shall Ye Reap,* p. 188.)

You are choice sons and daughters of God—precious souls sent to this earth at this special time for a special reason. God loves you, each and every one of His children, and His desire and purpose and glory is to have you return to Him pure and undefiled, having proven yourselves worthy of an eternity in His presence. ("Youth—Promise for the Future," BYU Graduation, Provo, Utah, 19 April 1986.)

Dating

Our Heavenly Father wants you to date young women who are faithful members of the Church, who encourage you to serve a full-time mission and to magnify your priesthood. (CR April 1986, *Ensign* 16 [May 1986]: 45.)

For many years the Church has counseled parents concerning their children in early dating and the dangers of "going steady" prematurely. Here again, you mothers have a critical role in seeing that this counsel is understood and accepted by your children. (London England Area Conference, 19–20 June 1976.)

Remember the importance of proper dating. President Spencer W. Kimball gave some wise counsel: "Clearly, right marriage begins with right dating. Therefore, this warning comes with great emphasis. Do not take the chance of dating nonmembers or members who are untrained and faithless. A girl may say, 'Oh I do not intend to marry this person. It is just a fun date.' But one cannot afford to take a chance on falling in love with someone who may never accept the gospel." (*Miracle of Forgiveness,* pp. 241–42.)

Our Heavenly Father wants you to date young men who are faithful members of the Church, who will be worthy to take you to the temple and be married the Lord's way. There will be a new spirit in Zion when the young women will say to their boyfriends, "If you cannot get a temple recommend, then I am not about to tie my life to you, even for mortality!" And the young returned missionary will say to his girlfriend, "I am sorry, but as much as I love you, I will not marry out of the holy temple." ("To the Young Women of the Church," *Ensign* 16 [November 1986]: 84.)

May I suggest some steps to avoid the pitfalls of immorality:

Avoid late hours and weariness. The Lord said to retire to your bed early (D&C 88:124), and there are good reasons for that. Some of the worst sins are committed after midnight. Officers in the wards and stakes, branches and missions, should not keep our people, especially our youth, up late at night even for wholesome recreation.

Keep your dress modest. Short skirts are not pleasing to the Lord, but modesty is. Girls, do not be an enticement for your downfall because of your immodest and tight-fitting clothes. (See Proverbs 1:10; James 1:14–15.)

Have good associates or don't associate at all. Be careful in the selection of your friends. If in the presence of certain persons you are lifted to nobler heights, you are in good company. But if your friends or associates encourage base thoughts, then you had best leave them.

Avoid necking and petting like a plague, for necking and petting are the concession that precedes the complete loss of virtue.

Have a good physical outlet of some sport or exercise. Overcome evil with good. You can overcome many evil inclinations through good physical exertion and healthful activities. A healthy soul, free of the body- and spirit-dulling influences of alcohol and tobacco, is in better condition to overthrow the devil.

Think clean thoughts. Those who think clean thoughts do not do dirty deeds. You are responsible before God not only for your acts but also for controlling your thoughts. So live that you would not blush with shame if your thoughts and acts should be flashed on a screen in your church. The old adage is still true that you sow thoughts and you reap acts, you sow acts and you reap habits, you sow habits and you reap a character, and your character determines your eternal destiny. "As [a man] thinketh in his heart, so is he" (Proverbs 23:7).

Pray. There is no temptation placed before you that you cannot shun. Do not allow yourself to get in positions where it is easy to fall. Listen to the promptings of the Spirit. If you are engaged in things where you do not feel you can pray and ask the Lord's blessings on what you are doing, you are engaged in the wrong kind of activity. (*God, Family, Country,* pp. 240–41.)

Youth Leadership

Never has the Church had a more choice group of young people than at present, and Satan is well aware of who they are. He is doing everything in his power to thwart them in their destiny. He knows that they have been sent to earth in this crucial period of the world's history to build the kingdom of God and establish Zion in preparation for the second coming of the Lord Jesus

Christ. Yes, our youth have an awesome challenge. ("Challenges for Leaders of Aaronic Priesthood," Young Men's General Presidency and Board, Salt Lake City, Utah, 19 September 1979.)

We must inspire our youth to look up, to face the world honestly, unafraid. They must be ready to carry the torch, to provide the leadership, to carry the load which will be theirs in the years ahead. (Boy Scouts of America, Region 12 Annual Meeting, Salt Lake City, Utah, 11 December 1963.)

I like to think of youth as a kind of savings bank. We put in our experiences of all kinds, the things we see and learn, the things we do—in the homes, in Church, in school, at work, at recreation —and all the rest of our lives we keep drawing on that savings bank of experience and knowledge. The wonderful fact is that the more we draw on the account, the larger it seems to grow.

There are some savings that all of our youth ought to have in their accounts. They ought to have some basic knowledge—some basic principles—to fit them for life. They must realize, first, that they have a duty to God. This includes reverence for sacred things, the observance of the Sabbath, the maintenance of the standards of the Church with which they are affiliated, faith that they can reach out and tap that unseen power. (*So Shall Ye Reap,* pp. 126–27.)

Now, as never before, the youth of this Church need the program of the Church. They cannot afford to be without it. They need the companionship of a good man and a good woman, and I hope, as officers and as fathers, we will provide that companionship, that we will put our arms around them and sustain them, help them, and direct them during this very crucial period. (CR April 1944, *Improvement Era* 47 [May 1944]: 325.)

There will be trials and disappointments to our young people, but I am convinced that any person who has real faith in God and a testimony of this work can endure anything and still keep his spirit sweet. We want our young people prepared so they can endure anything. (*Title of Liberty,* p. 205.)

Our youth are faced with temptations to compromise their character and standards, a bombardment of temptations the like of which has not been experienced by any other age in such intensity and sophistication. These temptations are constantly before them in literature, movies, radio, clothing, fashions, television, modern music, and barracks and dormitory talk. Today Satan—who I testify is real—uses many tools to weaken and destroy character. His thrust is directed at the youth and vitality of our nation. He masquerades sex perversion as something that is natural and harmless. He uses drugs (LSD, marijuana, and others), leading magazines, underground publications, television, movies, pornographic literature, and morally destructive paperback books, filthy and obscene talk—all in an effort to see young people compromise their integrity, sacrifice their morality, and spend their moral strength for the pleasure of the moment. (*This Nation Shall Endure,* p. 95.)

Could many of our ills today have resulted from our failure to train a strong citizenry from the only source we have—the boys and girls of each community? Have they grown up to believe in politics without principles, pleasure without conscience, knowledge without effort, wealth without work, business without morality, science without humanity, worship without sacrifice? Give a pig and a boy everything each wants, and you will get a good pig and a bad boy. ("Will America Be Destroyed by Americans?" Annual Boy Scouts Banquet, Commerce, Texas, 13 May 1968.)

Youth needs hope, not despair; visions, not clouds; models, not critics; inspired leaders to help them to be honest with themselves. Young people ask for a fair chance to succeed. Let us help provide wholesome challenges and opportunities, and they will complete the job of becoming well-adjusted, useful citizens. ("Youth—A Savings Bank," *Scouting* [May–June 1959]: 3.)

We love the youth of the Church and we know the Lord loves them. There isn't anything the Church wouldn't do that is right to help our young people—to save them. They are our future. We have faith in them. We want them to be successful in their chosen fields. We want them to be exalted in the celestial kingdom.

We say to them, you are eternal beings. Life is eternal. You cannot do wrong and feel right. It pays to live the good, wholesome, joy-filled life. Live so you will have no serious regrets—no heartaches. Live so you can reach out and tap that unseen power, without which no man or woman can do his or her best. (*God, Family, Country,* p. 246.)

I have confidence in the youth of Zion. I recognize the serious and crucial period through which the youth of Zion are passing, and I sincerely pray that we will throw around them every safeguard that is possible, in order that they can meet the temptations and overcome them. (CR April 1944, *Improvement Era* 47 [May 1944]: 325.)

Youth will need a sane spiritual foundation if they endure, if they are going to be able to live clean and to maintain the standards of the Church. God expects great things of them. He expects them to develop into noble characters, into good citizens—citizens which may eventually provide in part, at least, the leaven which may help to save this great nation. He expects them to live clean even in a wicked world. He expects them to grow up with a testimony of the gospel. He expects these young men to live so that they can receive the holy Melchizedek Priesthood and so that eventually they can be married in the temple of God to worthy companions for time and eternity. He also expects them to know the glorious blessings of honorable parenthood and eventually to be exalted in the celestial kingdom of God. (CR April 1951, *Improvement Era* 54 [June 1951]: 422.)

PART 5

COUNTRY

COUNTRY

America

This nation was established by the God of heaven as a citadel of liberty. A Constitution guaranteeing those liberties was designed under the superintending influence of heaven. We may liken our system to the law of Moses which leads men to the higher law of Christ. ("A Vision and a Hope for the Youth of Zion," in *1977 Devotional Speeches of the Year* [Provo, Utah: BYU, 1978], pp. 76–77.)

"Righteousness exalteth a nation" (Proverbs 14:34). This is the key to understanding our heritage and this is the key to maintaining it. The foundations of America are spiritual. That must never be forgotten nor doubted. Lest we forget, let us review those beginnings, looking for the spiritual moorings which underpin our nation. ("Righteousness Exalteth a Nation," Provo Utah Freedom Festival, 29 June 1986.)

When Columbus and his men sighted the lands of this hemisphere in October 1492, one of their first acts was to fall on their knees and give thanks to God. There is evidence that they were directed to these shores by the hand of Providence (1 Nephi 3:12).

The Pilgrims of Plymouth, the Calverts of Maryland, Roger Williams, William Penn—all had deep religious convictions that played a principal part in their coming to the New World. They too, I believe, came here under the inspiration of heaven. (1 Nephi 13:13.)

When Washington was desperately hard pressed at Valley Forge, his men found him on his knees praying for guidance and aid. Yes, this nation has a spiritual foundation. (American Association of School Administrators, Atlantic City, New Jersey, 14 February 1960.)

America as a nation has been built on prayer. It has a spiritual foundation, a prophetic history. When the God-fearing Pilgrims arrived in the Western Hemisphere, Governor William Bradford recorded these words: "Being thus arrived in good harbor and brought safe to land, they fell upon their knees and blessed the God of Heaven." (*God, Family, Country,* p. 115.)

In the early frontier days of this country, a special breed of men and women came here from all over the world, seeking not only opportunity, but freedom. They were strong, proud, and fiercely independent. They believed that the surest helping hand was at the end of their own sleeves. They shared one thing in common—an unshakable faith in God and in themselves. And that, without doubt, is the secret of success as viable today as it was yesterday. ("A Tribute to Pioneer Ideals," Sandy Utah Historical Marker Dedication, 14 September 1977.)

Do you realize that very, very few people in the history of this world have ever had the opportunity which we have? This last two hundred years has been a very short minuscule period in the history of mankind, where we have had a government with a Constitution—a Constitution endorsed by the Lord Jesus Christ. (Salt Lake Utah Emigration Stake Conference, 5 November 1978.)

We must teach our children about the spiritual roots of this great nation. We must become actively involved in supporting programs and textbooks in the public schools that teach the greatness of the early patriots who helped forge our liberties. We must teach our children that it is part of our faith that the Constitution of the United States was inspired by God (see D&C 101:77, 80). We reverence it akin to the revelations that have come from His hand. ("Righteousness Exalteth a Nation," Provo Utah Freedom Festival, 29 June 1986.)

Our nation, the United States of America, was built on the foundation of reality and spirituality. To the extent that its citizens violate God's commandments, especially His laws of morality — to that degree they weaken the country's foundation. A rejection and repudiation of God's laws could well lead our nation to its destruction just as it has to Greece and Rome. It can happen to our country unless we repent. An eminent statesman once said: "Our very civilization itself is based upon chastity, the sanctity of marriage, and the holiness of the home. Destroy these and Christian man becomes a brute." (J. Reuben Clark, Jr., CR October 1938, p. 137.) (*This Nation Shall Endure,* p. 97.)

When this nation was established, the Church was restored and from here the message of the restored gospel has gone forth — all according to divine plan. This then becomes the Lord's base of operations in these latter days. And this base — the land of America — will not be shifted out of its place. This nation will, in a measure at least, fulfill its mission even though it may face serious and troublesome days. The degree to which it achieves its full mission depends upon the righteousness of its people. God, through His power, has established a free people in this land as a means of helping to carry forward His purposes.

It was His latter-day purpose to bring forth His gospel in America, not in any other place. It was in America where the Book of Mormon plates were deposited. That was no accident. It was His design. It was in this same America where they were brought to light by angelic ministry. (See Book of Mormon Introduction.) It was here where He organized His modern Church, where He, Himself, made a modern personal appearance (see D&C 20:1; Joseph Smith — History 1:17).

It was here under a free government and a strong nation that protection was provided for His restored Church. Now God will not permit America, His base of operations, to be destroyed. He has promised protection to this land if we will but serve the God of the land (see Ether 2:12). He has also promised protection to the righteous even, if necessary, to send fire from heaven to destroy their enemies (1 Nephi 22:17).

No, God's base of operations will not be destroyed. But it may be weakened and made less effective. One of the first rules of war strategy—and we are at war with the adversary and his agents—is to protect the base of operations. This we must do if we are to build up the kingdom throughout the world and safeguard our God-given freedom.

We must protect this base of operations from every threat— from sin, from unrighteousness, from immorality, from desecration of the Sabbath day, from lawlessness, from parental and juvenile delinquency. We must protect it from dirty movies, from filthy advertising, from salacious and suggestive television programs, magazines, and books.

We must protect this base from idleness, subsidies, doles, and soft governmental paternalism which weakens initiative, discourages industry, destroys character, and demoralizes the people.

To protect this base we must protect the soul of America—we must return to a love and respect for the basic spiritual concepts upon which this nation has been established. We must study the Constitution and the writings of the Founding Fathers.

If we are to protect this American base, we must realize that all things, including information disseminated by our schools, churches, and governments, should be judged according to the words of the prophets, especially the living prophet. This procedure, coupled with the understanding which will come through the Spirit of the Lord, if we are living in compliance with the scriptures, is the only sure foundation and basis of judgment. Any other course of action leaves us muddled, despondent, wandering in shades of gray, easy targets for Satan. If we fail in these pressing and important matters, we may well fall far short of the great mission the Lord has proffered and outlined for America and for His divinely restored Church. (*Title of Liberty*, pp. 88–91.)

I have seen this great nation decline spiritually. What happens to a nation collectively is but the result of its citizenry departing from the fundamental spiritual and economic laws of God: making the Sabbath day a day of pleasure; individuals and businesses giving license to immorality; and politicians dignifying the coveting of others' possessions and property by stating, "We will take from the haves and give to the have nots." At first we resisted this philosophy; then consented; next, demanded; and now have legislated. Politically, we licensed coveting what others had earned!

("The Task Before Us," American Dairy Science Association, Logan, Utah, 26 June 1979.)

America needs greater spirituality. You can help provide it. "Ye shall know the truth and the truth shall make you free" (John 8:32). Freedom is an inherited, God-given principle. It has always been planned that God should have in His plan that men should be free. Our great system in the United States is based on the freedom of choice. (Munich, Germany High School Graduates, April 1964.)

I sometimes think that one of the greatest sins at the door of American citizens is the sin of ingratitude. We are inclined to take so much for granted—the blessings which are ours as American citizens. Most of us have never seen anything else. I have often wished that it would be in some way required that every American live abroad for two or three years as the average people over there live—not as tourists live, but as people live over there. Often I have wished we might be required to live for a few months in a nation where people no longer have their freedom—these basic things that are so important to us—in order that we might come back to these shores with a deeper appreciation for what we have as American citizens. ("Free Agency," Washington D.C. Stake Conference, 22 May 1960.)

If our blood-bought freedom is surrendered, it will be because of Americans. What is more, it will probably not be only the work of subversive Americans. The Benedict Arnolds will not be the only ones to forfeit our freedom. "At what point, then, is the approach of danger to be expected?" asked Abraham Lincoln, and answered, "If it ever reaches us, it must spring up among us. It cannot come from abroad. If destruction be our lot, we must ourselves be its author and finisher; as a nation of freemen, we must live through all time or die by suicide." (Springfield, Illinois, 27 January 1837.) ("Will America Be Destroyed by Americans?" Annual Boy Scouts Banquet, Commerce, Texas, 13 May 1968.)

If America is destroyed, it may be by Americans who salute the flag, sing the national anthem, march in patriotic parades, cheer

Fourth of July speakers—normally "good" Americans, but Americans who fail to comprehend what is required to keep our country strong and free, Americans who have been lulled away into a false security.

Great nations are never conquered from outside unless they are rotten inside. Our greatest national problem today is erosion, not the erosion of the soil but erosion of the national morality—erosion of traditional enforcement of law and order. ("The American Challenge," in *BYU Speeches of the Year* [Provo, Utah: BYU, 1970], p. 6.)

Now is the time for us to nail our colors to the mast and to stand up for God and those unequivocal principles of freedom and morality—the very foundations of this blessed land of America! ("Freedom—Our Priceless Heritage," Sons of the American Revolution, Salt Lake City, Utah, 22 April 1978.)

I testify to you that this is a choice land, that God held this hemisphere, as it were, in the palm of His hand for hundreds, yea, thousands of years in order that the great mission of this land might be undertaken and might be accomplished. (CR October 1954, *Improvement Era* 57 [December 1954]: 922.)

"Blessed is the nation whose God is the Lord; and the people whom he hath chosen for his own inheritance" (Psalm 33:12). The United States of America has been—and still is—a great nation. It has been great because it has been free. It has been free because it has trusted in God, and was founded upon the principles of freedom that are set forth in the word of God. To me, this land has a prophetic history. America is our beloved homeland. (*An Enemy Hath Done This,* pp. 113–14.)

This nation will be preserved so long as we retain the same quality of faith in God that our founders manifested. Personal righteousness is essential to our liberty. The burden of self-government depends on our supporting wise and good representatives, exercising self-restraint, and keeping the commandments of God. ("The Faith of Our Founding Fathers," in *Faith* [Salt Lake City: Deseret Book, 1983], pp. 25–26.)

With God's help, the light of high resolve in the eyes of the American people must never be dimmed! Our freedom must — and will — be preserved! It will continue to be a land of freedom and liberty as long as we are able to advance in the light of sound and enduring principles. (*The Red Carpet*, pp. 319–20.)

Prophecy Fulfilled

This is a great country and certainly this greatness was foreshadowed and foreseen by ancient prophets who lived here, prophecies made by the brother of Jared (Ether 13:8), by Lehi, by Jacob (2 Nephi 10:18–19), and by Nephi of old (1 Nephi 13:13–20). It is enough to know that this nation has a prophetic history. All of the great events that have transpired here, including the coming of Columbus and of the Pilgrim fathers, were foreseen by ancient prophets (1 Nephi 13:12–13). It was predicted that those who came to this great land would prosper here, that they would humble themselves before the Almighty, that the power of God would be with them, and that this nation would move forward to its great destiny. (See 1 Nephi 13:15–19.) ("Responsibilities of Citizenship," BYU, Provo, Utah, 22 October 1954.)

The prophet of the Jaredite colony, Mahonri Moriancumer, commonly referred to as the brother of Jared, spoke of this land as a choice land, a land choice above all other lands. He indicated that those people who live here should worship the God of this land if they were to enjoy the blessings of freedom and liberty and be free from bondage. Otherwise, if they failed, they were to be swept off. And he proclaimed that this is the everlasting decree of God. (Ether 2:8–10.)

Sixteen hundred years later the prophet Nephi was privileged to see a large part of the history of the establishment of this great nation. He spoke in no uncertain terms regarding its mission. He told that the Spirit of the Lord came down and wrought upon a man upon foreign shores, and that he went forth and discovered this land. He also saw other Gentiles follow to these shores under the influence of that same Spirit. And he saw that the Spirit of the Lord was here and that multitudes of people came to these shores and that God prospered them because they humbled themselves before Him; that He was with them and that His power was here, and that during times of struggle and conflict—referring to the Revolutionary War—that the Lord was with them and sustained them and bore them off victorious. (1 Nephi 13:12–19.) He further saw that this land was consecrated to those whom the Lord should bring and who would serve Him and keep His commandments; that it should be a land of liberty; that it should never be brought down into captivity unless it be because of the iniquity of the people. (2 Nephi 1:6–7.) (CR April 1948, *Improvement Era* 51 [May 1948]: 283.)

What is the essential message of the Book of Mormon that is so vital to our time? It is a witness to our generation. It prophesied the founding of this nation and how we may survive as a free country.

All nations who inhabit this land are bound by an everlasting decree from God, a decree that the inhabitants of this land shall serve God or they shall be swept off (see Ether 2:10). "This is a choice land, and whatsoever nation shall possess it shall be free from bondage, and from captivity, and from all other nations under heaven, if they will but serve the God of this land, who is Jesus Christ" (Ether 2:12).

The Book of Mormon chronicles the rise and fall of two mighty civilizations in America that failed to give heed to this decree, and thus met with destruction. The Book of Mormon declares that God deliberately kept the American continent hidden until the Holy Roman Empire had broken up and the various nations had established themselves as independent kingdoms. Keeping America hidden until this time was no accident. (See 2 Nephi 1:8.) ("Martin Harris—A Special Witness," Martin Harris Memorial Amphitheater Dedication, Clarkston, Utah, 6 August 1983.)

It was a divine way in which this nation began. The rules of conduct were taken from the Decalogue, from the Bible, from the Gospels and other scriptures. They kept a sacred Sabbath. They maintained other high standards. They frowned upon profanity and other vices. They prohibited gambling. They encouraged people not to keep bad company, to repeat no grievances. They emphasized the spiritual values.

Many years later when the nation was founded, Washington, echoing the feeling of the early Pilgrim fathers and others who had come from abroad, acknowledged God's direction and the importance of spirituality in the lives of our people and in this great country. ("Responsibilities of Citizenship," BYU, Provo, Utah, 22 October 1954.)

There are principles that may bring us back into heaven's favor again. The Ten Commandments came from God Himself to Moses, and form the foundation of civilized society. Designed by the Almighty, these laws plumb the depths of human motives and urges, and, if adhered to, will regulate the baser passions of mankind. No nation has ever perished that has kept the commandments of God.

Neither permanent government nor civilization will long endure that violates these laws. The conscience of all right-thinking people declares this to be so. "America cannot remain strong by ignoring the commandments of the Lord" (President Spencer W. Kimball, 3 June 1976). (*This Nation Shall Endure,* p. 105.)

Every American citizen should understand God's purpose for this great nation in which we live, and how we may avert the decadence and destruction suffered by other mighty empires. Here is what the Book of Mormon says about the founding of this nation and how we may survive as a free country.

God inspired "a man among the Gentiles" (1 Nephi 13:12) who, by the Spirit of God was led to rediscover the land of America and bring this rich new land to the attention of the people in Europe. That man, of course, was Christopher Columbus, who testified that he was inspired in what he did.

"Our Lord," said Columbus, "unlocked my mind, sent me upon the sea, and gave me fire for the deed. Those who heard of my enterprise called it foolish, mocked me, and laughed. But who can doubt but that the Holy Ghost inspired me?" (Jacob Wasserman, *Columbus, Don Quixote of the Seas,* pp. 19–20.)

God revealed that shortly after the discovery of America, this nation would be colonized by peoples of Europe—called Gentiles —who would desire to escape the persecution and tyranny of the Old World. Book of Mormon prophets foretold the time that the Gentiles would scatter and kill the inhabitants of the land whom we know today as the Indian nations (1 Nephi 15:17).

God revealed over twenty-five hundred years ago that the kingdoms of Europe would try to exercise dominion over the colonists who had fled to America, that this would lead to a struggle for independence, and that the colonists would win (1 Nephi 13:17–19). The Book of Mormon foretold the time when the colonists would establish this as a land of liberty which would not be governed by kings. The Lord declared that He would protect the land and whoever would attempt to establish kings from within or without would perish. (2 Nephi 10:11–14.) ("A Promised Lord—A Promised Land—A Promised People," Wichita, Kansas, 11 November 1976.)

I bear witness that America's history was foreknown to God; that His divine intervention and merciful providence has given us both peace and prosperity in this beloved land; that through His omniscience and benevolent design He selected and sent some of His choicest spirits to lay the foundation of our government (see D&C 101:80). These men were inspired of God to do the work they accomplished. They were not evil men. Their work was a prologue to the restoration of the gospel and the Church of Jesus Christ. It was done in fulfillment of the ancient prophets who declared that this was a promised land, "a land of liberty unto the Gentiles," and that is us (2 Nephi 1:7). (*This Nation Shall Endure,* p. 23.)

Challenges

We live in a great and glorious land. We have been the beneficiaries of great blessings from heaven. We must not ever forget the blessings that have been bestowed upon us. Our nation is still in deep need of the help of the Almighty. We need His inspiration. We need His guidance. We need His protection. When we as a people not only desire to do His will, but determine we will do it, we can expect that help from our God. ("Righteousness Exalteth a Nation," Provo Utah Freedom Festival, 29 June 1986.)

We are at the crossroads in American policy. We will build soundly for the future in a manner that leaves essential freedom of action in the hands of the individual American, or we will go the tragic other road—which is to encroach more and more upon the individual citizen's control of his own life, and end only with a fully socialized America. My words are not one whit too strong. This is our choice. This is the decision we face. (*The Red Carpet*, pp. 308–9.)

This nation came into being only through freedom of choice, sacrifice, labor, and struggle. Brave Americans gave their lives in the settlement of this nation—and in its preservation. Let us remember our heritage and recognize that the day of courage, labor, and sacrifice is never done. For the welfare of America, each citizen must develop a keener sense of responsibility for the solution of public questions—all public questions.

Our people must think. They must discuss. They must have the courage of their convictions. They must decide on a course of action and they must follow through. All this must be done freely, in the open, without government dictation or control. (*The Red Carpet,* p. 312.)

Let us examine our own lives and the life of our own beloved land. How richly we the people of the United States have been blessed! Truly ours is a land of great favors and opportunities. Yet, is it not true that these very blessings could prove to be our undoing unless our perspective is right and our idealism more concerned with eternal standards and values than with material gain and worldly honors? How does our nation stand? Are not many of us materialistic? Do we not find it well-nigh impossible to raise our sights above the dollar sign?

Are not many of us pragmatists—living not by principle but by what we can get away with? Are not many of us status-seekers—measuring the worth of a man by the size of his bank account, his house, his automobile? Are we not complacent, given to self-satisfaction, and self-congratulation—willing to co-exist with evil so long as it does not touch us personally. If the answer to these questions is yes—and who can honestly give a different answer?—surely these are among the many reasons why this is truly an era of peril. (*Title of Liberty,* p. 155.)

Rarely in the annals of human history has a nation of free people been more careless of their liberty than we Americans. We take our precious God-given freedom for granted. ("Freedom—

Our Priceless Heritage," Sons of the American Revolution, Salt
Lake City, Utah, 22 April 1978.)

There are some in this land, among whom I count myself,
whose faith it is that this land is reserved only for a righteous
people, and we remain here as tenants only as we remain in the
favor of the Lord, for He is the landlord as far as this earth is concerned. If we are to remain under heaven's benign protection and
care, we must return to those principles which have brought us our
peace, liberty, and prosperity. Our problems today are essentially
problems of the Spirit.

The solution is not more wealth, more food, more technology,
more government, or instruments of destruction—the solution is
personal and national reformation. In short, it is to bring our national character ahead of our technological and material advances.
Repentance is the sovereign remedy to our problems. ("A Promised Lord—A Promised Land—A Promised People," Wichita,
Kansas, 11 November 1976.)

You are witnesses to pronouncements of atheism, agnosticism,
and immorality in our midst. Sadly, you are witnesses to the truth
that as a nation we have forgotten God. I ask myself, How long
can we remain under heaven's benign protection? We tend to forget how America became the greatest, most prosperous and powerful nation in the world, blessed with an abundance of everything
needed for the good life. ("A Warning to America," Washington
D.C. Stake Independence Day Celebration, 3 July 1979.)

We need to search for the reasons for the decline in public
morals in this country, and I am sure if we look very closely these
are some of the reasons we will find. We will find that there is evidence in high and in low places that we have had a weak and vacillating leadership and it is not confined to any one party. There is
too much effort, too much action, based on expediency and not
enough on principles, eternal principles, which constitute the very
foundation of all we hold dear as a great Christian nation. ("Responsibilities of Citizenship," BYU, Provo, Utah, 22 October
1954.)

America was built upon a firm foundation and created over
many years from the bottom up. Other nations, impatient to ac-

quire equal abundance, security, and pursuit of happiness, rush headlong into that final phase of construction without building adequate foundations or supporting pillars. Their efforts are futile. And even in our country there are those who think that because we now have the good things in life we can afford to dispense with the foundations which have made them possible. They want to remove any recognition of God from governmental institutions. They want to expand the scope and reach of government which will undermine and erode our economic and personal freedoms. The abundance which is ours, the carefree existence which we have come to accept as a matter of course, can be toppled by these foolish experimenters and power seekers. By the grace of God, and with His help, we shall fence them off from the foundations of our liberty, and then begin our task of repair and construction. (*An Enemy Hath Done This,* pp. 142–43.)

In America, two days of historical significance to our country are observed closely together—Thanksgiving Day and Pearl Harbor Day. One serves to keep us ever mindful of the blessings that are ours. The other is a brutal reminder that these blessings cannot be taken for granted; they must be protected. They are this day as in 1941 in danger of being wrested from us by the forces of evil—internal as well as external.

We must constantly be on guard against the dangers from within—against those philosophies which would weaken our economy. We must protect our investment in the past and future of our nation just as assiduously as bankers protect the investments of their clients. (*The Red Carpet,* pp. 314–15.)

We need to recapture the strength of individualism and independence. We needn't be shaped by our environments. We should fight against it, live up to the ideals, and refuse to be moral copycats. We should recapture the hardness and discipline in our national life. We play too much. We work too little. We overeat, overdrink, and overplay. We are the richest people in the world, but not the sturdiest. We are at ease in America. And so we need to recapture the spirit of our parents and grandparents. We need to recapture the American challenge. We need to sell the American way of life, the basic fundamental principles upon which this nation has been built. We need to admit our failures and repent of our sins. ("New Year 1961," Washington D.C. Ward, 31 December 1960.)

Our complacency as a nation is shocking—yes, almost unbelievable! We are a prosperous nation. Our people have high-paying jobs. Our incomes are high. Our standard of living is at an unprecedented level. We do not like to be disturbed as we enjoy our comfortable complacency. We live in the soft present and feel the future is secure. We do not worry about history. We seem oblivious to the causes of the rise and fall of nations. We are blind to the hard fact that nations usually sow the seeds of their own destruction while enjoying unprecedented prosperity.

I say to you with all the fervor of my soul: We are sowing the seeds of our own destruction in America and much of the free world today. It is my sober warning to you today that if the trends of the past continue, we will lose that which is as priceless as life itself—our freedom, our liberty, our right to act as free men. It can happen here. It is happening here.

Our great need in America today is to be alerted and informed. When we have become alerted and informed, we will soberly sense the need for a reversal of the present trends. We will realize that the laws of economics are immutable. We will be convinced that we must return to a spirit of humility, faith in God, and the basic concepts upon which this great Christian nation has been established under the direction of Divine Providence.

The sad and shocking story of what has happened in America in recent years must be told. Our people must have the facts. There is safety in an informed public. There is real danger in a complacent, uninformed citizenry. This is our real danger today. Yes, the truth must be told even at the risk of destroying, in large measure, the influence of men who are widely respected and loved by the American people. The stakes are high. Freedom and survival is the issue. (*An Enemy Hath Done This,* pp. 90–91.)

Our crisis is a crisis of faith; our need is for greater spirituality and a return to the basic concepts upon which this nation was established. How much this country needs men in government who acknowledge their debt to the Almighty, men whose lives are a daily witness to the truth of the American motto "In God We Trust"!

The days ahead are sobering and challenging, and will require the faith, prayers, and loyalty of every American citizen. Our challenge is to keep America strong and free—strong socially, strong economically, and above all, strong spiritually, if our way of life is to endure. Indeed, it is America's only hope for life, liberty, and the pursuit of happiness! (*This Nation Shall Endure,* p. 80.)

Here in this privileged land we hold in our hands the best hope of mankind, and it will be to our shame and disgrace before God and man if we allow that hope to wither and die. ("Our Duty— Stand for Freedom," BYU, Provo, Utah, 3 April 1978.)

The history of men and nations clearly teaches that "those nations only are blessed whose God is the Lord" (see Psalm 33:12). Our duty as a nation is not to expediency or to national interest, but to the Lord of Hosts. ("God and Country," Frankfurt am Main, Germany, 1964.)

I have faith in the American people. I pray that we will never do anything that will jeopardize in any manner our priceless heritage. If we live and work so as to enjoy the approbation of a Divine Providence, we cannot fail. Without that help we cannot long endure. So I urge all Americans to put their courage to the test. Be firm in our conviction that our cause is just. Reaffirm our faith in all things for which true Americans have always stood. I urge all Americans to arouse themselves and stay aroused. (*The Red Carpet,* pp. 318–19.)

One of the most precious of our blessings in America is the right to speak out—the right of free speech. We have a duty to speak out for the things in which we believe. So I speak out for the kind of America I want.

I want an America that will meet the challenge of the present day, not with softness and complacency, but with the depth of faith, wisdom, and daring that characterized our forefathers. I want an America that will rally to meet this grave challenge of a godless, atheistic, cruelly materialistic system. I want an America whose citizens will demand that our government stand firm at all costs against any further expansion into the free world of alien philosophies that seek to destroy freedom and free men everywhere.

I want an America that will stand guard, not only in defense of the free world, but against those forces which would destroy freedom from within. I want an America in which the principles of freedom and the institutions based thereon are understood. I want an America which does not overtax its free system or lay on it burdens it was never intended to bear. I want an America composed of those who recognize the imperfections of our economic and social system, and seek wisely to repair them. I want an America that would strengthen the tree of enterprise rather than uproot it.

I want an America wherein no one asks for themselves privileges which they would deny to others. I want an America which cherishes the spark of celestial fire—freedom, faith, conscience —which has been planted in the heart of every one of us. I want an America composed of citizens who prize freedom above life itself, who are of strong moral courage, of high ideals and standards, and who will fight to the very last for the security of this nation I love. Together this makes for a mighty America. Such citizens make mighty company and to this end we will—we must—win the fight. (*The Red Carpet*, pp. 317–18.)

World Leadership

It is well to review the elements of our health and strength that we have acquired under our divinely inspired Constitution, the liberties it guarantees, and the free institution it sets up.

Few nations enjoy such freedoms—freedom to speak, freedom to own property and business or participate in ownership, freedom to worship, freedom to print, freedom to travel at home and abroad, freedom to censure even public officials, and freedom to have the privacy we desire. No country has been more concerned with due process in its judicial system than ours. The protection of human rights, as granted by our Constitution and Bill of Rights, is not just theory. History will record that we bent over backwards to protect the rights of the individual, sometimes even to a fault.

No other country has been so generous as America in terms of its money and food. No other nation has fought starvation and economic collapse and come to the rescue of nations struck by natural disaster as America has. There are many more blessings, but these are a few we might enumerate. Whence came these blessings? To those who would malign our country or system we ask, By what source did we receive such prosperity?

The power has come to us from God, because, to a great extent, we have been a God-fearing, Christ-worshiping people. There are some in this land who believe this is "a land choice above all other lands" to the Lord (1 Nephi 2:20), and that we shall remain here on this land so long as we remain in God's divine favor. (*This Nation Shall Endure*, pp. 49–50.)

Why can't we be proud of America as an independent nation and also have a feeling of brotherhood and respect for other peoples around the world? As a matter of fact, haven't Americans done just that for the past two hundred years? What people have poured out more treasure to other lands, opened their doors to more immigrants, and sent more missionaries, teachers, and doctors than we? (*An Enemy Hath Done This*, p. 156.)

It is heart-rending to see people who have lost their freedom of choice—their free agency—who feel no security; who have no home they can call their own, and who own no property; whose hearts are filled with hatred, distrust, and fear of the future. Yet among such people, many of them cold, hungry, and in rags, I found hope and faith that conditions would, with the aid of America and under the guidance of God, improve. It seemed that the common people who know our customs and understand our form of government look to America to show them the way to contentment and to peace. (Tribute to America Broadcast, Salt Lake City, Utah, 7 March 1949.)

The supreme test of any government policy—agricultural or other—should be, How will it affect the character, morale, and well-being of our people? We need—the world needs—a strong America in the critical years ahead. (*Farmers at the Crossroads*, p. 98.)

America must keep strong if she is to preserve herself and provide effective world leadership. This strength must come not alone from armaments and military might. It must be measured in the integrity, moral courage, economic strength, independence of spirit, and spirituality of her people. ("You Can Look Forward with Confidence," *Improvement Era* 57 [February 1954]: 96.)

Do we dare ask ourselves if the United States, though cast in the role of leader to preserve and strengthen world civilization, isn't itself tottering internally because too many of its citizens have abandoned the virtues that comprised the basic format of its own civilization? For instance, if spiritual faith, courage, and the willingness of our forebears to work hard were the sustaining virtues, and if, solely because of them, they were able to create our own civilization, can we now in the United States substitute for these virtues the human weaknesses of selfishness, complacency, apathy, and fear—and still hope to survive as a civilized nation? (*An Enemy Hath Done This,* p. 118.)

America will not be mighty unless her economy is healthy and sound. The people of this country, who have done so much to build a free and independent America, are a bulwark, a safeguard, a veritable fortress against foreign isms and dangerous ideologies that would strike at the very foundation of the traditional free American way of life. (*The Red Carpet,* p. 133.)

In this dark hour, the fate of the world seems to rest largely in our hands. We who live in this choice land have the opportunity, the responsibility, and the solemn obligation to stand firm for freedom and justice and morality—the dignity and brotherhood of man as a child of God. (*So Shall Ye Reap*, p. 88.)

God and our children will judge us for what we do with our land and our liberties. As Theodore Roosevelt said over half a century ago, we "hold in our hands the hope of the world, the fate of the coming years, and shame and disgrace will be ours if in our eyes the light of high resolve is dimmed, if we trail in the dust the golden hopes of men." (*Title of Liberty,* p. 177.)

I have lived all the past years of this, the twentieth century. I have witnessed great changes in our beloved land. I have seen us literally come from the horse and buggy days to our present state of marvelous technological advancements. I have traveled most of the countries of the world, on both government and Church assignments. To say that America is a blessed nation—a prosperous nation—is an understatement. Truly we live in a nation quite exceptional as compared to some other nations. Certainly God has prospered this people. ("The Task Before Us," American Dairy Science Association, Logan, Utah, 26 June 1979.)

Divine Destiny

Consider how very fortunate we are to be living in this land of America. The destiny of this country was forged long before the earth was even created. This choice land was set apart by God to become the very cradle of freedom. Men of unflinching courage established this nation and under God's guiding hand provided a Constitution, guaranteeing freedom to every one of its citizens. ("Freedom—Our Priceless Heritage," Sons of the American Revolution, Salt Lake City, Utah, 22 April 1978.)

The events that established our great nation were foreknown to God and revealed to prophets of old. As in enacted drama, the players who came on the scene were rehearsed and selected for their parts. Their talents, abilities, capacities, and weaknesses were known before they were born. As one looks back upon what we call our history, there is a telling theme that occurs again and again in this drama. It is that God governs in the affairs of this nation. As the late President J. Reuben Clark, Jr., said, "This is the great motif which runs through our whole history." (*This Nation Shall Endure*, p. 11.)

Long before America was discovered, the Lord was moving and shaping events that would lead to the coming forth of the remarkable form of government established by the Constitution. America had to be free and independent to fulfill this destiny. (*The Constitution: A Heavenly Banner*, p. 10.)

Many great events have transpired in this land of destiny. This was the place where Adam dwelt; this was the place where the Garden of Eden was; it was here that Adam met with a body of high priests at Adam-ondi-Ahman shortly before his death and gave them his final blessing, and the place to which he will return to meet with the leaders of his people (D&C 107:53–57). This was the place of three former civilizations: that of Adam, that of the Jaredites, and that of the Nephites. This was also the place where our Heavenly Father and His Son, Jesus Christ, appeared to Joseph Smith, inaugurating the last dispensation.

The Lord has also decreed that this land should be "the place of the new Jerusalem, which should come down out of heaven, and the holy sanctuary of the Lord" (Ether 13:3). Here is our nation's destiny! To serve God's eternal purposes and to prepare this land and people for America's eventual destiny, He "established the Constitution of this land, by the hands of wise men whom [He] raised up unto this very purpose, and redeemed the land by the shedding of blood" (D&C 101:80). (*This Nation Shall Endure,* p. 13.)

From the standpoint of numbers, equipment, training, and resources, the rag-tag army of the colonists should never have won the War for Independence. But America's destiny was not to be determined by overwhelming numbers or better military weapons or strategy. As John Adams purportedly declared: "There's a divinity which shapes our ends" (Shakespeare). God took a direct hand in the events that led to the defeat of the British. ("Righteousness Exalteth a Nation," Provo Utah Freedom Festival, 29 June 1986.)

Great promises have been made to this land of Zion, through the Book of Mormon prophets and through prophets in the latter days. And yet, I wonder sometimes if we, as members of this great land, recognize what is necessary for us to do in order that those promises might be realized. The fulfillment of those great promises is contingent upon our worshiping the God of this land, who is Jesus Christ. (CR April 1944, *Improvement Era* 47 [May 1944]: 287.)

This nation is God-ordained for a glorious purpose. It is ordained as an ensign of liberty to all other nations. That liberty will be maintained as we keep the commandments of God. (2 Nephi 1:7; Ether 2:12.) Righteousness, as the Book of Mormon states, is the indispensable ingredient to liberty. ("A Promised Lord—A

Promised Land—A Promised People," Wichita, Kansas, 11 November 1976.)

With all my heart I love our great nation. I have lived and traveled abroad just enough to make me appreciate rather fully what we have in America. To me the United States is not just another nation. It is not just one of a family of nations. The United States is a nation with a great mission to perform for the benefit and blessing of liberty-loving people everywhere. (*An Enemy Hath Done This,* pp. 27–28.)

Loyalty

Patriotism is more than flag-waving and fireworks. It is how we respond to public issues. If we ask only, "What is in this proposal for me? What do I get out of it?"—we are not patriotic and we are not very good citizens. But if we ask, "Is this right? Is it good for the American people? Would it preserve and strengthen our freedom?"—we deserve to stand in the company of Washington, Jefferson, and Lincoln. Patriotism is trying always to give more to the nation than we receive. It is selfless service. (Tribute to America Broadcast, 4 July 1960.)

This nation needs a revival of patriotism, a return to basic concepts, an awakening. We must become alerted and informed. With our national prestige at or near an all-time low, when will we act like men of courage? (*An Enemy Hath Done This,* p. 51.)

As watchmen on the tower of Zion, it is our obligation and right as leaders to speak out against current evils—evils that strike at the very foundation of all we hold dear as the true Church of Christ and as members of Christian nations.

In times as serious as these, we must not permit fear of criticism to keep us from doing our duty. In the crisis through which we are now passing, we have been fully warned. This has brought forth some criticism. There are some of us who do not want to hear the message. It embarrasses us. The things which are threatening our lives, our welfare, our freedoms are the very things some of us have been condoning. (*God, Family, Country,* pp. 358–59.)

By 1962 some American liberals had almost completely neutralized the resurgence of American patriotism. They had frightened uninformed citizens away from study groups and patriotic rallies. They had made it popular to call patriotism a "controversial" subject which should not be discussed in school assemblies or churches. (*Title of Liberty*, p. 32.)

I do not believe the greatest threat to our future is from bombs or guided missiles. I do not think our civilization will die that way. I think it will die when we no longer care—when the spiritual forces that make us wish to be right and noble die in the hearts of men. ("Will America Be Destroyed by Americans?" Annual Boy Scouts Banquet, Commerce, Texas, 13 May 1968.)

We should not be astonished when other nations view the United States as a "faltering democracy." How long would a basketball team that was ranked number one in the polls remain in that position if the student body, the school paper, and supporting faculty constantly pointed out its weaknesses? Soon the team would begin to lack confidence and fail. This is what we have been doing in our blessed country. Our heroes and institutions have been tarnished. We are constantly being reminded, via the press and other media, of what is wrong in our country. A recent editorial in the London *Daily Telegraph* appealed to us:

> The United States should know that her European cousins and allies are appalled and disgusted by the present open disarray of her public life. The self-criticism and self-destructive tendencies are running mad, with no countervailing force in sight. . . . Please, America, . . . pull yourself together. (As quoted in *U.S. News and World Report,* 26 January 1976, p. 20.)

It is the job of the historian and educator and Church leader to help us as a nation to pull ourselves together, to help us regain perspective and vision and the respect of all nations. This will not be done by showing that this is merely a phase through which we are passing. No, it will be done by men who possess a love of country, a vision of our country's future, and the assurance of her divinely guided destiny. (*This Nation Shall Endure,* p. 20.)

I would like to appeal to the Latter-day Saints that we seek to promote a spirit of humility throughout this great land, that we pray for the president of the United States. He is our president. He needs our faith and prayers. (CR April 1953, *Improvement Era* 56 [June 1953]: 415.)

Too often in recent years, patriotic symbols have been shunted aside. Our national heroes have been maligned, our history distorted. Has it become a disgrace to pledge allegiance to our flag, or to sign a loyalty oath, or to pay tribute to our national anthem? Is it shameful to encourage our children to memorize the stirring words of the men of '76? Has it become opprobrious to state "In God We Trust" when proclaiming love of country?

What we desperately need today is patriotism founded on a real understanding of the American ideal—a dedicated belief in our principles of freedom and a determination to perpetuate America's heritage. (*Title of Liberty,* p. 18.)

Certainly a true American cannot have too much patriotism. Surely Americans who have respect for our traditions, who support our freedoms and are willing to fight to preserve them have been called patriots from the very beginning of our nation.

I am proud to be called a patriot, for it correctly denotes one who loves his country. I love America's traditions and its freedoms and I believe they are well worth fighting for, against all that which threatens from within as well as from without. (*The Red Carpet,* p. 199.)

Any Christian constitutionalist who retreats from this battle jeopardizes his life here and hereafter. Seldom has so much responsibility hung on so few, so heavily; but our numbers are increasing, and we who have been warned have a responsibility to warn our neighbor (see D&C 88:81).

To His disciples, the Lord said that they should be of good cheer, for He had overcome the world—and so He had (see John 16:33). And so can we, if we are allied with Him. The wave of the future is freedom. There is no question of the eventual, final, and lasting triumph of righteousness. The major question for each of us is what part will we play in helping to bring it to pass. (*God, Family, Country,* pp. 332–33.)

There are some people who hesitate to get into this fight for freedom because it is controversial, or they are not sure if we are going to win. Such people have two blind spots.

First, they fail to realize that life's decisions should be based on principles—not on Gallup polls. There were men at Valley Forge who weren't sure how the Revolution would end, but they were in a much better position to save their own souls and their country than those timid men whose concern was deciding which side was going to win, or how to avoid controversy.

After all, the basic purpose of life is to prove ourselves—not to be with the majority when it is wrong. We must discharge responsibilities not only to our church, home, and profession, but also to our country. Otherwise we do not merit the full blessings of a kind Providence.

There are people today all over the world who in their own courageous and sometimes quiet ways are working for freedom. In many cases we will never know until the next life all they sacrificed for liberty. These patriots are receiving heaven's applause for the role they are playing, and in the long run that applause will be louder and longer than any they could receive in this world.

Which leads me to the second blind spot of those who hesitate to get into the fight. And that is their failure to realize that we will win in the long run, and for keeps, and that they pass up great blessings by not getting into the battle now when the odds are against us and the rewards are greatest.

The only questions, before the final victory, are, first, "What stand will each of us take in this struggle?" and second, "How much tragedy can be avoided by doing something now?"

Time is on the side of truth—and truth is eternal. Those who are fighting against freedom may feel confident now, but they are shortsighted.

This is still God's world. The forces of evil, working through some mortals, have made a mess of a good part of it. But it is still God's world. In due time, when each of us has had a chance to prove ourselves—including whether or not we are going to stand up for freedom—God will interject himself, and the final and eternal victory shall be for free agency. And then shall those complacent people on the sidelines, and those who took the wrong but temporarily popular course, lament their decisions. To the patriots I say this: Take that long eternal look. Stand up for freedom, no matter what the cost. Stand up and be counted. It can help to save your soul—and maybe your country. (*An Enemy Hath Done This*, pp. 61–62.)

The Constitution

The Constitutional Convention gave birth to the document that Gladstone said is "the most wonderful work ever struck off at a given time by the brain and purpose of man." I heartily endorse this assessment. I would like to pay honor—honor to the document itself, honor to the men who framed it, and honor to the God who inspired it and made possible its coming forth. God Himself has borne witness to the fact that He is pleased with the final product of the work of these great patriots. (*The Constitution—A Heavenly Banner,* p. 1.)

Our Creator endowed each one of us with certain rights at birth, among which are the rights to life, liberty, speech, and conscience, to name a few. These are not just human rights; they are divine rights. When these rights are not permitted expression by a nation, that nation becomes inhibited in its progress and development, and its leaders are responsible before God for suffocating sacred rights.

This native endowment is what separates man from the animals. It causes men to want to be good and to seek higher aspirations. It creates in man a desire to better his life and his station in life. ("A Spiritual Approach to Man-made Problems," Brigham Young University—Hawaii, 11 February 1983.)

It is time we recognize, as a people, that this country rests on divinely inspired and uniquely formulated principles. Until 1791, no nation had all basic rights guaranteed and recognized by written contract. That is what the Constitution is—a contract between a sovereign people and their elected officials. It is high time these principles are not just acknowledged, but carried out. Indeed this is the only real hope for our survival as a free nation. ("A Warning to America," Washington D.C. Stake, 3 July 1979.)

The Constitution of the United States was aimed to establish justice, insure domestic tranquility, provide for the common defense, promote the general welfare, and secure the blessings of liberty to ourselves and our posterity. ("The American Free-Enterprise System: Will It Survive?" Contemporary Issues Forum, Ogden, Utah, 18 January 1977.)

We must study and learn for ourselves the principles laid down in the Constitution which have preserved our freedoms for the last two hundred years. If we do not understand the role of government and how our rights are protected by the Constitution, we may accept programs or organizations that help erode our freedoms. An informed citizenry is the first line of defense against anarchy and tyranny. ("Righteousness Exalteth a Nation," Provo Utah Freedom Festival, 29 June 1986.)

How can people who are ignorant of the principles and guarantees of American government stand up in defense of it and our rights under the Constitution? The fundamentals and processes of free government should be known to every schoolboy and his parents. No free people can ever survive if they are ignorant of and fail to understand the principles of free government!

Unless our educational system in America turns out young men and women of character who know the basic facts of economics, history, finance, and government, and who have respect for law and an appreciation of the spiritual, that system will truly have been a failure. (*The Red Carpet,* pp. 202–3.)

We must instruct ourselves and others in the great spiritual values underlying our divinely inspired Constitution and our American free-enterprise system. One of the many sure ways of defeating our enemy is to instruct the people about the eternal verities of our own country. (*Title of Liberty,* p. 84.)

May we be worthy of the freedoms that have been provided us in our Constitution, and equal to the trials and tests that shall surely come. We truly have special and individual responsibilities to befriend and to defend that "glorious standard," our Constitution.

Our Heavenly Father raised up the men who founded this government (see D&C 101:80), thereby fulfilling the prophecy of His Beloved Son that the people "should be established in this land and be set up as a free people by the power of the Father" (3 Nephi 21:4). ("Remarks on the Constitution," Bicentennial Ball, Salt Lake City, Utah, 18 September 1987.)

May we pledge anew that the divine principles embodied in the divinely inspired documents that govern our country be written on the tablets of our own hearts. I pray that our eyes might be single to the will of God, that we might thereby bless our families and our country and that we shall, with increased devotion, work for less government, more individual responsibility, and, with God's help, a better world. (*God, Family, Country,* p. 407.)

Inspired Origin

The coming forth of the Constitution is of such transcendent importance in the Lord's plan that ancient prophets foresaw this event and prophesied of it. In the dedicatory prayer for the Idaho Falls Temple, President George Albert Smith indicated that the Constitution fulfilled the ancient prophecy of Isaiah that "out of Zion shall go forth the law" (Isaiah 2:3). He said:

> We thank thee that thou hast revealed to us that those who gave us our constitutional form of government were wise men in thy sight and that thou didst raise them up for the very purpose of putting forth that sacred document [the Constitution of the United States]. . . .
> We pray that kings and rulers and the people of all nations under heaven may be persuaded of the blessings enjoyed by the people of this land by reason of their freedom and under thy guidance and be constrained to adopt similar government systems, thus to fulfill the ancient prophecy of Isaiah and Micah that "out of Zion shall go forth the law, and the word of the Lord from Jerusalem." (*Improvement Era* 48 [October 1945]: 564.)

(*The Constitution: A Heavenly Banner,* p. 16.)

About two hundred years ago some inspired men walked this land. Not perfect men, but men raised up by the Perfect Man to perform a great work. Foreordained were they to lay the foundation of this republic. Blessed by the Almighty in their struggle for liberty and independence, the power of heaven rested on these founders as they drafted that great document for governing men —the Constitution of the United States. Like the Ten Commandments, the truths on which the Constitution were based were timeless; and also as with the Decalogue—the hand of the Lord was in it. They filled their mission well. From them we were endowed with a legacy of liberty—a constitutional republic. (*An Enemy Hath Done This,* p. 53.)

It is my firm conviction—no, more than that—it is my certain knowledge that the greatness of our beloved nation was foreshadowed and foreseen by ancient prophets who lived here. It is assuring to know that this nation has a prophetic history, that all of the great events that have transpired here, including the coming of Columbus, the Pilgrim Fathers, and the War for Independence, were foreseen by ancient prophets (see 1 Nephi 13:10–19).

It was predicted that those who came to this great land would prosper here, that they would humble themselves before the Almighty, that the power of God would be with them, and that this nation would move forward to its great destiny. When they came, they truly came with that spirit of humility. They were God-fearing, humble people. (See 1 Nephi 13:15–19.) (*The Red Carpet,* p. 107.)

Our earliest American fathers came here with a common objective—freedom of worship and liberty of conscience. The Pilgrim Fathers, the Puritans in New England, the Quakers in Pennsylvania, the Catholics in Maryland, the Lutherans in Georgia and the Huguenots in Virginia, all came seeking God and the enjoyment of God-given, self-evident rights based on eternal principles. Familiar with the sacred scriptures, they believed that liberty is a gift of heaven. They acknowledged their dependence upon God as they exhibited their humble faith in, and devotion to, Christian principles. (*The Red Carpet,* p. 103.)

The Constitution of the United States was ratified in 1789. The priesthood of God was restored in 1829. Between those two dates is an interval of forty years. It is my conviction that God, who knows the end from the beginning, provided that period of time so the new nation could grow in strength to protect the land of Zion. (CR October 1979, *Ensign* 9 [November 1979]: 31.)

The Constitution of this land, with which we should all be familiar, is the only constitution in the world bearing the stamp of approval of the Lord Jesus Christ (D&C 101:76–80). ("Be True to God, Country, and Self," Young Adult Fireside, Logan, Utah, 11 February 1979.)

During the Constitutional Convention of 1787—which in four months drew up the basic laws of our land—the Congress at one time was about to adjourn in utter confusion. The attempt to establish a lasting union had apparently failed. At this crucial moment, eighty-one-year-old Benjamin Franklin arose, and is reported to have said, "In the beginning of the contest with Great Britain, when we were sensible of danger, we had daily prayers in this room for divine protection. Our prayers, sir, were heard and they were generously answered. . . . I have lived a long time and the longer I live the more convincing proofs I see of this truth— that God governs in the affairs of men. If a sparrow cannot fall to the ground without His notice, is it possible that an empire can rise without His aid?" Then Franklin proposed that the Congress seek divine aid, and they should begin each session with a petition to the Almighty. (*The Red Carpet,* p. 105.)

The Constitution was designed to work only with a moral and righteous people. "Our Constitution," said John Adams (first vice-president and second president of the United States), "was made only for a moral and religious people. It is wholly inadequate to the government of any other."

In recognizing God as the source of their rights, the Founding Fathers declared Him to be the ultimate authority for their basis of law. This led them to the conviction that people do not make law but merely acknowledge preexisting law, giving it specific application. The Constitution was conceived to be such an expression of higher law. And when their work was done, James Madison wrote: "It is impossible for the man of pious reflection not to perceive in it a finger of that Almighty hand which has been so frequently and signally extended to our relief in the critical stage of the revolution" (The Federalist, no. 37). (*The Constitution: A Heavenly Banner,* p. 23.)

We must return to a spirit of humility, faith in God, and the basic concepts upon which this great Christian nation has been established under the direction of Divine Providence. We must return to a realization of the source of our strength. Then will we realize the truth of what President George Albert Smith said: "The Constitution of the United States of America is just as much from my Heavenly Father as the Ten Commandments'' (CR April 1948, p. 182). (*Title of Liberty,* p. 45.)

Founding Fathers

The Lord raised up the Founding Fathers. He it was who established the Constitution of this land—the greatest document of freedom ever written. (See D&C 101:77, 80.) This God-inspired Constitution is not outmoded. It is not an outdated "agrarian document" as some would have us believe. It was the Lord God who established the foundation of this nation; and woe be unto those —members of the Supreme Court and others—who would weaken this foundation. (CR October 1965, *Improvement Era* 68 [December 1965]: 1150.)

It is my firm belief that the Constitution of the land was established by men whom the God of Heaven raised up unto that very purpose (see D&C 101:80). It is my firm belief also that the God of Heaven guided the Founding Fathers in establishing it for His particular purposes. ("Freedom—Our Priceless Heritage," Sons of the American Revolution, Salt Lake City, Utah, 22 April 1978.)

Our earliest American fathers came here with a common objective—freedom of worship and liberty of conscience. They were familiar with the sacred scriptures, and they believed that liberty is a gift of heaven. To them, the idea of man as a child of God was not just an empty phrase, but the summation of their belief in the sacredness of the individual and the interest of a kind Providence in the affairs of men and nations. ("God and Country," Frankfurt am Main, Germany, 1964.)

George Washington referred to the Constitution as a miracle. This miracle could only have been performed by exceptional men. (*The Constitution: A Heavenly Banner,* p. 11.)

Washington acknowledged God's direction and stated, "Of all the dispositions and habits which lead to political prosperity, religion and morality are indispensable supports. . . . Reason and experience both forbid us to expect that national morality can prevail in exclusion of religious principles." (Farewell address.)

Lincoln knew that God rules in the affairs of men and nations. He solemnly declared: "God rules this world. It is the duty of nations as well as men to owe their dependence upon the overruling power of God, to confess their sins and transgressions in humble sorrow . . . and to recognize the sublime truths that those nations only are blessed whose God is the Lord."

The Founding Fathers knew that "where the Spirit of the Lord is, there is liberty" (2 Corinthians 3:17; see also Alma 61:15). The United States of America began and lives as a result of faith in God. The Bible has been and is the foundation for this faith. (*God, Family, Country,* p. 392.)

The Founding Fathers had no problems seeing the hand of the Lord in the birth of the nation. George Washington gave direct credit to God for the victory over the British in the Revolutionary War. But that did not end the need for inspiration and divine help.

A constitution was drafted. And thirty-nine of fifty delegates signed it. I would ask: Why is it that the references to God's influence in the noble efforts of the founders of our republic are not mentioned by modern historians?

The fact that our Founding Fathers looked to God for help and inspiration should not surprise us, for they were men of great faith. These men had been raised up specifically by the Lord so they could participate in the great political drama unfolding in America. ("Righteousness Exalteth a Nation," Provo Utah Freedom Festival, 29 June 1986.)

The Founding Fathers did not invent this priceless boon of individual freedom and respect for the dignity of man. That great gift to mankind sprang from the Creator and not from government. But the Founding Fathers with superb genius, I believe, welded together certain safeguards which we must always protect to the very limit if we would preserve and strengthen the blessings of freedom.

They were guided by allegiance to basic principles. These principles must be kept in mind always by those who are here today and reaping the benefits and the blessings which they so wisely provided. We must be careful that we do not trade freedom for security. Whenever that is attempted, usually we lose both. There is always a tendency when nations become mature for the people to become more interested in preserving their luxuries and their comforts than in safeguarding the ideals and principles which made these comforts and luxuries possible. ("Responsibilities of Citizenship," BYU Homecoming, Provo, Utah, 22 October 1954.)

The Founding Fathers, in order that their new experiment—establishment of a new nation of free men—make sense, had to turn to religion and to the scriptures. They turned to the prophecies, the Decalogue, the Sermon on the Mount.
Then when the time came for the establishment of the Constitution, and when the time came for them to issue their Declaration of Independence—a sacred document issued in white heat on the anvil of defiance—they appealed to the Almighty. Both at the opening of that document and at its closing they spoke of eternal truths. (*The Red Carpet,* p. 106.)

The founders of this republic had deeply spiritual beliefs. Their concept of man had a solidly religious foundation. They believed "it is not right that any man should be in bondage one to another" (D&C 101:79). They believed that men were capable of self-government and that it was the job of government to protect freedom and foster private initiative. (*The Red Carpet,* p. 102.)

The Founding Fathers recognized the importance of vital religion and morality in the affairs of individuals and governments, and they turned to religion in order to give their new experiment a sense of direction. They were well aware that the principles of moral, intellectual, and spiritual integrity taught and exemplified by the Savior are the perfect guide for the conduct of countries and of individuals. It is no accident that the principles of Christian religion are the foundation of the Constitution of the United States. ("God and Country," Frankfurt am Main, Germany, 1964.)

The Founding Fathers well understood human nature and its tendency to exercise unrighteous dominion when given authority (D&C 121:39–40). A Constitution was therefore designed to limit government to certain enumerated functions, beyond which was tyranny. (*The Constitution: A Heavenly Banner,* p. 21.)

The Founding Fathers understood the principle that "righteousness exalteth a nation" (Proverbs 14:34), and helped to bring about one of the greatest systems ever used to govern men. But unless we continue to seek righteousness and preserve the liberties entrusted to us, we shall lose the blessings of heaven. Thomas Jefferson said, "The price of freedom is eternal vigilance." The price of freedom is also to live in accordance with the commandments of God. The early Founding Fathers thanked the Lord for His intervention in their behalf. They saw His hand in their victories in battle and believed strongly that He watched over them.

The battles are not over yet, and there will yet be times when this great nation will need the overshadowing help of Deity. Will we as a nation be worthy to call upon Him for help? ("Righteousness Exalteth a Nation," Provo Utah Freedom Festival, 29 June 1986.)

I believe with all my heart the words of the American patriot Patrick Henry, who, on the eve of the American Revolution, said, "There is a just God who presides over the destinies of nations and who will raise up friends to fight our battles for us." Further, it is part of my faith that no people can maintain freedom unless their political institutions are founded on faith in God and belief in the existence of moral law. God has endowed men with certain inalienable rights, and no government may morally limit or destroy these.

The Founding Fathers of the United States seemed to have a clear realization that the new nation would need a reliance on the protection of God for their survival. In the Declaration of Independence there is an appeal to the "Supreme Judge of the world" and to "the laws of nature and nature's God." The document concludes with this affirmation: "And for the support of this Declaration, with a firm reliance on the Protection of Divine Providence, we mutually pledge to each other our Lives, our Fortunes, and our Sacred Honor." (*This Nation Shall Endure,* pp. 68–69.)

It seems highly significant, in retrospect, that our forefathers gloried in hard work while drawing liberally upon their prodigious spiritual reserves. They were not content to place their trust "in the arm of flesh" alone (Jeremiah 17:5; D&C 1:19). They sought to rely upon their cherished independence, their frugality and honest toil, nurtured and fortified by a kind Providence to whose service they were dedicated. History records that even the climate was tempered for their sakes and their humble, untiring efforts made "the desert to blossom as the rose" (Isaiah 35:1). (*The Red Carpet*, p. 287.)

I wonder what our Founding Fathers would do and say about America today if they were here. As they looked searchingly for the answers, they would observe evidence of weak and vacillating leadership in many places, not confined to one group or one party. They would find a tendency for men in high places to place political expediency ahead of principle. They would be concerned with the alarming growth of a something-for-nothing philosophy, a failure of people to stand on their own feet. They would find some bad examples by unscrupulous politicians and by delinquent parents, and possibly a weakening of religious training, and the substitution therefore of a faith-destroying materialism. (*The Red Carpet*, pp. 239–40.)

The Founding Fathers made it clear that our allegiance runs to the Constitution and the glorious eternal principles embodied therein. Our allegiance does not run to any man—to a king or a dictator or a president—although we revere and honor those whom we elect to high office. The Founding Fathers made that clear and provided well for checks and balances and safeguards in an attempt to guarantee this freedom. (CR October 1954, *Improvement Era* 57 [December 1954]: 920.)

Our Founding Fathers, with solemn and reverent expression, voiced their allegiance to the sovereignty of God, knowing that they were accountable to Him in the day of judgment. Are we less accountable today? I think not. I urge you to keep the commandments and to pray for our nation and its leaders. ("Righteousness Exalteth a Nation," Provo Utah Freedom Festival, 29 June 1986.)

Those who say that in this country one's religion should be relegated to his private life alone and never be allowed to "intrude" on his public activities should study the Founding Fathers. This nation has a spiritual foundation. Its wellsprings are themselves religious. Its life is deeply rooted in faith. (*Crossfire: The Eight Years with Eisenhower,* p. 587.)

When I became President of the Twelve and Spencer W. Kimball became President of the Church, we met, just the two of us, every week after our Thursday meetings in the temple, just to be sure that things were properly coordinated between the Twelve and the First Presidency. After one of those first meetings, we talked about the many sacred documents in some of the older temples. St. George was mentioned in particular because St. George is our oldest temple in Utah. I had a stake conference down there about that time, and it was agreed that I would go into the archives—the walk-in vault—of that great temple and review the sacred documents that were there. We were planning for the remodeling and renovating of the St. George Temple and thought that the records might possibly be moved to Salt Lake for safekeeping. And there in the St. George Temple I saw what I had always hoped and prayed that someday I would see. Ever since I returned as a humble missionary and first learned that the Founding Fathers had appeared in that temple, I wanted to see the record. And I saw the record. They did appear to Wilford Woodruff twice and asked why the work hadn't been done for them. They had founded this country and the Constitution of this land, and they had been true to those principles. Later the work was done for them.

In the archives of the temple, I saw in a book, in bold handwriting, the names of the Founding Fathers and others, including Columbus and other great Americans, for whom the work had been done in the house of the Lord. This is all one great program on both sides of the veil. We are fortunate to be engaged in it on this side of the veil. I think the Lord expects us to take an active part in preserving the Constitution and our freedom. (Sandy, Utah, 30 December 1978.)

The Founding Fathers of this nation, those great men, appeared within those sacred walls of the St. George Temple and had their vicarious work done for them. President Wilford Woodruff spoke of it in these words: "Before I left St. George, the spirits of the dead gathered around me, wanting to know why we did not redeem them. Said they, 'You have had the use of the Endowment House for a number of years, and yet nothing has ever been done for us. We laid the foundation of the government you now enjoy, and we never apostatized from it, but we remained true to it and were faithful to God.' "

After he became President of the Church, President Wilford Woodruff declared that "those men who laid the foundation of this American government were the best spirits the God of heaven could find on the face of the earth. They were choice spirits [and] were inspired of the Lord." (CR April 1898, p. 89.) (CR October 1987, *Ensign* 17 [November 1987]: 6.)

The temple work for the fifty-six signers of the Declaration of Independence and other Founding Fathers has been done. All these appeared to Wilford Woodruff when he was president of the St. George Temple. President George Washington was ordained a high priest at that time. You will also be interested to know that, according to Wilford Woodruff's journal, John Wesley, Benjamin Franklin, and Christopher Columbus were also ordained high priests at that time. When one casts doubt about the character of these noble sons of God, I believe he or she will have to answer to the God of heaven for it. Yes, with Lincoln I say: "To add brightness to the sun or glory to the name of Washington is . . . impossible. Let none attempt it. In solemn awe pronounce the name and in its deathless splendor, leave it shining on." (*This Nation Shall Endure*, p. 18.)

The restoration of the gospel and the establishment of the Lord's Church could not come to pass until the Founding Fathers were raised up and completed their foreordained missions. Those great souls who were responsible for the freedoms we enjoy acknowledged the guiding hand of Providence. For their efforts we are indebted, but we are even more indebted to our Father in Heaven and to His Son, Jesus Christ. How fortunate we are to live when the blessings of liberty and the gospel of Jesus Christ are both available to us. (Bicentennial Ball, Salt Lake City, Utah, 18 September 1987.)

Our forefathers gave birth to the ideal of freedom. Our fathers nourished and defended that heritage. Like them, we are resolved to make faith, morality, and freedom the vital forces of daily living, and because of this heritage and this resolution we shall climb through the years to new heights of well-being, strength, and peace. Then let us here and now rededicate ourselves to the unfinished "task remaining before us." This nation, under God, conceived in liberty, must and will "have a new birth of freedom." (*So Shall Ye Reap,* pp. 210–11.)

Elements

We have been blessed with a great heritage. I thank God for the priceless principles of free government. Our American way of life developed under the Constitution rests upon a deep spiritual foundation. President Woodrow Wilson said, "Our civilization cannot survive materially unless it is redeemed spiritually." You can help in that redemption.

Our Constitution and Bill of Rights guarantee to all our people the greatest freedom ever enjoyed by the public of any great nation. This system guarantees freedom of individual enterprise, freedom to own property, freedom to start one's own business and to operate it according to one's own judgment so long as the enterprise is honorable. The individual has power to produce beyond his needs, to provide savings for the future protection of himself and family. He can live where he wishes and pick any job he wants and select any educational opportunity. (*So Shall Ye Reap,* p. 151.)

The Constitution consists of seven separate articles. The first three establish the three branches of our government—the legislative, the executive, and the judicial. The fourth article describes matters pertaining to states, most significantly the guarantee of a republican form of government to every state of the Union. Article 5 defines the amendment procedure of the document, a deliberately difficult process that should be clearly understood by every citizen. Article 6 covers several miscellaneous items, including a definition of the supreme law of the United States, namely the Constitution itself, the laws of the United States, and all treaties made. Article 7, the last, explains how the Constitution is to be ratified.

After ratification of the document, ten amendments were added and designated as our Bill of Rights. To date, the Constitution has been amended twenty-six times, the most recent amendment giving young people the right to vote at age eighteen. (*The Constitution: A Heavenly Banner,* pp. 17–18.)

Our constitutional government is based on the principle of representation. The principle of representation means that we have delegated to an elected official the power to represent us. The Constitution provides for both direct representation and indirect representation. Both forms of representation provide a tempering influence on pure democracy.

The House of Representatives were elected for only two years by direct vote of the people on a population basis. This was balanced by the establishment of a Senate, originally elected by state legislatures for six years. This was an ingenious system whereby the Senate, not directly responsible to the people, could act as a restraining influence on any demagoguery by the House. No law could be passed without the majority approval of the House, whose members were directly elected by the populace; but also, a law had to have the majority concurrence of the Senate, who at that time were not elected by the people. In this way, the passions and impulses of the majority vote were checked. (*The Constitution: A Heavenly Banner,* pp. 21–22.)

Political and economic rights are the things we are inclined to take for granted as American citizens. These rights include the right to worship God in one's own way, rights to free speech and a free press, the right to assemble and freely to speak our own minds without any fear whatever. There are many countries of this world where you cannot do that today.

The right to petition for grievances, the right to privacy in our homes, the right to trial by jury and to know that we are innocent until we are proven guilty. The right to move freely at home and abroad, the right to own private property, the right to free elections and personal secret ballot. The right to work in callings and localities of our choice. The right to bargain with our employees and employers. The right to go into business, to compete, to make a profit. The right to bargain for goods and services in a free market. The right to contract about our affairs.

These are an impressive list of rights which lie at the very foundation of the American way of life and preserve the dignity of the individual. Our constitutional government desires to serve the people, and basic in our beliefs is our fundamental belief in God and in the eternal principle of free agency, the right of choice. (*The Red Carpet,* p. 266.)

Our most cherished rights and interests—freedom of religion, freedom of speech and of the press, right of assembly, right of petition, right of trial by jury, protection from search and seizure, and freedom of enterprise—are all a part of the American way of life. (*So Shall Ye Reap,* pp. 151–52.)

To safeguard these rights, the Founding Fathers provided for the separation of powers among the three branches of government —the legislative, the executive, and the judicial. Each was to be independent of the other, yet each was to work in a unified relationship. As the great constitutionalist President J. Reuben Clark, Jr., noted: "It is the union of independence and dependence of these branches—legislative, executive, and judicial—and of the governmental functions possessed by each of them, that constitutes the marvelous genius of this unrivaled document. . . . It was truly a miracle." (*Church News,* 29 November 1952, p. 12.)

In order to avoid a concentration of power in any one branch, the Founding Fathers created a system of government that provided checks and balances. Congress could pass laws, but the president could check these laws with a veto. Congress, however, could override the veto and, by its means of initiative in taxation, could further restrain the executive department. The Supreme Court could nullify laws passed by the Congress and signed by the president, but Congress could limit the court's appellate jurisdiction. The president could appoint judges for their lifetime with the consent of the Senate.

The use of checks and balances was deliberately designed, first, to make it difficult for a minority of the people to control the government, and second, to place restraint on the government itself. (*The Constitution: A Heavenly Banner,* pp. 19–20.)

The right to property is based on scriptural precept (see D&C 134:2; Alma 44:5; Matthew 5:5; Isaiah 14:1). It recognizes that the earth belongs to the Lord, that He created it for man's blessing and benefit. Thus, man's desire to own property, his own home and goods, his own business, is desirable and good. Utopian and communitarian schemes that eliminate property rights are not only unworkable, they also deny to man his inherent desire to improve his station. They are therefore contrary to the pursuit of happiness.

No property rights! Man's incentive would be diminished to satisfying only his barest necessities such as food and clothing. No property rights! No contractual relationships to buy and sell, since title to possessions of goods could not be granted. No property rights! No recognition of divine law that prohibits man from stealing and coveting others' possessions (see Exodus 20:15, 17). One cannot steal that which belongs to everyone, nor can he covet that which belongs to everyone, nor can he covet that which is not another's! No property rights! No possibility of the sanctity of one's own home and the joy that comes from creation, production, and ownership.

A free-market philosophy recognizes property rights as sacred. Because the individual is entitled to ownership of goods and property that he has earned, he is sovereign, so far as human law is concerned, over his own goods. He may retain possession of his goods. He may pass his wealth on to family or to charitable causes. Charity, that greatest of godly virtues, would never be possible without property rights, for one cannot give what one does not own.

James Madison recognized that property consisted not only of man's external goods—his land, merchandise, or money—but, most sacredly, he had title also to his thoughts, opinions, and conscience. A civil government's obligation, then, is to safeguard this right and to frame laws that secure to every man the free exercise of his conscience and the right and control of his property.

No liberty is possible unless a man is protected in his title to his legal holdings and property and can be indemnified by the law for its loss or destruction. Remove this right and man is reduced to serfdom. Former United States Supreme Court Justice George Sutherland said it this way: "To give [man] liberty but take from him the property which is the fruit and badge of his liberty, is to still leave him a slave." (Address to the New York Bar Association, 21 January 1921.) (*This Nation Shall Endure,* pp. 84–85.)

Church and State

A critic claimed that a person who serves in a church capacity should not comment on civic matters. He charged that the separation of church and state requires that church officials restrict their attention to the affairs of the church.

I also believe that the institutions of church and state should be separated, but I do not agree that spiritual leaders cannot comment on basic issues which involve the very foundation of American liberty.

In fact, if this were true, we would have to throw away a substantial part of the Bible. Speaking out against immoral or unjust actions of political leaders has been the burden of prophets and disciples of God from time immemorial. It was for this very reason that many of them were persecuted. Some of them were stoned; some of them were burned; many were imprisoned. Nevertheless, it was their God-given task to speak up. It is certainly no different today.

To Moses, God said, "Proclaim liberty throughout all the land unto all the inhabitants thereof" (Leviticus 25:10). To modern men God has said that the Constitution "should be maintained for the rights and protection of all flesh" (D&C 101:77). (*Title of Liberty*, p. 28.)

I support the doctrine of separation of church and state as traditionally interpreted to prohibit the establishment of an official national religion. But this does not mean that we should divorce government from any formal recognition of God. To do so strikes a potentially fatal blow at the concept of the divine origin of our rights, and unlocks the door for an easy entry of future tyranny. If Americans should ever come to believe that their rights and freedoms are instituted among men by politicans and bureaucrats, they will no longer carry the proud inheritance of their forefathers, but will grovel before their masters seeking favors and dispensations—a throwback to the feudal system of the Dark Ages. ("Freedom Is Our Heritage," LDS Business and Professional Men's Association, Glendale, California, 10 November 1970.)

States' Rights

The history of all mankind shows very clearly that if we would be free—and if we would stay free—we must stand eternal watch against the accumulation of too much power in government.

There is hardly a single instance in all of history where the dictatorial centralization of power has been compatible with individual freedom—where it has not reduced the citizenry to the status of pawns and mere creatures of the state. God forbid that this should happen in America. Yet I am persuaded that the continuation of the trend of the past could make us pallbearers at the burial of the states as effective units of government. ("Freedom Is Our Heritage," LDS Business and Professional Men's Association, Glendale, California, 10 November 1970.)

The individuality, initiative, and enterprise of the state tend to diminish in direct proportion to the centralization of power in federal programs. The money is not as wisely spent as if the states had participated financially. States not only have rights, but they have responsibilities. (*The Red Carpet,* p. 160.)

I am especially mindful that the Constitution provides that the great bulk of the legitimate activities of government are to be carried out at the state or local level. This is the only way in which the principle of self-government can be made effective. As James Madison said, before the adoption of the Constitution, "[We] rest all our political experiments on the capacity of mankind for self-government" (*Federalist,* no. 39). Thomas Jefferson made this interesting observation: "Sometimes it is said that man cannot be trusted with the government of himself. Can he, then, be trusted with the government of others? Or have we found angels in the forms of kings to govern him? Let history answer this question." (*Works,* 8:3.)

It is a firm principle that the smallest or lowest level that can possibly undertake the task is the one that should do so. First, the community or the city. If the city cannot handle it, then the county. Next, the state; and only if no smaller unit can possibly do the job should the federal government be considered. This is merely the application to the field of politics of that wise and time-tested principle of never asking a larger group to do that which can be done by a smaller group. And so far as government is concerned, the smaller the unit and the closer it is to the people, the easier it is to guide it, to correct it, to keep it solvent, and to keep our freedom.

It is well to remember that the people of the states of this republic created the federal government. The federal government did not create the states. (*An Enemy Hath Done This,* pp. 133–34.)

Sooner or later, the accumulation of power in central government leads to a loss of freedom. Everyone knows, also, it is hard to end undesirable government programs after they have been established. If power is diffused, such cannot happen. Every schoolboy knows that this is why the founders of our country carefully divided power between state and federal levels.

Our traditional federal-state relationship, we must never forget, starts with a general presumption in favor of state and individual rights. Under the constitutional concept, powers not granted to the federal government are reserved to the states or to the people. This is in the Bill of Rights. It is one of the first ten amendments to the Constitution, insisted upon by a number of the states as a condition of ratification of the Constitution.

The framers of our Constitution knew that many forces would be at work toward the concentration of power at the federal level. They knew that it somehow seems easier to impose "progress" on localities than to wait for them to bring it about themselves. Raids on the federal treasury can be all too readily accomplished by an organized few over the feeble protests of an apathetic majority. With more and more activity centered in the federal government, the relationship between the costs and the benefits of government programs becomes obscure. What follows is the voting of public money without having to accept direct local responsibility for higher taxes.

I know of no device of government which will lead more quickly to an increase in the number of federal programs than this. If this trend continues, the states may be left hollow shells, operating primarily as the field districts of federal departments and dependent upon the federal treasury for their support. (*The Red Carpet,* pp. 147–48.)

The thought that the federal government is wealthy and the states poverty-stricken is a dangerous illusion. It is difficult for the states to make a strong case for assistance from the federal government when anything the federal government spends must come from the states. There are no resources of consequence in the United States—no income of wealth which is not located within the borders of the states and subject to their taxing powers.

More local action means heavier financial responsibility, but, in the long run, local financial responsibility will be to the states' advantage. It is cheaper for the people to do more on the state level where the revenue originates. (*The Red Carpet,* p. 162.)

I have been a farmer in the private enterprise sector of our economy. I have worked with farmer cooperatives, in which private persons voluntarily associate themselves to improve their bargaining power. I have been stationed at a local unit of government as a county agricultural agent. I have worked at the state level and have been stationed at the federal level, where the problem of intergovernmental relations comes sharply into focus.

We do not have, under the Constitution, a form of government that is federal, regional, and state. Yet, in recent years, we have been rapidly building up some forms of regional organization with the result that there has been a weakening in the division of functions between federal and state authorities. State governments must be supported "in all their rights as the most competent administrators for our domestic concerns and the surest bulwarks against" tendencies that would weaken our form of government. (*The Red Carpet,* pp. 148–49.)

The typical American is inherently a states'-righter by inclination and by sentiment. Deep in their hearts, the American people instinctively know that great concentration of power is an evil and a dangerous thing. (*The Red Carpet,* p. 147.)

Unconstitutional Actions

At this bicentennial celebration we must, with sadness, say that we have not been wise in keeping the trust of our Founding Fathers. For the past two centuries, those who do not prize freedom have chipped away at every major clause of our Constitution until today we face a crisis of great dimensions. (*The Constitution: A Heavenly Banner,* pp. 24–25.)

Our Founding Fathers wisely established three branches of the federal government—the legislative, executive, and judicial—as partial checks against each other. Even the legislative branch was further subdivided into two parts—the House and the Senate—

each with different modes of election so that one would represent the people directly, and the other would represent the people indirectly through the states. Every conceivable precaution was taken to insure that the government which they had created would not be able to gather total political power into one place and become as venal and oppressive as the one from which they had separated.

If those who so carefully drafted the checks and balances into our Constitution could have looked into the future and seen what the Supreme Court of the United States would do to their masterpiece, they would have been dismayed. Through the process of supposedly "interpreting" the Constitution, the Court has twisted beyond recognition just about every conceivable clause to justify the transfer of all sovereignty from the states to the federal government, to broaden the powers of the federal government beyond any definable limit, and then to make it possible for all such powers to fall into the hands of the executive branch of government. We may still give lip service to the checks and balances of our constitutional republic, but the phrase is now quite hollow. (*An Enemy Hath Done This,* pp. 265–67.)

We, the people, have allowed the government to ignore one of the most fundamental stipulations of the Constitution—namely, the separation of powers. In recent years, we have allowed Congress to fund numerous federal agencies. While these agencies may provide some needed services and protection of rights, they also encroach significantly on our constitutional rights. The number of agencies seems to grow continually to regulate and control the lives of millions of citizens.

What many fail to realize is that most of these federal agencies are unconstitutional. Why are they unconstitutional? They are unconstitutional because they concentrate the functions of the legislative, executive, and judicial branches under one head. They have, in other words, power to make rulings, enforce rulings, and adjudicate penalties when rulings are violated. They are unconstitutional because they represent an assumption of power not delegated to the executive branch by the people. They are also unconstitutional because the people have no power to recall administrative agency personnel by their vote. (*The Constitution: A Heavenly Banner,* pp. 25–26.)

There is one and only one legitimate goal of United States foreign policy. It is a narrow goal, a nationalistic goal: the preservation of our national independence. Nothing in the Constitution grants that the president shall have the privilege of offering himself as a world leader. He is our executive; he is on our payroll; he is supposed to put our best interests in front of those of other nations. Nothing in the Constitution nor in logic grants to the president of the United States or to Congress the power to influence the political life of other countries, to "uplift" their cultures, to bolster their economies, to feed their people, or even to defend them against their enemies. ("America at the Crossroads," Jackson, Mississippi, 30 August 1969.)

To get some idea of how we are flaunting the Constitution, see how the Constitution defines treason (see Article III, section 3). Then observe what we are doing to build up the enemy, this totally anti-Christ conspiracy. If we continue on this tragic course of aid and trade to the enemy, the Lord has warned us in the Book of Mormon of the consequences that will follow (Ether 8). Thank God for the Constitution. And may God bless the elders of Israel that when, as President John Taylor said, "the people shall have torn to shreds the Constitution of the United States, the Elders of Israel will be found holding it up to the nations of earth and proclaiming liberty" (*Journal of Discourses*, 21:8). ("Jesus Christ —Gifts and Expectations," *New Era* 5 [May 1975]: 19.)

Support

I reverence the Constitution of the United States as a sacred document. To me its words are akin to the revelations of God, for God has placed His stamp of approval on the Constitution of this land (see D&C 101:76–80). I testify that the God of Heaven sent some of His choicest spirits to lay the foundation of this government, and He has sent other choice spirits—even you who read my words—to preserve it. (*The Constitution: A Heavenly Banner,* p. 31.)

From the time I was a small boy I was taught that the American Constitution is an inspired document. I was taught that we should study the Constitution, preserve its principles, and defend it against any who would destroy it. To the best of my ability I have always tried to do this. I expect to continue my efforts to help protect and safeguard our inspired Constitution. (*An Enemy Hath Done This,* p. 37.)

God placed a mandate upon His people to befriend and defend the constitutional laws of the land and see that the rights and privileges of all mankind are protected. He verified the declaration of the Founding Fathers that God created all men free. He also warned against those who would enact laws encroaching upon the sacred rights and privileges of free men. He urged the election of honest and wise leaders and said that evil men and laws were of Satan. (See D&C 98:5–10.) (*God, Family, Country,* p. 344.)

While the Gentiles established the Constitution, we have a divine mandate to preserve it. But unfortunately, today in this freedom struggle many Gentiles are showing greater wisdom in their generation than the children of light (Luke 16:8). (*An Enemy Hath Done This,* p. 277.)

A standard I use in determining what law is good and what is bad is the Constitution of the United States. I regard this inspired document as a solemn agreement between the citizens of this nation which every officer of government is under a sacred duty to obey. (*An Enemy Hath Done This,* p. 133.)

Men who are wise, good, and honest, who will uphold the Constitution of the United States in the tradition of the Founding Fathers, must be sought for diligently (D&C 98:10). This is our hope to restore government to its rightful role. (CR October 1979, *Ensign* 9 [November 1979]: 33.)

We pay lip service to the principles embodied in the Declaration of Independence and the Constitution without realizing what they are and the danger of ignoring them. (*So Shall Ye Reap,* p. 195.)

To every Latter-day Saint, we have a tremendous obligation to be good citizens, to uphold the Constitution of this land, to adhere to its basic concepts, to do all in our power to protect the freedoms and the liberties and the basic rights which are associated with citizenship. The Lord has said even in our day, through the Prophet Joseph Smith, that we have an obligation. He has not only spoken about the Constitution being inspired, he has said that if we are to be good Latter-day Saints, we also have to take an interest in this country in which we live and we are to see to it that good men are upheld and sustained in public office. The Lord taught the Prophet Joseph Smith:

> Now, verily I say unto you concerning the laws of the land, it is my will that my people should observe to do all things whatsoever I command them.
> And that law of the land which is constitutional, supporting that principle of freedom in maintaining rights and privileges, belongs to all mankind, and is justifiable before me.
> Therefore, I, the Lord, justify you, and your brethren of my church, in befriending that law which is the constitutional law of the land. . . .
> I, the Lord God, make you free. . . .
> Nevertheless, when the wicked rule the people mourn.
> Wherefore, honest men and wise men should be sought for diligently, and good men and wise men ye should observe to uphold; otherwise whatsoever is less than these cometh of evil. (D&C 98:4–6, 8–10.)

(Short Hills, New Jersey, 15 January 1961.)

What can we do to preserve our Constitution, and how can we avoid being misled into doing those things that would actually help to destroy it? During October 1963 conference I spoke on the subject "Be Not Deceived." I said there were three keys one could use to avoid deception: first, the scriptures; second, the words of the prophets, especially the President of the Church (particularly the living one); and, third, the Holy Ghost. (*Title of Liberty,* p. 80.)

Learn about the Constitution, the Declaration of Independence, and other basic documents of our great country so that you can sustain them and the free institutions set up under them. The greatest watchdog of our freedom is an informed electorate. ("The Ten Commandments," *New Era* 8 [July 1978]: 39.)

As an independent American for constitutional government I declare that:

I believe that no people can maintain freedom unless their political institutions are founded upon faith in God and belief in the existence of moral law.

I believe that God has endowed men with certain inalienable rights as set forth in the Declaration of Independence and that no legislature and no majority, however great, may morally limit or destroy these; that the sole function of government is to protect life, liberty, and property, and anything more than this is usurpation and oppression.

I believe that the Constitution of the United States was prepared and adopted by men acting under inspiration from Almighty God; that it is a solemn compact between the peoples of the states of this nation that all officers of government are under duty to obey; that the eternal moral laws expressed therein must be adhered to or individual liberty will perish.

I believe it a violation of the Constitution for government to deprive the individual of either life, liberty, or property except for these purposes: to punish crime and provide for the administration of justice; to protect the right and control of private property; to wage defensive war and provide for the nation's defense; to compel each one who enjoys the protection of government to bear his fair share of the burden of performing the above functions.

I hold that the Constitution denies government the power to take from the individual either his life, liberty, or property except in accordance with moral law; that the same moral law which governs the actions of men when acting alone is also applicable when they act in concert with others; that no citizen or group of citizens has any right to direct their agent, the government, to perform any act that would be evil or offensive to the conscience if that citizen were performing the act himself outside the framework of government.

I am hereby resolved that under no circumstances shall the freedoms guaranteed by the Bill of Rights be infringed. In particular I am opposed to any attempt on the part of the federal government to deny the people their right to bear arms, to worship, to pray when and where they choose, or to own and control private property.

I maintain that every person who enjoys the protection of his life, liberty, and property should bear his fair share of the cost of government in providing that protection; that the elementary principles of justice set forth in the Constitution demand that all taxes imposed be uniform; and that each person's property or income be taxed at the same rate.

I believe that each state is sovereign in performing those functions reserved to it by the Constitution, and it is destructive of our federal system and the right of self-government guaranteed under the Constitution for the federal government to regulate or control the states in performing their functions or to engage in performing such functions itself.

I consider it a violation of the Constitution for the federal government to levy taxes for the support of state or local government; that no state or local government can accept funds from the federal government and remain independent in performing its functions, nor can the citizens exercise their rights of self-government under such conditions.

I believe that no treaty or agreement with other countries should deprive our citizens of rights guaranteed them by the Constitution.

I consider it a direct violation of the obligation imposed upon it by the Constitution for the federal government to dismantle or weaken our military establishment below that point required for the protection of the states against invasion, or to surrender or commit our men, arms, or money to control of foreign or world organizations or governments.

These things I believe to be the proper role of government. We have strayed far afield. We must return to basic concepts and principles—to eternal verities. There is no other way. The storm signals are up. They are clear and omnious. (*God, Family, Country,* pp. 299–302.)

It may cost us blood before we are through. It is my conviction, however, that when the Lord comes, the Stars and Stripes will be floating on the breeze over this people. May it be so, and may God give us the faith and the courage exhibited by those patriots who pledged their lives and fortunes and sacred honor that we might be free. (*The Constitution: A Heavenly Banner,* p. 33.)

Elders of Israel

The Lord told the Prophet Joseph Smith there would be an attempt to overthrow the country by destroying the Constitution.

Joseph Smith predicted that the time would come when the Constitution would hang, as it were, by a thread, and at that time "this people will step forth and save it from the threatened destruction" (*Journal of Discourses*, 7:15). It is my conviction that the elders of Israel, widely spread over the nation, will at that crucial time successfully rally the righteous of our country and provide the necessary balance of strength to save the institutions of constitutional government.

If the Gentiles on this land reject the word of God and conspire to overthrow liberty and the Constitution, their doom is fixed, and they "shall be cut off from among my people who are of the covenant" (1 Nephi 14:6; 3 Nephi 21:11, 14, 21; D&C 84:114–15, 117). (*God, Family, Country,* p. 345.)

As we spread abroad in this land, bearers of this priesthood, men and women with high ideals and standards, our influence will spread as we take positions of leadership in the community, in the state, in the nation, in the world. We will be able to sit in counsel with others and we will be able to influence others in paths of righteousness. We will help to save this nation, because this nation can only be preserved on the basis of righteous living. ("The Greatest Leadership," BYU Student Leadership Conference, Sun Valley, Idaho, September 1959.)

The devil knows that if the elders of Israel should ever wake up, they could step forth and help preserve freedom and extend the gospel. Therefore the devil has concentrated, and to a large extent successfully, in neutralizing much of the priesthood. He has reduced them to sleeping giants. (*An Enemy Hath Done This,* p. 275.)

It is the devil's desire that the Lord's priesthood stay asleep while the strings of tyranny gradually and quietly entangle us until, like Gulliver, we awake too late and find that while we could have broken each string separately as it was put upon us, our sleepiness permitted enough strings to bind us to make a rope that enslaves us.

For years we have heard of the role the elders could play in saving the Constitution from total destruction. But how can the elders be expected to save it if they have not studied it and are not sure if it is being destroyed or what is destroying it? (*An Enemy Hath Done This,* p. 313.)

Here in America, the Lord's base of operations—so designated by the Lord Himself through His holy prophets—we of the priesthood, members of His restored Church, might well provide the balance of power to save our freedom. Indeed we might, if we go forward as Moroni of old, and raise the standard of liberty throughout the land. My brethren, we can do the job that must be done. We can, as a priesthood, provide the balance of power to preserve our freedom and save this nation from bondage.

The Prophet Joseph Smith is reported to have prophesied the role the priesthood might play to save our inspired Constitution. Now is the time to move forward courageously—to become alerted, informed, and active.

We know, as do no other people, that the Constitution of the United States is inspired—established by men whom the Lord raised up for that very purpose. We cannot—we must not—shirk our sacred responsibility to rise up in defense of our God-given freedom. (*An Enemy Hath Done This*, p. 321.)

The Lord's priesthood has a mission to perform for liberty-loving people everywhere. We cannot, any more than Jonah of old, run away from our calling. If the people shall accept the Lord's solution of the world's problems, even as those who listened to a repentant Jonah, then all shall be well with them. If they do not, however, they will suffer the consequences. Our responsibility, as in Jonah's case, is to see to it that the people have a chance to choose decisively after they have been shown clearly the Lord's way and what the Lord expects of them. (See Jonah 1–4.) (CR October 1954, *Improvement Era* 57 [December 1954]: 922.)

Only in this foreordained land, under its God-inspired Constitution and the resulting environment of freedom, was it possible to have established the restored Church. It is our responsibility to see that this freedom is perpetuated so that the Church may more easily flourish in the future.

The Lord said, "Therefore, I, the Lord justify you, and your brethren of my church, in befriending that law which is the constitutional law of the land" (D&C 98:6).

How then can we best befriend the Constitution in this critical hour and secure the blessings of liberty and ensure the protection and guidance of our Father in Heaven?

First and foremost, we must be righteous. John Adams said, "Our Constitution was made only for a moral and religious people. It is wholly inadequate to the government of any other." If the Constitution is to have continuance, this American nation, and especially the Latter-day Saints, must be virtuous.

The Book of Mormon warns us relative to our living in this free land: "Wherefore, this land is consecrated unto him whom he shall bring. And if it so be that they shall serve him according to the commandment which he hath given; it shall be a land of liberty unto them; wherefore, they shall never be brought down into captivity; if so, it shall be because of iniquity; for if iniquity shall abound cursed shall be the land for their sakes, but unto the righteous it shall be blessed forever." (2 Nephi 1:7.)

"And now," warned Moroni, "we can behold the decrees of God concerning this land, that it is a land of promise; and whatsoever nation shall possess it shall serve God, or they shall be swept off when the fulness of his wrath shall come upon them. And the fulness of his wrath cometh upon them when they are ripened in iniquity." (Ether 2:9.)

Two great American Christian civilizations—the Jaredites and the Nephites—were swept off because they did not "serve the God of the land, who is Jesus Christ" (Ether 2:12). What will become of our civilization?

Second, we must learn the principles of the Constitution in the tradition of the Founding Fathers. Have we read the Federalist Papers? Are we reading the Constitution and pondering it? Are we aware of its principles? Are we abiding by these principles and teaching them to others? Could we defend the Constitution? Can we recognize when a law is constitutionally unsound? Do we know what the prophets have said about the Constitution and the threats to it?

As Jefferson said, "If a nation expects to be ignorant and free . . . it expects what never was and never will be."

Third, we must become involved in civic affairs to see that we are properly represented. The Lord said that He "holds men accountable for their acts in relation" to governments "both in making laws and administering them" (D&C 134:1). We must follow this counsel from the Lord: "Honest men and wise men should be sought for diligently and good men and wise men ye should observe to uphold; otherwise whatsoever is less than these cometh of evil" (D&C 98:10). Note the qualities that the Lord demands of those who are to represent us. They must be good, wise, and honest.

Fourth, we must make our influence felt by our vote, our letters, our teaching, and our advice. We must become accurately informed and then let others know how we feel. The Prophet Joseph Smith said: "It is our duty to concentrate all our influence to make popular that which is sound and good, and unpopular that which is unsound. 'Tis right, politically, for a man who has influence to use it. . . . From henceforth I will maintain all the influence I can get" (*History of the Church,* 5:286).

I have faith that the Constitution will be saved, as prophesied by Joseph Smith. It will be saved by the righteous citizens of this nation who love and cherish freedom. It will be saved by the enlightened members of this Church—among others—men and women who understand and abide the principles of the Constitution. (CR October 1987, *Ensign* 17 [November 1987]: 6–7.)

I quote Abraham Lincoln: "Let [the Constitution] be taught in schools, in seminaries, and in colleges, let it be written in primers, in spelling books and in almanacs, let it be preached from the pulpit, proclaimed in legislative halls, and enforced in courts of justice. And, in short, let it become the political religion of the nation." We must become involved in civic affairs. As citizens of this republic, we cannot do our duty and be idle spectators. (*The Constitution: A Heavenly Banner,* pp. 28–29.)

You must keep your honor. You cannot yet speak officially for the country, but you can become informed. You can speak your mind. You may think you can do little about the national economy or the actions of our government and the moral weakness all about us, but we must all remember that the Lord has placed great responsibilities upon the elders of Israel in the preservation of our Constitution.

Many seem to excuse themselves from involvement with the expression "that's politics," but the Constitution was established by men whom the God of Heaven raised up unto that very purpose (see D&C 101:80). It is your charter. It is a charter belonging to every American. No, we may not be fully responsible for deception in others, but we are responsible for ourselves and our activities as citizens in using our influence to see that honest men and wise men are elected to office and that we will uphold "good men and wise men" as the Lord has commanded (D&C 98:10). ("Be True to God, Country, and Self," Young Adult Fireside, Logan, Utah, 11 February 1979.)

Part of the reason we may not have sufficient priesthood bearers to save the Constitution, let alone to shake the powers of hell, is because unlike Moroni, I fear, our souls do not joy in keeping our country free, and we are not firm in the faith of Christ, nor have we sworn with an oath to defend our rights and the liberty of our country (see Alma 48:17). (CR October 1966, *Improvement Era* 69 [December 1966]: 1145.)

The Prophet Joseph Smith saw the part the elders of Israel would play in this constitutional crisis. Will there be some of us who won't care about saving the Constitution, others who will be blinded by the craftiness of men, and some who will knowingly be working to destroy it? He who has ears to hear and eyes to see can discern by the Spirit and through the words of God's mouthpiece that our liberties are being taken. (*God, Family, Country,* p. 399.)

To all who have discerning eyes, it is apparent that the republican form of government established by our noble forefathers cannot long endure once fundamental principles are abandoned. Momentum is gathering for another conflict—a repetition of the crisis of two hundred years ago. This collision of ideas is worldwide. The issue is the same that precipitated the great premortal conflict—will men be free to determine their own course of action or must they be coerced.

We are fast approaching that moment prophesied by Joseph Smith when he said: "Even this nation will be on the very verge of crumbling to pieces and tumbling to the ground, and when the Constitution is upon the brink of ruin, this people will be the staff upon which the nation shall lean, and they shall bear the Constitution away from the very verge of destruction" (Church Historian's Office, Salt Lake City, July 19, 1840). (*The Constitution: A Heavenly Banner,* pp. 27–28.)

For All Flesh

The product of the Constitutional Convention was referred to as our God-inspired Constitution. They had incorporated within its sacred paragraphs eternal principles supported by the holy scriptures with which they were familiar. It was established "for the rights and protection of all flesh according to just and holy principles" (D&C 101:77–80). (*The Red Carpet,* p. 284.)

God has told us in modern scripture that the United States Constitution was divinely inspired for the specific purpose of eliminating bondage and the violation of the rights and protection that belongs to "all flesh" (D&C 101:77–80). If we believe in God and His works, it is up to each one of us to uphold and defend our Constitution, which guarantees our precious freedom. For God states unequivocally: "Let not that which I have appointed be polluted by mine enemies, by the consent of those who call themselves after my name; For this is a very sore and grievous sin against me, and against my people, in consequence of those things which I have decreed and which are soon to befall the nations" (D&C 101:97–98). (*This Nation Shall Endure,* p. 74.)

The United States Constitution has been in existence longer than any written constitution in history. It has been a blessing, not only to our land, but to the world as well. Many nations have wisely adopted concepts and provisions of our Constitution, just as was prophesied (D&C 101:77). ("Remarks on the Constitution," Bicentennial Ball, Salt Lake City, Utah, 18 September 1987.)

It is gratifying that the constitutions in many of the other lands of our neighbors in the Americas are patterned very much after this divinely appointed Constitution which the God of Heaven directed in the founding of this nation. It isn't any wonder, therefore, that Joseph Smith, the Prophet — a truly great American — referring to the Constitution, said, "[It] is a glorious standard; it is founded in the wisdom of God" (*Teachings of the Prophet Joseph Smith,* p. 147). (CR October 1954, *Improvement Era* 57 [December 1954]: 918.)

Declaration of Independence

This nation is unlike any other nation. It was uniquely born. It had its beginning when fifty-six men affixed their signatures to the Declaration of Independence. I realize there are some who view that declaration as only a political document. It is more than that. It constitutes a spiritual manifesto, declaring not for this nation alone, but for all nations, the source of man's rights.

The purpose of the declaration was to set forth the moral justifications of a rebellion against a long-recognized political tradition — the divine right of kings. At issue was the fundamental question of whether men's rights were God-given or whether these rights were to be dispensed by governments to their subjects. This document proclaimed that all men have certain inalienable rights; in other words, that those rights came from God. The colonists were therefore not rebels against political authority. Their contention was not with Parliament nor the British people; it was against a tyrannical monarch who had "conspired," "incited," and "plundered" them. They were thus morally justified to revolt, for as it was stated in the declaration, "when a long train of abuses and usurpations, pursuing invariably the same Object, evinces a design to reduce them under absolute Despotism, it is their right, it is their duty, to throw off such Government, and to provide new Guards for their future security." (*This Nation Shall Endure,* pp. 25–26.)

The doctrine of that crowning document — the Declaration of Independence — is this: That the Creator endowed all men with basic rights, and that governments derive their powers from the consent of the governed.

Until the American Revolution, a millennium of political tradition vested powers only in monarchs and dictators. The founders of our republic simply declared the truth—that God gave all men the right to life, liberty, and property. Man, therefore, was master over government rather than the other way around.

That is what the American Revolution was all about—not just a separation from England, but a separation from the historical tradition that made one man another's chattel and denied all men liberty and property. ("Righteousness Exalteth a Nation," Provo Utah Freedom Festival, 29 June 1986.)

The Founding Fathers of this great land, under the benign influence of a kind Providence, established a solid foundation aimed at guaranteeing a maximum of individual freedom, happiness, and well-being. "We hold these truths to be self-evident," they said in the Declaration of Independence, "that all men are created equal; that they are endowed by their Creator with certain inalienable rights; that among these are life, liberty, and the pursuit of happiness. That to secure these rights, governments are instituted among men, deriving their just powers from the consent of the governed."

This inspired document proclaims clearly that governments should be established on such principles as "seem most likely to effect" the "safety and happiness" of the people. ("The American Free-Enterprise System: Will It Survive?" Contemporary Issues Forum, Ogden, Utah, 18 January 1977.)

When the American patriot Patrick Henry shouted his immortal "Give me liberty or give me death," he did not speak idly. When at Philadelphia in 1776, the signers of the Declaration of Independence affixed their signatures to that sacred document, they, in a very real sense, were choosing liberty or death. Not one of them but knew full well that if the revolution failed, if the fight for freedom should come to naught, they would be branded as rebels and hanged as traitors. (American Institute of Real Estate Appraisers, Salt Lake City, Utah, 19 April 1974.)

The founders recognized that if the new nation were to survive, there must be reliance on the protection of God. The Declaration of Independence concluded with this affirmation: "With a firm reliance on the protection of Divine Providence, we mutually pledge to each other our lives, our fortunes, and our sacred honor."

("The Faith of Our Founding Fathers," in *Faith* [Salt Lake City: Deseret Book, 1983], p. 25.)

This Declaration was a promise that would demand terrible sacrifice on the part of its signers. Five of the signers were captured as traitors and tortured before they died. Twelve had their homes ransacked and burned. Two lost their sons in the Revolutionary War; another had two sons captured. Nine died from wounds or the hardship of the war. The Lord said He "redeemed the land by the shedding of blood" (D&C 101:80). Nephi recorded that the founders "were delivered by the power of God out of the hands of all other nations" (1 Nephi 13:19). (CR October 1987, *Ensign* 17 [November 1987]: 4.)

Economics

Free Enterprise

Nothing is more to be prized, nor more sacred, than man's free choice. Free choice is the essence of free enterprise. It recognizes that the common man will make choices in his own self-interest. It allows a manufacturer to produce what he wants, how much, and to set his own price. It allows the buyer to decide if he wants a certain product at the price established. It preserves the right to work when and where we choose.

In his first inaugural address, Thomas Jefferson said that the sum of good government shall leave citizens "free to regulate their own pursuits of industry and improvement, and shall not take from the mouth of labor the bread it has earned." (*This Nation Shall Endure,* p. 86.)

Enterprise, initiative, self-reliance! Called by whatever name, this dynamo for human betterment has been developed within the environment of freedom and responsibility laid down by our forefathers. This system has fed the body and nourished the spirit. It has released the creative power within each person. It has given this country an unprecedented degree of freedom, the richest blessing a nation can receive from the hand of God.

Not only that, our American farmers and business people, through their enterprise, have lifted the standard of living of this country higher than ever occurred before, in any land, at any time. The abundance which this enterprise has produced is shared more widely than ever, anywhere. I believe in the free-enterprise system. (*The Red Carpet,* pp. 216–17.)

Our abundant material blessings have come to us through an economic system which rests largely on three pillars: Free enterprise—the right to venture, to choose. Private property—the right to own. A market economy—the right to exchange. We must never make the catastrophic blunder of putting the chains of big government on our basic economic freedom. Yet there is that very danger today.

The pillars of our economic system are being threatened by a strange and unlikely coalition of subversives, do-gooders, and self-servers. There are, in this country, a hard core of subversives who hate the free-enterprise system and are dedicated to its overthrow. There is a host of do-gooders, who constantly criticize our free choice system, ready to solve all human problems with legislation, willing to impose their version of the millennium on you and me, unwilling to rely on the judgment of the individual. There are the self-servers, who view government as a way to gain an advantage, to restrain competition, or to obtain special favors.

But the most dangerous threat of all comes from the disinterested—that great group of otherwise intelligent people who shrug off any responsibility for public affairs. (*Title of Liberty,* pp. 147–48.)

No fair-minded person contends that the private-enterprise system is perfect. Many deplore the fact that a few of our corporate entities seem to lack that social consciousness proportionate to their power and the privileges granted them by the state. Some businesses apparently still fail to recognize that there are social and spiritual values as well as profits that should be considered in their operations. Neither do our needs always correspond to our demands under the free-enterprise system. (*The Red Carpet,* p. 119.)

Economic security for all is impossible without widespread abundance. Abundance is impossible without industrious and efficient production. Such production is impossible without energetic, willing, and eager labor. This is not possible without incentive. Of all forms of incentive—the freedom to attain a reward for one's labors is the most sustaining for most people.

Sometimes called the profit motive, it is simply the right to plan and to earn and enjoy the fruits of your labor. This profit motive diminishes as government controls, regulations, and taxes increase to deny the fruits of success to those who produce. (See G. Edward Griffin, *The Fearful Master,* p. 128.) ("America, a Choice Land," California-Hawaiian Region of the Elks, Anaheim, California, 8 November 1968.)

A free market operates in an environment of free enterprise and free competition. Here everyone has a chance to decide what is a fair price, a fair wage, and a fair profit, and what should be produced and in what quantities. (*The Red Carpet,* p. 221.)

Our freedom of individual opportunity permits us to draw upon our natural resources and upon the total brain and brawn power of the nation in a most effective manner. This freedom of individual choice inspires competition. Competition inspires shrewd and efficient management, which is conducive to the production of the best product possible at the lowest price. (*God, Family, Country,* p. 310.)

The individual has power to produce beyond his needs, to provide savings for the future protection of himself and family. He can live where he wishes and pick any job he wants and select any educational opportunity. He is, to a high degree, free through his own hard work and wise management to make a profit, to invest in any enterprise he may choose, and to leave a part of his accumulation to be inherited by others as he may, in large measure, determine.

He may enjoy the sacred rights of freedom of speech, freedom of assembly, freedom of the press, and freedom of worship. To this American entrepreneur his home is his castle, and in the event that he is accused of an offense against the laws established by the people, he has the right of trial by a jury made up of his own fellow citizens. Here is freedom guaranteed by the limitation of government through a written constitution. ("The American Free-

Enterprise System: Will It Survive?'' Contemporary Issues Forum, Ogden, Utah, 18 January 1977.)

We must realize that the growth of industry does not just happen. It takes the same vision, the same personal initiative and pioneering spirit that in an earlier day opened the continent. Any new business, particularly in a new field, is a pioneering effort. It requires imagination and courage, the risk of capital and the willingness to work hard. These are the things America is made of— and new industry is tangible proof that they are not dead among us. (*The Red Carpet*, p. 226.)

We have a responsibility to preserve our free economy, bequeathed to us as a great heritage by our forefathers who pioneered in this great land. We must also be pioneers in standing firm against proponents of unsound panaceas for all facets of our American economy that may be harmful not only to ourselves, but especially to our children and grandchildren. This modern-day challenge is every bit as demanding and forbidding as the frontier wilderness which spurred our forefathers to their successful efforts. (*The Red Carpet*, pp. 227–28.)

Profit is the reward for honest labor. It is the incentive that causes a man to risk his capital to build a business. If he cannot keep or invest that which he has earned, neither may he own, nor will he risk. Profit creates wealth; wealth creates more work opportunity; and more work opportunity creates greater wealth. None of this is possible without incentive.

There is another benefit to profit. It provides man with moral choices. With profit, man can choose to be greedy and selfish; he can invest and expand, thereby providing others with jobs; and he can be charitable. Charity is not charity unless it is voluntary. It cannot be voluntary if there is nothing to give.

Only saved profit, not government, creates more jobs. The only way government can create jobs is to take money from productive citizens in the form of taxes and transfer it to government programs. Without someone's generating profit that can be taxed, government revenue is not possible. (*This Nation Shall Endure*, p. 86.)

Students of economics know that a nation cannot spend itself into prosperity. Nor can we preserve our prosperity and our free-enterprise system by following a reckless policy of spending beyond our income in peacetime. Critics forget that our free-enterprise system is based on solvent government and sound money. This is the road of common sense, the road of a sound defense—a sound defense against the enemies and forces that endanger freedom both at home and abroad. (*The Red Carpet,* p. 167.)

Some say that free enterprise is aimless and unplanned. I doubt if there is as much planning in any other country on earth as there is here in the United States. But it is planning by individuals—millions of them—free planning, planning based on freedom of choice. It is not collectivist state planning. (*The Red Carpet,* p. 128.)

Some say the free-enterprise system is heartless and insensitive to the needs of those less fortunate individuals who are found in any society, no matter how affluent. What about the lame, the sick, and the destitute? Most other countries in the world have attempted to use the power of government to meet this need. Yet, in every case forced charity through government bureaucracies has resulted in the long run in creating more misery, more poverty, and certainly less freedom than when government first stepped in. (*This Nation Shall Endure,* p. 79.)

Our needs do not always correspond to our demands under the free-enterprise system. For example, the American male still prefers steak and potatoes and apple pie to a better balanced diet. Many American families often prefer housing below a decency level to the "indecency" of getting along without a family car. As a nation, we have spent twice as much money for liquor and tobacco as for medical care, about the same for movies as for the support of the churches, and almost as much for beauty parlor services as for private social welfare. Whether wise or unwise, these decisions on the part of individuals as to how they spend their money are the result of free consumer choice, which is a part of the free-enterprise system. With all of its weaknesses, our free-enterprise system has accomplished in terms of human welfare that which no other economic or social system has even approached. (*God, Family, and Country,* p. 310.)

The enterprise system is on trial today throughout the world, and in this country. All of us are a part of that private, free-enterprise system and are vitally concerned with the outcome of this struggle. If the enterprise system fails and if representative government should prove incapable of meeting its responsibilities, then fails a bright hope of the human race. Ours would be a gloomy page in history if this generation were to allow the highest aspirations of mankind to slip through our fingers. There is in this country a deep belief in freedom and responsibility. If we demonstrate as much ingenuity in organizing this belief as the opponents of freedom have demonstrated in attacking it, we stand well to win the battle. (*The Red Carpet,* p. 213.)

If reference is made continually to weaknesses of the private-enterprise system without any effort to point out its virtues and the comparative fruits of this and other systems, the tendency in this country will be to demand that the government take over more and more of the economic and social responsibilities and make more of the decisions for the people. (*This Nation Shall Endure,* p. 54.)

If the government were genuinely concerned about full employment and real prosperity, it could do much in bringing it about. It could support the proven and successful free-market system, the law of supply and demand, where the buying public, not the government, is the deciding factor in what shall be produced and marketed, including energy products. The bureaucrats ignore the lessons of American history that freedom works and that the ability of individuals to come to mutually beneficial agreements is the very essence of a free society. (*This Nation Shall Endure,* p. 78.)

Now, while the world is in commotion and turmoil over ideologies and political philosophies, is a good time to reflect upon the past. It is a good time to draw a few comparisons, to take stock, to sound a few warnings and to give some sound and vital counsel that will help us to realize that, just as past advances have been the fruit of our freedom—our free-enterprise system—so the progress of the future must flow from this same basic source—our freedom.

We have developed a productive plant and a way of life which have given the highest standard of living for the masses known to the civilized world. In the long run, a nation enjoys in the form of goods and services only what it produces. (*The Red Carpet,* pp. 116–17.)

Some who are engaged in the business of advertising and selling are doing a magnificent job of telling the story of freedom—and I commend them. They use advertisements to explain the meaning of capitalism and free enterprise. They present to their audiences such challenging and valuable statements as these—and I could mention many more: "More money for less work soon means no work." "We can't legislate happiness." "You can't vote yourself security." "America is 'opportunity unlimited.' " (*The Red Carpet,* p. 231.)

American ingenuity under freedom of choice has harnessed tremendous amounts of mineral energy to do physical work. Under our free-enterprise system there are good reasons to believe that the technological progress of the past will continue in the future, perhaps even at an accelerated rate. Then, too, our free-enterprise system allows for all necessary flexibility. No other economic program responds so readily to changes in wartime and peacetime demands. (*The Red Carpet,* p. 118.)

There are some in our midst who decry free enterprise, who would place business, agriculture, and labor in a government straitjacket. The fundamental reason that our economic order is better by far than any other system is that ours is free. It must remain free. In that freedom ultimately lies our basic economic strength. Let us work aggressively to correct any weaknesses, but let us never make the blunder of putting chains on our basic economic freedom. (*The Red Carpet,* p. 129.)

Our free-enterprise economic order is not perfect. Let us admit the weaknesses that exist. Let us work aggressively to correct them. If the face of our economy is dirty in places, let us wash it. But let us not subject it to unneeded amputations and plastic surgery. (*Crossfire: The Eight Years with Eisenhower,* pp. 578–79.)

Are we aware that all over the free and neutral world people are asking: Is the free-enterprise system really stronger, more productive, more fruitful than is the Communist system? Show us! We want to believe it, but show us! Are we ready to accept the challenge? Do we understand that we are face to face with our destiny and we must meet it with a high and resolute courage? Survival is not guaranteed. It must be won by sound thinking, hard work, and right living. (*The Red Carpet,* pp. 127–28.)

Past material advances have been the fruit of our freedom— our free-enterprise capitalistic system, our American way of life, our God-given freedom of choice. Progress of the future must stem from this same basic freedom. Because our forefathers— yours and mine—fought for the ideal of freedom; because our fathers preserved that ideal through the free competitive enterprise system under our God-given free agency; because they were willing to make religion the vital force of daily living, all of us have climbed through the years to new heights of well-being and inner strengths. (*An Enemy Hath Done This,* p. 17.)

I believe strongly in our free-enterprise system. And I would like to see that system preserved and strengthened for my children and my children's children, down to the last generation, and I am willing to do anything in my power, small though it be, to contribute toward the preservation and the strengthening of that system which I believe is built upon eternal principles: freedom of choice. (Conference of National Federation of Grain Cooperatives, Washington, D.C., 29 March 1955.)

I never travel across this great nation without experiencing a feeling of gratitude and thanksgiving for all that we have and are. As I see its broad, fruitful farms, its humming factories, its gleaming cities, certainly it is easy to realize that we have achieved unequalled material progress in this great country. It could not have happened under any other system of economy. (*The Red Carpet,* p. 120.)

Labor Unions

The right to life, liberty, and the pursuit of happiness is fundamental. It includes the right to earn one's living. This right should not be curtailed by man-made prohibitions. I have always felt that our system of government and way of life has succeeded so well because it has been based on freedom for the individual. It disturbs me that in our great nation it is necessary to vouchsafe this elementary principle by statute when it is embodied in the Constitution.

All of us will agree that a man has the right to join with others in forming a union to bargain collectively with an employer. A corollary of equal importance is the right not to join a union. A great religious leader, David O. McKay, has said: "It is understood, of course, that any person is free to join a union when to do so favors his best interest; but no one should be compelled to join, or be deprived of any right as a citizen, including the right to honest labor, if he chooses not to become a member of a union or specially organized group." (*The Red Carpet,* pp. 266–67.)

Freedom of association means that a man will be free to join or not to join a union, as he sees fit. This will not only give each man his freedom of choice, but will force labor bosses to be more considerate of the wishes and needs of the workingman. Poorly run unions or those that accomplish little except to spend the members' dues will have to improve or make way for better unions. Well-run, uncorrupted unions need never worry about membership. Only those that have little to offer the workers need the government to force people to join them. If a company wishes to negotiate a closed shop agreement with a union, it should be free to do so. But the power of government should never be brought to bear to force it one way or the other. (*An Enemy Hath Done This,* pp. 238–39.)

Individual rights of men are the very bedrock of our republic, and freedom of choice is certainly one of the cornerstones of a free society. I am fully sympathetic with the problems of the laboring man. His rights should be protected. When Congress has had under consideration important labor legislation, the right of a worker to walk off the job at will has been carefully protected. The right to walk on the job without the limitation of requiring that a worker join a union or any other organization should be equally protected.

Unions may be necessary to our complex society, but they are not an end in themselves. It is my firm conviction that a person should get and keep a job on the basis of his ability and performance. This is fair. It is the American way. (*The Red Carpet,* p. 267.)

My conscience forbids me to consent to granting exclusive privileges to either business or labor unions. Since I would not forcibly prevent anyone from entering any legitimate business or joining any union they desired, and since I could never bring myself to dictate to the buying public whom they could and whom they could not purchase goods and services from, I consider it wrong to ask government to do things on my behalf.

Economic wealth flows from thrift and productive investment. Many labor laws even hamper economic output and therefore cause poverty rather than wealth. (*An Enemy Hath Done This,* p. 237.)

The extent of government interference into labor-management relationships should be limited. Government has no business making up rules for the game and then forcing the players to follow those rules. If left completely alone, labor and management will work out their own agreements in the shortest possible time and with the least disruption to the economy. In time, a natural balance between the forces of supply and demand will result in the greatest benefit for business, for labor, and for the country. (*An Enemy Hath Done This,* p. 238.)

As a result of the natural forces and counterforces in the labor marketplace, without government interventions to aid or hinder either side, it is likely that the size of the labor union involved in a contract negotiation will equal the size of the management unit. In other words, instead of a giant nationwide industry intimidating a tiny union of employees at just one of its plants, or instead of a giant nationwide union intimidating a tiny company in just one community, there will tend to be a grouping and regrouping of unions and employers so that the forces on both sides will be approximately equal. While this could conceivably result in industry-wide negotiations between giant unions and giant employer associations, most of the natural economic pressures point in the opposite direction. Cost of living and cost of production factors vary so widely from one part of the country to the other that if a uniform compromise wage rate were set on a national basis, workers in the high-cost areas would form a local union for more realistic negotiations, and employers in the low-cost areas would form a local association for the same purpose. (*An Enemy Hath Done This*, p. 239.)

Voluntary unionism would put an end to the present practice in some of the larger unions of spending huge amounts of the members' dues for political action which is pleasing to the labor bosses but may or may not be for the membership. No man should be forced to pay through union dues for political campaigns or philosophies which he opposes. Political contributions should be strictly voluntary. Just as corporation funds should not be spent for political action by the president of that corporation, so, too, union funds should not be spent for political action by the president of that union. (*An Enemy Hath Done This*, pp. 239–40.)

Labor and management are equal partners in business. They should be treated as equals, with no special favors either way. Government, as a nonproductive entity that lives off the income of both labor and management, has no business meddling in their affairs, except to make sure that public order is maintained and that contracts are honored. (*An Enemy Hath Done This*, p. 240.)

Federal Monetary Policies

Few policies are more capable of destroying the moral, political, social, and economic basis of a free society than the debauching of its currency. And few tasks, if any, are more important for the preservation of freedom than the preservation of a sound monetary system. (*An Enemy Hath Done This*, p. 211.)

We must return to policies of fiscal responsibility which will regain the world markets we are losing and protect our private competitive economy. We must reverse our present dangerous fiscal policies. If we fail so to do, we will set off an international monetary debacle that could easily make the experience of the 1930s sink into insignificance.

The welfare state, towards which America is steadily moving, is not something new. History has recorded it in the ancient civilizations of Babylon, Greece, and Rome; and modernly in Mussolini's Italy and Hitler's Germany. It is the program of all of today's Communist countries. It not only fails to provide the economic security sought for, but the welfare state always ended in slavery—and it always will. (*The Red Carpet,* p. 308.)

Many of our problems and dangers center in the issues of so-called fair prices, wages, and profits, and the relationship between management and labor. We must realize that it is just as possible for wages to be too high as it is for prices and profits to be excessive. There is a tendency, of course, for almost everyone to feel that his share is unfair whether it is or not. An effort to adjust apparent inequities often calls for government subsidies. Too often these are authorized without asking the question, Who will pay for them? Much of our program of letting the government pay for it, "can be described as an attempt to better yourself by increasing your pay to yourself and then sending yourself the bill." (*The Red Carpet,* p. 221.)

The root of all evil is money, some say. But the root of our money evil is government. The very beginning of our troubles can be traced to the day when the federal government overstepped its proper defensive function and began to manipulate the monetary system to accomplish political objectives. The creation of the Federal Reserve Board made it possible in America for men arbitrarily to change the value of our money. Previously, that value had been determined solely by the natural interplay of the amount of precious metals held in reserve, the value men freely placed on those precious metals, and the amount of material goods which were available for sale or exchange. (*An Enemy Hath Done This,* pp. 213–14.)

The pending economic crisis that now faces America is painfully obvious. If even a fraction of potential foreign claims against our gold supply were presented to the Treasury, we would have to renege on our promise. We would be forced to repudiate our own currency on the world market. Foreign investors, who would be left holding the bag with American dollars, would dump them at tremendous discounts in return for more stable currencies, or for gold itself. The American dollar both abroad and at home would suffer the loss of public confidence. If the government can renege on its international monetary promises, what is to prevent it from doing the same on its domestic promises? How really secure would be government guarantees behind Federal Housing Administration loans, Savings and Loan Insurance, government bonds, or even Social Security?

Even though American citizens would still be forced by law to honor the same pieces of paper as though they were real money, instinctively they would rush and convert their paper currency into tangible material goods which could be used as barter. As in Germany and other nations that have previously traveled this road, the rush to get rid of dollars and acquire tangibles would rapidly accelerate the visible effects of inflation to where it might cost one hundred dollars or more for a single loaf of bread. Hoarded silver coins would begin to reappear as a separate monetary system which, since they have intrinsic value would remain firm, while printed paper money finally would become worth exactly its proper value—the paper it is printed on! Everyone's savings would be wiped out totally. No one could escape.

One can only imagine what such conditions would do to the stock market and to industry. Uncertainty over the future would cause the consumer to halt all spending except for the barest necessities. Market for such items as television sets, automobiles, furniture, new homes, and entertainment would dry up almost overnight. With no one buying, firms would have to close down and lay off their employees. Unemployment would further aggravate the buying freeze, and the nation would plunge into a depression that would make the 1930s look like prosperity. At least the dollar was sound in those days. In fact, since it was a firm currency, its value actually went up as related to the amount of goods, which declined through reduced production. Next time around, however, the problems of unemployment and low production will be compounded by a monetary system that will be utterly worthless. All the government controls and so-called guarantees in the world will not be able to prevent it, because every one of them is based on the assumption that the people will continue to honor printing press money. But once the government itself openly refuses to honor it —as it must if foreign demands for gold continue—it is likely that the American people will soon follow suit. This, in a nutshell, is the so-called "gold problem." (*An Enemy Hath Done This,* pp. 216–18.)

We have been feeling the exhilarating effects of inflation and have become numbed to the gradual dissipation of our gold reserves. In our economic stupor, when we manage to think ahead about the coming hangover, we have merely taken another swig from the bottle to reinforce the artificial sensation of prosperity. But each new drink at the cup of inflation, and each new drain on the gold supply of our bodily strength does not prevent the dreaded hangover, it merely postpones it a little longer and will make it that much worse when it finally comes. What should we do? We should get a hold on ourselves, come to our senses, stop adding to our intoxication, and face the music! (*An Enemy Hath Done This,* p. 218.)

When the going gets rough, we mustn't rush to Washington and ask big brother to take care of us through price controls, rent controls, guaranteed jobs and wages. Any government powerful enough to give the people all that they want is also powerful enough to take from the people all that they have. And it is even possible that some of the government manipulators who have brought us into this economic crisis are hoping that, in panic, we, the American people, literally will plead with them to take our liberties in exchange for the false promise of "security." As Alexander Hamilton warned about two hundred years ago: "Nothing is more common than for a free people, in times of heat and violence, to gratify momentary passions by letting into the government principles and precedents which afterward prove fatal to themselves" (*Alexander Hamilton and the Founding of the Nation,* p. 21). Let us heed this warning. Let us prepare ourselves for the trying time ahead and resolve that, with the grace of God and through our own self-reliance, we shall rebuild a monetary system and a healthy economy which, once again, will become the model for all the world. (*An Enemy Hath Done This,* pp. 220–21.)

There is no "happy" solution to our problems, but, if left to our own resources, the productive genius that is the product of the free-enterprise system, coupled with the initiative and drive of the American people, can successfully lead us through the trying readjustment period that lies ahead, and then on to higher levels of real prosperity and security than we have ever known.

While politicians will continue to insist that our economy is not in the slightest danger, lest they be accused of being "negative," or "spreaders of doom," there is a sound and realistic course of action that we can follow to prepare for the coming readjustment period and to lessen the shock. As a nation, we must stop giving away money to foreign nations as though we had it. We should demand repayment of our loans to other countries — especially those which are making the heaviest demands upon our gold supply. We should cease giving them our gold until they pay their debts to us. We must stop the federal government from deficit spending, and begin immediately to pay off the national debt in a systematic fashion. This, of course, means increasing taxes or decreasing the size of government. It is doubtful that the American people can absorb more taxes without further injuring the productive base of our economy, but there is no doubt that government can be reduced without any such risk. (*An Enemy Hath Done This,* p. 219.)

Inflation

It is important to understand that the wage-price spiral is not the cause of inflation. The rise of wages and prices are the result, not the cause. There is one and only one cause of inflation — expansion of the money supply faster than the growth of the nation's material assets. Whether those assets are gold and silver, or food, machines, and structures, the creation of money more rapidly than the creation of tangible items of value which people may want to purchase floods the marketplace with more dollars than goods and dilutes the accepted value of money already in existence.

In America, only the federal government can increase the money supply. Government can create inflation. The most common method of increasing the money supply today is by spending more than is in the treasury, and then merely printing extra money to make up the difference. Technically this is called "deficit spending." Ethically, it is counterfeiting. Morally, it is wrong. (*An Enemy Hath Done This,* pp. 209–10.)

Deficit spending and the inflation it produces constitute a hidden tax against all Americans—especially those who own insurance policies, have savings accounts, or who are retired on fixed incomes. Every time the dollar drops another penny in value, it is the same as if the government had counted up all the money that you and I had in our pockets, in savings, or in investments, and then taxed us one cent on each dollar. The tax in this case, however, does not show up on our W-2 forms. It is hidden from view in the nature of higher and still higher prices for all that we buy. (*An Enemy Hath Done This,* pp. 210–11.)

One of the first arbitrary and politically motivated interferences with the natural value of money was to peg the price of gold at thirty-five dollars per ounce. At first this made little difference because it was quite possible for men to mine gold profitably at this price. But as the government moved into a program of deficit spending, the motivation for fixing the price of gold became obvious. The artificial increase of the money supply caused the value of each dollar to decrease in relationship to the total supply of material goods which that dollar could purchase. This relative decrease in purchasing power, of course, is known as inflation. But if gold were not held by law at a fixed price, its value would have risen in direct proportion to the artificial increase in paper money, and as long as gold was guaranteed backing behind each dollar, the government wouldn't have been able to benefit one iota from deficit spending. (*An Enemy Hath Done This,* p. 214.)

Taxes are necessary for defense and for some needful services that none of us would begrudge. But at the same time all of us are concerned about the expense of operating the government with our money. We must not let inflation impose further crushing burdens of cheaper dollars. (*The Red Carpet,* p. 172.)

The tragedy of destroying fixed pension and savings is but one cruelty of inflation. Economists point out to us that it discourages savings, for why should people save, with the value of saved dollars being constantly lessened. Inflation, like big government, big debt, and deficit spending, need not be inevitable. Perhaps it is just the sad experience of a whole generation which leads people to expect that their dollars will always be worth less each year. (*The Red Carpet,* p. 173.)

We must stop inflation! It appears that will only come in the wake of an aroused public opinion. We can only do it by all working together. A balanced budget is of the utmost importance. (*The Red Carpet,* p. 175.)

Inflation is a serious threat to American industry and labor. We must understand that if inflation — even so-called creeping inflation — is permitted to take further root, it can destroy the future freedom and security of our children. This matter of inflation is of vital importance to all of us, but especially to our younger citizens. They will live under the hysteria of inflation through the rest of their lives if it is not checked now. They and their children will pay the bill that will inevitably be rendered by a continuing fiscal irresponsibility — and, it will, I fear, be a bill compounded in hardship and heartache. (*The Red Carpet,* pp. 174–75.)

Environment

A common problem is a concern for our environment. It is not likely that someone who does not love his neighbor will be concerned with his adverse impact on the environment. To love one's neighbor is a spiritual law. Just as physical laws are interrelated, so are spiritual laws. One dimension of spiritual law is that a man's self-regard and his esteem for his fellowmen are intertwined.

If there is disregard for oneself, there will be disregard for one's neighbor. If there is no reverence for life itself, there is apt to be little reverence for the resources God has given man. The outward expressions of irreverence for life and for fellowmen often take the form of heedless pollution of both air and water. But are these not expressions of the inner man?

You are among those who must undertake the task of alerting mankind to problems with regard to his physical environment, but do you not see that if you attempt to do this without giving heed to the spiritual law involved, you undertake an impossible task.

If we are not really the children of a Creator who placed us here by design and purpose, and if there are not absolute spiritual as well as physical laws which we violate at our peril, man must be appealed to on different grounds. And that task is next to impossible.

If we are merely transients in an unexplainable world, we will act more like tourists than residents! Men born into this planet are stewards. They have responsibility for their environment, but also stewardship for the moral laws of God.

Surely you can see the inconsistency in the individual who insists that we be good stewards and not pollute our environment, and yet who is unscrupulous in his personal life. Again, physical and spiritual laws are interrelated. Pollution of one's environment and moral impurity both rest on a life-style which partakes of a philosophy of "eat, drink, and be merry"—gouge and grab now, without regard to the consequences. Both violate the spirit of stewardship for which we will stand accountable. ("A Spiritual Approach to Man-made Problems," Brigham Young University—Hawaii, 11 February 1983.)

The Lord said: "Yea, all things which come of the earth, in the season thereof, are made for the benefit and use of man, both to please the eye and to gladden the heart; Yea, for food and for raiment, for taste and for smell, to strengthen the body and to enliven the soul. And it pleaseth God that he hath given all these things unto man; for unto this end were they made to be used, with judgment, not to excess, neither by extortion." (D&C 59:18–20.) What is lacking so often is not the engineering to produce what grows out of the world of technology, but the human engineering necessary to share that which we have. Sharing with generations yet unborn, however, is also rooted in brotherhood and love.

Whatever mortal reasons there are to be concerned about environment, there are eternal reasons, too, for us to be thoughtful stewards. President Brigham Young said: "Not one particle of all that comprises this vast creation of God is our own. Everything we have has been bestowed upon us for our action, to see what we would do with it—whether we would use it for eternal life and exaltation, or for eternal death and degradation." ("A Plea for America," White House Forum on Domestic Policy, Denver, Colorado, 21 October 1975.)

Stewardship in the Church is a very important matter. The Lord has mentioned it in the revelations. (See D&C 59; 104.) We are stewards over these earthly blessings which the Lord has provided, those of us who have this soil and this water. We have no moral latitude, it seems to me. In fact, we are morally obligated to turn this land over to those who succeed us—not drained of its fertility, but improved in quality, in productivity, and in usefulness for future generations.

I am sure our Heavenly Father expects us to use these precious natural resources wisely, unselfishly, and effectively—both our soil and our water. (Welfare Meeting, General Conference, Salt Lake City, Utah, 6 April 1957.)

The Church has urged its members to be efficient users of our resources, to avoid waste and pollution, and to clean up their own immediate environment or that over which they have control. It was Goethe who said, "Let everyone sweep in front of his own door and the whole world will be clean." We have made an appeal to all Church members to clean up their premises, to plant gardens and trees, and then to use efficiently what they grow. We have found that Church members have responded well to this appeal, thus becoming more self-reliant and responsibly concerned for their neighbors and their environment. (*This Nation Shall Endure,* p. 63.)

It is terribly important that we preserve and improve the great natural resources with which the God of heaven has so richly blessed us, that we may not follow the experience of some other nations that have come and gone because of the mismanagement of their natural and God-given resources. (Welfare Session, General Conference, 5 April 1958.)

The soil holds spiritual riches for all of us, besides being the source of what we eat and wear. As it greens up each year with the turning of the seasons, we see fulfillment of the promise of life eternal. ("Spiritual Riches," Washington, D.C., 1957.)

Some people ask me, as a Church leader, why we seek to change individuals when there are such large problems around us, such as the so-called urban crisis. Decaying cities are simply a delayed reflection of individuals suffering under a decadent attitude.

The laws of God give emphasis to the improvement of the individual as the only real way to bring about improvement in society. Until we focus on basic principles, little progress will be made. So much, therefore, depends on one's basic desires, attitudes, and self-discipline.

And self-discipline depends on having fundamental values to check one's appetites and passions. It has been said that we cannot tame our technology until we tame ourselves. We likewise cannot tame our environment until we tame ourselves. It is a truth of the universe that the control of outward things depends on inward commitments.

While the resources of our planet are both perishable and renewable, time cannot be recycled. We must be reminded that when time is spent in too much pleasure seeking, the serious and eternal things will be left undone. Self-centered, pleasure-seeking people will not only plunder our environment much more rapidly, but they will be less concerned about the needs of their fellow human beings. ("A Spiritual Approach to Man-made Problems," Brigham Young University—Hawaii, 11 February 1983.)

Let us strive for progress down the road of goodness and freedom. With the help and blessings of the Lord, the free people of the United States and the free world can and will face tomorrow without fear, without doubt, and with full confidence. We do not fear the phony population explosion, nor do we fear a shortage of food, if we can be free and good. The Lord has declared that "the earth is full, and there is enough and to spare" (D&C 104:17). We can accept this promise with confidence. (*God, Family, Country,* p. 361.)

Farmers and Agriculture

I have a great love for our rural people. If it were not for the new blood that moves into the cities from the rural communities and the farms of this country, many of the great cities would dry up and blow away. Our rural people are the salt of the earth. (Agricultural Recognition and Award Banquet, BYU, Provo, Utah, 17 March 1973.)

The Minutemen who fought and won the first battles of our country are most frequently depicted with one hand holding a musket and the other on the handle of a plow. George Washington, Thomas Jefferson, and others of the Founding Fathers were farmers, and proud of it. Jefferson's writings are full of the idea that there is a direct relationship between farming and freedom. As Jefferson saw him, the American family farmer — master of his own acres, with no landlord but himself — would always be both prosperous and free. This concept of political and economic independence, farm-bred and won by fighting farmers, was stamped on the new nation at its birth. (*Freedom to Farm,* p. 39.)

There is something basically sound about having a good portion of our people on the land. The country is a good place to rear a family. It is a good place to teach the basic virtues that have helped to build this nation. Young people on a farm learn how to work, how to be thrifty, and how to do things with their hands. It has given millions of us the finest preparation for life. (*Freedom to Farm,* p. 109.)

I have been impressed with the spirit of our rural people. I remember an incident that occurred in 1953 when we had that terrible drought through the Southwest and into the West. Down in Amarillo, Texas, we had held meetings with eight delegations from eight different states, each delegation headed by the governor of that state. One old rawboned, weather-beaten rancher from Texas came up to me, extended his hand, and said, "Mr. Secretary, it is so dry down where I am ranching that our water is only 20 percent moisture." Without smiling, he turned and walked away. I have been on those ranches and have seen them burning the spears off the cactus with blowtorches and then cutting up the cactus and feeding it to the cattle to keep them from dying, and I have seen these same ranchers refuse government subsidies and government price supports even during those very difficult days. There is a lot of that spirit in agriculture, and it is one of the great safeguards we have in this country. (Agricultural Recognition and Award Banquet, BYU, Provo, Utah, 17 March 1973.)

The farmer and Mother Nature have an alliance that frustrates efforts to weaken it. Nowhere has this been better illustrated than in the United States. Beginning in the 1930s a continuing series of programs attempted to maintain acreage controls and artificially high prices. But such prices stimulated production and impeded adjustment, while the advance of technology made controls largely ineffective. The technological revolution in agriculture cannot be repealed by legislation.

It is perfectly natural that farmers resist regimentation. I count their independence of spirit and action as one of our great strengths. Far from doing anything to weaken that independence, we should always look for opportunities to strengthen it. (*The Red Carpet,* pp. 248–49.)

Real and lasting prosperity is the joint product of the farmer and the city dweller. There is an abundance of evidence to support this contention. In our modern society we are completely interdependent. Every group is essential to the welfare of America. This should be accepted by every thinking man. (*The Red Carpet,* p. 268.)

We must move toward more freedom for farmers. Our freedom was not achieved, and it cannot be maintained, by simple shortcuts that attempt to bypass basic eternal truths. We cannot— we must not—ignore sound, basic economic principles. If our country, so blessed with opportunity and purpose, is to progress and prosper for the benefit of all, it cannot—it must not—replace integrity with cynicism, principles with catchwords, ideals with doles, and liberty with controls. (*An Enemy Hath Done This,* pp. 259–60.)

American agriculture is a giant without equal in any other agriculture in all history. Our farmers contributed tremendously to the success of the allied nations during World War II. In the ideological struggle of today, the productive genius of our farmers remains one of the free world's greatest assets. (*Farmers at the Crossroads,* p. 3.)

The greatest material contribution the industrialized nation can make to world peace and world progress is to join hands in helping the underdeveloped nations of the world help themselves. This cannot be done by giving away food surpluses indiscriminately— by destroying free competitive markets. It cannot be done by putting these nations on a food relief dole, which undermines their self-respect.

We and the other industrialized nations have a tremendous opportunity to use our abundance as capital to help the newly emerging nations develop their own agriculture and industry. (*Title of Liberty,* p. 139.)

Only in one fundamental way may the earth be persuaded to yield forth her abundance for the blessing of mankind. It can only result from a devoted, unselfish populace working energetically, purposefully, and happily upon the land, in the factories, in the marketplaces, and in the offices and homes. The necessary common ingredients are freedom, not compulsion; incentives, not threat of reprisal; human understanding and brotherhood, not suspicion and godless atheism. (*The Red Carpet,* p. 264.)

I look into the faces of some of the wonderful people I meet across this country—and they are wonderful people. Ofttimes I say to them, "You are the finest group of people I know anywhere outside the Mormon Church." They are a wonderful people. You cannot find better people, generally speaking, than those people who live on the land, close to the soil. They are not easily stampeded. They are pretty sound and solid citizens. And I thrill as I have the opportunity of mingling with them, working with them. Oh, they have their differences. Sometimes you will find groups with radical leadership that would like to lead agriculture down the road to a socialized industry, but on the whole, the rank and file of our farm people, regardless of their political affiliation, are solid, substantial citizens. ("The Greatest Brotherhood," Welfare Meeting, General Conference, Salt Lake City, Utah, 11 October 1958.)

As one who has been reared among farmers, served them and been served by them, I declare without fear of successful contradiction that our rural people are today the strongest bulwark we have against all that is aimed, not only at weakening, but at the very destruction of our freedoms in America.

It is gratifying to note that in recent years an increasing number of industrial, labor, political, and religious leaders have come to acknowledge this fact. It seems that man must get his feet in the soil to keep sane. In any event, no other segment of our population knows so well that "as ye sow, so shall ye reap" (Galatians 6:7; D&C 6:33). America and the world must learn this eternal truth. Failure to do so can bring only disappointment, suffering, and desperation.

Our rural people—men and women of faith and common sense—play an important part in teaching this all-important lesson. From our rural families must come much of the faith, courage, and leadership to face effectively the problems of tomorrow. (*The Red Carpet*, pp. 273–74.)

Freedom to Farm

Thanks largely to the trail-blazing of the free American farmer, it is now possible for men everywhere to live above the level of starvation and want. It remains only for us, through our God-given free agency, to use our intelligence and our efforts to lift ourselves into an era of peace and plenty that men of former centuries could only dream about.

In contrast to the darkness of the iron curtain, a light to the free world can shine from our nation because we have freedom of choice and recognition of the rights, responsibilities, and dignities of the individual. Because agriculture is a cornerstone of the American way, we must also have freedom to farm. (*Freedom to Farm*, p. 239.)

The farms of the United States cannot be run from a desk in Washington. In fact, the answer to farm and ranch problems caused or aggravated by the technological revolution and made worse by unwise government policy is to be found in the pursuit of four basic objectives: freedom, profit through efficiency, expansion of free markets, and wise use of abundance. Freedom is as fundamental to agriculture as soil and water. Agriculture does not flourish where the spirit of freedom is lacking. (*An Enemy Hath Done This*, pp. 252–53.)

I wish all other groups in the country were as alert to the threat against freedom as are our farmers. If the voices of 21 million farm people in the United States could be united in one voice, that voice I feel certain would say: Give us more freedom to plant—so that we can run our farms efficiently. Give us more freedom to market — so that we can increase our incomes. Give us more freedom to meet our competition — so that we can expand our markets. Give us more freedom from government interference — so that we may be independent and self-reliant. (*Title of Liberty,* p. 148.)

In a country with a representative government and a tradition of freedom, strict controls are not wanted. The plain truth is that when controls pinch too hard on volume, on income, on jobs, on efficiency, on the farm supply industry, on the rural community, or on the independent nature of our people, public opinion rises in opposition. Then come critical editorials, angry resolutions from farm groups, ominous letters to the congressmen, stern delegations calling on the Secretary of Agriculture, and telegrams of protest to the president. The machinery of representative government goes into action in behalf of individual freedom. And it is effective! This is fortunate for America — it is a safeguard to our God-given freedom. (*An Enemy Hath Done This,* p. 251.)

When will we learn that economic laws are just as immutable as moral laws or the laws of nature or the Ten Commandments. Interventionists and socialists vary by degrees. Some don't know what it is all about. Others do. We can't have agriculture partly free and partly controlled. (*An Enemy Hath Done This,* p. 258.)

We are the undoubted world leader in agriculture. How we exercise our leadership will have tremendous effect on the food and people problem. We must keep our agriculture free, dynamic, expanding — growing in efficiency and productivity. We cannot do this by strapping it more and more firmly into the straitjacket of government controls. (*Title of Liberty,* pp. 128–29.)

Whether we in this nation keep our freedom — the freedom to choose where we will go and how we will earn a living, what we will do with our savings, and how we will spend our leisure — may depend to a significant degree on how our government in the years ahead approaches the farm problem.

The fundamental economics of the farm dilemma is simple — it is the politics of the problem that is baffling. What farmers and ranchers want and need is not more but less government in the farming and ranching business — not more, but less politics in agriculture. (*An Enemy Hath Done This,* pp. 254–55.)

Future Progress

In 1920 the American farmer fed himself and eight others. In 1976 the American farmer fed himself and fifty-eight others! According to Dr. Richard Sandor, chief economist for the Chicago Board of Trade, American agriculture produces 23 percent of the world's food supply. Yes, we have come a long way from the days of the horse and mule. ("1977 — Year of Decision," Utah Cattlemen's and Woolgrowers' Association Convention, Salt Lake City, Utah, 3 December 1976.)

In the near future we shall probably be using sea water for irrigation and other uses — and in the not too distant future we will, if desirable, be able to farm the oceans. I believe that the answer to hunger is food. A decade, a generation, a century hence, the capacity to produce per capita abundance can, I believe, dwarf our most hopeful imaginings. But much will depend on our own economic and agricultural policies. (*Title of Liberty,* pp. 135–36.)

I am dedicated to freedom for the farmer. There are some politicians who will continue to farm the farmer — but a good administration will want the farmer to farm his own farm. My goal for agriculture has been stated many times. It is for an agriculture that is expanding, prosperous, and free — for the benefit of the entire American people. (*The Red Carpet,* p. 257.)

The freedom of our nation can only be as strong as each of its member groups. Our country is dependent upon a prosperous agriculture. Should the agricultural segment of our economy collapse, the United States would be a much weaker member of the family of nations. This is true of every country. The free peoples of the world can eat well, be properly clothed and sheltered.

Of one thing I am certain. The decisions which made this country great were characterized by neither timidity nor short-sightedness. American agriculture did not reach its present eminence because of any farm price support formula — rigid or flexible. If agriculture continues to make great forward strides, it will not be because of mere legislation. It will be because the people who live on the farms of the nation—together with the scientists in our colleges and our industries, and those who design and produce farm machinery—all push forward this march of progress which has made our agricultural plant one of the modern wonders of the world. (*The Red Carpet,* p. 270.)

Farmers want government at their side, not on their back. Surveys show that eight out of ten farmers are opposed to governmental regimentation and control. This nation will never reach its full strength until our farmers have more freedom to plant, to market, to compete, and to make their own decisions.

Economic and technological progress cannot be stopped with legislative blockades. The day will no doubt come when the rapid growth of our economy and population will call for all available farm production. When that day comes, our farmers must be free and strong and ready—but, above all, free. (*An Enemy Hath Done This,* p. 259.)

It will be increasingly valuable to have vocational skills—to be able to use our hands. The most essential temporal skills and knowledge are to be able to provide food, clothing, and shelter. Increasingly, the Lord, through His servants, is trying to get us closer to the soil by raising our own produce. ("In His Steps," in *1979 Devotional Speeches of the Year* [Provo, Utah: BYU, 1980], p. 62.)

Freedom and Liberty

There is a God in Heaven who is the sovereign power of the universe, and we are His literal offspring. He has endowed us with inalienable rights, among which are life, liberty, and the pursuit of happiness. This He has implanted in the human breast. This is why men cannot be driven indefinitely or led by despotic rulers to intellectual or physical slavery and bondage. Fear and despotism may rule for a generation or two or three, but in time the human spirit rebels, the spirit of liberty manifests itself, and its tyrannous hand is overthrown. Yes, as the offspring of God, we share a common paternity that makes us literally brothers, and thus a common destiny. When this truth sinks into the human heart, men demand their rights—life, liberty, and happiness. It is as the Apostle Paul told the Corinthians, "Where the Spirit of the Lord is, there is liberty" (2 Corinthians 3:17). (*This Nation Shall Endure,* p. 69.)

Contemplate this moment in man's history. Almost six millennia had passed since Adam's exile from Eden. The time for the gospel's restoration was soon to come to pass—but first, freedom must be established. Characters held in reserve for millennia were sent on the scene. Do you not think that the hosts of heaven stood by in glorious contemplation? Do you not think there was cause for great rejoicing?

Here was the moment Nephi had foreseen (1 Nephi 13:12–19). The leading characters in the drama were not just good and wise, but men jealous of their rights. Passive and subservient spirits would have been intimidated before the crises. You see, the issue before them was whether men had certain inalienable rights, God-given rights, or whether a despotic form of government was to dictate those rights. Freedom or slavery—that was the issue! ("The Crises of Our Constitution," Salt Lake Valley Utah Central Area Special Interest Lecture Series, 8 September 1977.)

Freedom's moments have been infrequent and exceptional. From Nimrod to Napoleon, the conventional political ideology has been that the rights of life, liberty, and property were subject to a sovereign's will, rather than God-given. We must appreciate that we live in one of history's most exceptional moments—in a nation and a time of unprecedented freedom. Freedom as we know it has been experienced by perhaps less than 1 percent of the human family. (*The Constitution: A Heavenly Banner,* pp. 3–4.)

Freedom should be our constant goal, not only for ourselves but for all men. What we seek is not a fitful, tenuous freedom based on compromise of principle and expediency, but a real and lasting freedom founded on the recognition of human rights. True freedom springs from within. It is born in the hearts of men and nurtured on more freedom. If we have freedom as our goal, we have a measuring stick against which to gauge our problems, our actions, and the trend of our times. (*The Red Carpet,* pp. 132–33.)

How strong is our will to remain free, to be good? False thinking and false ideologies, dressed in the most pleasing forms, quietly—almost without our knowing it—seek to reduce our moral defenses and to captivate our minds. They masquerade under various names, but all may be recognized by one thing that they have in common—to erode away character and man's freedom to think and act for himself. (*God, Family, Country,* pp. 360–61.)

What can you and I do to preserve our God-given free way of life? First, let us all prize the treasures we have in this country. This is a choice land—all of America—choice above all others (1 Nephi 2:20). Blessed by the Almighty, our forebears have made it so. It will continue to be a land of freedom and liberty as long as we are able and willing to advance in the light of sound and enduring principles of right. Second, let us all do our part to stay free; let us stand eternal watch against the accumulation of too much power in government. Here in our free land let us preserve a true climate in which man can grow.

Third, let us all reaffirm our patriotism, our love of country. It is how we respond to public issues. Let us rededicate ourselves as patriots in the truest sense. Fourth, let us all help to build peace: True peace springs from within. Its price is righteousness, and to achieve righteousness we must so conduct ourselves individually and collectively as to earn the loyalty and devotion of other men. Finally, let us all rededicate our lives and our nation to do the will of God. With each of you, I love this nation. (*Title of Liberty,* pp. 120–21.)

No nation which has kept the commandments of God has ever perished, but I say to you that once freedom is lost, only blood—human blood—will win it back. There are some things we can and must do at once if we are to stave off a holocaust of destruction. (CR October 1979, *Ensign* 9 [November 1979]: 33.)

We must put our trust in Him who has promised us His protection—and pray that He will intervene to preserve our freedom just as He intervened in our obtaining it in the first place. (CR October 1979, *Ensign* 9 [November 1979]: 32.)

Individual Freedom

The fight for freedom is God's fight. Freedom is a law of God, a permanent law. And, like any of God's laws, men cannot really break it with impunity. So when a man stands for freedom he stands with God. And as long as he stands for freedom he stands with God. And were he to stand alone he would still stand with God—the best company and the greatest power in or out of this world. Any man will be eternally vindicated and rewarded for his stand for freedom. (*An Enemy Hath Done This,* pp. 54–55.)

There is no excuse that can compensate for the loss of liberty. Satan is anxious to neutralize the inspired counsel of the prophet and hence keep the priesthood off balance, ineffective, and inert in the fight for freedom. He does this through diverse means, including the use of perverse reasoning.

For example, he will argue, "There is no need to get involved in the fight for freedom—all you need to do is live the gospel." Of course this is a contradiction, because we cannot fully live the gospel and not be involved in the fight for freedom.

We would not say to someone, "There is no need to be baptized—all you need to do is live the gospel." That would be ridiculous because baptism is a part of the gospel. How would you have reacted if during the War in Heaven someone had said to you, "Look, just do what is right; there is no need to get involved in the fight for free agency." It is obvious what the devil is trying to do, but it is sad to see many of us fall for his destructive line.

The cause of freedom is a most basic part of our religion. Our position on freedom helped get us to this earth and it can make the difference as to whether we get back home or not. (*An Enemy Hath Done This,* p. 314.)

I would rather be dead than to have to give up my freedom, my right of choice, this God-given privilege. And I say to you that no one can imagine the condemnation that will come upon men who deliberately take away from their fellowmen their freedom of choice. It goes contrary to everything that the gospel stands for. (Short Hills, New Jersey, 15 January 1961.)

Both religious conviction and personal experience have led me to believe that the power of a man's creative potential will be unleashed for inestimable good once he is given his freedom and the opportunity to solve his own problems.

Witness the great technological and scientific progress of the last two centuries. Does it not illustrate that such progress is possible only when man is given freedom to try, freedom to fail, and freedom to succeed. You must not fail to note this: The bulk of man's progress has come out of the free nations of the world! ("A Spiritual Approach to Man-made Problems," Brigham Young University—Hawaii, 11 February 1983.)

No one can delegate his duty to preserve his freedom. There are now thousands of businessmen behind the iron curtain who, if they had their lives to live over, would balance their time more judiciously and give more devotion to their civil responsibilities. An ounce of energy in the preservation of freedom is worth a ton of effort to get it back once it is lost. (*An Enemy Hath Done This,* p. 57.)

Can freedom triumph now? The answer to that question hangs on the answer to yet more crucial questions: What are we doing to keep freedom alive? The answer to that first question—can freedom triumph now?—is speculative; it is based upon the degree of man's temporary acceptance of an eternal principle. But the answer to the second question—what are we doing to keep freedom alive?—has eternal consequences to every soul, no matter what the temporary outcome. (Taipei Taiwan Area Conference, 13–14 August 1975.)

That divine duty to be a faithful fighter for freedom requires that those of us who have been warned do our duty to warn our neighbor, for our neighbor's involvement in this struggle can bless his soul, strengthen his family, and protect him from pitfalls while he helps his country. The blessings far outweigh the burden when we stand up for freedom. (*God, Family, Country,* p. 404.)

Study the scriptures and study the mortals who have been most consistently accurate about the most important things. When your freedom and your eternal welfare are at stake, your information had better be accurate. (*God, Family, Country,* p. 330.)

Study the writings of the prophets. Fortunately, the consistent position taken over the years by the prophets of the Church on vital issues facing this nation have been compiled in an excellent book by Jerreld L. Newquist entitled, *Prophets, Principles and National Survival.* (CR October 1964, *Improvement Era* 67 [December 1964]: 1068.)

Responsibility of Church Members

As important as are all other principles of the gospel, it was the freedom issue that determined whether you received a body. To have been on the wrong side of the freedom issue during the War in Heaven meant eternal damnation. How then can Latter-day Saints expect to be on the wrong side in this life and escape the eternal consequences? The War in Heaven is raging on earth today. The issues are the same: Shall men be compelled to do what others claim is for their best welfare or will they heed the counsel of the prophets and preserve their freedom?

We believe that the gospel is the greatest thing in the world; why then do we not force people to join the Church if they are not smart enough to see it on their own? Because this is Satan's way, not the Lord's plan. The Lord uses persuasion and love. (*God, Family, Country,* p. 384.)

The children of Israel were willing to sacrifice liberty and begged Samuel the prophet to give them a king. He pointed out the fallacy of their reasoning. Samuel, like other great spiritual leaders both ancient and modern, saw the results that would follow the surrender of liberty. (1 Samuel 8:5–22.) (*Title of Liberty,* p. 93.)

An old adage declares, "A society of sheep must in time beget a government of wolves."

In a general conference, President J. Reuben Clark issued this sobering warning: "I say unto you with all the soberness I can, that we stand in danger of losing our liberties, and that once lost, only blood will bring them back; and once lost, we of this Church will, in order to keep the Church going forward, have more sacrifices to make and more persecutions to endure than we have yet known, heavy as our sacrifices and grievous as our persecutions of the past have been. (CR October 1966, *Improvement Era* 69 [December 1966]: 1146.)

The devil knows that if the elders of Israel should ever wake up, they could step forth and help preserve freedom and extend the gospel. Therefore the devil has concentrated, and to a large extent successfully, on neutralizing much of the priesthood. He has reduced them to sleeping giants. His arguments are clever. Here are a few samples.

"We really haven't received much instruction about freedom," the devil says. This is a lie, for we have been warned time and again. No prophet of the Lord has ever issued more solemn warning than President David O. McKay.

"You want to be loved by everyone," says the devil, "and this freedom battle is so controversial you might be accused of engaging in politics." Of course, the government has penetrated so much of our lives that one can hardly speak for freedom without being accused of being political. Some might even call the War in Heaven a political struggle — certainly it was controversial. Yet the valiant entered it with Michael (Revelation 12:7). Those who support only the popular principles of the gospel have their reward. And those who want to lead the quiet, retiring life but still expect to do their full duty can't have it both ways.

"Wait until it becomes popular to do," says the devil, "or, at least, until everybody in the Church agrees on what should be done." This fight for freedom might never become popular in our day. And if you wait until everybody agrees in this Church, you will be waiting through the second coming of the Lord. Would you have hesitated to follow the inspired counsel of the Prophet Joseph Smith simply because some weak men disagreed with him? God's living mouthpiece has spoken to us — are we for him or against him? Where do you stand?

"It might hurt your business or your family," says the devil, "and besides, why not let the Gentiles save the country? They aren't as busy as you are." Well, there were many businessmen who went along with Hitler because it supposedly helped their business. They lost everything. Many of us are here today because our forefathers loved truth enough that they fought at Valley Forge or crossed the plains in spite of the price it cost them or their families. We had better take our small pain now than our greater loss later. There were souls who wished afterwards that they had stood and fought with Washington and the Founding Fathers, but they waited too long—they passed up eternal glory. There has never been a greater time than now to stand up against entrenched evil. And while the Gentiles established the Constitution, we have a divine mandate to preserve it. But, unfortunately, today in this freedom struggle many Gentiles are showing greater wisdom in their generation than the children of light (Luke 16:8).

"Don't worry," says the devil; "the Lord will protect you, and besides, the world is so corrupt and heading toward destruction at such a pace that you can't stop it, so why try?" Well, to begin with, the Lord will not protect us unless we do our part. This devil-ish tactic of persuading people not to get concerned because the Lord will protect them no matter what they do is exposed by the Book of Mormon. Referring to the devil, it says: "And others will he pacify, and lull them away into carnal security, that they will say: All is well in Zion; yea, Zion prospereth, all is well—and thus the devil cheateth their souls, and leadeth them away carefully down to hell" (2 Nephi 28:21).

I like that word *carefully*. In other words, don't shake them—you might wake them. The Book of Mormon warns us that when we see these murderous conspiracies in our midst, we should awaken to our awful situation (see Ether 8:24). Now, why should we awaken if the Lord is going to take care of us anyway? Let us suppose that it is too late to save freedom. It is still accounted unto us for righteousness' sake to stand up and fight. Some Book of Mormon prophets knew of the final desolate end of their nations, but they still fought on, and they saved some souls, including their own, by so doing. For, after all, the purpose of life is to prove our-selves, and the final victory will be for freedom (Abraham 3:24–25).

The last neutralizer that the devil uses most effectively is simply this: "Don't do anything in the fight for freedom until the Church sets up its own specific program to save the Constitution." This brings us right back to the scripture about the slothful servants who will not do anything until they are "compelled in all things"

(D&C 58:26). Maybe the Lord will never set up a specific Church program for the purpose of saving the Constitution. Perhaps if He set one up at this time it might split the Church asunder, and perhaps He does not want that to happen yet, for not all the wheat and tares are fully ripe (D&C 86:5–7). (CR April 1965, *Improvement Era* 68 [June 1965]: 537–39.)

National Heritage

The Lord recognized that truth will only prosper where religious freedom exists. Religious freedom cannot be fully enjoyed without a full measure of political freedom. So before the gospel was restored, wise and inspired men in North, Central, and South America were raised up who proclaimed the sovereign truth that all men—not just the privileged, the rich, or the rulers—but all men have divine rights. Among these rights are life, liberty (which includes our freedom to worship), and right to property. (See D&C 101:79.) (Puerto Rico, 12–17 December 1980.)

Freedom is the rock on which our great land is founded. The fervent search for freedom brought our Pilgrim forefathers to these shores. Through the years freedom has been guarded by patriots of high and low station, without regard for personal well-being. They who today protect us on the land, on the sea, and in the air stand ready to maintain that freedom at any cost against any foe of our freedom. Each of us as citizens shares the grave responsibility of protecting our precious heritage. We must be aware of the insidious forces in the world today that may strike either from within or from without—that may even strike unseen at the core of our vitality as a nation.

Freedom is not always lost on the battlefront. We must not compromise ideals so hard won, or adopt or be blindly led into any course which would erode away our freedom. (*The Red Carpet,* p. 134.)

The one great revolution in the world today is the revolution for human liberty. This was the paramount issue we all faced in the great Council in Heaven before this earth life. It has been the issue throughout the ages. It is the issue today. It is difficult for Americans to understand the danger to our liberty. It is generally outside the range of our experience.

Never before in the history of our country has there been a greater need for all of our people to take time to discover what is happening in the world. Every day decisions are being made affecting the lives of millions of human beings.

We as a people have never known bondage. Liberty has always been our blessed lot. Few of us have ever seen people who have lost their freedom—their liberty. And when reminded of the danger of losing our liberty and independence our attitude has usually been —it cannot happen here. (*Title of Liberty,* pp. 92–93.)

The freedoms which the Constitution guarantees and which our fathers and forefathers have bequeathed to us—the freedom to explore new paths and reap the blessings of our own efforts, the freedom to think, act, and speak as we will—have brought us material blessings and opportunities for spiritual, intellectual and material development unmatched anywhere in the world. ("God and Country," Frankfurt am Main, Germany, 1964.)

Faith, courage, and freedom represent the life elements of growth—either in man or a nation. Spiritual faith and courage were the bone and sinew of the first freedom our people enjoyed on this continent. Then, as free hard-working Americans, our growth to abundance was only a matter of time. It is most significant that during this uphill struggle by Americans to create a civilization with an abundance for all, they gave no thought to the word *ease* as it might apply to their own way of life. People who are imbued with a strong spiritual faith, which in turn endows them with the courage to fight and win their battles for freedom and abundance, would view with contempt any person seeking an easy way through life. ("Will America Be Destroyed by Americans?" Annual Boy Scouts Banquet, Commerce, Texas, 13 May 1968.)

Freedom is a costly prize. Each new generation must assess its benefits and preserve it anew. Its preservation cannot otherwise be guaranteed. Some people have not appreciated what they once had until they lost it. It is well for you to carefully assess the comparative fruits of the system you live under versus other systems. ("The American Free-Enterprise System: Will It Survive?" Contemporary Issues Forum, Weber State College, Ogden, Utah, 18 January 1977.)

The Lord revealed to the prophet Nephi that He established the Gentiles on this land to be a free people forever; that if they were a righteous nation and overcame the wickedness and secret abominations that would rise in their midst, they would inherit the land forever (1 Nephi 14:1–2). (*God, Family, Country,* p. 345.)

We should support our government in keeping the flame of liberty burning in the souls of the oppressed—wherever they may be throughout the world. (*Title of Liberty,* p. 101.)

Our problems today call for greatness and courage just as insistently as did the era of 1776. Just as then, a new age is dawning today. The world has suddenly become so small that all nations and all men are next-door neighbors. Just as our forefathers stood proudly for freedom in their new-dawning era, so today we must steel ourselves to the building of a new era in which liberty can truly live.

Here in our free land let us preserve a true climate in which men can grow. Here with Lincoln we should always be able to say: "As I would not be a slave, so I would not be a master." And here we can add, "But I will be free—free to worship, free to speak, free to grow." (*The Red Carpet,* p. 97.)

The men who wrote the Declaration of Independence, the Constitution, and the Bill of Rights were under no illusion that their work was done. They were confident that we of succeeding generations would carry on.

Along with the political freedom so dearly won came a climate which challenged man's intellect and ingenuity. People began to move freedom forward along lines possibly not envisaged by the men who drafted the Declaration of Independence, the Constitution, and the Bill of Rights. Freedom from backbreaking toil came with the invention and development of labor-saving devices in factories and on farms.

In the political climate created by Jefferson and Hamilton and Washington and Franklin and all the rest, ideas could be planted and nourished into full bloom. Men were not afraid to venture across new frontiers, whether they were geographic or in the human mind. There was freedom for the Daniel Boones to invade the wilderness, and for inventors, equally bold, to explore the unknowns of science—to bring forth the cotton gin, to harness electricity, to develop the internal combustion engine, and at last to smash the atom.

Freedom moved forward with the development of all these inventions. It moved forward when it became possible for a mechanized agriculture to free the larger portion of the nation's working force from the production of food to devote energy and talents to other worthwhile pursuits.

We have yet to reach the summit of political and economic freedom. There is unfinished work to be done—but it must be done within the framework of our Constitution. We have won the freedom to produce an abundance of all the material things we need. We have won the freedom—and must push it forward—to develop the spiritual values which are sometimes overlooked in our striving for political and economic attainment.

To use a phrase from the Declaration of Independence—"appealing to the supreme Judge of the world for the rectitude of our intentions"—we cannot fail in our resolve that "freedom must move forward." (*The Red Carpet,* pp. 94–95.)

Nations that truly love freedom love God. We in this land have a heritage of freedom. It has rewarded us beyond our brightest dreams. Our God-given freedom, a basic principle of religious truth, is still the most powerful force on the face of the earth. (*Title of Liberty,* p. 121.)

In the World

The thirst for freedom is universal. Freedom and peace are the two great yearnings of mankind. The important dates of history, whether those of the United States or of the many other nations of the free world, are those concerning the struggle for, and the winning of, freedom and peace. Freedom is a precious thing. "No emotion is more deeply imprinted in man than the desire for liberty," wrote the Danish leader Colbjornsen. (*The Red Carpet,* p. 87.)

Freedom can be killed by neglect as well as by direct attack. Too long have people of the free world, generally, stood by as silent accessories to the crimes of assault against freedom — assault against basic economic and spiritual principles and traditions that have made nations strong. (*God, Family, Country,* p. 361.)

Freedom from aggression is a justifiable concern. As historians have pointed out, however, great nations do not usually fall by external aggression; they first erode and decay inwardly, so that, like rotten fruit, they fall of themselves.

The history of nations shows that the cycle of the body politic slowly but surely undergoes change. It progresses from bondage to spiritual faith, from spiritual faith to courage, from courage to freedom, from freedom to abundance, from abundance to selfishness, from selfishness to complacency, from complacency to apathy, from apathy to fear, from fear to dependency, from dependency to bondage. Every nation yearns for liberty, but too frequently its own self-indulgence precludes the possibility of freedom. (*This Nation Shall Endure,* p. 68.)

It is not pleasing to the God of Heaven whenever a spirit of coercion and force and intimidation is used in place of freedom of choice. I tremble when I think of the great calamity which will befall nations whose leaders refuse to recognize this principle of freedom as an eternal principle. (*The Red Carpet,* pp. 287–88.)

On the way to the airport our last night in Moscow [in 1959], I mentioned again to one of our guides my disappointment that we had had no opportunity to visit a church in Russia. He said a few words to the chauffeur, the car swung around in the middle of the avenue and we eventually pulled up before an old stucco building on a dark, narrow, cobblestone side street not far from Red Square. This was the Central Baptist Church.

It was a rainy, disagreeable October night with a distinct chill in the air. But when we entered the church, we found it filled; people were standing in the hall, in the entry, even in the street. Every Sunday, Tuesday, and Thursday, we learned, similar crowds turn out.

I looked at the faces of the people. Many were middle-aged and older but a surprising number were young. About four out of every five were women, most of them with scarves about their heads. We were ushered into a place beside the pulpit.

A newsman who was present described what happened: "Every face in the old sanctuary gaped incredulously as our obviously American group was led down the aisle. They grabbed for our hands as we proceeded to our pews which were gladly vacated for our unexpected visit. Their wrinkled, old faces looked at us pleadingly. They reached out to touch us almost as one would reach out for the last final caress of one's most-beloved just before the casket is lowered. They were in misery and yet a light shone through the misery. They gripped our hands like frightened children."

The minister spoke a few words, and then the organ struck a chord or two and began a hymn in which the entire congregation joined as one. Hearing a thousand to 1,500 voices raised there became one of the most affecting experiences of my entire life. In our common faith as Christians, they reached out to us with a message of welcome that bridged all differences of language, of government, of history. And as I was trying to recover balance under this emotional impact, the minister asked me, through an interpreter who stood there, to address the congregation.

It took me a moment of hard struggle to master my feelings sufficiently to agree. Then I said, in part, "It was very kind of you to ask me to greet you.

"I bring you greetings from the millions and millions of church people in America and around the world." And suddenly it was the most natural thing in the world to be talking to these fellow Christians about the most sacred truths known to man.

"Our Heavenly Father is not far away. He can be very close to us. God lives, I know that He lives. He is our Father. Jesus Christ, the Redeemer of the world, watches over this earth. He will direct all things. Be unafraid, keep His commandments, love one another, pray for peace and all will be well."

As each sentence was translated for the congregation, I saw the women take their handkerchiefs and as one observer put it begin to "wave them like a mother bidding permanent goodby to her only son." Their heads nodded vigorously as they moaned, "Ja, ja, ja! (yes, yes, yes!)." Then I noticed for the first time that even the gallery was filled and many persons were standing against the walls. I looked down on one old woman before me, head covered by a plain old scarf, a shawl about her shoulders, her aged, wrinkled face serene with faith. I spoke directly to her.

"This life is only a part of eternity. We lived before we came here as spiritual children of God. We will live again after we leave this life. Christ broke the bonds of death and was resurrected. We will all be resurrected.

"I believe very firmly in prayer. I know it is possible to reach out and tap that Unseen Power which gives us strength and such an anchor in time of need." With each sentence I uttered, the old head nodded assent. And old, feeble, wrinkled as she was, that woman was beautiful in her devotion.

I don't remember all that I said, but I recall feeling lifted up, inspired by the rapt faces of these men and women who were so steadfastly proving their faith in the God they served and loved.

In closing I said, "I leave you my witness as a Church servant for many years that the truth will endure. Time is on the side of truth. God bless you and keep you all the days of your life, I pray in the name of Jesus Christ, amen."

With that I brought this broken little talk to an end, because I could say no more, and sat down. The whole congregation then broke into a favorite hymn of my childhood, "God Be with You Till We Meet Again." We left the church as they sang and as we walked down the aisle, they waved handkerchiefs in farewell—it seemed all 1,500 were waving at us as we left.

It has been my privilege to speak before many church bodies in all parts of the world, but the impact of that experience is almost indescribable. I shall never forget that evening as long as I live.

Seldom, if ever, have I felt the oneness of mankind and the unquenchable yearning of the human heart for freedom so keenly as at that moment.

Ten members of the American press who were present felt it, too. Without exception they told me later what a moving experience it had been. One of them wrote in the next issue of his magazine: "The Communist plan is that when these 'last believers' die off, religion will die with them. What the atheists don't know is that God can't be stamped out either by legislated atheism or firing squad. This Methodist backslider who occasionally grumbles about having to go to church, stood crying unashamedly, throat lumped, and chills running from spine to toes. It was the most heart-rending and most inspiring scene I've ever witnessed."

On the drive to the airport one of the interpreters, a young
Russian girl who had never known any life save that under communism, said, "I felt like crying."

So did I. (*Crossfire: The Eight Years with Eisenhower,* pp.
485–88.)

Government

We should fully recognize that government is no plaything. As
George Washington warned, "Government is not reason, it is not
eloquence—it is force! Like fire, it is a dangerous servant and a
fearful master!" It is an instrument of force, and unless our conscience is clear that we would not hesitate to put a man to death,
put him in jail, or forcibly deprive him of his property for failing
to obey a given law, we should oppose it. (*God, Family, Country,*
p. 288.)

We need to keep before us the truth that people who do not
master themselves and their appetites will soon be mastered by
government. I wonder if we are not rearing a generation that seemingly does not understand this fundamental principle. Yet this is
the principle that separates our country from all others. The central issue before the people today is the same issue that inflamed
the hearts of our Founding Fathers in 1776 to strike out for independence. That issue is whether the individual exists for the state
or whether the state exists for the individual.

In a republic, the real danger is that we may slowly slide into a
condition of slavery of the individual to the state rather than entering this condition by a sudden revolution. The loss of our liberties
might easily come about, not through the ballot box but through
the abandonment of the fundamental teachings from God and this
basic principle upon which our country was founded. (*This Nation
Shall Endure,* pp. 29–30.)

History reveals why the great Roman Empire fell. These are the
major reasons. Note them carefully and try to determine in your
mind if there is anything in evidence in our own country today
which smacks of these causes, which the historican Will Durant
asserts were largely responsible for the fall of the great Roman
Empire.

The first group of causes he lists as biological. These he considers the most fundamental. Mr. Durant claims they began with the educated classes, and started with the breakdown of the home and the family—the limitation of children, the refusal to assume the obligations of honorable parenthood, the deferment and avoidance of marriage. Sexual excesses were indulged in outside the marriage covenant. The practices of contraception and abortion became prominent; reduced fertility resulted. Sex ran riot and moral decay resulted.

Second, he mentioned the waste, among other things, of natural resources—mining, deforestation, erosion, neglect of irrigation canals. Most important he considered the negligence of harassed and discouraged men, the failure to teach high moral principles to the youth of the land—those principles which make for the building of character—and the sad neglect of our greatest single asset, our boys and girls.

Third, he lists rising costs of government—armies, doles, public works, expanding bureaucracy, a parasitic court, depreciation of the currency, and absorption of investment capital by confiscatory taxation. Is there anything suggestive in this summary? (*The Red Carpet,* pp. 238–39.)

For man to exercise fully the agency God has granted to him, his God-given natural rights must be recognized and protected. It has only been recognized within the past four hundred years that these rights inherently belong to man. (*This Nation Shall Endure,* p. 5.)

Every government system has a sovereign, one or several who possess all the executive, legislative, and judicial powers. That sovereign may be an individual, a group, or the people themselves. Broadly speaking, there are only two governmental systems in the world today. One system recognizes that the sovereign power is vested in the head of state (a monarchy or dictatorship) or a group of men (an oligarchy). This system is as old as history and rests on the premise that the ruler grants to the people the rights and powers he thinks they should have. It is the basis of Roman, or civil, law.

The other system is that which had its historic origin in 1776, the year of the American independence. The Founding Fathers were men who understood the tyranny that can come out of the system of civil law. They had been indoctrinated in a different system of thought, that of common law, which is premised on the idea that true sovereignty rests with the people, under God. Believing this to be in accord with truth, they inserted this imperative in the Declaration of Independence: "That to secure these Rights [life, liberty, and the pursuit of happiness], Governments are instituted among Men deriving their just Powers from the Consent of the Governed."

Later, when the young nation had won her independence through the Revolutionary War, a free people's representatives drafted a second document, the Constitution of the United States.

Here the people were speaking. They recognized their sovereignty, not that of a king, emperor, or oligarchy. All rights and powers not granted specifically to the government were retained by themselves. This is the difference between freedom and despotism! (*This Nation Shall Endure,* pp. 70–71.)

Police should not be encumbered by civilian review boards, or asked to be social workers. They have their hands full just trying to keep the peace. Soft-on-crime decisions of the Supreme Court which hamper the police on protecting the innocent and bringing the criminal to justice should be reversed. Persistent cries of "police brutality" should be recognized for what they are—attempts to discredit our police and discourage them from doing their job to the best of their ability. Salaries should be adequate to hold onto and attract the very finest men available for police work. But, in questions of money, great care should be taken not to accept grants from the federal government. Along with federal money, inevitably there will come federal controls and "guidelines" which not only may get local police embroiled in national politics, but may even lead to the eventual creation of a national police force. (*An Enemy Hath Done This,* pp. 198–99.)

Before we can set the affairs of the nation in order, we need to set our own houses in order. We must return to the fundamental standards of integrity and morality—honesty, industry, thrift, modesty, chastity, cleanliness of mind and body. ("God and Country," Frankfurt am Main, Germany, 1964.)

The burden of self-government is a great responsibility. It calls for restraint, righteousness, responsibility, and reliance upon God.

If we fail in these, we fail as a people. ("The Crises of Our Constitution," Salt Lake Valley Utah Central Area Special Interest Lecture Series, 8 September 1977.)

Functions of Government

I should like to outline in clear, concise, and straightforward terms the guidelines that determine, now and in the future, my attitudes and actions toward all domestic proposals and projects of government. These are the principles that, in my opinion, proclaim the proper role of government in the domestic affairs of the nation:

[I] believe that governments were instituted of God for the benefit of man; and that He holds men accountable for their acts in relation to them.

[I] believe that no government can exist in peace, except such laws are framed and held inviolate as will secure to each individual the free exercise of conscience, the right and control of property, and the protection of life.

[I] believe that all men are bound to sustain and uphold the respective governments in which they reside, while protected in their inherent and inalienable rights by the laws of such governments. (See D&C 134:1–2, 5.)

(*The Constitution: A Heavenly Banner,* pp. 4–5.)

It is generally agreed that the most important single function of government is to secure the rights and freedoms of individual citizens. But what are those rights? And what is their source? Until these questions are answered there is little likelihood that we can correctly determine how government can best secure them.

Starting at the foundation of the pyramid, let us first consider the origin of those freedoms we have come to know as human rights. There are only two possible sources. Rights are either God-given as part of the divine plan, or they are granted by government as part of the political plan. Reason, necessity, tradition, and religious convictions all lead me to accept the divine origin of these rights. If we accept the premise that human rights are granted by government, we must be willing to accept the corollary that they can be denied by government. I, for one, shall never accept that premise. As the French political economist Frederic Bastiat phrased it so succinctly, "Life, liberty, and property do not exist because men have made laws. On the contrary, it was the fact that life, liberty, and property existed beforehand that caused men to make laws in the first place." (*An Enemy Hath Done This*, pp. 127–28.)

A government is nothing more nor less than a relatively small group of citizens who have been hired, in a sense, by the rest of us to perform certain functions and discharge responsibilities which have been authorized. It stands to reason that the government itself has no innate power nor privilege to do anything. Its only source of authority and power is from the people who have created it. This is made clear in the Preamble of the Constitution of the United States.

The important thing to keep in mind is that the people who have created their government can give to that government only such powers as they, themselves, have in the first place. Obviously, they cannot give that which they do not possess, so the question boils down to this: What powers properly belong to each and every person in the absence of and prior to the establishment of any organized governmental form? A hypothetical question? Yes, indeed! But, it is a question which is vital to an understanding of the principles which underlie the proper function of government. (*An Enemy Hath Done This,* pp. 129–30.)

The proper function of government is limited to those spheres of activity within which the individual citizen has the right to act. By deriving its just powers from the governed, government becomes primarily a mechanism for defense against bodily harm, theft, and involuntary servitude. It cannot claim the power to redistribute money or property, or to force reluctant citizens to perform acts of charity against their will. Government is created by the people. No individual possesses the power to take another's wealth or to force others to do good, so no government has the right to do such things either. The creature cannot exceed the creator. (*The Constitution: A Heavenly Banner,* p. 9.)

In general terms, the proper role of government includes such defensive activities as maintaining national military and local police forces for protection against loss of life, loss of property, and loss of liberty at the hands of either foreign despots or domestic criminals. It also includes those powers necessarily incidental to the protective function, such as the maintenance of courts where those charged with crimes may be tried and where disputes between citizens may be impartially settled; the establishment of a monetary system and a standard of weights and measures so that courts may render money judgments, taxing authorities may levy taxes, and citizens may have a uniform standard to use in their business dealings. (*An Enemy Hath Done This,* pp. 131–32.)

A category of government activity which today not only requires the closest scrutiny but which also poses a grave danger to our continued freedom is the activity not within the proper sphere of government. No one has the authority to grant such power as welfare programs, schemes for redistributing the wealth, and activities which coerce people into acting in accordance with a prescribed code of social planning. There is one simple test. Do I as an individual have a right to use force upon my neighbor to accomplish my goal? If I do have such a right, I may delegate that power to my government to exercise on my behalf. If I do not have that right as an individual, I cannot delegate it to government, and I cannot ask my government to perform the act for me. (*An Enemy Hath Done This,* p. 135.)

In a primitive state, there is no doubt that every individual would be justified in using force, if necessary, for defense against physical harm, against theft of the fruits of his labor, and against enslavement by another.

Indeed, the early pioneers found that a great deal of their time and energy was spent defending all three—defending themselves, their property, and their liberty—in what properly was called the "lawless West." In order for people to prosper, they cannot afford to spend their time constantly guarding family, fields, and property against attack and theft, so they joined together with their neighbors and hired a sheriff. At this precise moment, government is born. The individual citizens delegate to the sheriff their unquestionable right to protect themselves. The sheriff now does for them only what they had a right to do for themselves— nothing more. (*The Constitution: A Heavenly Banner,* p. 8.)

History records that eventually people get the form of government they deserve. Good government, which guarantees the maximum of freedom, liberty, and development to the individual, must be based upon sound principles. We must ever remember that ideas and principles are either sound or unsound in spite of those who hold them. (*This Nation Shall Endure,* p. 93.)

Citizenship

We all have a special citizenship responsibility. As the Prophet Joseph Smith said, "It is our duty to concentrate all our influence to make popular that which is sound and good, and unpopular that which is unsound." We must elect men to public office with a mandate higher than the ballot box. Yes, read what the Lord has said on this important subject in the ninety-eighth section of the Doctrine and Covenants and then read what He has said regarding our inspired Constitution in the one hundred first section. The days ahead are sobering and challenging and will demand the best within each of us if we are to preserve our freedom. ("Be True to God, Country, and Self," Young Adult Fireside, Logan, Utah, 11 February 1979.)

History teaches that when individuals have given up looking after their own economic needs and transferred a large share of that responsibility to the government, both they and the government have failed. At least twenty great civilizations have disappeared. The pattern of their downfall is shockingly similar. All, before their collapse, showed a decline in spiritual values, in moral stamina, and in the freedom and responsibility of their citizens. They showed such symptoms as excessive taxation, bloated bureaucracy, government paternalism, and generally a rather elaborate set of supports, controls, and regulations affecting prices, wages, production, and consumption. (*The Red Carpet,* pp. 168–69.)

Only an alert and informed citizenry can insure that the "sentinels on the country's watchtower" do their duty. If we continue to sleep—as we have been doing—we may one day awake to find that the sentinels have been overpowered and replaced by the godless soldiers of the enemy. We must never cease to exercise our God-given rights as citizens to criticize, to suggest alternatives, and to vote new men into office. ("God and Country," Frankfurt am Main, Germany, 1964.)

Some leaders may be honest and good but unwise in legislation they choose to support. Others may possess wisdom but be dishonest and unvirtuous. We must be concerted in our desires and efforts to see men and women represent us who possess all of these good qualities. (See D&C 98:10.) (*The Constitution: A Heavenly Banner,* p. 30.)

Pray for civil magistrates and leaders even when you do not agree with them. Obey the laws of your country; rebel not against civil authority. Do your duty as citizens. "Do not yield to the bad, but always oppose it with good" (Virgil). (CR April 1978, *Ensign* 8 [May 1978]: 34.)

Let us seek to take an active part in our local, state, and national affairs. We are commanded by the Lord to do so. It is as binding on us as any of the Lord's commandments. Actually it is when good men do nothing that evil flourishes. (CR October 1954, *Improvement Era* 57 [December 1954]: 922.)

If a government is really the sum of its people, it follows that they must be watchful, vigilant, and informed lest their liberties become gradually usurped by naive or unscrupulous leaders and they awaken to find their liberty gone. Despotism does not arise on the platform of totalitarianism or anything resembling it. It is voted into office on platitudes of "democracy," "freedom," promises of what the government will provide the people, or "something for nothing." (*This Nation Shall Endure,* p. 72.)

Let those who call for unity and the elimination of hate be sure they are not merely trying to silence the friends of freedom. These are they who respect their leaders and resist them only when it is felt they are headed for a catastrophe. What patriotic American would wish to stand silent if he saw his president verging on a blunder because of bad advice or a mistaken judgment of the facts? I believe one of the most serious mistakes a president could make would be to weaken the Constitution. (*Title of Liberty,* pp. 27–28.)

It is doubtful if any man can be politically free or even morally free who depends upon the state for his sustenance. An uncorrupted citizenry builds a great state. No state ever built an uncorrupted citizenry. (*The Red Carpet,* p. 146.)

Critics of independence, self-help, and self-reliance have their own theory. These critics believe that the national government can do most things better for the people than they can do for themselves as individuals or through their state and local governments. I believe the closer to home you keep government the more effective it will be—and it will cost less.

These critics also believe that federal employees in Washington know more about your school, your farm, your business, your job, than you, the people, do in your own communities, on your farms, in your businesses. You and I know that is not true—and we do not believe it. (*The Red Carpet,* pp. 158–59.)

We must make our influence felt by our votes, our letters, and our advice. We must be wisely informed and let others know how we feel. We must take part in local precinct meetings and select delegates who will truly represent our feelings. (*The Constitution: A Heavenly Banner,* p. 30.)

If we lose our freedom, it will be to this strange and unlike coalition of the well-intentioned, the slothful, and the subversives. It will be because we did not care enough, because we were not alert enough, because we were too apathetic to take note while the precious waters of our God-given freedom slipped—drop by drop—down the drain. (American Institute of Real Estate Appraisers, Salt Lake City, Utah, 19 April 1974.)

Edmund Burke once said, "All that is necessary for the triumph of evil is for good men to do nothing." It is not enough that we wring our hands and moan about conditions in America. We must become responsible citizens and carry out our civic duty. We should be "anxiously engaged" in good causes and leave the world a better place for having lived in it (D&C 58:27). ("Righteousness Exalteth a Nation," Provo Utah Freedom Festival, 29 June 1986.)

I think the Lord wants us to be good citizens of this country. I believe He wants us to keep our economic and social thinking straight and not be influenced by policies and programs that strike at the very foundation of all that we hold dear in this country.

We have a measuring rod that no other group has. We have the revelations of the Almighty to indicate to us whether a thing is right or wrong. The Lord has spoken. He has placed a responsibility upon us to see that our form of government is preserved and that good men and honest men are elected for public office. His counsel is found in the Doctrine and Covenants (see D&C 98; 101). We are not left to move in the dark. (*God, Family, Country,* p. 194.)

Counsel of God

Our governmental system, like the systems of ancient Israel and biblical Christianity, recognizes man as a special creation of God. He is not, as some theorists reason, a product of chance or merely an educated animal. His paternal origin is from God. Thus, man inherently possesses God-implanted attributes and potential: reason, free agency, judgment, compassion, initiative, and a personal striving for perfection. (*This Nation Shall Endure,* p. 84.)

Where the first worldly government began as a theocracy, Adam's descendants soon departed from this perfect order and degenerated into various political systems. The result has been human misery and—for most of humankind—subjugation to some despotic government. ("The Crises of Our Constitution," Salt Lake Valley Utah Central Area Special Interest Lecture Series, 8 September 1977.)

The Ten Commandments and the Sermon on the Mount are the foundation principles upon which all civilized government and our present civilization are built (see Exodus 20:1–17; Matthew 5–7). To disregard them will lead to inevitable personal character loss and ruin. To disregard them as a nation inevitably will lead that nation to destruction. ("On My Honor," Explorer Presidents Conference, Ogden, Utah, 4 March 1978.)

The Lord counseled the Saints in the early days of the Church that they should accept their hardships in patience, that they should also befriend the law of the land, and that they should choose honest men to administer the laws, for He said concerning the laws of our land: "That law of the land which is constitutional, supporting that principle of freedom in maintaining rights and privileges, belongs to all mankind and is justifiable before me" (D&C 98:5). (*So Shall Ye Reap,* p. 225.)

We should measure all proposals having to do with our national or local welfare by four standards: First, is the proposal, the policy, or the idea being promoted, right as measured by the gospel of Jesus Christ? I assure you it is much easier for one to measure a proposed policy by the gospel of Jesus Christ if he has accepted the gospel and is living it.

Second, is it right as measured by the Lord's standard of constitutional government? (See D&C 98:5.) Whether we live under a divinely inspired Constitution, as in the United States, or under some other form of government, the Lord's standard is a safe guide.

Third, we might well ask, Is it right as measured by the counsel of the living oracles of God? It is my conviction that these living oracles are not only authorized, but are also obligated to give counsel to this people on any subject that is vital to the welfare of this people and to the upbuilding of the kingdom of God.

Fourth, what will be the effect upon the morale and the character of the people if this or that policy is adopted? After all, as a Church, we are interested in building men and women and in building character. (*God, Family, Country,* pp. 278–79.)

As Latter-day Saints we should pray for our civic leaders and encourage them in righteousness. (*God, Family, Country,* p. 320.)

We must live the higher law—for that purpose we were sent. That means we "forsake [our] sins, . . . wicked ways, the pride of [our] hearts, and . . . covetousness, and all detestable things"

(D&C 98:20). You will not design to receive what you have not earned by your own labor. Government owes you nothing. You do owe a debt to preserve what preceding generations made possible for you. You will keep the laws of the land, for in Lincoln's words, "to violate the law is to trample on the blood of his father, and to tear the charter of his own and his children's liberty." ("The Crises of Our Constitution," Salt Lake Valley Utah Central Area Special Interest Lecture Series, 8 September 1977.)

When the Prophet Joseph Smith outlined the Articles of Faith, he set forth in clear, unmistakable terms the foundations of our worship and of our relationships with one another. In view of the troubled times which the nations of the earth are experiencing at present, it is well for us as members of the Lord's kingdom to understand clearly our responsibilities and obligations respecting governments and laws as declared in the twelfth article of faith: "We believe in being subject to kings, presidents, rulers, and magistrates, in obeying, honoring, and sustaining the law."

In it is a declaration requiring obedience, loyalty to, and respect for duly constituted laws and the officials administering those laws. In justifying such loyal compliance, however, the Lord also promulgated certain safeguards and conditions which must be observed if freedom and liberty are to be preserved and enjoyed. These are emphasized primarily in sections 98 and 134 of the Doctrine and Covenants. How I wish these fundamental concepts were emblazoned on the hearts of all our people! (*God, Family, Country,* p. 277.)

American Government

When the thirteen colonies formed our federal union, they had two very important factors in their favor, neither of which are present in the world at large today. First, the colonies themselves were all of a similar cultural background. They enjoyed similar legal systems, they spoke the same language, and they shared similar religious beliefs. They had much in common. The second advantage, and the most important of the two, was that they formed their union under a constitution which was designed to prevent any of them, or a majority of them, from forcefully intervening in the affairs of the others. The original federal government was authorized to provide mutual defense, run a post office, and that was about all. (*An Enemy Hath Done This,* p. 159.)

If Americans should ever come to believe that their rights and freedoms are instituted among men by politicians and bureaucrats, they will no longer carry the proud inheritance of their forefathers, but will grovel before their masters seeking favors and dispensations—a throwback to the feudal system of the Dark Ages.

Since God created man with certain inalienable rights, and man, in turn, created government to help secure and safeguard those rights, it follows that man is superior to government and should remain master over it, not the other way around. As said so appropriately by Lord Acton:

"It was from America that the plain ideas that men ought to mind their own business, and that the nation is responsible for the acts of the State—ideas long locked in the breast of solitary thinkers, and hidden among Latin folios—burst forth like a conqueror upon the world they were destined to transform, under the title of the Rights of Man. . . . and the principle gained ground, that a nation can never abandon its fate to an authority it cannot control." (*The History of Freedom and Other Essays*, 1907, pp. 55–56.) (*This Nation Shall Endure*, p. 29.)

"That government is best which governs least." So taught the courageous founders of this nation. This simple declaration is diametrically opposed to the all too common philosophy that the government should provide for one from the cradle to the grave. (*So Shall Ye Reap,* p. 161.)

Every right carries with it a responsibility. Every opportunity is a challenge. Just as we in the United States have been the most favored of any nation in our heritage, so we bear the greatest responsibility to protect and to pass on these blessings to others. (*The Red Carpet,* p. 214.)

The governments—both state and federal—by making grants and giving exclusive licenses to railroads, banks, and public utilities, created artificial government monopolies. Free competition in these fields was prohibited by law. One had to possess a certificate of convenience and necessity to enter business and these were given to only a select few.

The results were only to be expected. With no competition to keep these monopolies in line, prices and rates were raised until the public clamor to halt these abuses brought about the antitrust laws. The correct remedy, of course, would have been to withdraw all exclusive privileges and allow anyone who had the desire to enter into these fields of economic activity.

If every member of society and every group is allowed to compete, and if the consuming public is left completely free to select those with whom they do business, the public will always be served by those who offer the best product at the cheapest price. When the exclusive power to make or break business concerns rests in the hands of the consumers, we may rest assured there will be no monopolies. Public opinion can break a business overnight unless the government steps in and forcibly prohibits competition. (*An Enemy Hath Done This*, p. 236.)

We must expose to the light of public inquiry those forces which would destroy our country and our way of life. We should pay no attention to the recommendations of men who call the Constitution an eighteenth-century agrarian document—who apologize for capitalism and free enterprise. We should refuse to follow their siren song of increasingly concentrating the powers of government in the chief executive, of delegating American sovereign authority to non-American institutions of the United Nations and pretending that it will bring peace to the world by turning our armed forces over to a United Nations worldwide police force. (*Title of Liberty*, p. 16.)

The open and covert management of the news in this country is frightening in its implications. One high government official has made the appalling statement to the effect that it is all right for the government to lie to the people if it serves the government's purpose to lie. Certainly lies can take place by omission as well as by commission. (*Title of Liberty*, p. 79.)

We must resolutely refuse to exchange principles for government handouts. We must realize that giving without earning, rights without responsibilities, and freedom without vigilance are but figments of an imagination gone wild. Never must this choice nation be permitted to fall prey to a mammoth, centralized, paternalistic government on the pretext that such a government can by decree create and dispense health, wealth, and happiness to a subservient people. (*So Shall Ye Reap,* p. 331.)

In a discussion of big government in America, let us realize that the cure for our ills is not to give the patient another dose of what made him sick in the first place. And yet that is precisely what some are urging today in demanding more and more government controls. (*The Red Carpet,* p. 151.)

There is only one way to reverse this greatly increasing expenditure of money by the federal government and that is to have an awakening to the dangers of excessive spending, and start eliminating programs which require these huge funds. Our government cannot continue to overspend its annual income indefinitely any more than your family or mine can do it.

We must balance the budget and reduce the overall indebtedness. We must not allow demagogues to get away with political promises and proposals requiring fantastic—yes, unbelievable—federal expenditures. (*The Red Carpet,* p. 171.)

If the preservation and strengthening of our military, economic, and political independence is the only legitimate objective of foreign policy decisions, then, at last, those decisions can be directed by a brilliant beacon of light that unerringly guides our ship of state past the treacherous reefs of international intrigue and into a calm, open sea. (*An Enemy Hath Done This,* p. 153.)

Ever since World War I, when we sent American boys to Europe supposedly "to make the world safe for democracy," our leaders in Washington have been acting as though the American people elected them to office for the primary purpose of leading the entire planet toward international peace, prosperity, and one-world government. At times, these men appear to be more concerned with something called world opinion or with their image as world leaders than they are with securing the best possible advantage for us, with showing that they are not "nationalistic" in their views, that they are willing to sacrifice narrow American interests for the greater good of the world community. Patriotism and America-first have become vulgar concepts within the chambers of our State Department. It is no wonder that the strength and prestige of the United States has slipped so low everywhere in the world. (*An Enemy Hath Done This,* p. 150.)

Civic Responsibility. The Constitution of the United States was prepared and adopted by courageous men acting under inspiration from the Almighty. The eternal moral laws must be adhered to or individual liberty will perish. It is the responsibility of government to punish crime and provide for the administration of justice, and to protect the right and control of property.

But today these basic principles and concepts are being flaunted, disregarded, and challenged, even by men in high places. Through the exercise of political expediency the government is condoning the breakdown of law and order. (*An Enemy Hath Done This,* pp. 4–5.)

We must study the inspired Constitution and become involved in the political process ourselves. I quote the First Presidency statement that was read in sacrament meetings on Sunday, 1 July 1979: "We encourage all members, as citizens of the nation, to be actively involved in the political process, and to support those measures which will strengthen the community, state, and nation —morally, economically, and culturally." (Letter from the First Presidency, 29 June 1979.) (CR October 1979, *Ensign* 9 [November 1979]: 33.)

We must become involved in civic affairs. As citizens of this republic, we cannot do our duty and be idle spectators. It is vital that we follow this counsel from the Lord: "Honest men and wise men should be sought for diligently, and good men and wise men ye should observe to uphold; otherwise whatsoever is less than these cometh of evil" (D&C 98:10).

Note the qualities that the Lord demands in those who are to represent us. They must be good, wise, and honest. We must be concerted in our desires and efforts to see men and women represent us who possess all three of these qualities—goodness, wisdom, and honesty. ("The Constitution—A Heavenly Banner," BYU Devotional Assembly, Provo, Utah, 16 September 1986.)

Our heritage of freedom is threatened by self-seeking men who see in government legislation a way to obtain special privileges for themselves or to restrain their competitors. They use demagoguery as a smokescreen to deceive. These people have no love for freedom or enterprise. They would learn the value of freedom only after it was gone. (*An Enemy Hath Done This,* p. 25.)

We Americans have strayed far from sound principles—morally, constitutionally, and historically. It has been getting us into a quagmire of trouble all over the world, and especially here at home. Americans at the grassroots level have sensed that their way of life is being threatened. During the last several years there has been a rising tide of resistance to the prevailing political trend. Compromises with communism abroad and flirtations with socialism at home have stirred up opposition in both political parties. If this has led to disunity, by all means let us return to a program of sound constitutional principles on which we can unite. (*Title of Liberty,* p. 25.)

At this particular moment in history the United States Constitution is definitely threatened, and every citizen should know about it. The warning of this hour should resound through the corridors of every American institution—schools, churches, the halls of Congress, press, radio, and television, and so far as I am concerned it will resound—with God's help.

Wherever possible I have tried to speak out. It is for this very reason that certain people in Washington have bitterly criticized me. They don't want people to hear the message. It embarrasses them. The things which are destroying the Constitution are the things they have been voting for. They are afraid of their political careers if these facts are pointed out. They therefore try to silence any who carry the message—anyone who will stand up and be counted. (*Title of Liberty,* p. 30.)

In this time of deadly peril we must choose men and women to represent us in our government who have attained an inner attunement of mind, heart, and soul with God. Only these people have anchors firmly rooted and strong enough to withstand the slings and arrows of outrageous fortune. They only have the inner sense of direction, stability of spirit, and firmness of character essential to our survival.

We must not place in positions of trust cheap opportunists who will sell their souls for a mess of pottage. Rather we should place in public office men and women who place the love of God first in their lives and who, as a consequence, can serve their fellowmen with true wisdom.

Not cheap politicians but statesmen are needed today. Not opportunists but men and women of principle must be demanded by the people. In this time of great stress and danger we must place only those dedicated to the preservation of our Constitution, our American Republic, and responsible freedom under God. "Oh, God, give us men with a mandate higher than the ballot box." (*Title of Liberty,* pp. 84–85.)

Each priesthood holder should use his influence in the community to resist the erosion which is taking place in our political and economic life. He should use the political party of his choice to express his evaluation of important issues. He should see that his party is working to preserve freedom, not destroy it. He should join responsible local groups interested in promoting freedom and free competitive enterprise, studying political issues, appraising the voting records and proposed programs, writing to members of Congress, promoting good men in public office, and scrutinizing local, state, and federal agencies to see that the will of the people is carried out. He should not wait for the Lord's servants to give instruction for every detail once they have announced the direction in which the priesthood should go. Each member should exercise prayerful judgment and then act. (*Title of Liberty,* p. 192.)

We should study the records of our Congressmen—how they vote, not what they say only—to help determine whether or not we maintain an administration dedicated to freedom and free enterprise. The record we are making—the record we will make with the election of good representatives and senators obviously must include the preservation of peace and freedom. We must provide for the security of our nation. With fine representation in Congress we can win the battle for freedom. (*The Red Carpet,* p. 236.)

Honest legislators will not spend money they do not have, thereby mortgaging future generations to debt. Honest legislators will remember the words of Jefferson: "We shall all consider ourselves unauthorized to saddle posterity with our debts."

Honorable legislators will not permit government to print money, creating the cruelest tax of all, inflation. They will not vote themselves pay increases without consent of the governed. They will refrain from demagoguery (promising what they can't deliver or pandering to the covetousness of those who demand what they have not earned). In short, elected officials will not assume prerogatives they do not have and which you have not expressly granted to them.

When you have wise, good, honorable representatives, you have effective constitutional government. When you don't have this kind of representation, constitutional government will fail. It is as Edmund Burke said, "Men of intemperate habits cannot be free. Their passions forge their fetters." ("A Warning to America," Independence Day Celebration, Washington D.C. Stake, 3 July 1979.)

Seldom are men willing to oppose a popular program if they themselves wish to be popular—especially if they seek public office. Such an approach to vital political questions of the day can only lead to public confusion and legislative chaos.

Decisions of this nature should be based upon and measured against certain basic principles regarding the proper role of government. If principles are correct, they can be applied to any specific proposal with confidence.

Unlike the political opportunist, the true statesman values principle above popularity, and works to create popularity for those political principles which are wise and just. (*An Enemy Hath Done This,* p. 126.)

It was not just incidental nor was it mere political platitude that the name of God was mentioned in the Declaration of Independence four times, and that our adopted national motto became

"In God We Trust." From the life of our illustrious founder, George Washington, we have an example of rectitude worthy of emulation by all public servants, an example that demonstrates a consistency between his private morality and public behavior. In light of past and present indiscretions by public officials, it would seem that this is a lesson that needs to be relearned. (*This Nation Shall Endure,* pp. 104–5.)

It is right politically for a man who has influence for good to use it. (CR October 1954, *Improvement Era* 57 [December 1954]: 922.)

America's choice each election day is either to elect price fixers and the forces of regimentation, or to vote for a program under enlightened leadership aimed at an expanding, prosperous, and free economy under the free-enterprise system.

America's choice on election day is to either support the drive for punitive legislation aimed at undermining private enterprise, or a conscientious Congress and president dedicated to the protection, promotion, and strengthening of the free-enterprise system.

America's choice is either a program of spending, taxing, deficits, and runaway inflation, or a prudent government dedicated to fiscal integrity, a stabilized dollar, balanced budgets, and a greater proportion of the tax revenue expended at the state and local level.

America's choice by free ballot is either a centralization of control in the federal government with an increasing dose of bureaucratic paternalism, or for an administration fostering greater responsibility in state and local governments and less domination from those desks in Washington. The time for decision is always with us. Americans, regardless of political affiliation, can and must help in this fight for the preservation of our free way of life. (*The Red Carpet,* p. 235.)

I presume in America we will never lose those freedoms and those blessings of liberty by force from an outside power, but we may very easily lose them because of our indifference, because of our failure to exercise our franchise, because we permit men who are unworthy to rise to positions of political power. (*So Shall Ye Reap,* p. 230.)

Let history bear witness that when the infamous extermination order was issued by the governor of the state of Missouri, and when twelve thousand defenseless citizens who had done no wrong were exiled from their homes, they sought refuge elsewhere and then sought formal redress of the injustices done against them through the courts of the land, even to the president of the United States. We did not then urge our people to revolt against unjust persecution, corrupt public officials, or their civil government, but to seek redress through constitutional means. We urge the same process for all minorities today. (*This Nation Shall Endure,* p. 62.)

We should help those who have been deceived or who are misinformed to find the truth. Unless each person who knows the truth will "stand up and speak up," it is difficult for the deceived or confused citizen to find his way back. (*God, Family, Country,* pp. 354–55.)

I know that many of our brethren today are facing responsibilities as we go to the polls. Many of them will be elected to legislative bodies; others will be chosen as chief executives in municipalities, to positions of trust in counties and states. We honor you because of your interest in political affairs, and we have confidence that you will always remember that no political power or office which may ever come to you will even approach in importance the great blessing and honor which came to you when you were ordained to the holy priesthood of God. (CR October 1952, *Improvement Era* 55 [December 1952]: 942.)

We must be devoted to sound principles in word and deed: principle above party, principle above pocketbook, principle above popularity. (*God, Family, Country,* p. 379.)

I wonder what our Founding Fathers would do and say about America today if they were here. As they looked searchingly for the answers they would observe evidence of weak and vacillating leadership in many places, not confined to one group or one party. They would find a tendency for men in high places to place political expediency ahead of principle. They would be concerned with the alarming growth of a something-for-nothing philosophy, a failure of people to stand on their own feet. They would find some bad examples by unscrupulous politicians and by delinquent parents, and possibly a weakening of religious training and the substitution therefore of a faith-destroying materialism.

As American citizens, we need to rouse ourselves to the problems which confront us as a great Christian nation. We need to recognize that these fundamental, basic principles—moral and spiritual—lay at the very foundation of our achievements in the past. (*The Red Carpet,* pp. 239–40.)

Monroe Doctrine. Here was the situation that called forth this policy known as the Monroe Doctrine in 1823. Several of what are now the Latin American republics had by force of arms newly won their independence from Spain and Portugal. Among them were Colombia, Mexico, Chile, and Brazil.

Meantime, a number of the sovereigns of Europe were seeking to enforce the "divine right of kings" with the express purpose of putting "an end to the system of representative government." France, accordingly, had proceeded to restore the rule of Ferdinand VII in Spain. Now these countries proposed to overthrow the new and independent governments in Latin America.

This our government refused to permit. It said so plainly in the celebrated Monroe Doctrine. The heart of the Monroe Doctrine consisted of these words: "The American continents, by the free and independent condition which they have assumed and maintained, are henceforth not to be considered as subjects for future colonization by any European power."

And the Doctrine went on to spell out clearly just what was meant as follows: "The political system of the allied powers is essentially different . . . from that of America. . . . We owe it, therefore, to candor, and to the amicable relations existing between the United States and those powers, to declare that we should consider any attempt on their part to extend their system to any portion of this hemisphere as dangerous to our peace and safety." (*The Red Carpet,* pp. 189–90.)

The Monroe Doctrine is based upon the principle, long recognized in international law journals, that a nation has a right to interfere in the affairs of another nation if such interference is within the framework of self-defense. In other words, if the establishment by a foreign power of unusually heavy military installations is observed on a nation's frontier, and if that nation has good reason to believe that those installations eventually are going to be used as part of an offensive attack against it, it is justified in taking the initiative in destroying those installations, without waiting for the actual attack. Such action, although aggressive by itself, is viewed as part of a generally defensive maneuver. (*An Enemy Hath Done This,* pp. 242–43.)

Constitutionalism. I want to be known as a constitutionalist in the tradition of James Madison—father of the Constitution. Labels change and perhaps in the old tradition I would be considered one of the original Whigs. The new title I would wear today is that of conservative—though in its original British connotation the term *liberal* fits me better than the original meaning of the word *conservative.*

To show how labels can change or be stolen, a liberal today believes in greater government intervention and less personal freedom for the people, which is practically the opposite of what the old liberals believed years ago. (*The Red Carpet,* pp. 206–7.)

As a conservative I believe we must continually seek progress. We must prepare for progress, strive for it, insist on it. But this does not mean that we must accept every proposed change on the assumption that all change is progress. Change is a two-way street. We can follow it forward or we can travel it backward. It is the reactionary who resists all change.

However, I have never felt that constantly stirring things up and changing policy by continually presenting new emergency programs to the people is the solution. I have great faith in the free-enterprise system, which is based on the choice of the people, and I would be slow to interfere in the workings of that system. To me this has nothing to do with turning back the clock. (*The Red Carpet,* pp. 207–8.)

In politics I am a conservative, in agriculture a conservationist. To be so, I do not have to wear two hats. The two just naturally go together. The conservationist seeks to preserve, develop, and improve the natural resources of soil, water, minerals, and timber that made and that keep this country materially rich. The conservative seeks to preserve, develop, and improve the political resources that made and that keep this country free. To me, the political resources of this land are no less important than its natural resources. As a conservative and a conservationist, I want to preserve both, develop both, improve both.

Conservatives are said to be more interested in property rights than in human rights. This statement is meaningless; it obscures the truth that the right to property is a human right. Property as such has no rights. Only human beings have rights, and among these is that of acquiring and owning property. As a conservative, I deplore as a violation of human rights the efforts to place more and more of the functions of private business and free enterprise in the hands of government. Few people realize how far this trend has already gone. As a conservative I deplore this trend because I am for the human right of human beings to acquire and own property. (*The Red Carpet,* pp. 208–9.)

The conservative has faith in the human person to make his own decisions. The liberal has faith in the ability of Washington to make more and more decisions for us. The liberal would impose on the people his version of progress whether the people want it or not. Conservatives believe that the best way to achieve progress in our country is through individual effort and not government force, which in the end will destroy all progress and all freedom. In the long run we do things better for ourselves than the government can do them for us. Government serves best when it protects the freedom of the individual. But the moment the government steps in and dictates the economic or agricultural life of the nation, the individual's rights begin to diminish and are in danger ultimately of vanishing. (*The Red Carpet,* p. 211.)

The greatest right humans possess is the right of free choice, free will, free agency. This above all is what today's true conservative strives to preserve for his fellowmen and for himself. Ironically, it is this very objective that has helped to give credence to the myths. Because the conservative fervently believes in human freedom, he is slow to tell everybody else how to run their lives. It goes against the conservative grain to be a political, social, or economic busybody, and especially to beat the drums for government action on virtually every existing problem. (*The Red Carpet,* p. 210.)

As a conservative, I say let us respect and remain true to our constitutional system, to our freedoms, to our American way of life. Let us pledge ourselves to integrity and unselfishness, to courage in defense of our blessed rights and privileges. Let us always discharge our responsibilities in accordance with the principles we are pledged to uphold. (*The Red Carpet,* p. 212.)

Statism

We cannot afford to minimize the threat of socialism in America. We must be on guard against unsound theories and programs which strike at the very root of all we hold dear. We have lived too long under a government of controls. Government by control has extended into almost all of our economy and even invaded many of our personal freedoms. We must be made aware of this and be awakened to its dangers.

This major effort is to keep left-wing, bureaucratic planners away from control of our national government. They are leading us today toward more and more socialization of our entire economy, a weakening of the free-enterprise system, and an increase in the regulation and domination of the people of America. (*The Red Carpet,* p. 311.)

Today's Socialists—who call themselves egalitarians—are using the federal government to redistribute wealth in our society —not as a matter of voluntary charity, but as a so-called matter of right. One Housing, Education, and Welfare official said, "In this country, welfare is no longer charity; it is a right. More and more Americans feel that their government owes them something." (*U.S. News and World Report,* 21 April 1975, p. 49.) President Grover Cleveland said—and we believe as a people—that though the people support the government, the government should not support the people. ("A Vision and a Hope for the Youth of Zion," in *1977 Devotional Speeches of the Year* [Provo, Utah: BYU, 1978], p. 77.)

Yes, we have traveled a long way down the soul-destroying road of socialism. (You young men and women today little realize that the federal government has taken over what once was the exclusive domain of the local government or the individual citizen.)

How did it happen? Men of expediency ascended to high political offices by promising what was not theirs to give, and citizens voted them into office in the hopes of receiving what they had not earned. You can, therefore, see how the violation of one commandment—Thou shalt not covet—has weakened our entire system of government and led to a partial loss of liberty. ("Be True to God, Country, and Self," Young Adult Fireside, Logan, Utah, 11 February 1979.)

There is an evidence in our beloved country of certain trends and tendencies which strike at the very foundation of all we hold dear. The outlook for free enterprise in the world has never seemed so uncertain as now. A world survey by the *New York Times* shows that nationalization is growing rapidly, especially outside the Western Hemisphere. Many nations have a mixed economy brought about by an increase in state control and a corresponding weakening of the private-enterprise system. The seriousness of the situation demands careful reflection by all interested in the preservation and perpetuation of our system of individual free enterprise, predicated as it is on a democratic capitalistic economy under a republican form of government. ("Cooperative Goals," American Institute of Cooperation, Madison, Wisconsin, 22 August 1949.)

I fear for the future when I realize that our once-free institutions—political, economic, educational, and social—have been drifting into the hands of those who favor the welfare state, and who would "centralize all power in the hands of the political apparatus in Washington. This enhancement of political power at the expense of individual rights, so often disguised as 'democracy' or 'freedom' or 'civil rights,' is 'socialism,' no matter what name tag it bears." (Admiral Ben Moreell.) (*Title of Liberty,* p. 62.)

How is it possible to cut out the various welfare-state features of our government which have already fastened themselves like cancer cells onto the body politic? Isn't drastic surgery already necessary, and can it be performed without endangering the patient? In answer, it is obvious that drastic measures are called for. No halfway or compromise actions will suffice. Like all surgery, it will not be without discomforts and perhaps even some scar tissue for a long time to come. But it must be done if the patient is to be saved, and it can be done without undue risk.

Obviously, not all welfare-state programs currently in force can be dropped simultaneously without causing tremendous economic and social upheaval. To try to do so would be like finding oneself at the controls of a hijacked airplane and attempting to return it by simply cutting off the engines in flight. It must be flown back, lowered in altitude, gradually reduced in speed and brought in for a smooth landing. Translated into practical terms, this means that the first step toward restoring the limited concept of government should be to freeze all welfare-state programs at their present level, making sure that no new ones are added. The next step would be to allow all present programs to run out their term with absolutely no renewal. The third step would involve the gradual phasing-out of those programs which are indefinite in their term. In my opinion, the bulk of the transition could be accomplished within a ten-year period and virtually completed within twenty years. Congress would serve as the initiator of this phase-out program, and the president would act as the executive in accordance with traditional constitutional procedures. (*An Enemy Hath Done This*, pp. 141–42.)

With little but raw courage and indomitable purpose, those intrepid pioneers set forth into the unknown by covered wagon, on horseback, and sometimes on foot. The land demanded iron men with steel in their backbones. Nature did the weeding out. But they didn't whine or bleat because things were tough. They asked no favors from any man. They knew what they were up against and they accepted the challenge. All they wanted was to be left alone to do what had to be done. They were wrenching a civilization out of the wilderness.

America soon blossomed into a rich, fertile, productive nation. Individual initiative — free enterprise — paid off, and American ingenuity flourished in a climate of freedom. Very soon our technology, our inventiveness, and our business know-how became the envy of the world. America had reached maturity, a giant among nations, a glowing example of free enterprise in action, and a perfect demonstration of what free men can do when they are left alone to do it.

But, as those affluent years slipped by, voices were heard in the land singing the siren songs of socialism. And many Americans tapped their feet to the beat of the music. Politicians were already promising something for nothing—that elusive free lunch. Thus, gradually, the people let the government infringe upon their precious freedoms and the preliminary signs of decay began to appear in our young republic.

Our economic situation is precarious. Reality has descended on us. Inflation, like an insidious disease, is weakening us. We got to this position because we lost our national pride, our sense of independence. When we wanted something, we went crawling to the government instead of doing it ourselves. We, like Esau of old, exchanged God-inspired principles, for a mess of shoddy values. No wonder our structures of freedom are cracking. ("A Warning to America," Independence Day Celebration, Washington D.C. Stake, 3 July 1979.)

World Government

God raised up wise leaders among your progenitors which afforded Latin American countries political freedom and independence. I only mention the names of a few whom God raised up to accomplish His holy and sovereign purposes: Jose de San Martin, Bernardo O'Higgins, and Simon Bolivar. These were some of the "founding fathers" of your continent.

I believe it was very significant that when independence came to the countries of South America, governments were established on constitutional principles—some patterned after the Constitution of the United States. I believe this was a very necessary step which preceded the preaching of the gospel in South America. ("The Righteous Need Not Fear," LaPaz, Bolivia, 10–18 January 1979.)

Many well-intentioned people are now convinced that we are living in a period of history which makes it both possible and necessary to abandon our national sovereignty, to merge our nation militarily, economically, and politically with other nations, and to form, at last, a world government which supposedly would put an end to war. We are told that this is merely doing between nations what we did so successfully with our thirteen colonies. This plea for world federalism is based on the idea that the mere act of joining separate political units together into a larger federal entity will somehow prevent those units from waging war with each other. The success of our own federal system is most often cited as proof that this theory is valid. But such an evaluation is a shallow one. (*An Enemy Hath Done This,* pp. 156–57.)

Sovereignty for a nation is hard to come by and even more difficult to retain. It cannot be shared, for then sovereignty becomes something else, and, for want of a better word, when sovereignty is lessened the end-product is internationalism. Sovereignty is neither more nor less than self-government. American self-government is blueprinted in the Constitution. (*An Enemy Hath Done This,* p. 99.)

To protect our people from international theft, we must enter into agreements with other nations to abide by certain rules regarding trade, exchange of currency, enforcement of contracts, and patent rights. To protect our people against involuntary servitude or the loss of personal freedom on the international level, we must be willing to use our military might to help even one of our citizens, no matter where he might be kidnapped or enslaved. (*An Enemy Hath Done This,* p. 152.)

The world is smaller, you say? True, it is, but if one finds himself locked in a house with maniacs, thieves, and murderers — even a small house — he does not increase his chances of survival by entering into alliances with his potential attackers and becoming dependent upon them for protection to the point where he is unable to defend himself. Perhaps the analogy between nations and maniacs is a little strong for some to accept. But if we put aside our squeamishness over strong language, and look hard at the real world in which we live, the analogy is quite sound in all but the rarest exceptions. (*An Enemy Hath Done This,* pp. 154–55.)

Do you realize that a great republic, Greece, provided a great degree of freedom and a high standard of living but it vanished? Rome came along with a great republic. Roman citizenship was cherished — yes, it was sought, it was bought. But Rome, falling into the throes of cheap politics, began to tax everything that could be taxed and to regulate everything that could be regulated — even to the load that could be carried on an ass. And what was the result? They began to put names on the public payroll until a third of the citizens of Rome were on the national payroll, and that republic collapsed. A dictatorship followed until the fat accumulated during the days of the republic had been consumed, and then the empire fell — and great was the fall thereof. It ushered in a period known as the Dark Ages, lasting a thousand years. Should our American private free-enterprise system fall, what will be the result? Would this usher in a period again comparable only to the fall of Rome?

Channing Pollock observed that most democracies last for about two hundred years. They are conceived and developed by simple, vigorous, idealistic, hard-working people who, unfortunately, with success become rich and decadent, learn to live without labor, depend more on the largess of big government, and end by trading domestic tyrants for foreign tyrants.

With the end of the second century of our republic, it appears very much in order to examine its political, social, and economic structure to ascertain whether it contains a unique charter which makes it impervious to the lessons of history. (*An Enemy Hath Done This,* pp. 115–16.)

Even among free nations we see the encroachment of government upon the lives of the citizenry by excessive taxation and regulation, all done under the guise that the people would not wilfully or charitably distribute their wealth, so the government must take it from them. We further observe promises by the state of security, whereby men are taken care of from the womb to the tomb rather than earning this security by the "sweat of their brow" (Moses 5:1); deception in high places, with the justification that "the end justifies the means"; atheism; agnosticism; immorality; and dishonesty. The attendant results of such sin and usurpation of power lead to a general distrust of government officials, an insatiable, covetous spirit for more and more material wants, personal debt to satisfy this craving, and the disintegration of the family unit. Yes, we live today amidst the times the Savior spoke of, times when "the love of many shall wax cold, and iniquity shall abound" (Matthew 24:12). (*This Nation Shall Endure,* p. 8.)

United Nations

I have in my possession a copy of an unpublished manuscript on the United Nations Charter prepared in 1945 and given to me by that eminent international lawyer and former Under Secretary of State, J. Reuben Clark, Jr.

President Clark's declaration on this, as on other subjects, emphasize more and more with the passing of time his vision and statesmanship. Commenting on the United Nations Charter and the "travesty on exhaustive consideration" as the charter was hastily approved by the Congress under urging from the State Department, he continues with a devastating analysis and a sober warning to the American people that there will be a day of reckoning. I believe that day is near at hand. The hopes and the aspirations of the people have been betrayed. I hope this scholarly, unpublished memorandum by President Clark with its penetrating analysis will someday soon be available in full. Meantime, I urge all to read the solid volume *Stand Fast by the Constitution,* which embodies much of J. Reuben Clark's timely instruction. (*Title of Liberty,* pp. 78–79.)

On the surface, the United Nations Charter and the structure of its various departments bears a strong resemblance to those of our own federal government. But the similarity goes no further than outward form. Whereas the United States is founded on the concept of limited government, the United Nations concept is one of unlimited government power with virtually no meaningful restraints to protect individual liberty.

For instance, article 4, section 4 of our Constitution states: "The United States shall guarantee to every State in this union a Republican form of government." This means a government with limited powers. The framers knew that the Union would not last if the individual states were allowed to become despotic and unrestrained. To provide protection against the creation of a super-federal government, the ninth amendment further stipulates: "The enumeration in the Constitution of certain rights shall not be construed to deny or disparage others retained by the people." And more of the same in the tenth amendment: "The powers not delegated to the United States by the Constitution, nor prohibited by it to the States, are reserved to the States respectively, or to the people.''

Compare this with the ideological foundation upon which the United Nations is built. Instead of insuring that all member states have limited forms of government, the United Nations assumes that most of them have unlimited power over their subjects. The United Nations is not the least bit concerned over the fact that a majority of its members are governments which rule with police-state methods. Instead of assuming that any power not specifically mentioned in the Constitution is reserved to the individual citizens or their smaller governmental units, the United Nations operates under the doctrine that its charter is sufficiently vague and broad so as to authorize doing absolutely anything. (*An Enemy Hath Done This,* pp. 203–4.)

Even if we assume that all of the people at the United Nations representing the various nations were of the highest moral caliber and prompted only by the most pure and selfless motives, there still is every reason to believe that the concentration into their hands of the absolute power of a nuclear monopoly, plus a military land, air, and naval force superior to any nation, would be a mighty tempting influence. In time, the flesh could weaken, even the best of men would be caught up in the inevitable struggle for world power, and finally, the whole planet would be subject to an unchallengeable dictatorship of the few over the many. True, such a development conceivably might not materialize for years, but it would materialize. The only legitimate question open to speculation is how soon. (*An Enemy Hath Done This,* p. 178.)

History

The history of men and nations clearly teaches that only that nation is blessed ''whose God is the Lord'' (Psalm 33:12). God is still at the helm. He rules in the affairs of men and nations. As a nation we have been kept in the hollow of God's hand. But what of the future? In our history—ancient and modern—is the answer. Serve the God of this land who is Jesus Christ (see Ether 2:8–10). There is no other course of safety. May we accept His guidance before it is too late. Real security can come in no other way. (*The Red Carpet,* p. 298.)

Secular scholarship, though useful, provides an incomplete and sometimes inaccurate view of our history. The real story of America is one which shows the hand of God in our nation's beginning. ("God's Hand in Our Nation's History," Sons of Utah Pioneers, Salt Lake City, Utah, 23 August 1986.)

History is not an accident. Events are foreknown to God. His superintending influence is behind righteous men's actions. And though mortal eyes and minds cannot fathom the end from the beginning, God does. ("The Crises of Our Constitution," Salt Lake Valley Utah Central Area Special Interest Lecture Series, 8 September 1977.)

Great moments in history are made by colliding influences: the personalities in the drama, an issue or crisis, and a timing which synchronizes these influences into an event. The birth of this nation was such an event. ("The Crises of Our Constitution," Salt Lake Valley Utah Central Area Special Interest Lecture Series, 8 September 1977.)

Today we are almost engulfed by a tide of self-criticism, depreciation, and defamation of those who served our country honorably and with distinction. I know the philosophy behind this practice is "to tell it as it is." All too often those who subscribe to this philosophy are not hampered by too many facts. When will we awaken to the fact that the defamation of our dead heroes only serves to undermine faith in the principles for which they stood, and the institutions which they established. Some have termed this practice as "historical realism" or moderately called it "debunking." I call it slander and defamation. And I repeat, those who are guilty of it in their writing or teaching will answer to a Higher Tribunal. ("God's Hand in Our Nation's History," Sons of Utah Pioneers, Salt Lake City, Utah, 23 August 1986.)

Lest there be some who get the impression that I am an antagonist to the discipline of history and historians, let me declare my feelings about that noble profession. I love to read history and historical biography. I have great respect for the historian who can put into proper perspective events and people, and make history come alive. I believe the maxim that "those who do not understand the lessons of the past are doomed to repeat those errors anew." I love history books that tell history as it was — as the Book of Mormon tells it — with God in the picture guiding and directing the affairs of the righteous. I love to read history for its timeless lessons and the inspiration I can gather from the lives of great leaders. I have been privileged to know many in my lifetime who have made history both in the world and in the Church. ("God's Hand in Our Nation's History," Sons of Utah Pioneers, Salt Lake City, Utah, 23 August 1986.)

The lessons of history stand as guideposts to help us safely chart the course for the future. ("A Voice of Warning to the Nations of the World," New Zealand and Australia Area Conferences, 25 November 1979 and 2 December 1979.)

The lessons of history should serve as wise counselors. Too frequently, however, we seem to disregard or forget them. It is wisdom for us to sharpen our vision and fortify our courage to face the future by considering carefully the costly, yet priceless, lessons of the past. The man who cannot learn from the past will be a poor steward of the future. (*So Shall Ye Reap,* p. 307.)

Peace

To those who yearn for peace, we announce that it may be found with the Prince of Peace. Even in these tumultuous times the individual who turns to Christ can find the inner peace that surpasses understanding. ("First Presidency — Christmas Message," *Church News* [15 December 1985]: 3.)

The whole spirit of the gospel is one of peace and brotherhood. The Lord has made it very clear in the revelations. This is what the Lord said to His Church in this day, and these revelations were intended for the entire world. This is what He says about peace: "Therefore, renounce war and proclaim peace, and seek diligently to turn the hearts of the children to their fathers, and the hearts of the fathers to the children" (D&C 98:16). ("Free Agency," Washington D.C. Stake Conference, 22 May 1960.)

The precepts of men would have you believe that by limiting the population of the world, we can have peace and plenty. That is the doctrine of the devil. Small numbers do not insure peace; only righteousness does. After all, there were only a handful of men on the earth when Cain interrupted the peace of Adam's household by slaying Abel. On the other hand, the whole city of Enoch was peaceful; and it was taken into heaven because it was made up of righteous people.

And so far as limiting the population in order to provide plenty is concerned, the Lord answered that falsehood in the Doctrine and Covenants when He said: "For the earth is full, and there is enough and to spare; yea, I prepared all things, and have given unto the children of men to be agents unto themselves" (D&C 104:17). (*God, Family, Country,* pp. 257–58.)

The only real peace—the one most of us think about when we use the term—is a peace with freedom. A nation that is not willing, if necessary, to face the rigors of war to defend its real peace-in-freedom is doomed to lose both its freedom and its peace! These are the hard facts of life. We may not like them, but until we live in a far better world than exists today, we must face up to them squarely and courageously. (*An Enemy Hath Done This,* pp. 161–62.)

Despite the world's crises—Korea, Indochina, Lebanon, Quemoy, and Berlin—the greater crisis by far is that we might forget the Lord. How much protection would our missiles and nuclear weapons prove to be if we did not take at face value the Lord's injunction: "Thou shalt love the Lord thy God with all thy heart, and with all thy soul, and with all thy strength, and with all thy mind; and thy neighbor as thyself"? (Luke 10:27.) (*Crossfire: The Eight Years with Eisenhower,* p. 441.)

The outlook for the world is not encouraging, but we know what the answer is. There is only one answer, and that is the gospel of Jesus Christ. Peace must come from the heart. Men's hearts must change, and righteousness must rule in the lives of the people of the world before peace can come. May God hasten the day. May the message of the restored gospel go forward in great force, by increasing numbers, that God's children may escape the calamities which are impending. (CR April 1947, *Improvement Era* 50 [May 1947]: 296.)

It is our hope and prayer that people throughout the world will incorporate into their daily thoughts and actions the principles espoused by Jesus. To do so would most assuredly lead to less war and more peace, less turmoil and more serenity, less unrest and more stability, less crime and sin and more self-respect and happiness.

If greed and lust and the quest for power and dominion were to be replaced by commitments to pattern lives after the example of the Prince of Peace Himself, how blessed the world would be! It is our prayer that during this Easter season and hereafter, there will be progress toward that worthy goal. ("First Presidency — Easter Message," *Church News* [23 March 1986]: 1.)

Ours must be a crusade for clean, purposeful living. Only those who steadfastly pursue such a course ever experience real peace, real freedom. Those fettered by insatiable appetites for things destructive of man's noblest qualities never know either real freedom or the sweet fruits of inward peace. ("Purposeful Living," *Listen, A Journal of Better Living* [January–March 1955]: 19.)

The price of peace is righteousness. Men and nations may loudly proclaim, "Peace, peace," but there shall be no peace until individuals nurture in their souls those principles of personal purity, integrity, and character which foster the development of peace. Peace cannot be imposed. It must come from the lives and hearts of men. There is no other way. ("Purposeful Living," *Listen, A Journal of Better Living* [January — March 1955]: 19.)

Peace for America

We must keep our hearts free from hatred and remember ever that we should carry with us always a love for the children of men. We should renounce war and declare peace. The Lord has commanded us so to do. (D&C 98:16.) Our message is a message of peace. We are followers of the Prince of Peace, and we should re-dedicate our lives to the spread of truth and righteousness and the preservation of the liberty and freedom which have been vouch-safed to us as American citizens and as Latter-day Saints. (CR April 1948, *Improvement Era* 51 [May 1948]: 343.)

We should seek peace—without appeasement. We should seek prosperity—without war. We should seek progress—without so-cialism. To reach this sublime objective, we must be constantly alert to the forces and changes operating in our economy. We must be everlastingly devoted to the God-given freedom that is our priceless heritage. (*The Red Carpet*, p. 215.)

Until all nations follow the concept of limited government, it is unlikely that universal peace will ever be realized on this planet. Unlimited, power-grasping governments will always resort to force if they think they can get away with it. But there can be peace for America. As long as our leaders faithfully discharge their duty to preserve and strengthen the military, economic, and political inde-pendence of our republic, the world's petty despots will leave us alone. What more could we ask of United States foreign policy? (*An Enemy Hath Done This,* pp. 162–63.)

God bless us, as Latter-day Saints, that we may wield our influ-ence to the very maximum in promoting peace, in promoting spiri-tuality among the people of this great nation, that this great coun-try of which we are a part may be preserved, and may continue to be, through all the days to come, a beacon and an inspiration to liberty-loving people everywhere. (CR April 1953, *Improvement Era* 56 [June 1953]: 415.)

Peace for the World

There are those who act as though they do not believe in eter-nity or a resurrection. They cower at the thought of nuclear war, and to save their own bodies they would have peace at any price.

Yet the best assurance of peace and life is to be strong morally and militarily. But they want life at the sacrifice of principles. Rather than choose liberty or death, they prefer life with slavery. But they overlook a crucial scripture: "Fear not them which kill the body but are not able to kill the soul; but rather fear him which is able to destroy both soul and body in hell" (Matthew 10:28). The Lord could, I suppose, have avoided the War in Heaven over free agency. All He needed to do was to compromise with the devil, but had He done so He would have ceased to be God. (CR April 1964, *Improvement Era* 67 [June 1964]: 504.)

People do want peace—everywhere. People long to be free. In their hearts they yearn to be brothers. The spirit of freedom, the spirit of brotherhood, and the spirit of religion live on and on even under immense difficulties. We are charged with a responsibility, all of us who are now members of the Church, to carry this gospel message to our Father's children because this is the only message that will bring about peace and happiness—inner peace as well as peace among the nations of the earth. There is no other way. (San Diego California Stake Conference, 7 December 1969.)

Let us apply this lesson to our own lives—and to the world in which we live—this lesson that man to man we must act not as acquaintances occupying the same star in space, nor even as friends living on the same continent, but as brothers under the fatherhood of one God. (*So Shall Ye Reap,* p. 272.)

It is my conviction that the world needs, as it needs no other thing, the gospel of Jesus Christ, and the people of the world want what the gospel will give, but they do not realize it. They want the anchor which the gospel provides, which gives them the answers to the problems that face them; which brings them a feeling of security and a feeling of inner peace. The gospel is the only answer to the problems of the world. We may cry peace. We may hold peace conferences. And I have nothing but commendation for those who work for peace. But it is my conviction that peace must come from within. It cannot be imposed by state mandate. It can come only by following the teachings and the example of the Prince of Peace. (*Title of Liberty,* pp. 213–14.)

War

I fully realize that the Lord has predicted wars and rumors of wars (D&C 45:26). I recognize that only true repentance can stay the destructive forces of war and calamity. Nevertheless, I fervently hope and pray that a spirit and influence will come into the lives of the Latter-day Saints which will enable them to be a leaven, as it were, to raise the spirituality and faith of the people amongst whom they live. (Bern Switzerland Stake Creation, 3 May 1981.)

The Mormon servicemen, not only from the United States but other parts of the world, performed a great service to the Church during the Second World War and immediately following the war. We felt very badly that we had to curtail our missionary work during the war, but I think in reality we had more missionary work during the war than at any other time, because our servicemen held the priesthood. Many of them had been missionaries, and almost without exception they had a testimony of the gospel. Then, too, there were many civilians who served in the military service after the war who also rendered great service to the Church. ("The Church," Paris, France, 7 August 1960.)

Too often we bask in our comfortable complacency and rationalize that the ravages of war, economic disaster, famine, and earthquake cannot happen here. Those who believe this are either not acquainted with the revelations of the Lord, or they do not believe them. Those who smugly think these calamities will not happen, that they somehow will be set aside because of the righteousness of the Saints, are deceived and will rue the day they harbored such a delusion. The Lord has warned and forewarned us against a day of great tribulation and given us counsel, through His servants, on how we can be prepared for these difficult times. Have we heeded His counsel?

Be faithful, my brothers and sisters, to this counsel and you will be blessed — yes, the most blessed people in all the earth. (CR October 1980, *Ensign* 10 [November 1980]: 34.)

Subject Index

Scripture Index

OLD TESTAMENT

NEW TESTAMENT

BOOK OF MORMON

DOCTRINE AND COVENANTS

PEARL OF GREAT PRICE